ALSO BY DOUGLAS WALLER

Wild Bill Donovan: The Spymaster Who Created the OSS
and Modern American Espionage

A Question of Loyalty: Gen. Billy Mitchell and the Court-Martial
That Gripped the Nation

Big Red: The Three-Month Voyage of a Trident Nuclear Submarine

Air Warriors: The Inside Story of the Making of a Navy Pilot

The Commandos: The Inside Story of America's Secret Soldiers

THE WORLD WAR II MISSIONS
OF THE CIA DIRECTORS WHO
FOUGHT FOR WILD BILL DONOVAN:

ALLEN DULLES,

RICHARD HELMS,

WILLIAM COLBY,

WILLIAM CASEY

DISCIPLES

DOUGLAS WALLER

Simon & Schuster

New York London Toronto Sydney New Delhi

Simon & Schuster
1230 Avenue of the Americas
New York, NY 10020

First Simon & Schuster hardcover edition September 2015

SIMON & SCHUSTER and colophon are
registered trademarks of Simon & Schuster, Inc.

For information about special discounts for bulk purchases, please contact Simon & Schuster Special Sales at 1-866-506-1949 or business@simonandschuster.com.

The Simon & Schuster Speakers Bureau can bring authors to your live event. For more information or to book an event contact the Simon & Schuster Speakers Bureau at 1-866-248-3049 or visit our website at www.simonspeakers.com.

Interior design by Joy O'Meara

Manufactured in the United States of America

10 9 8 7 6 5 4 3 2 1

Library of Congress Cataloging-in-Publication Data

Waller, Douglas C.
    Disciples : the World War II spy story of the four OSS men who later led the CIA: Allen Dulles, Richard Helms, William Colby, William Casey / Douglas Waller.
        pages   cm
    Includes bibliographical references and index.
    ISBN 978-1-4516-9372-0 (hardback : alkaline paper)—ISBN 978-1-4516-9374-4 (trade paperback : alkaline paper)—ISBN 978-1-4516-9376-8 (ebook)   1. Dulles, Allen, 1893–1969.   2. Helms, Richard.   3. Colby, William Egan, 1920-1996.   4. Casey, William J.   5. Donovan, William J. (William Joseph), 1883-1959—Friends and associates.   6. Spies—United States—Biography.   7. World War, 1939-1945—Secret service—United States.   8. United States. Office of Strategic Services—Biography.   9. Espionage, American—Europe—History—20th century.   10. United States. Central Intelligence Agency—Biography.   I. Title.
    D810.S7W34   2015
    940.54'86730922—dc23   2014039395

ISBN 978-1-4516-9372-0
ISBN 978-1-4516-9376-8 (ebook)

To Alex, Annabel, and Nathan

CONTENTS

CAST OF CHARACTERS

Terence Airey. British Field Marshal Harold Alexander's chief intelligence officer and his representative in the "Sunrise" negotiations for a German surrender in North Italy.

Harold R. L. G. Alexander. The British field marshal in command of Allied forces in Italy.

Gerhard Van Arkel. An OSS officer who recruited spies among European labor organizations in New York and later in London. He also worked for Allen Dulles in Bern.

Mary Bancroft. She worked for Allen Dulles in Switzerland during World War II and became his mistress.

Roger Bardet. A key aide to Henri Frager, leader of the Donkeyman French Resistance network. Bardet betrayed Frager to the German Abwehr.

Ludwig Beck. A retired German general and former army chief of staff who was a leader in the conspiracy to topple Adolf Hitler.

Hugo Bleicher. One of the Abwehr's most skilled counterintelligence operatives in France who infiltrated the Donkeyman Resistance network with informants like Roger Bardet.

Alphonse Blonttrock. Radioman for the OSS spy team "Doctor" who went by the alias Jean Denis.

David K. E. Bruce. The OSS station chief in London.

Wilhelm Canaris. The admiral in charge of the Abwehr. Canaris supported the German plot to overthrow Hitler.

Franklin Canfield. The OSS officer in charge of recruiting and training the Jedburgh commandos.

Sophia Kurz Casey. William Casey's wife.

William Joseph Casey. The head of the OSS London station's secretariat, then the agency's chief of secret intelligence for Europe. Casey was CIA director from 1981 to 1987.

Wally Castelbarco. An Italian countess and daughter of Arturo Toscanini. She aided Italian partisans and had an affair with Allen Dulles.

Leo Cherne. The head of the Research Institute of America, where William Casey worked as an analyst.

Colonel Chevrier. The code name for Adrien Sadoul, a French Resistance commander in the Yonne Department.

Barbara Heinzen Colby. William Colby's first wife.

Sally Shelton Colby. William Colby's second wife.

William Egan Colby. An OSS Jedburgh commando who parachuted into France and later led the NORSO team that infiltrated into Norway. Colby was CIA director from 1973 to 1976.

Claude Dansey. The deputy chief of Britain's Secret Intelligence Service (MI6) who oversaw its Swiss operations from London.

André Dewavrin. Charles de Gaulle's intelligence chief who went by the code name "Passy."

Otto "Ole" Doering Jr. A senior Donovan aide who interviewed William Casey for a job at the OSS.

William J. "Wild Bill" Donovan. The director of the World War II Office of Strategic Services.

Allen Welsh Dulles. The OSS station chief in Bern, Switzerland, during World War II and later CIA director from 1953 to 1961.

Clover Todd Dulles. Allen Dulles's wife.

John Foster Dulles. Allen Dulles's brother and secretary of state in the Eisenhower administration.

Erich Fellgiebel. The chief of German army communications and a member of the conspiracy plotting to oust Hitler.

François Flour. Radioman for the OSS spy team "Painter" who went by the alias François Fouget.

Henri Frager. The leader of the Donkeyman Resistance network in France. Frager was captured and killed by the Nazis.

Friedrich Fromm. The general who commanded Germany's Replacement Army.

Gero von Schulze-Gaevernitz. An international financier and son of a Weimar legislator who became a key World War II operative for Allen Dulles in Bern.

Hans Bernd Gisevius. An Abwehr officer who slipped information to Dulles and became a conduit to German conspirators trying to oust Adolf Hitler.

Carl Goerdeler. A former Reich Prices Commissioner and Leipzig mayor, who was part of the conspiracy to topple Hitler.

Arthur Goldberg. Goldberg worked for Allen Dulles organizing spying for the OSS by European unions and later began an operation out of the London station to infiltrate agents into Germany.

Ides van der Gracht. A lieutenant colonel who was Richard Helms's boss in the postwar Germany mission's intelligence production division.

Franz Halder. The German general who succeeded Ludwig Beck as army chief of staff and became a part of the conspiracy to topple Hitler.

Charles Hambro. The World War II chief of Great Britain's Special Operations Executive.

Georg Hansen. Hansen ran the Abwehr's military intelligence functions after Admiral Canaris was fired. Hansen also supported the German conspirators plotting against Hitler.

Leland Harrison. The head of the U.S. legation in Bern during World War II.

Wolf-Heinrich Graf von Helldorf. Berlin's police chief and a member of the conspiracy to topple Hitler.

Cynthia Helms. Richard Helms's second wife.

Julia Helms. Richard Helms's first wife.

Richard McGarrah Helms. William Casey's assistant in London, chief of the Berlin spy base just after the war, and CIA director from 1966 to 1973.

Max Egon Hohenlohe von Lagensberg. A Liechtenstein national and Heinrich Himmler agent who tried to cultivate Dulles.

J. Edgar Hoover. The FBI director and William Donovan rival during World War II.

Max Husmann. The head of a private school near Lucerne who served as an intermediary in the "Sunrise" negotiations for the surrender of German forces in North Italy.

Henry Hyde. An OSS officer who infiltrated agents into southern France and later into Germany.

Ernst Kaltenbrunner. The SS general who was chief of the Reich Main Security Office and the second most powerful man in the SS.

Milton Katz. William Casey's deputy when Casey served as chief of secret intelligence for Europe.

Albert Kesselring. The field marshal who commanded German occupation forces in North Italy.

Ernst Kocherthaler. The German intermediary who introduced Fritz Kolbe to the Americans in Bern.

Fritz Kolbe. A German Foreign Office bureaucrat who supplied Dulles with intelligence on the Third Reich. Dulles gave him the code name "George Wood."

Camille Lelong. A French Jedburgh officer who was a member of Colby's Team Bruce. His code name was Jacques Favel.

Lyman Lemnitzer. An American general who was Field Marshal Harold Alexander's deputy chief of staff and representative in the negotiations for a German surrender in North Italy.

Paul Lindner. An agent with the OSS spy team in Berlin code-named "Hammer."

André Marsac. An agent in the Donkeyman French Resistance network who was arrested by the Germans.

Ferdinand "Ferd" Mayer. Mayer was in charge of the German desk at OSS headquarters and oversaw Allen Dulles's penetration of Germany from Bern. His code name was "Carib."

Gerald Mayer. The Office of War Information representative in the Bern legation who worked closely with Allen Dulles.

John McCaffrey. The British Special Operations Executive representative in Bern during World War II.

Stewart Menzies. The World War II chief of Great Britain's Secret Intelligence Service (MI6).

Gerald Miller. The London OSS station's special operations chief who hired William Colby to lead the Norwegian Special Operations Group (NORSO).

Helmuth James Graf von Moltke. A Silesian count and leader of the Kreisau Circle, a German opposition cell plotting to overthrow Hitler.

George Richard Musgrave. The second British commander of Milton Hall, where the Jedburghs trained.

Frederick Oechsner. United Press's Berlin bureau chief in the mid-1930s and Richard Helms's boss. Oechsner later served in the OSS.

Friedrich Olbricht. The general who was deputy to Friedrich Fromm (commander of Germany's Replacement Army) and part of the conspiracy to oust Hitler.

Hans Oster. The deputy chief of the Abwehr and one of the German conspirators plotting to overthrow Hitler.

Luigi Parrilli. An Italian baron who served as an intermediary for the peace talks SS General Karl Wolff had with Allen Dulles.

George Pratt. Pratt served under Arthur Goldberg in the OSS New York office and later became William Casey's Intelligence Procurement Division chief in the London station.

Rudolf Rahn. The German ambassador to the puppet regime the Nazis established in North Italy for Mussolini after he was ousted in 1943.

Karl Ritter. The head of the German Foreign Office's political-military affairs department and Fritz Kolbe's boss.

Anton Ruh. An agent with the OSS spy team in Berlin code-named "Hammer."

Arthur Schlesinger Jr. A research analyst in the London OSS station and later for the agency's mission in postwar Germany. Schlesinger served in the Kennedy administration and became a noted historian.

Whitney Shepardson. Donovan's chief of secret intelligence in Washington. His code name was "Jackpot."

Peter Sichel. An OSS officer who ran an espionage unit for Helms in postwar Berlin and cleaned up corruption in the unit.

John Singlaub. A Jedburgh commando who served with William Colby in the OSS.

Hans Skabo. The OSS lieutenant colonel who was William Colby's immediate boss for the NORSO mission.

Jan Smets. Intelligence agent for the OSS spy team "Doctor" who went by the alias Jan Bloch.

Frank Spooner. The first British commander of Milton Hall, where the Jedburghs trained.

Claus Schenk Graf von Stauffenberg. A Wehrmacht colonel and leader of the July 20, 1944, plot to assassinate Hitler.

William Stephenson. Britain's intelligence officer in the United States who advised William Donovan on setting up the OSS.

Henning von Tresckow. A German general on the Eastern Front who plotted to overthrow Hitler.

Gerhard Van Arkel. A labor lawyer who worked for Arthur Goldberg in the OSS New York office and later for Allen Dulles in Bern infiltrating agents into Germany.

Emil Jean Van Dyck. Intelligence agent for the OSS spy team "Painter."

Heinrich von Vietinghoff. The general who succeeded Albert Kesselring as commander of German forces in North Italy.

Roger Villebois. The French Jedburgh radio operator on Colby's Team Bruce. His code name was "Louis Giry."

Eduard Waetjen. A German lawyer in Switzerland who became a conduit for Dulles to the German resistance movement.

Max Waibel. A Swiss military intelligence major who helped Dulles in the "Sunrise" negotiations for a surrender of German forces in North Italy.

Frank Wisner. A Navy commander in the OSS who was Allen Dulles's secret intelligence chief in the postwar German mission.

Erwin von Witzleben. The German general commanding the Berlin military district and a member of the conspiracy plotting to overthrow Hitler.

Karl Wolff. The Waffen SS general for North Italy who negotiated the German surrender there.

If ye continue in my word, *then* are ye my disciples indeed;
And ye shall know the truth, and the truth shall make you free.

JOHN 8:31–32

DISCIPLES

PROLOGUE

The Cathedral of St. Matthew the Apostle on Rhode Island Avenue was among the capital's most impressive churches, shaped in the form of a Latin cross, its interior walls covered with shimmering Italian Renaissance–styled murals, its large copper dome in the center atop an eight-sided lantern rising two hundred feet. Appropriate for Washington, D.C., Matthew was the patron saint of civil servants. Funeral masses for Catholics who had risen to the highest levels of the U.S. government had been celebrated inside its nave, which could seat about one thousand. On this Wednesday morning, February 11, 1959, as light from the chilly day outside streamed through translucent alabaster windows, nearly every space in the pews was filled with veterans of the two world wars, captains of New York finance, lawyers with Washington's power firms, barons from publishing, high clergy from the archdiocese, Georgetown and Virginia horse country matrons, senior officers from the Pentagon, representatives from the White House—and spies. Many spies.

The body of General William "Wild Bill" Donovan rested in the flag-draped coffin before the white marble table of the Eucharist in the sanctuary. The funeral home had dressed him in his tailored Army uniform with his rows of combat ribbons pinned to it. Donovan's had been the life of "medieval legend," an editorialist wrote: an Irish kid who escaped the poverty of Buffalo's First Ward, who quarterbacked his college football team, graduated from Columbia Law School with Franklin Roosevelt, was awarded the Medal of Honor for heroism in World War I, and who made millions as a Wall Street attorney. At the dawn of America's entry into World War II, Roosevelt had made him his spymaster—the director of what became known as the Office of Strategic Services. Donovan, who had earned his nickname "Wild Bill" as a hard-driving commander in the First World War, assembled for the Second a force of more than ten thousand espionage agents, paramilitary commandos, propagandists, and research analysts, who waged battle in the shadows against the Axis from stations all over the world—a remarkable achievement considering he began his intelligence organization with just one person. Wild Bill.

When the choir from Catholic University had finished singing and the rustling in the congregation had quieted, Monsignor John Cartwright climbed the steps to the ambo to deliver the eulogy.

> *"The citizen and soldier of whom we are taking leave today filled an exceptional role in the lives of multitudes of people," he began in a booming voice that echoed through the nave. "This gathering testifies both by number and character how great a role that was . . ."*

Allen Dulles sat near the front on the left side with a contingent of his clandestine officers in the pews around him. The CIA director's secretive nature, even with the obvious, could be maddening to outsiders—"you ask him if it was raining outside, he'd laugh at you," said one—but his agents revered him. Dulles had a talent for getting men and women to risk their careers and lives for him. He had become an international celebrity by 1959, his Central Intelligence Agency popular among Americans and a formidable instrument of foreign policy. Dulles could pick up the phone and call leaders and secret service chiefs all over the world, many of whom he had known personally for years. (Although, technologically inept, he always struggled with the switch on the handle of his scrambler phone, which had to be pushed to talk and released to listen.) Dulles understood power, how to play power games, and he loved to play them. An adoring CIA analyst penned a clumsily written poem about the director:

> *So Mr. D.*
> *Went by land, air, and sea*
>   *Round the length and breadth of the world*

The craft he was in
Ranged from choppers at Hua-bin
    To a yacht that had its spinnaker unfurled

Mr. D. worked all day
While others would play
    Yet he seldom let loose his thunder.
He's a man that his troupe
All felt as a group
    Mighty glad and proud to be under.

To friends, Mister D looked like the headmaster of an upper-class English boarding school, dressed usually in bow tie and tweed sport coat, his wiry gray hair slightly mussed, his mustache carefully trimmed, a pipe almost always clenched between his teeth (sometimes more for effect, they suspected, than for smoking), gray-blue eyes that sparkled with interest behind steel-rimmed glasses, and a soft voice that invited people to pour their hearts out to him. The laugh. It seemed to be with him always—occasionally hearty when he was genuinely amused, but more often a mirthless "ho-ho" he turned on when trying to ingratiate himself with a stranger or deflect a question he did not want to answer. Colleagues could see that the country gentleman routine also masked a fierce competitor not willing to give up a single point on the tennis court, "a back alley fighter" as one put it, a devious man who sized up other men and women based solely on whether they could be useful to him, an introvert at heart whose true agenda could be unfathomable behind the veneer he erected.

Dulles, who had been Donovan's station chief in Switzerland during World War II, had had—as many men did—a complicated relationship with the general. That Donovan was a skilled intelligence officer Dulles would never publicly deny. Donovan after the war had hailed Dulles as his top spy, which was the case. But Donovan always suspected that Dulles thought he could have better managed the OSS and that he wanted his job, which was also the case. Yet for all his private disdain of Donovan's leadership, Dulles now ran the CIA much as Donovan would have. Like Donovan, Dulles believed gentlemen behind closed doors could undertake unsavory missions and violate ethical strictures for a higher cause. He had recruited for his CIA, as Donovan had for his OSS, America's brightest, most idealistic, most adventuresome minds—self-assured men and women sent out to the world, with broad latitude from headquarters, to secretly battle communists in the Cold War as Donovan had fought the Nazis in World War II. Like Donovan, Dulles loved to swap stories with his spies in the field, to micromanage the covert operations that interested him, and largely ignore the ones that didn't. Like Donovan, Dulles was willing to undertake clandestine missions others would shrink from as reckless and be unfazed if he met with failure. "If one stops gathering intelligence because some day something should be a little out of place," Dulles once rationalized, "you wouldn't be doing anything." Donovan would have said the same. Dulles looked back on World War II as his best years. Although he never explicitly stated it, his OSS experience shaped his character for life.

"General Donovan bore an illustrious part in the two great wars that have filled so much of our century. No less illustrious were the services he rendered in our years of anxious and troubled peace . . ."

Sitting with the CIA contingent was Richard Helms, an officer nearing middle age whose rise in the agency had been respectable yet blocked at times by other men Dulles valued as more daring. Helms instead stood out for his administrative skills, an attribute Dulles considered "useful" (always his favorite adjective for Helms) yet boring. As he had been in Donovan's OSS, Helms in the CIA was a purist of the trade, far more interested in quietly collecting and keeping secrets on an enemy than in actually fighting him in the shadows. Unlike Donovan and Dulles, he distrusted covert operations that presidents could deny, believing that if anything could go wrong with them it would. The seamier aspects of clandestine warfare— such as assassination—gave him pause, not for moral reasons but because he thought them crude tools and often ineffective.

Helms was the consummate spy with his Mona Lisa–like smile, hair always slicked back neatly, and an aloof personality. He did not make friends easily and when he did he remained deliberate in his friendships, always restrained, rarely letting down his inhibitions. "An open mouth gathers no

information," he liked to tell his children. There were plenty of stories circulating in the CIA on its colorful characters. No one could think of a good
anecdote about Helms. The consummate intelligence operative, he left no
trail behind. Men had to strain to come up with something to say about him
because he made so little impression on them. Women thought him tall and
handsome, which he was, but little else came to mind. He detested drawing
attention to himself, grew furious with relatives who revealed even innocuous details about his job. At parties he was a good dancer and a charming
conversationalist, but he rarely drank more than one martini so his head
remained clear and was the first to leave early so he'd be fresh for the office
the next day. Or, if the gathering was at his house, he would shoo out guests
when his bedtime neared.

Yet family members could detect a twinkle in his eye. He took teasing
well from them and enjoyed the ironies of life. He was attentive to his
children when they became adults and they could converse with him on
his level. He grew sentimental and teary-eyed delivering family toasts. He
always sent handwritten thank-you notes and expected them in return. He
had a prodigious memory, an obsession with accumulating the tiniest details in his head (who at a party had crowns in his teeth, who bit his nails),
was fluent in French and German, and could be fanatical about proper spelling and punctuation in reports he read. He loved to play a who-leaked-it
game with his wife when he read a revealing story in *The Washington Post*
on intelligence. He enjoyed spy novels except for John le Carré's, which he
found too darkly cynical about his profession.

He also had his distinctive features if you looked hard. He smoked two
packs of Chesterfields a day for most of his life. Though otherwise a tightwad, he was always immaculately tailored—his expensive suits bought from
Lewis & Thomas Saltz in Washington, his shoes specially made for his small,
high-arched feet at $700 a pair from Peal & Co. in London. He wore his belt
with the buckle on the side of his waist instead of at the front. He never left
home without a tiepin at the bottom of his tie and a white handkerchief
tucked neatly into his jacket pocket. And he strutted out to the tennis court
always in long white trousers.

As he did with everything, Helms viewed his service in the OSS as a
young Navy lieutenant with clinical cool dispassion, never with nostalgia.

Donovan's "league of gentlemen," as the general had called them, contained its share of social register misfits and bored Wall Street businessmen looking for action, Helms knew, many of them now hangers-on in the CIA. Helms thought the OSS had only had a minimal effect on World War II's outcome. "The war would have been won without the OSS," he once said. But Donovan deserved credit for being a visionary, if somewhat chaotic, leader, Helms thought. The general had introduced the Pentagon and Americans to unconventional warfare practiced on a global scale. And the OSS had taught Helms how to be a spy.

> *"His record of achievement and honor has been much reviewed since the day of his death and will always be remembered in the pages of our history. But his life of combat and of leadership, of service and example is ended now . . ."*

In the back of the cathedral with the focal mosaic of St. Matthew's looking down on him, Bill Casey sat numbed by grief, as a son would be over the loss of a father. Donovan had been not just a boss but also a mentor to Casey, who served as his secret intelligence chief for all of Europe during the war when he was only thirty-one years old. The two shared similar backgrounds—descendants of poor Irish Catholic immigrants who had worked their way through law school—and since the war Casey had set out to follow Donovan's path to power, climbing the ladder of Republican Party politics and bankrolling his love of international affairs with a fortune earned on Wall Street. In the fourteen years after the war, Casey was now, as Donovan had been, a multimillionaire. He worshipped everything about the general—his charisma, his drive, his intellect. He kept a miniature bronze statue and photos of Donovan in the study of his Long Island mansion. The two had kept in close touch after the war, dining out frequently, exchanging letters on foreign policy issues, and sharing a love of books. Donovan would send Casey volumes he had read with notations on the pages. Casey reciprocated with his favorite books, except he rarely ever wrote in the margins.

Casey did not have the patience for notating. He once wrote a lengthy article on how to consume a nonfiction book "and save a lot of time." Casey usually read back to front, starting with the index and source notes to select what he thought he needed to know and to bypass the rest. With a photographic memory, he could retain passages almost verbatim of journal articles he seemed to be just flipping through; he would become incensed with subordinates who wasted his time in meetings repeating what they had written to him in lengthy memos many months earlier.

He had always made a bad first impression on others, even more so in middle age—tall and lumpy, with a jowly face, thick lips, eyes bulging, wisps of graying hair on his balding head, an expensive suit always rumpled, his tie often stained from what he had eaten for lunch, and frequently mumbling when he spoke as if he had marbles stuffed in his mouth. The acquaintances he made usually ended up being either lifelong friends who worshipped him or skeptics who could not escape an uneasy feeling that he was a devious operator working business or political deals they would rather know nothing about.

The slovenly appearance, however, covered a body constantly on the go, incapable of sitting down for a long talk over drinks. His mind was insatiably curious. On family vacations in Europe he would vacuum the timetable brochures at train stations and study them in his hotel room at night to recite from memory itineraries for his companions the next morning: "If you're travelling from Nice to Avignon on a Tuesday at 2 p.m. and miss your train, you'd have to wait for three hours for the next one to arrive at the station." Little did not interest him. On subjects remote from his daily life he would ask hundreds of questions. James Jolis, the son of a family friend, recalled Casey showing up out of the blue at a nightclub where his rock band was playing; after listening for a set, he walked backstage to interrogate him. "How does this band work?" Jolis recounted him asking. "How do you get paid? How do you store your equipment? In five minutes he had ascertained how to run a rock band better than I could."

As with Donovan, making millions in New York would never be as exciting or fulfilling for Casey as his war years with the OSS. Never again would he know such responsibility at such a young age, commanding scores of espionage agents sent to penetrate the Third Reich. His most cherished friendships had been formed in the general's organization. His proudest moments had been with the OSS. It was the high point of his life.

"He has gone from the scene of his success to meet his final judgment, his final reward, his final destiny . . ."

February 8, the day Donovan died and the first day of the Vietnamese celebration of the Tet New Year, William Colby stepped out of the Pan Am Stratocruiser into a blast furnace of heat at Saigon's Tan Son Nhut Airport. He was soon wilting in his drip-dry suit, bow tie, and polished shoes—although his only concession to Vietnam's perpetually broiling sun, which he made that day and for the next three years in the country, was to take off his jacket but keep his bow tie in place. Behind him, his wife, Barbara, herded their children, exhausted from the long flight. A CIA officer from the Saigon station shepherded the family through customs in the dirty, faded terminal and bundled them into a staff car. Colby was the new deputy chief of the CIA station, which numbered only forty at that point and was relegated mostly to collecting intelligence on the communist Viet Minh.

Barbara and the kids gazed out the automobile's windows as it sped quickly south on Ngo Dinh Khoi Road, which was lined with teeming squalid shanties interrupted occasionally by high-walled villas where the rich quarantined themselves. Across Saigon's boundary line, the road's name changed to Cong Ly, for "Justice," and more white- and cream-colored tropical houses for the wealthy appeared along the way. The heavily guarded homes reminded Colby of villas he'd seen in the south of France. But he looked up at them only briefly. The lengthy secret cable on his lap now consumed his attention. At the airport, he had been handed the urgent message that bore his first crisis—an informant the CIA had placed in Prince Norodom Sihanouk's army had been nabbed and the Cambodian leader was furious with the agency and the United States.

Past the former palace of the French governor general, now the residence of South Vietnam's strongman Ngo Dinh Diem, the CIA driver wheeled the staff car into the courtyard of Colby's new quarters, a high-ceilinged, French colonial-styled villa shaded by tall trees. Inside, the house was filled with servants bowing with their hands together as if praying. In the entrance hall on a table sat another cable, which Dulles had sent out to all his stations announcing that Donovan had died.

Barbara could see that Colby, who could be severe about keeping his emotions always in check, was grief-stricken. Before they had boarded a plane in Washington for their flight to Southeast Asia, they had visited Donovan at the Walter Reed Army Medical Center and had come away heartbroken. Donovan had spent the last seventeen months in the hospital dying slowly from arteriosclerotic atrophy of the brain, a severe form of dementia. Colby had served as one of Donovan's commandos in the OSS. The general treasured his special operations guerrillas who parachuted into enemy territory, as Colby had, to fight the Nazis. Colby's first job out of law school after the war had been in Donovan's firm as his assistant. Donovan took the couple to professional football games in New York on weekend afternoons and enjoyed flirting with Barbara at parties. Eventually bored with the law, Colby joined the CIA and traveled the world with Barbara and the kids as a covert operative. Donovan, who visited the family occasionally at their overseas posts, was the kind of warrior-intellectual that Colby wanted to be. His months behind enemy lines living by his wits as a paramilitary operative fighting the enemy had been exhilarating. He naturally gravitated to the covert operations side of the CIA where he believed the action was, fighting communism as he had Nazism with a sureness that his cause was righteous. Colby's secret world of espionage and sabotage, for all the dirty things that went on in it, was a pristine one in his mind.

When asked one time for his definition of the best kind of spy, Colby answered with the obvious: "The one you don't see." He looked like a man who could be overlooked—slightly built, pale dull eyes behind horn-rimmed glasses, his hair always parted neatly at the side. A private man, he could nevertheless be warm and friendly around friends and strangers. He was unfailingly polite with refined manners. He made a point of serving others drinks at parties, almost never uttered a mean-spirited or petty sentence, and rarely showed anger. He was not a frivolous man. He paid no attention to what he wore, repaired plumbing and performed carpentry work around the house. Yet he had what for him were his guilty pleasures. He enjoyed a good bottle of Sauvignon Blanc, drove a red Fiat sports car on weekends, loved to sail, and appreciated beautiful women (though there is no evidence he ever acted on what he noticed). He was intrigued by classical Greek and Roman heroes. He had three favorite movies: *Lawrence of Arabia* (Peter O'Toole's portrayal of one of his heroes, T. E. Lawrence), *The Bridge on the*

River Kwai (about a British colonel's misplaced loyalty), and *The Third Man* (a mystery written by Graham Greene). He told a family member he had never had a nightmare—never even dreamed for that matter.

His sons—he always called them "sport"—found his inner drive and courage intimidating. He never bragged about the combat he had seen in the OSS; only an occasional aside that let them know it had been intense at times. In fact, during the war he had been coolly analytical about its dangers, willing to take what he called "calculated risks." He kept his secret world carefully walled off from his family. And even inside the OSS and later the CIA, colleagues recalled Bill Colby as a dedicated soldier-priest, but a loner they never really knew. An informal poll once circulated among nearly sixty retired CIA officers with two questions. If you were shipwrecked on a pleasant deserted island with plenty of food and liquor "and every hope a ship would pass by," who would you choose to be with? Dulles won handily over Colby because he would be far better company while they were stranded. Second question: If you were stuck on a miserable deserted island with little food or hope for survival and you badly wanted to escape, who would you choose to be with? Colby easily led Dulles because he would know how to build a boat to get them off the island, one voter noted—and he would make sure the boat was big enough for two.

> *"Each of us has his purpose, fulfilled on Earth but planned by God for us, to carry out a human ministry. He who does well serves God and can look for God's reward."*

For all their differences in personality, a common thread ran between Allen Dulles, Richard Helms, William Casey, and William Colby. They were all smart—indeed, intellectuals in one sense because they were voracious readers, thoughtful, curious, and creatures of reason—but they were not the ivory tower types who would sit for long in doubtful introspection. These were strong, decisive, supremely confident men of action, doers who believed they could shape history rather than let it control them. They returned from World War II not emotionally drained or scarred by what they had experienced but rather invigorated and ready for the next battle. The OSS, which had interrupted their lives, now delineated them, they became regulars at postwar reunions of Donovan's agency, but they talked little about their OSS experience and preferred not to dwell in the past. They were always more interested in the future than in what they were doing at the moment or had done before.

Helms, Colby, and Casey would become CIA directors as Dulles was now. Eventually all four men would resign as controversy engulfed their agency. Dulles's downfall would come after the CIA debacle attempting to land anti-Castro guerrillas at Cuba's Bay of Pigs. Helms, always the loyal keeper of secrets, would later be convicted of lying to Congress over the CIA's role in the coup that ousted President Salvador Allende in Chile. Colby would become a pariah among old hands in the agency for releasing to Congress what became known as the "Family Jewels" report on CIA misdeeds during the 1950s, 1960s, and early 1970s. (Helms would reserve a special loathing for Colby because he also turned over to the Justice Department the evidence of Helms's perjury.) Casey would nearly bring down the CIA—and Ronald Reagan's presidency—from the scheme to secretly supply Nicaragua's contras with money raked off from the sale of arms to Iran in exchange for American hostages in Beirut.

But that would be in the future. On this chilly February morning in 1959, their thoughts were with the old man whose body lay in repose at St. Matthew's Cathedral and on the good war they had fought for him.

"May his soul rest in God's peace. And may those whom he has loved and the many whom he has served be worthy to know him again in the communion of saints."

PART ONE

PREPARATION

CHAPTER 1

ALLEN WELSH DULLES

He was born in Watertown, New York, on the morning of April 7, 1893, with congenital talipes equinovarus, commonly called a clubfoot. The medical profession since Hippocrates had treated the condition with slow mechanical pressure to bend the foot back out. With the advent of anesthesia doctors began surgically repairing the damage by the late 1860s. The parents found a Philadelphia orthopedist who successfully performed the operation on the baby. Even so, the family treated Allen Welsh Dulles's deformity at birth as a dark secret not to be revealed to outsiders.

Edith Foster Dulles had worried about having a third child. The births of John Foster in 1888 and Margaret just fifteen months later had been difficult and doctors had warned her a third might kill her. Edith, however, found celibacy unbearable; she delivered two more daughters after Allen—Eleanor in 1895 and Natalie in 1898. Though the births did weaken her and she suffered migraines and bouts of depression, Edith remained a determined and domineering woman, active in social work and fluent in French and Spanish. "She was a person who said, 'Now let's stop fussing around, and let's get this done,'" recalled Eleanor.

Edith Foster had been born during the Civil War into what became diplomatic aristocracy. Her father, John Watson Foster, rose from major in the 25th Indiana Volunteers to a field commander for the Battle of Shiloh and to a Union general on retirement. After the war, the tall, erect officer, with his billowy white muttonchops and Harvard law degree, became President Ulysses S. Grant's minister plenipotentiary to Mexico. More diplomatic postings followed—ambassador to the court of St. Petersburg under Tsar Alexander II in 1880, envoy to Spain in 1883. The family accompanied him overseas and Edith traveled throughout Latin America, Europe, and even Asia. In the waning months of Benjamin Harrison's administration, Foster, who had become known as the "handyman of the State Department," reached his pinnacle as secretary of state in 1892. He would not be the family's only one. Edith's sister Eleanor married Robert Lansing, a handsome lawyer-diplomat with a perpetually tanned face, who perfected an English accent, dressed like a dandy, and would become Woodrow Wilson's secretary of state in 1915.

The first time she met Allen Macy Dulles at a Paris soiree in 1881, Edith had not been terribly impressed by the slender young man, with his wide eyes and a soft boyish face, who had played on Princeton College's football team and just graduated from its theological seminary. Dulles, then twenty-six, fell instantly in love with the eighteen-year-old girl and spent the next five years resolutely courting Edith until she agreed to marry him in 1886. He could claim distinguished lineage as well. His mother's family had joined the Plymouth colony from the second voyage of the *Mayflower* in 1629. The ancestors of his father, Rev. John Welsh Dulles, fought in the Revolutionary War. One of seven children, Allen Macy had attended Philadelphia's Hastings Academy, whose harsh discipline his brothers worried would kill him. Allen Macy survived and later thrived at Princeton, where in addition to playing what was then considered the brutal game of football he sang tenor in the glee club, excelled in philosophy, and became president of the Nassau Bible Society. After graduating in 1875, he taught briefly in Princeton's prep school, then entered its seminary. He had been on a tour of Europe and the Middle East after graduation when he met Edith.

When he returned to America, Allen Macy Dulles was ordained by the Presbytery of Detroit and installed as pastor of the city's Trumbull Avenue church. A year after their marriage, he moved to Watertown, a fast-growing trade and industrial center near Lake Ontario in upstate New York, to be pastor of its more upscale First Presbyterian Church. He first installed his growing family into a white clapboard parsonage nearby on Clinton Street, and later built a roomier manse with long colonnades on Mullins Street, where the church was also located. Dulles was a contemplative, imaginative, and, for his times, a liberal minister. He spent hours in his third-floor study crafting tightly written sermons so they would last no more than twenty minutes. No souls were saved after that, he believed. Twice he was nearly expelled from the church, for officiating the marriage of a divorced woman and for publicly questioning the Virgin Birth. Though he never earned more than $3,500 a year to support a family of seven, he was generous to a fault, often letting the town drunk, when he was down on his luck, sleep in a room in the house.

His was a happy home. Children from other families in the congregation found it fun hanging out at the house of this warm-hearted religious man because it was so welcoming. His own children had contests to see who could sing the most hymns. Reverend Dulles required them to bring a pencil and pad to church every Sunday to take notes on his sermon. The kids did not find this an onerous chore. They took what they had scribbled to Sunday dinner to discuss the sermon; if what they had written was not clear, Allen Macy always blamed himself for delivering his message poorly.

The Dulles children were all "live wires," as one family member described them. Among the girls, Eleanor, who wore wire-rimmed glasses and usually had her nose buried in a book, was the intellectual dynamo. The oldest, John Foster, whom the family called Foster, had the strongest personality and an imperious look to him even as a boy. He was the leader of the five. Allie, which is what the family called his younger brother, was devoted to Foster and followed him everywhere when they were children.

Allie, who had his father's eyes and soft features, was obsessively curious about others around him. As a young boy he listened intently to adult conversations on domestic and foreign policy issues of the day and, when he could write, began jotting down notes on what he had heard. He also developed at an early age a fixation with making others like him—although his sister Eleanor noticed that the irresistible charm her brother displayed could be interrupted at times by overpowering rage.

John Watson Foster, who preferred to be addressed as "General" even as secretary of state, was always the dominating presence in the Dulles family.

In 1894, he built a red clapboard cottage for the clan with a circular porch that reached over the shore of Lake Ontario at a cove called Henderson Harbor. "Underbluff," his name for this simple house, had a large living room and kitchen with wood-burning stove, a tin bathtub for scrubbing the children, kerosene lamps for light, and a hand pump for water because it had no plumbing or electricity. Allie and the other kids loved this summer retreat, where they swam, sailed, and fished for smallmouth bass in the lake and crowded around John Watson along a long wooden bench at night to listen to his Civil War stories. The General doted on Allen Macy's children and "borrowed" each one of them to enjoy a winter season with him in Washington, when he could give the child a more sophisticated education than he thought his son-in-law could provide. He brought in tutors and governesses and allowed each grandchild to eavesdrop on the salons he hosted with the capital's powerful at his stately town house on 18th Street near other foreign embassies. Allen Macy came to resent these abductions, but Allie could not have been more excited when it was his turn. General Foster introduced him to foreign affairs.

At age eight, Allie made his grandfather a proud man. Listening to the debates in the General's dining room, the youngster had become interested in what was then a hot foreign policy topic in Washington circles—the second Boer War. It had erupted two years earlier when the British Empire attempted to wrest control of the pastoral Orange Free State and gold-rich Transvaal, two Boer republics in South Africa held by rebellious Dutch settlers. Britain's brutal tactics included a scorched-earth campaign to starve out guerrillas and the herding of civilians into concentration camps where thousands of women and children perished. The United States government remained neutral, but Americans became keenly interested in the far-off conflict with many joining each side to fight. Though his family backed the United Kingdom, Allie thought the British were taking unfair advantage of the Boers. Without telling the General he began clipping news articles, jotting down notes from what he heard at his grandfather's dinner table, and finally wrote in his childish scrawl a short book titled *The Boer War: A History.* "It was not right for the british to come in and get the land because the Boers came first and they had the first right to the land," Allie wrote, laying out his case for the settlers in seven chapters.

John Watson Foster sent the manuscript to a publisher, who corrected only a few of the misspelled words and printed seven hundred copies of the thirty-one-page book, which was sold for 50 cents a copy. (Allie donated the $1,000 he earned to the Boer Widows and Orphans Fund.) Newspapers around the country published stories on the eight-year-old author. "A most interesting little book," noted *The Washington Post*. The speaker of the house, who had seen a review in a Chicago paper, bought a copy. Edith was ecstatic—"We are very proud of our dear little boy," she wrote her son—and sold five copies to her friends. A more subdued Allen Macy, who considered the Boers "a noble, if perhaps mistaken, people," ordered Foster, who also sympathized with the British, not to argue the subject with his younger brother. Foster dutifully congratulated Allie on his book—although he told other family members he thought the volume was "infantile."

Two years after the publication of Allie's book, Reverend Dulles moved his family eighty miles south in 1904 to assume the chair of Theism and Apologetics at Auburn Theological Seminary. He had no intention of leaving the education of his children up to the General or to Auburn High School, which Allie attended. He hired a live-in governess to tutor all of them properly in Greek and Latin. Rather than memorizing the rules of grammar he wanted their hours of homework spent reading fine literature to soak up its style. And if he had to go hungry he would scrape up the money to send them abroad for their finishing school. Allie, who enjoyed history the most, was sent to live with family friends in Lausanne, Switzerland, to learn French (he broke away briefly with his father and Foster to climb the Diablerets in the Bernese Alps) and later to the cutting-edge École Alsacienne on the Rue Notre-Dames-des-Champs in Paris. His report card for the 1908–09 trimester noted that he had an "excellent intellectual and moral disposition," though he averaged no better than B– because of a low grade in French composition.

In the fall of 1910, Allie enrolled in his father's alma mater, Princeton. Its deeply discouraged president, Woodrow Wilson, had just been forced by the trustees to resign as he ran for governor of New Jersey—despite the reforms he had instituted to make the New Jersey school nationally on par with Harvard and Yale. Because of Wilson's energy, the Princeton Allie entered had seen its administration reorganized, the deadwood in its faculty replaced by academic stars, its curriculum revamped, admission standards hiked, and new Gothic-styled classroom buildings erected thanks to rejuvenated fund-raising. The seventeen-year-old at first showed no appreciation for the improved education he was receiving. Nearly six feet tall and beginning a mustache, Allie enjoyed playing tennis, chasing girls, shooting dice in the dorm, and spending weekends in New York enjoying musical comedies and champagne. His father grew furious with the mediocre report cards his son brought home. Allie finally buckled down his senior year, improving his grades enough to be elected to Phi Beta Kappa and graduating ninth in a class of ninety-four.

Much later in life, Allen Welsh Dulles would look back on June 1914 as the beginning of the path he took that eventually led to a career in intelligence. His class would be the last to graduate for some years into a peaceful world. Allie was offered a fellowship to remain at Princeton through 1915 but he considered it "a useless thing to wait around here another year," he wrote his father. He had also been offered a teaching job in India, which he decided to take, sailing east through Europe to see the world along the way. On June 20, he boarded the RMS *Olympic*, a grand-sized vessel with seven decks, four elevators, a squash court in the gym, an elegant restaurant called the Ritz, and plenty of college girls whom he quickly met. He arrived in Paris on June 28, checking into the Hôtel de l'Opéra. While sitting with Princeton friends at an outdoor café on the Avenue des Champs-Élysées his lazy Sunday afternoon was interrupted by newsboys hawking extras on the street with the headline that Archduke Franz Ferdinand and his wife had been assassinated in Sarajevo by a Serbian nationalist.

As Europe inched toward war, Allie took the train to Venice, then a boat to Trieste, where he boarded a steamer that carried him through the Suez Canal and the Red Sea and into the Arabian Sea. He reached Bombay on July 20 and checked into the elegant Taj Mahal Palace Hotel. (Young Dulles by then had acquired a taste for traveling in style, which he would not abandon for the rest of his life.) Three days later, after a comfortable ride in a first-class train car, Allie, dressed nattily in a cream-colored silk suit he bought in Bombay, finally arrived at his destination, dusty Allahabad in northeast India, to begin his job as an English teacher at Ewing Christian College.

He found a cobra curled up one time in the bathroom of his apartment, a large monkey hiding under his dining table, and the heat so oppressive he often slept outside under a mosquito net instead of in his bedroom. But the work at the missionary school, located on the banks of the Yamuna River near where it joined the Ganges, was easy. He awoke each day at 6 a.m. for toast and tea, studied Hindi until 10 a.m. when he had brunch, taught English classes to Indian teenagers from 11 a.m. to 4 p.m. using the works of Plato and Shakespeare as his texts, then after tea time he headed to the tennis courts for a couple of sets with the missionaries, and had his dinner dished out by his servant promptly at 8:30 p.m. He paid the servant $2.50 a month.

Allie found Allahabad's English newspaper to be one of the best he had ever read and by fall the paper was printing two editions a day with stories on Europe spinning out of control. A week after he had arrived in India, Austria-Hungary declared war on Serbia. Germany declared war on Russia on August 1 and on France two days later. After Germany invaded Belgium, the United Kingdom became a belligerent on August 4. Woodrow Wilson, who had assumed the presidency in 1913, announced that the United States would remain neutral. With the first Battle of the Marne in early September the two sides began grinding trench warfare that would see the slaughter of millions to gain what ultimately amounted to little territory over the next four years. Allie interviewed a wounded Sikh soldier returned to Allahabad from the Western Front who told him "the Germans couldn't shoot very well but were up to date with every mechanical device," he wrote his mother. In another letter to her, he worried that if the British began diverting too many of their colonial troops from India to the European theater "there might be trouble" in this colony from nationalists agitating for a break from the empire. Otherwise, the only impact the war had on him at this point was the discovery soon that his letters from America were being opened and read by British censors in Calcutta. It did not particularly bother him, except for the fact that the censors seemed to be slow readers, which meant the arrival of his mail was delayed for another week.

By December 1914, Allie planned to cut short his tenure at Ewing and return home early the next year. Although he admired the missionary college's noble work, he had decided he was not particularly good at teaching

English, a subject that interested him little. He was never sure how much of his lectures on Plato's *Apology* his students actually understood, "and I don't know much more about English syntax and parsing than they do," he admitted in a letter to his mother. With $160 in American and British gold coins, $300 in American Express checks, and a bank draft for 200 Chinese taels in his valise, Dulles set sail from India in mid-March 1915. He decided to travel east to complete his circumnavigation, stopping in Singapore, Hong Kong, Shanghai, Nanking, Peking, Seoul, Kobe, Kyoto, Yokohama, and Tokyo for sightseeing. He mailed home to his mother long travelogues with an eye for detail that an intelligence officer would appreciate. He also had his grandfather cable letters of introduction to the U.S. embassies along the way so he could meet their ambassadors. Sailing the Pacific on the SS *Manchuria*, he finally touched American soil in San Francisco toward the end of July.

Allie returned to Princeton for a year of postgraduate studies in international affairs, using the time more for agonizing over what he wanted to do with his life than preparing for academia. He tried out for a job at J. P. Morgan & Co. and after a day realized the investment bank wanted to make him a glorified clerk translating French contracts. When it was also clear to Morgan at the end of the day that this applicant could not type beyond hunting and pecking, a supervisor told him not to return. He toyed with a career in law "yet I have always rather fought against the idea as I don't like the technicalities and evasions which seem to be inevitably connected with it," he wrote his father. Allen Macy made no secret that he hoped his son would follow his footsteps and enter the ministry. General Foster and "Uncle Bert" (Allie's name for Robert Lansing, who had just become Wilson's secretary of state) had succeeded in talking him out of the clergy and nudging him toward the State Department. His father huffed that the diplomatic service was more an avocation than a respectable career.

Allie, who was not completely sold on the idea, told his father he saw no harm in taking the foreign service exam. If he passed, then he could decide whether he wanted to work in the State Department for a year or so. Allie took the test in April 1916 and had no trouble passing. His decision about what to do next was made easier by the alternative that would be forced on him if he did not join the diplomatic service. While at Princeton he had enlisted in the New Jersey National Guard. Simultaneously with the arrival of the letter telling him he had passed the foreign service exam came the notice that his Guard company was being deployed to the Mexican border to join General John "Black Jack" Pershing's Punitive Expedition hunting Pancho Villa, whose revolutionary band had been attacking Americans. Allie convinced his local draft board that he would be more valuable to the country as a diplomat than a ground soldier. He joined the State Department on May 22.

CHAPTER 2

WILLIAM JOSEPH CASEY

Bill Casey's ancestry mirrored Wild Bill Donovan's—a fact Casey was proud of in later years. His grandfather, George C. Casey, had landed in Queens, New York, in 1849 at age two, the son of a shoemaker who had escaped the poverty of Daingean in County Offaly, Ireland. Donovan's grandfather, Timothy, who was in his early twenties, ended up in Buffalo about the same time, a refugee from Skibbereen in Ireland's County Cork. Both were scrappy men. George Casey fought as a seaman in a Union gunboat during the Civil War and survived to open a saloon in Astoria, in the borough of Queens, which he called Casey's Place. Timothy became a scooper shoveling grain from the holds of ships at Buffalo's Lake Erie port and rail yard. Friday nights he could be found at his corner pub, although sipping only a ginger ale because he was a teetotaler.

The first of George Casey's three children, William Joseph, was born in 1882. Like Timothy Donovan's son Timothy Jr., who escaped the rail yard to become "lace curtain Irish" as a Buffalo cemetery secretary, William Joseph Casey had no intention of tending bar in his father's saloon. He worked his way up the Tammany Hall Democratic machine to finally land a supervisor's job in the borough's street cleaning department. A self-taught pianist, William Joseph also worked weekends in the theater playing the accompaniment when silent movies arrived.

Blanche A. Le Vigne, who was six years younger than William Joseph, had arrived in New York from Ontario, where her French Canadian father had worked as a chef. She was shy and deferential toward others, but a stylish dresser who loved to travel and who knew enough about fashion to rise from sales clerk to comparison shopper for the May Department Stores Company. Blanche met William Joseph while roaming New York City's department stores to check if May's prices were competitive. The two married in 1910 and moved from Astoria to Queens's more upscale Elmhurst neighborhood, which was almost exclusively Jewish and Italian save for the few Irish interlopers like the Caseys.

Blanche delivered her first baby three years later on March 13, 1913, setting a family record she would have preferred not to have set. The boy arrived weighing a staggering fourteen pounds. They named him William Joseph after his father. (The family and son, however, would never attach "Jr." to the end of his name.) A little more than a fortnight later, baby William, whose bright blue eyes at birth remained that color the rest of his life, was baptized at the Church of Our Lady of Sorrows in nearby Corona.

Whereas the Dulles family orbited around Presbyterianism and the Republican Party, the center for the Casey family was Roman Catholicism and the Democratic Party. The next five years, Blanche delivered Dorothy, then George. A fourth baby survived only a day. Just as the Dulles siblings did with Foster, Dorothy and George looked up to Bill, who in later years would pay for George's college. By 1920, William Joseph had made another important move up the Tammany Hall ranks, assigned to organize and help manage New York City's pension system. He bought a Model T Ford and moved the family once more, this time to the southern shore of Queens and into an even nicer Dutch colonial on Midwood Avenue in the Bellmore neighborhood. Young Bill took the bus to St. Agnes School just west in Rockville Centre, where he scored high enough on his placement test to skip a grade and enter the eighth grade at age twelve. Every Sunday he made his parents even prouder serving as an altar boy at ten o'clock mass.

He was a bright child, but early on determined to educate himself as he saw fit. He hated the St. Agnes nuns who taught him and they became infuriated with him when he acted smart-alecky. His Latin teacher once halted class when she thought she had caught him not paying attention and announced: "Mister Casey, what did I just say?" Casey stood up and smugly recited her lecture practically word for word. The dime he was given each Saturday for the movies he usually took to a bookstore to buy a book. He said it would give him far more enjoyment than a one-hour film. The bookstore owner complained that he spent his Saturday hour in the shop pawing through the pages of many books before deciding on the one to buy. He would return home and Blanche would serve him bread and butter for a snack as he perused his purchase. Casey never lost his love of buying books, but he came to hate bread and butter because he had it so many Saturday afternoons.

St. Agnes had no sports program, so Casey's parents agreed to move him to Baldwin High, a public school that did. Casey was in love with baseball, although he was far better at remembering the statistics of professional players than at actually playing the game. By age sixteen, he had grown six feet tall, but it was a gangling and totally uncoordinated six feet, with no physical gift for athletics, only determination. His teammates called Casey "Cyclone" because he did hustle, even though his fielding, throwing, and hitting were subpar. He could barely utter a sentence in front of a girl because he was so shy. Friends also found that Casey had a hot temper. He pummeled an Italian boy who called him a "mick bookworm" in the cafeteria. He was fired from a summer job with the Long Island State Park Commission when he was seventeen after he cussed out a nurse who worked there. Different stories circulated about what caused his mumbling. One held that it started after he was punched in the neck during a boxing match, which damaged his throat muscles. Another: that the damage to his throat came after being hit with a baseball. Later in 1941, doctors cauterized a growth inside his nose, which they thought might be impairing his speaking voice.

Originally known as St. John's College, Fordham University had been founded in the Bronx by the Archdiocese of New York in 1841—the first Catholic school of higher education in the Northeast, established primarily to train priests. Edgar Allan Poe had lived a few blocks from Fordham on the Grand Concourse, striking up a friendship with the Jesuits who ran the school—his 1845 poem "The Bells" is believed to have been inspired by the bells of the university church. In September of 1930, the intellectual turmoil of communism, socialism, and other isms sweeping through

American colleges had been kept at bay from Fordham's gated campus with its close-cropped lawns, bricked paths, gray fieldstone buildings, and Jesuit rectitude. It suited Bill Casey, who enrolled in Fordham that month and found the Jesuits' self-assurance and rationale for Catholicism an anchor in the moral turbulence he saw around him. The first in his family to attend college, Casey commuted from home and worked part-time to pay for what his scholarship did not. One of his jobs to make money was not particularly ethical—writing term papers for other students.

He thought he wanted to be a doctor. His first semester of biology, which he almost flunked, disabused him of that notion, particularly after he gagged dissecting a cat. Instead, Casey majored in philosophy and science but he proved to be a harder partier than studier. Though Prohibition was still in force, he managed to find the booze to get roaring drunk on weekends and wake up the next morning not remembering what he had done the night before. His grades were erratic the first three years—As in physics and religion, Ds in English and French. He ran track and cross-country but gave them up at the end of his sophomore year. His only brush after that with athletics came his senior year when he won a position in the university's powerful Athletic Association, which set rules for student participation in sports. He campaigned in that election "using real high pressure methods," he admitted.

His freshman year, Casey met the girl who would eventually tame him into being a responsible student, although it would take her more than three years. Sophia Kurz (she pronounced her first name "Soph-eye-a") was the oldest of eight children of Henry Kurz, an Alsatian American who had been a successful Long Island builder until he lost his money in the stock market crash of 1929, and Mary MacCadden, a Brooklyn girl whose parents had emigrated from Rathowen, Ireland. Sophia, who had been born in Brooklyn a year after Casey, was working as an telephone operator on Long Island when two Fordham men arrived one weekend in 1930 at the family's home in West Hempstead. Casey had borrowed his father's Model T to drive him and a classmate to the Kurz house, where his buddy promised there would be other girls besides the one he was dating, Sophia's sister Loretta.

When Casey met Sophia, it was as if he had been smacked in the throat again and couldn't give voice to a complete sentence. She was petite with an angelic face, short brown hair with curly locks that drooped over her fore-head, and a gentle inviting manner that had her many other suitors babbling their hearts out to her within minutes. Soon Casey was showing up at the West Hempstead home practically every weekend for card parties—taking tea and sugared toast with Sophia in the living room and occasionally walk-ing down to the basement with her father where Henry Kurz kept a still and offered Bill a nip from his latest batch of liquor.

By his junior year, Casey worshipped Sophia. He begged her to take Sat-urdays off from the phone company so she could be with him at Fordham. He called her "Toots" and with her encouragement began dressing sharper. "All my actions," he wrote her, "can be traced, in the ultimate analysis, to you." He worried constantly that he was smothering her with attention and she was too polite to tell him to back off. He tried not to interrupt conversa-tions she was having with others when he walked up, for fear of appearing possessive. "You are so darn good I feel like a dog for taking advantage of your goodness," he wrote. By the fall semester of his senior year, Bill Casey was hopelessly in love. "The more I think of you the more highly I regard you," he wrote her in another love note with stiff prose. "Toots, I think your face is beautiful not because of any harmonious physical configuration, although that is present, but because there seems to be a beautiful sympa-thetic, understanding, saintly light shining from it."

Their courtship had its rocky moments. Sophia, who went to mass every morning, was indeed a kind and gentle soul, but it masked a steely will and she did not appreciate a suitor with a wild streak who got drunk on a date and stumbled off her front porch, as Casey once did. He was always pro-fusely sorry when he'd had too much to drink or when he ignored her or was inconsiderate or argued with her—although he thought Sophia could be "super sensitive" at times. Usually after a short period of moping from one of their spats, Casey would grovel for forgiveness. "Whenever I have the slightest disagreement with you, Toots, I am utterly miserable for days," he wrote in one of numerous apologetic notes. "The realization that I am invariably at fault and that anybody, who finds trouble in getting along with a person of your affable and easy going disposition, must be unbalanced somewhere, inflicts on me torments which make me suffer more than any physical punishment which I can imagine."

Casey's grades improved to As and Bs during his senior year. He joined the debate team, impressing the coach with his ability to assemble facts to bolster his arguments but not with his mumbled delivery. He practiced against his roommate and boozing pal, Cornelius "Red" Cassidy, a liberal who usually bested him with polished elocution rather than facts, Casey thought. Red "is the most pigheaded individual I have ever come across," he complained to Sophia. "He has opinions about everything and he understands nothing." In June 1934, Casey graduated cum laude from Fordham.

No doubt influenced by his father's work in New York, Casey had become interested in the social sciences and had taken four education and psychology courses during his last semester at Fordham. He had been captivated by Edward M. House's memoir and told a friend he wanted one day to be a key White House aide behind the scenes whispering advice into a president's ear on public policy as Colonel House had once been for Woodrow Wilson. After graduation, Casey screwed up his courage and told his father he would not remain in the city and find a job, as the family wanted him to. He was moving to Washington, D.C., to pursue a master's degree in social work through a fellowship he had won from Catholic University of America. "I want to dedicate my life to remedying the crying injustices of our blind economic and social system," he declared to Sophia.

Casey arrived in the District of Columbia in the fall of 1934, with a somewhat racist delusion that it would be a capital with folks just like him and "composed of splendid white structures and rolling lawns plus a few Japanese cherry trees," he wrote Sophia. He had never pictured in his mind a city still wracked by the Depression and filled with African Americans, rows of tenement houses, and gin joints. Nevertheless, Casey believed he would enjoy Catholic University's new School of Social Work, which had attracted students from all over the country, most of them priests. The new dean of the school, located off Michigan Avenue in northeast Washington, was Father John O'Grady, a learned gentleman, Casey thought, who had written many books on social work. Even so, Casey was embarrassed to have friends in New York know that he was attending a school of social work, fearing it might appear to be an unmanly course of study, so he instead told them he was working on a master's degree in sociology.

He was also disappointed in his first semester of classes, considering many of them—such as social casework and child welfare—"sissy stuff." He was more interested in courses on industrial ethics to improve the workplace environment or classes on gentrification "to alleviate poverty, spread the population and clear slums," he said. He soon found pleasurable diversions in Washington, such as cheap beer that he could wash down from a huge mug for just 10 cents and tennis courts at the university where he was learning to play. (After a few lessons, he thought he already had a fierce backhand.)

Casey missed Sophia terribly. He wrote her long newsy letters and was crushed when she replied with only short notes. Every weekend that he could break free, he took the overnight bus on Fridays to New York, arriving the next morning sleepless yet overjoyed to be with his girlfriend. They crammed as much as they could into their Saturdays—one time a "heavenly evening," according to Casey, dancing at a club to Guy Lombardo's band. Or they just sat all day holding hands in a movie house. Casey fashioned himself a film critic. "They used to figure that a liberal supply of smutty cracks plus a bedroom scene or two was all the public wanted," he said of Hollywood. "They neglected the dramatic qualities of their productions." Sunday mornings he climbed back on the bus, in a grumpy mood, for the long trip back to D.C.

Among the innovative programs Father O'Grady instituted for the new school: having the graduate students live at Washington's public welfare institutions to appreciate the plight of the poor. It had the opposite effect on Casey. He was assigned to the National Training School on Bladensburg Road, which housed juveniles convicted of federal crimes. They were hardly juveniles, Casey thought, but rather a bunch "of young Dillingers," he wrote Sophia. From now on, he sarcastically told her, his letters would be filled with "real good" news of "negroes, bloodhounds, guards, sirens, etc."

By the beginning of 1935, Casey had begun to hate Washington and the fact that he was so far from Sophia. Because of a heavy class load and the time he had to spend with what he soon began calling the "brats" at the National Training School, it was six to eight weeks between visits to her in New York. He started drinking hard liquor heavily and alone at Washington bars. He began to grow disillusioned with Catholic University as well. He had begun reading books about the quarter million minors roaming the country homeless during the Depression and had interviewed many who were now adult hobos passing through Washington and whose "outlook on life is desolate and hopeless," he wrote Sophia. "They might as well be dead for all they can look ahead to is a pint of Bay Rum at sixteen cents a bottle. . . . A social and economic system that permits such conditions is positively immoral and indefensible." Yet he rejected communism, socialism, or fascism as alternatives and was opposed to liberal utopian notions of a welfare state that would redistribute income to the poor, particularly the undeserving poor. Casey had no objections to a class system in America based on wealth that had been earned through hard work. "Perhaps depressions, etc., are not entirely bad," he opined in one letter. "They sober a frivolous world."

Casey tried to remain dutiful in his class work because he really did admire the professors Father O'Grady had recruited to teach the graduate courses. But by the end of spring 1935 his grades began to drop as he skipped classes for longer weekends with Sophia in New York. He also spent more afternoons watching sessions of Congress, which he thought were "a riot," or the Supreme Court, which he thought had far more "magnificent minds." It took Casey several visits to O'Grady's office before he finally summoned the courage to break the news to the dean that he would not return for the fall semester. He was moving back to New York to take a job in the city's welfare department.

He began his New York assignment as an investigator in July. It paid $1,620 a year. His job was to audit case files and make spot visits to the homes of recipients to ensure they deserved the financial assistance they were receiving. It didn't take Casey long before he hated the work. Even when the paperwork was in order, he often thought New York's welfare money was being wasted. He came to view the hard-core poor as mostly cheats and loafers and to despise Roosevelt as a bleeding-heart liberal, whose New Deal Casey deemed out of control. By fall he had joined the Bellmore Republican Club and soon began campaigning against Roosevelt's reelection. His father, who was an ardent New Dealer, did not live to see his son reject all he believed in and embrace Republican conservatism. William Joseph senior died of a heart attack on October 27, at the relatively young age of fifty-three.

Casey's visits to the Supreme Court had made an impression on him. With a law degree he could do anything, he thought. It would open doors to careers far more interesting and high-paying than being a welfare cop. So simultaneously with joining New York's welfare department Casey enrolled in night classes at St. John's Law School in Brooklyn. He had to learn to budget his time, working a full day in the welfare office and spending nights and weekends attending class or studying. He mastered speed-reading his law books. Even so, his grades at St. John's were mediocre. He never scored higher than a B and even received a D in his class on mortgages. Yet he managed to graduate in a little more than two years.

After clerking in a New York law firm for seven months to learn how a partnership was set up, Casey formed his own with three other young attorneys. They took on tax and labor relations cases and Casey made as much as $6,000 annually—a hefty sum considering the practice soon became part-time work to a day job that would eventually pay him twice that at $12,000 a year. The Research Institute of America cranked out analytical reports to help businessmen land federal contracts among the hundreds of New Deal programs Roosevelt had launched. The institute, which had been started in 1936, soon developed a reputation for producing studies so accurate and chock-full of insider information about programs such as Social Security and the Works Progress Administration that customers believed RIA was a secret arm of FDR's administration. It was not. RIA just had dogged investigators talented at digging into federal programs to produce clear-eyed forecasts of where lucrative contracts lay.

The institute was run by Leo Cherne, the son of Russian émigrés, who had graduated at the top of his New York Law School class and was barely a year older than Casey. Shorthanded at the time, Cherne had placed a help-wanted ad in a law journal and Casey had walked in to interview for a job. Cherne was impressed. Behind his thick New York accent, Casey seemed to Cherne to have the makings of an intellectual, so he hired him to be a tax analyst for one of RIA's publications. Casey knew little about the subject but proved to be a quick study and adept at boiling down complex tax code into concise, readable paragraphs that businessmen could understand. Cherne's operation soon expanded to both New York and Washington offices filled with more than four hundred researchers, whose personal politics ranged from socialists on the left to Republicans like Casey on the right. Office debates between Casey and RIA's liberals usually devolved into shouting matches. Casey, who would back Wendell Willkie in the 1940 presidential race, often went lively rounds with Cherne, a Roosevelt admirer. "I would win the debates," Casey later insisted, "but Leo always won the election."

By spring 1939, Cherne and RIA's other managers were convinced there would be war in Europe, and the United States would inevitably be drawn into it. William Donovan, who was a prominent Wall Street attorney and outspoken member of the Republican Party's internationalist wing, believed the same and backed the defense buildup Roosevelt was beginning. Cherne had sent Casey to Washington to open RIA's office there and to start collecting data on war production requirements that industry would be called on to fulfill. He soon was overseeing a staff of sixty analysts and editing the *Business and Defense Coordinator*, a dense RIA publication on contract regulations for weapons programs with such chapters as "How to Sell to the Army" and "What the Medical Corps Buys." Casey quickly became a key number cruncher on business opportunities in the buildup, with a wide range of contacts in Washington's growing military-industrial community. Government officials began phoning him for advice on how to simplify complex weapons procurement rules to make them more business friendly and to speed up the delivery of arms from assembly lines. Word of Casey's *Business and Defense Coordinator* came to the attention of Donovan, a New York friend of Cherne's and soon a behind-the-scenes adviser to Roosevelt on war matériel Great Britain needed from America.

The work Casey was performing may have been arcane and designed primarily to help businesses turn a war buck. But it was hugely important for the country. The day Germany invaded Poland on September 1, 1939, which also happened to be the day Casey's *Business and Defense Coordinator* was released, the United States Army was only the seventeenth largest in the world, just below Romania's. Washington soon faced a monumental job reorganizing practically the entire U.S. economy so it would begin producing more tanks, planes, and warships than washers, sewing machines, and Chevrolets. Mobilizing American business and fitting all its pieces together into a powerful and efficient war machine, as he was helping to do, would be key to an eventual Allied victory. But if the United States joined the fighting in Europe, Bill Casey did not intend to remain in Washington pushing paper.

CHAPTER 3

RICHARD McGARRAH HELMS

Richard McGarrah Helms was born in St. Davids, Pennsylvania, a small town on the Main Line fifteen miles out of Philadelphia. He arrived shortly after noon on March 30, 1913—a little more than two weeks after Bill Casey. Any similarity in the early years of the two boys ended there.

The baby's middle name came from his maternal grandfather, Gates Mc-Garrah, as towering a presence in the Helms family as John Watson Foster was for the Dulleses. Tall and rotund with a close-cropped mustache and an oval face, McGarrah started as an eighteen-year-old clerk in the Goshen, New York, National Bank. He moved to New York City in 1883 to work in the teller's cage of the Produce Exchange National Bank. By his late thirties, McGarrah had risen to president of the Leather Manufacturers' National Bank—one of the youngest chief executives of a major financial institution in the United States. He built a grand mansion at the southwest tip of Cape Cod near Martha's Vineyard and soon would be named the first chairman of the Federal Reserve Bank in New York, with *Time* magazine calling him "Magnificent McGarrah." From then on the family would call him "Governor."

McGarrah was not pleased when the younger of his two daughters, twenty-year-old Marion, announced in early 1910 that she had accepted a marriage proposal from Herman Helms, who was six years older. The tycoon suspected the young man was just after his money. His full name was Herman Heinrich Adolf Helms, the son of a middle-class German Lutheran family, which had emigrated to the United States from a village near Bremen. Herman anglicized Heinrich to Henry and dropped the "Adolf" in the 1930s when it became practically a dirty word because of the Nazi dictator. An austere man who loved opera, Helms was an attentive yet stern father to Richard. He possessed a Germanic obsession with order and structure—to the point of insisting that the vegetables, potatoes, and meat he ate at meals be served on separate plates. Herman was also a manic-depressive who would lie by himself in rooms with the shades drawn and later write darkly introspective letters to his oldest son. Richard would say after his father died only that "he was a fair man." He did not attend his funeral.

Herman, who had become a mechanical engineer, clearly had married above his social rank. Marion McGarrah was a warm, fun-loving, and gregarious woman who had not let wealth spoil her caring nature. She also would suffer from bipolar disease, but did her best to keep the depression hidden from her children, occasionally checking herself into the Silver Hill psychiatric hospital in Connecticut to have nervous breakdowns treated. Richard, who became far closer to Marion than to Herman, struggled as a young boy to understand this mysterious illness no one talked about but had his mother missing for periods.

Two years after Richard was born, Herman moved the family to nearby Merion, where they remained while he served as an Army captain during World War I. As the war neared its end, they moved once more, to New York City, where Richard entered first grade at the private Lawrence Smith School. By then, two more siblings had arrived: Elizabeth in 1915, whom the family nicknamed "Bets," and Pearsall in 1917, whose nickname was "Pear." Marion would have her fourth child in 1924—Gates, named after her father, whom the other children called "Wuz." As if they were quadruplets, Dick (whom the family called Richard) and his siblings shared the same personality and many of the same mannerisms (each, for example, always kept a hand over the cheek when reading a book). They also became close to one another as they grew up—forced to because constant moves often left them with few outside friends.

In 1919, Herman relocated the family once more, this time to South Orange, a New Jersey village whose spacious homes on large lots had become a refuge for New Yorkers escaping cramped apartments. Herman moved there to be closer to his job in Newark with Alcoa, the Aluminum Company of America, where he worked as a district manager. More of his income, however, was soon coming from the stock market, thanks to his wife's fortune that he had available to invest and to shrewd trading helped by tips from his father-in-law.

Later in life, Richard Helms would say that his childhood had groomed him to be a spy. Perhaps. He was a loner as a young boy, inclined often to do strange things, like taking the train to attend dog shows—although he never wanted to own a dog. Though he respected his father he idolized his grandfather, who had the family spend summers with him at his Woods Hole retreat on Cape Cod, next to a mansion owned by the Mellon family. Gates McGarrah, who treated Dick practically as an equal as he grew into a teenager, encouraged his interest in international affairs.

His year at Lawrence Smith prepped him well for his second private school, Carteret Academy in West Orange, which was a half hour bike ride for him from the family's home on Tillow Road. Dick was allowed to skip a grade and enter the exclusive school as a third grader. He remained at Carteret until his junior year of high school. Except for Latin, his grades were excellent, but he was too skinny for football and thought he'd be killed by an errant puck as hockey goalie, so he settled for team manager.

In the spring of 1929, Herman quit his Alcoa job and bundled his family aboard the SS *Lapland* to spend a year in Europe. For a quality education, the children must be exposed to cultures abroad and receive a solid grounding in French and German, their father believed. Probably due more to blind luck than prescience, Herman cashed out his stocks and closed his margin account five months before the market crashed. Dick was enrolled that fall in Le Rosey, an avant-garde and pricey boarding school founded in 1880 in a medieval château near Rolle, Switzerland, to provide children of the world's wealthy a rounded education in academics, the arts, and sports. Young Helms, who attended Le Rosey through June of 1930, had to cram to keep up with the other students. He scored high in German and French, much lower in geometry. His Swiss roommate, a future diplomat for his country named Jacques Mallet, helped him with French in return for Helms tutoring Mallet in English. Helms played goalie on the soccer team and crewed a four-man rowing shell on Lake Geneva. During the winter months the school relocated to a fashionable Gstaad resort in the canton of Bern so Dick and the other students could perfect their skiing.

His year at Le Rosey made him a far more cosmopolitan young man with close friendships struck among boys who stood to inherit fortunes far larger than he ever would. "Living in a different environment and with people of other nationalities develops a side of one's personality which is usually neglected or underdeveloped, namely that of perspective," he wrote his brother, Wuz. Le Rosey also enabled Dick to grow closer to the Governor. In 1930 Gates McGarrah had been named the first president of the Bank of International Settlements and had moved to Basel, where the secretive financial institution was housed in a former hotel. The BIS had been set up to manage the onerous reparations payments forced on Germany after World War I, but soon evolved into a clearinghouse where the world's central bankers could deposit gold and convertible currencies for settling international payments without having to move the funds between countries. The central bankers' bank also intended to bring order to the growing international financial crisis. It proved largely a failure on both counts: the Nazis would successfully undermine BIS to weasel out of reparations payments and the bank was too small to impose financial stability in the world depression. While at Le Rosey, Dick began a lively correspondence with McGarrah, who shared with him confidential details on BIS's operations along with his private pessimism about the organization succeeding in its mission. (McGarrah did become enchanted with the new Nazi regime, which seemed to him "pretty smart" at restoring financial discipline to Germany.) Dick, whom McGarrah trusted not to divulge his secrets, was proud of his grandfather and mailed him letters with news clippings he collected on the Governor. McGarrah's notes sparked an interest in world finance that would stay with his grandson for the rest of his life.

Henry moved his family back to the United States in the summer of 1930, but quickly discovered the Depression had dried up job prospects there, so they all returned to Europe, settling this time in Freiburg im Breisgau, a university town on the western edge of the scenic Black Forest in southern Germany. That fall Richard enrolled as a guest student in the Realgymnasium for what in effect was a junior year of high school. "Education in the Weimar Republic was a dead serious activity," Helms wrote later. There was little time for sports or extracurricular activities. Students attended classes nonstop morning until late afternoon and spent their evenings and nights studying for the next day. The coursework was far too advanced for the young American, but Helms at least mastered German during the year. Herman also hired an affable Freiburg academician to tutor his son in Latin, a required language for college when he returned to the United States. The old professor, always formally clad in tailcoat, knew enough English to understand Richard's translations of Virgil's *Aeneid*. He delivered his corrections in French, which both of them spoke well.

On a family trip to Italy during his Easter recess in 1931, Richard contracted a virulent case of chicken pox. To protect his family from what was a serious disease in those days he was packed off to the Governor's home in Basel and quarantined in a bedroom. So he wouldn't infect his grandparents walking by them, a ladder was installed from his window to the garden for when he wanted to venture outside. Helms managed to put his time bedridden and itching to good use, reading textbooks for the European history examination he also had to pass to enter college that fall.

Herman and Marion wanted Richard to go to Princeton. He thought that university too close to the home in New Jersey, to which the family had returned. Helms instead chose, sight unseen, Williams College, one of the "Little Ivies" nestled in the Berkshires of northwestern Massachusetts at the village of Williamstown. The loner from grade school was now a tall, strikingly handsome, meticulously groomed young man, and soon the "undisputed monarch of the campus" with many girlfriends, as a college magazine article described him. During his four years at Williams, Helms became editor of his college newspaper and yearbook, class orator and president, the leader of his fraternity and the school's elite Gargoyle Society, and a member of Phi Beta Kappa.

Classmates were struck by qualities in Helms that he would later find useful as a spy—"an unparalleled ability," the magazine article noted, not to irritate anybody. "He has the knack of giving his allies a mental slap on the back without so much as raising his voice and with his invariably disgruntled opponents he has the popular bedside manner, cooling them off and soothing them." Helms also worked his charms with school administrators, talking them into letting him have a major that combined English literature and history—unheard of at the time. With T. C. Smith, a favorite history professor and biographer of President James A. Garfield, Helms took what he later believed was his "first small step" on his path toward a career in intelligence. Smith instructed his students with what Helms called the "problem method," posing a "historical episode" and having them troop to the library to read "sources on both sides" of the issue to decide on their own the best course of action.

After graduating magna cum laude—and voted by his classmates "most respected," "most likely to succeed," "class politician," and the student "who has done the most for Williams"—Helms, with a head somewhat swollen, applied for a Rhodes Scholarship. Thinking he was a shoo-in, he didn't bother to prep for the interview. He was not awarded the scholarship. It taught him a valuable lesson. Never again would he walk into any situation unprepared.

The two paths he now considered after the Rhodes rejection were Harvard Law School (a Williams graduate with his grades would have no trouble being accepted) or journalism. Helms chose journalism. Owning a newspaper one day might be nice, he thought. A fraternity brother's father, who was a top Scripps Howard executive, whetted his interest in the business. United Press offered him a job in its London bureau if he could pay his own way to England. Herman paid for his cruise line ticket as a graduation gift.

Helms arrived in London on September 17, 1935, and checked into the Raglan Hotel on Upper Bedford Place. The United Press office in the News of the World building on Bouverie Street a dozen blocks away was frenetic with activity. Helms was put to work immediately, updating obituaries on celebrities, scanning London papers for "brighteners" (feel-good stories he could boil down to fill small news holes in American papers), and fielding phone calls on the news desk from European correspondents. He picked up the line one morning and an Italian clerk in the Rome bureau blurted: "Flash! Webb Miller reports the Italian Army invaded Abyssinia today." This was heady journalism, he thought.

But the thrill would not last long in London. The British Home Office did not look kindly on foreigners taking jobs that could be filled by its citizens and in late November summarily ordered Helms out of the country within three days. United Press decided to transfer their eager cub reporter to Berlin with a hike in his weekly salary to $35 to cover the amount he would lose converting his paycheck to marks. "This all sounds brutal, but not meant that way," his London boss told him. "You're a real Unipresser, and for good if you continue as you have been going." The Berlin bureau was eager to have the extra body. "And, by the way, how is your German?" his boss asked.

Throughout the Roaring Twenties and early 1930s, Berlin was the city Europeans flocked to for culture, the arts, concerts, nightlife, films, theater, and sex. It had sixteen thousand bars, coffee shops, and dance halls, more than nine hundred dance bands, eight hundred dramatists and authors, 149 newspapers, and four hundred magazines. Cabarets flourished. Garden theaters were jammed with smokers. Aeroplane racing was popular. Nude sunbathing was the rage and many of the most upscale clubs staged topless reviews.

Adolf Hitler was as contemptuous of the city's freewheeling ways as Berlin's sophisticates were of this provincial rabble-rouser. After he was appointed Reich chancellor on January 30, 1933, the city was emptied of its best actors, movie technicians, film producers, writers, and directors. Museums were closed, books burned, the 149 newspapers shut down. The Nazis censored all forms of entertainment, banned Jewish composers, and frowned on jazz. Berlin became a schizophrenic city. For the party faithful or those who did not ask questions prosperity reigned. Restaurants remained full, movie houses flourished with propaganda films, light comedies and some operettas were allowed, grand hotels hosted swanky parties for Nazis with government-approved starlets hanging on to them, and cabarets whose acts did not insult National Socialism continued to flourish. For those who did not fit the Nazi mold, there was terror.

Foreign diplomats and saner German heads could not imagine that Hitler and his gang would survive for long. It was wishful thinking. The fact that up to 40 percent of Germans voted for a lawless demagogue in 1933 demonstrated that a large part of the nation's population was infected with violent nationalism. During the next two years industrial production doubled, the country's colossal unemployment dropped thanks to massive public works projects, production of consumer goods shot up, the hated reparations payments from World War I were ended, rearmament was accelerated, and German pride had been restored. Hitler cleansed the nation of independent political parties, clubs, and societies. Dissidents within his own ranks, the Sturmabteilung (SA), were crushed in a bloody purge on June 30, 1934, which saw at least one thousand SA storm troopers and assorted other political dissidents murdered in the Night of the Long Knives.

By the time Helms arrived in Germany near Thanksgiving 1935, Adolf Hitler was wildly popular, mobbed wherever he went with women screaming like teenagers. Berlin was a city of more than four million, all its citizens seeming to rush along sidewalks, full of nervous energy. He found the metropolis he had left five years earlier almost sterile in its cleanliness and still laced by rivers, lakes, parks, and forests with wild game. Berlin's industrial districts, crammed with aging apartment blocks for workers, still ringed an imposing city center with buildings no taller than five stories, the Tiergarten zoo the size of New York's Central Park, the majestic Brandenburg Gate, and the mile-long Unter den Linden, a wide avenue lined on each side with exclusive shops, cafés, luxury hotels, corporate headquarters, and Baroque structures built centuries earlier. Hitler, who believed Berlin was still "nothing but an unregulated accumulation of buildings," was now intent on making it the premier capital of the world. He had appointed his young architect Albert Speer to renew the city with grand building plans and a new name, "Germania."

Helms found a one-room apartment at Bayreutherstrasse 34 near Wittenbergplatz, a major shopping square in western Berlin with the huge Kaufhaus des Westens (Department Store of the West). He paid 65 reichsmarks a month in rent and ate out most every night at an Italian restaurant, Die Taverna, which other correspondents enjoyed, or at a café around the corner from his apartment, which served cheap beer and borscht. Wittenbergplatz also had one of Berlin's oldest U-Bahn stations, whose subway Helms hopped on each morning for the ride to the United Press office on Unter den Linden.

Its bureau chief was Frederick Oechsner, a thirty-three-year-old veteran newsman from New Orleans who earned a law degree from Tulane University, spent most of the last decade reporting in Europe, and spoke three other languages besides German. Helms became fascinated with the cast of colorful characters working under Oechsner. They included Edward Beattie, a heavyset, cynically irreverent foreign correspondent who enjoyed fine dining and expensive wines, and Paul Kecskemeti, a small, hunched-backed Hungarian Jew who could translate Hitler's speeches as fast as the führer said the words and wrote treatises on mathematical logic in his spare time. Oechsner handed Helms small assignments at first: translating German speeches and documents to be cabled to UP's important clients in Latin America, rewriting articles in the Nazi-controlled press if they contained important policy statements, covering award ceremonies and funerals for German generals. Helms needed the seasoning. Naively, he at first thought that not much had changed in Berlin since he was there as a student five years earlier. Gradually it dawned on him that the Germans had become frosty to foreigners, less willing to chat with him informally. His social life, therefore, was confined to the American community in Berlin—the diplomats in the U.S. embassy and other foreign correspondents who covered Hitler.

The best in the news business had come to Berlin—like the savvy H. R. "Red" Knickerbocker of the *New York Evening Post*, the well-traveled Ralph Barnes of the *New York Herald Tribune*, and Louis Lochner, the Associated Press bureau chief and dean of the city's foreign press corps. Young Helms was thrilled to be mingling among them. William Shirer, Universal News Service's aggressive correspondent, could be prickly at times—or at least Helms thought so—but Shirer took a liking to the new UP man, who unlike other cub reporters seemed to be well grounded in European history and the German language before he arrived. He formed what would be a lifelong friendship with Wallace Deuel, the *Chicago Daily News*'s Berlin correspondent, won over by the Helms charm and intelligence that had worked its magic in college. Sigrid Schultz, a fearless reporter for the *Chicago Tribune* who infuriated the regime with her stories on Nazi brutality, took in Helms for a Christmas meal.

Their favorite hangout, which Helms now frequented, was the bar at the luxurious Hotel Adlon on Unter den Linden. The Adlon, considered a palace with its enormous lobby, interior garden, grand ballrooms, and bellhops

wearing blue tunics and white gloves, was the social hub for foreign journalists and government officials, conveniently located near the Chancellery
and Reich ministries. Hitler's guests stayed in Adlon rooms, bugged by the
Gestapo. The Foreign Press Association hosted its annual dinner and ball
there, when top Nazis girded themselves for a night of clinking glasses with
reporters they despised.

Helms also became a frequent invitee at receptions U.S. ambassador
William Dodd hosted for American and British reporters at his chancery
on Bendlerstrasse near the Tiergarten. Soon Helms was infatuated with the
erudite envoy's twenty-seven-year-old daughter, Martha, who was alluring
and decidedly oversexed. Helms took her out for dinner one night, but Martha paid him no more attention after that, no doubt because her stable of
lovers was already too full to take on another. Martha's bedmates included at
different times a Hitler press aide, a third secretary in the French embassy,
a Gestapo chief, and a Russian diplomat who turned out to be an NKVD
agent. At one point, Hitler's press aide even tried, unsuccessfully as it turned
out, to hook her up with the führer.

Though a few were Nazi sympathizers, most American correspondents
courageously reported on Hitler's preparations for war and his regime's brutality toward Jews, communists, and political opponents. It was hard not to.
Paramilitary gangs roaming Berlin streets routinely carted off in broad daylight Germans considered undesirable or assaulted foreigners who did not
acknowledge their Nazi salutes with a right arm raised. Journalists leaving
Friedrichstrasse's nightclubs could not help but hear the screams of torture
victims in the nearby SA building. Joseph Goebbels set up a massive propaganda operation to impress American visitors and schmooze with reporters.
For correspondents considered too hostile, the regime came down hard,
expelling more than two dozen. Those allowed to remain were blasted on
the pages of government newspapers for stories the Nazis deemed offensive
or they were beaten up or, as happened to the UP's Kecskemeti, kidnapped
by government thugs until the U.S. embassy could talk authorities into releasing them.

Curiously, Helms admitted years later that he never witnessed "the
frightening aspects" of Berlin, as he put it. He was summoned once to the
propaganda ministry, where a press "referee" chided him over an inconse-

quential story under his byline about the German movie industry, which had appeared, of all places, in a Caracas, Venezuela, newspaper. He was not particularly alarmed by the episode. Helms found Hitler, and the Germany he now led, difficult to understand, as many Americans at the time did. It was clear to Helms, as he wrote in a 1938 article after leaving Germany, that Hitler had "crushed" his opposition, rigged his reelection, was now a "war-wolf," and had "pet bugaboos—Jews and Bolshevists." Yet he considered Hitler a cold and calculating politician rather than a madman. For the moment Helms showed more curiosity about the dictator than the moral outrage some of his colleagues had begun to feel.

His first big story came March 7, 1936, when he was assigned to cover Hitler's noon address to the Reichstag, whose six hundred deputies, all handpicked by the führer, had gathered in the Kroll Opera House. (A mysterious fire seriously damaged the nearby Reichstag building three years earlier. Hitler blamed communists but many suspected the Nazis arranged the arson to spark a crackdown of the opposition.) Helms passed through black-uniformed SS paramilitaries with snarling dogs at the theater's entrance. Inside, the tension was palpable. The deputies had not been given advance notice of what Hitler would say. Helms sat in the balcony with some fifty of his news colleagues. Hitler, his voice beginning low and hoarse, then rising to a shrill rant, harangued his audience for more than an hour on the injustices of the Versailles Treaty and the dangers of Bolshevism. "I will not have the gruesome Communist international dictatorship of hate descend upon the German people!" he screamed. Helms raced to write down every word. Reporters never received advance copies of Hitler's speeches and his salivary glands seemed to Helms to become overactive when he got wound up causing him to slur his words, making it difficult to understand him.

Helms noticed Hitler passing a handkerchief back and forth between his hands underneath the open lectern. His face grew pale. Leaning over the lectern, he began to slow his speech. Finally, he declared in a soft voice soon returned to a roar: "The German government has re-established, as from today, the absolute and unrestricted sovereignty of the Reich in the demilitarized zone. . . . At this moment German troops are crossing the Rhine bridges and occupying the Rhineland!" The Versailles and Locarno treaties after World War I had permanently demilitarized Germany's Rhineland region in the west; it was now in violation of those accords. The deputies leaped to their feet, chanting "Sieg Heil!" dozens of times, "their eyes, burning with fanaticism, glued on the new god, the Messiah," Shirer scribbled in his notebook. Helms sat stunned by the oratory power of this man.

Other choice reporting assignments came Helms's way. He covered the 1936 Winter and Summer Olympics, which were both held in Germany that year. Hitler, who had been reluctant to host games he claimed were "inspired by Jews," eventually realized their propaganda value and whitewashed his capital for the world. A massive new sports complex was built, Unter den Linden was draped with swastika banners, lavish parties were hosted for many of the 1.2 million foreign visitors, some seven thousand high-priced call girls were allowed back on the streets, and the terror campaign against Jews was suspended. Helms was enchanted by the beauty and grace of Norwegian Sonja Henie on the ice rink and thrilled when Swedish grand master Ulrich Salchow gave him an impromptu tutorial on figure skating. The day Jesse Owens won the 200-meter race, Helms sat in the press box atop the Olympic Stadium, which seated a hundred thousand and had the airship *Hindenburg* floating above it throughout the games. He watched how Hitler, who would lean over the railing in his government box and become giddy when German athletes won, had a stone-cold look on his face when the African American bested the field. Helms afterward discovered that the Germans had not cornered the market on racism. When he asked an American coach in an interview how the U.S. team was faring, the man answered with Owens in mind: "We're doing fine in the monkey sports."

After the Olympics, Oechsner had assigned Ed Beattie to cover the annual Nazi Party Congress in Nuremberg during the second week in September, but Beattie had to bow out at the last minute because of family problems. Helms was sent as a replacement, which proved a stroke of luck for him. When he walked through the lobby of Nuremberg's Hotel Württemberger Hof on Saturday, September 12, a young SS officer approached stiffly and handed him an envelope. The note inside said a staff car would pick him up at seven the next morning, drive him to Luitpold Arena for the Sunday rally, and afterward take him to Nuremberg Castle on a hilltop outside the city for a "light luncheon" with the führer. Helms immediately phoned his bureau with the news. Hitler had received few foreign visitors and until now kept reporters from overseas papers at a healthy distance.

The next morning at the appointed time, a black Mercedes with the top down pulled up to the entrance of the Württemberger. Alfred Rosenberg, who had inspired the Nazi racial laws the party announced at the previous year's Nuremberg rally, sat in the backseat with a Polish reporter. Helms climbed into the front seat beside the SS driver. What he saw when the car arrived at Luitpold took his breath away. The arena was actually a large open meadow. A massive stone podium, with three long swastika banners as backdrop, was filled to capacity with party faithful at one end and faced tens of thousands of SS paramilitaries standing at attention in tightly packed columns. Helms found the führer in full form as usual. "The wonder of this age is that you have found me—an unknown man among millions," Hitler declared to the vast assemblage, which erupted into thunderous "Sieg Heils." At the end of his speech the huge crowd drew dead silent, the chirping of birds over the meadow and the muffled drumbeat from the SS band the only sounds to be heard. The heels of his jackboots clicking on the stone, Hitler walked slowly down the steps of the podium, pausing at the bottom, where he bowed his head, then delivered two Nazi salutes to twenty-three black pylons, each representing a storm trooper killed during the 1923 Beer Hall Putsch. "It was a perfectly executed and stage-managed political pageant," Helms later wrote.

Afterward, Helms and a half dozen other reporters, mingling with Deputy Führer Rudolf Hess, Ambassador Joachim von Ribbentrop, and other Nazi dignitaries, stood on the parapet of the medieval castle in the warm autumn sun, gazing out at the city's red-gabled roofs and beyond them the Frankonian plain. A throaty voice behind them interrupted. "That is certainly a lovely view." Helms and the others spun around to see Hitler stepping onto the battlement. An SS aide introduced the dictator to each of the correspondents, who formed a half circle around him. Helms found the hand he shook soft and delicate with tapered fingers, not the hand of a worker but of someone who held a pen all day. His hair in the bright sunlight had a russet tone to it and Helms thought the blue eyes everyone claimed were hypnotic were actually a dull slate blue protruding somewhat from his head and perfectly ordinary. In fact, everything about Hitler up close seemed commonplace to Helms, from his brown mustache flecked with a little gray to his pasty white face tinged slightly pink to the gold that filled many of his teeth. The dictator who had been mesmerizing before thousands that morning seemed to Helms to be ill at ease in this small group, his knees rocking back and forth when he talked. But Helms was struck by how he spoke in a moderate voice like a man supremely self-assured in what he was saying—straightforward, emotionless, offering certainties in his mind rather than opinions, never beginning a sentence with "I believe" or "I think." For an hour Hitler gave concise, thought-out answers to the reporters' questions. Helms was impressed with his command of facts, even if they were his version of the truth, and with the frank insights he had on the people he ruled. "I know the German bureaucrat very well," Hitler said at one point. "If he is due to come in at 8 a.m. he arrives at 8 a.m. He hangs up his coat, hat, washes his hands, does this and that, so that by the time he gets to work, it's twenty minutes after eight. At the end of the day, he starts at twenty minutes to five and does all those things in reverse so that he leaves at 5 p.m. We are never going to get anywhere in Germany with people working that way."

After an hour, Hitler grew weary of the reporters and hungry for his lunch. Before they retreated to the dining room, where a dish of milk chocolates had been set at the führer's table place, one of Helms's colleagues asked: "Why do you hold these Nazi Party conferences every year?" A slight smile crept across Hitler's face for the first time. "The party units all over Germany work hard for me and for the cause all year long," he replied. "What should I do? Money prizes would break the Treasury. So I bring the most effective leaders here for a couple of days, give them this show and a chance to meet us all. They pay their own expenses. If they can't afford it, the local party units help them out. They go home stimulated, ready to work for me again. Besides," he added matter-of-factly after a brief pause, transporting tens of thousands of SS men and party workers to the Nuremberg rally "is exactly the kind of exercise the German railways would be required to perform in the event of war."

"That last word—*Krieg*—hung in the air," Helms wrote later. The lunch left two impressions in his mind. Hitler might later become maniacal, but he appeared coolly rational to Helms on that Sunday afternoon—"a man very clear in his head, what he was up to and where he was headed." And it was obvious to Helms that he was headed toward war.

His assignment in Berlin had taught Helms the discipline of struggling daily to get the news first, to be accurate, to pay attention to detail, to report what he had found clearly and succinctly—all skills he would find useful later as an intelligence officer. But a month after the Nuremberg rally Helms wrote his father that he was ready to leave Germany and United Press. Herman, who had been coaxing his son since March to return to the United States, was delighted; he considered news reporting, particularly overseas where his son was out of sight and mind, a career cul-de-sac. If you stay in the newspaper business you should become an editor or publisher, Herman advised. Richard agreed. He had done far more interesting work as a UP man in Berlin than any of his Williams classmates, but "I've about had enough of this place," he wrote his father. He now wanted to make "money as fast as possible."

It was June 1937 before Helms managed to break free from Berlin. Upset over losing a man they knew had the makings of a top-flight foreign correspondent, UP's managers had talked him into remaining at least that long. Helms arrived in New York with ambitious plans for earning his fortune. They ran smack into an economy still crippled by the Depression. To survive while job hunting he submitted pieces to magazines like *Esquire* and *Cosmopolitan* but they found his writing unremarkable. Wally Deuel urged his *Chicago Daily News* bosses to give his Berlin colleague a look but they took a pass, and his grandfather (who detested using his business connections to find family members jobs) proved to be no help. Finally, after working the connection he had with his college fraternity brother's father who was a Scripps Howard executive, Helms managed to land an entry-level position in the advertising department of the chain's Indiana paper, the *Indianapolis Times.*

Helms started a long way from his goal now of owning a newspaper. Working out of a run-down office on Maryland Street in Indianapolis, he phoned local retailers or walked door-to-door struggling to convince them to place small ads in the newspaper. It was the hardest job he had ever had. Helms was not a natural salesman or backslapper. He bought self-help books on how to act charming and dress for success. After six months, he debated whether he should return to United Press, which was eager to have him back. His Scripps Howard managers urged him to tough it out; none of their ad men were doing well in this miserable economy but things were bound to pick up, they assured him. Helms persevered. By the end of 1938 he began exceeding his sales quotas. After two and a half years in the bowels of retail advertising, he was promoted to the paper's executive ranks and made the national advertising manager for the *Times*. As he had in college, Helms became a pillar of Indianapolis, joining the Athletic Club, Woodstock Club, Contemporary Club, Traders Point Hunt Club, and the Literary Club (where he gave a talk on his meeting Hitler). He became a regular at the Indianapolis 500 each year and was considered one of the city's most handsome and eligible bachelors.

Julia Bretzman Shields was a beautiful, fashionable, and fastidious Indianapolis divorcée with two children and a small fortune from her settlement. She had also been a Phi Beta Kappa student at Butler University in the city and would become a talented sculptress, studying under nationally renowned artists. Her father, Charles Bretzman, had emigrated from Germany at the turn of the century. A press gang at Ellis Island hijacked him to a Kansas sheep ranch. He eventually stole a horse and made it as far as Indianapolis, where he set up a successful photography studio. Julia, who also could be intense, demanding, and direct with people, married Frank Shields, who was fifteen years older and had become a millionaire turning the Barbasol Company into a national business. Shields, who put his wife up in an opulent estate raising and showing horses, turned out to be an alcoholic and serial womanizer.

As Julia left the divorce court, her lawyer told her that there was a handsome young man just arrived in Indianapolis from Europe whom he wanted her to meet. The last thing that interested Julia was a rebound affair, but she reluctantly agreed to have dinner with him that night. She found Richard Helms, who was six years younger, indeed handsome and urbane. He was also the most determined man she had ever met. They became a hot item in Indianapolis high society—both were superb dancers—and soon fell in love. On September 9, 1939, the two married. After a short honeymoon, which amounted to only a long weekend at a lakeshore cottage in southern Michigan, Helms settled in with Julia and an instant family. He did not know how to act around Julia's young son, James, and daughter, Judith. Helms showed no interest in children then and he wouldn't become a kid person three years later when he and Julia had a boy they named Dennis.

Though he was now a man of some prominence in Indianapolis, Helms continued to look beyond its horizon. His colleagues at United Press sent him long notes on what they were witnessing in Europe. Increasingly their news was disheartening. A little more than a week before he and Julia had married, Germany invaded Poland. England and France declared war on the Third Reich two days later. From his lunch with the führer, Helms was sure the conflict would only grow.

CHAPTER 4

WILLIAM EGAN COLBY

Fierce Yankee individualism was embedded like DNA in Elbridge Colby. He proudly traced his lineage to eleven sailing vessels the Puritan lawyer John Winthrop commanded in 1630 with more than seven hundred migrants escaping religious persecution in England. In the dank, chilly hold of Winthrop's command ship, the *Arbella*, which had set sail from the Isle of Wight on April 8, huddled Anthony and Susanna Colby. Anthony had been born about 1605, perhaps in Lincolnshire near Sempringham, the seat of the Earl of Lincoln, where his name is found in local registers. Susanna Haddon Colby, who was about twenty-two when they embarked on their voyage, was listed as a daughter of one of the "Old Families of Salisbury." The *Arbella* landed at Salem on June 13 and Winthrop eventually settled his Massachusetts Bay Colony—the third from England after Jamestown and Plymouth— on the Shawmut Peninsula and what would become Boston. A First Church member and freeman, Anthony lived with his wife for three years in Boston, then moved west to Cambridge where he owned two houses and six acres of land on Brattle Street. By 1639 he had sold his Cambridge property and moved northeast, becoming a successful planter in Salisbury and Amesbury near the Massachusetts coast and leaving his wife and seven children a modest estate when he died in 1660.

Successive generations of Colbys remained in Massachusetts variously as planters, a pub owner, a blacksmith, an Indian fighter, Revolutionary War soldiers, shipbuilders, abolitionists, one banker, and, according to a genealogy, a black sheep "fined for abusing a wench." The first intellectual Colby came in the fourth generation. Born in 1855, Charles Edwards Colby was a child prodigy interested in electricity and chemistry who studied abroad and eventually became a renowned organic chemist at Columbia College in New York. His promising academic career, however, was snuffed out early when he died at age forty-two of kidney disease. His young widow, Emily Lynn Carrington Colby, who was a tough New Englander, took a job in the registrar's office of New York's Hunter College, scrimping to feed and educate her son and two daughters.

It was nine months after his birth in 1891 that Charles and Emily finally decided on a name for their son: Elbridge Atherton Colby. Elbridge, who was six years old when his father died, was a bright child, as were his two older sisters, Sabra and Dorothea. The boy soon became painfully aware that his mother was scraping to get by. (For the rest of his life, the specter of destitution haunted him.) Though he was the youngest, Elbridge soon became the man of the house, working part-time during high school to supplement his mother's meager salary and to put himself through Columbia, where he excelled as an English major, champion hurdler, and long-distance swimmer. Elbridge graduated summa cum laude with a Phi Beta Kappa key in 1912 and remained at the school for another year to earn his master's degree. While at Columbia, he became something of an Anglophile, devouring the books and poems of Rudyard Kipling, admiring Robert Baden-Powell (the British founder of modern scouting), and becoming a Catholic (swept up by the conversion movement among the British intellectual class at the time). That last interest infuriated his Congregationalist mother and sisters—even more so because Elbridge, like many converts, became a more ardent Catholic than those born to the religion.

After Columbia, he moved to St. Paul in 1914, where he taught as an instructor at the University of Minnesota while studying for a Ph.D. in English. Within a year, the war in Europe distracted him as it did many young progressives in America. Elbridge volunteered for the Serbian Expedition of Mercy, driving ambulances and delivering relief supplies to refugees in the Balkans. With the Serbian Red Cross's Gold Medal in his pocket, he returned to Minnesota in 1916 to resume his teaching and his romance with a carefree and pretty English major he had met before he left. Margaret Mary Egan was the daughter of a well-off Irish Catholic family in St. Paul. Her father, William H. Egan, had run away from home, traded with the Sioux Indians in the Dakotas, and eventually became a successful coffee merchant in St. Paul, buying a small mansion on Summit Avenue. Egan was not a hidebound Catholic and encouraged Margaret and her brothers to attend secular universities instead of religious schools. Even so, he was not pleased when his daughter married a Catholic convert in 1917. Neither was the Congregationalist Colby family.

When America entered the war, Elbridge enlisted in the Army, hoping to be sent to France with the American Expeditionary Forces. He was bitterly disappointed when his orders arrived for Panama, where he would serve in a dashing white uniform on glorified guard duty. Margaret became pregnant in Panama and Elbridge sent her back to their Lincoln Avenue home in St. Paul to have the child. She delivered a boy on the evening of January 4, 1920, at St. Luke's Hospital. They named him William Egan Colby. He would be their only child.

After the Armistice, Elbridge returned to the University of Minnesota and his teaching duties. Though he had money, his childhood fear of poverty lingered and he soon worried that his salary as a struggling writer and underpaid professor would not be enough to support his family. The interwar military was in a decrepit state but at least offered economic security to the soldiers who remained in it, Elbridge thought, so he applied to return to the Army, which this time granted him a commission as a second lieutenant since he had an advanced degree. Elbridge would spend the next twenty-eight years in the Army, rising to the rank of colonel. But for the military, he was somewhat of an intellectual misfit. While in the service he wrote more than a half dozen books—an odd assortment that included *English Catholic Poets* (covering Chaucer to Dryden), a biography of Theodore Winthrop (the first Union officer to die in the Civil War), and a dictionary of soldier slang titled *Army Talk*—along with numerous scholarly articles, reviews, and impassioned letters to the editor, often on subjects beyond the arcane. He once published a lengthy article badgering the government to restore the apostrophe to Thompsons Point, Vermont.

Elbridge was a dour and hidebound father to his only son—a Victorian disciplinarian, erect, full of spit and polish, somewhat of a martinet, who held Bill to high standards. He later would be an ornery curmudgeon to his grandchildren, who always addressed him as "Colonel" and found him not much fun to be around. For love and emotional support, Bill's refuge was Margaret, a charming, soft-hearted Irish woman, with an eye for beautiful art objects and furnishings and a personality the polar opposite of Elbridge's. Margaret adored her son more than she did her husband. Yet though his heart belonged to his mother, Bill was intellectually closer to his father. Deeply patriotic and a diehard Democrat, Elbridge instilled in his boy independent and unorthodox thinking, curiosity about all things around him and beyond, a rigid sense of military duty, and the rectitude of Old Yankee stock. From his mother Bill inherited an outwardly warm personality. Yet he shared his father's stern outlook on the world as well as his inclination not to let others grow too close to him.

From his life as an Army brat, Bill learned volumes. The moves from one duty station to another every few years made him a perpetual outsider in neighborhoods and at schools, but he adapted. In 1923, the Army sent Elbridge to Fort Benning, which trained infantrymen just outside Columbus, Georgia. Elbridge served as a press officer, but two years into his tour he stirred up publicity his commanders would have preferred not to see. A black soldier from the post had been shot dead by a white man in nearby Americus for refusing to step off the sidewalk to let him pass. The all-white jury predictably found the killer not guilty. An ardent integrationist (he had sent his son to an elementary school on post rather than a segregated institution in Columbus), Elbridge was outraged and penned an angry letter in the post newspaper (which the liberal *Nation* magazine reprinted) denouncing the murder and verdict. The black press hailed his protest. Georgia's newspapers and congressmen excoriated him. The Army, an organization as racist as the state at the time, shunted Colby to duty its white officers considered a dead-ender, assigning him to the post's all-black 24th Infantry Regiment. Elbridge considered it a badge of honor, but his military career never recovered from his speaking out. In later years Bill could not have been more proud of his father.

Elbridge Colby's next posting, to the Army's 15th Infantry Regiment in

Tientsin, China, in 1929, was considered exotic duty for an American officer. The family found the three-year assignment exciting. Since the Boxer Rebellion of 1899–1901, the 15th Infantry had been among the foreign armies occupying this gateway city of nearly a million off Bohai Bay and just southeast of Peking. By the time the Colbys arrived, the regiment, many of whose families now occupied the portion of the international quarter the Germans vacated after World War I, was assigned to protect American interests as the civil war between Chiang Kai-shek's Nationalists and Mao Tse-tung's communists intensified. Captain Colby found a large house to rent in the foreign quarter on Race Course Road near the Japanese legation. It came with a staff of a half dozen low-paid servants, one of whom was a nanny for his son. Nine-year-old Bill, clad in a uniform with a belt whose silver buckle had a snake stamped on it, attended the British Tientsin Grammar School, whose regimentation he hated. Elbridge, who was required to learn Chinese as all American officers were, supplemented his son's schooling with a tutor who came to the home to instruct the boy and Margaret in the language.

Young Bill proved to be a brash and adventuresome child, which often got him into trouble. His father spanked him one time for clapping to summon a servant, which Elbridge considered rude. Soon, without his nanny at his side, he began exploring the open-air markets and streets of this exotic city, which teemed with rickshaws adorned with brass lamps, electric trams, and automobiles. He had a girlfriend in the quarter and shimmied down the drainpipe outside his top-floor room at night to visit her. Another time, he disobeyed his father's strict instructions to walk directly from school to home each day and wandered to the Bohai Bay port, where a crewman for an American submarine tethered at the dock gave him a tour of the vessel. For three months, Elbridge withheld his Christmas present (a rifle mail-ordered from the United States) as punishment. Bill Colby would later claim that this experience in China prepared him "for the exoticism of Asia" when he returned to the region as an adult. That may be a stretch. He was, after all, no older than eleven at the time. But his three years in Tientsin did open a window to a world unlike any he had ever experienced.

After a temporary assignment back at Fort Benning, in August 1933 Elbridge was transferred to the University of Vermont for what his Army peers would consider another less than desirable job as an instructor in its Reserve Officers' Training Corps detachment. But for Elbridge and his family, it was a return to their New England roots. They relished it as they had Tientsin. Elbridge bought a yellow Victorian house on Maple Street in Burlington, the small rural town on the eastern shore of Lake Champlain, which at the time boasted little more than the university. He taught English at the college in addition to his military science classes. Most summer week-ends, the family loaded up the car and drove to a spacious cottage on the lake, which Elbridge owned with his mother and sisters. For Bill, Vermont served as an anchor the rest of his life. As a teenager he was a short five foot seven and a scrawny 135 pounds, but he enjoyed the outdoors. He learned to ski during the winter months and one summer paddled a canoe on Lake Champlain for nine days, camping each night on the shore. On another adventure when he was just fifteen, Bill and a friend rode their bicycles 753 miles through five New England states over fifteen days.

He attended Burlington High, which for a public school had an academ-ically elite group of students, most of whom went on to prestigious universi-ties. Bill more than held his own in the classroom. His yearbook tagged him with the nickname "The Brain," which was apt. He graduated in June 1936 at age sixteen, a year ahead of schedule.

Early on, young Colby assumed he would follow his father and make the military a career. But nearsightedness and the fact that at sixteen he was too young to apply kept him out of the U.S. Military Academy at West Point, his first choice. Dartmouth University was his second choice for the skiing, but Elbridge took a dim view of that being a reason for attending a school and practically ordered him to enroll in Princeton. The university had become an expensive institution for the rich, the town of Princeton's suburbs around the image-conscious campus had turned fashionably upscale, and the col-lege's eating clubs, which Woodrow Wilson had tried so hard to dismantle when he was university president, continued to be snobby bastions for well-off students. The Depression-era students who entered Princeton with Colby were not as politically apathetic or blasé about their studies as their predecessors from the Roaring Twenties. Even so, the gentleman's C culture persisted. A quarter of Colby's classmates had been admitted solely because their fathers were alumni. More than three-fourths arrived from elite private schools or expensive college prep academies. Colby could hardly have been more out of place—a middle-class public school student on scholarship who waited on tables at an eating club instead of joining one, a Catholic among an overwhelmingly Protestant student body, and a skinny shy kid with glasses who appeared noticeably younger to the other freshmen.

Colby, however, was content to go his own way at Princeton. Instead of the eating clubs he attended the Catholic chapel serving as an altar boy and joined the ROTC, rising eventually to the rank of cadet captain. The intellectual hothouse that bored many of his classmates stimulated him. He became immediately intrigued his freshman year with an anthropology course. He inhaled the constitutional law classes of noted professors Edward S. Corwin and Alpheus T. Mason. In the new School of Public and International Affairs he did independent study on the problems of black education, the Cuban sugar trade, and civil liberties in New Jersey. He was thrilled the first time he encountered Albert Einstein shambling across campus in a tattered black academic gown. A classmate had nudged him, pointing to the old scientist and saying: "There goes the most intelligent man on the planet."

Like Helms's father, Herman, Elbridge did not consider a gentleman's education complete until he had spent time abroad to learn French, so in August 1939 he sent his son to live for a month with the Govare family in the city of Blois in central France's Loire Valley. Once more Colby hopped onto a bicycle and rode among the region's grand châteaus and vineyards, stopping in farm villages along the way to sample the local wines in their cafés. On a longer trip, he biked south with a friend he had met in Loire to the Pyrenees mountain range on Spain's border and interviewed bedraggled leftist refugees who had fled fascist General Francisco Franco's victorious nationalists in the Spanish Civil War.

Colby fell in love with France. His idyllic month was jarred, however, by the German invasion of Poland as he left. He crossed the channel to England with two French army mobilization posters tucked in his bags that he would hang in his dormitory room and boarded an armed British ship, which zigzagged its way across the North Atlantic to avoid German submarines.

Colby returned to Princeton for his senior year a determined interventionist, committed to the liberal ideals of Roosevelt's New Deal at home and to the war against Nazism and fascism abroad. He used the interview notes he had taken in the Pyrenees for his senior thesis condemning the failure of

France and other Western democracies to support the valiant Spanish Republicans against Franco. His paper stopped short of siding with the Soviets, who backed the Republic. Colby equally detested communism.

After graduating with honors from Princeton, Colby spent the summer of 1940 in Washington, living with his father who had been transferred to Army headquarters. He found a job pumping gas at a station on 21st and M Streets, and soon was helping the local Oil Workers' Union organize station attendants, which his boss, John Hardy, did not much appreciate. Colby, however, had become infected by the labor movement. Still a year shy of being old enough for an Army commission from his ROTC work, he decided to enroll in Columbia's law school with visions of a career as a labor attorney and later perhaps in liberal politics. While at school, he rang doorbells in the evening for local Democratic candidates.

During Colby's first year at Columbia, a law school buddy named Stan Temko arranged a blind date for him at the Gold Rail on Broadway near the school. It was with a Barnard College girl Temko knew, who was smart and popular enough with the boys that she didn't really need blind dates. But she had agreed to this one. Colby was stunned when he walked into the bar and met Barbara Ann Heinzen. She looked to him like the movie starlet Barbara Stanwyck. The Barnard senior did not find anything Hollywood about Colby during their first date—he was barely taller than her and about as thin, not the kind to sweep a girl off her feet—but this law student did seem to her to be a good conversationalist. He was Roman Catholic as she was. And they shared the same ideas on politics and social issues, she thought. Both out to save the world.

Barbara had been born about eleven months after Bill in Springfield, Ohio, where her father, Karl Heinzen, had started as a journalist. Heinzen drifted into public relations and advertising, eventually ending up in Scarsdale, New York, as the Bayer Aspirin Division president for Sterling Drug. An only child like Colby, Barbara had been an outgoing high school student who won a scholarship in 1938 to the prestigious Wellesley College for women in Massachusetts. Karl, however, was stricken with a ruptured appendix that year so Barbara switched to Barnard in New York to be nearer to her father, who was struggling to recuperate in the city. Karl died of coronary thrombosis during Barbara's freshman year at Barnard. Her mother,

Annette Chmelitzki Heinzen, whose parents had emigrated to the United States from Austria, remained in New York and paid her daughter's Barnard tuition with the money she earned from Montgomery Ward as a fashion consultant arranging photo shoots of sportswear models for its catalogue.

Throughout 1940 and the first half of 1941, Bill and Barbara dated pretty much steadily, "racing around New York, dancing, partying, endlessly arguing politics with our friends," he later wrote. The couple watched in disgust as communist demonstrators at Columbia (during the time when Germany and the Soviet Union were still allies) marched around campus carrying mock coffins to protest Lend-Lease aid to Great Britain, which Roosevelt had approved in March 1941. Ever since the German invasion of France in the spring of 1940, Colby believed America needed to build up its military for a war with Hitler, which he thought was coming soon. Or at least he hoped it would be soon.

CHAPTER 5

WAR CLOUDS

Allen Dulles sat in an armchair by the radio on the morning of June 14, 1940, with his head in his hands weeping as he listened to the broadcast on German forces marching into Paris. For two decades he had dreaded that this day would come. The start of World War II and the fall of France had not surprised him.

· · · ·

A month after joining the State Department in May 1916, Dulles had set sail for Europe aboard the merchant steamer *Philadelphia* to his first assignment in Vienna. He felt guilty that he had abandoned his National Guard unit. The State Department fended off the Army's attempts to keep him, insisting he was more valuable to his country serving as a diplomat than lugging a rifle. The department paid its newly minted foreign secretary $1,500 a year. His grandfather supplemented that meager salary with $200 a month from his checkbook. Allen arrived in Vienna on July 18 and was immediately loaded up with work. Vienna had been a sleepy outpost—now five secretaries with his arrival—but the world war suddenly made it a busy mission. Dulles processed passport applications, deciphered coded diplomatic cables, and offered what little help he could to Americans stranded there with no money because of the war. He took an immediate dislike to Frederic Courtland Penfield, an amiable Connecticut newspaperman hopelessly out of his depth as U.S. ambassador to Austria-Hungary. When Penfield one day asked his most junior clerk to carry his suit to the cleaners, Dulles haughtily replied: "I may be your third secretary, but I am not your valet." Dulles could afford to be insubordinate; Penfield could not afford to retaliate against the boss's nephew. A year earlier Robert Lansing had replaced William Jennings Bryan as Wilson's secretary of state. Allen was not shy about using that connection. Throughout his State Department career he kept up a back channel to Uncle Bert with private memos to raise issues he thought Lansing was not being briefed on through regular channels or to denigrate poor-performing diplomats like Penfield.

Sandwiched among the long hours, Dulles enjoyed Vienna's world-renowned symphonies. He found the city's operas and theaters high quality and fine dining at its restaurants far less expensive than in Paris. He honed his tennis—the game became a lifelong passion—and played in local tournaments. Though exhausted by evenings, he made time to take German lessons. (He had mastered French as a child but struggled with German for the rest of his life.) Dulles also was not content to remain chained to the paperwork piled on his desk. Penfield showed little interest in intelligence gathering. Dulles began dabbling in it on his own, striking up friendships with Austro-Hungarian officials and other foreign diplomats to milk them for information he could cable to Washington.

By the second week of April 1917 Dulles was waiting impatiently in Paris. After repeated U-boat attacks on American merchant and passenger ships, Wilson, who had campaigned for reelection in 1916 on the slogan "He kept us out of war," finally gave up on American neutrality and obtained from Congress a declaration of war against Germany on April 6. Though war against Austria-Hungary (allied with Germany, Turkey, and Bulgaria as the Central Powers) would not be declared until December 7, the State Department ordered the Vienna embassy evacuated the night of April 6. "Unless I get a post where I can really be of some usefulness I think that it would be better to get into the Army," Dulles wrote to his mother from Paris. Uncle Bert came to the rescue. He mailed his nephew orders to take the train to neutral Switzerland to join the U.S. legation at Bern.

The Swiss capital, on a plateau just west of the country's center with the Aare River snaking around its Old City, was now flooded with thousands of refugees fleeing war zones. Dulles encountered what he called "an ever changing crowd of notables" traipsing through: Greek royalty, Spanish duchesses, the Prince Consort of Holland, the Prince of Hohenlohe. Though he found the city picturesque, its old Bernese families and aristocracy struck him as medieval in their thinking, "too proud and self-satisfied to have anything to do with us foreigners," he wrote. Far more fascinating and congenial, he discovered, were its diplomats from Britain, France, Spain, and even Russia. Within a year, twenty-five-year-old Dulles had been promoted to second secretary and his salary had increased to $3,555 annually, but he found it barely enough to live off of, even with profits from his U.S. stocks that his father adroitly managed. Bern was an expensive city with food shortages, particularly in butter, cheese, and sugar. Affordable housing was in even shorter supply. Dulles was forced to live for a year at the expensive Hotel Bellevue Palace until he found a seven-room apartment in the Old City that he shared with the legation's military attaché.

The American outpost, housed in a modest home in the Old City's Hirschengraben, was designated a legation because it had a much smaller staff than an embassy—unfortunate for this tiny band at the outset because with the United States now at war and Switzerland at the vortex of Europe's belligerents Bern became even more hectic than Vienna's embassy had been. Dulles joined a staff with not much more experience than he had. Several of them—such as Hugh Wilson (the legation's efficient number two man) and Frederic Dolbeare (who came with Dulles from Vienna)—would be his OSS colleagues in the next war. The legation's chief was Pleasant Stovall, another likable newspaperman and Wilson political crony who was even more incompetent than Penfield had been in Vienna. Dulles was soon filling Uncle Bert's in-box with memos trashing Stovall.

With reinforcements arriving, the legation rented a second, roomier house in the Old City. Dulles worked in its palatial, wood-paneled dining room now filled with desks. His twelve-hour days left little opportunity for the endless parties on the diplomatic circuit, but he did carve out time on weekends for tennis, golf, climbing the Finsteraarhorn (the highest mountain in the Bernese Alps), and chasing girls. Dulles became somewhat of a fop on the social circuit, trying to impress others with stylish clothes and highbrow manners.

Because no one else was available, by default Dulles became the legation's intelligence officer. He found Bern filled "with all sorts of outlandish people" peddling information, he wrote in letters to home—Czechs, Albanians, Montenegrins, Ukrainians, Lithuanians, Poles, Russians from any number of sects, liberal Austrians, and turncoat Germans. It was almost impossible to walk the city's streets and not bump into one of these "questionable characters." Or they turned up at the legation office asking for American help "and we use them for information." Most legations had far larger staffs than the Americans'. The German embassy, by Dulles's count, had "several hundred," a majority of whom devoted their days to vacuuming intelligence. At the Bellevue Palace, where Dulles stayed his first year, maids and bellhops on the payroll of foreign envoys routinely searched the rooms of guests to snatch documents their secret employers might find useful. In the hotel's main dining room diplomats from the warring powers filled their stomachs and strained their ears to pick up conversations at other tables.

Hugh Wilson, whom Stovall let run the diplomatic operation, assigned Dulles to be the legation's point man for reporting on Austro-Hungarian and Balkan affairs. The young second secretary could not have found a better perch than Bern for that mission. Swiss papers were full of useful tidbits about Austria and Germany. Aides with the legation of Spain, which remained neutral throughout the war, slipped him cables on the Central Powers. On one typical day, Dulles breakfasted with a Polish source who brought him a long memo on "internal conditions" in Austria, spent an hour in his office with a Southern European acquaintance discussing reactionaries in Hungary, and then consumed the rest of his day editing a report for Washington prepared by a "private source" on "German plans for the commercial and political domination of Switzerland."

Dulles's Bern assignment began teaching him how to be a spy. He cultivated other intelligence officers, particularly the Swiss, who shared their estimates on German defenses. He found journalists in the region valuable for insights that had not appeared in their stories. He mastered the use of intermediaries—called "cutouts" in the espionage trade—to obtain information from other sources who did not know the Americans would be the recipient. He learned to write accurate and clear intelligence reports with "expressive English," as he put it, which impressed State Department officials reading them. Dulles also discovered that a spy had to be flexible and creative. He began combining intelligence gathering with vacations, using, for example, a weekend golfing trip to Vevey on Lake Geneva's north shore to meet with a nearby Polish source with helpful intelligence on German political and military advances into Russia. He had his brother, Foster, mail him a dozen tennis balls each week, which he used as gifts for Swiss officials addicted to the sport as he was. Tennis balls, which were scarce in Bern, became not only useful barter for information; when an Austrian diplomat applied for membership in the city's best tennis club, the Swiss blackballed him for fear of losing their supply from Dulles.

He found his secret war against Germany exhilarating. "We see the boche from all angles and occasionally are able to slip a little over on him as well as to find out his habits and his haunts and his plans," Dulles wrote to a friend. "I never have had such interesting work or come into contact with so many interesting characters." But quickly he grasped that a good intelligence officer must contend with an onslaught of information and the people trafficking it. "We are buried with rumors and stories" of impending German military attacks, of political machinations among the Central Powers, of peace feelers from enemy countries, he wrote his mother. "We have to sift and investigate and try to get at the truth." He suspected that salted among the hundreds of German, Austrian, and Turkish dissidents who approached him with information were double agents reporting back to their spy services. Dulles had to learn—painfully as it turned out—that in sorting through the deluge of leads a good intelligence officer also must never close the door to potential sources.

The American legation had an unstated policy of showing the exit to Russian Bolshevists visiting its offices. That may explain why Dulles had no intention of giving up his tennis date with a pretty French girl to meet a communist who had phoned the legation and, speaking German with a heavy Russian accent, insisted that he must speak to someone there that afternoon. Dulles, who had recently arrived in Bern and was stuck answering phones that afternoon as duty officer because the others had left early, told the man to come the next morning when the legation was open. Tomorrow will be too late, the Russian insisted. He must talk to the Americans that afternoon. Sorry, Dulles starchily replied, it will have to be tomorrow. He hung up. The Russian was Vladimir Ilyich Ulyanov, better known as Lenin, who had been exiled in Switzerland. The next morning, he boarded a train in Bern and made his way back to his homeland, helped by German officials eager to have the communists take Russia out of the war. Lenin may have intended to alert the Americans that he would do just that. In later years Dulles would repeat that anecdote over and over in his welcome lectures for new CIA officers with the admonition: never turn down a meeting even with those most suspicious.

Consorting with the shady, however, did have its hazards, Dulles also discovered. He was shocked to learn that a Czech woman, who worked at the U.S. legation and whom he had begun dating, was a German agent. While walking the girl home after their last dinner, Dulles, on instructions from his superiors, stopped at a street corner. Two officers from the British embassy, which had a score to settle with the spy as well, appeared out of nowhere and whisked her away. Dulles never learned what happened to the woman. Then there was the case of Rasmus Rasmussen, who showed up at the legation in the fall of 1917 claiming he had just arrived in Europe on a ship bearing other repatriated German internees from the United States. Rasmussen told Dulles and Hugh Wilson that German agents in Bern had recruited him to return to the United States to spy for Berlin. Believing Rasmussen's story that he hated the Germans and thinking that he could be an ideal double agent, Dulles and Wilson paid him to find out everything he could about what enemy intelligence officers wanted him to do in America, then arranged for him to be shipped back to the United States. Rasmussen, however, turned out to be mentally unbalanced, which did not take immigration officers at Ellis Island long to discover after he disembarked. They locked him up in an insane asylum. Convinced the Bern legation had set him up, Rasmussen finally talked his way out of the facility and vowed to hunt down Dulles and Wilson and kill them with a pistol he had bought. Dulles was terrified of the "Wild Man," as he had begun to refer to Rasmussen in memos, and made sure the State Department never gave him a passport to get anywhere near Switzerland.

Dulles always began his morning coffee with the *Frankfurter Zeitung* delivered to his apartment. What he read in the German newspaper the first week of November 1918 astounded him—hostile stories on Wilhelm II, Germany's emperor. News from other papers he scanned had been just as positive. The Americans neared victory in their month-long Meuse-Argonne offensive. Austria-Hungary, Turkey, and Bulgaria had already signed separate armistices. "The war is won," Dulles wrote his mother on November 5. When Germany did sign the Armistice six days later, he was convinced that Bern would return to insignificance as a diplomatic assignment. Weakened with influenza, which had swept the world in the 1918 pandemic, Dulles summoned enough strength to lobby Uncle Bert to allow him to join President Wilson and the some four hundred Americans in his delegation who would soon arrive in Paris for the Peace Conference. Lansing agreed to Allen serving as one of his aides there. He also approved having Foster, now a fast-rising attorney for the prestigious Sullivan & Cromwell law firm in New York, join his staff to work on German reparations.

It took Dulles little time to become indispensable in the French capital. He helped draw new borders for countries like Czechoslovakia, coordinated the distribution of thousands of intelligence reports among the U.S. delegation's members, and passed notes with advice to the president during plenary sessions. By November 1919, the portfolio of issues he oversaw had grown so wide Dulles was being called his delegation's "universal expert." But he was ready to leave Paris. The power plays he witnessed among prime ministers behind closed doors the past year had jaded him. He thought the reparations demanded of Germany unrealistic. The new boundaries he had helped draw for Central Europe moved people around like "vegetables" in a store, he wrote to a friend. He was even more disappointed with his own country, where opposition in the Senate to the Versailles Treaty and the League of Nations was building.

Though homesick, Dulles decided to accept a three-month assignment in Berlin at the end of November—"a sadder but wiser man after a year of the Peace Conference," he wrote a colleague. Housed in a stately if somewhat dilapidated building at 7 Wilhelm Platz, the American Commission had been set up to establish relations with Germany's new Weimar government. It quickly became one of the most challenging diplomatic posts. Dulles was delighted to be reunited with old Bern comrades such as Hugh Wilson and Fred Dolbeare. Food was in short supply, thieves stole anything not nailed down, and people strolling along Berlin's best streets were routinely mugged, but Dulles found the city luxuriously affordable with the dollar trading for 100 marks and servants (paid the equivalent of $2 a month) attending to his every need.

Assigned as the mission's deputy, Dulles once more became the de facto intelligence officer. He motored throughout Germany jotting down his observations for cables to Washington on the industries he saw, the farm crops that were planted, the physical appearance of cities (Leipzig did not look as dirty and unkempt as Berlin, he noted). He sat with communists in their cell meetings, interviewed government officials in Munich ("a much easier going place than Berlin"), and discussed politics with radical socialists ("possibly the Germans that are most mentally honest"). He struck up a friendship with a Freiberg economist and Weimar legislator he found perceptive: Gerhart von Schulze-Gaevernitz. You should one day meet my son, Gero, who is away at the university studying international banking, Gaevernitz told him. Dulles made a mental note to do just that.

Within weeks after the 1918 Armistice, an uneasy feeling had gnawed at Dulles, as it did with many senior American military officers, that the Germans would not accept responsibility for the war and their defeat. Walking the streets of Berlin now, Dulles was sure of it. He witnessed angry protests over the Paris conference's demand that Germany's war leaders, such as Paul von Hindenburg, chief of the General Staff, be surrendered as criminals. German workers appeared to him pacifistic, but the military certainly was not. Dulles watched as several thousand soldiers marched on Berlin to try unsuccessfully to overthrow the Weimar Republic in what became known as the Kapp Putsch. He learned that in one of Berlin's nicer hotels belligerent former Reichswehr officers threw French officers out of a ballroom for refusing to stand when the band played "Deutschland Über Alles." Dulles left Germany at the end of April 1920—convinced the nation felt it had been cheated.

For twenty-five-year-old Martha Clover Todd, the work in the YMCA's Paris canteen serving the American delegation was pedestrian; the excitement came when she could slip away to the Hôtel de Crillon and catch glimpses of busy delegates to the Peace Conference scurrying off for meetings. Clover—as she was known—never bumped into Dulles, who had an eye for lovely ladies (he became a regular at Montparnasse's luxury Le Sphinx brothel) and would have noticed the slender, stylish, and hauntingly beautiful New Yorker with her high cheekbones and doe-eyed look always serious in photos. Clover had a soft cultivated voice, an eye for anything first-class, plus an otherworldly quality to her. Her family had a history of depression. Intrigued by the unknown and mystical, Clover would have sudden outbursts. When Dulles did meet her—at a house party in Water-town the summer of 1920 after he had returned to the United States—they fell instantly in love and he proposed to her three days later. Their whirlwind romance shocked both families. Clover's father, Henry Todd, was a prom-inent Columbia University academic and a snob. He assiduously checked Dulles's background, impressed when he found in the Columbia library's card catalogue a book written by the young man on the Boer War. (He never realized the author was eight years old.) Even so, Dulles went to great lengths to convince the Todd family, particularly his future mother-in-law, that he would make a good husband. Clover had early hints that might not be the case. When Dulles took her to Princeton for a weekend, he ignored her to play tennis with Foster.

The Todds reluctantly announced the engagement in the New York papers on August 4. A little more than two months later, Clover and Allen were married in her grandmother's Baltimore mansion. Less than a month after that, the newlyweds set sail on the SS *Olympic* for France, where they boarded the Orient Express for a leisurely train ride to Dulles's next diplo-matic posting: Constantinople, now occupied by British, French, and Italian troops. Dulles had been designated the deputy in the embassy's U.S. High Commission to look out for American oil interests in the Ottoman Empire. His other, more important job: keeping watch on some 130,000 Russian refugees roaming inside Turkey plus the Bolshevik forces just outside its border in the Caucasus. Under his supervision, the embassy set up a wireless station to intercept Bolshevik radio messages to the region from Moscow, which Dulles had a team spend hours each day trying to decode. Clover, whom Dulles enjoyed showing off at embassy parties, thrived in Constanti-nople. She bought new furniture and Persian rugs for their rustic house with its small garden and spectacular view of the sapphire-blue Bosporus and gave English lessons in the afternoon to White Russian soldiers wounded in their civil war.

Clover was blissfully happy her first year in Constantinople, but strains in their marriage surfaced after her pregnancy with their first child. Dulles was an extrovert who enjoyed hobnobbing with the rich and powerful. The shy Clover had no interest in that. Dulles was absent long stretches for work and when he traveled with his wife, he often abandoned her to pursue his own interests, which would leave her in tears. And there were his women friends. Dulles had many. His relationships with Betty Carp, an efficient High Commission secretary skilled as a "fixer," and Fanny Billings, an American missionary in Constantinople, were platonic; Clover was good friends with both of them. But she could not be sure of others. Allen wrote her long letters when he was away, promising to be a better husband when he returned. Clover soon realized that would not be the case.

They returned to Washington in March 1922. Dulles became the head of the State Department's Near Eastern Division. Soon he and Clover led separate lives. He was away constantly on foreign trips. His letters when they were apart often told her of his nights on the town dancing with other women at parties, which Clover, caring for their first daughter (Clover Todd, whom they called Toddie) and pregnant with their second child, did not appreciate. When Dulles was home, his nose was buried in textbooks. Foster had talked him into enrolling in evening classes at George Washington University Law School. Dulles admitted to Clover in a letter that after four years of marriage "I have been getting worse and worse." He felt guilty. But not enough to change his ways. Clover became more drawn to her children and, her husband thought, more erratic in her behavior—temperamental and unpredictable at times, wasting money on spending binges, or walking out of the house to wander aimlessly.

By September 1926, Foster had convinced his brother, who now had his law degree, to give up the penurious life of a foreign service officer and join Sullivan & Cromwell, one of the most powerful law firms in the world with fifty attorneys headquartered at 49 Wall Street. Soon, Allen earned a six-figure salary, largely drumming up business for the firm from his international contacts. It was enough to buy a posh summer home in Lloyd Neck on Long Island's North Shore and to never again worry about his wife draining his bank account.

Allen, who nurtured dreams of one day being secretary of state like his grandfather and uncle, continued to dabble in foreign policy. He joined the

Council on Foreign Relations writing tracts for its journal *Foreign Affairs* and became a regular at "The Room," an informal confab of top New York financial men who gathered at an East 62nd Street apartment to share intelligence they picked up on overseas trips. The State Department also hired him in 1927 as a part-time legal adviser for its delegation involved in international conferences to limit the number of warships among the world's naval powers. Today, working as a counsel for the department and a private law firm, particularly one with so many foreign clients, would be considered a clear conflict of interest. At the time muckraking columnist Drew Pearson questioned the propriety of Dulles having both jobs. His foreign work also soon came to the attention of J. Edgar Hoover's agents, particularly with people the FBI suspected of being communists or engaged in espionage. The agents concluded Dulles was innocent of any wrongdoing. Hoover nonetheless opened a file on this young attorney, which he kept filling with agent reports for the rest of Dulles's life. The short-staffed State Department, however, depended on outside experts like Dulles. Sullivan & Cromwell, realizing the doors it opened for the firm, was only too happy to give Dulles the time off to tour Europe with American disarmament delegations.

It was on one such mission in 1933 that Dulles spent an hour and a half with Adolf Hitler. Franklin Roosevelt had dispatched Norman Davis, a Wall Street banker and diplomat, to Europe's capitals for another stab at what had so far been a futile effort to curb the continent's arms race. Dulles accompanied Davis and sat quietly taking notes in the Chancellery on Wilhelmstrasse the afternoon of April 8 as the new German leader harangued the two Americans on the oppressiveness of the Versailles Treaty. Germany believed in disarmament, Hitler insisted, but "had no intention of leaving herself as defenseless as she now is," Dulles wrote in his notes. Davis left the meeting publicly optimistic—the führer is a "dynamic force," he told reporters—but privately he worried about the dangers of the Nazi revolution. Dulles was strangely quiet afterward. Unlike Helms, who talked often about his lunch with Hitler, Dulles in later years hardly said a word about meeting the dictator. Three days after his Berlin visit he wrote to Clover only that it was an "interesting interview"—and to note that the hour and a half convinced him that Germany will make any progress in disarmament "much more difficult than it was before." Only later in October 1933, after he had returned to the United States from Europe and Hitler had announced that Germany was pulling out of the League of Nations, did Dulles begin to worry that the Nazis posed a serious threat to peace in Europe. Germany would not start a war immediately, he wrote in one memo, but she could "a couple of years hence."

When Dulles returned from his mission with Davis in October 1933 he had been away from Clover and his three children for nine of the previous twelve months. After Toddie, Joan had been born in 1923 and Allen Macy in 1930. Theirs was a warm and pleasant house, with servants and nannies to attend to the family and parents who never fought in front of the children. The only thing missing was the father. Dulles was rarely at home and when he was he showed little interest in the children beyond briefly looking up from his newspaper for perfunctory questions about their day. Joan later thought he would at least grow close to Allen Macy, a brilliant student and Dulles's intellectual equal, but he ignored "Sonny" (his nickname for the boy) as well. By 1930, Clover knew her husband was having many affairs. Dulles loved his wife. Neither of them ever considered divorce. But as he admitted in one letter, "I am rather too fond of the company of other ladies." (He never detailed his extracurricular jaunts beyond those hints.) The problem came to a head in the 1930s when Clover learned of his torrid romance with a Nordic blonde who was his mixed doubles partner in tennis. The children found out as well. Furious, Clover went on an expensive shopping trip to make him pay. More seriously, she and Toddie suffered bouts of depression, and Allen Macy became deeply troubled by his father's absences.

• • • •

Two weeks after Dulles heard the distressing news of Germany's invasion of France, he sat in a hotel bar near Philadelphia's Convention Hall at 34th and Spruce, where Republicans were nominating their 1940 presidential candidate to run against Franklin Roosevelt, who was seeking an unprecedented third term. Wild Bill Donovan, who rarely drank, nursed a cocktail with him. The two men had known each other in Washington during the 1920s, when Dulles was at the State Department and Donovan had been an assistant to the attorney general in Calvin Coolidge's administration. They had run into each other in New York law circles and occasionally played tennis together, but they were not close. Donovan found Dulles to be a fierce competitor on and off the court, which tended to irritate him. The two men talked about the war in Europe and American unpreparedness if drawn into it—a subject on which both men saw eye to eye. Donovan, a prominent member of the GOP's internationalist wing, secretly favored New York industrialist Wendell Willkie, a dark-horse candidate who supported American aid to the British. Dulles liked Willkie as well, but Foster had pressured him to back Manhattan district attorney Thomas E. Dewey, who was an isolationist. Willkie upset Dewey and won the nomination.

Allen had always been conflicted in his politics. A wealthy Wall Street lawyer, he was expected to be a Republican, as Foster was. Allen remained a GOP stalwart for the most part, working in New York party functions and even making a failed run for a Manhattan congressional seat in 1938 as a Republican. But he had worked for and worshipped Woodrow Wilson, a Democrat, and supported Roosevelt's initiatives to increase defense spending and supply Great Britain with arms. By the late 1930s, Allen had become a committed internationalist, calling for America to fight dictatorships that threatened democracy. He pressured Sullivan & Cromwell to close its Berlin office, which partnered with an old Prussian law firm, because of Hitler's persecution of the Jews, some of whom, from leading financial families, were Sullivan & Cromwell clients. That did not sit well with Foster, who deprecated internationalists like his brother as alarmists and believed there was still business to be done in Germany.

Though the two had clashed in New York politics, Roosevelt saw common cause with Donovan on foreign policy and sent the wealthy lawyer, whom Republicans had talked up as a future presidential candidate, to Europe in the summer of 1940 and winter of 1940–41 on fact-finding missions. Donovan reported back that Great Britain could survive German attacks if the United States stepped up its help. He also recommended that America needed a foreign intelligence service. Roosevelt, who had no spy agency to speak of, agreed. The tiny foreign intelligence units in the Army and Navy were often a dumping ground for poor-performing officers. In July 1941, FDR signed a vaguely worded executive order designating Donovan as head of the Coordinator of Information. The organization would be renamed the Office of Strategic Services a year later. Dulles had picked up rumors that Roosevelt had made Donovan chief of some nefarious spy group with unaccounted-for funds the White House controlled and that it had sparked a bureaucratic firestorm in Washington. Which was true. Hoover, whose hatred of Donovan would be matched only by how much Donovan despised him, saw this new agency as a threat to intelligence gathering by the FBI. General George C. Marshall, the Army chief of staff, feared Donovan was trying to set himself up as a czar controlling Army and Navy intelligence. Dulles decided to keep his distance from the Coordinator of Information, and see what else might be open to him if the United States joined the war. He did notice, however, that a number of his friends had gone to work for Donovan—such as Fred Dolbeare from Bern and David K. E. Bruce, an aristocratic Virginian who had married into the Mellon family.

Donovan liked to say that he started his intelligence agency from "minus zero," which was certainly the case. He began with a handful of trusted advisers, looking for agents and operations practically off the street. Flipping through personnel memos in his Washington headquarters in early September 1941, he stopped at the dossier that James Warburg, a New York banker now on the COI payroll, had compiled on the Dulles brothers. Foster wanted to volunteer his services, but Donovan and his senior aides were wary. Foster "is rather inclined to be an appeaser," Warburg noted. Allen, however, had compiled a notable record in Bern, the dossier noted, particularly in psychological warfare activities against the Germans. "He might be useful as a consultant," Warburg's memo advised.

As six Japanese aircraft carriers steamed east to the Hawaiian Islands, Dulles still played hard to get. Bruce, who occasionally played tennis with Dulles in Washington, had lost interest in him as a COI prospect. In a December 1, 1941, memo, he told Donovan that Dulles "for one reason or another had been eliminated" from consideration among the former State Department diplomats who might be useful to their spy agency.

PART TWO

WORLD WAR II

CHAPTER 6

WASHINGTON

Shortly before 8 a.m. Hawaiian time on December 7, the first wave of 181 Japanese torpedo bombers, dive-bombers, high-altitude bombers, and fighters swarmed over Oahu. The second wave of 170 enemy warplanes arrived just before 9 a.m. Most of the some ninety American battleships, cruisers, destroyers, and smaller vessels were nestled quietly in their piers at Pearl Harbor, their sleepy duty crews just awakening for Sunday morning chapel services. The U.S. vessels and most of the planes, parked wingtip to wingtip at a half dozen nearby airfields, could hardly have been easier targets. The two-hour raid left twenty-one Pacific Fleet ships damaged, more than 347 aircraft destroyed or disabled, and 2,403 Americans dead. Barely five months old, the Coordinator of Information escaped much of the blame that came after the sneak attack. For Navy and Army intelligence, Pearl Harbor was a monumental failure.

Donovan, who was attending a Sunday afternoon professional football game at New York's Polo Grounds, learned of the strike when a voice over a stadium loudspeaker summoned him to a phone and an aide on the line told him the president wanted him back at the White House immediately. In nearby Bellmore, where he was spending a weekend at his mother's house with Sophia, Bill Casey listened to reports of the attack on the radio. He was just finishing up a Research Institute of America study for Leo Cherne titled "Your Business Goes to War." Through early 1941, as he organized RIA's Washington office, Casey had rented a room in the Carroll Arms Hotel at 1st and C Streets, practically the only decent accommodation he could find in a capital city becoming more crowded as the government prepared for war. Sophia took the train down from New York on most weekends for visits. During weekdays, Bill set up a numbering system to keep track of Sophia's letters to him and his responses to her. After February 22, he needed the mail tracking less; they finally were married and Sophia moved to Washington permanently. They would have wed sooner but they decided to wait out the Depression, or at least until Casey's finances were secure enough for him to support a wife during the slow recovery. The young couple found a town house at 2500 Q Street in northwest Washington. Soon Sophia was pregnant. Bernadette, their only child, would arrive in 1943.

Casey was desperate to join the fight. His Long Island draft board expected as much, classifying him 1-A. Cherne was just as desperate, however, to retain him to produce RIA studies and papered the government with letters trying to keep Casey out of the Army. His RIA work was not considered vital enough to win a deferment, but Cherne managed to have him reclassified 3-A, which kept him in Washington because leaving supposedly would pose a hardship to his family. Casey went along with the deferment, but it felt humiliating; his younger brother and brother-in-law were in the service and other men with wives and children were being drafted. For more than a year he continued writing industrial mobilization reports for Cherne. He also helped RIA advise the War Production Board on priorities for U.S. manufacturers and served as a consultant for the Board of Economic Warfare (set up to try to strangle Axis economies). But by the spring of 1943, Casey could no longer stomach being stateside. He convinced Cherne to use his lobbying prowess, this time to get him into the military.

Casey, however, did not impress the armed forces as officer material. He took a physical and applied for a commission in the Army Air Forces, believing he could be valuable producing planes, but the Army thought he was too old at thirty and would offer him only a job as an enlisted man perhaps on an assembly line. The Navy was no more impressed with him. Officers who interviewed Casey found him well qualified for research work but slovenly dressed, unmilitary-looking, and difficult to understand because of his mumbling. Moreover, Navy doctors ruled that he was physically unfit for sea duty because of astigmatism in both eyes and "marked kyphosis" (a curvature of the spine commonly called a hunched back). Casey pleaded his case, inundating the service with recommendation letters from friends. The Navy finally found a home for him with its Office of Procurement and Material, which seeing the value of his RIA experience for its shipbuilding programs ordered personnel officers to ignore his physical defects and make him an officer immediately. Pushing his luck, Casey asked that he skip two ranks and be brought in as a full lieutenant. The Navy thought that a bit too much and agreed to allow him to enter on April 26, 1943, as a lieutenant junior grade, one step above the lowest commissioned rank of ensign.

He looked jaunty in his crisp new uniform with the one and a half gold stripes on his sleeves. But Casey soon discovered that sitting behind a desk in the Navy procurement office on Constitution Avenue was not much different from working for RIA. He spent his days unsnarling bottlenecks in the production of landing craft—a job more important than he realized. The Allies desperately needed more of the small amphibious vessels for the invasion of France. But Casey found the work boring. His claim that he "itched for action" was likely a hollow boast. He was, after all, physically unfit for combat. But there had to be work in the war more exciting than this, he thought.

Casey noticed that a number of wealthy young men who wangled commissions had found jobs with a secretive organization a former Wall Street lawyer ran out of a converted Public Health Service building on Navy Hill at 25th and E Streets. Donovan's OSS indeed had attracted officers from America's best families—a fact that had not gone unnoticed by newspaper reporters, who sometimes snickered in their columns that OSS stood for "Oh So Social" and that the agency's Navy Hill headquarters was the "bad eyes brigade" because so many of its staffers wore glasses or were otherwise physically unfit for combat. Casey knew little about intelligence gathering beyond interviewing a few German Jews on the RIA payroll about how the Nazis mobilized their war industry. He had also picked up gossip that the OSS was FDR's pet project, but he set aside his distaste for Roosevelt and began looking for ways to get a foot in the door.

The only connection Casey could find with the OSS—and it was a remote one at that—was Jerome Doran, a lawyer in Donovan's Wall Street firm. Casey had parked cars with him one summer at Jones Beach when the two were in college. Doran agreed to contact Otto "Ole" Doering Jr., a former law partner in Donovan's firm and now one of his top aides in the OSS, to see if he would agree to an interview. At the end of August 1943, Casey walked past commandos practicing hand-to-hand combat on the front lawn and up the steps past the marble pillars to the entrance for the headquarters building OSS officers had nicknamed "the Kremlin." After checking his identification with a visitors' log, a security guard phoned for an escort to take Casey to Doering's small first-floor office down the hall from Donovan's. Men and women, many carrying files with SECRET stamped on them, almost knocked him over as they darted through corridors, talking quickly among themselves in whispered conversations.

Sitting behind his desk when the escort ushered Casey in, Doering wore an Army major's uniform and appeared to Casey to be cheerful and self-effacing. This demeanor masked a ruthlessly efficient general counsel, who had helped Donovan assemble and collate massive amounts of information for the law firm's complex antitrust cases and who now handled administrative chores in the OSS and watched Donovan's back for countless bureaucratic enemies trying to sabotage his organization. After the briefest of small talk, Doering quickly got to the point. He had organized a secretariat for Donovan's Washington headquarters and was looking for someone to do the same at the OSS station in London. Casey wondered if the major was talking about a piece of furniture. Doering explained. The secretariat was a concoction the Joint Chiefs of Staff had adopted from the British and had urged complex organizations like Donovan's to set up. It was a coterie of eager administrative aides around the OSS director who helped smooth relations between the agency and other military organizations, who served as Donovan's eyes and ears tracking the multitude of units under his command, and who ensured the spy organization's rank and file faithfully carried out his many orders. Doering needed an energetic young man like Casey to set up a secretariat in the London station, now run by David Bruce. He told Casey to report back to headquarters at ten o'clock the next morning, September 1, for another round of interviews.

As he did in so many of his job interviews, Casey made a poor first impression the next day. Sophia had starched and pressed his summer khakis so the uniform would hold up in the stifling heat that oppressed Washington each September. Casey seemed to the first interviewer bright, unusually well qualified, and eager to join the spy service for the adventure. But his appearance and military bearing were underwhelming, the interviewer thought. Clearly Casey wasn't suited for leading saboteurs in the field. His next interviewer—Colonel Charles Vanderblue, a former New York manufacturer who now served as a headhunter for Donovan—was more favorably disposed. The analytical and organizational skills Casey had acquired at RIA made him ideal to head a secretariat, Vanderblue thought. He confided to the junior lieutenant that the OSS London station was an organizational mess. Bruce was a good big-picture man, but as erratic an administrator as Donovan was. Doering needed a secretariat there to clean up the bureaucratic chaos Bruce left in his wake as the secretariat in Washington did for Donovan. Casey was fascinated by the prospect of going abroad. But he realized he was not the unanimous choice for the job, so he ginned up another one of his recommendation letter campaigns, this time aimed at Doering and Vanderblue. Then he waited.

It took a month for Doering and the others to make up their minds, but the OSS finally delivered a request to the Navy to have Casey transferred to the spy service's headquarters to prepare for an "urgent" assignment in London. The Navy, which had grown irritated with Donovan poaching its officers, agreed only to loan Casey for the time being. He was sent to the Kremlin on October 13. Cherne generously agreed to continue paying him his $12,000-a-year RIA salary while he served with the OSS, which meant Casey and Sophia lived well.

After a quick background check for his security clearance, Casey spent the next two months in the Washington headquarters roaming quietly from office to office, taking copious notes on how Donovan's far-flung agency operated. Casey performed odd jobs for the secretariat to learn its inner workings. He toured the secret camps the OSS ran in southern Maryland to observe how the agency trained its spies and commandos. Sitting in on conferences just to listen, it did not take Casey long to realize that in the fall of 1943, with the United States almost two years into the war, Donovan and his senior aides still spent "an inordinate amount of time," as Casey later wrote, fending off bureaucratic enemies in the Pentagon, State Department, and FBI. He could also see that chaos reigned most days atop Navy Hill—Casey could never tell if it was organized or not—with bodies in the headquarters building in constant motion. Casey marveled at the diverse assemblage Donovan had recruited for his organization—the best and brightest from academia, the scientific community, finance, law, journalism, even the sports world, along with an assortment of circus stars, race car drivers, safecrackers, lock pickers, forgers, break-in artists, and an occasional Mafia thug—most of whom appeared to have little more experience in espionage or sabotage than he did. But no one captivated Casey's attention more than the sixty-year-old lawyer, now plump around the middle with his hair turned white, who presided over this aggregation of talent.

Doering placed Casey on the corridor Donovan occupied, sitting at a small desk in the office of Edwin Putzell, another Donovan law colleague who now managed his schedule and the flow of memos and intelligence reports to him. From that vantage point Casey could witness Donovan's office routine: At 9 a.m. he convened a half-hour senior staff meeting to review the intelligence that had come in overnight or deal with sudden emergencies that had cropped up overseas. The next hour he quickly waded through the mail, foreign cables, and memos stacked on his desk, using a lead pencil to scrawl comments, correct mistakes, or demand more information from the documents he speed-read. By 10:30, he was ready to plunge into one meeting after another with military generals, diplomats, cabinet officers, branch chiefs in his organization, spies and commandos on home leave, and an occasional journalist for an off-the-record session. Casey saw that he rarely ate a breakfast, lunch, or dinner without an aide briefing him as he wolfed down his food. And after Donovan's workday ended, often at 11 p.m., Casey saw, as he locked his own safe and prepared to return to Sophia and his baby daughter, that Donovan walked to the chauffeured car that took him to his Georgetown home usually lugging a briefcase full of reports his research and analysis section had produced on Axis military capabilities.

Occasionally, Donovan—as he was prone to do with anyone walking by—would wave Casey into his office just for a chat. The director had a talent for making an OSS officer—even a junior one like Casey—feel as if he were the most important person in the organization and an intimate friend and adviser—though Donovan actually had few of them. Casey was enthralled. Never had he been in the presence of a man—with his soft voice and gentle manner—who exuded such power and charisma. He found Donovan to be a quick study, able to grasp the essence of problems rapidly and to make decisions fast. Casey intensely studied Donovan's management style, which often drove his branch chiefs half mad. Donovan delegated authority in headquarters "but kept his fingers on everything," Casey later wrote. He ignored organizational charts and the chain of command, leap-frogging senior officers to phone underlings for information. He gave his station chiefs overseas broad authority, but would often swoop in and make snap decisions to upend spy missions. "His watchword," Casey wrote, "was 'the perfect is the enemy of the good' and he used it as he moved about improvising and implementing operations which in any other part of the American war machine would have required months for study, debate and clearance." It was the kind of leadership Casey intended to practice if ever given the chance.

By the end of October, Doering was convinced he had the right man to organize the secretariat in London. Casey had extraordinary administrative talent, he thought. The junior lieutenant was able to write clear, succinct reports and to get things done. Donovan was impressed as well and agreed that the former RIA analyst should be sent to Bruce. In early November 1943, Casey received his orders to fly to London. The Navy finally released him to the OSS. Unlike Dulles, who was never bothered by long absences from his family, Casey dreaded leaving his beloved Sophia and Bernadette. But the Washington headquarters just processed paper. The real intelligence work happened overseas and the most important station in Donovan's grow-ing spy empire was London. Casey wanted to be there.

CHAPTER 7

JEDBURGH

Bill Colby liked to quote Napoleon's standing order for his troops: "March to the sound of the guns." Since the Pearl Harbor attack, it seemed to him as if he was marching in the opposite direction—further and further away from that sound. Colby quit Columbia Law School after a year. He was finally old enough at twenty-one to be commissioned in August 1941 as an ROTC second lieutenant. The Army packed him off to muggy hot Fort Bragg, just outside Fayetteville, North Carolina, where he languished for six months in a replacement unit for new officers awaiting assignment. In February 1942, he finally received orders to Fort Sill, another desolate Army post near Lawton, Oklahoma, to begin his training as an artillery officer. Colby's punishment for being a good student—or at least he considered it bad luck—was being selected after he graduated to remain at the post as an instructor teaching other students how to fire the howitzers, instead of shipping off to the front with a combat unit. He began to worry that he would miss this war as his father had the last one.

Four months into the boring job, he one day spotted a notice posted on a bulletin board that the Army wanted volunteers to test an idea the War Department had recently approved to parachute artillery pieces and their gunners out of planes. The notice also stated that Fort Sill's commanders could not block any officer who wanted to join an airborne artillery battalion. Seeing it as his best chance to escape Oklahoma and get into the fight, Colby volunteered. The only problem: his poor eyesight, which had kept him out of West Point, might bar him from being a paratrooper, he worried. When the time came for his physical, he made sure to sit down next to the eye chart to undress so he could memorize the lines of letters. He read them off with no problem during the exam.

"Now do it backwards," ordered the doctor, suspicious his patient was cheating.

Colby stumbled with his answer.

"You really want to be a parachutist," the physician said.

"You're damn right I do," Colby answered.

"I think you'll be able to see the ground okay" after jumping out of a plane, the doctor said with a chuckle and approved his application.

Fort Benning, which took up more than 180,000 acres of rolling pine-covered hills along the Chattahoochee River in west Georgia, was home for the infantry. It advertised itself as "the most complete Army Post in the continental United States," producing each week some one thousand new lieutenants, who were quickly shipped off to combat platoons at the front. Colby arrived in September 1942 because Fort Benning also trained paratroopers in a tent city set up on the west side of the Chattahoochee in Alabama. The more he studied it, the more he thought the idea of airborne artillery battalions laughable. The heavy 75-millimeter howitzers he fired were each shoved out of a cargo plane in nine separate parachute packs, none of which arrived in the same place when they landed on the ground—or at least not in the drops practiced at Fort Benning. Invariably the gunners could find only eight of the nine packs. Colby, nevertheless, was eager to give it a try if it brought him closer to the war. Running double-time to each class for four weeks, he practiced jumping from a mock-up aircraft, dangling from a suspended harness to simulate floating down, free-falling under a billowing parachute canopy from a 250-foot-high steel tower, and learning to roll when he landed to soften the impact of hitting earth.

Bad luck continued to dog him, however. On his second practice jump from a plane, Colby broke his right ankle. It took six months for the ankle to heal so he could finish his parachute training and be assigned as an assistant operations officer in an airborne artillery battalion in April 1943. But just before the battalion was to ship out to North Africa with the 82nd Airborne Division its lackluster commander was relieved and the lieutenant colonel who replaced him brought in his own personal staff, including an assistant operations officer to take Colby's job. Once more the Army shunted him to a replacement pool, this time at Camp Mackall, an outpost in what had once been wilderness just west of Fort Bragg, but now had 1,750 buildings, erected since the start of the war. Again, he waited and watched enviously as other officers in the pool received orders to join parachute units.

One day in mid-October, Colby noticed that tacked to a camp bulletin board was a sheet with OSS stamped at the top, advertising that if you spoke French and were looking for adventure overseas, call this number. From his month in France the summer after his junior year, Colby spoke French, although it was not perfect. (A friend called it "creative French"; if he did not know a word he made it up.) Colby had no idea what OSS stood for, but it sounded a hell of a lot more interesting than hunting on the ground to put nine pieces of a howitzer back together. He called the phone number on the sheet.

· · · ·

Few in the OSS knew the details of the top secret project. Even its code name was classified. A senior Donovan aide had ordered recruiters to canvass the United States for suitable men. Clutching secret memos with detailed specifications, they fanned out to Fort Benning, Fort Bragg, Camp Mackall, and other Army posts, flashing security badges to bewildered unit commanders so they could root through their personnel files to round up a hundred junior officers who spoke French. From that pool the recruiters wanted fifty of the most reliable ones to be commando team leaders— preferably first lieutenants and captains, but they would take majors if they were young and aggressive. The other fifty would be assigned to staff jobs for the project. The recruiters also wanted fifty enlisted radio operators, whom they were most likely to find at Camp Crowder in southwest Missouri or Fort Monmouth near the New Jersey shore, where the Army trained them. At Camp Crowder, OSS agents locked themselves in an empty office and screened the files of 1,200 names. The radio operators did not have to be as highly qualified as the officers. They needed only a fair working knowledge of French. Even so, Signal Corps trainers told these mysterious OSS operatives they would have an easier time finding prospects if they accepted French-speaking men who tapped out Morse code at slower speeds. The recruiters eventually picked sixty-two soldiers, with at least fifteen-words-a-minute speed. By the end of November, they had found 109 officers, many from parachute regiments.

On October 20, Colby walked into a bare room at Camp Mackall with only a desk and two metal chairs. A man, who identified himself as Shelly, sat behind the desk with a pen and notepad. Colby never heard Shelly's first name if he ever told it. Recruiters had met prospects in diners and hotel lobbies to make their pitches, or they gathered them in conference rooms for presentations. Sometimes the rooms emptied afterward save for a few who remained to sign up. The bulletin board pitches also attracted a number of questionable characters—thrill seekers, men mentally unbalanced or escaping bad marriages. The OSS was not interested in them. The recruiters wrote down short notes with their gut feelings on each man. The comments could be brutal. "Nit wit—I think. Critical of everything but himself," a recruiter scribbled down for one captain. "Brilliant Phi Beta Kappa," the notation for a major read, "but questionable type for any duty . . . too damn talkative." Foreign-born officers fluent in European languages and culture were prized, but they often came with complicated pasts that had to be examined more closely. A German Jew dismissed from grade school when the Nazis came to power had made his way to America and was now "in a definite vengeful mood" and eager "to take a crack at the Hitler system without regard for his own safety," a recruiter's memo noted. They decided he was a good candidate. An Austrian émigré whose mother had been married three times appeared "reserved" during his interview "and gives evidence of unplumbed depths," according to the memo. He claimed to be "bitter" toward the Nazis. "I have no specific suspicions," the OSS interviewer noted, but "it seems to me that a reasonably clever actor might have memorized the explanations he gave me."

Shelly warned Colby not to repeat anything spoken in this meeting. The OSS, he said, was looking for daring young men with proven leadership skills, men who were adept with small arms, who could speak and understand French (although "scholastic proficiency and accent" were "not essential," he recited from a memo), and men who were in superb physical condition. The officers should also be experienced in handling soldiers, preferably from prior combat, and they should be prepared to parachute in uniform behind enemy lines and operate on their own in "a highly hazardous mission." Colby nodded, asked a few questions, but Shelly enlightened him little on the spy agency the recruiter represented. Shelly was also under orders not to tell Colby the code name of the OSS unit he would join, nor its mission, nor the country into which he would parachute.

Colby had no combat experience and precious little time commanding troops, but Shelly marked in notes that the young captain appeared to be highly intelligent, he looked sharp, he definitely had "military bearing," and he gave the impression of being a self-starter and a competent leader. Colby did not want to join for revenge or money or any other questionable reason. He just "wants action," the interview report stated. Shelly wrote that if he were his commander he would sign up Colby for a simple reason. He seemed "dependable."

Heroism, Colby always thought, came not in the heat of battle with shells exploding around you and bullets aimed at you. A soldier's training kicked in then. He fought simply to survive, to protect his comrades or out of anger or fear of looking like a coward. Real courage came in a peaceful room thousands of miles from the sound of the guns, as he was in now, when a man made the quiet decision to risk his life. He told Shelly he wanted to join.

Colby received secret orders the next day instructing him to report to the OSS headquarters in Washington between October 22 and October 24. The orders also told him to come with his bags packed for Europe. The same set of instructions was telegraphed to the other 108 officers, although recruiters expected only fifty of them to eventually make the trip abroad. Colby was determined never to return to Camp Mackall. He was smart enough to deduce where this mysterious unit wanted him to drop into if Shelly was so interested in how well he spoke French. From his summer abroad he had fallen in love with France. But it was now a troubled nation.

. . . .

The German invasion on May 10, 1940, had been swift and efficient. It took just six weeks for the Wehrmacht's blitzkrieg to conquer the country, aided in good measure by the failure of the French military. The defeat, which left

French men and women stunned, was catastrophic. The only success for the humiliated Western armies—more than 330,000 British and French soldiers managed to evacuate from Dunkirk. The France they left behind began its "Dark Years," as they came to be called.

The armistice terms Hitler's emissary signed on June 22 with a French representative were simple, harsh, and terribly convenient for the Germans. The French army that remained after Dunkirk demobilized, save for 100,000 soldiers used to maintain internal order. The navy docked its fleet. The German army occupied the northern half of the country including Paris. Because it saved Wehrmacht manpower, Hitler found it to his advantage to leave the southern half unoccupied and run by a government Marshal Philippe Pétain set up. When American and British troops successfully invaded North Africa in November 1942—and a foul-mouthed, pro-Nazi admiral named François Darlan agreed to switch sides and have his French forces in the region join the Allies—an enraged Hitler sent his army into the rest of France to occupy it. He left Pétain—now even more a figurehead—in office to administer the southern half from the quiet summer resort town of Vichy.

Pétain believed Germany had defeated France because she was soft, rotted to her core by feckless politicians, and now in danger of being taken over by communists. The eighty-four-year-old marshal—vain and cunning yet universally revered by his countrymen for his defense of Verdun during World War I—viewed Great Britain as more the enemy than Germany. He vowed to bring a "new order" to his country. Pétain's collaborationist prime minister, the far more detested Pierre Laval, became his enforcer, obsessed with keeping the Nazis calm, even openly calling for their victory in the war.

Hitler's occupation policy was premised on terror. For every German victim of a guerrilla attack, the Gestapo or SS executed fifty to a hundred French civilians. France's industry—and ultimately about 650,000 of its workers—was drafted to feed the Nazi war machine with military vehicles, planes, locomotives, weapons, and champagne. The fascist Vichy regime, through its hated paramilitaries called the Milice française, became as repressive as the Nazis, aiding in the execution of some 30,000 resisters and cooperating in the deportation of 75,000 Jews to the Auschwitz concentration camp where they perished. The 25,000 to 30,000 Milice thugs were aided by even more French collaborators, up to 220,000 by one rough count—among them traitorous snitches, right-wing extremists, greedy businessmen, opportunistic entrepreneurs, shady middlemen, outright criminals, and prostitutes (the "horizontal collaborators").

After the fall of France, British prime minister Winston Churchill adopted a three-pronged strategy: bomb German cities from the air, quarantine the enemy with the still formidable British navy, and stir revolt in the countries Hitler had conquered. To set occupied Europe "ablaze," the prong Donovan enthusiastically supported, Churchill established the Special Operations Executive, an unconventional warfare organization of commandos and saboteurs, headquartered in several tightly guarded town houses on Baker Street in London. It became known by such nicknames as "the Old Firm" and "the Racket." A unit inside SOE, called the F Section, was created to stir up sabotage operations in France.

The F Section got off to a slow start. For at least the first year and a half, a large majority of the French public, focused more on day-to-day survival and believing the Germans would win the war, remained passive toward the occupation, preferring *attentisme* (wait and see). Stray attacks did occur—a few occupation officials assassinated, freight cars loaded with supplies for the Third Reich misdirected, an enemy weapons depot raided—and an occasional British bomber dropped in SOE agents with radios and explosives. But it all amounted to little more than vandalism for the 850,000 Germans stationed in the country. Most French citizens thought such attacks were futile.

As Pétain made his peace with the Nazis in June 1940, a newly promoted and largely unknown French general with an unspectacular military career, "a head like a pineapple and hips like a woman's" (a British diplomat's description of him), set up his exile office near Buckingham Palace and declared himself chief of the provisional French government. Dulles believed Charles de Gaulle stood as the only viable leader of a future French resistance, but that view was decidedly in the minority. Churchill thought de Gaulle might be crazy and kept a "frog file" on him, Roosevelt remained dubious of the French general throughout his presidency, and Dwight Eisenhower, the Supreme Allied Commander in Europe, thought he had a "Joan of Arc complex." Among the colorful characters de Gaulle assembled in his makeshift headquarters was Colonel André Dewavrin, his intelligence chief, who went by the code name "Passy." Donovan thought he could work with the colonel, who was deeply suspicious of the British, but U.S. Army intelligence considered him a right-wing thug. Passy would later be accused of torturing captured enemy agents in the basement of his London headquarters.

Soon, however, mounting German atrocities and Vichy police repression roused French citizens from their apathy. By spring 1943, clandestine guerrilla networks—the SOE called them "circuits"—had sprung up throughout France, their membership growing to the tens of thousands. Thousands more young Frenchmen fled to the foothills of the French Alps to escape being drafted as German slave labor. They formed armed bands known as the Maquis—the local word for a scrub bush that survives in the island of Corsica's hills, as these resisters did in France's remote countryside. Aided by the SOE, saboteurs cut telephone lines, derailed trains, destroyed electric power transformers, damaged factories supplying the Third Reich, ambushed German soldiers, and assassinated Gestapo collaborators. France reached "a serious turning point" in 1943, Field Marshal Gerd von Rundstedt, the occupation commander, wrote in a memo; it was becoming "impossible to dispatch single members of the Wehrmacht, ambulances, couriers or supply columns without armed protection."

The French Resistance, however, was more a collection of three poorly armed and loosely organized factions—the communist Francs-Tireurs et Partisans (FTP), disaffected Vichy soldiers of L'Organisation de résistance de l'armée (ORA), and de Gaulle's Forces Françaises de l'Intérieur (FFI)—all fighting the Germans on their own and feuding with one another in the field. Donovan considered them a mixed blessing. Eisenhower's staff found them poorly coordinated, often working at cross-purposes. De Gaulle— initially as suspicious of the disparate guerrilla groups as they were of him— eventually succeeded in uniting them under his FFI by the end of 1943. But the three factions remained wary of one another throughout the war and whatever authority the politically ambitious de Gaulle had over them held together with baling wire and sleight-of-hand. "Only a small minority of adult French" identify themselves with de Gaulle, an OSS report concluded. Very few regard him "as a possible head of a future government."

The Resistance's early battlefield successes also proved short-lived. The Germans recognized that the most effective way to combat the insurgency was to infiltrate it. For that task they had a vast security apparatus in France beyond what the Milice provided: the military's counterintelligence arm (Abwehr III), the Nazi Party counterintelligence service (the Gestapo), the Sicherheitsdienst or SD (a spy service working closely with the Gestapo), and an assortment of military police units. French informers—the Abwehr and Gestapo called them "V-men"—wormed their way into the commands of many circuits. In June 1943, the Nazis sprang their trap. Mass arrests were carried out, hundreds of Resistance leaders were carted off to torture chambers or grisly executions, and arms caches were captured. The nation-wide raids decimated the Resistance—but did not wipe it out. The Germans had not discovered all the weapons stores. The V-men penetrations gave the SOE valuable intelligence on what the enemy knew about the networks so holes in security could be plugged. The circuits rebuilt. By the end of 1943 the resilient Resistance had resumed its expansion with Abwehr, Gestapo, and SD resources now stretched thin to stanch it. But SOE's commanders recognized that even if the Germans could no longer roll it back, the Resistance desperately needed an infusion of leadership from London if it was to make any meaningful contribution to the Allied invasion of France.

. . . .

Franklin Canfield, a recently commissioned OSS captain who had been a Dulles law partner in Sullivan & Cromwell's Paris office, sat quietly in a British command center in London late on the night of March 3, 1943, watching as SOE staffers began to answer radio calls and rush to large maps to mark the positions of commando teams with colored pins. Canfield had been asked to join the SOE officers to be "properly indoctrinated," as one classified British memo he would never be shown put it. Delighted with the invitation—SOE officers had largely ignored him since he arrived in London two months earlier to organize OSS commando operations into occupied Europe—the thirty-two-year-old Army officer needed little enticing. He now observed the unfolding of "Spartan," the code name for a nationwide war game hundreds of thousands of British and Canadian troops were staging to practice the invasion of continental Europe. The SOE was testing the idea of parachuting in eleven three-man commando teams ahead of the invading force to link up with resistance groups (played in this case by Royal Welsh Fusiliers), which were leaderless. As the British forces marched north across the chalk plateau of southern England's Salisbury Plain, the three-man teams—made up of an SOE officer, a foreign guide, and a radio operator—were assigned to lead the local guerrillas in mock raids, such as blowing up targets, attacking enemy headquarters, and cutting phone lines. Canfield and several French and Belgian officers had been invited to the command center for a little persuasion because the SOE did not have enough commandos for at least seventy three-man teams it wanted to parachute into France and possibly occupied Belgium and Holland. The British needed French-speaking natives as guides and they were willing to make the OSS a partner in the operation if the Americans would provide officers as team leaders along with radio operators.

The Special Operations Executive had been brainstorming the idea since spring 1942. The three-man teams—consisting of a British or American officer, a foreign officer from the country to which they were headed, and a radioman—would parachute deep behind enemy lines on or just after the invasion of France. They would be the Allied high command's liaisons with the Resistance networks, passing along London's orders to them and arranging for arms and other supplies to be airdropped to the circuits. Wearing their uniforms—the SOE believed it would boost French morale and reinforce the message that the local guerrillas were now part of the Allies' broader war strategy—the commandos would help lead Resistance attacks to disrupt train travel, cut telephone lines, ambush German officers in cars, raid enemy supply depots, cripple Luftwaffe planes at airfields, disable power plants the Wehrmacht used, destroy bridges needed for their convoys, and radio back intelligence on their troop concentrations for Allied bombers.

Ever since he formed his spy agency in July 1941, Donovan had been angling to have commandos be a part of it. In fact, if FDR would have let him, Donovan was ready to lead the unconventional warriors into battle himself. Roosevelt deferred that kind of decision to George Marshall, who would not hear of it, but the Army chief of staff did allow Donovan to form what became known as the Operational Group, a two-thousand-man commando force skilled in guerrilla attacks that officers far younger than he would lead

behind enemy lines. Exercise Spartan, which ended on March 11, demonstrated that the three-man teams, parachuted in at the eleventh hour, could
organize unorganized Resistance fighters to launch attacks that aided the
conventional army's invasion. Some senior aides thought Donovan's agency
should stick to spying and leave guerrilla warfare to the military while others were leery of peeling off the commandos the OSS did produce to join the
British in an operation as risky as this one. Indeed, it was a bold plan at a
time in 1943 when the outcome of Europe's war was far from certain and the
Allies did not know if the German army would throw their invaders back
into the ocean after they landed on the coast of France. But Donovan liked
the idea of infiltrating multinational teams and lobbied the Joint Chiefs
of Staff and American commanders in Europe to approve it. Five months
after the Spartan exercise, they did. The SOE gave the program a randomly
generated code name, which also happened to be the name of a town in
Scotland—Jedburgh.

Promoted to major, Canfield was given the job of recruiting and training the one hundred commandos the OSS promised for the operation. He
rushed back to the United States in early September with high-priority orders from Donovan to scour the military for the best men.

•   •   •   •

American and British commanders ordered that Colby and the other recruits be kept ignorant of the planning that led to Jedburgh. Secrecy was
paramount. The third week of October, Colby wandered the halls of the
Munitions Building on Constitution Avenue in Washington hunting for
Room 1048. He found it and inside a roly-poly Army major with a limp salute, whose sole job was to confirm that Colby's identity matched the name
he had on the pile of personnel files in front of him. It did. The bored major,
barely looking up from his paperwork, wrote down the address for the Q
Building in the OSS headquarters complex on Navy Hill, handed him the
slip of paper, and told him to report there the next morning.

Colby arrived at Navy Hill as instructed. A guard at the entrance to the
Q Building checked his name off a list Canfield had provided and directed
an escort to take him to the Special Operations Branch. For the rest of the
day, Colby underwent another physical, filled out a lengthy personal his-

tory form, answered intimate questions about his finances so OSS security officers could have the credit agency, Dun and Bradstreet, run a check on him, and sat through more interviews with Canfield and other officers running the Jedburgh program. They told him that a World War I hero named Bill Donovan led the OSS, that the agency worked for the president of the United States, that Colby would be extensively trained before being thrown into the dangerous combat, and that he should keep his mouth shut when friends and family now asked him what he did in the military. No mention was made of the Jedburgh name or the country in which Colby would fight. At the end of the day, they told him to check out of the temporary quarters the OSS had provided at nearby Fort Myer and be standing at the entrance to the Q Building the next morning with his bags packed.

Two-and-a-half-ton trucks with canvas tops lined up at the Q Building and scores of young officers milled about when Colby arrived the next morning. He tossed his bag into the back of one of the trucks and climbed in. John Singlaub, a Californian who had studied French and Japanese at UCLA and was serving in a parachute infantry regiment at Fort Benning when OSS recruiters talked him into giving it up, climbed in behind Colby.

"Where are we going?" Singlaub shouted to the driver in the front.

"The Congressional Country Club," the driver shouted back.

Singlaub, Colby, and the other officers crowded onto benches in the back laughed. Must be some joke. A private folded down the back flaps to the canvas so they could not look outside.

After a half-hour bumpy ride the truck came to a stop. The driver walked to the back and opened the flaps. To their surprise, Colby and the others, squinting from the bright light, discovered that he had not been kidding. They climbed out into the circular driveway at the Congressional Country Club.

Located off River Road on four hundred acres just northwest of the District of Columbia line in Bethesda, Maryland, the club had fallen on hard times by 1943 with its membership shrunk after the Depression. Donovan rescued it from foreclosure when he agreed to lease the facility for $4,000 a month and repair any damages after the war ended. Its open fairways, streams, and thick woods were perfect for training spies and saboteurs, plus Congressional was close enough to the capital so that he could drive congressmen and senior government officials to it to show off how the OSS trained its secret warriors. The agency designated it Area F. Rows of tents for the students were planted around the clubhouse, which looked like a grand hacienda with a red-tiled roof. Loudspeakers were nailed to the walls outside so the recording of a bugler blowing reveille could blast them out of their cots in the morning. Inside, the charming main dining room was converted into a dreary GI mess hall, the spacious ballroom with its crystal chandeliers hanging from its ceiling was partitioned into classrooms, the wood-paneled bar became an officers' lounge, and the indoor pool was drained and boarded over so desks could be placed on top. An obstacle course was constructed near the first tee. The fuselage of a cargo plane was placed near its putting green along with a half dozen suspended harnesses so parachutists could practice jumping out into a sand trap. Firing ranges, demolition pits, and simulated minefields dotted other fairways. Robert Kehoe, a young radio operator who had dropped out of college after two years, called Area F "a luxurious shock."

Colby and other recruits spent the next two weeks, early morning often to midnight, engaged in what the instructors told them was the beginning of their commando training. That was a cover story for testers who wanted to weed out the men who did not possess the qualities needed to be commandos. They endured miles of cross-country running and hours on the obstacle course for physical conditioning. They were sent out on guerrilla exercises often with no sleep the night before to test how they reacted under stress. Instructors divided the students into groups of a half dozen, with one designated as the leader, and gave them mock missions, such as sneaking up on a guard, blowing up a bridge over a fairway's water hazard, or simply moving a heavy object from one spot to another to test their ingenuity. All the while psychologists lurked nearby, asking the recruits seemingly innocent questions and marking notes on clipboards.

Sometimes men they had never seen before posed as lazy or overaggressive students and infiltrated the groups to see how they reacted to someone not pulling his weight or taking too many chances. Or, to test their ability to make quick decisions, they were locked in a dark cellar, a guard outside slipped a note under the door with instructions on how to escape, and the students had to decide whether to risk fleeing or to stay put. They were assigned impossible tasks. During one exercise, instructors ordered Colby and a comrade to climb up greased ropes. The comrade reached higher but fell to the ground sooner than Colby, who held on for as long as he could, then finally said, "I can't do it," and let go. His friend washed out, probably, Colby believed, because he gave up sooner than the instructor expected.

Many of the recruits came to despise the two weeks of screening with the psychologists spying on them constantly, trying to trip them up with creepy questions that could send them packing if they gave an answer the shrinks didn't like. Colby found his Country Club sojourn delightfully fun. Often he was in the same test group as Singlaub, who thought his New England accent amusing the few times Colby spoke. Airborne infantry officers like Singlaub tended to be a boisterous bunch. Colby was one of the quiet ones. The fact that this artillery officer had qualified as a paratrooper even though he had bad eyes impressed Singlaub. Only much later did he learn that Colby had graduated from Princeton. He did not wear his Ivy League credentials on his sleeve.

At the end of the two weeks, a bus took each man back to the Kremlin for a private interview with Donovan. Colby walked nervously into the director's corner office in Room 109 (which also became Donovan's code number on OSS documents). He saluted and said stiffly: "Major Colby reporting as ordered." Though it was early November and the weather had turned chilly, Donovan, as always, kept open his window with its view of the Potomac. Though middle-aged, his bright blue eyes and the Irish charm he could turn on when he spoke still made him irresistible to women. Promoted to brigadier general eight months earlier, his new uniform came immaculately tailored from Wetzel in New York with just his Medal of Honor ribbon sewn to the jacket—a not so subtle reminder in meetings with other flag officers draped in rows of ribbons that he had the only award that counted. Donovan waved Colby to a hard-backed chair in front of his desk, which on one corner had two telephones with direct lines to the White House and Pentagon and on the other an in-box piled high with classified documents.

Donovan asked the question he posed to practically all the Jedburgh candidates: "What makes you think you're qualified to serve in this unit?" When the candidate recited the training and jobs he had had in the military, as Colby did, Donovan always interrupted him: "Yeah, I know all about that." And he did. Donovan carefully read the personnel file of each man before he walked in. Colby had to answer the more difficult question of what in his soul made him want to risk his life for a dangerous operation whose details he knew nothing about. Colby stammered out an answer about wanting to serve his country and taste adventure. It was not eloquent, but enough for Donovan to approve his continuing to the next phase of training.

Trucks took Colby and the other candidates who had made the cut at Congressional to a camp in the Catoctin Mountains near Thurmont, Maryland. Desperate for training areas near big cities, the Army had taken over nine thousand acres of National Park Service recreational land there and in the fall of 1942 had turned over part of it, a former camp for handicapped children called Greentop, to the OSS. Donovan set up three schools to train commandos in guerrilla combat and psychological warfare. Among the new OSS buildings: a "spook" house trainees entered with a pistol to fire at Nazi cardboard cutouts that popped up in darkened rooms. Camp Greentop now became known as Area B. Residents around it volunteered as "spotters" to watch for enemy planes. Area B's most distinguished neighbor was Franklin Roosevelt. With German U-boats now patrolling the Atlantic coast, the presidential yacht became too dangerous for excursions and FDR's Warm Springs, Georgia, retreat too far from wartime Washington for weekend getaways. The Park Service offered the White House a plot of land in the Catoctins that already had cabins and a swimming pool. The retreat, which Roosevelt named Shangri-La (and a later president, Dwight Eisenhower, renamed Camp David after his father and grandson), was completed by July 1942 and kept secret from the public for fear that Axis planes or saboteurs might attack it. Roosevelt worked on his stamp collection there. Occasionally Donovan showed up with his guerrilla fighters to show off their paramilitary skills to the president. And occasionally the secret warriors arrived uninvited. Marine guards at Shangri-La had had no qualms about firing over the heads of OSS students who wandered accidentally onto the grounds surrounding the compound before yelling at them to halt.

The radio operators who had been screened for the program now joined Colby and the other officers—delighted to be in pine-paneled cabins with plumbing instead of flimsy tents for the winter months. The enlisted radiomen, some of whom had as much education as the officers, also enjoyed

Area B's egalitarian atmosphere. Taught that they should look out for their men, the officers did not expect salutes and always stood at the back of the mess hall line to let the privates and corporals eat first. On weekends the enlisted men played the officers in tackle football, which could get rough. For that matter, the trainers now treated all the Jedburgh candidates as soldiers of value, a cut above the regular Army. Colby and the others felt proud to be volunteers.

They would need that self-confidence the next six weeks. The training at Area B was rigorous. Instructors, many of them British and French officers, drilled the men in firing and cleaning the foreign weapons they might encounter in the field, including German arms. They crawled through dangerous obstacle courses, where live rounds whizzed over their heads and explosives detonated near them. They practiced killing a man at close range with three quick pistol shots, driving a stiletto into his kidneys, or strangling him with their bare hands. They learned how to live off the land if they had to, how to break into buildings and steal or photograph documents from offices, how to send messages to headquarters in code and decode the ones that came back on their radios. They launched guerrilla attacks at night on floodlit shacks, set up shoot-and-run ambushes, and slapped plastic explosives to trees, concrete slabs, and steel beams to gauge their power when detonated. For Colby, who had been trained to fire big artillery pieces, guerrilla warfare with small arms was a lot to learn, but Singlaub was impressed that his New England friend proved to be a quick study.

Thankfully, the trainers were generous with leave for the Jedburgh students. On November 6, Colby hopped aboard a northbound train for nine glorious days in New York with Barbara. He told her nothing about his OSS training when he arrived at the three-story walk-up on 9th Street just above Washington Square, where she lived with her mother. The two were not engaged. Barbara, who was finishing her senior year at Barnard, saw other men. But when Colby was in New York on leave, they dated steadily and at one point he took her to Vermont to meet his parents.

For Thanksgiving the cooks at Area B served a feast with the mess hall's tables groaning under baked turkeys and all the fixings. The 109 officers selected for the Jedburgh program by then had been whittled down to about fifty—Colby among them. An equal number of radiomen also remained.

They were the oddest collection of characters Colby had ever seen. They included a former Hollywood stuntman, writers, a public relations agent, and assorted adventurers. In addition to Singlaub, Colby became close friends with Bernard Knox, a British expat and Cambridge classicist who had been wounded in the Spanish Civil War, and Douglas Bazata, a red-haired soldier of fortune the recruiters almost rejected because they had trouble sorting out his foreign background, who contemptuously called all colonels "Sugar." The other would-be commandos had a good feeling about Colby. Not a stuck-up East Coast elitist, they thought, more a trade school type of guy.

If Colby and the other officers at Area B shared qualities, it was that they all had become first-rate leaders, they respected one another but remained wary of outsiders, they disliked soldiers who bragged about their exploits, they were each "a healthy animal, all of one piece" and disdainful of introspection (as one psychological study described them), and they hated being kept waiting or having others waste their time. After too many VIPs had begun arriving to interrupt their training with useless inspections or to bore them with windy speeches about winning the war, they developed a weird chant in front of the bigwigs, which embarrassed their trainers. "Forty-eight," one man would call out. "Forty-nine," two others would respond. "Fifty," a half dozen would shout. Then all of them would roar: "Some shit!"

By December, snow had begun to fall on the Catoctin Mountains. As Christmas approached, the loudspeaker in Area B's orderly room played Bing Crosby's "I'll Be Home for Christmas" again and again until a lieutenant broke into the room with the phonograph and smashed the record— to the relief of Colby and the others. The men still had not been told where they were headed, but they were all now certain it was France. Canfield fretted that while all the officers had become skilled guerrilla fighters, some still did not speak French well enough to function in the field. He hoped they would learn enough of the language between now and D-Day.

At 2 a.m. on a mid-December morning, Canfield's aides rousted Colby and the other officers from their beds and ordered them to pack their gear. They boarded trucks that took them to a northbound train with the curtains in its cars drawn. The train deposited them at New York's Grand Central Terminal. From there the fifty commandos marched to 42nd Street, lugging full packs on their backs, to another fleet of trucks that carried them to nearby Fort Hamilton, an embarkation post for troops preparing to sail for Europe. On the chilly night of December 13, they took the ferry up the Hudson to Manhattan's West Side passenger terminal and the next morning boarded the Cunard-White Star's superliner, the RMS *Queen Elizabeth*. The British had repainted the outside of the 83,000-ton passenger ship camouflage gray and stripped the luxury accoutrements inside to fit it with row after row of steel bunks so fifteen thousand American soldiers could be hauled at a time. The radiomen arrived at the port nine days later and boarded her sister ship, the *Queen Mary*.

Colby shared a cramped stateroom with a dozen other officers from Area B. They all had removed the parachute badges and commando insignias from their uniforms so they looked to others like ordinary GIs. Cruising at a speedy thirty knots and zigzagging to avoid German U-boats, the *Queen Elizabeth*'s voyage across the Atlantic proved to be maddeningly dull for Colby and the others. The *Queen Mary* plowed through far stormier weather, leaving the seasick radiomen retching into buckets or wading across decks covered in seawater, discarded food, and vomit.

CHAPTER 8

TRADECRAFT

Richard and Julia Helms had finished lunch at the home of Hubert Hickam, a prominent Indianapolis lawyer, and had settled into couches in the living room to enjoy the New York Philharmonic's Sunday concert on the radio when an announcer interrupted to report that Pearl Harbor had been attacked. What a sad coincidence, Hubert told the couple. Hickam Field, which the Japanese fighters also bombed and strafed, had been named after his brother Horace, an Army Air Corps lieutenant colonel who had died in a plane crash seven years earlier. Helms had closely followed the war in Europe. He had not paid attention to Asia, never considering the possibility of the Japanese bringing the United States into the conflict. Always thinking several moves ahead like a chess player, Helms began churning in his mind—as they put on their coats to leave—what he would do after the Japanese raid.

Helms made that decision in March 1942. He took a leave of absence from the *Indianapolis Times*, packed up their household goods, and moved Julia and the children from Indianapolis to South Orange, New Jersey, where his parents still resided, so he could commute into New York. He took a volunteer job in the public relations office there of the Navy Relief Society. Helms hoped his work for the Relief Society, which raised money for the families of sailors killed at Pearl Harbor, would burnish his credentials to land a commission in the Navy. He had little else in the application he submitted on March 12 to impress the service with his seamanship, save for the fact that he had sailed small boats in a lake. Careful as always not to leave any loose ends, Helms attached to his application recommendation letters from a half dozen *Indianapolis Times* executives, city fathers, Relief Society officials, and former United Press colleagues.

The Navy was not impressed. The day after he submitted his application, Helms flunked his physical. He had high blood pressure, too rapid a heartbeat, and at six foot one he was thirty-one pounds underweight with a flat chest. Not fit to serve on a warship.

Helms persevered and found a senior officer—the commander of the Navy's Eastern Sea Frontier headquartered in New York City—to intervene and convince the service's personnel office to overlook his physical defects. They would not impair the young man for the job the Eastern Sea Frontier had in mind for him—charting the movement of German submarines off the East Coast from its office in the Big Apple. The Navy reconsidered and three months later approved his commission as a lieutenant junior grade (skipping the first rank of ensign as Casey had). He later gained weight, but his blood pressure never dropped.

Just twenty-four hours after Julia gave birth to their son, Dennis, Helms boarded a train to Cambridge, Massachusetts, on July 1 for sixty days of officer indoctrination training at the Naval Training School at Harvard University. When Julia had recovered from the delivery, she took the children to Harvard, but she hardly saw her husband there—and for that matter the next four years—because work so consumed him. The Navy exempted him from further courses so he could join his unit sooner and get busy tracking subs.

At the Eastern Sea Frontier headquarters in New York City, Helms sat at a desk in the Ship Plot Department, hunched over navigation charts, plotting courses American vessels could take to England to avoid U-boat wolf packs—whose positions Helms also did his best to guess. Occasionally he had the opportunity to interrogate captured German submariners for clues as to how their boats operated—giving him his first taste of wheedling intelligence out of an enemy. The work was tedious, but Helms performed it well. His superiors gave him top scores on his efficiency reports and in less than a year promoted him to full lieutenant—although they did note in the reports that he should be more forceful as an officer. Helms asked to be transferred to a battleship in the Pacific, where he thought the Navy was doing the real fighting. His bosses ignored the request.

Early in December 1942 the phone at his desk rang with Fred Oechsner, his old UP boss, on the line. He asked Helms to meet him for a drink after work at the Overseas Press Club in the city. Oechsner had joined the OSS a week earlier—just shy of his fortieth birthday. Wallace Deuel, the *Chicago Daily News* reporter who had been a Helms colleague in Berlin and was already with Donovan's outfit as a roving political and propaganda consultant, had talked Oechsner into signing up and doing the same. Oechsner did not need much convincing. For almost half a year, while still working for UP, the bureau chief had been slipping the OSS notes from his reporting in Berlin. Taking a healthy pay cut, Oechsner was now assigned to put together a propaganda and psychological warfare branch for Donovan called Morale Operations. Psyops dated back to the tale of the Trojan horse the Greeks convinced the citizens of Troy to pull into their city, but Oechsner would soon find it an uphill climb convincing the modern Army and even skeptics within the OSS who questioned what business an intelligence gathering agency had dabbling in such black arts. Donovan, however, was enthusiastic about Morale Operations. And Oechsner thought his protégé from Berlin was a perfect fit for it.

The men ordered their cocktails and found two secluded chairs at the end of the press club bar. Oechsner got right to the point. "Donovan, the head of the Office of Strategic Services, has asked me to build a new section known as Morale Operations," he began almost in a whisper. "This is highly secret and I do not want you to repeat what I am telling you to anyone."

Helms had never heard of Donovan or the OSS, but he promised to remain silent. He waited for Oechsner to continue.

"MO will be responsible for the black propaganda," the former bureau chief said, but saw that Helms had a blank look on his face. He obviously didn't understand what Oechsner was talking about.

"Black propaganda—misinformation," Oechsner explained in a louder voice. "Stuff that will deceive and confuse the enemy."

Helms nodded. What else did this OSS do? he finally asked.

Oechsner looked down the bar to see if anyone was listening in. "Sabotage, espionage, building paramilitary guerrilla armies, resistance operations, counter-espionage," he said, leaning over closer to Helms and again in a soft voice. "But I want you to join us in black propaganda—MO." With Helms's understanding of German culture and his fluency in the language, "you're a natural," Oechsner told him.

Helms was not so sure about that. He had begun to enjoy the cat-and-mouse game he played with German U-boats. Helms had never been particularly close to Oechsner during their Berlin days and did not know if the spy tale he was spinning for him now was credible. One thing he did know. The United States Navy had been around for more than a century and a half. This OSS a little more than a year. His head in a whirl, Helms told his former boss he wasn't interested.

He thought nothing more of Oechsner's offer until one Sunday morning in early August 1943 when he ambled into the Eastern Sea Frontier office for weekend duty and met his angry commander, who gruffly summoned him into his office.

"What the hell is this?" the Navy captain barked, tossing a cable across his desk at Helms. "I'm the one who decides if you like it here, not you!" The cable stated that OSS headquarters in Washington needed Helms "immediately" for a "special billet."

"Why do you want to leave this command?" the captain asked him, truly mystified.

"But I *don't* want to leave," Helms sputtered.

Neither the lieutenant nor his captain had any say in the matter, however. Only later did Helms discover he had been the victim of the Navy personnel office's IBM computer. A former Madison Avenue ad executive who had joined Oechsner's Morale Operations Branch sent a request to the Navy for a German and French speaker who had lived in Europe and worked as a reporter. The computer spit out three punch cards. Two of the officers were stationed overseas. Helms, whose name was on the third, was the only one available in the United States.

The second weekend of August, Helms, lugging his bags, climbed aboard a Pennsylvania Railroad train for the ride to Washington. Over the next year and a half, commuting back to his family in New Jersey when he could break free on weekends, Helms would become intimately familiar with every twist and turn of its track.

The OSS had instructed Helms to arrive at Navy Hill on Monday morning, August 16, ready to begin a new life in anonymity. He was ordered to wear a drab business suit instead of his uniform. Before he left New Jersey, Julia had combed through the suit, his shirts, socks, and underwear to remove labels, tags, monograms, or laundry marks—anything that might identify the clothing's owner or from where it came. She was mystified as to why he wanted her to do this. The OSS cable Helms received ordered him not to tell family or friends he was being transferred to the OSS. Just say you are starting a new job in Washington and you "do not know any details yet." The agency gave him a post office box in the District where Julia could address her letters. Helms had also left behind watches, rings, cuff links, and all other jewelry with his initials or personalized inscriptions engraved on them.

Sitting in a nondescript training office in the OSS headquarters, Helms listened as an agency officer behind a desk read slowly to him from a three-page Indoctrination Memo.

"You are going to proceed to a two-week basic course in OSS training," the officer said with a deadly serious look on his face. "Your clothes will be checked in at the school and you will be issued fatigue clothing and GI shoes."

The officer gave Helms his student name that he would use when filling out documents or talking to others at the school. It will be simply "Dick." "It's not necessary for the instructors or other students at the school to know your full name, your hometown, occupation or anything else about you," he explained. "On the contrary, it may be dangerous to the organization itself if you and your fellow students know such facts about each other." For two weeks you should refrain "from talking about yourself and your personal history," the officer said. "Remember this: If you use the word 'I' or 'My,' some fact about yourself will follow it. For example, a man who says, 'My daughter told me . . .' has already told you several facts about himself—whether he realizes it or not. Now don't be conspicuous by not talking. Be friendly, even communicative. Just always think first before speaking."

Create a cover story for yourself—"what you want others to think you have been or are. But you cannot build such an impression by telling a false story all at once. No one will believe you. Don't try to give the impression that you were a bricklayer or fisherman if you have soft office-worker hands. Choose a personality that is not too far from your real life" and build your cover slowly "by dropping hints."

A "game" will be played at the school "as if it were a matter of life and death," the training officer said finally. Each student will conceal his identity from the others, but each student will try his best to uncover the identity of the others. People might try to trip you up in a casual conversation, or search your room for clues, or even try to pick your pocket. At the end of the two weeks, Helms and his classmates will announce what they have learned about one another at a graduation dinner.

The indoctrination session over, the training officer asked Helms if he understood everything just said. Helms said he did. A staff car is waiting outside in the driveway to take you to your school, the officer told him.

The car whisked Helms to the countryside north of Baltimore. Late Monday afternoon, the automobile finally pulled to a stop an eighth of a mile off a main road at the secluded Nolting Manor estate near the town of Glencoe. The OSS had rented the vacant property for $4,000 a year—an ideal spot for training spies and saboteurs with its eight bedrooms in a wood and stone farmhouse, another eight rooms in an adjoining house, and a four-car garage, all set on a four-acre landscaped yard surrounded by forests. The trainers also pitched tents on the estate so they could accommodate at any time as many as two dozen students, who were instructed outside or in the half dozen living rooms, dining rooms, and parlors on the ground floors of the two buildings that had been converted into classrooms.

Nolting Manor, part of a complex designated as Area E, was one of some twenty secret training sites the OSS had in Maryland, Virginia, Pennsylvania, Illinois, and California. A month before the Pearl Harbor attack Donovan had hurried up a training program for his secret agents, sending an OSS captain to England to observe Secret Intelligence Service—MI6—spy schools. The aide returned impressed with the three months of classes MI6 gave its students in such shady tactics as stalking Germans, sabotaging factories, and "silent killing." MI6 provided Donovan with curriculums, espionage manuals, and lecture notes and allowed OSS instructors to attend the spy school it ran near Toronto. Donovan largely adopted the British training system for his own—with one exception. Nolting and the other country manors the OSS acquired were bare-bones. To toughen them, Donovan wanted his agents trained in rustic farmhouses or tents, not at plush country estates like the British students attended.

A reception officer in Nolting Manor handed Helms his fatigues, boots, and a two-inch-thick stack of manuals (all stamped SECRET) on basic spy tradecraft, how the OSS was organized, and the makeup of the German army. Helms took the cash out and handed over his wallet with his driver's license and other identification cards. The officer had more instructions for Helms: he would be charged 60 cents a day for his meals, plus 10 cents daily to tip the orderly and waiter who attended to him. Do not speak to the servants or tip them further. "Liquor and beer will be available at the bar," the officer said. "The hours of sale are rigidly observed." Making telephone calls or sending telegrams to the outside must be kept "to an absolute minimum" and only in case of emergency. "The entire period of your stay will be taken up with the work at hand," he said. "It will be difficult to plan any time away from camp in the evenings or on weekends."

The reception officer told him to begin memorizing the manuals' contents and directed him to a second-floor bedroom where he would sleep for the next two weeks. In the hallway upstairs, Helms noticed another recruit—obviously well off and taking seriously the OSS order to show up incognito—who walked by with a hole in the left breast of his custom-made shirt. The shirt's monogram had been there, he explained.

Classes started promptly at eight o'clock the next morning. Every hour until late into the evening was booked for the next two weeks. The instructors at Area E were looking for definite qualities in recruits like Helms, which they had detailed in a ten-page secret memo. Agents of the OSS must be emotionally stable, with no "trouble-making traits, uncontrolled weaknesses (liquor, women), phobias, crippling egotism, lack of emotional control, uncontrolled dominating prejudices, conspicuous eccentricities," according to the memo. Spies must be self-motivated, prepared to work long hours without friends, neighbors, or colleagues patting them on the back for it—in other words, willing "to lead a difficult life alone . . . under more or less complete anonymity." They must solve problems with unorthodox methods but not be the "slapdash, snap judgment type," the memo continued. Thoroughness and attention to detail were prized. Covert operatives must be sociable, good mixers at parties, self-confident, savvy judges of others, "have highly developed powers of observation," and, above all, be discreet. Courage also was "necessary in considerable degree [for] all bona fide agents," the memo concluded.

Helms learned the basics of the subversive war Donovan's agents now waged in Europe and Asia. He had classes on how to build a cover story to hide his identity, how to evade house raids, searches, or shadowing by Gestapo agents, and how to act if captured and interrogated. He learned how informants were recruited for information, studied how foreign officials should be blackmailed for secrets, and practiced picking locks and burglarizing an office if he had to steal the documents himself. Instructors taught him how to install wiretaps on phones, read maps to find his way around in a foreign country, how to code and decode messages, and how to draw sketches of enemy military installations with details the U.S. Army would find useful. Technicians from Donovan's research office also arrived to show the students a sample of the spy gadgets they had developed: pistols with silencers; incendiary pencils to detonate charges; small bombs shaped like lumps of coal and nicknamed "Black Jo" to disable a locomotive; explosive flour, called "Aunt Jemima," that could be kneaded into dough for bread or to blow through thick steel; a variety of invisible inks for writing secret messages; a K tablet to slip into an enemy's drink to knock him out; a suicide pill, called an L tablet, that a spy could chomp down on and swallow to quickly kill himself before being captured and interrogated.

Outside the farmhouse amid the tents, Helms and the two dozen other recruits stood in a circle one afternoon around a short, slightly built, middle-aged man with graying hair, horn-rimmed glasses, a slit for a mouth, and a thick British accent. He looked more like a country vicar than the instructor who was about to teach them how to fight dirty. William Ewart Fairbairn, however, was well acquainted with his trade. Major W. E. Fairbairn, as his spy colleagues all knew him, had been the assistant commissioner of the Shanghai Municipal Police Command from 1925 to 1940, during which he had chased drug smugglers, busted up vice rings, shot it out with kidnappers and armed robbers, and hit the streets some two thousand times with riot squads to quell angry mobs in the city's British sector. Since 1940, he had taught close combat to commando units in the British army until Donovan talked the Special Operations Executive into lending him to the OSS in April 1942 to instruct his spies and commandos in "gutter" fighting with pistols, knives, and judo. The low-key and polite Fairbairn, who displayed a morbid exuberance for killing and maiming at close range, traveled the circuit of OSS training camps in the United States giving his ghastly classes.

"This is war," Fairbairn now told Helms and the other Area E students. "You have to size up your opponent and attack within a split second. If you let him attack first, you are on the defensive and you are in for it." Fairbairn started with knives or anything else they could find that was sharp. "Always hold a knife pointed forward and stab that way," he explained. "Holding the point down may slash *you* if you miss your target." If they were caught in a bar fight, "don't reach for a stool. Just grab a bottle, break it on the bar edge, and go for the face of your opponent with that ragged edge."

If they were foolish enough to be "without a pistol or a knife," Fairbairn had a menu of crippling blows they could deliver, such as the "Tiger's Claw" to gouge eyes, the "Chin Jab" driving the heel of the right hand up the jaw, or the "Edge of the Hand Blow," a karate chop an inch below the Adam's apple to kill instantly. Some of the moves made Helms wince. To silence a hysterical woman, "grab her lower lip," Fairbairn advised. If that doesn't shut her up, slap her across the face while holding on to the lip.

To demonstrate each maneuver, Fairbairn called out a student as a foil. He pointed to Helms and ordered him to the center of his makeshift ring. Helms stood almost a head taller than his teacher, but he hated being singled out like this. He had never been much of an athlete or a fistfighter. He managed to win a letter sweater at Williams College, but that was as a goalie on his freshman soccer team, which didn't require much physical exertion.

"Grab my privates," Fairbairn ordered.

Helms reached out tentatively for the good major's groin as if he were touching the hot handle of a frying pan.

"Not good enough," Fairbairn shouted. "*Go* for me!"

Helms grabbed. How it happened, he never knew. But in less than a split second, he was flat on his aching back in the grass looking up at a smiling Fairbairn.

Toward the end of the second week, Helms was sent out on two "schemes"—the term the OSS used for a training exercise in which students tested their newly acquired espionage skills by trying to worm their way into a local government facility or defense plant to steal an important document, such as a company's recent war production figures. If plant workers or the local police caught them, all the better; it gave the students the opportunity to try to talk their way out of a jam. The schemes, however, had become a sore point between Donovan's agency and their victims. Top officials at the White House and cabinet agencies became furious when they learned that enterprising students tried to gain access to plants using phony government stationery with their forged signatures. When an enraged Hoover heard that one OSS student posed as an FBI Academy graduate he threatened to prosecute any schemers his agents caught. Police also grew tired of being called out for these pranks. The year before Helms arrived, Baltimore police complained to the Army after they nabbed five Area E students trying to break into different facilities. It took only a few whacks with a wet towel for the cops to get one of their prisoners to confess and give them the emergency phone number for the OSS camp. Donovan directed his trainers to alert local authorities when the exercises were conducted in their jurisdictions and he ordered that students no longer use White House stationery to gain access. But he refused to let other agencies bully him into halting the schemes.

For his first outing, a one-day affair, Helms was given $5 and sent to Baltimore with orders to walk into an ammunition factory and apply for a job, using a false name and carrying no identity documents in his pockets. His palms sweating, his stomach knotted, and his throat so dry he could barely speak, Helms filled out forms and answered routine questions from a company personnel officer. All his answers were lies. The plant, like most in the United States, was desperate for male employees, however. The personnel officer asked for no identification and told Helms to show up the next day to begin work.

His second scheme lasted three days. A trainer drove Helms, this time with $18 in his pocket, to Pittsburgh, where he had to sneak into a steel plant and purloin details on the types of war goods it manufactured, their rates of production and shipping routes, as well as information on worker morale, plant security, and the facility's vulnerability to sabotage. Fortunately for Helms—although he didn't realize it at the time—security at this factory was weak, as it was for most defense plants across the country. He had little trouble talking his way in, scooping up handfuls of company advertising brochures and stock reports from unattended desks, making a few sketches, and then slipping out past inattentive guards who never checked what he had under his arm.

Two weeks at Area E hardly made Helms a competent spy. Before being sent into the field, he would have had to take advanced courses at other OSS camps and likely attend a "finishing school" in England with American and British instructors. But the crash course was enough to give Helms a sense of how to direct other spies as a staff member in headquarters, which is what the OSS now wanted him to do instead of being a propagandist as Oechsner envisioned. Helms retuned to the Kremlin to join the planning staff, which dreamed up operations espionage agents and saboteurs could launch around the world.

He was fascinated—and somewhat overwhelmed—by the talent Donovan had recruited to this busy headquarters. Calvin Hoover, a Duke University professor and noted economist who managed operations in Sweden, became one of Helms's early mentors. He struck up a friendship with Julia McWilliams, a bright young Smith College graduate overqualified for her job as a junior researcher near Donovan's office. (After her marriage, she would later be known to culinary enthusiasts around the world as Julia Child.) His office mate in the planning staff room was John Gardner, a Marine Corps lieutenant using his skills as a psychologist to evaluate recruits. (Gardner later founded Common Cause.)

On the planning staff, Helms and other aides conjured up operations to sap morale among Wehrmacht troops, to form a peace group among German women called a "Mother's Organization," to clog enemy rail traffic in Slovenia by blowing up bridges, to sabotage Sumatran oil fields and refineries supplying aviation fuel to Tokyo, and to spread rumors among Japanese soldiers in Burma that the war was nearly over. Helms also fielded suggestions from outsiders, like one from a New York man recently emigrated from Upper Silesia who knew how German rail yards there could be sabotaged. His superiors gave Helms high marks on his efficiency report. But after seven months on the planning staff, he grew bored with brainstorming. Helms also realized that OSS stations around the world, stretched thin for agents, paid little attention to the grandiose plans the staff hatched.

Ferdinand Lathrop Mayer rescued him in March 1944. Mayer had been a widely traveled American diplomat since 1919, with postings in London, Geneva, Berlin, and Peking. Allen Dulles had been a close friend when they served together in the State Department. A Republican like Dulles, Mayer had resigned as ambassador to Haiti in 1940 because he strongly disagreed with Roosevelt's New Deal. He retired to Bennington, Vermont. After Pearl Harbor, however, Ferd Mayer set aside his political differences with FDR and begged the White House to take him back. His bridges at the State Department were burned by then, but the OSS, believing his foreign policy experience could be valuable in organizing spy operations, finally hired him in late 1942. The agency assigned him the code name "Carib."

In August 1943, Whitney Shepardson, Donovan's chief of the Secret Intelligence Branch, which was responsible for spying worldwide, tapped Mayer to attempt some coordination of the disparate operations scattered throughout the OSS that struggled with a Donovan priority—penetrating Germany with agents. Mayer's tiny program, code-named "Zombie," had identified eight cities as launching pads for agents—Stockholm, London, Lisbon, Madrid, Tangier, Algiers, Bern, and Istanbul—but the OSS was only in the earliest stage of sending men and women into Germany from any of these places. The London station as yet had no German Desk, Stockholm was still looking for Danish refugees and visiting European seamen who might be infiltrated, and OSS officers in Madrid had begun only preliminary probes to penetrate the German embassy there. The mission ahead was formidable, Mayer recognized. "Germany is a fortress," he wrote to his superiors four months after launching Zombie, "a besieged fortress—an inner core with an outer ring of satellite or occupied countries which have to be traversed." From headquarters, Mayer thought he could help the overseas stations by cabling suggestions for spy initiatives, keeping them informed of the missions of other stations, and smoothing the ruffled feathers of ambassadors upset when OSS operations disrupted their diplomacy. Carib also kept $5,000 in his office safe to pass out to German expats or other Europeans traveling overseas, whom he expected to return to Washington with useful information on the Third Reich.

One of three dozen officers in the Secret Intelligence Branch fluent in German, Helms joined Mayer to be, in effect, his operations officer, helping coordinate intelligence collection on Germany. "At last I was learning a bit about what was going on in the real world," he later wrote. "And it was not much, at least as far as penetrating Germany was involved."

Helms fielded other odd jobs—one of them coming when his superiors learned he also spoke French and had been a newspaperman. Anxious to launch future operations in France with André Dewavrin, de Gaulle's spymaster, Donovan with Eisenhower's blessing invited the infamous colonel to the United States for a tour to butter him up. The OSS chief knew full well Passy's odorous reputation. Hoover, who referred to him as "de Gaulle's Himmler" in memos, was up in arms over Dewavrin being allowed into the country. Donovan had to personally plead with Undersecretary of State Edward Stettinius for a visa. Stettinius held his nose and granted it—but on the condition that there be no publicity in the United States about Passy's trip. The OSS assigned Helms to the escort team squiring the French colonel around the country with the mission of keeping his name out of the newspapers.

On November 1, 1944, Donovan stood on the tarmac of the New York Municipal Airport–LaGuardia Field with Helms and the rest of the OSS delegation behind him as Passy's plane came to a stop. Helms gingerly approached his boss.

"General Donovan, what about publicity in connection with this visit?" he asked.

"We don't want any," Donovan grunted as steps folded out from Passy's plane.

"I know, but what if some newspaperman asks me whether it is true that Colonel Passy is in this country?" Helms pressed.

"That's what *you're* here for, lieutenant," Donovan answered with a slight smile and turned to greet the colonel, who walked down the steps in full dress uniform with a swagger stick.

In other words, lie.

The OSS pulled out the stops to entertain Passy and two of his aides the next three weeks. An Army Air Forces plane flew the Frenchmen, Helms, and the other OSS escorts to see the sights in Chicago, San Francisco, Los Angeles, Miami, and New Orleans. They were treated to an expensive night out at Antoine's Restaurant in New Orleans. In Hollywood, movie executives arranged for high-priced call girls to entertain Passy and his aides in their hotel rooms. (One of the aides complained to Helms the next morning that his hooker "had only one arm." Studio moguls assumed it would be the kind of evening a Frenchman would enjoy.)

Helms succeeded in keeping that tidbit and everything else about the trip out of the newspapers.

After three months as Mayer's aide, Helms moved to the Secret Intelligence Branch's Central European and Scandinavian section. He still looked for ways to penetrate Germany, just not under Mayer's direct supervision. Helms had come to the conclusion that Mayer was past his prime. His operation to infiltrate Germany with spies seemed listless to the young Navy lieutenant. What's more, though Mayer spoke German and had spent time in Berlin, Helms believed he did not really understand the country. Helms soon had a top secret clearance that gave him access to the OSS's most sensitive operations dealing with Germany. He had three safes in his Q Building office crammed with classified documents on those operations. Helms soon began reading closely the cables arriving from a former State Department pal of Mayer's now posted in Switzerland, whom Mayer considered the top performer of all the station chiefs Donovan had spying on the Germans: Allen Dulles.

CHAPTER 9

SWITZERLAND

Early Sunday, Clover and Allen Dulles bundled their daughter Joan into a train crowded with soldiers and bound for Cambridge. She was beginning her second semester as a Radcliffe College freshman. The couple had planned to spend the rest of the day recovering from their hangovers when the radio interrupted with the news that the Japanese had bombed Pearl Harbor. The night before, Clover and Allen had hosted Joan's coming out party and danced into the wee hours at a high society debutante ball in New York's Hampshire House. Pearl Harbor ended the debate between the two Dulles brothers over American intervention. In the weeks that followed, Allen and Clover occasionally motored to an airfield on Long Island to watch fighter planes take off for eventual shipment to England.

At the beginning of February 1942, David Bruce telephoned Dulles to inquire once more if he had any interest in joining the Coordinator of Information. Donovan was scrambling to put together a credible spy agency. In the days after the Japanese attack, his six-month-old organization had precious little besides research papers and propaganda broadcasts to fire at the enemy. Donovan had a hundred analysts working out of cramped offices on Navy Hill with borrowed material from the Library of Congress. A Foreign Information Service, staffed with former newsmen and radio technicians, had a broadcast station in San Francisco beaming propaganda messages to the Far East. His Oral Intelligence Division had begun interviewing refugees and returning overseas travelers for shards of information from abroad. But he had few spies or saboteurs in the field and none in Germany or Japan.

Two days after the attack, Allen's brother, Foster, had sent out a pointed memo to Sullivan & Cromwell's attorneys hoping that patriotic fervor would not infect too many of them. The firm, he warned, could not guarantee that their jobs would be available when they returned from military service. The threat did not faze Allen. After several more phone calls from Bruce, Dulles agreed to join the COI—and to become another prominent Republican added to Donovan's agency. (The accumulation of them soon made White House aides and Democratic hacks nervous, although Donovan insisted his organization was bipartisan.) Dulles quickly and quietly tidied up pending cases at Sullivan & Cromwell. He told Clover only that he would be doing some work for Donovan. He kept secret from his family and friends what kind of work it was. Not until seven months later did it leak to the press that he had joined the spy service.

Dulles started on February 4. Already wealthy from his law practice, he agreed to take no government salary. His orders from Bruce: organize a major outpost in New York to collect and analyze overseas intelligence as well as to hatch covert operations that might destabilize Germany or Japan. Donovan believed that within its city limits abundant, and so far untapped, resources awaited his agency. New York was the business, banking, and legal center for the country, as well as for much of the world. Scholars and organizations interested in foreign affairs populated it. The city was fertile ground for finding future foreign agents and saboteurs. Immigrants poured in from Ellis Island. European expats, members of deposed royal dynasties, representatives, or at least professed representatives, of underground move-ments, plotted their return to their homelands in Manhattan salons. Dulles was ideally suited for the New York job, Donovan thought. His law firm, one of the city's leading, had foreign connections all over the world. Dulles knew many lawyers and bankers who did business overseas. And from his time as a State Department diplomat he knew how to plumb discreetly for secrets.

New York remained tense after Pearl Harbor, its residents fearing they might be the targets of a second wave of Axis attacks. Donovan shared that worry, sending Roosevelt a February 17 memo with a warning from an informant that "the next move of the Nazis will be [a] frontal attack on New York." Using unaccounted-for money Donovan received from a secret White House fund, Dulles ran his secret operation for a couple of weeks first out of his office at Sullivan & Cromwell and then in a midtown hotel apartment. On February 16, he signed a lease for a small suite of offices on the thirty-sixth floor of the International Building at 630 Fifth Avenue in Rockefeller Center. Its previous tenant, the Japanese government, had been evicted after the Pearl Harbor attack. At $3.25 a square foot, the space was pricey real estate, whose rental the OSS staff wanted to keep secret, if for no other reason than taxpayers would howl if they found out.

Dulles inherited a handful of programs Donovan already had under way in the city, such as the Oral Intelligence Division, which had begun interviewing thousands of war refugees streaming into New York, and a highly secret project to collect information on German companies operating in Latin America and elsewhere overseas, which was code-named "George." Dulles moved quickly to expand the New York operation, making it an intelligence organization that rivaled Donovan's in Washington. Within a few months he had it collecting and analyzing mounds of information pouring into the city from overseas. He set up contacts with New York corporations operating abroad, dispatched liaison officers to work with the intelligence bureaus the FBI, Army, and Navy had set up in the city, arranged for the Post Office to alert him to suspicious letters coming in, and reached out to the British, Free French, Polish, Czech, Belgian, and Dutch information services whose headquarters were in New York. He also began organizing "special projects," as he called them, to send his own agents into Axis or Axis-occupied countries.

By the end of 1942, Donovan's New York office had sixty-nine staffers, more than half of whom reported directly to Dulles in his section of the Secret Intelligence Branch. Dulles hired attorneys, businessmen, ex-diplomats, and academics too old for the draft but with expertise in all parts of the world. He mixed them with young assistants fluent in multiple languages. Spencer Phenix, a former State Department colleague, became his action officer for Central Europe. Murray Gurfein, who had served as an assistant U.S. attorney, handled Switzerland and the Balkans. Lithgow Osborne, a New York State conservation commissioner who had spent time in Berlin as a third secretary in the U.S. embassy, supervised Scandinavian operations. Betty Carp, Dulles's fixer from the embassy in Turkey, signed up and was soon cultivating the Soviet ambassador's secretary for gossip on Moscow. Alexander Lipsett, a multitalented lawyer, economist, and college professor educated in Germany, inundated the office with research papers on worldwide topics. Hans Simon, a former Austro-Hungarian official recommended by Dulles's sister Eleanor, analyzed the personalities of German civil servants. Sigrid Schultz, the *Chicago Tribune*'s aggressive reporter who had worked in Berlin with Helms, fished out the dirt from her notebooks and wrote long exposés for Dulles on the corruption of top Nazis like Hitler deputy Hermann Göring.

Dulles's operation eventually expanded to three more floors—the thirty-first, thirty-fifth, and thirty-eighth—which meant more tenants, such as the Polish consulate and talent agent Myron Selznick's New York office, had to be evicted. (Donovan's agency, renamed the OSS in June 1942, paid for Selznick's moving expenses so he wouldn't complain publicly.) The public entrance, with a guard at the door night and day, was located on the thirty-fifth floor, which housed the Oral Intelligence Division. The thirty-eighth floor had an engineering laboratory for spy devices. Offices, large vaults, and a reproduction plant that printed phony documents for agents took up the thirty-first and thirty-sixth floors. Two private phone lines, with encryption devices attached to them to scramble the calls, were installed so New York could be in instant contact with OSS headquarters in Washington. Dulles, who occupied a corner room on the thirty-sixth floor, had one of the direct lines, which patched him to a phone in Donovan's office whenever he lifted it.

At first, the cover story for the New York office was that a group of financial consultants occupied it. That ruse soon became unworkable. Outsiders noticed that only the Rockefellers took up more space at the center than these mysterious financial consultants. With reporters beginning to sniff around, Dulles changed the cover name to the "Statistical and Research Office for the Coordinator of Information," which sounded bland enough. He still kept any listing of the office out of telephone or building directories.

One tenant not kicked out as Dulles expanded in the International Building was the British government. In the summer of 1940, Churchill had dispatched Canadian-born William Stephenson, a millionaire entrepreneur who had been a British fighter pilot in World War I, to the United States to take command of His Majesty's intelligence operations there. Before the Japanese attack, Stephenson had a three-fold mission: mount covert actions to discredit American isolationists opposed to sending aid to Britain, ensure that Nazi agents in the United States did not sabotage war goods before they were shipped overseas, and, even more important, help Churchill with his diplomatic campaign to bring America into the war. Stephenson soon realized that Donovan, an outspoken interventionist, could be useful for the third job and set out to cultivate the New York lawyer. When Roosevelt signed the executive order creating the Coordinator of Information in the summer of 1941, Stephenson and other British security officials fed Donovan a steady stream of intelligence reports along with advice on how to organize his agency. Stephenson, however, soon ran afoul of Hoover and senior State Department officials, who became increasingly irritated as they uncovered evidence of his spying in the United States. They tried to shut him down. Knowing such a move would end vital British aid to his operation, Donovan ran interference with Roosevelt to keep Stephenson in business and now working closely with Dulles. The affable Canadian's espionage organization—using an innocuous-sounding cover name, the British Security Coordination Office—was also located in the International Building in a suite adjoining Dulles's on the thirty-sixth floor. Donovan's New York spy chief lost no time in establishing a pipeline to his British neighbors, who began feeding him a steady diet of "most secret" reports.

One of Dulles's most energetic intelligence operatives was a slightly built labor lawyer with dark wavy hair, whom Donovan had found on Chicago's gritty West Side. The son of a Jewish peddler who had fled Ukraine's Russian pogroms in 1890, Arthur Goldberg toughened quickly as a child with neighborhood bullies taunting him for being a "kike" and his father dying at fifty-one. He left a family of seven to fend for itself. Goldberg, however, excelled as a student and by high school already knew that he wanted to be an attorney. He graduated from Northwestern University and its law school with honors in 1929 and eventually set up shop as a liberal labor lawyer committed to Roosevelt's New Deal. When Hitler invaded France, Goldberg, alarmed over the Nazi threat to Jews and the rest of humanity for that matter, joined an interventionist group and campaigned for FDR's reelection. After the Pearl Harbor attack, Goldberg made up his mind to join the Marines or Army despite the fact that he was married with two young children and had bad eyes. Only the Army would take him for deskwork. Goldberg, who had crossed paths with Donovan during a Milwaukee antitrust case, mailed him a raft of ideas on how the besieged labor movement in occupied Europe could be mobilized for espionage and sabotage. Donovan sent him to New York in March 1942 to organize the overseas unions for Dulles's secret war.

The savage purge of unions in Germany and European countries the Nazis occupied had not entirely wiped out the labor movement. Hitler's Wehrmacht could not run all the trains or operate every factory. Workers, whether in Germany or conquered nations, had to be used and many harbored a deep hatred for Nazism and fascism. Remnants of labor unions remained underground eager to sabotage the Axis war machine and ready to send out valuable intelligence to the Allies. Goldberg believed Donovan's agency was better suited to reach out to these left-leaning organizations than the FBI or Army and Navy intelligence, which the labor leaders tended to distrust. Senior Donovan aides from Wall Street, who were no friends of the New Deal or big labor, became leery of Goldberg and his background as a lawyer for liberal causes. Some hard-liners thought he was soft on communism. Dulles, however, was convinced like Goldberg that the European labor movement could be "among our surest allies" against the Nazis, as he wrote Donovan. With Dulles's blessing, Goldberg's Labor Division, located on the thirty-sixth floor near the boss's corner office, launched a wide-ranging program to make contact with the underground labor organizations and begin supplying them with money, radios, and sabotage devices.

Goldberg hired labor activists and attorneys who made Donovan's Republican aides even more jittery, but whom the Chicago lawyer knew were best suited for dealing with unions. George Pratt, a pipe-smoking Yale Law School graduate and former chief trial examiner for the National Labor Relations Board, became the division's second in command. Goldberg hired two other NLRB attorneys as well: David Shaw, a Harvard Law graduate, and Gerhard Van Arkel, who had been the labor board's assistant general counsel. The team began working with the AFL-CIO, whose contacts with overseas unions were extensive, with the International Transport Workers'

Federation (before the war, it had affiliates in Germany and fifty-four other countries), the clandestine New Beginning Group in Germany (which still maintained contact with labor activists in Europe and the United States), the underground Polish labor movement (one of the best organized in Europe), and the Jewish Labor Committee (it had lines into Europe's garment workers). In a nondescript shop at 42 Broadway, Goldberg also set up the Ship Observer Project, whose officers fanned out to New York's docks interviewing merchant seamen aboard neutral ships for intelligence on military ports they might have visited or enemy vessels they might have spotted at sea. A young Swedish mariner recounted bleak conditions he witnessed at Hamburg's port on the Elbe River. A Polish sailor on a Swiss boat sketched for Goldberg Nazi shore defenses at Genoa, Italy.

Working often through intermediaries—cutouts—Dulles cast a wide net for agents or informants. Most were amateurs and he had mixed results with them. He recruited a cranky and indiscreet college professor with a bad eye to visit Ireland—the country of his expertise. The biased reports the professor filed proved worthless. Dulles hatched a plan for a *Chicago Sun* reporter to be sent to Switzerland or Sweden and spy for the New York office on the side. The plan fizzled. The reporter turned out to be a lackadaisical student during spy training. By the fall of 1942, the New York office had grown into such a hodgepodge of different operations that headquarters in Washington had difficulty accounting for all of them. Security officers, and even Donovan, began to worry about Dulles hiring people without proper background checks. Administration did not appear to be Dulles's strong point, senior OSS officers soon concluded.

As his operation grew so too did Hoover's dossier on him. A month after he had signed on with Donovan, Dulles showed up at the door of the FBI's New York office, promising to be cooperative and to pass along information he picked up that the bureau might find useful. By June 1942, Dulles was regularly supplying the FBI with leads his operatives uncovered on possible Axis espionage activity in New York. Hoover was impressed, but not enough to stop spying on him. The FBI director's informants warned that Donovan used Allen as a hollow log to leak secrets to his brother, Foster. FBI agents continued to probe Dulles's prewar business ties with clients the bureau considered suspect. In the summer of 1942, Donovan rang up Dulles on their private line to alert him that Hoover's agents were now snooping on his sister Eleanor, who they thought was having an affair with a Polish translator. Donovan had a mole in the FBI who regularly alerted him to the director's shenanigans. It did not take long before Dulles suspected that the FBI had planted its own snitch in the OSS's New York office and was tapping their phones. Hoover was convinced Dulles had communist and Nazi sympathizers on his payroll.

As far as Hoover was concerned, the shadiest character working for Dulles was Donald Chase Downes. A European-roaming, former Cape Cod schoolmaster, always wrapped in a tight corset for a bad back—with phobias for snakes, stray dogs, and yellow paint, to name a few—Downes had been rejected by Army and Navy intelligence when he applied in 1940 to be a spy. So he approached MI6 officers. They put him to work under Stephenson tailing isolationists and casing Axis embassies in Washington for British agents to burgle before the United States entered the war. About the time Dulles moved into the offices at the International Building in February 1942, Downes showed up as well, recovering from amoebic dysentery and fish tapeworm. Dulles hesitated to bring him aboard because of the baggage he brought. American citizens were prohibited by law from spying in the United States for a foreign government and FBI agents had already picked up Downes's trail when he worked for Stephenson. Their reports to Hoover always referred to him as the "sex deviate." Downes's biographer suspects he was gay, although Downes never admitted it. That alone hardly disqualified him as a spy, but in every other respect Downes truly was an oddball. None of that bothered Donovan, who thought he could be of value when Downes came to him in Washington asking if he could switch to the American team. He sent the schoolmaster to work for Dulles, who installed him in an office blocks away from the International Building—hoping to keep a semblance of separation between the eccentric and Donovan's agency.

Distance did not deter Donald Downes. He wormed his way into Goldberg's program interviewing merchant seamen and hatched a panoply of operations himself, such as the Library Project to infiltrate a Yale professor into Istanbul spying under the cover of an academic researcher. Downes held a cynically dark view of spying. "To do our type of work requires living in its atmosphere in a strange netherworld of refugees, radicals and traitors," he wrote in one memo. "There is room for neither gentility nor protocol in this work. Utter ruthlessness can only be fought with utter ruthlessness." For all his wariness of Downes, Dulles agreed with the schoolmaster.

Together they began diving deep into New York's netherworld—again with mixed results. Baron Wolfgang von und zu Putlitz, a Prussian Junker and ex–foreign ministry officer who loathed Hitler, had barely managed to escape capture in 1939 when Gestapo agents uncovered his collaboration with British intelligence. Putlitz ended up in New York, where FBI agents soon began tailing him, reporting to Hoover that he "frequented haunts of sex deviates." Downes recruited the baron to emcee a radio show beaming propaganda broadcasts into Germany. Dulles considered Putlitz more valuable for the thumbnail biographies he wrote on top German officers such as General Erwin Rommel and Abwehr chief Admiral Wilhelm Canaris. He sent the profiles to Donovan. Dulles was even more enthusiastic about another Downes recruit: Paul Hagen, a handsome Austrian author who proposed to infiltrate comrades into Germany, Austria, and France and link up with underground movements. But Hagen proved worthless as a clandestine operative after he had a public spat with other exiles, who accused him of being a communist Don Juan. Dulles and Downes thought they had their best chance of organizing a revolt in the Third Reich with Gottfried Treviranus, a Weimar Republic minister before Hitler came to power who had ties to anti-Nazi terrorists among the Freikorps (paramilitary bands of ultranationalist soldiers from World War I). The project became known as the T-Plan. Downes moved Treviranus and his family from Canada to an apartment on East 63rd Street, near where he lived, and promised him $10,000 a year to begin organizing an insurrection. Backbiting, however, continued among New York's expatriates. Hagen and Putlitz complained that Treviranus had no following in Germany and had, in fact, been chummy with the Nazis. Treviranus also proved to be too talkative, bragging to friends before he left Canada that he was organizing a coup for the Americans in Germany. Headquarters ordered the project shut down and Treviranus was paid $3,750 to keep him quiet.

Stephenson's officers in New York fretted that their American cousins were naively "falling into all the German émigré traps which we have so studiously tried to avoid here," according to one British memo. Even OSS research analysts in Washington concluded that New York's exiles "are not true samples of the European bodies politic from which they have come," according to a memo sent to Donovan. Dulles ignored the warnings. Like the Washington headquarters, the New York office became a laboratory for almost limitless experiments in intelligence gathering. Dulles funneled money to the French Resistance, organized a project to counterfeit enemy currency, and bought clothes from European refugees his men interviewed so OSS agents infiltrating enemy territory could wear the garments to blend in. He even started a secret unit to tap into records American insurance companies held on Axis business clients before the war. The files often contained blueprints of buildings, which Allied air forces found useful for determining how they should be attacked. If an idea didn't pan out, Dulles was no more bothered than Donovan.

• • • •

One country Dulles began targeting almost from the moment he took over spy operations in New York was Switzerland. Donovan knew that penetrating a totalitarian state like Germany directly with agents could take years. He did not have that kind of time. Instead, he decided to set up intelligence operations in neutral European countries to serve as his portal into Germany. The most important neutral—centrally located on the European continent and bordering Germany, Austria, Italy, and France—was Switzerland. Senior OSS officers began referring to it as "Shangri-La" in their memos.

Yet for all the brainstorming Dulles and his men had done on setting up a network inside Switzerland they had little to show for it by fall 1942—four informants there of varying reliability, two pedestrian OSS officers in the U.S. legation operating under diplomatic cover, and a handful of corporations like IBM and ITT willing to slip Dulles information from trips their executives made to the country. Dulles decided Switzerland was too important to leave to freelancers. It needed a high-powered operative—him. Donovan had talked to Dulles about moving to the London station to serve as deputy to David Bruce, who thought the OSS's New York man was "one of the chosen ones of the earth," as he wrote in his dairy. Dulles did not feel the same about Bruce, whom he considered junior to him, as well as a potential rival. In Switzerland, Dulles could run his own show with little meddling from Bruce in London or from Donovan and his staff in Washington. Agreeing to continue not taking any salary and peppering Washington with memos on how he would operate in the neutral nation, Dulles convinced Donovan to approve the transfer.

Getting there would not be easy. The head of the American legation in Bern, the Swiss capital, was Leland Harrison, an old friend of Dulles's from their days together at the Paris Peace Conference. But the State Department, and even Harrison, were nervous about Dulles coming and making Swiss authorities more suspicious of the U.S. legation than they already were. Everyone assumed the Swiss, and Germans for that matter, had read press stories that Dulles had joined the OSS. To mollify the State Department, and to try to fool Nazi intelligence, the OSS spread the cover story that Dulles had had a falling out with Donovan and was returning to the diplomatic service as Harrison's special assistant.

On November 2, Dulles boarded a packed Pan Am Clipper Flying Boat at New York Municipal Airport for the first leg to Bermuda. The plane would refuel there and head across the Atlantic to Lisbon. In addition to Switzerland and Portugal, his diplomatic passport had visas stamped for France, Ireland, Britain, and Spain in case he needed to make stops elsewhere. In his suitcase he had packed dozens of letters of introduction for Swiss officials plus long lists of useful contacts, potentially helpful sources, friendly foreign spies, and the names of Nazi sympathizers to avoid. To jump-start his mission, the bag also had a $1 million letter of credit to a Swiss bank.

As they did for all clandestine operatives sent abroad, dispatchers at the Washington headquarters had reviewed an Agent's Check List with Dulles before he departed. It contained forty-five items. It was agreed that his code name would be "Burns" and his code number on cables he sent out would be "110"—one above Donovan's, which was 109. The exchange of passwords he memorized so a foreign agent could confirm his identity was: Question: "Where did you have dinner the last evening that you were in Washington, D.C.?" Answer: "The Metropolitan Club." The dispatchers finally asked Dulles for a mark on his body that they could write on the Check List as further identification. The scar on the inside of his left foot, he told them.

The Clipper made it to Bermuda in six hours and after refueling took off for the Azores, the next stop before Lisbon. Bad weather, however, grounded the amphibious plane on the Portuguese islands for two days. Dulles waited, becoming more nervous by the hour because he knew a secret none of the other passengers did. American and British forces would soon be landing in North Africa for the invasion code-named "Torch." When that happened Dulles was sure the Germans would respond by occupying the rest of Vichy France, making his journey through the southern part of the country to reach Switzerland extremely hazardous if not impossible. The Pan Am plane finally reached Lisbon late on November 5. The next morning Dulles caught a flight to Barcelona and from there boarded a train that chugged slowly along Spain's Mediterranean coast to the town of Portbou near the French border. Stalled once more—this time by an interminably long passport check at Portbou—he lunched in a station café midday on November 8, when a Swiss passenger he had met on the train ran up to his table. "Have you heard the news?" he said excitedly. "The Americans and British are landing in North Africa!" Dulles faced a tough decision—to remain in neutral Spain or continue on the train through France, gambling that it would take several days before Hitler's army moved in.

He stayed on the train as it rumbled across the border into France. If the Germans stopped them at any point, Dulles decided he would climb off and slip away into the countryside, praying to God that he might hook up with a French Resistance band. He doubted his diplomatic passport would get him past a Gestapo checkpoint. They would probably pack him off to an internment camp for the rest of the war or, if they put the pieces together from the suspicious material in his suitcase, haul him off to a torture chamber or a firing squad. To his relief, at the train's first regular stop in the town of Verrières he was met not by German security but deliriously happy Frenchmen who thought he was the advance party for Americans come to liberate them. The next morning, November 9, the train had reached its last stop in France at Annemasse, near the Swiss border. Bleary-eyed from little sleep the night before, Dulles climbed off with the other passengers to have their passports checked by French authorities before reboarding at noon for Geneva. Dulles had been told in Washington to expect a Gestapo man at the border checkpoint. He had little trouble picking out the agent in black fedora and tailored business suit standing behind the Vichy gendarme checking the passengers' papers.

Dulles was the only passenger not waved on. The Gestapo officer jotted in a notebook the particulars of his diplomatic passport and whispered words to the gendarme that Dulles could not hear. A few minutes later the gendarme approached Dulles and explained that orders had come from Vichy to detain all Americans and British at the border and report their appearance directly to Marshal Pétain. Dulles pulled the policeman aside and in the most impassioned French he could muster implored the officer to let him pass, invoking Pershing, Lafayette, and any other figure of Franco-American solidarity he could think of. He then pulled out his wallet to let him gawk at the Swiss thousand-franc notes stuffed in it that could be his. Unmoved, the gendarme walked off to make his phone call to Vichy. Dulles nervously paced the platform, casing the area around it. He could grab his bag and run across the field surrounding the station, hope to make it across the Swiss border. But it would not be easy. So he waited.

When the clock in the station struck noon, the Gestapo officer, as was his Germanic habit every day at precisely that time, walked to a nearby pub to enjoy his lunch and a beer. The train's whistle blew to signal it was about to leave. The gendarme hurriedly walked up to Dulles and motioned him to board it. The policeman had made his perfunctory call to Vichy, but once the Gestapo agent had left he felt free to act on his own. Handing Dulles his passport, the gendarme whispered, *"Allez passez. Vous voyez que notre collaboration n'est que symbolique."* ("Go ahead. You see that our collaboration is only symbolic.") Within minutes Dulles was across the border and in neutral Switzerland—one of the last Americans to do so legally from France until that country's liberation two years later.

The next evening, on November 10, Dulles, using his code name, Burns, sent his first cable from the American legation in Bern to "Victor," the code name for the OSS radio relay station just west of London. He recounted how he had talked his way past the authorities at Annemasse. The cable also contained Dulles's first intelligence report from Switzerland—his observations on French morale from talking to citizens at train stops through the Vichy zone. A little more than a fortnight later he finally wrote Clover. He could not say much, only that "I got in here by the skin of my teeth." At their first meeting, Dulles and Leland Harrison went through the required sign-countersign exchange agreed to in his Agent's Check List—a silly exercise, both men thought, since they had known each other for years. Harrison was truly happy to see his old friend and lent Dulles a comfortable room in his residence for a month until he could find permanent quarters. The two dined and played bridge regularly in the evenings.

About half the size of the state of Maine with twenty-eight natural lakes, spectacular snow-covered mountain ranges, and the scenic River Aare that flowed from them through the capital, Switzerland had a people devoted to fitness and making every minute of their leisure time productive. It was also a nation proud to be the world's oldest democracy—so many questions came before its citizens that practically every Sunday was consumed with voting—and obsessed with guarding its self-serving neutrality, which infuriated both the Allies and the Axis. Soviet dictator Joseph Stalin called the Swiss "swine" for playing both sides in the war. Roosevelt would not go that far, but the Alpine Republic's trade with the Nazis angered him as much. The isolated Swiss supplied the Third Reich with finished steel, precision machine parts, and discreet banking services in exchange for much-needed German coal, iron ore, and petroleum. When Dulles later sent Washington evidence of Switzerland laundering Reichsbank gold for Swiss francs and selling Berlin militarily important ball bearings, an angry FDR ordered the State Department to try to shut it down. Swiss public attitude toward the war was schizophrenic. The country had pockets of resident Germans sympathetic to Hitler along with eight right-wing parties mirroring Nazi ideology, yet a vibrant anti-Nazi and pro-American sentiment prevailed among its citizenry and Swiss businesses managed to smuggle some precision military instruments to the Allies. The Swiss government nevertheless had strong reason to reach accommodation with Hitler. His generals had laid plans to invade the tiny country. The idea was eventually abandoned—with its mountainous terrain and practically every able citizen armed and ready for military call-up, the "porcupine," as the Germans called Switzerland, would have been tough to cage—but the Wehrmacht kept invasion plans on the shelf.

The Bernese Dulles returned to twenty-five years after his first diplomatic posting shivered with the onset of winter for lack of adequate heating fuel and appeared thinner because of food rationing. The capital maintained its medieval quality with families still strolling by beautiful old homes along arcaded streets, the great bell of the Zytglogge clock tower in the city center still chiming hourly, the grand and venerable Hotel Schweizerhof across from the railway station still booked with visitors, and the ornate fountain on Kornhausplatz still pouring water with its Kinderfresser (the mythological ogre who gobbled up children). Yet the once contented Federal City now functioned on edge with residents fearing German rocket bombs might rain on them at any time and many of its young men pulled away from shops for army duty constructing fortifications just north.

Dulles could not have found more ideal territory for spying than Switzerland and its capital. Bern had become an espionage haven with a cottage industry of political refugees, asylum seekers, escaped war prisoners, deserters, resistance representatives, disaffected German officials, deposed royalty, business travelers, embassy workers of all stripes, and, for lack of a better category, professional snitches trading information among the Germans, British, and Americans. Often the same secret was passed to the first in the morning, to the second in the afternoon, and to the third in the evening. MI6 had identified 425 Axis agents in Switzerland. Saturday nights many of the spies gathered at the Hotel Bellevue Palace as they had during the First World War to drink, sup, and snoop. The German legation, located in a villa at Willadingweg 78, had become a major spy station with Abwehr agents operating under business cover and some Gestapo operatives who had sneaked across the border posing as Jewish refugees. German intelligence officers had heavily penetrated the Swiss spy service and foreign ministry, where sympathetic officials passed along information, mostly political tidbits picked up making the rounds of foreign embassies. Hitler's agents also staked out Allied outposts and routinely followed their diplomats throughout the city. Other services kept active as well. The British legation closely tracked the Germans and ran smuggling rings to spirit Swiss military technology back to London. The GRU (Soviet military intelligence) set up networks of undercover agents to feed Moscow information on the Germans. The Vichy French tried to penetrate American codes—unsuccessfully, the Americans believed, or at least hoped.

Donovan had given Dulles a straightforward mission in Bern: penetrate Germany for intelligence and exploit what was left there of the underground movement opposing Hitler. As he had in New York, Dulles did much more, soon making his OSS station a central intelligence agency in its own right.

He not only collected information but also funneled millions of Swiss francs to resistance cells in France and Italy, organized paramilitary operations among hundreds of agents there, and sent millions of propaganda pamphlets into Germany. Dulles also became a self-appointed foreign policy adviser, delivering Washington long tracts with his opinions on grand strategy for the war. When Roosevelt, for example, announced at the Casablanca conference with Churchill in January 1943 that the Allies would accept only "unconditional surrender" from the enemy, Dulles flooded headquarters with critical cables warning that Goebbels would exploit the "meaningless slogan" to harden German morale for a fight to the bitter end.

Within a few weeks after his arrival in Bern, a widely read Swiss newspaper reported that Dulles had come as "the personal representative of President Roosevelt." Friends suspected that Dulles leaked the story. Rather than operating in secret, he practically hung a shingle on his door saying informants were welcome. The British secret services thought Dulles's advertising as FDR's envoy an appalling breach of security. "It served only to attract the dross," sniffed one SOE report. But before Dulles had left Washington, Donovan had told him not to bother trying to remain under deep cover. It would be futile with Nazi surveillance in the city so heavy. Dulles also did not have time to establish a network of informants in secret. Far better just "to let people know you were in the business of intelligence and tell them where they could find you," he later wrote.

Where snitches could find Dulles was at Herrengasse 23, a spacious apartment on the ground floor of a four-story late Baroque structure off a busy cobblestoned street in Bern's Old City. He began renting it in December 1942. Dulles convinced city officials to turn off the street lamps in front of the building to make it difficult for Axis agents to identify his visitors at night. The apartment also had a more discreet entrance for informants in the back with its two vineyard terraces and a spectacular view of the River Aare and the Bernese Alps beyond. The front entrance opened into a large reception room with a living room, dining room, kitchen, bedrooms, and servants' quarters branching off of it. To put sources at ease, Dulles ushered them into a cozy wood-paneled study with red drapes over the windows, a table that served as a bar, two comfortable armchairs, and a sofa drawn around a working fireplace he enjoyed tinkering with. A silver-framed portrait of Clover hung over its mantel.

For a legation assistant, he lived in grand style. The apartment came with a butler named Jacques and a first-class cook from one of Bern's finer hotels. He also was assigned a Ford automobile with a French chauffer named Edouard Pignarre and was permitted to drive on weekends when other legation employees couldn't because of gas rationing.

Leland Harrison—whose small legation had offices scattered in three private homes—was as much a socialite as Dulles. The crystal highball glasses in his residence had pigs engraved on them from his membership in Harvard's tony Porcellian Club. The ambassador also fashioned himself a spy aficionado and had been running his own aggressive operation to collect information on the Axis. Dulles quickly latched on to Harrison's staffers who dabbled in intelligence, such as finance officer Charles Dyer and Brigadier General Barnwell Legge, Harrison's military attaché. His most important collaborator in the legation soon became the multilingual Gerald Mayer, a dapper German American with a thin mustache who had arrived in Bern eight months earlier to be the representative for the Office of War Information, a propaganda agency that operated alongside Donovan's psyops teams. To maintain the fiction that he was a legation assistant, Dulles kept a desk in Mayer's OWI office at Dufourstrasse 24.

Dulles soon began cobbling together his own staff from European refugees and Americans living in Bern. He leased space next door at Number 26 for the near dozen he hired. Betty Parsons, a New Yorker transplanted from Italy to Bern, joined as his chief secretary. Dulles found Royall Tyler, a Massachusetts historian and Paris Peace Conference colleague, to be his expert on Hungarian and East European affairs. Max Shoop, a former Sullivan & Cromwell attorney from its Paris office, joined to funnel money to resistance groups and handle the military intelligence they sent back; Dulles, who knew little about what information was valuable to the Army, paid him handsomely. A former British butler named Henry Baldwin became Dulles's fixer untangling bureaucratic snarls with the Swiss; the OSS assumed he was an MI6 mole as well. Some 1,500 American airmen were forced to make emergency landings in Switzerland or had escaped to the country after being shot down over enemy territory. (When apprehended by the Swiss they were interned for the rest of the war.) Short of clerical help, Dulles arranged for a half dozen of them to join his unit performing the laborious job of coding and decoding messages.

Within days of arriving in Bern, Dulles began scouring the city for informants and cabling their tidbits to the Victor station in London, which promptly relayed the messages to OSS headquarters in Washington. Doing his best to make them understand his often mangled French and German, he interrogated Swiss and even Reich businessmen working the Bern–Berlin sales circuit, questioned Protestant and Catholic representatives in touch with their churches in the Fatherland, and found friendly sources in the Hungarian embassy and among Italian, Polish, and French intelligence officers. Elizabeth Wiskemann, a temperamental English journalist and historian working as a press and propaganda attaché for the British legation, had a trove of old sources in Germany. Dulles charmed their reports out of her with flowers, flirty notes, and fancy meals his cook prepared.

Bouquets, however, did not work so well with his other British cousins. Sir Claude Edward Marjoribanks Dansey, the number two man in Britain's Secret Intelligence Service who oversaw its Swiss operations from London, did little to hide his contempt for the OSS. Dulles complained that John "Jock" McCaffrey, the Special Operations Executive representative in Bern, was just as much "a son of a bitch." Jock and "Uncle Claude" (subordinates who revered or detested Dansey called him that) became apoplectic when Dulles began recruiting sources the SOE and MI6 considered theirs. "The Americans 'splashed money' and had large houses, offices and fleets of cars," griped one secret SOE report. Snitches had begun to flock to Dulles instead of to the British services. McCaffrey groused to London that Bern's new OSS chief was doling out 800 Swiss francs a month to an Italian socialist and giving a French labor activist a whopping 1,800 Swiss francs monthly—both of whom were already on the SOE's payroll. Dulles, who quickly wearied of British attempts to monopolize spy assets and contacts with Europe's resistance movements, believed he could glean more information from these two informants. He eventually reached an agreement with the British on sharing some sources. But he refused to dial back his aggressive recruiting, even when it meant big-footing Dansey and McCaffrey.

Dulles arrived in Bern sporting a mustache and tweed jacket. The pipe-puffing, shabby professor look put sources at ease, he thought. A month later he bought English cloth for another winter suit in the same style. A skilled intelligence officer was like a "good fisherman," Dulles said.

He prepared meticulously for his catch, scouted patiently the waters in which his sources swam, remained inquisitive and open-minded, but he was always aware that the person he hooked might be an enemy double agent intent on deceiving him. Dulles improvised clandestine techniques for his operations. An agent crossing the Italian border to Lugano, Switzerland, for example, called his handler at the Hotel Splendide from a public phone booth using the password "Pocatte." He should watch his every move through the city for Swiss police or the Gestapo following him and deliver his intelligence always by courier. "The phones are not secure." Washington eventually stocked the OSS station with matchbook cameras, microfilming equipment, and briefcases with concealed spaces for agents to hide documents. Dulles also kept a loaded revolver in the drawer of his bedside table, although he had no real need for it. His spying was a genteel affair. No one ever shot at him, and he avoided traveling too close to Switzerland's borders with France, Germany, or Italy to give anyone the opportunity.

On a typical day, using American slang to confuse foreigners listening in, Dulles phoned morning instructions to key aides from his Herrengasse quarters before driving to the Dufourstrasse office with his locked, hard-bottomed briefcase at his side and newspapers and documents stuffed in the pockets of his rumpled gray overcoat. He lunched with other intelligence officers at the Theater Café (where the waiters knew him by name), spent the afternoon composing cables for Washington, dined at the Bellevue Palace with foreign diplomats in the evening, or hosted private suppers with sources in his apartment.

Being surrounded by the enemy made communicating with the outside a problem. Coded diplomatic messages could be sent from the legation over Swiss commercial radio but they had to be short. Longer documents, maps, and photographs were first microfilmed, then delivered to a rail employee who hid the rolls in the engine box of a train, which carried the precious cargo to Lyon, France, to be dropped off with a secret courier, who bicycled it to Marseille, where a ship sailed it to Corsica, then a plane flew it to Algiers, where the OSS station delivered it to London and the film was processed and flown to Washington. The entire trip could take more than two weeks. After over eight months of negotiations, AT&T also finally agreed to install a radiotelephone line at Herrengasse 23 (the service cost $1,000 a month) so each night at eleven o'clock Dulles (using the name Bertram L. Johnston) could call Charles B. Jennings, the pseudonym for OSS headquarters in Washington. Reading from a script that he wrote longhand on stationery, Dulles kept his messages, called "flashes," confined to ten minutes of analyzing news in the papers. AT&T required that the installation be cleared with the Swiss, who insisted that their speech-scrambling device be used for the line. So Dulles assumed they, and perhaps the Germans, could easily unscramble his flashes to listen in.

He found spy work grueling yet "quite thrilling," as he wrote to Clover. His first four months in Bern he did not take a single day off and suffered occasional bouts of painful gout from the stress. But his years in Switzerland would be the best of his life. And for Clover they would be too many years. He wrote to Clover in early March 1943 that they would likely be separated only several more months. It proved to be a naive prediction.

As in New York, Dulles rarely rejected out of hand an informant with a suspicious background (the arrogant British lost many a good lead because of that, he thought). In his first month in Bern he struck up an acquaintance with Egon Winkler, a gimlet-eyed Austrian financier he suspected of working for the Abwehr. Eduard Schulte, a wealthy and vain German mining executive who hated the Nazis, analyzed Reich economic data for him, provided him intelligence on Hitler's V-1 rocket and alerted him to mass executions of Jews. The British and even Washington warned him that Eduard Waetjen, a Berlin lawyer sent to Zurich as a diplomat, was a dangerous double agent, but Dulles found him valuable as a conduit to the German resistance movement. Another Sudeten German Dulles soon realized was pimping for SS *Reichsführer* Heinrich Himmler was Prince Max Egon Hohenlohe von Lagensberg, now a Liechtenstein national who tried to sell him the line that the SS chief was the best man to preserve order and fight communism in a post-Hitler Germany. Dulles nevertheless believed Prince Max could be useful for intelligence. His best information, Dulles always insisted, came from walk-ins off the street. That was why he would talk to practically anybody.

Ten days after arriving in Bern, Dulles had met Gero von Schulze-Gaevernitz, the son of the Weimar legislator he had befriended during his Berlin assignment in 1920. Gero was finishing his Ph.D. when Dulles first met his father, Gerhart, and after graduation he moved to New York to study banking. He became an American citizen and wealthy in his own right as an international financier. The onset of World War II caught him in Switzerland tending to a seriously ill sister at her country estate in Ascona. Unable to leave, he was forced to manage his international business from Zurich, where he fattened his fortune further as a currency trader. Tall, suave, and handsome with warm blue eyes and polished manners that attracted confidants, Gaevernitz, now in his early forties, soon became Dulles's prized door opener. He introduced the American to some of the most valuable intelligence assets and German resistance contacts he would have during the war. Gaevernitz's playboy image belied a strong conviction that Hitler was leading his nation to ruin. Assigned the code number 476, Gero became like a son to the OSS station chief. So close that Hungarian intelligence agents thought they were sleeping together. A Hoover memo to the White House claimed Gaevernitz "had a rather unsavory reputation." Two of his investment trusts during his time in New York "had gone more or less on the rocks while his personal affairs seemed to be prospering."

Mary Bancroft's Zurich parlor had become a sought-after gathering place for many of Switzerland's avant-garde writers, scholars, and journalists. She was not a glamorous brunette, but she was gregarious and extroverted, "one of the let-it-all hang out types," as a friend described her. Bancroft had attracted an eclectic group of acquaintances since moving to Switzerland—from writer James Joyce's wife to psychiatrist Carl Jung, who diagnosed her frequent sneezing fits as psychosomatic. She had been a wildly imaginative and insatiably curious child—"almost an adult" by age nine, she once wrote—whose father deposited her with her millionaire grandfather in Cambridge when her mother died of an embolism hours after she was born. After a boring three years at Smith College, she married Sherwin Badger, a United Fruit Company executive, who eventually bored her as well. She pursued an affair with a pianist and composer. That romance soon petered out, but Mary divorced Badger and in 1935 married Jean Rufenacht. He was a heavyset and balding French Swiss financier fourteen years her senior yet worldly and intriguing, or so Mary thought. Soon after their wedding night, she realized she had made a terrible mistake. Rufenacht turned out to be an insanely jealous husband who became surly and abusive when he was drunk, which was often. Mary stuck it out, though, and moved to Switzerland with her daughter from the first marriage to join Rufenacht, a roving European auditor for Credit Suisse.

Among her many American visitors: Rebecca Stickney Hamilton, a *Harper's Bazaar* editor and estranged wife of a Morgan family heir, who used Bancroft's apartment on the Stockerstrasse for rendezvous with her secret lover, William Donovan. Becky gave the excuse that she was visiting her girlfriend in Zurich to set up trysts there with Donovan when he toured Europe in the late 1930s. After one assignation, she sent Mary a glamorous black lace nightgown as a thank-you gift. Thinking the present was from a Bancroft lover, an enraged Rufenacht burned it in the incinerator.

Mary's early visits to Nazi Germany with her husband on his business trips convinced her Hitler was intent on world war. Still eager to trade with the Third Reich, Rufenacht thought her naive. Emotionally shattered and feeling encircled by the enemy after the fall of Paris and the Japanese attack on Pearl Harbor, Bancroft, who had written feature articles on American life while overseas, began working for Gerald Mayer planting more of the pieces in Swiss papers and analyzing Hitler's speeches for the Office of War Information. In early December, Mayer invited Bancroft to join him for afternoon drinks at Zurich's Hotel Baur au Lac to meet a newly arrived embassy assistant, for whom she might want to do some work.

She guessed that the man she met in the Baur au Lac's bar, with his thin mustache and keen blue eyes behind rimless spectacles, was about ten years older than her and certainly nobody's assistant. Bancroft was instantly struck by Dulles's hearty laugh over a sign at the bar's window warning in broken English: "The seagulls making to [sic] much noise, please do not feed them." (Dulles later decided to use the line as a code during phone calls.)

That night she told Jean about her meeting with the new man at the embassy. He already knew about him and what he really did. "You Americans," he said with a sigh. "Everyone knows Dulles is the head of your intelligence service here—except, of course, you Americans." Rufenacht had no problems with her working for the spy. In fact, he thought it would add to his prestige on overseas sales calls if it became known that his American wife was employed by such an important man. "But please be discreet, will you?" he cautioned. "Remember, the Swiss will know everything you do."

Several days later, Dulles phoned her to see if she could dine with him the next evening in Bern. Mary eagerly accepted and boarded the afternoon train to the capital. After Herrengasse's butler took her coat, Dulles ushered Mary into his study, where she nibbled on hors d'oeuvres and sipped a martini while he fussed with the fire. Supper in the dining room was delicious—Dulles was obviously a gourmet, she thought—and Mary began to sense at different points during the meal that this man was attracted to her. Dulles was, though that evening he stuck to detailing the job he wanted her to do: continue analyzing the speeches of top Nazis but now send the reports to him instead of to Mayer, and meet visitors from neighboring countries who could not see him because it would be too dangerous if enemy agents spotted them. After their second dinner, this time at the Veltlinerkeller in Zurich, Dulles lit his pipe as they strolled through a nearby park and finally blurted out with obvious delight that their relationship "should work out quite well. We can let the work cover the romance—and the romance cover the work!" Startled, Mary at first thought he was joking because in the next instant he informed her in all seriousness that he would pay her only the minimum.

She soon realized though that he was intent on her sharing his bed. Mary fell madly in love, thrilled with a man who operated so coolly under pressure. Donovan, who cheated on his wife almost as often as Dulles did on his, quickly learned of the affair and pressed his old go-between for details. Mary told him none, though the details were steamy. After his nightly radiotelephone call to Charles B. Jennings—Mary now typed the script for Dulles—they would rush to his room for torrid sex before she scurried back to her hotel in the blackout. One time, knowing Jean and her daughter were away, Dulles raced to her Zurich apartment. "Quick!" he commanded. "I've got a very tricky meeting coming up. I want to clear my head." She serviced him on the living room couch.

Rufenacht, who was on the road much of the time, posed no impediment to Mary's affair. She told him she wanted a divorce, but instead of beating her, Jean uncharacteristically begged her to remain in the marriage, arguing that it would afford her protection under Swiss law while she worked for her lover. Mary reluctantly agreed. She thought Dulles also was in love with her, but he soon made it clear he would never divorce Clover to marry her, so she accepted being his wartime mistress.

Six months into their separation, Dulles wrote Clover a cheery note telling her he was glad he decided to come to Bern because "I am doing something useful." Not what Clover wanted to hear. She kept busy working as a forewoman in a Manhattan factory assembling electronics for the military. But she sank into a deep depression from Allen's absence. Occasionally flowers arrived that he managed to wire. But letters were rare—some bounced back to Dulles or when they reached Clover they had been heavily censored. One arrived in an envelope whose writing was not her husband's. Clover assumed someone had read it and put it in a new mailer. On top of that, she faced difficulties with Sullivan & Cromwell drawing money from her husband's account and began running short of cash. Finally in July 1943, distraught with her nerves strung out, Clover went to the OSS New York office and unloaded on senior aides her frustration at being cut off from Allen. To improve communications, the State Department had her microfilm her letters, which could be sent faster by diplomatic pouch. Even so, mail from Allen remained intermittent, which continued to deeply depress her.

Though he professed constantly in his letters to miss his family, Dulles was delighted to be far away—particularly from the OSS in Washington. He never invited Donovan to visit him in Bern—though it would have been next to impossible for the OSS director to slip into Switzerland if the invitation had been extended—and he always believed that agents in the field like him should *not* keep headquarters too informed about what they were doing. Dulles would dash off testy cables to Donovan if he thought he was second-guessing his decisions in Bern. Top Donovan aides like Secret Intelligence chief Whitney Shepardson would fire back with angry memos, such as one admonishing Dulles for being "indiscreet" in a nightly radio-telephone call, which he knew the Swiss monitored. After six months of backbreaking work scrambling to find sources and cabling to Washington what they revealed, Dulles received a snide memo from Shepardson, which Donovan cleared, advising him that "all news from Bern these days is being discounted 100% by the War Department." The criticism stung. But Dulles had been consorting with characters of questionable reliability. Many of his early cables did have flawed information or they rushed to injudicious conclusions.

But Dulles's output improved. The military intelligence he raked from operatives, once scorned by the War Department, soon began to receive better ratings for reliability. The services started using it to confirm information London received through its Ultra program, which intercepted and decrypted German radio messages. Dulles sent cables, some of which Donovan also relayed to Roosevelt, on German technological advances with submarines, fighter planes, V-1 flying bombs and V-2 rockets, atomic research, chemical and biological weapons, even with artificial fog (pumped into the air to conceal targets during the day). He was one of many agents who supplied information on the Nazi missile production facility at Peenemünde, which British aircraft eventually attacked. He sent reports on Wehrmacht troop movements in Italy and France, on arms factories in Berlin and other German cities to strike, and, when he could find it, on the damage the air raids had done. As senior military officers grew more confident of Dulles's intelligence, they began sending him long lists of questions on German, and even Japanese, arms development. Dulles tried to answer them all. He vacuumed practically anything—from a treatise on the measurement of electricity he thought Einstein in Princeton might find useful to a report on a German ring smuggling in liver extract from Argentina to treat diseases. And he continued not to be shy about passing along rumors, unverified reports, wild stories, or misinformation that poured into his station. He did not have the staff to check out everything. So he often left the sorting of fact from fiction to Washington.

It did not take long for German intelligence to add Herrengasse 23 to the list of American diplomatic buildings its agents staked out. The Abwehr and Gestapo assumed all employees at Allied diplomatic missions around the world were spies. The fact that the Swiss press had identified Dulles as an important adviser to Roosevelt made him a prime target. The Germans had broken one of the codes Harrison's legation employed and which Dulles had used. They decoded an account he had cabled to Washington of one of his meetings with Prince Hohenlohe—not a particularly spectacular find since the prince already kept the SS briefed on his visits. German intelligence—which kept extensive files on the OSS's global organization, a surprising number of them filled with erroneous information—assumed incorrectly that Dulles was focused on gathering merely economic-related material for the legation. The Gestapo dispatched bogus informants to his door to feed him disinformation. One of the Abwehr's V-men, a wealthy German lawyer in Bern identified in its reports only as "Wuttich," ingratiated himself with Dulles and sent back to his handlers rumors the American passed along on Allied strategic planning—which the Abwehr already could read about in newspapers. A man identified in an SS memo as "Dr. Schüddekopf" reported on his long talks with Dulles, who probed him on German resistance contacts he might have. Dulles was expansive during their chats, but shared only harmless diplomatic gossip with him and stuck to his cover story that he was FDR's representative. The SS captain reading the report did not believe otherwise.

Though they never had a clear picture of exactly what Dulles was doing in Bern, the Germans were not averse to playing hardball with him. German agents provocateurs posing as French Resistance operatives showed up at his door; suspicious, Dulles sent them on bogus missions to France, where cells quickly executed them. To try to scare off his sources, German agents spread rumors that they had broken Dulles's OSS code and could identify them. They also pressured Swiss authorities to investigate Dulles's operation and arrest his contacts. Dulles accepted the spy-versus-spy games more as an irritant than a threat. "The Abwehr didn't have its heart in its work," he told an OSS historian. But Donovan, who had approved his operating more or less in the open, soon worried about Nazi agents watching Dulles too closely and urged him to be more careful. A postwar CIA evaluation of the Bern operation concluded that Dulles was "careless" and "naive" about security, not only against Nazi penetration but also from the Soviets. Like Donovan, Dulles had no qualms about working with communists if they helped in the war against Hitler. Russian espionage agents closely monitored Dulles's contacts with German resistance elements (Stalin was paranoid the resistance was angling for a separate German peace with the Americans) and even kept tabs on his family back home, cabling Moscow when his daughter Toddie went to work for the OSS as a clerk. The NKGB (the People's Commissariat for State Security) considered anything they could find for the Russian dictator on what Dulles was up to in Bern valuable intelligence.

People who should have been allies spied on Dulles as well. Showing a healthy respect for Swiss neutrality, he took pains not to anger them with his espionage and worked diligently to cultivate their secret services. Even so, the Swiss counterintelligence service, which could be ruthless with for-eigners spying in the country, tapped his phones, often tailed his car, and watched him in the hotels and restaurants he frequented. The FBI was far away, but Hoover also tried his best to keep tabs on Dulles's activities in Bern. In addition, rival senior officers in U.S. Army intelligence formed a secret espionage unit behind Donovan's back led by a quirky major named John "Frenchy" Grombach, whom Donovan had earlier dismissed from the OSS for being too conspiratorial. Nicknamed "the Pond," Grombach's tiny unit spied not only on the Axis, it also collected information on Donovan, his officers, even the wives of his officers. Grombach looked for dirt on Dulles, keeping a dossier on him and having his snitches in Bern report to him on his movements. His agents were convinced Dulles's operation was also a front for looking out for old Sullivan & Cromwell clients in Germany when the war ended.

Hans Bernd Gisevius was a hulk of a man, six foot four with shoulders that seemed as wide as a doorway and a countenance always stern—a stiff Prussian who shunned chitchat, preferred to keep to himself, and was not nearly as smooth or socially adept as his friend Gaevernitz. In January 1943, the thirty-eight-year-old Abwehr officer approached Dulles offering to betray his country. The son of a judge, Gisevius was a law school graduate who became a committed conservative nationalist and aspired in 1933 to be chief of the Prussian Gestapo. But in bureaucratic warfare raging within the German counterespionage service at the time, Gisevius came out on the losing end. He was derailed to lesser police jobs in the Reich's interior min-istries, blocked from advancement by Gestapo leaders who considered him suspect. Gisevius drifted into the camp of dissident German officers con-spiring against Hitler in the late 1930s. By then the Gestapo reject saw the Nazis as enemies of the state—his driving ambition was now to destroy the fanatical Hitler and his murderous regime. When war broke out, one of the dissident officers, General Hans Oster, who was deputy chief of the Abwehr, arranged for Gisevius to be drafted into the military intelligence service and dispatched to the German consulate in Zurich. Working under the cover of a vice-consul, but with no intelligence duties to perform, Gisevius's real job was to make contact with foreign services that might be helpful to the Ger-man resistance. Admiral Wilhelm Canaris, the Abwehr's cunning chief who had also become disillusioned with Hitler, protected Gisevius from other German officers in the consulate who quickly became suspicious that this new man consorted with the Allies.

Gaevernitz arranged Dulles's meetings with Gisevius, first in Zurich and later at his Herrengasse apartment. The German financier insisted that his Abwehr friend was a genuine regime opponent. Dulles checked him out ahead of time on his own. Church leaders in Geneva also vouched for Gisevius—the one person who could give you the inside story of the German underground, they said. Dulles assumed Gisevius had investigated him as well.

A meeting between enemy intelligence officers—each obviously intent on using the other—was fraught with danger, both men knew. Dulles took every precaution he could devise, conferring with Gisevius only at night under the cover of the Swiss blackout. It took a while for the two men to warm to each other. The Prussian literally looked down his nose at Dulles because he was so tall and squinted through thick tortoiseshell glasses due to being severely nearsighted. Dulles tried to put Gisevius at ease by insisting at the outset that he call him Allen. The German told Dulles that a victorious Hitler would mean "the end of Christian civilization, and of Western culture in Europe and possibly in the world." He was not betraying his country by consorting with the OSS, Gisevius told Dulles. He was saving it.

British intelligence, whom Gisevius had first approached, believed the Abwehr man was a plant—"compromised to the point where he cannot be redeemed," according to one secret OSS cable—and turned him away. About three years earlier, the SS kidnapped two MI6 officers at the Dutch-German border, lured there by Nazi double agents with the dangle that they would meet regime opponents in the German military. London believed Gisevius was another trap and warned Dulles to back off. Convinced the British were wrong once more, Dulles again refused to be bullied. He gave Gisevius the code name "Tiny"—apropos of his size—and assigned Mary to babysit him. The Abwehr officer, whom he introduced to Mary only as Dr. Bernhard, had written a tell-all book on the Third Reich, which he wanted to publish in the West after the war. Bancroft's job was to translate his 1,415-page manuscript into English and use their sessions together to milk him for more information. "I want you to report to me everything he says to you—*everything*,"

ordered Dulles. "He may be off his guard and say things to you that contra-
dict the story he is telling me." Two hundred pages into the book, Mary discovered the true identity of this Dr. Bernhard, who came on to her as Dulles
had. She declined a second romance, though Dulles saw no problem with it
if Gisevius spilled more secrets.

Tiny proved to be extremely valuable. He provided Dulles with his early
information on development of the V-1 and V-2, alerted him to German
naval reports of fewer Allied ships being sunk by U-boats, delivered him
data on Third Reich shortages in scrap iron, and sent him intelligence on
meat rations for German households being shortened further. Dulles discovered that his Abwehr informant had scruples, so to speak. He would not
share information he thought might get German soldiers killed. Yet he had
no qualms about burning the Abwehr's assets. He alerted Dulles to the fact
that the Germans had broken one of the American legation's codes. Dulles's
stomach suffered as a result of another of his tips, that Herrengasse's cherished cook was a Nazi informant. He immediately fired the woman. Most
importantly, in the months that followed their first meeting Gisevius kept
Dulles posted on progress with the plot to topple Adolf Hitler.

· · · ·

Richard Helms was earning high marks for his work as an operations officer
in the Central European and Scandinavian section of Secret Intelligence. As
was the case with his superiors at the Navy's Eastern Sea Frontier, his OSS
bosses still thought he could be more forceful. Helms, however, had tired of
deskwork in Washington. He wanted to be in Europe. Wading through the
stack of overseas cables he faced each day, Helms became fascinated with
the ones Ferd Mayer had forwarded to him from Dulles on an obscure official he had recruited in Berlin's Foreign Office. Carib believed he was so far
the OSS's "best penetration" of Germany.

A short man no taller than five foot seven, Fritz Kolbe had a round
Slavic-like face easily forgettable in a crowd. His head was mostly bald with
a fringe of brown hair around the side, his gray-blue eyes somewhat beady
and wide apart, his nose large, and his small ears protruding out. He did not
smoke, rarely drank, and was obsessed with physical fitness. His shoes were
always polished, his conservative suits neatly pressed, his manner charming

yet unobtrusive. The perfect Foreign Office bureaucrat. Born into a middle-class Pomeranian family, Kolbe fell into the antiauthoritarian Wandervögel (roughly translated "Wandering Free Spirit") movement as a teenager, a Boy Scout–like group antithetical to the later Hitler Youth. He soldiered in a World War I engineering battalion, and eventually ended up in the Foreign Office as a consular officer, serving in posts worldwide and finding ways to avoid joining the Nazi Party by pretending to be too simpleminded for politics.

By 1941 Kolbe nursed a deep revulsion over Hitler's conquests, but playing the obtuse yet efficient bureaucrat, he realized, accomplished nothing except to protect himself. Assigned to the Foreign Office in Berlin, he began minor acts of defiance, joining old Wandervögel comrades to write anti-Nazi leaflets secretly circulated among the capital's cafés and businesses. Kolbe by then had risen to the position of personal assistant to Karl Ritter, an unlikable Bavarian ambassador who headed the ministry's political-military affairs department and harbored a private contempt for his boss, Foreign Minister Joachim von Ribbentrop. Kolbe's job—screening hundreds of diplomatic cables, memos, and high-level meeting transcripts each day for the important ones that Ritter should read—made him one of the best-informed officials in the Foreign Office and gave him access to highly classified documents on German foreign and military policy. The irony that such an ardent anti-Nazi could assume so sensitive a post was not lost on the civil servant.

Believing his country must lose the war for the Nazi regime to fall, in the spring of 1943 Kolbe began saving copies of some of the more important documents he saw for the Allies. To deliver them, he had finally talked a Wandervögel friend in the ministry's mail office into assigning him as a courier carrying diplomatic pouches to Bern. A distracted Ritter approved his side trips, buying Kolbe's story that he needed to visit Switzerland for personal business.

Monday afternoon, August 16, 1943, Kolbe checked into the Jura Hotel near the train station in Bern's Old City. The Swiss capital struck him as idyllic compared to wartime Berlin, except for the fact that all the signposts stood stripped of their road signs. Swiss police had taken them down to confuse the Germans if they invaded. Kolbe's head throbbed from staying awake all night worrying on the train whether he would be tripped up by the many security searches along the way in Germany. The journey, however, proved uneventful. The courier orders and diplomatic passport he carried in his jacket pocket enabled him to breeze through the checkpoints with no searches of his locked leather briefcase or his person. In his modest room, Kolbe laid the case on the bed. The thick wax-sealed envelope inside it was filled with cables and memos he would deliver to the legation as part of his courier duties. He took off his pants and untied the cords that tightly wrapped documents around both thighs. He would take those papers to the Allies.

Late the next morning, Ernst Kocherthaler, who was a Jewish petroleum merchant Kolbe had befriended during an early posting in Madrid and who had relocated to Bern in 1936, walked up to the British legation on Thunstrasse and asked the guard at the door if he could speak to the ambassador. Ernesto, as Kocherthaler was also called because he had been born in Germany but became a Spanish citizen, clutched sixteen Foreign Office telegrams Kolbe gave him earlier that morning. The ambassador was not available, the intermediary was curtly told. Eventually Colonel Henry Antrobus Cartwright, the legation's military attaché, came down the stairs with a look on his face that told Kocherthaler he did not have much time for uninvited visitors. The petroleum merchant hurriedly told Cartwright he was an intermediary for a friend from the German Foreign Office, who was offering to share material with the British. Cartwright was unimpressed. Kocherthaler would not divulge the name of this mystery diplomat ready to pass secrets for free. After about fifteen minutes Cartwright politely showed the man the door. The army colonel did not bother to notify the legation's intelligence section of what he considered an inconsequential encounter. When Cartwright ran into Dulles later that evening near his Dufourstrasse office, he mentioned to him in passing to "be on the lookout" for a suspicious character—he could not remember his name—who would likely show up at his shop offering supposedly valuable information. Kocherthaler left the British legation fuming. He pondered whom in the American legation he might now contact.

Shortly after nine o'clock Wednesday morning, Kocherthaler sat in front of the desk of Gerry Mayer, whom he did not know. A mutual friend had arranged the meeting. Kocherthaler spoke hurriedly in English not knowing if the Americans would give him the brush-off as the British had. He offered to set up a meeting with a friend in the German Foreign Office who was "a devoted anti-Nazi" prepared to deliver intelligence to the Allies. If the Americans wanted to meet him it would have to be before noon on Friday when his friend planned to return to Berlin. Mayer nodded noncommittally. Kocherthaler reached into his coat pocket and pulled out the documents Kolbe had given him. He shoved the papers across the desk to Mayer, who began leafing through them. The stamp on the first mimeographed cable— *Geheime Reichsache* ("Top Secret")—immediately caught his attention. Mayer asked the man to wait a moment and scampered upstairs with the papers to Dulles's office. Dulles listened to Mayer's story, then quickly scanned the documents. Routed to Ritter, many of the telegrams were signed by Ribbentrop or his ambassadors. They looked to Dulles like typical diplomatic cables, dealing with such subjects as German operatives sent behind the lines in North Africa, problems with the resistance in occupied Czechoslovakia, and British agents infiltrating into Turkey.

As Mayer had instructed, Kocherthaler showed up at his apartment in the Kirchenfeld district precisely at midnight. Standing next to him was a short, bald-headed man in a black leather coat, which looked to Mayer like it had been borrowed from a movie set and, for August, likely left the poor fellow sweating. Kolbe reached into his coat pocket. Mayer tensed, fearing he might be pulling out a gun. But Kolbe had retrieved a large brown envelope with the red wax seal on it broken. It was stuffed with more documents. He set it on a table near the divan. As Mayer was examining the material— more reports on German troop morale at the Russian Front, sabotage damage by the Resistance in France, and on the Japanese ambassador's visits to Ribbentrop—Dulles arrived a half hour later. The OWI representative introduced him to Kocherthaler and Kolbe as "Mister Douglas." Mayer mixed highballs for everyone, but the drinks did little to ease the tension in the room. Acutely aware that he might be facing a clever Nazi plant on a mission to flush out his OSS operation in Bern, Dulles had huddled with Cartwright once more that day to have him repeat everything about his meeting with Kocherthaler and had tasked Mayer to learn all he could about the German Spaniard before they gathered at the apartment. Gaevernitz later reported that his reputation was spotless. Over the next few months, OSS and British counterintelligence agents would comb for every detail they could find on Kolbe. He was, in fact, employed by the Foreign Office, they confirmed. Kolbe's first wife died at an early age and left him with a son he now rarely saw. He drifted apart from his second wife (a Nazi sympathizer, it turned out) and had begun taking a mistress.

Kolbe cut to the first question he knew the Americans had on their minds. "You gentlemen will ask whether these dispatches are authentic and if so how I was able to get them," he said in a pleasant voice. Dulles's first impression: this man appeared rather unsophisticated and unworldly to be a diplomat or a spy. Kolbe explained his job with Ritter. Mayer and Dulles glanced at each other. They knew the man.

For almost three hours, they talked. Kolbe fleshed out the material in the envelope, detailed his hatred of the Nazis, and recounted more insights on life in Berlin. He revealed the cryptographic system the Foreign Office used to conceal its messages and sketched out a map of the buildings in Wolf's Lair, Hitler's East Prussia headquarters that he had visited on errands for Ritter. Dulles finally raised the suspicion that lingered with him. "We have no way of knowing that you are not an agent provocateur," he said bluntly, but with a smile.

"You would be naive if you did not suspect that," Kolbe responded. "I cannot prove at this moment that I am not. If I were, however, I would hardly have been so extravagant as to bring you the contents of so many documents. Two or three would have sufficed." Good point, Dulles thought. He asked how much money Kolbe wanted for his information. The courier said none. Dulles and Mayer were incredulous.

Past three in the morning, Kolbe finally stood up to leave. He could safely stay no longer. Dulles remained with Mayer after their visitors departed, the two poring over the documents and comparing notes on what Kolbe had told them. Their informant seemed too good to be true, they agreed, which made them all the more suspicious they were being played by a double agent.

Dulles, however, did not intend to make the same mistake he had with Lenin during World War I. The four reconvened at Mayer's apartment Friday morning for an hour-and-a-half meeting before Kolbe boarded his noon train to Berlin. Kolbe recounted information he had picked up at the legation the day before on the Nazi spy network in Bern. Though the German did not want money, Dulles handed him 200 Swiss francs to cover travel expenses and pay for gifts to bring back to his Berlin bosses. Kolbe handed Dulles a letter to be delivered to his son, Peter, in case the Gestapo captured and executed him. Dulles worked out with Kolbe the multiple passwords they would use for his further trips outside of Germany. If he returned to Bern he would identify himself as "George Winter." If he reached neutral Sweden his name for the OSS man in Stockholm would be "George Sommer." To verify his identity his password would be "25900," a simple contraction of his birthday, September 25, 1900.

The next day, August 21, Dulles fired off a cable alerting headquarters to the midnight meeting. In that message and the hundreds of subsequent ones, he gave Kolbe another code name, "George Wood," along with two code numbers, 674 or 805. Mayer and he were scrambling "to verify Wood's bona fides," Dulles wrote. So was MI6. Meanwhile, "every existing safeguard must be observed" to keep Wood's identity secret. His intelligence "may have vast consequences." In follow-up cables Dulles transmitted tantalizing highlights from the documents Kolbe had given him so far, such as the battle damage from Allied bombings of the Ruhr, the rendezvous point for German and Japanese submarines off South Africa's Cape of Good Hope, and the 2 million gold marks in "bribe money" just shipped to the German embassy in Buenos Aires. Washington set up special handling procedures for Dulles's cables on Kolbe; they were code-named "Kappa" with only about a half dozen people cleared to read them. After the cables arrived, headquarters analysts reorganized the take by subject matter and designated it the "Boston Series." To confuse enemy agents if they ever intercepted and decoded his Kappa messages, Dulles used an elaborate array of code words for the names, places, and organizations mentioned in them. The Nazi consul in Bern, for example, was referred to as "Waldo." Budapest became "Latte." The German Foreign Office—"Grand."

Back in Berlin, Kolbe set up a routine for stealing material. After Ritter had initialed Foreign Office telegrams to indicate that he had read them, the copies went to Kolbe, who was supposed to destroy them. He did for innocuous cables, but the important ones he stashed in his safe for Dulles. Sometimes using friends traveling to Bern as witting or unwitting couriers, Kolbe delivered letters to Kocherthaler with the telegrams enclosed and he passed them on to Dulles. If Dulles had a specific request, say for intelligence on Japan's military, he had a Swiss woman pretending to be Kolbe's girlfriend mail him a postcard with a short note that a friend who owned a shop in Bern wanted to know if Berlin stores stocked particular Japanese goods. Dulles eventually slipped Kolbe a miniature camera to make microfilms of the material. He spent sleepless nights at his apartment photographing documents, then secreted the microfilm to Dulles in watchcases.

On October 8, 1943, George Wood arrived in Bern for his second visit. The trip this time had been more harrowing; a stray British Mosquito plane strafed the train and bombed the track. In a separate envelope in his courier pouch he had two hundred pages of telegrams dealing with a wide range of economic, diplomatic, and military topics, as well as two gold rings to repay Dulles for the 200 Swiss francs from the first trip. Kolbe traveled a circuitous route to sneak into the Herrengasse apartment the next three nights so he could brief Dulles on his documents by the fireplace. To convince the German legation that his nocturnal absences were for sex, he spent several hours at a Bern brothel so the whores would remember him if the Gestapo checked, and he visited a doctor who treated venereal diseases to obtain a bill that he could show if interrogated. Dulles cabled headquarters that "weeks will be needed" to process and transmit this load.

But that fall few people in Washington who mattered were reading the treasure Dulles had unearthed with Fritz Kolbe. Claude Dansey found it inconceivable the OSS officer could snare such a spectacular source. Almost from the instant he learned of it, Uncle Claude led what ultimately became an unsuccessful MI6 campaign to discredit the German as another double agent likely in cahoots with Gisevius. Washington remained suspicious as well that George Wood was a plant. Though they had no evidence it was happening, counterintelligence officers at OSS headquarters spun elaborate scenarios for how the German might be duping the agency. The Kolbe telegrams Dulles retransmitted to headquarters in code, so went one notion, were being intercepted by the Abwehr, which already knew their texts and could use the cables to decipher the OSS encryption system. Helms, who now had access to the Kappa cables, was as confounded as Ferd Mayer by the narrow-mindedness in Washington and London. "How could such a volume of messages possibly be manipulated and distorted?" Helms later wrote. George Wood's intelligence was too good and too damaging to German interests to be "chicken feed"—spy jargon for harmless secrets a double agent feeds the enemy to ingratiate himself. Dulles became increasingly angry that the Kappa cables were being denigrated and stuck on the desks of counterintelligence officers like a museum piece instead of distributed to consumers in the field who could use the information. "I'm ready to stake my reputation on the fact that these documents are genuine," he wrote headquarters in one angry cable. At one point headquarters prepared a list of questions for Dulles to send to George Wood in order to test his credibility. Dulles balked. Communications with Kolbe put him in too much danger to be wasted on playing such games.

Kolbe, who kept a revolver in a drawer at home and planned to use it if the Gestapo knocked on the door, did have his share of close calls. One time while photographing documents in his office a secretary phoned that Ribbentrop wanted that file for a conference with Himmler. Kolbe raced to replace the papers in the cabinet before anyone noticed them missing. Another time, a security agent in the courier office began rooting through a trunk of clothes he planned to ship to Bern. Kolbe gripped the pistol in his overcoat, ready to kill as many Nazis as he could before shooting himself. Microfilm was stashed in the pockets of some of the garments. Another official entered the room distracting the inspector, who let the trunk pass.

Kolbe arrived once more in Bern shortly after Christmas with another two hundred pages of telegrams, many with Fritz's penciled notes on the margins to explain them. Not bothered by his assistant wanting to make so many trips to Switzerland, Ritter asked him to bring back a box of Brazilian cigars from a local store. The small Bern staff worked around the clock translating the documents and transmitting summaries of them as well as of the oral reports Kolbe delivered during his fireside chats with Dulles. Over the course of the war, Kolbe brought out for the OSS some 1,600 Foreign Office cables and memos from more than forty German diplomatic outposts around the world. They alerted the Allies to eight thousand Italian Jews moved out to be "liquidated," disclosed what German intelligence knew about British airfields being readied for the invasion of France, revealed Nazi aircraft losses over England, pinpointed the locations of German arms factories for bombing, and provided statistics on Japanese war plane production. Kolbe's secrets also turned up weaknesses in Allied security. His messages unmasked "Cicero," the Nazi code name for an Albanian who spied for the Germans in the British embassy in Turkey, and helped expose "Josephine," a Swedish naval attaché in London aiding the Germans. Paired with what Dulles had accumulated since August, Kolbe's Christmas delivery finally convinced the lords of American and British intelligence that he was the genuine article—although doubts about him lingered throughout the war. The U.S. Army's military intelligence wing carefully scrubbed the Boston Series and concluded it was mostly authentic. Some material the Army could not verify but assumed it was true. The service found only "one piece of bad fish," according to an OSS memo—a dispatch on the Wehrmacht's Italian front deemed erroneous. British intelligence grudgingly conceded it could find only 4 percent of Kolbe's reports to be inaccurate. Bill Stephenson, Britain's New York station chief, later concluded that the Wood traffic was "one of the greatest secret intelligence achievements of this war."

Five months after Kolbe handed his first telegrams to Dulles, the War Department finally began disseminating the German's information to the field. Donovan began sending George Wood reports to Roosevelt. On Christmas Eve, Ferd Mayer and his boss, Whitney Shepardson, whose code name was "Jackpot," cabled season's greetings to Dulles. "Your accomplishments during the past year have been outstanding, and have been a source of inspiration to all of us," the message read. His start had been bumpy, but since October, Dulles had been receiving better reviews from headquarters for all the reports he sent. Even transcripts of his "flashes"—his nightly radiotelephone calls with unclassified information and foreign policy advice—were being read by a "rapidly growing number of people," another cable advised. If he had "an especially interesting conversation piece," headquarters asked that he let aides know several days ahead of time so they could arrange for Donovan to listen in on the call. Within a year, Shepardson proudly noted in a secret internal memo, Dulles had turned Bern into "the hub of intelligence from Germany, Italy, occupied countries, and the Balkan satellites."

But headquarters still kept a what-have-you-done-for-me-lately attitude. In a December 30 cable, which surely must have irked Dulles, Jackpot and Carib wrote that Fritz Kolbe was not good enough. He needed to plant more agents inside the Third Reich who could organize networks of more spies to send even more intelligence back to Switzerland.

CHAPTER 10

LONDON

Bill Casey landed in bitter cold Prestwick on the southwest coast of Scotland shortly after eight o'clock on Sunday night, November 14, 1943. He hefted fifty pounds of luggage off the plane. The OSS London office had warned him to pack heavy. British ration coupons would not be enough for a shopping spree when he arrived. A crowded bus took him across desolate flatland to the station, where he bought a ticket for the train to London. He was starving. His flight from Washington to the United Kingdom had begun more than twenty-four hours earlier, with a stop at Newfoundland, and all he had to munch on during the trip were two Spam sandwiches and an apple. The best he could find in the Prestwick station was a wafer and cup of tea. On the train he rooted around in one of his bags for the only other nutrition he could muster: a vitamin tablet and a cough drop.

As the end of 1943 neared, the Washington bureaucratic battles that had engulfed the OSS subsided; Casey was sure Donovan's organization would survive. He was glad now to be overseas. If he didn't count short vacations in Canada and the Caribbean, this would be his first time abroad. Casey, who knew only a little Spanish and French and garbled most of what he did know, arrived in London realizing full well he was a neophyte—both to the espionage the British had long mastered and the scars their prized capital had suffered.

The empire's greatest city had become the greatest target with the start of World War II. The Luftwaffe had dropped almost 50,000 tons of bombs on London during the Blitz of 1940 and 1941, destroying some 300,000 homes, damaging 4.5 million others, killing 20,000, prompting the eventual evacuation of more than 600,000 children, and leaving the nerves of the adults who remained behind badly frayed. Most of the treasured icons had been struck—the House of Commons chamber, Big Ben, Westminster Abbey, the Tower of London, Madame Tussauds Wax Museum, Buckingham Palace (the attack on the king and queen, in residence at the time, served only to boost British morale). Inside behind closed doors and drawn curtains, dance halls and West End pubs remained jammed at night and movie theaters still filled with viewers who booed lustily when newsreels showed Hitler. Outside, London had become a dark and silent city. The war brought out the best and worst among its dwellers. Stiff-upper-lip good humor, which British propagandists made much of, could indeed be found; psychiatrists reported relatively few cases of shell shock or nervous breakdowns during the Blitz. Yet one-third told pollsters they were exhausted with less than four hours sleep nightly because of the bombing, and practically every resident had become testier.

Bone tired from his trip, Casey checked into a hotel and slept for a day. The OSS station had told him not to bother to come in the first twenty-four hours. The London station had also told Casey to lie to customs officers at Prestwick when they asked where he would be working in England. The train had taken him through multiple defense rings around the city. Immediately he found "everything about" London "intriguing," he wrote Sophia. Though the intensity of the early bombing had passed, it still felt to him like a city under siege. Barbed wire and sandbags ringed many government buildings with soldiers perched atop fortifications manning heavy machine guns. A thousand barrage balloons had sprouted during the Blitz to force the Luftwaffe to bomb at higher altitudes. Searchlights and antiaircraft guns dotted parks and open areas, the shrapnel and unexploded shells from the AA fire posing another deadly threat to Londoners when they fell back on the city from the sky. By the time Casey arrived, a dozen or so German bombers continued to raid the metropolitan area several times a week, causing far less damage but still serious casualties. Rumors swept through

London that these attacks were a prelude to a more devastating retaliatory air weapon coming.

Soon Casey became as adept as seasoned dwellers in recognizing the sounds of war—the warbling air raid siren signaling an imminent attack, the more steady blare to signal all clear, the throbbing beat of distant German plane engines, the difference in the whine and swish of falling bombs depending on their weight, the tinny plinking sound of antiaircraft shrapnel falling back to earth. He learned to make his way around the city's streets with a flashlight at night, the blackout restrictions having been eased some. But in the soupy fog blanketing many nights he could walk into a lamppost and knock himself out if he wasn't careful. When the enemy bombers roared overhead Casey also became nimble, as other Londoners were, at doorway hopping in a half walk, half run until he found an air raid shelter. By the time Casey arrived in London, conditions in the Underground facilities, which early in the war had been filthy, fetid, and disease-ridden, had improved greatly with latrines, sinks for washing, canteens offering drinks and hot food, even library books and gramophones playing classical records.

The city was becoming bitter cold with winter's onset in 1943. Coal for heating homes was in short supply and Londoners had already begun scrounging ingredients for their Christmas dinners, which would be meager as they had been for past holiday meals except for the usual supply of mutton. Food rationing combined with a previous summer drought meant other meats, along with potatoes and green vegetables, were in short supply. No one was starving, but none were fat and happy or washing down meals with wine or whiskey. The OSS station had given Casey a list of three dozen decent restaurants in town, but they were crowded and expensive, their menus limited, and their portions skimpy. He found better fare at Red Cross canteens and the London club set up for American officers.

By late 1943, London had tidied up some with shattered windows boarded over and rubble cleared from many neighborhoods. But parts of the capital remained uninhabitable because of bomb damage. The rest of the city still had a shabby, battered, and drab gray look to it, Casey thought. Londoners' clothes appeared old and worn, few houses had fresh coats of paint, even many mansions had gone to seed. The city was also infested with millions of rats, thanks to a not-well-thought-out program in 1940 that destroyed about 400,000 of its cats. The people were worn out from four years of conflict, Casey could see. A jaded cynicism afflicted them. Though the British appeared to him outwardly pleasant, the mass of Americans in uniform come to end this wretched war drew a mixed reaction from them. Most were delighted to have the United States on the Allied side, but the influx of officers and enlisted men crowding Londoners out of scarce real estate and dating their women grated on many. The popular refrain Casey soon heard from the locals: the Americans are "over-paid, over-sexed, and over here." The retort Casey's comrades gave: the British are "under-paid, under-sexed, and under Eisenhower."

The near unanimous opinion of OSS officers who knew David Kirkpatrick Este Bruce: he was the most handsome, sophisticated, charming, discreet, and smooth-operating man they had ever met—aristocratic even in his colonel's uniform. So immensely self-controlled and self-assured was David K. E. Bruce that few knew it masked a man always nervous on the inside. A Princeton classmate of F. Scott Fitzgerald's and a lawyer who won a seat first in Maryland's, then Virginia's House of Delegates, Bruce had married Ailsa Mellon, the spoiled hypochondriacal daughter of Pittsburgh multimillionaire Andrew Mellon. Also the treasury secretary for Republican administrations, Mellon made his son-in-law wealthy as his financial adviser and fine art buyer.

Bored with investment banking, Bruce joined Donovan's agency in October 1941 to start his nascent Secret Intelligence Branch. He arrived in London, a city he knew well from a previous stint there as an American Red Cross representative, in February 1943 to take over a growing OSS station that had already been through two chiefs Donovan found wanting. The patrician Bruce proved a perfect fit for schmoozing the British government and its upper crust. He collected expensive antiques to decorate his flat at 3 Lees Place and proved resourceful as a treasure hunter at finding fine bottles of wine in London. Bruce also shared many of his boss's traits. Like Donovan, he enjoyed touring Europe's front lines and remained open to unconventional and even wacky ideas. He offered to pay Edward R. Murrow under the table for OSS propaganda work; CBS's London correspondent declined but was willing to help occasionally for free. Bruce also proposed a million-man parachute attack on Germany instead of a landing at Normandy; the War Department ignored the idea.

Casey arrived at Bruce's office with a letter from Ole Doering, Donovan's senior counselor, assuring him the young lieutenant was "thoroughly trained in his work." Bruce had told Doering he did not need any more officers with no intelligence experience just warming seats in his station. Casey was hardly an experienced espionage operative—neither was Bruce, for that matter—but he did arrive with a list of nine suggestions for how Bruce could set up a secretariat in the station to better manage the paper flow and help him oversee his vast enterprise. Bruce, however, showed no interest in the list or the secretariat Washington had sent Casey to organize. He left Casey adrift to wander around his headquarters with no assigned duties.

The courtly station chief had little in common with the in-your-face New Yorker. Casey soon noticed their personal lives also could not have been more different. By Thanksgiving, Casey was painfully homesick and desperate for the family photos Sophia enclosed in her notes. "Tootsie, I can't tell you how much I miss you," he wrote her that holiday. He became emotional when he saw baby girls in London about Bernadette's age. He and Sophia even numbered their letters to make sure they missed none. Bruce ignored his daughter, and his marriage to Ailsa had effectively ended by this point. Casey and other aides could not help but notice a stunning, twenty-nine-year-old brunette with hazel eyes who sat at a desk outside Bruce's office and appeared to have an unusually close working relationship with the boss. Donovan had sent Evangeline Bell, a widely traveled Radcliffe graduate who spoke flawless French, to London to serve as an administrative assistant to the previous station chief. Bruce, who enjoyed being around beautiful women, began a wartime romance with Miss Bell. He would divorce Ailsa after the war and marry his assistant.

London's was the largest overseas OSS station in Donovan's organization, with nearly 1,300 Army, Navy, and civilian staffers when Casey arrived. It occupied space in Grosvenor Square, which had become an American enclave with the U.S. embassy, Eisenhower's headquarters, the U.S. Army and Navy headquarters, and the main office for the American Red Cross. Some 333 houses and hotels around what soon became known as "Eisenhower Platz" were also commandeered as living quarters for GIs. Donovan's operation began on the top floor of the U.S. embassy at No. 1 Grosvenor Square but soon expanded into several Georgian and neo-Georgian town houses branching from it. The OSS also rented downtown flats and country houses outside the city to entertain sources and give agents secluded spots to recu-perate after missions. Casey had to walk around with a pocketful of passes to be admitted into all of them. In his wallet next to his OSS badge he also kept a "For God and Country" card with a Bible verse.

Bruce put Casey at a desk near Evangeline's in the five-story brick town house he made his command post at 70 Grosvenor Street. A six-page memo lay on Casey's chair the first day with detailed security instructions: "Noth-ing that is learnt within this office should be spoken of outside the office," don't brag about what you do or know, assume the enemy listens in on all your phone calls, "one should not appear to be doing secret work or arouse curiosity by appearing suspicious." Just tell others "you are working with the embassy."

The station's "rarefied atmosphere" impressed him, he wrote Sophia. In adjoining offices sat banking heir Junius S. Morgan, who managed clan-destine operations money, and Chicago meatpacker Lester Armour, now a Navy commander whose job, he told Casey, was to "screen the bullshit" among operations. Casey found misfits as well. The son of an MGM ex-ecutive who was a Donovan pal eventually had to be sent home because he was a drunk and a ne'er-do-well. Casey also formed otherwise unlikely bonds among Bruce's staff, such as with a young liberal historian named Arthur Schlesinger Jr., who worked as a research analyst on European pol-itics. Schlesinger later wrote that Casey concealed a "steel purpose under a shuffle of mumbles." Both men realized the irony of what became a lifelong friendship. The conservative Casey would later despise the administration of John F. Kennedy, which Schlesinger served.

Casey had to first settle for a pricey hotel room ($20 a day with a break-fast of cold porridge and a mush-filled sausage) until he could find an apart-ment. By 1940 wealthy Londoners had vacated many well-appointed flats, one of which Casey found that had been owned by a Lady McMahon. He shared it with another officer until he was forced to move out. He shared his next apartment, a seven-roomer on Alford Street near Grosvenor Square, with three other officers, who quickly discovered he was a sloppy roommate. Though he managed to splurge for a membership in the Navy wine mess he had trouble living off the per diem the OSS gave him because London was so expensive.

By 1940, most senior British civil servants regularly worked twelve-hour days and kept cots in their offices for when it was not worth going home. The men and women in Britain's clandestine services stayed even busier and Casey soon found they did not suffer fools gladly—particularly what they considered the naive American variety. To Bruce's annoyance, the American high command early on also viewed the OSS London station as an unruly collection of civilians and refused to challenge the British monopoly on European spy operations. After a year of haggling with Stewart Menzies, MI6's secretive director who controlled all plane services from England into occupied Europe, Donovan in the summer of 1943 finally managed to pry loose some of those aircraft to fly in the OSS's spies. He also worked out an agreement with Sir Charles Hambro, a former international banker and now SOE's chief, which divided up the world for each agency's guerrillas and saboteurs. Even so, Casey could see that their cousins still tried to hamstring OSS operations. Dansey, for one, complained that Donovan was sending "a great many dubious characters" to London for missions into the continent. In his first months with the station, Casey could also see that British clandestine operations were far superior to any that Bruce could mount. But the junior partner was catching up and Casey realized Bruce's charm was critical to overcoming British aloofness and hostility toward the Americans.

He decided not to press his new boss on Doering's demand that a secretariat be set up in London. Casey wanted to fit in and forcing such a unit down Bruce's throat would not be the way to do that. Instead, he floated around the station for the first month and a half, learning how it operated and suppressing the nagging feeling that he was not being useful. "He couldn't sit still," recalled Hugh Montgomery, who worked with him in London.

Casey finally decided that if Bruce would not appoint him the head of a secretariat he would make himself a de facto one. He put his writing talent to work drafting letters Bruce sent to Donovan and operational plans delivered to Eisenhower. He brainstormed long-range intelligence projects for the station, organized joint field exercises for American and British operatives, became a troubleshooter for Bruce, and set up a registry system to route the thousands of cables, memos, and reports pouring into the station so the right people read them. Bruce already had an executive committee consisting of his senior advisers. Casey wormed his way into the group. It enabled him to dabble in practically every London operation—from making recommendations on the distribution of OSS reports to Army units, to coordinating how OSS commandos in the field received intelligence from the French Resistance, to keeping Bruce posted on progress with the Jedburgh training. Casey, in effect, became Bruce's one-man talent pool that he could draw from to tackle odd jobs, such as devising an insurance policy for officers to meeting with a *New York Times* editor on the work the OSS performed. The eager lieutenant also found time to edit a reference book Leo Cherne's RIA published in Washington.

By February 1944, Casey was swamped with work, which he found "damn interesting," he wrote Sophia. Days became a blur of endless staff meetings, long lunches, working dinners, then back to the office, sometimes until midnight. Bruce assigned him an assistant. Colleagues discovered that Casey wasn't afraid to speak his mind—"you could not *not* pay attention to him," said Montgomery—and that he became a hothead at times. When a Navy lieutenant commander ordered him to fetch a chair, Lieutenant Junior Grade Casey barked back: "Get it yourself!" Superiors talked the officer out of demanding that Casey be brought before a captain's mast for insubordination, for good reason. Casey's writing and administrative skills honed at RIA were becoming invaluable to the London station.

Bruce was won over. Seven months after Casey arrived in London he officially designated him what he had already become—chief of the station's new secretariat. Casey quickly put together a group of "bright young men" as he called them to control the paper avalanche to Bruce, to make sure the ballooning bureaucracy under him followed his orders, and to supervise any special projects that might pop up. Casey, in particular, began working with the exiled governments that had taken refuge in London, evaluating for Bruce which of their resistance groups in occupied Europe should receive OSS support. Belgium's intelligence service, he decided, would be important as the Allied invasion of France neared. The Nazis had virtually wiped out the Netherlands' spy networks, he found. The Danes had anti-Nazi operatives unmatched in skill and dedication, he told Bruce. The exiled Polish government also maintained an aggressive and efficient intelligence service inside its country. But Casey discovered, as others already had, that the French had the most important espionage and guerrilla assets. He struggled with Bruce to understand de Gaulle and to cultivate Colonel Dewavrin. Casey began taking French lessons, although they only marginally improved his command of the language.

Casey also began reading—with considerable admiration—copies of cables that passed through the station from Allen Dulles, whose tiny Bern operation, he thought, rivaled London's in terms of its importance to the OSS. He observed as a fly on the wall the firestorm Dulles had sparked behind closed doors with Uncle Claude over a German agent Casey knew only by his code name, George Wood. He also became one of the regular transcript readers of Dulles's flashes with their foreign policy advice to Washington. He tended to agree with the Bern chief's criticism of FDR's unconditional surrender announcement. Casey considered it an "albatross" hanging over any Allied effort to convince the Germans to give up. Dulles, the junior lieutenant could see, had become a star in the OSS. Casey wanted to be one as well.

He started hatching his own programs to undermine Germany. One of his ideas: sneak into neutral nations the leaders of top companies, such as General Motors and Standard Oil, who had worked with German firms before the war. The American executives would infiltrate into countries like Spain and Sweden, renew old German acquaintances, and begin enticing them to subvert the Nazi regime so business that had flourished between them before the war could resume after Hitler was toppled. Bruce backed the idea, but senior Donovan aides dismissed it as wildly impractical. For one, no president of a top corporation would likely take time off from business to play secret agent for the OSS. If he did, he would be violating the Trading with the Enemy Act, which prevented "any conversations of a business nature between Americans and Germans as long as the war is in progress," a headquarters letter to Bruce pointed out. Even if that not so minor legal hurdle could be cleared, Germany's top businessmen "are not fools," the note continued. "They require no instructions from us on how to get rid of their leaders." Donovan eventually gave Casey the green light for a less ambitious project, code-named "Harvard," to publish a weekly four-page newsletter titled *Handel und Wandel* and containing legitimate world economic news sprinkled with defeatist propaganda; it was circulated in Sweden among visiting German industrialists. Casey also recruited Stockholm businessmen traveling to Germany to report back to him on plants they visited, so Allied planes could bomb them.

Among the many distractions Bruce had to deal with was Donovan constantly dropping in on the London station, often unannounced. After November, the OSS chief began to notice the busy young naval officer, perpetually restless like him, showing up everywhere as Bruce's right-hand man. Into the early morning hours Donovan would hold court with Casey and other OSS staffers at the prestigious Claridge's Hotel near Grosvenor Square, with its ornate rooms, restaurant grill still stocked with a sumptuous smorgasbord, and doormen who greeted guests in livery and top hats, only now next to sandbags. Donovan—always "brimful of new ideas" for operations, as Casey recalled—used a suite of rooms at Claridge's as his command post when he visited London. The spymaster began dispatching Casey to Bumpus Bookshop on Oxford Street to buy the latest tomes on military issues and politics—a chore Casey enjoyed. He also prowled the city's bookstores for what had become an increasingly scarce commodity. Libraries were short of volumes and the Blitz had practically decimated paper stocks so few new books were published, and those that were sold out quickly. Famished from too little reading material, Casey had Sophia mail him American magazines.

Though spy work consumed him almost every waking moment, Casey made a point of attending mass every Sunday at the nearest Catholic church he could find. Late at night when he returned exhausted to his apartment he tried to wedge in time to write to Sophia. Along with the books he wanted her to mail (Jan Karski's war memoir of the Polish underground and Edgar Snow's *Red Star over China*), he nagged her in one letter for news clippings about himself from the local newspapers. "You know how vain I am," he admitted. He also peppered Sophia with detailed instructions on stocks he wanted her to buy or sell for his portfolio. The war—or at least what he saw of it in the skies overhead and the shadow operations of the OSS—left him contemplative in the free moments when he scrawled notes home. He sent a touching one on February 21, 1944, to little Bernadette after he received a Valentine's card Sophia had sent from her:

Some day you'll understand why your daddy has been exported from his wonderful life with you and transplanted to the British Isles. All the men of his age have a rendezvous with history and a job to do in making the world a safe place where people like you and your mom and your pop can live quietly and peacefully according to their own conscience and wishes. Whenever anybody starts pushing other people around we'll have to all gang up and stop him because if we don't he'll get powerful enough to push us all around so that instead of living the way we think we should we'll be living the way he thinks we should.

After your pop has done his very small part in putting out this fire there are a lot of things he plans for us.

After four months in London Casey thought his secret war had changed him. "This experience is teaching me a great deal about how things are done and how political organizations operate," he wrote Sophia. "No, it won't harden me. I think I'm steadily becoming more mellow and more tolerant." He did have big plans when he returned home. He wanted them to live in New York instead of Washington, he told her, in a penthouse apartment until Bernadette turned four or five years old. "Then I'd like to get a house with lots of sprawling lawn—on the North Shore in Westchester [County, New York] or Connecticut near the water so we can have a boat and I can use my Navy training," he wrote her. After the war, Casey was convinced "that, God willing, I can be a very big guy."

CHAPTER 11

MILTON HALL

Two days before Christmas 1943, tugboats nudged the *Queen Elizabeth* bearing Bill Colby and the fifty-four other Jedburgh officers to the dock pilings at Gourock, a port town up the Firth of Clyde and northwest of grimy Glasgow. Colby and the thousands of other GIs aboard jostled for space at the deck railings to catch glimpses of land, which in Gourock's case was scarred by redbrick warehouses, rusted cranes, and rubble farther away because of the Blitz. Soldiers from different countries crowded the piers. Camouflaged destroyers and corvettes steamed out for battle on the high seas. The *Queen Mary* arrived December 29 with the radiomen, delighted to escape the miserable ship yet furious over the final indignity—all their duffel bags were lost after debarking. Frigid skies gray with coal smoke and dust greeted all the Jedburghs on the Scottish coast. Within a week, most had come down with colds, which they attributed to the smutted air they inhaled.

Elbridge Colby, now chief of information and in charge of civil affairs for the European Theater Forces headquartered in London, had been following his son's OSS training from afar. He hoped to see him in the city soon. The Jedburgh planners originally hoped that would be the case. After a week's layover in London the Americans would be sent north to a nicely appointed country estate in Peterborough to join nearly two hundred British and

French commandos for their final training. But because of maddening bureaucratic delays the country estate would not be ready until the first week of February. Instead of London, two battered lorries trucked Colby and the others to a dingy warehouse in Glasgow, where they were broken into groups of about three dozen each, then shuffled like foster children from one temporary training site to another around Scotland and England.

At one point, while the radiomen attended a communications school to learn British procedures, a train took the Jedburgh officers to a Stodham Park estate in southern England's village of Liss, where His Majesty's psychiatrists spent a week rooting through their brains. The British Special Operations Executive was not satisfied with the Americans' psychological screening at the Congressional Country Club and demanded that its Student Assessment Board have a crack at them too. At the "booby hatch"—the not so affectionate name the American officers gave the Stodham Park estate—the board's SOE trainers and shrinks poked and probed with many of the same tests, like the Rorschach, and outdoor practical exercises to measure ingenuity that Colby and the others had suffered at Congressional. The British called theirs "groupstacles." Their screeners also looked for the same qualities in a Jedburgh that their American counterparts sought—smart, battle-savvy commandos, skilled with many weapons, well versed in the French Resistance movement, who would be good leaders in guerrilla combat—but they had a tough grading system to measure them: A for outstanding, B for good, C for fair, and D for indifferent. None of the Americans received an A. Eighteen flunked—one for not sticking to his cover name over drinks with an SOE trainer, another for joking around during his ink blot test. The British psychiatrists had no sense of humor. Colby was among the thirty-seven who passed. His evaluator gave him a B on his report card, which listed thirty-two criteria for the grade. "A quiet and extremely intelligent officer who showed good powers of leadership," the evaluator noted, "although not of the aggressive type." Also not as self-confident as the SOE would prefer. But Colby "should do extremely well as a Jedburgh."

The booby hatch put the Americans in an ugly mood. The humiliation of so many of their comrades not making the British cut—combined with the fact that the SOE schools they were attending to mark time turned out to be grueling—left the U.S. Jedburgh contingent "extremely perturbed," as one British memo delicately put it. Meanwhile, Major Canfield, the man in charge of the American contribution to Jedburgh, scrambled to find replacements for the men who had washed out.

The next diversion did not lift their spirits. Though Colby and most of his American comrades had their parachute badges, they were dispatched in small groups once more to Ringway, a parish in southern Manchester, for a quick course in the British way of jumping out of planes. The three days there proved unnerving. The SOE commandos bailed out of aircraft traveling faster than American ones and from lower altitudes—five hundred to six hundred feet. The American Jedburghs were shocked to discover their British chutes did not come with spares in case the first one failed. Dropping from such low altitudes there was no time to deploy a second one. "Our parachutes always open," an instructor assured them. "If not, bring it back and we'll give you another one." The Americans didn't find the joke funny.

On February 5, more than a month after they landed in Great Britain, Colby and the other commandos were bused to their permanent home in Peterborough—a country estate known as Milton Hall. The men were finally told the name of their unit—Jedburgh—but little more. Milton Hall was always referred to as Area D or ME-65 in secret internal documents and to outsiders it was known simply as the "Allied Commando School." For security reasons, the SOE and OSS still wanted to keep Colby and the other trainees as ignorant as possible of the overall clandestine operation for Europe and their role in it. They had good reason to be paranoid. The Gestapo interrogated Allied guerrillas they captured about their training. German intelligence tried to monitor the schools MI6 and the SOE ran. They had already identified Ringway and some of the communications training centers and had collected information on instructors.

Some ninety miles north of London, Peterborough began as a Saxon village in the seventh century with wool weaving its main business by the late Middle Ages. Mary, Queen of Scots, was buried in its Gothic cathedral after her execution in the sixteenth century. By the onset of World War II, Peterborough's expanding industry, manufacturing cast iron and tools, made it an inviting target for occasional Luftwaffe missions. But Milton Hall and its some twenty thousand acres four miles west of the city remained untouched and unnoticed by enemy bombers.

The convoy of British Army trucks carrying Colby and the other Jeds motored down a thin dirt road with sheep and cattle grazing the pastureland on each side, past the stone Gate Lodge, then the larger bricked Gothic Lodge, then the rustic Chauffeur's Lodge and through open white gates into the five-hundred-acre park where the grand mansion with its several hundred rooms sat. Actually it was three mansions grafted to one another over more than four hundred years. Sir William Fitzwilliam, the first baronet, bought the property in the early sixteenth century during the reign of Henry VII. Sir William the third, a noted Elizabethan, built the north front in Tudor style during the late 1500s, followed by the first Earl Fitzwilliam, who added a stable block and clock tower at the east end of Milton designed in the early 1700s by an associate of the famed architect Christopher Wren. In the mid-eighteenth century Georgian-styled additions were attached to the Tudor and Wren structures. During World War I, Milton Hall was turned over to the British Army as a convalescent home for officers, with rows of beds filling the Pillared Hall, Smoking Room, Long Gallery, and Peterborough Rooms. For this war, the SOE requisitioned the entire estate. Army Captain Tom Fitzwilliam, Milton's current owner, retained small bachelor quarters in the west end of the hall that he used when not away on deployment.

Everything to manufacture a guerrilla warrior had been installed at Milton Hall. A staff of 236 had been brought in to train the students, drive them, cook for them, and care for the estate. Nissen huts lined the lawn off the north front as student quarters. Farther out, obstacle courses, race car and motorcycle tracks, a soccer field, and tracts for combat maneuvers in the pastures and forests had been laid out. A large climbing wall was built off one corner of the mansion. The kitchen garden off the south front had been converted into a pistol range (bullet holes soon pockmarked the nearby stable clock tower). The mansion's basement housed the armory, equipment stores, and an indoor range. Chin-up bars were planted in the lawn stretching from the clock tower on the south front. Staff offices were set up in the carriage stables and a boxing ring was erected in its courtyard. The large halls on the first floor, with fine art and Fitzwilliam family portraits hanging from their walls, were used for group lectures and to show training films, while rooms on the second level became classrooms with radios and weapons on tables, and sabotage devices and spy gadgets hanging from their walls for demonstration. Milton Hall boasted other amenities, though bathwater wasn't one of them (the men had to share it as part of a British conservation measure). A bar was set up in the main foyer during evenings for students to mix with instructors. Pretty women, many from titled British families and serving in FANY (the First Aid Nursing Yeomanry), taught Morse code. Even batmen (the British version of an orderly) were assigned to officers to shine their boots, polish their brass buckles, and wake them gently each morning with a cup of tea in hand.

But in little more than a week after they moved into Milton Hall, the American Jedburghs began inching toward mutiny. They had accumulated a long list of grievances, starting with their previous month of itinerant purgatory (the British instructors had been brutal and many of them unqualified to teach special operations, they thought). Promised promotions and extra pay for being parachutists had not come through. The lowliest private from Milton Hall's support staff was allowed into Peterborough for a pint at the pub, but the Jedburgh officers were confined to quarters as a security measure. The Americans were fed up with being kept in the dark about their mission—they had heard outlandish rumors that three-man teams would be assigned to attack an entire Panzer division—and they wanted a war room placed near the bar in the foyer with maps tacked up tracking what was happening in the European conflict, which seemed to them a world away. They became irritated by the steady stream of London visitors, clueless about guerrilla operations, who interrupted training for dog-and-pony shows from the students. And their stomachs found British cooking indigestible— plates practically every day of gray mutton or greasy lamb stew, bland boiled potatoes, mushy turnips, cabbage overdone, or brussels sprouts that one officer said swam "in a pale and scummy juice."

The Americans also developed a deep dislike for the British commandant of Milton Hall. Lieutenant Colonel Frank Spooner was a stiff, unimaginative martinet with little understanding of covert warfare who liked snappy salutes, morning parades, and strutting about with a snarling chow dog named Mister Wu. The U.S. officers, who came to despise Wu as much as Spooner, kicked the animal when it strayed from its master.

Cultural tensions also simmered. The British instructors routinely denigrated loudmouth Americans as latecomers to a war they had been fighting for four years. Colby thought the Brits at Milton Hall "crusty," as he later told a son, quick to appear exasperated with him and the other Yanks. Anti-British sentiment percolated among the Americans as well. Konrad Dillow, a U.S. lieutenant, got drunk at the foyer bar one night and in front of the English officers lambasted the British people and their army.

Alarm bells began ringing in London and Washington. The American Jedburghs were all volunteers. They could un-volunteer and the program would be crippled. The radio operators had become lazy and inattentive in class. Instructors feared they would not be ready by D-Day. The U.S. officers were muttering among themselves that with so many administrative foul-ups thus far perhaps this entire Jedburgh plan—whatever it was—might be a failure; if so, they wanted out. High morale was critical to the success of this hazardous mission, Canfield realized. If properly handled, an internal OSS memo predicted, the Jedburghs "may be the backbone of the Resistance movement after D-Day"—a critically important part of the shadow war Donovan and the SOE's leaders envisioned for France. But that strategic asset was now in danger of evaporating before their eyes.

Canfield rushed an investigator to Milton Hall to assess the damage. He returned with a grim report. "Morale is bad," the investigator wrote. Senior American and British officers moved quickly into damage control. Spooner was fired and replaced by Lieutenant Colonel George Richard Musgrave, a handsome British officer with a jet-black mustache who had been a big-game hunter before the war. Musgrave did away with spit and polish and became far more popular among the men. Food rations improved and better cooks came. The Jedburgh officers were allowed into town. The red tape was untangled for promotions and parachute pay. The higher ranks would also have a practical benefit in the field, commanding more respect among French Resistance leaders. Colby soon became a major.

On February 24, the three hundred Jedburgh officers and their radio operators crowded into the main first-floor hall. Brigadier Eric E. Mockler-Ferryman, an upper-crust British SOE officer, had arrived from London to finally explain to the men their mission.

"I want to tell you about the future," Mockler-Ferryman began, clearing his throat, as the commandos settled in their chairs and quieted. "I know you have had a difficult start and that things have not been going too well." But the brigadier was quick to add, "I don't want anyone to feel that he is going into this show half heartedly. After my talk, when you have heard what it is all about, anyone is at liberty to say that he does not wish to go. We shall think none the worse of him."

Mockler-Ferryman outlined their mission. Most of the men will parachute into occupied France shortly after D-Day. A handful of Dutch and Belgian officers who had joined the training will be sent to the Low Countries. All the men will link up with resistance groups on the ground, call in airdrops to supply them with arms, organize them into an effective military force that can help Ike's conventional army, pass on to them orders from London, and help lead them in guerrilla attacks. It will be a difficult mission, Mockler-Ferryman warned. Some of the resistance bands "are well organized and led, others not so well" and most are short of arms. Mockler-Ferryman next dropped a minor bombshell. To impress the partisans, the Jedburghs will be dropped in uniform. Perhaps it will afford them some protection under the Geneva Convention's rules for captured soldiers, but it will definitely make them stand out. Later, if they need to blend in, they can change to civilian clothes. "But no one will be ordered to wear plain clothes unless he is willing," the brigadier added. A capture in civilian clothes guaranteed a Jedburgh he would be executed as a spy.

"I hope you realize what a vital part you will have to play in the battle," Mockler-Ferryman said in closing. He apologized for all the disappointments and waiting they had endured, but he added, like a parent gently scolding spoiled children, "if you think of the even longer wait and the more bitter disappointment of those in Occupied Europe, I think you will always agree that you have no real grouse."

One of the American officers raised his hand for a question. "How many Germans are there in France?"

"Not many," the brigadier said nonchalantly, "over a half million."

"Oh, that's all," the American muttered. Colby and the others laughed nervously.

Morale improved, as well as Anglo-American relations. The British officer Konrad Dillow had insulted decided to let the matter drop. A chastened Dillow gratefully accepted his punishment from his American superiors: a weekend pass denied and no more booze at the foyer bar. He could have been kicked out of the program.

The final seventy French volunteers for Jedburgh arrived at Milton Hall in March. They were polite to a fault, always pleasant with the American and British commandos, but they remained standoffish. To protect their families in France if they were caught, they came with noms de guerre. Colby and the others never knew their real names and they were ordered not to delve into the past of their French comrades, or of any officer for that matter. The instructors drilled into their heads secrecy and compartmentalization of information. The Jedburghs became content to live in the here and now; they took one another as they showed up at Milton Hall, ignored where they had come from. The quick read others had on Colby was that he was likable, cool, and calm, certainly not hyper like some of the Brits—in sum, quite ordinary. No one tried to analyze him much beyond that.

With tensions eased, the Jedburghs plunged into polishing their guerrilla skills. They practiced knife fighting, slitting a sentry's throat, tying up and gagging a prisoner, demolishing rail lines and arms depots, stalking a subject, ambushing a patrol, setting up a drop zone for weapons parachuted in and burying the caches, indentifying different Wehrmacht and Nazi Party security services, coding messages to be radioed to London. In case they ran out of rations, they were taught how to catch and cook rats, birds, frogs, snails, dogs and cats (their livers were nutritious), grass snakes and lizards (skin and boil for ten minutes), sheep, hedgehogs, and horses. They trained in how to make a quick and accurate reconnaissance of an area: focus your eyes on the site like a camera, clear your head of any thought, "allow the image to engrave itself on your brain," Singlaub recalled, "as if it were photographic film." Over and over they practiced "instinctive firing"—get the first shot off immediately, don't worry about accuracy, it will throw off your target no matter where the round lands, then more carefully aim the second for the chest. Soon they became proficient killers with every imaginable weapon. The trainers called them the "Milton Hall animals."

The instruction became more intense and pressure-packed—live ammunition was used often in exercises—but Colby loved every minute of it. His months at Milton Hall, he would tell his sons much later, were the best of the war for him. Gallows humor circulated, which always got a laugh out of Colby—the sergeants in the training cadre taught the men how to fight, one joke went, the officers taught them how to die. Musgrave dispensed with all the saluting. Informality prevailed—even for pesky dignitaries who continued to visit. When a general from London showed up to inspect a group of men, Colby, the only officer around, strolled up and shouted: "Fall in a column of bunches, men."

Off duty, the commandos hung out some evenings at the Fox and Hounds pub on Thorpe Road about a mile from Milton Hall, where hard liquor was scarce but beer was not, though too warm for the American throats. The brass at first ordered the Jedburghs to strip their uniforms of insignias so they would not stand out when away from Milton Hall; they soon relented when it became obvious to townsfolk that these soldiers were some kind of commandos. One Jedburgh pickup line with girls at the bar: the SF on British-designed special forces wing badges stood for "Sexually Frustrated." Fights sometimes broke out with the local men who resented the flirting.

Colby and Barbara exchanged letters frequently, although he told her nothing about Milton Hall or what he was doing. Barbara continued to write advertising copy for a firm in New York. After work she also stood guard as a plane watcher for the local civil defense force in case Axis aircraft attacked the city. She did not sit at home and pine for Bill. She liked him. So did her mother. But Barbara had other boyfriends. Several proposed to her though she was not ready for a formal engagement in any of the relationships. Bill hardly remained chaste in England. He spent his weekend passes in London with the other commandos hunting for pubs with good liquor and available women. Working-class girls tended to be the ones willing to go out with them; the women from well-off families shunned GIs. Colby soon found a British Red Cross volunteer he liked—nothing serious but he dated her almost every weekend he could make it to London. When he was not partying, Colby, like Casey and Donovan, also prowled London's bookstores. His favorite book, which he found at Foyles, was *Seven Pillars of Wisdom* by T. E. Lawrence, the unconventional British Army officer who fought alongside Arab guerrillas against the Ottoman Turks. Colby fantasized himself becoming a Lawrence of Arabia in France.

Mid-March, Musgrave gathered the Jedburghs in the first-floor hall for an announcement. It was time for them to form their three-man teams. Neither he nor London wanted to pick the men for each team. "You chaps go ahead and make your own marriages," he announced. The courtships began for the next two weeks. Each team had to have a Frenchman who knew his way around the country so the American and British officers did most of the courting. Officers could marry, divorce if the chemistry didn't work, and get engaged again until they found the partner they liked, then the couple would together pick a radio operator of any nationality. Colby did not really know any of the French officers, and none of their real names. But one did catch his attention—a dashing French lieutenant who looked like Clark Gable and who routinely cleaned out the Americans in their high-stakes poker games. His cover name was Jacques Favel.

His real name was Camille Lelong. He never went to college, but he was street smart, skipping grades in school, and had an impressive command of languages: he spoke German, Italian, Spanish, and English. His English was meticulous, spoken with just a clip of an accent. He enjoyed the *New York Times* crossword puzzle in later years and spotting spelling and grammar errors in American newspapers. He was good with numbers, which made him dangerous at the card table. Lelong's passion was poker. He focused on each hand like a laser and grew irritated with talkers who interrupted his concentration during games. Women swooned over him, he enjoyed twirling them on the dance floor, but he drank wine sparingly, hated drunks, was not wild or flamboyant, and he never suffered fools lightly.

He was born in 1915 in the French town of Perpignan along the Mediterranean coast near the Spanish border, into a wealthy Catalan family of businessmen and military officers. His grandfather had been a general, his great-grandfather a successful cigarette manufacturer. His beautiful mother, a tall woman with dark hair and olive skin that she passed on to Camille, died when he was five. Camille and his brothers were bundled off to boarding schools near Paris while his father, a World War I combat veteran, moved to America to buy land in north Louisiana. Lonely for his father, Camille, when he became a teenager, sailed to New Orleans in the 1930s, enrolling in a high school where he perfected his English. At eighteen, he enlisted in a French cavalry regiment stationed in Morocco. He served three years, after which he mustered out and returned to southern France. After his country declared war on Germany in 1939, he was drafted back into the French army. Wounded slightly from shrapnel, Lelong eventually fled to Algiers after the Nazi invasion of France and by 1943 was commissioned a lieutenant working in de Gaulle's secret service. He arrived in England about the same time Colby had, more or less ordered to the Jedburghs because his near perfect English made him an ideal fit for any British or American team.

Lelong found the Milton Hall training not much more taxing than Colby had. He wasn't above showing ingenuity to make it easier. During one exercise, when he was dropped twenty-five miles away from Milton Hall and told to make his way back on foot through forests and pastures, he found the nearest road and flagged down a bus that took him most of the way—the passengers staring at this strange creature in fatigues with camouflage paint smeared on his face. Behind the card-playing ladies' man, Colby found an officer as practical-minded as he was. They were both quiet men, not given to showing emotion. Colby liked that. Lelong also had charisma that drew people to him—important for commanding the respect of the Resistance in the field, Colby knew. Though he outranked Lelong, Colby thought it best that the Frenchman lead the team when they reached France. Soon the two began palling around in London on weekends. Lelong had no problem finding girls. Colby thought he would have better luck sporting one of Camille's berets with his Army uniform. American MPs (Military Police) patrolling the streets of Piccadilly ordered him to take off the hat.

For their radio operator, Colby and Lelong picked a sergeant also from de Gaulle's Free French whose pseudonym was Louis Giry. His real name was Roger Villebois. He had a gentle face, high forehead, and hair swept to the side. Villebois had been a workman in Nancy before the war. He was no-nonsense like his two new comrades and Colby thought skilled at operating a radio, their lifeline to London. By the time they parachuted into France, Louis Giry would be promoted to lieutenant.

A sixteen-page glossary with hundreds of code names and code words had been assembled for the commandos. Each team had a randomly assigned code name, which was either the name of a man, a medicine, or the make of a car. Colby's team was designated "Bruce." Villebois's personal code name was "Piastre." Lelong's was "Galway." Colby became "Berkshire."

The Jedburgh teams, some now married, others still dating, began rehearsing the types of missions they expected to carry out in France. They began with schemes lasting one to three days. They practiced raiding mock targets at night and withdrawing afterward to hideouts. Royal Air Force bombers flying at low altitudes dropped them into remote areas of Scotland

and Wales; the teams, with no money in their pockets, had to make their way back to Milton Hall without being caught by Home Guards or Scotland Yard, which had been alerted. The teams soon graduated to larger weeklong exercises, with code names like "Spur" and "Spillout" and "Megrin," where they divided into Partisan, Gestapo, and Jedburgh groups and fought one another. In Spur, the Nazis occupied land around Milton Hall and the Jedburghs had to organize the ambush of a German general. Colby played the role of a French partisan in Spillout. For Megrin, the Milton Hall instructors used completely untrained civilians in nearby Northamptonshire (shop owners, Boys Scouts, girl guides), whom the Jedburgh teams had to organize in an attack on the rail lines.

Donovan dropped by Milton Hall. He loved mingling with his commandos and, unlike the other VIPs who pestered them, the Jedburghs were delighted to see the old man, who they suspected would have grabbed a parachute and jumped in with them if the powers that be let him. As David Bruce's eyes and ears in the London secretariat, Casey also visited Milton Hall that spring. He arrived already well briefed on its training program— so much so, in fact, that commandos like Singlaub, whom he questioned, assumed incorrectly that he was some kind of Jedburgh case officer. Casey, who came in a civilian suit instead of his Navy uniform, slouched in a chair in the foyer with Singlaub and other officers and detailed for them his best read on the politics of different Resistance factions in France. The Jedburgh mission was important, Casey thought. It was one of the reasons he tracked their training so closely for Bruce. The guerrilla factions desperately needed these men in uniform to guide them.

On May 2, fifteen teams left Milton Hall with their gear and boarded a ship for an OSS base in Algeria. Ten more teams would join them later. When the order came, they would parachute into southern France to link up with Resistance groups there. Colby and the other commandos remained in England, where they would launch for points in northern France. By late May, their formal training had ended, save for occasional exercises to keep their skills honed. There was more time to relax—not that they could. The mood in Milton Hall turned tense. The men, excited and on edge, waited for their orders.

CHAPTER 12

D-DAY

Japan's advance in Asia had been stanched. American and British forces had begun a grinding naval and land campaign to reverse her gains. Pacific islands had been retaken, Merrill's Marauders had moved on Burma, Indian and British troops had driven the Japanese back in Southwest Asia, General Douglas MacArthur's army was gaining ground in New Guinea. On the Eastern Front, the Germans were retreating. Odessa and Sevastopol had been recaptured and Soviet forces had launched a major offensive through Ukraine. By the end of May 1944, however, the attention of Washington and London—and Hitler in Berlin—was focused on the impending Allied invasion of Western Europe. The amphibious landing at the northern French coast of Normandy would be the largest an army and navy had ever attempted. For more than a year and a half, Eisenhower, who was now smoking eighty Camels a day, had been planning and debating strategy with his top U.S. and British commanders and assembling his forces in England, 1.5 million of whom were American.

Dulles cabled from Bern the latest intelligence he had from Fritz Kolbe on the many spots the Nazis speculated that a landing could take place besides northern France—perhaps along France's Mediterranean coast, near Antwerp at the mouth of the Scheldt River, or Norway. Hitler had decided to hold the Italian Front as far south as possible, keep the Eastern Front as far east as he could, and concentrate on defeating the Allied invasion in the west. In France (the country his generals believed most likely for the main attack) the führer had increased Field Marshal von Rundstedt's infantry and Panzer divisions to fifty-eight.

London felt under siege once more. Since January the Luftwaffe had begun increasing its sorties over the city. St. James's in the central district had been badly damaged. Twenty thousand books were lost in an attack on the London Library. Incendiary bombs rained on the city. It was nothing like the early Blitz, but the raids, which had been heavy through April, crushed spirits that had weathered so many bombs the past four years. Looting during what became known as the "Little Blitz" increased.

The OSS station, which had grown to more than two thousand people in nine houses around London, was a madhouse. Weary staffers, operating on adrenaline, rushed about overseeing the dispatch of spies into France and the monitoring of final training for commandos like the Jedburghs. Tempers grew short from pre-invasion pressure; David Bruce found himself mediating more turf battles among squabbling aides. Casey, his de facto fixer, became adept at untangling bureaucratic snarls among Bruce's intelligence and special operations branches as well as with the U.S. Army and de Gaulle's secret service. He helped organize OSS intelligence detachments to travel with the American armies entering France and to serve as liaison with Resistance spy networks that lay ahead of them. By April he had two secretaries working for him. Casey developed a reputation around the station as a boss impossible to please. He had already fired two other sergeants competent by Army standards but not up to his. In May, the toll of twelve-hour workdays seven days a week finally caught up with him: he dragged himself to sick bay for three days to recuperate from exhaustion and a nervous stomach that had him vomiting.

Casey bounced "back in shape" after the "good rest," he wrote Sophia. By mid-May the London station's D-Day operations "were taking concrete shape," he believed. Agent reports—tapped out as Morse code radio messages or flown to London in pouches also filled with maps, drawings, and documents sneaked out of France—began flowing into the station on German troop concentrations, supply depots, and rail movements. Academics in Bruce's research and analysis section sent the Army and Navy topographic studies of Normandy's coast. His economists versed in French and German industry advised the Eighth Air Force on targets to bomb. Geographers and cartographers helped map the French countryside for the invaders. Psychological warriors in his Morale Operations Branch beamed propaganda to German soldiers from a transmitter in Woburn, England, with singers like Marlene Dietrich serenading between messages. Tons of leaflets were dropped on the Wehrmacht troops, one claiming their wives and girlfriends had joined a fictitious League of Lonely German Women to have sex with comrades back home on leave. Rumors (the British and OSS also called them "sibs" from Latin's *sibilare*, to hiss) were spread on the continent that top Nazis had fled to Argentina.

A good bit of Casey's time was also preoccupied with "Sussex," the code name for London's operation to infiltrate spies into France. Bruce had hammered out an agreement with MI6 to launch a joint British, American, and French operation that would send into the country some fifty two-man teams, each consisting of a spy collecting information and a radio operator transmitting it back. By the time Casey arrived in London at the end of 1943, three-fourths of Bruce's Secret Intelligence staff was laboring to train thirty-two Sussex agents. The spies—many of them refugee French farmers, shop clerks, and army soldiers—tended to be in their late thirties or mid-forties so the Germans would be less likely to draft them for work gangs. They would parachute near enemy railway centers, motor parks, headquarters, airfields, and equipment repair centers to observe and report back. In addition to monitoring Sussex training for Bruce, Casey performed odd jobs for the program, such as preparing a classified film documentary on it.

On February 8, the first advance-party agents, called "Pathfinders," were slipped into France to scout out landing sites and local espionage networks that might receive three Sussex teams (two controlled by MI6 and one by the OSS), which parachuted in two months later on April 9. By the end of May, the OSS and MI6 had thirteen Sussex and five Pathfinder teams in France. Bruce set up an operations room in the OSS's town house at 72 Grosvenor Street to process the messages the Sussex agents radioed to the Victor receiving station. The first intelligence report (in this case with the location of two munitions dumps) arrived on May 16 from the team code-named

"Jeanne," which had parachuted into Orléans south of Paris. The report would be the first of 170 Jeanne would radio on Wehrmacht troops and V-1 flying bombs being transported through France.

. . . .

From the outset the strategic question facing the planners had been a stark one. "Overlord," the code name for the Allied invasion of France, would boil down to a race to concentrate power at the beach. The first troops landing will be fighting "with their backs to the sea," a British memo, stamped "Most Secret," outlined in May 1943. If the Allies can overcome coastal defenses and build a force quickly at the beachhead, "we win," the memo concluded. If the Germans prevent the Allies from gaining a foothold and rush in reinforcements "to drive us back to the sea . . . then the enemy wins." As simple as that. Early Overlord planning assumed "a reasonable chance of success," according to another "Most Secret" British memo that May. Ike and his invasion commander, British General Bernard Law Montgomery, later insisted on a beefed-up landing force and a broader front to give them a fighting chance at Normandy. Their probability of success would also improve immeasurably if the Allies could drive off or slow the arrival of German reserves. It would be impossible to hide from Nazi intelligence services the massive pre-invasion buildup of troops and landing craft on England's southern coast, but Ike's planners thought they stood a good chance of keeping the Germans in the dark on where the concentrated blow might fall between Brittany in the northwest and the Belgian coast in the northeast. The Allied command assumed its forces at the beach would be vulnerable the first two to three months and that along with Luftwaffe counterattacks the Germans would rush Panzer divisions to the landing site to drive back the invaders.

Eisenhower settled on a three-pronged plan: a deception operation, code-named "Fortitude," to convince Hitler and his generals that Normandy was not the landing site; a second invasion, code-named "Anvil," at France's Mediterranean coast to pin down Wehrmacht forces in the south, and airpower along with the French Resistance to keep German reserve divisions from rushing over roads, rails, and bridges to the Allies' beachhead. Ike's third prong was called the "Transportation Plan" and by the time Casey arrived in London a debate still raged within the Allied command over how much the French Resistance could contribute to it. Was the Resistance "as good and as important as the OSS and SOE said it was," Casey recalled, or was it an "illusion" that might "not materialize in the crunch?" Aerial bombardment, he knew, could dump far more explosives on German reinforcements than could the guerrillas, whose attacks would prompt savage Nazi reprisals against the French population. American and British commanders also worried that delivering the Resistance more weapons to fight Germans would also make its factions better armed for a civil war among one another. But with aerial bombing came heavy collateral damage. The French public, which would suffer fifteen thousand civilian deaths from Allied bombing in the months leading up to the invasion, was in no mood for British and American warplanes killing more innocents after D-Day. Even Allied air marshals realized well-trained guerrillas in many instances could cut rail lines, blow up tunnels, and block highways with far less explosives and collateral damage than attacks from the air.

French Resistance leaders finally convinced Allied commanders that a better equipped underground could mount effective sabotage attacks after D-Day and at the same time keep German reprisals largely in check. The OSS and SOE opened the spigot. Between January and June 1944, nearly 3,500 tons of small arms, mortars, ammunition, incendiaries, and explosives, packed in over 36,000 sturdy boxes or sausagelike canisters, were airdropped to the Resistance. Donovan sent Roosevelt a memo with the typical load an American cargo plane carried—four machine guns, forty-four rifles, fifty-five Sten guns, 41,000 bullets, along with packages of "hand grenades, explosives, food and clothing."

Coded messages were radioed to Resistance cells with the hundreds of targets Eisenhower wanted attacked to slow the Panzer divisions and undermine German morale: rail tracks and stations, choke points on key roads, isolated Wehrmacht headquarters and small troop patrols, fuel depots, telephone and telegraph lines, electrical grids. Also radioed to the Resistance: the names and addresses of German railway officials in France whom the Allied command wanted assassinated. French partisans, who were already settling scores with Pétain's Milice agents, were only too happy to add the enemy civilians to their hit list. Yet despite the high hopes of Casey and others in the OSS station, Ike and his staff did not consider the untested

Resistance critical to their plans before or after the invasion. Allied bombers would have the main job of slowing the advance of German reserves. The Resistance was viewed as a bonus.

. . . .

In the lead-up to invasion, Dulles kept a steady stream of cables flowing to London and Washington—more than one a day by mid-May—on anything he could uncover about enemy defenses in France. He reported on the re-positioning of German infantry, Panzer, and Waffen-SS divisions as June neared. During one of his radiotelephone calls in March he passed along a report from an unnamed "neutral correspondent" plugged into German military circles. Field Marshal Erwin Rommel, commander of the Atlantic Wall defenses to repel a landing, had declared that Allied "air supremacy will triumph over any German fortification system, no matter what point is chosen by the enemy." For another "flash" in April, Dulles passed along gossip that "some months ago" German officers on the Western Front had given the Wehrmacht a 70 percent chance of driving back an invasion. But with improvements in Allied strength and tactics they now put the invaders' chances of success at "about 50–50." Washington cabled Dulles that "on the whole" the War Department had found his intelligence on German troop movements accurate and it wanted more. The Navy was also desperate for anything he could dig up on German defenses off the French coast or at its ports.

In addition to his Bern base, by spring 1944 Dulles had outposts in Ge-neva, Zurich, Basel, and Lugano with a total of five OSS officers handling agents or analyzing intelligence for him, a dozen airmen or secretaries coding messages or performing clerical chores, and more than one hundred informants feeding him information. Donovan now regularly forwarded Dulles's cables to Roosevelt on subjects ranging from Nazi mistreatment of Soviet prisoners to the appearance in Germany of a mysterious Himmler stamp the Interior Ministry printed instead of the post office. (Donovan had all his station chiefs send him foreign stamps and news on the latest releases to butter up the White House's philatelist-in-chief.)

Kolbe arrived in Bern on April 11 for his fourth visit. He was worn out. German intelligence had alerted the regime that information from Hitler's headquarters had made its way to neutral countries so the Gestapo began searching couriers and their pouches at checkpoints. Kolbe made it to Bern without a search but his nerves were frazzled. Dulles cabled Washington that day that George Wood had arrived "with more than 200 highly valuable Easter eggs."

Indeed they were. The two hundred documents, which totaled about four hundred pages, revealed that Berlin had been forced to move some twenty divisions to shore up the Eastern Front and the Wehrmacht had become increasingly worried that lack of fighter aircraft was making Germany more vulnerable to daylight bombing raids. The Easter eggs also contained a lengthy report on Japanese bases in Asia and the key members of the German espionage network in Sweden. Excited Dulles staffers worked around the clock to prepare the documents for transmission, this time under the code name "Kapril." Kolbe boarded the train three days later, terrified his luck would run out and Gestapo agents would arrest him. They didn't, but when he arrived in Berlin it was clear he would be trapped there. The Foreign Office planned to cut back on courier trips and Swiss authorities had become less willing to accept German visitors. Kolbe had made contact with the German resistance and now wanted to work with them to oust Hitler. Dulles thought that was a terrible idea and talked his valuable spy out of risking exposure by joining the coup plotters. Kolbe agreed to remain undercover, but felt increasingly unappreciated by the Americans and angry with them for not following his advice on targets to bomb.

For a year, Dulles had been making predictions in his cables that Germany's defeat was inevitable. "A knockout offensive in the USSR" was no longer "possible for Germany," he cabled Washington on May 19, 1943. German manpower along with tank and airplane production was "no longer adequate to meet a two front war." Assuming Russia kept up the pressure, Germany would surrender "well within a year" after an Allied landing at France—a prediction that turned out to be close to the mark. But after Kolbe's fourth visit in April 1944, Dulles grew even bolder with his forecast. In their fireside chats at Herrengasse 23, Kolbe told Dulles he believed his country's collapse "is imminent." The German was engaging in wishful thinking, but after scanning the four hundred pages Kolbe had brought with him, Dulles became convinced as well that the Nazi regime was in its "final deathbed contortions"—which were the words he cabled to Donovan on April 12. Germany's diplomatic and intelligence apparatus were in a state of chaos, he continued. The documents Kolbe had delivered presented "a picture of imminent doom and final downfall."

Startled, Donovan immediately forwarded Dulles's message to Roosevelt, Secretary of State Cordell Hull, George Marshall, Chief of Naval Operations Admiral Ernest King, and Eisenhower. He included a cover memo vouching for Dulles as a seasoned European expert and Kolbe as a credible source. The Bern station chief's latest intelligence, which contradicted a flash Dulles delivered just three months earlier that German morale had "stiffened," had monumental consequences for Overlord. If Germany indeed was now on the brink of caving in, the Allies' invasion might be a cakewalk. Cooler heads among Donovan's German experts urged caution. "Although the fortress of Europe may be cracking, Hitler himself is not," advised Ernst "Putzi" Hanfstaengl, a former Nazi press aide who had defected to the Allies and now analyzed the führer's speeches for the OSS. Expect "much hard fighting" in the months to come. Marshall's skeptical intelligence staff notified the Army chief that it had no evidence to back up Dulles's wild prediction. "It would be extremely unwise from the military viewpoint to count on an imminent collapse of the Nazis," a memo to Marshall concluded. Eisenhower certainly wasn't counting on it.

Dulles's forecast was making Donovan somewhat of a laughingstock in Washington. The OSS chief fired off a cable to Dulles asking him to review his April 12 message to see whether "on reflection" he wished "to modify any of its language." Dulles backpedaled in an April 17 cable—but only somewhat. He claimed, not too convincingly, that he never meant to say "that the morale of the entire Nazi Army . . . has yet reached the point of collapse." They will fiercely fight "any attempt to invade." But he continued to insist that "the collapse of Germany might follow a very few months" after the Allies gain a foothold in France—a prediction that would also prove to be erroneous. Donovan forwarded Dulles's qualifier to Roosevelt and Marshall, who by then had sent the whole series of communications to their pile of paperwork to be ignored.

In his defense, Dulles had been egged on by Washington in believing an imminent German collapse was a sound forecast. Headquarters had ordered him on February 1 to begin preparing lists of "trustworthy" Germans to run their government after defeat. Later in August both U.S. and British intelligence would conclude Germany's "strategic situation" had deteriorated so rapidly that "organized resistance" would cease by the end of 1944—again wishful thinking. Yet in April Dulles was guilty of letting his enthusiasm over the two hundred Easter eggs Kolbe had just delivered get the better of his judgment—or at least Casey thought so. Along with others in the London station, Casey read closely Dulles's Kapril cables. He did not believe for a minute that Hitler's generals in France would quit on him.

• • • •

By the beginning of May, Casey was receiving regular reports from the London station's special operations branch on the strength of the Resistance in France. The estimates varied, but the most conservative ones put it at roughly 165,000 with a potential of reaching as high as 400,000. Radio messages arriving at Casey's desk from Sussex agents in the field indicated that Resistance and Maquis bands were taking over an increasing number of towns and villages. By the end of May, the OSS and Britain's SOE calculated that they had dropped enough weapons and supplies into France to arm 125,000 fighters. Allowing for equipment damaged during the drops or breaking down after it arrived or scooped up by the Germans, "it is reasonable to suppose that some 100,000 men are ready for immediate action," an internal military memo concluded. They were prepared to sabotage rail lines at 417 points. Five thousand fighters were ready to disrupt telephone and telegraph communications by cutting trunk lines. The guerrillas were set to bury 1,460 antitank mines in roads to slow enemy convoys. Other fighters— perhaps as many as 85,000—would harass German soldiers marching west with raids and ambushes.

But would they? Resistance networks were still haphazardly organized and their fighting quality varied wildly from circuit to circuit. Senior German commanders in France did not consider the Resistance strong enough for them to alter any of their defense plans; Hitler dispatched only two or three extra divisions to the country to deal with the partisans. A hopeful sign for Casey and others in the London station: by April the Gestapo and Abwehr had stepped up their penetrations, but they were now not enough to crush the Resistance. Replacements were quickly found for those swept up by German security. And help was on the way. A notification went to SHAEF, the Supreme Headquarters Allied Expeditionary Force: ninety-seven Jedburgh teams were trained and ready to be dropped into France and the Low Countries.

Londoners did not have to be detectives to deduce that the invasion was near. By the end of May the city practically emptied of soldiers. The American officer and enlisted clubs closed, taxis became easy to find, theaters were nearly deserted. Restaurants normally packed, such as Claridge's and The Connaught, had only a handful of customers. Three days before the invasion, Casey bought a half dozen books from a London store, but he had time only to skim parts of them late at night before he fell asleep. Donovan arrived mid-May and was making "the fur fly" with orders and new programs for Bruce's station, he wrote Sophia. "I'll be racing around picking up the pieces. But it's fun and I'll watch the body." The body, however, disappeared on the night of May 30. Casey knew what happened to it. With Bruce in tow, Donovan had taken a train to Plymouth in southern England to board a Navy ship he hoped would deposit them at one of the Normandy beaches with the invaders.

Monday night, June 5, the BBC broadcast coded messages signaling the French Resistance to launch its attacks the next day. Parachute landings later that night by the British 6th and American 82nd and 101st airborne divisions generally succeeded in securing flanks behind the beachheads, although not without heavy casualties, and many soldiers scattered. Early Tuesday morning the first of nearly seven thousand ships, landing craft, and barges peeked up from the horizon off the Normandy coast. The British and Canadian landings at the eastern beaches designated Gold, Juno, and Sword and the American landing at the western beach designated Utah proceeded better than expected. A seasoned German division, however, had just arrived at Omaha Beach east of Utah and turned its shoreline into a murderous killing field that left nearly three thousand dead, wounded, or missing by the first day.

Tuesday morning Dulles cabled London and Washington the latest intelligence his sources had fed him on the positions of German infantry and Panzer divisions east of Normandy as well as on the rail and telephone lines the Resistance had severed. "Communications in northern France are nearing the point of utter paralysis," he reported, while the Nazis have sent special trucks along rail lines to repair cuts the guerrillas made and have dispatched as many as eleven thousand of their own railwaymen to operate trains. That night for his radiotelephone call he had the evening dispatch from a Zurich newspaper's Berlin correspondent to read to Washington. Berliners only learned of the invasion in the afternoon, the correspondent wrote, which to Dulles suggested that the landing caught the regime by surprise and the Nazis "waited to give the news until they had their line of propaganda." Berlin's Reich-controlled newspapers claimed the invasion was "on orders from Moscow"—a "desperate attempt of the Anglo-Americans to obtain some real success . . . in the interest of Bolshevism."

Donovan and Bruce made it to Utah Beach Wednesday afternoon after the first wave and marched on their own several miles inland to look for OSS spies. They found none, but their Sussex agents in other locales were filling up the London station's in-box with intelligence reports. All told, the OSS managed to parachute into France twenty-six two-man Sussex teams that radioed back some eight hundred messages on German troop positions, storage depots, airfields, and V-1 launch sites for Allied warplanes to bomb—an impressive number but the agency eventually concluded that over the six-month life of the program only about a quarter of the operations could actually be considered successful. "None of the teams were given much time before D-Day to get themselves 'in position,' " a confidential internal report explained. The Gestapo discovered six Sussex agents and executed them on the spot; a seventh was sent to a concentration camp, never to be heard from again. Communications also became a problem with many radio sets broken or lost when the teams landed. While Team Jeanne's operation in Orléans was the most productive with over two hundred pieces of information radioed, Team Cure, for example, became "totally useless" after it was dropped near Tours in northwest France on June 1, according to an after-action report. The team's radio, stashed in an abandoned building, had been "hastily removed by friends" who feared the Germans would search the hideout and "dumped into a well," leaving Cure no way to talk to London.

Casey and most everyone else in the station did not sleep Monday night as agent reports poured in ahead of Overlord. As Tuesday wore on they worried whether the invaders would be "swept back into the English Channel," he later wrote. So did Donovan, although at Utah Beach he was impressed that the Navy's big guns offshore appeared to be keeping the German army from overrunning the beachhead for the moment. Would the Allies hold their position? Casey was not sure that first day.

CHAPTER 13

FRANCE

One of the largest exercises staged for the Jedburghs, code-named "Lash," began May 31 in the hilly countryside near Leicester, which was west of Milton Hall. The teams had been given a particularly knotty assignment to organize guerrilla attacks with untrained civilians, played in this case by Leicester factory workers, in an area infested with Germans who have turned the local population against the commandos. British Home Guards, airmen from a nearby Royal Air Force base, and local police played the enemy, which meant they were everywhere. Late Monday night, June 5, Colby lay exhausted outside in an encampment near Milton Hall when the roar of planes blanketing the sky above woke him and the other Jedburghs in the exercise. They easily guessed that the invasion had started and what flew over them now were aircraft for the early wave.

Earlier in the day, a trainer had walked up to British captain William Crawshay and whispered an order to gather the two French officers in his team (code-named "Hugh") along with all their gear and sneak away to a truck waiting for them at Milton Hall. They would be taken to London. As paratroopers rained down just beyond the Normandy coast in the early hours of June 6, a lone aircraft carried Team Hugh farther south to a drop zone near Châteauroux, where guerrillas from the local Resistance circuit met the three commandos after they hit the ground.

Day after day through the month of June, three-man Jedburgh teams disappeared from Milton Hall at a painfully slow trickle. "Men would be called to Colonel Musgrave's office," recalled Jedburgh Stewart Alsop, who became a prominent Washington columnist after the war, "and would come downstairs to the bar, looking serious, trying not to look frightened, saying nothing." No good-byes. Just empty bunks the next day. Colby and the others left behind still went out on exercises, but they felt overtrained and stale; they continued their high-stakes poker games and evening trips to the Fox and Hounds, but tension replaced cheery moods. As they watched pins designating divisions moved on a map of France in the main foyer, they felt overlooked, unwanted, and deeply frustrated. By the end of June, only thirteen Jedburgh teams had been dropped into France; only twelve more would be sent in July. Colby and the others fumed that they should have infiltrated before D-Day. Eisenhower, however, did not want Jedburghs sent early and sparking a premature Resistance uprising the Germans could crush before the invasion. And after the landing, SHAEF intended to be careful and deliberate in deploying the teams ahead of the Allied army and not waste their expensive training on suicide missions. Casey, who continued to visit Milton Hall, agreed. The Jedburghs were an operational reserve not to be used precipitously.

· · · ·

The Normandy invaders were not driven back into the channel as Casey and others in the London station had feared. It took Eisenhower's force about half a day "to crack the Atlantic Wall" and establish a beachhead on France's northern shore, although it was a sliver of beach. After a week, more than 300,000 Allied soldiers and two thousand tanks jammed the coast. Wehrmacht strategy the rest of June was to keep them bottled up at the beach with defenses and counterthrusts while Hitler hoped for fanatical Nazi resistance and new wonder weapons to win the war. It was a plan not far from the propaganda Goebbels foisted on Germans, which Dulles reported in his radiotelephone call three days after the landing. The invasion, Dulles quoted from Berlin's spin, offered the Wehrmacht "the great opportunity to come to grips with the Western powers." He cabled Donovan on June 10 that his sources were telling him "the prevailing opinion" in German military circles "is that the battle for France will be lost if the Allies are successful in creating a number of strong bridgeheads." The Allies were headed in that direction. Their planes had dropped 71,000 tons of bombs by D-Day, knocking out most of the eighty key rail installations targeted for the invasion. Naval gunfire that had so impressed Donovan could hit Panzers fifteen miles inland while Allied aircraft kept troop trains more than 120 miles from the beachhead. Helping as well: German incompetence, delays, and miscalculations in moving reinforcements to Normandy, all encouraged by a successful Allied deception campaign to convince Hitler and his generals that the main attack would still come at Pas-de-Calais farther east.

From a Norwegian source in France, Dulles confirmed the trouble Allied airpower made for the enemy, exacerbated "by the lack of gasoline," he cabled Donovan, which had forced "large numbers of Nazi troops . . . to halt south of Paris en route to the front." But rail targets like the Paris beltline had to be hit again and again, his sources warned him, because Germans rushed to repair them after each raid. Dulles also alerted Donovan to the feud Hitler was having to referee between Rommel, who wanted all German reserves rushed to Normandy, and Rundstedt, who insisted on keeping mobile divisions near Paris prepared to counterattack a main Allied offensive wherever it occurred. Washington cabled Dulles to begin spreading a rumor in Switzerland that Hitler had canceled a public appearance after D-Day because he suffered from demophobia—a morbid fear of crowds.

The Resistance carried out its color-coded plans with a vengeance. Guerrillas cut rails at over eight hundred points from June through August (the Green Plan). More than a hundred phone and telegraph lines were severed (the Violet Plan), forcing the Wehrmacht to communicate over radio, which Britain's Ultra program could intercept and decode. The telecommunications cable from Paris to Berlin was out for two weeks in mid-July. Five German divisions, by Casey's count, had their march to Normandy slowed by Resistance and air attacks (the Tortoise Plan). The 2nd SS Panzer Division, dubbed "Das Reich," was ordered to leave Toulouse in southern France on June 7 expecting to reach Normandy by June 10, but warplanes bombed bridges ahead of it and guerrillas harassed the division along the way. The first elements of Das Reich did not arrive at the beachhead until June 23. The OSS estimated that guerrilla small arms fire, grenades, mortars, and mines killed or wounded more than seven thousand enemy soldiers during the three months. The Germans were forced to divert the strength of ten divisions by one OSS count to deal with this scourge. Wehrmacht columns took to spraying the sides of roads with random machine gun fire hoping to clear out ambushers. Resistance attacks began to have a demoralizing effect on German troops, their commanders complained. "We have the feeling that each fern is firing at us," one captured officer told the British.

All told, however, the Resistance was more a headache for the Wehrmacht in France than a strategic threat those first few months. Guerrilla attacks on German train convoys became a problem, they infuriated Hitler, who demanded detailed reports on them, but the sabotage, though increasing, was actually not as high as the command had expected and not enough for the Wehrmacht to significantly modify its defense plans. Some German divisions arrived late at the Normandy front as much because of their generals' indecision over where to send them as from guerrilla raids. Partisans controlled many French towns and villages by the end of July, but only the ones the Nazis considered not worth the effort to keep; the Germans had no trouble holding on to what they wanted and crushing the partisans, who could never win a pitched battle with them. In the fight to keep enemy reinforcements from Normandy the Resistance played a supporting role, not a decisive one.

Yet its "multitude of pinpricks," as one official Army history termed it, surpassed what SHAEF expected—largely because its expectation had been so low. General Walter Bedell Smith, Eisenhower's chief of staff, pronounced himself "agreeably surprised." Though he would have second thoughts after the war, Donovan sent Marshall a glowing report on July 12 on the Resistance, claiming the OSS investment in its force had been "well repaid."

Among the skeptics, however, was Casey, although he never told Donovan. Casey made it to the Normandy beachhead with Bruce on June 25. He looked about as unmilitary as an officer could be with a borrowed helmet, leather jacket, an ascot tucked behind his shirt collar, and his Navy pants bloused in boots. They trekked to a farmhouse near Carentan, which Army paratroopers had captured at the base of the Cotentin Peninsula. The OSS officers assigned to General Omar Bradley's 1st Army had gathered there to brief them, but there was not much to report. "The coastal area had been so thoroughly evacuated and the lines in the closely confined bridgehead were so tight," Casey recalled, there were no Resistance units just ahead of the Allied lines. He much later confided to a friend that while French guerrillas may have contributed to slowing the arrival of German reserves he did not think their role was critical. The deception effort to convince the Germans that Normandy would not be the main landing site was far more important in delaying reinforcements than Resistance sabotage or paramilitary attacks, he believed.

But with D-Day and the partisans' pinpricks new recruits poured into guerrilla base camps, swelling their ranks to 300,000. "Frenchmen are flocking to the known Maquis areas," a June 20 memo to Churchill declared. Many were mockingly called *Resistant de '44*—townspeople and villagers who had sat on the sidelines but now claimed they had been resisters all along. Eisenhower ordered airdrops to the guerrillas increased—the OSS delivered 8,914 containers to them in July, double the amount in June—but the fighters remained acutely short of arms. And as the Allies had feared, the expanding unconventional force was met with growing Nazi brutality. The SS now deemed the Resistance a murderous terror movement and hunted relentlessly for its known leaders. Maquis fighters found the body of one of their comrades with his legs burnt to the knees and his tongue cut out—a common torture they soon discovered. A French woman was raped by seventeen German soldiers while a Wehrmacht doctor checked her pulse to make sure she didn't collapse before the line finished. Another woman had her guts carved out of her stomach and wrapped around her neck. David Bruce was sickened by a report he received that Panzer division soldiers cut the testicles, gouged the eyes, and pulled the teeth of twelve French teenagers before they executed them. One reason the Das Reich division was two weeks late in arriving at Normandy was because it had been ordered to interrupt its northern march to brutalize partisans along the way. In retaliation for civilian attacks on Germans, Das Reich commanders hung ninety-nine men, boys, and women from house balconies, trees, and lampposts in the town square of Tulle and murdered 642 people in Oradour-sur-Glane—its men machine-gunned, its women and children burned alive in a church. Dulles radioed a report on the two massacres to Donovan, who passed it along to Roosevelt.

Discipline broke down on the other side as well. Resistance fighters sometimes murdered civilians to settle private scores, carried out senseless vengeance attacks against German soldiers, and summarily executed many taken as prisoners. "The Resistance partisans are not lenient to their prisoners," Bruce wrote in his diary. They "do not encumber themselves with many of them." He admired the courage of the French but admitted he found them at times "somewhat irritating" or "absolutely maddening."

It was the job of the Jedburghs now parachuting into France to harness the burgeoning Resistance capability—and carnage—in a direction that aided the Allied advance. Vermont captain Paul Cyr's Team George slipped away from Milton Hall on D-Day and parachuted near Redon on the Brittany Peninsula west of Normandy, where the jubilant village men hoisted them on their shoulders while the women toasted them with bottles of champagne and showers of kisses. They immediately set about the serious business of arming and training five thousand Resistance fighters to battle Germans fiercely defending their naval bases and key ports on the peninsula. Horace "Hod" Fuller, a battle-hardened Marine major who had been wounded in the Guadalcanal campaign, led Team Bugatti, which mounted its own little war in the Hautes-Pyrénées near the Spanish border. Soon changing into civilian clothes, Fuller and his teammates organized an underground force to cut rail and power lines, sabotage an oil refinery at Peyrouzet, fend off an attack by five hundred Germans near the village of Arbon without losing a man, and eventually capture over six hundred enemy soldiers when his band liberated the commune of Tarbes.

Soon after the Normandy landing, however, reports of Jedburgh casualties began to reach Colby and the others left at Milton Hall. Radio operator Jesse Gardner died when his parachute failed to open during Team Veganin's jump into Drôm the second night after D-Day. Late July, Germans ambushed a car carrying Team Ian in the Pleuville commune in southwestern France. They split up, running through back alleys. American major John Gildee and French captain A. Desfarges escaped, although Desfarges had his jaw smashed by a bullet. The Germans caught up with Canadian radio operator Lucien Bourgoin, pumped three rounds into him, and dumped his body into an unmarked grave. Illinois major Cyrus Manierre with Team Dodge had succeeded for over a month organizing sabotage attacks in the

Rhône Valley near Saint-Rambert. His luck ran out August 6 when the Milice grabbed him in his car. The French agents beat him for three days, then turned him over to the Gestapo, which tortured him for another three days. Manierre never talked and miraculously survived French and German prison camps until he was liberated near the end of the war in Europe.

For Colby and the rest of the overeager commandos, Milton Hall became a gilded cage. They stood with their French comrades in formation before the mansion on July 14 to raise the *Tricolour* in honor of Bastille Day—many with grim looks on their faces. On warm nights Colby and the others slept outside under the stars. OSS spies who had returned from France visited Milton Hall with advice for working there unobtrusively. In restaurants and bars, sit with your back to a corner so you have a view of anyone walking in or out, they advised, and always with both feet planted on the floor, as Frenchmen do, not with your legs crossed. Hold your fork in your left hand, learn the patois and gestures of the region you infiltrate. Trust no one completely, but if you have to, priests, railroad workers, and mailmen were the best. Never the police.

Casey returned as well. "Things are getting rough over there," he told a clutch of officers sitting in the mansion's foyer. Nazi reprisals against civilians in the areas which they would infiltrate had turned grisly. "A couple of weeks ago Wehrmacht headquarters in Berlin ordered all German units in France to execute anyone captured outside what they call the 'zone of legal combat,' who's taking part in resistance operations," he said in a flat tone, fixing them with a stare. "They emphasize this applies to all parachutists no matter what nationality or uniform." Casey left unsaid the obvious, that executions would follow torture.

But he did add: "If any of you want to be issued an L tablet [the suicide capsule OSS spies carried] now's the time to ask for it."

Colby wondered if he would ever see the terror and intrigue being described to him.

CHAPTER 14

BREAKERS

Shortly after Gisevius first approached Dulles in January 1943, he began his real mission in Switzerland. The Abwehr agent broached the subject of the German opposition movement with the OSS officer. "He stressed the importance of receiving encouragement that if the Nazi leaders eliminated Hitler there could be negotiations for a durable peace with the United Nations," Dulles recounted their conversation in a January 13 cable to Washington. The alternative was alarming, as Tiny saw it: Hitler would cut a deal with the Soviet Union and "turn to bolshevism." Gisevius's friends in Berlin "did not see any reason to risk their lives" unless the movement had "some hope" of succeeding in ousting the dictator and bringing an end to the war.

Other opposition emissaries arrived on the heels of Gisevius to lobby Dulles. Gaevernitz introduced him to Adam von Trott zu Solz, a German Foreign Office diplomat in his mid-thirties who had been making the rounds in neutral countries to drum up support. It was essential, Trott told Dulles, that the West differentiate between Nazis who were the enemy and Germans who could be allies; the movement felt downtrodden because the Americans and British so far had not. Dutch theologian Willem Adolph Visser 't Hooft, whose Geneva apartment became a favorite haunt for visiting German dissidents, dropped by Herrengasse 23 to warn that Western indifference was prompting "a strong tendency of the opposition to turn

East" and align with the Soviets. Dulles remained skeptical. "I, myself, doubt very much whether this movement is, as yet, organized seriously," he cabled Washington.

The dissidents were further along than Dulles realized. And as the war deteriorated for Germany in 1943 the opposition was presented with its best opportunity to act. But it was a movement in peril.

Organizing a widespread popular revolt against Hitler was impossible. After assuming power in 1933, the Nazis nearly wiped out opposition among communists, Social Democrats, trade unionists, and rightists, leaving just fragments of their organizations that had gone underground. Only Catholic and Protestant church opposition stiffened. It took from 1934 to 1938 for like-minded Germans in government, business, education, the clergy, the arts, and the military to slowly gather together in small, secretive, and loosely organized opposition cells, called "circles." Among the more prominent was the Kreisau Circle, made up of civil servants, professional people, labor leaders, and dissident army officers, who met near the Silesian country estate of their leader, Count Helmuth James Graf von Moltke, a well-educated international lawyer and scion of one of Germany's most revered military families.

Ultimately hope for a coup lay with Hitler's generals. But any so inclined could not count on the enlisted men under them to follow orders for a putsch; the rank and file remained fiercely devoted to their führer. The tyrant had also cleverly bought the loyalty of top commanders with such bribes as cash bonuses and richly appointed mansions. Moreover, German officers, culturally averse to mutiny as most military men are, had taken a second personal oath to Adolf Hitler, which they were equally loath to break. Yet none of Germany's leading generals wanted war—most in 1938 believed it not possible or winnable. By 1939 when it became clear that this was Hitler's intent, some in the senior ranks began quietly discussing how to seize the reins of power. They formed their own compartmentalized cells, speaking in code when they talked with one another. The conspirators included retired general Ludwig Beck, the deliberative army chief of staff who had resigned in quiet protest in 1938 and became a leading plotter; the stolid general Franz Halder, who always laid a handkerchief on his knee when crossing his legs so as not to crease the red stripe down his pants and who succeeded Beck as chief of staff; the handsome and energetic general

Hans Oster, the Abwehr's deputy chief and a Canaris confidant, who always referred to Hitler in private conversations as "the swine"; General Erwin von Witzleben, the no-nonsense commander of the Berlin military district; and the independent-minded general Henning von Tresckow, a cast-iron Prussian on the Eastern Front who became disgusted with Nazi atrocities. Among their civilian allies: the intense Carl Friedrich Goerdeler, who was a former Reich prices commissioner and mayor of Leipzig; Dr. Hjalmar Schacht, an early Reichsbank president and economics minister for Hitler, who had been forced out of the regime in 1937; and Wolf-Heinrich Graf von Helldorf, who held a key post like Witzleben as Berlin's police chief. Gisevius became one of the plotters' key staff men and their envoy overseas.

In such a rigidly controlled totalitarian state launching a coup was a dauntingly complex undertaking, full of imponderables that made the Wehrmacht's plotters, used to precise battle plans, jittery. Surprise was critical. Generals commanding large forces in strategic places had to move on top Nazis and their security apparatus in careful choreography. Gisevius gauged they had a twelve-hour window to act, after which "in this age of the airplane and the radio" Hitler would strike back and crush the revolt. But for the coup to get off the ground, "the generals must act," Gisevius wrote in his memoirs, and for the next four years they proved maddeningly indecisive—Halder one of the biggest equivocators. Hitler's stunning victories in Czechoslovakia, Poland, Norway, Denmark, France, and the Low Countries made him wildly popular among Germans. After each invasion the rebel generals judged the time not ripe for a coup and backed off.

After the 1939 invasion of Poland, Schacht, Moltke, and other conspirators in the army and Foreign Office began sending out peace feelers to the West. All met with suspicious indifference from Great Britain and the United States. Donovan had begun his war wary of them. A memo forwarded to him three weeks after the attack on Pearl Harbor recommended that the OSS begin strategizing for how the Roosevelt administration should react if Germany or Japan tried to foist peace proposals to weaken the resolve of the Allies. But it did not stop Donovan from brainstorming ideas to turn the tables and weaken Axis resolve, by enticing Berlin to surrender early. "Somehow or other there must be a way out" other than the Germans fighting "to the bitter end," he wrote to an aide in March 1942.

By the spring of 1943, British and American war planners had a contingency plan, code-named "Rankin," in case Germany suddenly collapsed and Allied victory came early in Europe. It was not a possibility anyone seriously considered. What *was* more possible, the Allies feared, were peace plots to dismember the Alliance. Stalin remained paranoid that Churchill and Roosevelt would stab him in the back and cut a separate deal with Hitler. The OSS stayed on watch for just the opposite—Stalin trying to hatch a separate arrangement with the Germans.

As 1943 drew to a close, German dissidents with peace feelers had begun to back up at the OSS director's door. Paul Leverkühn, a Berlin lawyer Donovan had known before the war, sent him a letter proposing that opposition members would persuade German army and Luftwaffe commanders not to contest an Allied invasion of France in exchange for the West negotiating peace with the movement after it had staged a coup. Donovan thought the offer worth exploring but Roosevelt showed no interest. Donovan was more ambivalent when Count von Moltke showed up at his OSS station in Istanbul during the summer of 1943 with the Kreisau Circle's peace proposal. Dubbed the "Hermann Plan" by the OSS, it was similar to Leverkühn's offer, although far more "anti-Russian," an agency analyst concluded. Moltke's conspirators proposed to overthrow Hitler, then help the Allies quickly invade both France and Germany, all the while shifting the Wehrmacht's forces east to hold the Soviet army at a defense line in Poland. Donovan and his advisers knew the names of no one else in the Kreisau Circle besides Moltke's. How could this seemingly amorphous group move the entire German army in France, the Low Countries, and inside Germany to the Eastern Front? The Hermann Plan smelled to some in the OSS like a Nazi plant to split Churchill and Roosevelt from Stalin. Donovan ordered his Istanbul station not to pursue the peace proposal, just keep in touch with Moltke to see if he could provide any intelligence helpful for Overlord.

Throughout 1943 Dulles relayed to Washington bits and pieces of information he gleaned from Gisevius and others on the German dissidents. They were an uncoordinated lot, he thought. As best as he could determine they were divided into two camps—those like Moltke who wanted to open "the door to the Anglo-Saxon occupation forces," he messaged to headquarters, and those who wanted to strike a deal with the Soviets. By August, Dulles was certain, based on his conversations with Gisevius, that retired general Beck was considered in army circles "to be the only person who possesses the necessary stature" to lead a military government after a coup, he cabled Donovan.

Senior State Department officials, meanwhile, became increasingly nervous about all the German peace feelers drifting into neutral nations and spies like Dulles being sucked into negotiations that more experienced diplomats should be conducting. Under orders from Cordell Hull, Donovan instructed his station chiefs in Bern, Stockholm, Madrid, Lisbon, and Istanbul to report "immediately" any offers to their ambassador. Dulles assured Donovan he was already doing that with his good friend Leland Harrison.

London remained just as wary of Dulles freelancing. Whatever opposition existed in Germany, British intelligence was convinced Gisevius was not a trustworthy emissary for it. "Broadway" (the Americans' code word for MI6) lobbied the OSS to dump Gisevius. Dulles stood by his Abwehr informant, although in the beginning, he confided to Mary Bancroft he wasn't sure that everything Tiny told him about the conspirators was true.

Dulles, however, was sure that a hidden hand behind the plot was Gisevius's boss, Admiral Wilhelm Canaris. His Abwehr was the Wehrmacht's spy service separate from the Nazi Party's rival intelligence organizations, the Gestapo and SD. The military's secret service had a mixed record; it aggressively vacuumed intelligence but often misread what it collected. Dulles considered most of the espionage agents and saboteurs in the Abwehr dangerous enemies, but it had this coterie at the top, led by Canaris and his deputy, General Oster, who appeared to him to be maneuvering against Hitler. The more he thought about it the more Dulles believed that the Abwehr was "the ideal vehicle for a conspiracy," he later wrote. Its members, like Gisevius, could "travel about at home and abroad under secret orders, and no questions are asked. Every scrap of paper in the files, its membership, its expenditure of funds, its contacts, even enemy contacts, are state secrets."

Dulles called him the "Little Greek" because of his Hellenic last name, although Canaris's early ancestors traced back to Italy. Fairly fluent in English, prematurely gray, an insomniac and a pessimist by nature, Canaris had commanded a submarine in World War I but in the interwar years he was deemed better suited for shore duty as an espionage director. He proved to be a cunning intelligence officer, with a nasty side. Gisevius found him perplexing. One memo to Donovan called him Germany's "most dangerous and mysterious wire-puller behind the scenes." Abwehr III, the counterespionage arm of his organization, had ruthlessly rooted out Allied spies left behind in the occupied countries, even arresting a consular clerk in the U.S. embassy in France who was considered an undercover British agent. Donovan soon tried to track every move made in Europe by Canaris, who like him was a travel bug.

A right-wing nationalist, Canaris had been an early Hitler supporter but had grown disenchanted with the führer and the war after England entered the conflict. He decided to remain in the Abwehr, however, believing he could prevent worse things from happening to his country as a spymaster. Canaris collected intelligence on the Allies that he thought would convince Hitler war was hopeless. He had his analysts color and even falsify reports to dissuade the dictator from what he considered the more insane military ventures and, when he could, he tried to frustrate Nazi orders to exterminate Poles, Russians, and Jews. Canaris was careful to avoid any direct involvement with Germany's dissidents. He left that to his deputy, Oster, who plotted with the cabal and set up a network of confidential Abwehr agents in neutral countries to make contact with the Allies. By November 1943 Dulles was closely tracking Canaris's visits to Bern, assigning him the code number 659 in his cables to Washington. Dulles also gained access to Canaris's mistress in Switzerland. Polish and British intelligence agents kept her on their payrolls for anything the admiral might divulge during his visits. The British assumed the crafty spy chief knew his pillow talk would not remain in the bedroom so he told her only what he wanted the enemy services to hear.

. . . .

Winter struck Bern with a vengeance early 1944, with snow piled high on city streets that could be cleared. "This should not be very helpful to the Germans in getting their war material over the mountain passes down to Italy," Dulles predicted during one of his evening radiotelephone calls to Washington. In the cramped offices he shared with Gerald Mayer on Dufourstrasse, Dulles kept boxes stuffed with hundreds of five-by-seven-inch index cards—his "Personality File" alphabetized with notations on cables he had written about key Germans, friendly or not, or sightings that had been made of them in Switzerland. His number of personality cards on the Reich's dissidents grew by the week. He continued to receive skeptical reviews of the opposition from some visitors arriving from Germany. A Swedish friend dismissed the movement as "negligible" and those few in it acting "rather childishly." But by that winter Dulles became convinced that some type of underground existed in Germany, even if he did not know its scope. In January, Eduard Waetjen, the Berlin lawyer sent to Zurich under diplomatic cover, began taking over many of Gisevius's courier duties from the dissidents. Dulles gave him the code name "Gorter." Mary Bancroft called him "Homer" in her phone calls because Waetjen liked to amuse himself by translating the *Odyssey* from its original Greek into German.

Whitney Shepardson and Ferdinand Mayer in Washington continued to question whether Waetjen was honest. Dulles thought he was, although he knew Waetjen, like Gisevius, would hold back or slant some information as long as the Allies remained standoffish toward the dissidents. Were the dissidents Waetjen and Gisevius represented really German rightists aligned with Göring, Jackpot and Carib asked? If so, the code name for them would be "Falstaff," after the comical Shakespeare character. No, Dulles responded, "Fat Boy" (his cover name for Göring, which wasn't far from what Germans called the *Reichsmarschall* behind his back) "commands no support in reputable opposition circles." Dulles asked that his dissident contacts be referred to as "Breakers."

Dulles assigned code names to the Breakers conspirators he knew so far. General Beck became "Tucky," Halder became "Ladder," Goerdeler was "Lester," Helldorf "Bobcat." By the end of January, Dulles had a clearer picture of the conspiracy from his conversations with Gisevius and Waetjen and he cabled it to Shepardson and Mayer in Washington. Breakers was "composed of various intellectuals from certain military and government circles," he wrote to headquarters, with "a loose organization among themselves." They "maintain their foreign contacts and communications through 659," the code number for Canaris. Gisevius and Waetjen served as their "intermediaries here in Bern." He realized headquarters still had its doubts about the two men but he trusted them, and Waetjen in particular gave him a direct line "to Breakers which we think can be used now for staying in close touch with events."

Dulles had not told British intelligence about Breakers and he did not want anyone else in the OSS alerting Broadway, which had been so hostile to Gisevius. It was not until June that he gave Bruce the okay to broach the subject with MI6 in London. Bruce did, but demanded that the British send him their intelligence on German dissidents "in return for our valuable 'Breakers' material," he wrote in his diary. What the cousins delivered was "lamentably weak," Bruce complained, mostly retreaded reports from other foreign services that he had already read.

Though the dissidents broke into pro-West and pro-Soviet factions, as near as Dulles could determine the two groups "keep in touch" with each other, he wrote to Washington on January 27, and they "are very eager to obtain political ammunition from our side." What is American policy toward the German resistance, Dulles asked Shepardson and Mayer? What could he offer Breakers? Casey, who was reading Dulles's cables as they passed through London, thought some type of conspiracy was "mushrooming" in the Third Reich. But from Washington, Shepardson and Mayer could pass along no guidance. The Roosevelt administration, they admitted, had no policy toward the dissidents except to be wary that they were Nazi plants conniving to divide the Alliance. Headquarters was delighted Dulles had made contact with an underground movement in "Nabors," their code word for Germany. But the only advice Jackpot and Carib could give him was be cautious, don't promise Breakers anything, just listen to what they have to say.

By March, Dulles had begun picking up intelligence that Germany's opposition was taking casualties. Canaris lost a bitter bureaucratic battle with Himmler. Hitler placed the SS commander in charge of the Abwehr and packed Canaris off to retirement. Oster was put under surveillance and forbidden to travel. The only saving grace: Himmler left Colonel Georg Hansen to run the Abwehr's military intelligence functions for him, not knowing that Hansen also sympathized with the opposition and kept Waetjen as his courier for information passed to the OSS in Bern. But more bad news arrived. Dulles learned on March 5 that the Gestapo had arrested Helmuth von Moltke. He received disturbing intelligence warning that Himmler suspected Halder's loyalty and was laying a trap for the army staff chief. Were Breakers' members now being rolled up? Dulles could not tell, but it appeared to him to be the case.

General Beck worried as well that Himmler was closing in. He ordered

Gisevius to lobby Dulles even harder on gaining U.S. support for the conspirators. By this point Beck believed the American in Bern was far more sympathetic to the dissidents' cause than the British, who wanted only to exploit the opposition for intelligence. In long talks at Herrengasse 23, Gisevius tried to convince Dulles that halting Soviet expansion worldwide was now more important than winning the war. He pleaded for a peace deal with the West that would enable Germany's army to continue the battle in the east. Out of the question, Dulles replied. Roosevelt would not act behind Stalin's back. Although he did not tell Gisevius, Dulles also feared the cabal's two apparent leaders, Beck and Goerdeler, might now be too well known as conspirators and the Gestapo, aware of the plot, was lying in wait to break up the gang.

Dulles nevertheless relayed Gisevius's plan to Washington. Breakers was ready to eliminate Hitler and oust his regime, he messaged on April 6 and 7; it was the only group, as far as Dulles could see, that had the power, the army, and the weapons, plus access to Hitler and other top Nazis in order to capture or kill them. The plotters, most of whom did not want a postwar Germany dominated by the Soviet Union, were ready to act if the United States and Great Britain could assure them that once they overthrew Hitler they could negotiate a separate peace with the West, not with Moscow. The window for a successful coup, the conspirators warned, "is quickly drawing to a close," Dulles reported. American support must come soon. Shepardson and Mayer replied quickly. They would discuss the proposal with the State Department. In the meantime, keep the line to Breakers open but don't give the plotters any false hope, they ordered Dulles.

The Breakers plan went nowhere in the U.S. government. Donovan, who had heard this same proposal from Moltke, feared Gisevius was laying a trap. Even Casey, who by then had become an ardent anticommunist, was cool to the idea of the Allies cutting a deal with the Germans so they could hold off the Soviets in the east. Adding to the complicated mix: Shepardson and Mayer alerted Dulles that their officers in Stockholm had sniffed out intelligence that Russian intermediaries might have been sending peace feelers to German representatives there. Dulles cabled Donovan: "I am completely aware of the delicacy of the situation and I am going ahead with the greatest care."

On May 13, Dulles delivered a classified message to headquarters with the final details Gisevius and Waetjen had just presented to him on the Breakers plan. Its audacity, particularly in what it demanded from the United States, was breathtaking. The group could not guarantee that an Allied landing in northern France would go unopposed because for the moment "they cannot count on Rommel for any cooperation," Dulles wrote. But the conspirators, who claimed their ranks now included the overall western commander Rundstedt and General Alexander von Falkenhausen (head of the military government in Belgium), "were ready to help our armed units get into Germany under the condition that we agree to allow them to hold the Eastern Front." Specifically, local German commanders would allow three Allied airborne divisions to parachute into a spot near Berlin. The Americans and British would also be allowed to make a major amphibious landing on Germany's North Sea coast near Bremen and Hamburg. Meanwhile Munich forces loyal to the conspiracy would isolate Hitler, Göring, and other high Nazi officials at their retreats in Obersalzburg. Before he even discussed the plan with Dulles, Gisevius sent a message by courier back to Beck that the Allies would never agree to it. When they met, Dulles assured him that would be the case, particularly "the plan for parachuting troops into Germany," he said. The Americans "would probably think that . . . was a Nazi ruse."

Donovan circulated the latest Breakers proposal at the highest levels of government in Washington. On May 16 his office delivered to Secretary of State Hull a six-page report, stamped SECRET and summarizing all the overtures Germany's generals and senior civilians had made to Dulles the past five months culminating with this final offer. The next day Mayer and Shepardson cabled Dulles that he was correct in telling Gisevius and Waetjen that the United States would never sell out the Russians. The latest Breakers plan was dead on arrival in Washington. With Overlord just three weeks away, the Allies were not going to spend much time considering such a wild scheme.

The conspirators couriered a message back to Gisevius: do nothing more with the Americans. The opposition would act on its own. Breakers went silent on Dulles.

Early July, Mary Bancroft noticed that Gisevius appeared extremely nervous. He could not sit still. He motored constantly from Bern to Zurich to Basel to Geneva. He telephoned her occasionally but began skipping their regular sessions to translate his manuscript. On July 8, Theodor Strünck, whom Gisevius had recruited into the Abwehr to run errands for Oster, arrived in Switzerland with an important message for his old friend. Gisevius happened to be vacationing in the mountains. Strünck, whose Berlin apartment had become a safe house for Goerdeler and other conspirators, tracked down a phone number for Gisevius and called. He must see him at once, was all Strünck would say over the line. When the two met, the nervous Abwehr captain pumped Gisevius's hand once and immediately launched into the message Hansen, his new boss, had asked him to deliver. The collapse of Germany's Army Group Center in Russia along with the successful Allied beachhead at Normandy had emboldened the conspirators. They believed Colonel General Friedrich Fromm, the powerful commander of the Replacement Army that trained and supplied fresh troops for the front, would now join them. More worrisome for Gisevius, Strünck warned, Himmler, now their Abwehr commander, had ordered him back to Berlin. If he didn't come voluntarily, Gestapo agents would kidnap him.

Are the conspirators ready to act? Gisevius interrupted.

"Yes and no," Strünck answered precisely. "The assassination is supposed to take place any day now, but you know how often we have been strung along with promises."

Strünck passed along Hansen's orders that Gisevius pretend to be ill so he could not return to Berlin. But Gisevius, who saw clearly that the conspirators were finally about to stage their coup d'état, "decided that it would be absolute madness" for him "to stay away from Berlin" and "watch it from afar in Zurich," he wrote in his memoirs. On July 11, he boarded a train in Bern with Strünck that would take them north to Berlin. When he arrived in the city he planned to disappear.

Before Tiny left, he dropped off a lengthy memo to Waetjen that he wanted delivered to Dulles after his departure. The twenty-page note, whose German Bancroft translated, assumed the assassination attempt would succeed and listed his recommendations for how the Allies should treat his country afterward.

Waetjen filled Dulles in with snippets of what Strünck had brought from

Berlin—that the Normandy invasion and Germany's deteriorating Eastern Front had invigorated Breakers, that Fromm may have joined their ranks. The updates were cabled to Donovan, who forwarded them to Hull. Dulles, however, continued to attach the caveat that he could not predict success for the plotters. "Without any doubt, the Gestapo is keeping its eye on developments," he wrote. "Moreover, it is quite probable that the military men, whose action is indispensable to the achievement of these ends, will lack the 'intestinal fortitude' to act, just as they have earlier." Kolbe managed to slip a message to the Bern station that "heads are starting to roll now." Dissidents were being rounded up in Berlin to be executed. Kolbe had heard that Goerdeler would soon be arrested. Something, Dulles decided, was about to happen in the next few weeks—good or bad.

On July 12, the day after Gisevius left for Berlin, Dulles cabled Shepardson and Mayer. If all his sources in Breakers were "to be trusted," he wrote Jackpot and Carib, "there is a possibility that a dramatic event may take place up north." The warning was immediately relayed to Roosevelt and Hull.

CHAPTER 15

VALKYRIE

Their overnight train had little trouble making its journey north and by the morning of July 12 had reached Potsdam just at the Berlin city limits. Gisevius decided to get off there. He didn't know whether the Abwehr officers who would meet Strünck at the main Berlin station were friendly or Himmler's thugs waiting to grab him, so he decided to show up on a different train. He raced through the underground tunnel to the commuter platform and hopped aboard another train just about to pull out. At Berlin's western borough of Wannsee he changed trains again, this one's tracks winding by the neighborhood where he had lived. He gazed down a smashed street and spotted his bombed-out house. A year later Gisevius returned to the address to find it little more than a blackened hole with torn, rain-soaked family photos scattered about.

His first meeting that afternoon was with a Breakers conspirator whose name had been told to Dulles, but it was a name Dulles had paid no attention to—Claus von Stauffenberg. Gisevius had never been introduced to Stauffenberg, but he quickly learned that with Oster out of action this Wehrmacht colonel with a patch over his left eye had become the driving force behind the plot to topple Hitler.

Their meeting in Strünck's apartment did not go well. Stauffenberg was a large man, but on closer inspection, Gisevius judged him a pitiful cripple.

His right arm, mangled by a war wound, hung limp with a stump at the end. With his left hand, which was missing two fingers, he lifted the patch over his missing left eye frequently to dab it with a cotton ball. Stauffenberg slumped into a wooden chair, opened the jacket of his uniform, and, Gisevius thought, rudely demanded that Strünck's wife, Elisabeth, fix him a cup of coffee. Gisevius instantly disliked the man—an arrogant general staff officer, he thought, the kind Hitler favored, perhaps consciously or unconsciously now trying to overcompensate for his mutilated body by acting like a boorish swashbuckler. After an hour of talking to him Gisevius was convinced Stauffenberg was a callow opportunist who wanted the führer assassinated not to establish a democracy afterward but so military men like him could create a true National Socialist dictatorship, free of Hitler's incompetent and corrupt gang. Gisevius also believed Stauffenberg was a leftist who would accommodate the Soviets.

Gisevius was being unfair, his disdain for the colonel tinged by jealousy and the fact that he saw him as a postwar rival. Claus Schenk Graf von Stauffenberg was made of sterner stuff. Born into Swabian nobility, he had risen through the ranks as a cavalry officer suffering severe wounds from an air attack during the Africa campaign in 1943, which left him without an eye and a hand. Though initially sympathetic to Nazi ideology, Stauffenberg, who studied Greek philosophy intently and enjoyed debating politics, was too educated an officer not to question Hitler's methods. By the time he reached major he often referred to the führer as "the wallpaper hanger"; he also thought the top Nazis around him were crooks, and he had begun bravely suggesting to superiors that the regime should be toppled. Returning to Berlin moody and intense after his wounds, Stauffenberg believed he must now do something to save his country from ruin. He joined the conspiracy in late summer 1943 and soon moved to take control of it as others equivocated or were detained by the Gestapo. Stauffenberg was more a pragmatist than the communist sympathizer Gisevius suspected. When it was clear Washington would provide no support he decided the plotters must act on their own. After the coup, Stauffenberg recognized the obvious: Breakers would have to negotiate with Stalin, whose Red Army would soon reach the gates of Berlin. But contrary to what Gisevius may have thought, the colonel had never specifically said he would negotiate *only* with the Soviets.

It was no secret to Hitler that he was in constant danger of assassination and that any plot would likely have generals behind it. All told, more than two dozen attempts would be made on his life, seven of which he knew of. In 1939, a lone communist assassin planted a bomb set to go off in Munich's Bürgerbräukeller during the führer's speech; Hitler left the room minutes before it detonated. With General Tresckow's help, on March 7, 1943, officers placed British-designed bombs disguised as two Cointreau bottles in a compartment of Hitler's plane, but they failed to go off while he was aboard. A fortnight later Tresckow enlisted a despondent army colonel to stand next to Hitler during a Heroes Memorial Day ceremony in Berlin and detonate an explosive hidden in his large overcoat. But the suicide bomber could never get close to the dictator, who practically ran through the event.

Hitler—often wearing a bulletproof waistcoat and cap, the conspirators thought—always surrounded himself with SS bodyguards in addition to a gaggle of trusted Wehrmacht aides. Nearby rail traffic halted when his private train, guarded by machine-gun-toting SS men, passed through. Four armored motorcades were positioned at different places in Germany to drive him, always in his own car with his personal chauffeur rather than ones the army provided. Twenty-four hours before a public event, Gestapo and the police swept the site of suspicious persons, placed all approach routes to it under surveillance, and had technicians search the venue for explosives. So many assassination attempts had been tried and failed, it seemed as if Hitler could smell danger. He would suddenly change his motorcade route or the time he showed up at an event or left it.

Stauffenberg and the other conspirators eventually decided the military unit for their coup would be the nearly two million men of the Replacement Army commanded by Friedrich Fromm. The colonel general had been cagey about whose side he was on. If he did not join the plotters, his deputy, General Friedrich Olbricht, who *was* part of the conspiracy, promised to force Fromm to act. Stauffenberg fortuitously was now in a position to help make it happen; in October 1943, Olbricht made him his staff chief with access to "Valkyrie."

It was the code word for a highly secret mission the Replacement Army had besides supplying field commanders with fresh troops—suppressing internal revolt in Germany among its citizens, millions of foreign workers, or saboteurs the Allies infiltrated. The Valkyrie plan detailed how units in the Replacement Army's military districts around the country would be activated to quell any disturbance and protect Nazi assets. Stauffenberg, who oversaw Valkyrie for Olbricht, realized it was the perfect cover for moving troops in Berlin and other key cities to be in a position not to protect Hitler but to topple him. As the staff chief he also now knew Hitler's whereabouts at all times. All the conspirators needed was a commander to issue the orders under Valkyrie. If Fromm wouldn't, Olbricht intended to arrest him and do it himself. Stauffenberg set about formulating and even rehearsing the Valkyrie directives that would have to be sent to launch the coup.

What to do with Hitler? The conspirators had been debating since 1939 whether he should be killed or captured and tried in a court. Gisevius favored killing him. So did Stauffenberg, who decided the weapon should be an explosive device rather than a pistol. A shooter could not be guaranteed a clean shot. Stauffenberg looked for someone to plant the bomb. The conspirators had not considered him a suitable assassin. He was crippled and did not have access to Hitler. Moreover, it would be difficult for him to kill Hitler, perhaps in his Wolf's Lair headquarters, and also run the coup in Berlin. But he could find no one else willing or suitable for the job and, more importantly, in June 1944, Stauffenberg could now get close to Hitler. Fromm had taken him from Olbricht and made him his chief of staff, which gave the colonel access to the dictator for briefings Fromm could not attend. Stauffenberg decided he would be the one to kill Hitler.

The conspirators planned for Stauffenberg to assassinate the führer at Wolf's Lair in East Prussia, which would then be isolated for at least a few hours so the Berlin cabal could begin moving units to take over the government without Hitler's entourage that remained at the field headquarters interfering. For the job of quarantining Wolfsschanze they had the fearless and highly educated chief of army communications, General Erich Fellgiebel. It was impossible to cut off all messages out of the Rastenburg compound. But Fellgiebel, who thought Hitler was a military incompetent, intended to disrupt its communications by ordering loyal officers to switch off repeater stations in East Prussia that carried all Wolf's Lair telephone and teleprinter traffic. At the same time his men would control exchanges in other parts of the country to allow the conspirators' orders instead of the regime's to get through. But for the plan to be successful Hitler first had to be killed.

Early July, Stauffenberg believed they had to hurry. In addition to Canaris, Oster, and Moltke out of action, Dr. Julius Leber, a former Reichstag deputy who was a member of the Kreisau Circle, had been arrested. Soon Goerdeler went into hiding because the Gestapo was after him. Rumors also had begun circulating in Berlin that some type of coup was brewing. It was only a matter of time, the plotters worried, before loyal Nazis closed in on them. Himmler, it turned out, was aware of the coup rumors but knew no details of the Valkyrie preparations. An informer from a communist group had betrayed Leber and the Gestapo had earlier planned Goerdeler's arrest for July. The strain on the conspirators now became almost unbearable. Stauffenberg looked like a nervous wreck to Beck, the retired army staff chief. Helldorf, Berlin's police chief, grew pessimistic that he could pull off the coup. Stauffenberg meanwhile squabbled with others over the makeup of a post-Hitler government.

During two führer briefings he and Fromm attended in Hitler's Bavarian Alps retreat near Berchtesgaden, Stauffenberg scoped out his quarry. When he returned to the Berghof the third time on July 11, he had the bomb in his briefcase but decided not to set it off because Himmler did not attend the briefing. The conspirators wanted to kill the SS chief and if possible Göring (who disgusted Stauffenberg when he appeared at an earlier briefing wearing makeup), so they could not crush the revolt after Hitler's demise. His second opportunity came at a Wolf's Lair briefing on July 15. Stauffenberg held off once more; Himmler was again absent and Stauffenberg had no chance to activate the time-delayed fuse for his bomb before the session with Hitler.

A muggy heat draped over Germany on July 20. Stauffenberg was summoned to Wolf's Lair that Thursday morning. Fromm could not come so his chief of staff had been ordered to brief the führer by himself on two Volksgrenadier divisions the Replacement Army would activate to throw at the Red Army advancing through Poland. Shortly before the 12:30 p.m. session, Stauffenberg asked to be excused so he could freshen up in a lavatory. He slipped into a nearby waiting room instead, where he and his nervous aide, Lieutenant Werner von Häften, set the fuse for one of two bombs in his briefcase using special pliers Stauffenberg could manipulate with the three fingers remaining on his left hand. He left the second bomb with Häften because two proved too bulky for his briefcase and rushed to catch up with other officers walking to the briefing hut. As they neared the hut, Stauffenberg asked a Wolfsschanze staffer: "Could you please put me as near as possible to the führer so that I can catch everything I need for my briefing afterwards?"

Hitler had arrived promptly at 12:30. Himmler and Göring were not there but Stauffenberg decided to proceed with the assassination without them. Some two dozen senior officers and aides stood in the room, including Field Marshal Wilhelm Keitel, chief of the Supreme Command of the Armed Forces, and Lieutenant General Adolf Heunsinger, the new chief of the General Staff of the Army, who was briefing Hitler on the status of the Eastern Front when Stauffenberg and two other aides slipped in. Hitler, who stood hunched over a long wooden table, both hands propped on maps, looked up. He did not recognize Stauffenberg, who had been among a crowd of officers in previous briefings with him. Keitel introduced him as Fromm's staff chief who would deliver the presentation on the home guard divisions. Hitler awkwardly shook Stauffenberg's left hand and turned back to Heunsinger to continue his briefing. One of the staffers who entered with Stauffenberg ushered him to a spot to the right of the führer, asking an admiral to make room because this colonel was so handicapped. The admiral willingly obliged. Stauffenberg placed his briefcase under the table in front of the place where the admiral had stood near the right-hand corner. But Heunsinger's aide, who was standing next to Stauffenberg, found the briefcase in his way and pushed it to the right of a heavy table support, which now stood between the bag and Hitler.

Stauffenberg excused himself, telling an officer in the passageway outside the room that he had to return a phone call from General Fellgiebel, the communications chief also in the Wolf's Lair compound. No one took notice. Officers walked in and out of the briefing room constantly to receive or deliver messages. But instead of placing the call, Stauffenberg exited the briefing hut to hunt for Häften and the car waiting to take them to the nearby Rastenburg airfield. As he was talking to Fellgiebel before climbing into a Horch sedan with Häften and a driver, a loud explosion sounded from the briefing hut. Stauffenberg ordered the driver to speed them to Guard Post 1, where sentries who had also heard the blast eventually opened the barrier to let the Horch pass. Stauffenberg convinced them the führer had ordered him to the airfield at once. He had arranged ahead of time for a Heinkel He 111 to be waiting at the strip to fly him and Häften back to Berlin. Buckling his seat belt in the speedy bomber, Stauffenberg was sure no one had survived the explosion, including Hitler.

But Hitler did survive. The bomb explosion, which left a hole in the floor where the briefcase had stood, destroyed all the furniture inside, engulfed the room in a bright yellow and blue flame, and sprayed glass and wood splinters everywhere, but the heavy table support that stood between Hitler and the briefcase protected his abdomen from the blast's full impact. Moreover, the briefing was held this day not in one of the compound's bunkers with concrete walls but rather in a wooden barracks. So instead of the explosion's force being contained inside the conference room, and likely killing everyone, its pressure escaped out the hut's walls and ceiling. Four officers died, a dozen were severely injured. Hitler, who had his right elbow leaning on the table when it collapsed and heaved up, suffered a contusion on his lower right arm and had his pant legs shredded, his skin and hair singed, splinters embedded in his body, and an eardrum perforated. Aides carried out their dazed yet agitated führer, who kept mumbling that he always knew traitors surrounded him and complaining that his new trousers had been ruined.

Fellgiebel proceeded with his plan to control communications from Wolfsschanze, aided, it turned out, by close Hitler aides who for the moment ordered a blackout, save for messages summoning Himmler and Göring, so the field headquarters could sort out what had happened. Shortly after 2 p.m., Hitler's inner circle strongly suspected the assassin had been Stauffenberg, who had gone missing, and by 3 p.m. the Wolf's Lair blackout had been lifted with Himmler's consent. Fellgiebel ordered the repeater stations in East Prussia switched off to halt telephone and teleprinter traffic out of Wolfsschanze, but he succeeded only in temporarily impeding communications to Berlin. Much of it was restored by late afternoon.

At 4:30 p.m., Stauffenberg finally reached the conspirators' headquarters, which was also the Replacement Army's headquarters on Berlin's

Bendlerstrasse. Gisevius showed up with police chief Helldorf a half hour later. Chaos reigned. Indecision paralyzed the generals. Fellgiebel had already phoned. "Something fearful has happened," he said only over the line, "the führer's alive." Their coup had been premised solely on Hitler dying; they had no contingency plan for his surviving the explosion. Stauffenberg could not believe the blast he saw did not kill Hitler and for a while convinced the others at Bendlerstrasse that the dictator was no longer among the living. Beck as well pleaded for solidarity. "For me this man is dead," he solemnly declared. Stauffenberg and other senior officers struggled mightily to mobilize the Replacement Army's Berlin force plus military districts across the country under Plan Valkyrie and to move on the regime and arrest top Nazis like Goebbels. They succeeded only briefly. Fromm, soon realizing the wind was not blowing with the conspirators, refused to cooperate. Olbricht, at first weak-kneed, eventually joined Stauffenberg in having officers detain Fromm for a while, but the Replacement Army chief later regained control. With Wolfsschanze communications fully restored by 4 p.m., Hitler and Keitel in East Prussia and Goebbels in Berlin succeeded, along with other key aides, in countermanding the conspirators' orders and announcing on nationwide radio by 6:30 p.m. that the assassination attempt had failed. The führer was still alive.

Troops loyal to the regime surrounded the Bendlerstrasse headquarters by nightfall and eventually moved in. Meanwhile, Beck put a gun to his head but after two unsuccessful tries remained a wounded heap on the floor until Fromm had an aide finish him off with a final bullet. Next, after a quickie kangaroo court Fromm staged to cover his tracks (he had, after all, dallied with the plotters), Stauffenberg, Olbricht, and two other officers were marched to the courtyard around midnight. With automobile headlights glaring at them they were executed by a hastily assembled firing squad. With his last breath, Stauffenberg shouted: "Long live Holy Germany!"

Gisevius, who had left Bendlerstrasse earlier, fled to the safety of Theodor and Elisabeth Strünck's apartment. After midnight, the three of them huddled around the radio to listen numbly as the canned music stopped and the voice of Adolf Hitler rang out defiantly. "German men and women! I do not know how many times an attempt on my life has been planned and carried out. If I address you today I am doing so for two reasons: first so you shall hear my voice and know that I personally am unhurt and well and, second, so that you shall hear the details of a crime that has no equal in German history." The failed assassination attempt, he boasted, was "a clear sign of providence that I must carry on with my work." The führer was not so confident in private. His personal secretary told Allied officers after the war that July 20 left him "a broken man," practically deaf for several months, his knees shaking when he stood too long, one hand trembling so violently he had to steady it with the other.

Exhausted from work with Dulles, Mary Bancroft had rented a vacation cottage for herself and her daughter on the shore of Lake Maggiore near the southern Swiss border with Italy. Just as she started a scrambled egg dinner for them the evening of July 20, the radio in their living room reported that an attempt had been made on Hitler's life. She kept turning the dial the rest of the night hunting for updates. Gisevius's name was not mentioned among the conspirators identified so far but she knew he must be in danger.

Back in Bern, Dulles had also heard the evening report of the assassination attempt. Shortly afterward he typed out his script on stationery for his radiotelephone call, making a few edits with his pen to what he had written, and dialed for Washington. At this point he did not have much more than what the radio and wire services were reporting and even if he did he would not have added more information to his call. He knew the Swiss and likely the Germans were monitoring it. "The attempt on Hitler's life is, of course, the outstanding item of news this evening," he began from his script. Dulles knew of several assassination attempts over the years. "The man seems to have a charmed life," he told Washington, "but possibly an all-wise Providence is saving him so that he may himself see the complete wreckage of the Germany he has led to destruction." He intended the last sentence as a propaganda message for his unwanted listeners. "As yet we have no reports other than the press and radio," Dulles said at the end. He had also typed that he had "no information as to the authors of this attempted coup." He crossed that out before he picked up the phone. He knew who was behind the putsch, but he was not about to divulge it over an open line.

The next morning Dulles began his scramble to find out all he could about what Breakers had attempted at Wolf's Lair and its consequences for the German opposition movement. Within days of the attack *The New York*

Times and other international news outlets ran photos of Hitler inspecting the bomb damage with Benito Mussolini, who had arrived at Wolfsschanze for a previously scheduled meeting with the führer after his midday briefings. Dulles studied the photos closely, particularly one showing Hitler extending his left hand for the Italian dictator to shake. It "may indicate that Hitler's right hand has been wounded," he cabled Washington. Also, he noted that only the left side of the dictator's face was shown in the shots "giving rise to the supposition that possibly the right side of the face is wounded." Donovan forwarded the speculation to Roosevelt.

Headquarters in Washington and Bruce in London were desperate for anything Dulles could uncover about the plot. Each scrap he cabled was rushed to the White House, State Department, and Pentagon. Dulles shook every tree he could find for intelligence, although much on how the assassination attempt came about he already had in his files.

Early Friday afternoon, July 21, he sent a coded cable to Donovan with more information collected overnight. Gisevius, as far as he could tell, was missing in Berlin, and Waetjen, who had remained in Switzerland, could glean only shards of information. Weak and timid by nature (Dulles found him useful only as a courier), Waetjen now grew indignant and emboldened by what had happened to his comrades in Berlin. Dulles could confirm that Breakers, the group he had been reporting on for seven months, had carried out the assassination attempt. Stauffenberg appears to have been a key player in the plot, Dulles cabled. Earlier that morning he had rooted through notes he had taken during conversations with Gisevius and discovered a brief mention Tiny had made of the colonel. Stauffenberg may have been a "liaison" between senior Wehrmacht officers and the younger members of Moltke's Kreisau Circle, Dulles speculated. "Of course the blood purge will be ruthless," Dulles acknowledged, but he remained optimistic. The coup may still succeed (Dulles at that point did not know it wouldn't), all depended on the loyalty of the Replacement Army (Dulles didn't know that force was now firmly under Himmler's control), and Hitler's midnight radio address followed by Göring's indicated "the revolt was not stamped out at once" (true, but the movement was pretty well dead after Thursday).

Dulles recommended psychological operations to bolster the opposition holdouts. Propaganda leaflets should be dropped on German soldiers.

Allied air forces should bomb Hitler's stronghold around Berchtesgaden to signal that the Nazi hierarchy was still under siege. SHAEF began the leaflet drops, but Eisenhower deferred any decision on bombing Berchtesgaden to FDR and Churchill.

Friday evening, Dulles ignored the other ears who were likely listening in on his radiotelephone call and filled Washington in on more intelligence he had picked up, although he admitted it still gave him "no very clear picture of the situation in Germany." The coup attempt "did not come as a great surprise," he began, except that he had always wondered if the senior officers "would have the courage to act." But apparently they realized "time was growing short," as he had reported to Washington in early July. "Possibly the Putsch was staged prematurely, probably because the action of the Gestapo forced the hand of those who were plotting to remove Hitler." To succeed, the plotters needed several key Wehrmacht divisions to seize "certain strategic points. . . . If they had, it would have seemed likely that certain powerful radio stations would be in the hands of the revolters." The fact that Dulles heard no broadcasts from the insurrectionists led him to believe the plot was doomed. Even so, "what has just taken place in Germany represents the one and only major attempt the past eleven years to overthrow the Hitler government." Wehrmacht morale has been delivered "a severe shock." In army circles, General Beck was highly respected. The officer corps will be jolted by his death. But Dulles concluded sadly that no other opposition group now existed in Germany powerful enough to stage a coup like Breakers. "If this attempt has failed, the Germans will probably have to wait for the complete military collapse of Germany to rid themselves of the Nazis." His prediction would prove true.

Dulles finally decided to tell his cousins in Switzerland what he knew about Breakers—although he couldn't help but point out to headquarters that "Zulu" (the OSS code word for the British) turned its nose up at Gisevius, who had been more than willing to let them in on the secret. The American ambassador to the Court of St. James's, John Gilbert Winant, also met with Churchill the night of July 23 to brief him on Dulles's negotiations with the German opposition. Afterward, Bruce sat down with Claude Dansey to break the news. Shepardson wrote Dulles he expected the "little Zulus" to raise "little stinkos" that he had been secretly talking with Breakers. The Brits, however, were not particularly upset about being kept out of the loop. Dulles wondered if it was because they already had advance notice of the plot. It turned out that MI6 had been picking up pieces of information on the plotters from Waetjen, whom their agents had known since 1942. But they also had kept their American cousins out of the loop.

What to do with the Russians? Dulles recommended that they be kept in the dark about Breakers. Donovan agreed. So did Ambassador Winant, fearing forthrightness would only stoke Stalin's paranoia that the Americans had been dealing behind his back. Stalin, however, already knew about Dulles's contacts with Breakers. An NKGB mole in the OSS's Washington headquarters tipped off the Soviets before July 20 that the Bern station had been working with the opposition. Dulles also feared that after the failed coup, the Soviets would now try to move in by co-opting German generals defeated on the Eastern Front to negotiate a separate peace with them. Donovan passed the worry on to Roosevelt, but it proved unwarranted. Moscow never hatched a deal.

From all he could learn from Waetjen and other sources, Dulles came to the grim conclusion two days after the assassination attempt that the regime had crushed the revolt. There was no hope for the plotters. "Breakers are breaking," he cabled Washington. For the next two weeks he struggled to produce a postmortem for headquarters. Rumors drifted into the station of last-minute dissent among the conspirators—Goerdeler and Beck wanting to reach a settlement with the West after Hitler was ousted, Stauffenberg determined to deal with the Soviets. But it was a moot point at this stage because Hitler had not been ousted. Dulles continued to find it disheartening that radio stations were never seized to deliver propaganda and the revolt never gained traction after Hitler survived the bomb blast. He became even more convinced the Gestapo had been tipped off to the plot and was just waiting to strike. But he still had no hard evidence of it—or, for that matter, of practically anything else that had happened. Newspapers circulated the same rumors he heard. If only Gisevius were back to fill in the blanks. Gisevius, he knew, was up to his neck in this plot. Dulles desperately hunted for any information that Tiny had survived and could escape Germany.

Yet even though all appeared lost, Dulles remained convinced the Allies stood to benefit "a good deal" from the failed coup, he told Washington in one of his radiotelephone calls. "This attempt at revolt should help to undermine the will of the German Army to keep up the struggle." Casey, who was reading Breakers cables that came through London, was not as sanguine. The Allied high command also did not find a silver lining. With the Normandy invaders still cooped up near the beachhead, some on Ike's staff noted that the Nazis now had time to bolster their regime and mop up any remnants of the German resistance.

Hitler did just that with a vengeance. He gave Himmler command of the Replacement Army, making him the most powerful man in the Reich after the führer. A week after the failed coup, Donovan's research analysts in Washington produced a secret study correctly predicting that Nazi Party control of the Wehrmacht would now be tightened, "the collapse of Germany may be retarded," and that Hitler would use the failed plot as an excuse for "a large-scale purge" of dissidents remaining in the armed forces, civil service, and industry. Dulles received a report that Himmler had a list of fifty thousand in the government and private sector he suspected were opposition sympathizers.

Dulles's suspicion that the Gestapo knew about the plot all along proved unfounded. Himmler bragged after July 20 that he expected this kind of attack, but his counterespionage service, in fact, was nowhere near to uncovering the coup. The Gestapo made up for its intelligence failure, however, by spending practically the rest of the war ruthlessly and efficiently unraveling how the plot came about and identifying the conspirators or anyone even remotely connected with them. "It would seem that the net is being pulled tighter around the Breakers group," Dulles cabled Donovan on August 5. Fellgiebel, Witzleben, Oster, Hansen, Helldorf, Halder, Schacht, Fromm, and the Strüncks were arrested. A one-million-mark bounty was placed on the heads of Goerdeler and a fellow conspirator, criminal police commander Arthur Nebe; both had gone into hiding. "The Gestapo is now certain" that Abwehr members "were employed in the Breakers matter," reported Dulles, who by the beginning of September cabled Washington with confirmation that "our 659 [Canaris] had been apprehended." The retired admiral, whom the Gestapo arrested on July 23, had not taken part in the coup attempt but knew of the preparations for it.

The conspirators were not prepared for the bestial cruelty Hitler unleashed. Instead of a firing squad's bullet, senior officers like Fellgiebel were tortured for weeks, then hung naked by wire or thin rope from meat hooks for an agonizing twenty-minute death with sound cameras recording for Hitler to enjoy the film later. Many were paraded before show trials Goebbels staged in front of a fanatical judge. Cattle trucks carted those given prison sentences to concentration camps. From newspaper stories and informant tips, Dulles filed reports to Washington throughout the summer and fall on those arrested and executed. The totals he compiled in Bern and MI6 calculated in London were inflated. Most of the some five thousand eventually executed were on old lists of suspects Himmler wanted eliminated and had no connection with the July 20 plot; perhaps two hundred to six hundred of those killed had been involved in one way or the other with Breakers. Dulles's Berlin informants had initially told him that Stauffenberg's wife, children, brother, and sister-in-law were among those executed. He learned at the end of the year that was untrue. Stauffenberg's family, along with over 140 relatives of other conspirators, had been packed off to Dachau.

Mid-August, a courier finally delivered to Dulles a coded letter from Fritz Kolbe. He was safe. Miraculously, the Gestapo dragnet had not swept him up. His bosses in the Foreign Office continued to give him high job ratings, even promoting him to the rank of secretary of the chancellery. On August 11, more joyous news came to the Bern station. Another courier arrived and informed Dulles he had just seen Gisevius, who was hiding in Berlin. The morning after the failed attempt, the Abwehr officer had left Strünck's apartment and for the next three weeks had been moving from one friend's home to another in and around the capital, fearful always that his tall frame made him stand out when he rode subways or scurried along sidewalks. Dulles ignored dark warnings from MI6 that Gisevius now must surely be a Nazi plant and began plotting how he could help his friend escape Germany.

Germans bearing peace feelers and stories of plots to oust Hitler continued to show up at Dulles's door throughout the fall and winter of 1944. Dulles forwarded their offers to Washington, but headquarters by then had soured on the dissident movement in Germany. Donovan's top research analyst even speculated in one report that Hitler may have staged the July 20 coup attempt to enhance his stature and tighten his grip on Germany—a notion Dulles found laughable. Shepardson wrote Donovan that Breakers was "an unbelievable collection of zealous and stupid Germans who seem to have had not the slightest conception of how to carry on conspiratorial activities." Dulles didn't argue the point with Jackpot.

Donovan ordered Dulles to have no more involvement with other coup plotters or the remnants of Breakers. "I consider that, if the Germans battle it out inside Germany without help from us, it will be of more benefit to humanity," the OSS chief wrote. Dulles agreed to follow orders—albeit reluctantly. He still suspected the Russians would not play by the same rules. At the very least, he argued to Donovan, the United States should not work against any "anti-Nazi action of Western oriented tendency, even if we do not identify ourselves with them in any way."

Though Breakers' plot had failed, Dulles's reputation in Washington soared for predicting it and providing such detailed intelligence on it afterward. Praise poured into the Bern station. "Your results are sensational," Shepardson cabled.

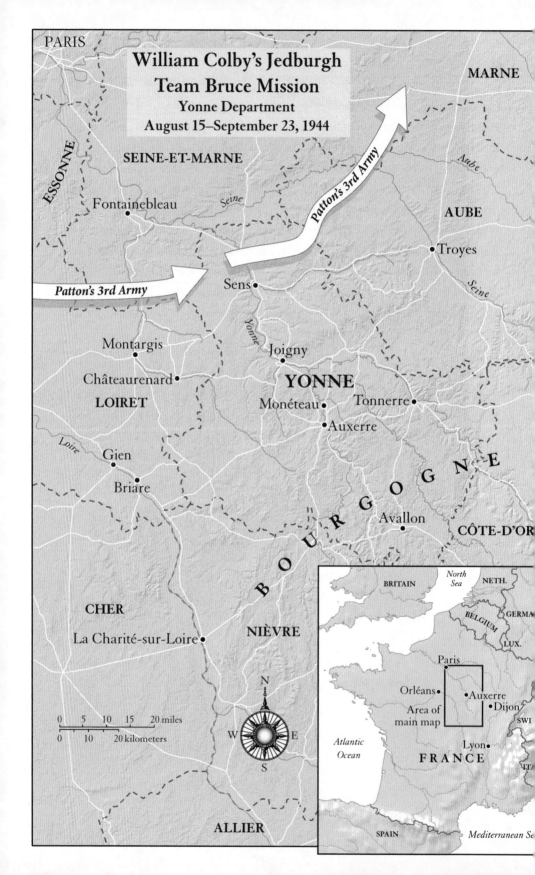

William Colby's Jedburgh Team Bruce Mission
Yonne Department
August 15–September 23, 1944

PARIS

MARNE

SEINE-ET-MARNE

ESSONNE

Fontainebleau

Seine

Aube

AUBE

Troyes

Patton's 3rd Army

Sens

Seine

Patton's 3rd Army

Yonne

Montargis

Joigny

YONNE

Châteaurenard

Monéteau

Tonnerre

LOIRET

Auxerre

Loire

Gien

B O U R G O G N E

Briare

Avallon

CÔTE-D'OR

CHER

NIÈVRE

La Charité-sur-Loire

0   5   10   15   20 miles

0   10   20 kilometers

N
W   E
S

ALLIER

North Sea

BRITAIN

NETH.

BELGIUM

GERMA

LUX.

Paris

Orléans

Auxerre

Dijon

Area of main map

SWI

Atlantic Ocean

Lyon

FRANCE

ITA

SPAIN

Mediterranean Se

CHAPTER 16

THE YONNE DEPARTMENT

After two months of Team Bruce sitting and waiting impatiently, their mission to jump into France descended upon them quickly. London's Special Forces Headquarters delivered the warning order to Milton Hall by scrambler phone on Saturday morning, August 12. Colby, Lelong, and Villebois must be ready to move out of the country estate by six that evening. A team often might have two to three days' notice before it parachuted into France—their mission briefings in London conducted at a somewhat leisurely pace, with time at night for a fine dinner, perhaps drinks afterward. But lines on the battlefield in France now moved faster than the Allies had anticipated. Team Bruce's London briefing would be speeded up to just one day. They would parachute in Sunday night.

Because of the time crunch, the team's equipment for the mission was sent ahead to the airfield. Pack civilian clothes in those bags, the three men were told. Colby had strained his left knee ten days earlier. It still throbbed a bit. But he had no time to dwell on the pain, nor on the reason for the order to bring civilian clothes.

Promptly at 6 p.m., a Dodge truck pulled up at Milton Hall's entrance. Colby, Lelong, and Villebois climbed into the back and the vehicle sped off for London.

. . . .

By the beginning of July, one million Allied soldiers had come ashore to a beachhead only six miles deep in some places along the Normandy coast. A combination of the most tenacious of the Wehrmacht's force just ahead of them, high crisscrossing walls of gnarly hedgerows south of Bradley's army known as the "bocage," plus heavy storms that delayed the off-loading of equipment to break through defenses the Germans and Mother Nature had erected kept Eisenhower's force bottled up for much of July in the "Normandy pocket." By the end of the month, however, Sherman tanks fitted with hedge cutters began slicing through the bocage while a bold thrust code-named "Cobra" enabled the Allies to finally break out of the pocket. Lieutenant General George S. Patton Jr., whose 3rd Army was activated on August 1, had been ordered to send his VIII Corps west to clear the Brittany Peninsula so the Allies could use the ports at its tip to off-load arms and equipment. Jedburgh teams and British Special Air Service commandos had dropped in to organize some twenty thousand French Resistance members to attack ahead of VIII Corps and protect its flanks. From a special forces war room in London, Casey monitored their bloody, fierce battles, which ultimately proved to be a wasted effort. The Allies never used Brittany as a major port.

Meanwhile, the rest of Patton's 3rd Army and Lieutenant General Courtney Hodges's 1st Army pointed east in a race toward the River Seine, while Lieutenant General Alexander Patch's 7th Army landed on France's southern Riviera coast August 15 to march north. Hitler's mission for the Wehrmacht after the Normandy breakout: slow the Allied advance through France at least into September to buy him time. But Patton, whom a reporter once labeled a "roaring comet" and a West Point classmate called a "gamecock with brains," refused to be slowed. "Too many battles have been lost because of stopping on the wrong side of the river," he told his men. The 3rd Army would advance relentlessly, throwing everything it had at the Germans so they would have no time to organize a defense. Patton had palled around with Donovan in Virginia's horse country outside Washington, where the two men owned estates, and was among a handful of ground commanders who appreciated the type of unconventional warfare the OSS fought. Third Army planes and artillery would shower German soldiers with more than 31 million propaganda leaflets during its campaign. Patton was open to any help Donovan's saboteurs like the Jedburghs offered.

The success of French Resistance units so far encouraged Allied planners to dial up their missions for Patton's force driving east and Patch's moving just as rapidly north. On August 8, French general Marie-Pierre Koenig, whom Eisenhower had made commander of espionage and guerrilla agents in France, ordered twenty-six Jedburgh teams, including Colby's, to prepare to jump in quickly and organize Resistance forces ahead of the 3rd and 7th Armies.

Saturday night, August 12, the Dodge truck with Team Bruce inside pulled up to a nondescript row house at 46 Devonshire Close in central London. The three men noticed geraniums in the flower boxes of the flat across the narrow street. They bounded up the front steps to a dimly lit door opened by a heavyset older man with a service ribbon pinned to his civilian suit indicating he had fought in the last war. Inside the cramped town house a beehive of overworked British and American officers, female secretaries, and academic-looking men in tweed jackets and bow ties rushed up and down stairs and into and out of rooms with folders stamped SECRET under their arms and strained looks on their faces. Jedburgh teams were now being processed into and out of the "Briefing House" like cars on an assembly line. A woman in a British Army uniform curtly introduced herself to Colby and his comrades and told them she would be their "conducting officer" to watch over them until they boarded the plane for France. They could deposit their overnight bags in the bedrooms on the third floor, she told them, then head down to the second floor where the briefings would start immediately.

After dropping their bags on beds, they found the second-floor briefing room, set up like a classroom with small desks, tactical and Michelin maps covering all the walls and stacked on a conference table, and a blackboard with "Team Bruce" and their three code names written on it. They worked late into that night and resumed the next morning at 9 a.m. One briefing team after another trooped in with intelligence summaries, signal plans, code pads, country reports, photographs, and more maps (some printed on silk so they could stuff them into their pockets). The material began to pile up around the pot of tea and cups on the conference table. No question Bruce's members had would be left unanswered. A tall, gray-haired British lieutenant colonel from the Jedburgh office in London slipped in from time to time to observe from the back of the room.

They would be the thirty-first team dispatched from England, the briefers told them. Colby, Lelong, and Villebois will parachute into the Yonne Department southeast of Paris Sunday night. They would arrange for supplies to be delivered to the local Resistance network and guide its guerrillas in blowing bridges and rail lines, blocking roads, and ambushing German patrols, all to help Patton's 3rd Army closing in from the west.

Yonne, whose gentle rolling pastureland and vineyards once produced a rich bounty, now strained under food shortages and long lines for scarce goods in mostly empty village shops. The hungry wolves around its prefecture of Auxerre in the department's center had begun eating grapes from the vines as they did during previous famines. Townsfolk suspected the lethargic packs they saw suffered from the fruit juices fermenting in their stomachs.

The police state the Germans imposed on Yonne could not have been more oppressive. The Wehrmacht set clocks to Berlin time, imposed an 8 p.m. curfew, demanded identity papers and frisked citizens on streets at any time, required pedestrians to step off sidewalks when German soldiers passed by, draped red and black swastika flags from public buildings, required bicycle headlights be painted blue for nighttime blackout, ordered cinemas to show German newsreels, and forbade Frenchmen from listening to the BBC, singing the "Marseillaise," or raising carrier pigeons (a favorite Yonne pastime but the Nazis did not want them secreting out messages). The department, part of the Burgundy region, attracted the interest of Goebbels and other top Nazis who loved the fine wines from its vineyards. To keep his inner circle lubricated, Hitler put German wine merchants in uniform to buy the best bottles at wholesale prices. The French called them "weinführers."

Yonne and the neighboring Côte-d'Or Department to the east had a powerful Resistance circuit, a British briefer told Colby and his comrades. Its code name was "Donkeyman." Henri Frager, who went by the pseudonym "Jean-Marie," ran it. A former French captain in Algeria who had sneaked to the coast of Marseille aboard a British submarine in 1941, Frager was a slender, soft-spoken Alsatian with hair prematurely gray and a kind, almost feminine, face that grew animated when the passion in his voice rose. First helping to organize networks in southern France, Frager eventually moved north in 1943 to take over the Donkeyman Circuit, which after D-Day had seven hundred men in Yonne cutting roads, blowing bridges, and gumming up production in factories the Germans had commandeered. Frager would have a reception committee waiting for them at their parachute drop zone, Team Bruce was told. His two key aides in the circuit, the briefer said, looking through his file to find the names, were André Marsac and Roger Bardet.

Colby scribbled notes on his pad but stopped to raise his hand for a question. "What should we do if we fail to make contact with Frager or his men?" he asked. The British officer seemed flummoxed by the query. The staff had not planned for that problem. An aide rushed out of the room and returned later with the address for a safe house the team could use if Donkeyman's men couldn't be located at first.

More briefers filed into the room. Team Bruce would be flown in when there was no moon to illuminate the ground for the pilots. That would make it more difficult for them to find the drop zone. The air forces also would not fly too far north in France during moonless nights the rest of the month, which meant London might have difficulty keeping the team properly supplied. Signal officers told Villebois he would have only one radio set for the drop. If it's lost or damaged, they promised to send a replacement quickly. They told him to establish radio contact as soon as he could after landing. He received a schedule of times he could radio his reports, which differed depending on whether he was transmitting on an even- or odd-numbered day. A finance officer arrived and passed out canvas money belts for the men to strap around their waists. Colby's and Lelong's belts each had 100,000 francs. Villebois's had 50,000 francs. Their password when they finally met advance elements of Patton's army arriving in Yonne would be "Nancy."

Counterintelligence officers arrived to outline the dangers the team would face from the Gestapo, SD, Abwehr, and Vichy's Milice. Colby had read enough reports at Milton Hall on the enemy security services and their treatment of captured Jedburghs to know what to expect. The CI men said, however, that some captured British agents had been thrown off guard by Abwehr officers offering them afternoon tea across a table to lure them into talking. Among the torture techniques being reported to SOE were beatings with fists and clubs, electric shocks to the genitals, and dunks naked in ice-cold water until the prisoner thought he would drown. London will assume that if you are caught you will break, they were told. The dangers for Team Bruce would also be compounded by the fact that Resistance security was generally poor, the commandos would have no cover story if they were caught, and if they were apprehended in civilian clothes they surely would be shot. Colby was fearless but not foolhardy. He prided himself on taking sensible risks. The three men already had decided that wearing civilian clothes was sensible so they packed them in the bags sent to the airfield.

The rushed briefing ended late Sunday afternoon, August 13. Colby, Lelong, and Villebois grabbed their bags on the third floor, stuffed them with the maps, notes, and money belts they had collected at Devonshire Close. With their conducting officer they piled into the Dodge truck waiting outside. During the two-hour drive north to Station 61 she continued to read them updates for the mission. Station 61 was an ivy-covered country house just outside Northampton and about a dozen miles from the airfield. Heavily guarded, it served as a holding pen for espionage agents and commandos like the Jedburghs ready to drop into France. Busy officers in battle dress and cheery Auxiliary Territorial Service girls greeted the three men after they climbed out of the truck. They strolled into the manor's high-ceilinged lounge with flags, maps, and a dartboard on the walls, magazines and books stacked on shelves, and a phonograph, radio, and Ping-Pong table standing in corners.

After a sumptuous late evening supper in the dining hall, however, Team Bruce had distressful news to digest. Rain and low clouds closing in over the Burgundy region forced their flight to be canceled that night. No one else among Station 61's staff was surprised. Bad weather over France held up more parachute drops than Germans on the ground. The team would try again Monday night.

Early the next evening, August 14, the advancing Allied force on the ground struggled to close the Falaise Pocket trapping German Army Group B some 190 miles west of the Yonne Department. Above them the weather over France cleared. A large black American sedan with drawn curtains on its side window carried Team Bruce to Harrington Field. Their conducting officer, wedged between two of the men in the backseat, had an important update she received from London overnight. The Abwehr had arrested Henri Frager. His deputy, Roger Bardet, was now in charge of the Donkeyman Circuit and would be Team Bruce's key contact when they arrived. The news did not particularly bother the commandos in the car. It was "as though our announced hostess had taken sick and was replaced by a cousin," Colby later wrote.

The ride took about a half hour. With the sedan's light off for the blackout the driver had to crawl slowly along narrow country roads. Harrington Field, north of Northampton, was ideal for launching clandestine flights—three crisscrossing runways marked off on vast pastureland, all roads leading to them barricaded to keep out the curious, a damp wind almost always sweeping over the grassy fields muffling the roar of nearly fifty bombers and transport planes taking off or landing each night. What amounted to a small town of more than three thousand aviators, aircrewmen, and ground personnel occupied the field, housed in a tent city north of the runways. A guard post at the south end let in the black sedan, which drove past camouflaged bomb dumps and fuel tanks, then around the east–west runway to a Quonset hut where OSS dressers waited for Team Bruce.

The dressers took over when the three men arrived. All the pockets of the commandos' fatigues were first searched for any telltale items that might give away their unit. Each man then strapped around his waist the money belt issued at Devonshire Close, wrestled on a heavy vest, and climbed into a canvas skeletal webbing with hooks for carrying equipment attached to their bodies: a Colt .45 pistol in holster, an Army .30 caliber carbine rifle with a folding stock, a magazine pouch, canteen, binoculars, knife, parachute shovel, flashlight and a side haversack filled with a mess kit, two packets of dehydrated rations, washing and shaving kit, spare socks, high-neck sweater for when it turned chilly in fall, maps, compass, protractor, matches, whistle, water purifying tablets, morphine, a beret, a cap, field message pad with pencil, and a small flask of rum. A separate leg bag, which would be attached by a fifteen-foot rope to the commando's ankle and dropped out when he jumped, was packed with more rations, spare boots, extra ammunition, underwear, a sleeping bag, Hexamine cooker, first-aid kit, two candles, and toilet paper. Separate cylindrical containers with more equipment, explosives, Villebois's radio, and their civilian clothes (headquarters kept records of all their sizes for resupply) would be dumped out of the plane with them as well. Before helping the Jedburghs into their parachutes, three dressers fitted a waterproof parachute smock over each man so none of the equipment hanging from him would snag on the lines. That done, Colby, Lelong, and Villebois placed British parachute helmets on their heads and buckled the chinstraps.

They could hardly walk they were so stuffed with gear. The dressers pushed the three Jedburghs into a station wagon that drove them and their British escort to the runway, where a B-24 Liberator bomber had begun turning over its engines. Colby, Lelong, and Villebois pried themselves out of the wagon. Their conducting officer wished them good luck but the men couldn't hear her for all the noise from aircraft taxiing around the field. She would wait at Harrington Field until the B-24 returned, hopefully with news that the parachute drop had succeeded.

The commandos waddled like penguins to the plane. The Liberator crewmen chuckled as they hoisted the bulky bodies through the bomber's bottom hatch. Before he climbed aboard, Colby noticed *Slick Chick II* painted on the side of the Liberator under the cockpit window.

Slick Chick II belonged to the Army Air Forces' 492nd Bombardment Group, made up of four squadrons that dropped OSS commandos and spies into occupied France. They were called the "Carpetbaggers" after the code name for their operation. The aircrew for *Slick Chick II* did not know the names of the Jedburghs in Team Bruce and didn't want to know them. All the airmen were under strict orders not to talk to the agents they dropped or even to learn the names of other Carpetbagger crews at Harrington Field; that way, German intelligence could learn nothing from them if they were forced to bail out over enemy territory.

The airmen on this Liberator looked young and scared to Colby. Which was true on both counts. Roderick Ewart, the bomber's pilot, who hailed from Wyoming, was just shy of his twenty-second birthday. The other seven crewmen were in their early twenties as well. After more than two dozen missions, they all had good reason to be terrified with each new flight. Air defenses over Germany and German-occupied countries became so murderously thick the first six months of 1944 that for every one thousand American heavy bomber crewmen serving during that period, 887 were killed, wounded, or missing. Dropping agents instead of bombs posed its own special risks. Crews debated which was more dangerous. For a bombing raid the Liberators simply had to follow the lead plane in formations often protected by fighter aircraft. Bomber crews could talk to one another after their missions. Carpetbagger missions were lone-wolf operations planned meticulously by pilots and their navigators with only the machine guns on board to protect them if they got in trouble. There was also no camaraderie to enjoy after a mission—just the relief of surviving another flight.

As Ewart and his copilot, Walter Saline, ran through their checklists in the cockpit, dispatcher Sidney Kagan busied himself buckling Colby, Lelong, and Villebois to hard wooden benches in the cabin and tying down their gear. The mass-produced B-24 bomber was an ugly beast, painted black for these missions, with four engines on its wings—hard for pilots to handle yet speedy, reliable, and durable with a three-thousand-mile range. Standard equipment in the cockpit and flight deck had been replaced with special radios and navigation gear for low-level flying at night. Much of the hardware in the rest of the Liberator's fuselage had been stripped so it could carry agents and their containers. Plywood had been placed over the plane's corrugated metal floor for passengers and crew to walk on, strong hooks were bolted to the sides for parachute static lines, and red and green jump lights had been installed along with handrails for operatives and the dispatcher to clutch when they moved to ready for a jump. All the plane's armaments had been removed save for .50-caliber machine guns in the upper and tail turrets. Instead of a ball turret underneath the fuselage, smooth metal lined a forty-four-inch-wide hole. A circular plywood door atop it, divided and hinged in the middle, could be opened in flight. This was the "Joe hole" Colby, Lelong, and Villebois would jump through to parachute out of the aircraft.

At 10:21 p.m., Ewart and Saline pushed the throttles forward and the Liberator rumbled down the runway. A dim orange-yellow light glowed in the cabin. Tattered blackout curtains covered the fuselage's tiny windows so Colby and the others could see nothing outside. Kagan plugged the intercom line into his headset and throat mike, then handed Colby and Lelong headsets so they could listen to the cockpit chatter. The engine roar made talking in the cabin next to impossible.

The skies over England as *Slick Chick II* sped south were like a freeway at rush hour with aircraft going to and from France. The Liberator reached

Littlehampton on Britain's southern coast at 11:01 p.m. The trip across the English Channel took another twenty-seven minutes. Ewart, who had been flying at nine thousand feet, dipped the B-24 to around two thousand feet to avoid German radar. Colby and the others felt their ears pop during the descent. Bombardier George Boes, sitting in a swivel seat in the glassed nose turret, radioed the cockpit when he spotted their first checkpoint at Életot on the French coast north of Le Havre. Ewart took a roundabout route his navigator, George Habor, had plotted to Yonne, banking sharply right or left to avoid searchlights and antiaircraft batteries along the way. The pilots never flew the same route to anywhere in France so German air defenses would not detect a pattern. Boes's hunt for landmarks on the ground to guide the plane was made more difficult this night, however, because no moon illuminated them. An occasional Luftwaffe fighter still lurked in the French skies. If one stumbled on *Slick Chick II*, the pilot would dive to two hundred feet or head for clouds hopefully to escape. Otherwise, the only threat Ewart and Saline expected tonight was stray ground fire from Wehrmacht soldiers who might hear them coming. Fortunately, by the time an excited trooper unslung his rifle to shoot, their bomber usually would be long gone.

Shortly after 1 a.m., Colby and Lelong heard through their headsets the navigator and bombardier alerting Ewart that they were approaching the drop zone at empty farmland around Joigny, just northwest of Auxerre in the Yonne Department. Ewart banked the plane and descended to hunt for the lights the Donkeyman reception committee on the ground would illuminate to signal the location of the drop zone—for this night, three bonfires blazing in a triangular pattern. The voices on the intercom took on a nervous edge, Colby could tell. Reception committees often had notoriously poor security. A noisy bomber circling overhead alerted everyone within hearing distance. Sometimes, Germans set bonfires on the ground to lure a plane into an antiaircraft ambush. Ewart dropped *Slick Chick II* to begin a circle at about five hundred feet, dangerously close for ground fire. He lowered his wing flaps to slow to 130 miles per hour, just barely above the speed at which the plane could stall and plunge to earth.

The red light in the cabin flashed signaling that the Jedburghs should prepare to jump. Kagan shouted, "Action stations!" and lifted the plywood cover off the Joe hole. The roar from the engines outside became almost deafening. With their static lines hooked, Colby, Lelong, and Villebois, clutching leg bags, shuffled forward to sit around the lip of the opening, their dangling legs buffeted by the onrushing wind. The bombardier and pilots spotted the fires on the ground five minutes later during the pass.

The red light extinguished. A green light flashed. Kagan shouted, "Go!" and patted each man on the shoulder. One by one, Lelong, Colby, then Villebois jumped through the hole, the static line attached to each parachute opening it automatically. Ewart and Saline glanced out their windows and saw three billowing chutes. The pilot circled for a second pass so Kagan could shove out the dozen supply containers to parachute down after the team.

Ewart flew a different zigzag course back to the English Channel, dropping propaganda leaflets for another mission at Boissy-lès-Perche and Ypreville-Biville at the French coast. Reaching England's coast the *Slick Chick II* crew remained tense. British antiaircraft batteries might mistake their black bomber for a Luftwaffe plane and shoot it down. Kagan fired flares out an open window with a prearranged color to signal this was a friendly aircraft. The crew prayed the AA batteries recognized the signal.

Landing back at Harrington shortly after 3 a.m., Ewart reported to his superiors and Team Bruce's conducting officer that the mission had been successful. The reception committee's light signal on the ground was "clearly flashed" and the crew saw the three parachutes open with no problem.

• • • •

Many years later, Colby would say in half jest that he spent the rest of the war looking for the pilot who dropped him into France.

Even with helmet and goggles on, the blast in the face from the slipstream hit him like an onrushing lineman. The harness jerked his shoulders. He heard the rustle of silk, looked up, saw his chute spreading open. Instinctively in the next second he yanked down hard on the front risers, held his feet together, pulled his knees up, closed his elbows to his body and looked down to prepare for the landing he knew would come quickly in a five-hundred-foot jump.

Something was wrong. Seriously wrong. Instead of empty farmland rushing to him Colby saw the rooftops of an obviously crowded urban area. Instead of three bonfires arranged in a triangle that the pilots thought they saw, Colby saw a single line of fire. (He learned later it was a train burning on a track in a marshaling yard, shot up by Allied planes several nights earlier and then attacked by Resistance saboteurs.)

No time to think. He swung his legs out of the way so they wouldn't hit a tile roof with chimney pots. He crashed into a backyard, grazing a chicken coop. Feathers flew. Hens began squawking. It sounded to Colby like every dog in France was now barking. Lights turned on in homes around him. People rudely awakened opened window shutters and shouted in French.

Villebois and Lelong, who was nearly impaled on a picket fence, had landed nearby. They quickly climbed out of their parachute harnesses and ran down the street to a front yard where Colby crouched. "Where are we?" Colby whispered to Lelong, although there was not much need to. The dozen supply chutes banged on rooftops or clattered down cobblestone streets, pretty much waking the entire town. A group of bleary-eyed villagers in bathrobes and nightcaps now closed in on them. They gathered around Lelong and in rapid-fire French informed him that the team had landed on the outskirts of Montargis, a town over twenty miles west of their drop zone in Joigny. Montargis was a medieval commune in the Loiret Department west of Yonne, laced with so many canals and bridges it billed itself as a mini Venice. Lelong worried more about the latest addition to Montargis, a German garrison the crowd in the front yard told him was just a few hundred yards up the main street and was surely roused by their noisy landing.

There was no time to gather the supply canisters scattered all over town. The men had to flee with the sidearms and few supplies they had on their backs. Villebois had radio crystals in his jumpsuit pocket. Lelong and Colby had codes, maps, and mission instructions in theirs. The containers with more arms and supplies for the Donkeyman Circuit, Villebois's radio, plus their civilian clothes—they would have to abandon all of it. The SOE had precise timelines for what a Jedburgh team like Bruce should accomplish, down to each half hour after they landed. Colby, Lelong, and Villebois had to throw that out the window and run for their lives. Lelong flipped open his compass to determine his direction. "We've got to go south-southeast," he said, pointing the way.

The three men ran to the railroad track past the burning cars and followed it until they reached the countryside. There they decided to leave the track (they feared it might be guarded ahead) and cut across wooded farmland. They were about six miles out and about fifty yards from a road headed west to Montargis when early dawn began to lighten the sky Tuesday morning, August 15. The Germans from the garrison had searched practically every home in the commune looking for parachutists and had begun sending hunting parties into the countryside. Colby, Lelong, and Villebois decided to hide in a shallow ditch near the road, covering themselves with leaves, and to stay there until nightfall when they could move more freely. Occasionally they peeked out of the leaves and saw on the highway truck and armored vehicle convoys of Wehrmacht divisions retreating east from the Normandy battlefield, along with smaller patrols they assumed the Montargis garrison had dispatched to hunt for them. Colby wondered, as they lay there all day, "how in the world I had gotten into this," he recalled later.

When night fell, the team climbed out of the ditch and began walking on a compass bearing toward the Donkeyman safe house London had given them for the Yonne Department. At midnight a ferocious summer thunderstorm erupted turning fields into muddy swamps and making it difficult for them to see more than a few feet ahead. Colby, Lelong, and Villebois tied their pistol lanyards to one another so they wouldn't become separated and lost. By 2 a.m., wet and miserable, they had not slogged far. Suddenly they heard faint voices ahead, perhaps laughter. A German patrol? French farmers? A flash of lightning illuminated a lone farmhouse just ahead. They crept up to it. Lights appeared to be on inside. Curious, Colby thought. It was far too late for farmers to still be awake. Lelong decided to chance it and knock on the door. He ordered Colby and Villebois to cover him with their pistols from nearby bushes.

Lelong tapped gently on the door. It opened slightly and the barrel of a rifle pushed out pointed at his nose.

"Qui est là?" a voice inside asked.

"Un français," Lelong replied.

The gun barrel motioned him inside and the door closed.

Colby and Villebois tensed. A minute later—it seemed to them like an hour—Lelong emerged. "It's all right," he called out to them with a wave of his hand. "Come on in."

As luck would have it, this cottage, named La Fourmilloire and located just north of the town of Châteaurenard, was a Resistance radio post. One of the two Frenchmen inside had parachuted in from England eight days earlier. La Fourmilloire's radio operator sent a short message to England that Team Bruce had arrived, but in the wrong spot. Exhausted, Colby, Lelong, and Villebois slept in the cottage the rest of the day.

The next morning, August 17, as Patton's XII Corps secured Orléans some seventy miles west of them, the three commandos, dressed in worn-out farm clothes their hosts provided, climbed into a beat-up Citroën a nearby doctor with the Resistance provided. Its gasogene engine burned charcoal because of the fuel shortage. At one point having to wait as a German convoy passed a crossroads, the Jedburghs were driven the last fifteen miles of their journey to the safe house in Yonne. Donkeyman operatives passed them through their network until they ended up later that afternoon in Sommecaise, a village outside of Auxerre where Roger Bardet kept his headquarters.

The Citroën stopped in front of Sommecaise's only café. Colby, Lelong, and Villebois climbed out of the car and hurried inside. Seated at a table in the corner before a bottle of red wine and a plate of food was Bardet, a tall and wiry man in his early thirties with jet-black hair, and, Colby thought, small, dark, beady eyes that darted about restlessly. Colby saw that he had several armed bodyguards around him who eyed the three of them suspiciously. Bardet, who operated under four different cover names, stood up with a blank look on his face and shook their hands. He had his minions fetch chairs so everyone could sit and snapped his fingers for a waiter to serve the Jedburghs food.

"Where have you been?" Bardet asked impassively. "We've been waiting three days. We had the signal fires but no plane came."

Lelong recounted their calamitous jump and narrow escape from Montargis. The food arrived while Bardet explained his setup. Tiny Resistance bands were scattered all over Yonne, the former French air force lieutenant told the commandos in a low voice, their ranks swelling as a result of a call to arms he issued three days before. He could count on about five hundred armed fighters now, but a half dozen other Resistance warlords in the department controlled other guerrillas. The Germans had garrisons of about five hundred soldiers each in two or three large towns here, while retreating Wehrmacht convoys moved through Yonne under light guard.

"We're here to help you fight the Germans," Colby said, pulling a map out of his coat pocket and spreading it out on the table. He began firing questions at Bardet about his network and the units other chiefs ran. "These are the things we need to know so we can bring in more arms, coordinate our actions with the invading Allied armies, and hurt the enemy as much as we can." The team had been briefed in London that the Donkeyman Circuit had been told to lie low until orders came for attacks in full force. But Bardet now seemed not particularly eager to begin the battle. He looked to Colby more like a petty civil servant going through the motions instead of a forceful and dynamic guerrilla leader.

Practically all the Jedburghs had parachuted into complicated situations. Reports came back to Colby while they waited at Milton Hall that teams had encountered Resistance chiefs who were poor leaders, insubordinate, or had their own agendas. Britain's SOE had begun with ironclad rules that no one would be brought into one of their French circuits until Baker Street had thoroughly vetted the operative, but by spring 1944 with Resistance ranks ballooning quickly there was no time for elaborate checks. France had become a nation of prisoners, deprived on the ground of life's basics by a brutal occupier and bombed from the air by Allies come to liberate them; some rationalized collaboration as the only way to survive. Espionage agents in France sometimes operated under their own moral compass. If cornered by the Nazis some found no problem working for them, trying to do as little harm as possible with the information they delivered, then returning to the Allied side as soon as they could, to pass along what they had learned working for the enemy. London received warnings some operatives had come under German control but often imprudently discounted them.

Something didn't feel right to Colby about Roger Bardet. For every initiative they suggested that afternoon in Sommecaise, the Frenchman had a reason why it couldn't be done. What Colby did not know, and would not learn until after the war, was that Bardet was a traitor—a dangerous double agent under the control of the Abwehr.

. . . .

Bardet had been turned by one of the most skilled and cunning German counterintelligence agents in France—Hugo Bleicher, who went by seven pseudonyms and was responsible for some of the most serious damage done to the Allies' clandestine networks in France. Hardly an impressive man—he was going bald and wore thick black glasses over a beak nose and puffy red face—Bleicher nevertheless had an innate talent, he liked to say, for convincing French agents to betray their country "on the pretext of serving a noble cause."

Nothing in his background before the war suggested Bleicher would be one of the Nazis' master spy catchers in France. A minor Hamburg businessman with a dull marriage that had produced one child, Bleicher, at age forty, had been drafted to be a low-level policeman in France after the invasion. Like many Germans in the country, he soon took a mistress—his was named Suzanne Laurent, an attractive bar owner in Caen who remained with him the rest of the war. He was recruited by the Abwehr in spring 1941 and quickly showed a gift for reading the French mind, enticing collaborators, and disrupting Resistance networks near Normandy. By December 1942, he had taken on expanded counterintelligence duties with the promise that he would be made an officer. The promotion never happened, which left Sergeant Bleicher bitter. He often introduced himself to potential informants as "Colonel Henri" so they would believe he was a big shot in the Abwehr. Briefly he also flirted with the idea of defecting to the Allies. But he soon resolved himself to serving what he expected to be a lost Axis cause. In 1943, working out of an office on Avenue Henri-Martin in Paris, Bleicher took over the Abwehr's most ambitious operation to break up the SOE's networks in France. Under the code name "Grossfürst" (for Grand Duke) he set out to penetrate Donkeyman and other big Resistance circuits.

His infiltration of Donkeyman began in March 1943 when he arrested André Marsac, one of its operatives. Visiting his cell at Fresnes prison south of Paris for hours each day, Bleicher convinced the tall, thin, and gullible Marsac that he too hated the Nazis and now wanted to defect. Won over, Marsac spilled details on the circuit including the name of its leader, Henri Frager, and a key lieutenant, Roger Bardet, whom Bleicher let visit his comrade in prison to begin cultivating him. Bleicher next had SD thugs arrest Bardet and throw him in Fresnes. The unscrupulous Bardet wasted no time when Bleicher paid his first visit. "Let me go free and I will work for you," he told Colonel Henri. The Abwehr sergeant arranged for him to escape from Fresnes.

The SOE normally distrusted Resistance agents who fled enemy custody, assuming the Nazis let them go to spy on their old employer. Some British officers, as well as OSS counterintelligence agents, found Bardet's escape from heavily guarded Fresnes extremely suspicious and wondered if he had become a double agent. But London had no evidence he was now passing secrets to the Germans. More importantly, Frager naively believed Bardet's escape story and promoted him to be his deputy for Donkeyman.

Bardet became a highly valuable informant, delivering to Bleicher more details on Donkeyman's organization and personnel, copies of its messages, schedules for supply drops to the circuit, and updates on Frager's movements throughout France. Abwehr agents seized many parachuted containers when they hit the ground and arrested or shadowed other Donkeyman operatives. Among the valuable tidbits Bardet turned over: the key given to Frager for decoding last-minute instructions the BBC would broadcast to the Resistance when the Normandy invasion began. Fortunately for the Allies, the Wehrmacht ignored the intelligence when the Abwehr passed it up the chain of command. Bleicher rewarded Bardet with a raise in the monthly salary he slipped him—from 6,000 to 10,000 francs. To help gather his intelligence haul, the Abwehr agent also assigned him one of his other turncoats—Raoul Kiffer, aka Kiki, who had been a French air force sergeant.

In a café off Paris's Champs-Élysées, Bardet in August 1943 set up the first of three meetings Bleicher would have with Henri Frager. As it did with others, Colonel Henri's charm worked its magic on the Donkeyman leader. Bleicher convinced Frager he was a closet anti-Nazi, sweetening his pitch by revealing the name of another French guerrilla leader collaborating with the SD. (Bleicher despised the Nazi Party intelligence service and didn't mind burning one of its informants). Frager, who had first introduced himself as Bardet's uncle who was not active in the Resistance, felt he had bonded with the Abwehr man. He revealed to him his true identity.

After the successful Normandy invasion, Bardet, as well as Kiki, could clearly see the tide of battle changing. The two traitors began to distance themselves from their Abwehr handler. Bleicher found it more difficult to get in contact with them. Meanwhile, senior SD officers in Paris, fed up with all the games they thought Bleicher had been playing with the Donkeyman Circuit, pressured him to arrest Frager, which he did on July 2, 1944, at a Paris Métro station on Boulevard du Montparnasse. A few days later at the Gestapo's prison on Rue des Saussaies, where Frager was being held, Bleicher told him of Bardet's betrayal and promised that he would get even for him. It was clear to Bleicher by this time that Bardet was switching sides once more.

Frager, however, set a new record for magnanimity. "I have always looked on Roger as a son," he told Bleicher. "I beg you, let us settle all this after the war."

Bleicher never saw Frager again—nor Bardet for the rest of the war. The Frenchman had moved to Yonne to take command of the Donkeyman Circuit and wait for a Jedburgh team London had promised would be arriving within weeks. With his mistress, Bleicher relocated to Auxerre. By early August, however, he became suspicious that Bardet wanted to trap him and turn him over to the Allies to cover his tracks. He took Suzanne and moved southeast to Dijon in the next department.

· · · ·

After their meeting in the Sommecaise café, Villebois borrowed the radio set of an SOE operator who had infiltrated into Yonne in May to provide Donkeyman with a communications link to London. Promptly at 4:30 that afternoon (his prearranged transmission time) Team Bruce's radioman quickly tapped out in Morse code a telegraph message beamed to a receiving station designated Charles that the SOE and OSS had set up for Jedburgh traffic in Poundon, a hamlet in southern England. Station Charles had a large British and American staff skilled in quickly deciphering coded messages, even if they arrived partly garbled, and relaying them to London.

Team Bruce's lone radio, known as a "Jed Set"—a clunky thirty-two pounds of shortwave transmitter, receiver, and accessories that was a modified version of a Type B Mark II—was somewhere in Montargis, likely being picked apart by a German soldier. Fortunately, when he landed in the commune Villebois had in his jacket pocket his pad with code sheets used one time only, which was identical to the pad at Station Charles so he and the station could encipher and decipher messages arranged in randomly selected five-letter groups. He also had saved from the jump his signal plan, written on silk in English and French, which included the times and frequencies for his sending radio messages and the three-letter call signs he should use.

Transmitting wireless telegraphy always put a Jedburgh team in danger. Villebois had to assume the Germans were listening in and with skilled radio-direction-finding teams they could be at his doorstep within a half hour if they picked up his signal. So he used the radio as little as possible, transmitted at random times (often in the middle of the night) and kept his transmissions short to give the enemy less opportunity to triangulate his signal. Before he left Milton Hall, Villebois recorded a taped message with his style of tapping out each letter of the alphabet—called his "fist"—so Station Charles could determine if the message they were receiving from Team Bruce was from him or a Nazi radioman pretending to be him. If the Gestapo captured Villebois and forced him to send a message, he had pre-arranged codes, like a deliberate spelling mistake, to slip into the message alerting the station he was transmitting under duress.

"Arrived safely," Villebois's clipped message to Station Charles began. "Burning train taken for committee. All equipment dropped in town. Send new radio. Are now with Roger." He described the forces Bardet had but cautioned that German garrisons around them were "thick north and east of Auxerre." He ended his transmission with a plea for more arms.

"Delighted to hear you at last," Station Charles radioed the next day. "Sorry about bad dropping. Will send radio equipment." It will arrive August 19, Charles said, hopefully at the spot where the team should have landed near Joigny.

Bardet never betrayed Team Bruce to the Abwehr, realizing that with Patton's tanks barreling across France he would be on the wrong side if he did. The clever Frenchman now tried to straddle the fence, not helping the Germans but at the same time not angering the Germans by helping the Americans. When he was with the Jedburghs he talked a good game about fighting the Nazis, but did little else.

Others in the Donkeyman Circuit had their suspicions. In April 1944, Peggy Knight, a petite twenty-one-year-old English typist who spoke flawless French, had parachuted into Yonne to serve as an SOE courier for the circuit, easily talking her way through German checkpoints to deliver messages to guerrilla outposts. Bardet, she said, always looked "like a hunted man." She began to suspect his loyalties when he didn't show up at an agreed-upon rendezvous one night, but a Nazi patrol did. "Nicole" (Peggy's code name) barely escaped the enemy roundup. When Colby arrived, she confided to him her doubts.

Colby, however, had no evidence to suggest that Bardet actually was a traitor. Years later, he would tell his sons the Frenchman might have had at least one opportunity to turn him over to the Nazis. In late August, before Patch's 7th Army had captured Lyon in the south, Bardet had driven Colby to France's third-largest city, once a hotbed for Resistance activity but still a regional center for the Gestapo. Mounting bicycles when they arrived, the two had ridden dangerously close to a building Bardet identified as the Gestapo's headquarters. Colby grew uneasy and biked down another street with Bardet following. The tense moment passed.

But after their first meeting in the Sommecaise café, Colby thought he was simply stuck for now with a lackadaisical and somewhat incompetent Resistance leader. He would have to make the best of it, he decided, since the only radio the team had at the moment to communicate with London belonged to Bardet and the Frenchman was not generous with it. Lelong and Colby immediately began hunting for better guerrilla leaders. They thought they had found one two days later. Adrien Sadoul was a sixty-year-old lawyer from Metz and a former French army reserve officer. Flamboyant, charismatic, and a bit imperious, Sadoul, who went by the pseudonym "Colonel Chevrier," could deliver spellbinding speeches to troops and claimed that de Gaulle had appointed him the Resistance commander for the Yonne Department. Colonel Chevrier's only problem—he had few troops under him. Bardet led the larger force—although he didn't seem to Colby and Lelong to command the respect of his soldiers that Chevrier did—and he claimed that he had been appointed chief of Yonne as Frager's replacement.

Colby and Lelong immediately began sorting out the chain of command and acting as intermediary between the two rival leaders, though they believed Chevrier would be the better combat commander. Villebois radioed Station Charles on August 19 that the team had "met Chevrier" and was more impressed with him. Headquarters in London messaged back the next day that it wanted Team Bruce to "work with all elements willing to take up arms with the Germans, whatever their political ideas." Colby and Lelong quickly found that the factions were many. Cunin Bernard, a guerrilla leader who went by the name "Georges," had about four hundred Maquis fighters southeast of Auxerre. Jean Chapelle, a young and energetic Parisian whose code name was "Vernouil," had six hundred armed men in Quarré-les-Tombes at the southern tip of Yonne. And "Yvon" (code name for Guy Charles) oversaw three hundred French communists throughout the department. All the commanders told Colby and Lelong they could put more men in the field if they had more arms.

Villebois, who received his replacement radio from England on August 19, began firing off radio messages to Station Charles requesting arms for the different factions. For his "men pouring in," Bardet's alone needed one thousand rifles and 2 million francs, the Jedburgh telegraphed. Resistance spies reported that remnants of the Germans' 192nd Infantry Regiment were fleeing east through Yonne, ripe targets for guerrilla harassing attacks. "Our men anxious for big action," Villebois messaged London.

Carpetbagger bombers began flying over Yonne parachuting supplies to secluded fields Chevrier selected. A dozen air deliveries came during the next two weeks. Villebois listened for nonsense phrases that followed Beethoven's Fifth Symphony on the BBC nightly news broadcast to France. They contained the code for the field in Yonne that would receive the air-drop at midnight. Colby, Lelong, and a receiving party crouched behind bushes. When they heard the sound of the plane they lit signal fires set in a prearranged letter pattern in the field to designate the drop zone. Then they ducked to avoid the heavy sausagelike containers crashing down on their heads in the dark.

The two Jedburgh officers began training the new guerrilla recruits in how to shoot and clean their weapons and advising their commanders on how to organize companies to launch attacks. It was a difficult job. The soldiering skills of even the veteran guerrillas were poor. Maquis fighters, for example, liked to fire up the entire clip in their machine guns rather than delivering short bursts and conserving ammunition. But within weeks, Yonne's irregular army had tripled in number by Colby's estimate.

He and Lelong began going out on missions with the guerrillas they trained to ambush German patrols, harass road convoys, and blow up enemy supply depots. A Luftwaffe fighter was forced to land in a field after it ran out of fuel. Colby led a company of guerrillas to seize the plane and the pilot. He learned quickly his fighters were no match for a Wehrmacht company, which also arrived at the scene. His guerrillas managed to shoot up the plane but had to flee in the face of overwhelming firepower from the Germans, who set fire to the aircraft so the Resistance couldn't use it. "Straight fighting job ahead," Villebois telegraphed London on August 21. But the team now urgently needed mortars, bazookas, and smaller portable antitank weapons called "Piats" for infantry assaults. Colby and Lelong soon realized those assaults had to be hit-and-run raids, aiming first for Wehrmacht officers in a convoy or patrol, then every man flees in a different direction to escape a counterattack. Their guerrillas were mauled when they tried to fight it out with battle-hardened and still-well-armed German soldiers.

Colby, Lelong, and Villebois quickly settled into a routine of distributing weapons, training men, venturing out on missions, and haggling with Resistance leaders. Their war became a lonely, exhausting one, interrupted by brief moments of horror. They tried to maintain military bearing, but baths and shaves were rare, and most of the time they wore shabby civilian clothes with their ranks pinned to a collar. To gain the trust of the guerrillas, they had to live like them, which meant primitive meals around campfires, tobacco a luxury, roasted acorns substituted for coffee. They did not suffer a conventional infantryman's day-to-day slugfest forward; they struck quickly and escaped. Fortunately, the enemy could not be everywhere in Yonne so they often could travel in their civilian clothes for distances and not confront a German soldier and if they did they could usually count on being smarter than the trooper and talking their way out of the encounter. But they had no unit to back them up, no cavalry to come to the rescue, no rear echelon they could return to for rest and relaxation. There was little time for uninterrupted sleep. Messages with encouragement from headquarters were rare. Mail drops were infrequent at best. They fought alone. They spent as much time watching their backs among the French guerrillas as they did forming lasting friendships. For camaraderie Colby, Lelong, and Villebois had just one another.

Yet the mission invigorated the three commandos. They were ready for bolder action. A Resistance leader arrived from Paris on August 21 and asked for airdrops to embattled guerrillas in the Hôtel de Ville. No German antiaircraft batteries remained in the city to threaten Allied planes, Villebois radioed headquarters the next day. The Jedburghs recommended that small arms and antitank weapons be parachuted night or day to nearby Île de la Cité, an island on the Seine in the city center where Notre-Dame Cathedral stood. "We realized that this was an unprecedented idea," Colby later wrote in his after-action report, "but considered the publicity and morale effect extremely large and worth the chance of the operation." London never responded. The brash members of Team Bruce did not realize the bigger issues at play. Not wanting to interrupt his drive toward Germany, Eisenhower originally intended to bypass Paris—thus avoiding costly street fighting and having to feed a city of five million. The Nazis, he reasoned, would have to surrender the city anyway after the Allied armies cut their northern supply lines. Further fueling a Paris insurrection at this point, as Team Bruce proposed, was not in Ike's game plan. Relentless pressure from de Gaulle had finally forced him to approve liberation of the city. Two days after Team Bruce sent its message, Major General Jacques Philippe Leclerc's French 2nd Armored Division, backed up by America's 4th Infantry Division, marched on Paris.

On August 26, Chevrier's guerrillas liberated Auxerre. That day Colby crossed the American lines to visit Patton's 3rd Army headquarters near Orléans and west of Yonne. Berlin no longer controlled combat operations in France. Its troops there were burned out, its senior field generals ignored the more unrealistic of Hitler's Führer Orders, and did their best to organize a fighting retreat to defenses at the German border. The only reprieve for Wehrmacht forces near Yonne: Patton's speedy advance, breathtaking up to this point, was now slowed by supply and fuel shortages. Colby and Lelong had been given a set of passwords at Harrington Field to exchange when crossing through American lines but it was still a risky maneuver. Allied units had been running into stay-behind German agents dressed in American uniforms so the 3rd Army's lead elements were automatically suspicious of this scruffy-looking man in civilian clothes who claimed he was an OSS major. An armed guard hustled Colby to the OSS detachment assigned to Patton's headquarters, where a security officer confronted him with a prearranged question to determine if he was legitimate.

"Do you know a girl named Rusty Allen?" the security officer asked.

"Yes, she is in the WAVES," Colby responded with the correct answer.

He updated the detachment officers on the different Resistance factions in Yonne, whose total number had swollen to more than six thousand. The OSS men at 3rd Army had news for him: London had picked Chevrier to be the overall leader for the department.

Colby and Lelong had been sending spies, including the fearless Peggy Knight, to towns like Montargis west of Yonne to scout enemy concentrations ahead of the 4th Division in Patton's army and report their locations to its intelligence officers. When the 3rd Army, with fuel in its tanks once more, began pushing east and northeast, the two Jedburghs decided their mission should be organizing harassing raids against German troops to keep them as far away as possible from Patton's right flank as his force plowed through Yonne. One of the reasons they were now visiting Patton's headquarters was to obtain written orders to protect the 3rd Army's right flank. Patton, whose eyes pointed only forward, declared: "Let the other son of a bitch worry about flanks." He had reason to be cocky. Ultra intercepts had revealed to him that the Germans were intent on retreating, not nipping at his side. If any danger did materialize from the south he was content to let airpower and French guerrillas deal with it so he could save his force for the offensive. Lieutenant Colonel Robert "Rip" Powell, a former New York architect and now the OSS detachment leader, handed Colby an order from Patton to defend his right flank.

. . . .

Several days later, Casey arrived at Patton's headquarters—appearing as unmilitary as Colby had been with mismatched fatigues and an ill-fitting helmet. He enjoyed portraying himself in letters to Sophia as an "old field soldier," but he was hardly that. What Casey had become was a senior Bruce adviser, promoted to full lieutenant (it boost his monthly paycheck by $50) and responsible for investigating problems not only in London but also on the continent. In addition, Donovan had made Casey one of his eyes and ears for Europe and sent him on a month-long August tour of France, Italy, and North Africa. He became at times a tourist, obtaining rosaries touched by Pope Pius XII to mail to Sophia, punishing his sensitive stomach with three-hour Italian lunches, and writing home that their cities were like "any Italian section of any American city." With a locked briefcase full of classi-fied documents chained to his wrist practically all the time, Casey showed a keen administrative eye for how spying should be conducted. Taking a microscope to OSS operations in Italy, he cabled Donovan lengthy reports on espionage, propaganda, and sabotage initiatives that could be improved. OSS intelligence officers in uniform are wandering about Rome vacuuming political secrets "a good newspaperman will get in the course of his rounds," he noted in one report. Their work should be married with research analysts sent to do the same. Meanwhile, Britain's MI6 is infiltrating spies into the liberated city under business cover to ferret economic information. "We should certainly get intelligence on this," he advised. Donovan circulated the recommendations among his senior staff.

In France, Casey toured Lyon and other southern cities that Patch's 7th Army had liberated, impressed with the spy networks Henry Hyde, another young agent who was a Donovan favorite, had organized there. He flew to Paris on August 28 as OSS officers poured into the city requisitioning rooms in the finest hotels for their offices. Several days later he motored to Patton's command post for a briefing from its OSS detachment on the operations to protect his flank. Rip Powell filled Casey in on an aggressive Jedburgh named Colby who was organizing a guerrilla guard south of the 3rd Army.

• • • •

The human toll of the French campaign had been heavy by the end of August. The Americans had suffered 134,000 dead, wounded, missing in action, or captured. The British, Canadian, and Polish casualties: 91,000. French Resistance killed would eventually number 24,000, French civilian deaths as many as 67,000. German casualties exceeded 400,000. The Allies now had two million men in France, twice as many as the Germans, twenty times more tanks. In the north on a broad front from Le Havre to Troyes, Field Marshal Montgomery's 21st Army Group and Bradley's 12th Army

Group had surged across the Seine with Patton's 3rd Army jutting farthest on the right. Meanwhile from the south, Patch's 7th Army and General Jean de Lattre de Tassigny's 1st French army marched relentlessly north up the Rhône Valley and past Lyon. The number of OSS agents and commandos spying on or attacking Germans ahead of the Allied advances had doubled to 225 in August. With General Koenig now calling for a mass guerrilla uprising, Jedburghs all over the country directed ambushes on retreating convoys, radioed bombing targets to air forces, rescued airmen for evacuation to London, and when overrun by Allied armies served as guides and intelligence officers for their advance.

By the beginning of September, Colby and Lelong had all of Yonne's Resistance factions, which amounted to a regiment of guerrillas Chevrier led out of Auxerre, operating off a common battle plan protecting Patton's right flank. As with everything having to do with the Resistance, the path to a unified command had been bumpy. On August 30, the faction leaders briefly revolted and demanded that a committee replace Chevrier as the department's leader, an impractical idea Colby and Lelong quickly talked them out of.

Haggling with OSS headquarters bureaucrats became maddening for Colby as well. On August 27, the day after Chevrier's forces entered Auxerre, Colby had Villebois radio London asking for a C-47 Dakota transport to land at its airport with supplies. For the next two weeks he got such a runaround it "destroy[ed] what faith we had in" headquarters, Colby wrote in his after-action report. He had carefully inspected and measured the Auxerre airport and radioed London it could handle a Dakota landing. London radioed that it heard a rumor the airfield had been mined. Colby radioed back that he had personally driven all over it to make sure it was clear. London dispatchers radioed they would not send the plane unless a trained air traffic controller was brought in to guide it. (Landing at makeshift fields the Resistance set up could be dangerous for pilots.) Colby radioed back that he had that training. More conditions came for the field's landing lights and signals. Colby met them. Bureaucratic delays or foul-ups from headquarters in sending supply drops were a constant headache for Jedburgh teams in the field. Requests overwhelmed London air staffers so sometimes messages pleading for arms went unanswered. Some teams were deluged with weapons, others received little or nothing, while still others opened containers to find the wrong stuff. One team that requested a shipment of sleeping bags got lamp shades instead. The American commandos who were shortchanged lost face with French guerrillas. Frustrated with the foot-dragging Colby finally called off the arms drop.

Colby could see the war moving quickly through their department. Patton's 3rd Army surged across Yonne's northern half; his headquarters ordered guerrilla units along the way to keep traffic lanes through cities open for his supply convoys, to protect bridges they needed to cross, and to mop up pockets of resistance the Germans left behind. From Auxerre and below, German troops from the west and south now rushed east and north to the Fatherland. The main highway stretching north from Dijon groaned with "much German traffic," Villebois radioed Station Charles. Wehrmacht soldiers and their officers were now focused singly on escaping France. Colby and Lelong did not have to worry about them stopping for battles with the Resistance. The two Jedburghs nudged Chevrier to have his guerrilla units become more aggressive in harassing the enemy as it retreated. When German defenses proved too strong, as they were at Nevers to the south, Colby called in air strikes to pound them. Small Werhmacht units traveling on back roads became easy prey for Team Bruce's guerrilla ambushes. It forced the Germans to move on main roads in large convoys with security patrols protecting them and at night to avoid Allied air strikes.

As enemy garrisons evacuated Yonne's towns, Chevrier's guerrillas moved in quickly to replace them and set up defense networks with roadblocks and barriers, forcing German convoys following from the south to lose time driving around these new Resistance centers. Colby and Lelong sometimes had to rush to villages to referee squabbling factions that had entered them. But eventually they had a picket line of guerrilla-occupied towns guarding Patton's flank from Briare on the Loire River in the west through Auxerre and to Tonnerre in the east. For some municipalities, Chevrier's defenders prevented enemy forces from returning to loot them. Past Monéteau just north of Auxerre, some three hundred White Russians drafted by the Werhmacht circled back with machine guns and several mortars to drain the town's petrol tanks for their vehicles. One hundred and fifty guerrillas, armed only with Bren light machine guns, put up such a stiff fight the marauders decided the extra gas was not worth the casualties and continued their flight north.

The first week of September, Colby and Chevrier set out on their own to scout bridges crossing the Loire for the portion of the river that snaked west of the Yonne Department from Gien in the north to La Charité in the south. Rip Powell, the OSS detachment chief for the 3rd Army, wanted the bridges blown so retreating Germans could not cross them and move closer to Patton's right flank. Colby and the French guerrilla chief sneaked up to each bridge along the forty-seven-mile stretch, crawling on their bellies the last leg to see if the span had already been knocked out or needed an attack to cut it. For some bridges, like the one crossing at Sancerre, they had guerrillas set demolitions. For others, like the one at La Charité that was camouflaged and still heavily guarded by Germans, they radioed for air strikes.

The scouting foray, for all intents and purposes, became their last combat mission. The German evacuation had grown more chaotic by the day. Enemy soldiers stole everything they could along the way—cars, bicycles, liver pâté, Burgundy wine—and in some instances began fighting among themselves. Colby radioed an account of a pitched battle he and Chevrier witnessed at the La Charité bridge between Wehrmacht and Waffen-SS units. By the second week in September, however, the fighting was over in Yonne. Save for lone stragglers, the enemy had cleared out of the department. Third Army's OSS detachment estimated that guerrillas in Yonne and the adjoining Aube Department to the northeast had killed two thousand Germans and captured five thousand prisoners. On September 11, Colby and Lelong helped bring together advance elements of Patton's 3rd Army and Patch's 7th Army for a linkup of the two forces just southeast of Yonne. From Switzerland to the North Sea, the Allied front now joined for the inexorable march east to Germany's border.

Team Bruce left Yonne on September 23, under orders from London to motor to the Hôtel Cecil in Paris where an OSS officer would arrange for their flight back to London. They lingered in the French capital, however, for almost three weeks, checking into the Hôtel Powers off the Champs-Élysées and partying with other Jedburgh survivors enjoying leave in the city. Fresh from the most intense combat many would ever see, the Jedburghs were emotional time bombs, draining wine bottles and brawling in bars. Colby had a brief reunion with his father. Elbridge was in Paris serving on the staff of Hodges's 1st Army. Colby and Lelong also managed to commandeer a black Cadillac to drive around the city and, for several days, make an excursion southwest to Lelong's home in Perpignan so the Frenchman could reunite with an old girlfriend.

Instead of all returning to England, Team Bruce broke up on October 10. Lelong was sent to an American headquarters, where he served as a French liaison officer. Villebois also returned to the French army and was transferred to Indochina, where he died in a firefight with the Japanese on March 9, 1945.

Colby flew to London and took the train north to Milton Hall for rounds of debriefings on his mission. He was ordered to keep his mouth shut outside the estate—no war stories or bragging at the Fox and Hounds. Security officers panicked when they learned that some OSS officers returned to the United States with photographs of French guerrillas executing German prisoners. The agency was horrified at the thought of the photos leaking to the press.

Administrative headaches awaited many of the returning commandos. The money they spent on missions had to be accounted for. One Jedburgh officer was hauled before a court of inquiry to explain how 250,000 francs had gone missing. Scratching the numbers on a sheet of paper Colby could account for all of Team Bruce's funds. The three men spent 226,630 of the 250,000 francs they had in their money belts—about 75,000 to pay agents and informants, the rest on food for the team and Resistance units or for clothes to replace the ones lost in the drop. Colby had 8,090 francs from his pocket to turn in, along with 15,280 francs Lelong and Villebois had given him to take back to England.

· · · ·

As many as a half million French men and women eventually joined in the Resistance. Quantifying their value has always been difficult. German casualty numbers attributed to the guerrillas are squishy. Clandestine warfare does not lend itself to exact body counts. Overall, one historian has estimated that Resistance forces by themselves liberated only 2 percent of the country's 212 urban centers. Most were freed either by the Allies overrunning them or the Germans simply abandoning cities when they fled east. If there had been no Resistance, the Allied force would still have conquered France. Its armies would have suffered more casualties in doing so, but they still would have driven out the Nazis.

Senior commanders gave the Resistance mixed reviews. Eisenhower claimed—a bit overgenerously—that the guerrillas equaled fifteen combat divisions in the field. "Without their great assistance the liberation of France and the defeat of the enemy in western Europe would have consumed a much longer time and meant greater losses to ourselves," he wrote in his memoirs. Patch's staff credited the Resistance with capturing 42,000 Germans during the 7th Army's drive from the south. Montgomery, however, barely mentioned the Resistance in his autobiography. Although Patton's staff was impressed with the guerrillas' protection of the 3rd Army's flank, he wasn't particularly. "Better than expected and less than advertised," he responded curtly when a reporter asked him how much support he received from the Resistance. In private, even Donovan voiced criticism. Behind closed doors he told a group of officers that often the intelligence the Resistance supplied "could not be trusted." After the Normandy landing, guerrilla ranks swelled with latecomers whose military effectiveness "was quite variable," he confided. "In some of the mountain regions they were magnificent. In other places their value was nil."

But the guerrillas did save Allied lives. Perhaps more would have been saved if Ike and his commanders had more faith in the Resistance and understood better how unconventional warriors could be used. Just as important, the Resistance restored French pride, so trampled during the occupation. It reminded collaborators as well that a day of reckoning would come after the war.

A total of 523 OSS special operations agents, Jedburghs, and other commandos fought behind the lines in France; eighty-six of them were killed, wounded, captured, or went missing. Britain's Special Operations Executive sent in 480 agents, 106 of whom died in combat or were executed by the Nazis. Eisenhower's staff concluded that the Resistance would have been useless for their military plans if the Jedburghs had not arrived. The ninety-three teams that infiltrated into France succeeded most places in uniting politically diverse guerrilla factions into a force that could attack key rail lines, harass Germans retreating, cut (or when needed keep intact) bridge crossings, and guide advancing Allied soldiers. The teams brought in supplies, communications with London, training for unskilled soldiers, and leadership for their missions. They also replenished guerrilla morale.

In the quiet of Milton Hall, Colby sat down and wrote his report on the operation in Yonne. His OSS superiors were delighted with Team Bruce's results. The Jedburghs jumped into a department under divided Resistance control and with persistent persuasion forged the factions into a unified force to blow bridges, occupy towns, and prevent retreating Germans from interfering with Patton's right flank. "A successful liaison mission," a head-quarters report concluded. Colby agreed, although he made the point at the end of his report that "far more work could have been accomplished had the mission been sent earlier." It was a common refrain from other Jedburgh teams: they arrived too late. If Team Bruce had been dropped in two weeks earlier "numerous German columns would not have escaped to play their part in today's battles," Colby wrote. Seven months later he penned another thoughtful memo to his superiors with recommendations for how small special operations units could be inserted overseas to train guerrillas in future conflict. What he envisioned was remarkably similar to today's U.S. Army Green Beret teams.

But long after the war, when he was in his sixties, Colby conceded in an interview that the decision not to send the Jedburghs too soon was "very intelligent." It would have sparked a premature uprising, he realized. The Germans would have "cleaned out" the guerrillas. With one of his sons, Colby was also harsh in his appraisal of Team Bruce's mission. They had been dropped into the middle of two powerful forces at play—Patton's army moving east and the German army retreating just ahead. Three Jedburghs and several thousand French guerrillas had only a marginal effect on these trajectories. "We didn't really do much," he told his son.

For what they did do, fifty-three of the American Jedburghs received decorations for combat heroism. Colby and Lelong were awarded the Bronze Star. Sixteen of the commandos died in combat, twenty-one were wounded, four taken prisoner, and one was missing in action. A few of the Jedburghs who returned to Milton Hall also suffered from posttraumatic stress disorders. Many more, like Colby, found the combat exhilarating. "It was an explosive, exciting time," he wrote in his memoirs, "and, though it didn't seem so then, remarkably brief."

He did not want his war to end now.

. . . .

Henri Frager was executed on October 5, 1944, at the Buchenwald concentration camp.

After the war, Marshal Pétain was imprisoned and his hated prime minister, Pierre Laval, dragged off to a firing squad. Justice for others proved uneven. Heavy reprisal for the nation's traitors did not serve the postwar political interests of de Gaulle, who preferred to portray French citizens as united against the Nazis. Resistance guerrillas summarily executed about nine thousand collaborators before, during, and immediately after the liberation of France. As many as thirty thousand French women had their heads shaved for alleged horizontal collaboration. In Yonne, one woman was spared the shaving so she could be dragged through the woods by the hair, then shot in the head. After the war, 311,263 collaboration cases deluged French courts, which adjudicated a little more than half of them; of those brought to trial, three-fourths received sentences.

By late September after the German army passed through Yonne, Roger Bardet lay low. French police finally arrested him in January 1945 but he soon wiggled out of custody. Convinced he was a traitor, Britain's SOE wanted him tried in a French court and shot. De Gaulle's security service was not as sure of Bardet's guilt. He spun an elaborate tale for his French interrogators, claiming he was a triple agent actually working for Frager and against Bleicher. The French service believed Bardet and released him in February.

In early June 1945, British agents finally caught up with Hugo Bleicher in Amsterdam. They hustled him to a plane that flew him to London, where MI5 counterintelligence agents drove him to Camp 020 at Latchmere House, an interrogation center in the southern part of the city, and began grilling him. Bleicher turned out to be as astute a prisoner as he had been a spy catcher. He told his questioners everything about his elaborate operation in France and Bardet's part in it. French agents rearrested Bardet in July 1945.

Three months later, MI5 put Bleicher on another plane, which flew him to Paris so French Interior Ministry officers could depose him for the rest of the year on Bardet's treachery. At one point the Abwehr man had a reunion in Fresnes prison with his haggard-looking double agent. In December 1949, Bardet was finally tried for treason and condemned to death. His sentence, however, was later commuted to twenty years and he was released from prison in 1955. He disappeared after that, living under a different name.

In June 1975, after Colby had been named CIA director, he had an "Addendum" clipped to his Team Bruce report in the OSS files. Bardet's treachery had been "unknown" to Team Bruce at the time of its mission, Colby wrote. It "undoubtedly explained Roger's lack of energy" when the Jedburghs fought in Yonne.

CHAPTER 17

FORTRESS GERMANY

The thunder of artillery from the west could often be heard in Bern, rattling teacups when it became intense. With the Allied advance, the border opened by the end of August, making it easier for Dulles to send reports to Washington and for the OSS to pour in reinforcements. Bern's tiny, secluded spy outpost soon grew into a major station with more than sixty people. Intelligence officers to manage missions arrived, along with research analysts to study and assess informant reports, counterespionage agents to vet spies, secretaries and clerks to type and encode messages, communications technicians to transmit cables. Newcomers included Gerhard Van Arkel, a thirty-seven-year-old from the London station's labor desk, to infiltrate agents into the Reich; Paul Blum, born in Japan and fluent in five languages, to organize counterintelligence operations, and Captain Tracy Barnes, a Harvard-educated lawyer who had made two parachute jumps into France and was now sent to Bern under the diplomatic cover of a legation clerk. The border's opening also enabled Dulles to cross into France for the first time in twenty months—not only to spy but also to have a reunion with his boss.

When Patch's 7th Army invaded France's Mediterranean coast August 15, Donovan, who liked to go in on amphibious landings, had waded ashore with troops at the beach near Saint-Tropez. With a jeep and driver he followed the Allied force north, impressed by the fighting quality of Resistance guerrillas he saw along the way. During his swing through southern France for his August fact-finding trip, Casey stopped in Grenoble, where the burned-down Gestapo headquarters smoldered and reports from firing squads executing collaborators still rang out. He found Donovan on the outskirts of the ancient city, comfortably ensconced in a stately château his OSS officers had found, with a spectacular view of the French Alps from its tree-shaded terrace. Over a delicious meal and several bottles of excellent Burgundy the estate's French chef had hidden from the Nazis, Casey and Donovan brainstormed a mission the spymaster had been mulling for quite a while—the penetration of Germany.

Since November 1943, Donovan had been prodding his staff in Washington and Bruce in London to come up with plans to infiltrate OSS spies and saboteurs into Germany. His aides had produced little so far, which frustrated him. As he made his way north through France, Donovan planned to energize a man he felt would be key to making his vision of a Germany swarming with OSS agents a reality—Allen Dulles. Donovan had been lobbying his Bern station chief on the idea since the beginning of August. The time has come to reorient the OSS from its secret warfare in France and other Nazi-occupied countries to clandestine operations inside Germany, he cabled Dulles on August 2. We "should bring all our skill and ingenuity to bear on the problem." Donovan proposed that the Bern station act "as a salient" for these intelligence and subversive missions with Dulles organizing teams of spies and special forces commandos to slip into Germany for snooping and creating havoc. It called for a "rebirth" of OSS operations "in their truest sense," Donovan wrote enthusiastically, "that of bold raids and nicely carried out attacks from hideouts, of patrolling by small groups, of destroying industrial installations."

Dulles thought the idea was ridiculously unrealistic. It also irritated him that Donovan appeared to be ignoring all he had accomplished with Fritz Kolbe and Hans Gisevius and was blithely launching this fool's errand. In polite but pointed memos he raised practical objections. The Bern station's small staff was already "pushed to the limit and beyond," he cabled Donovan. He did not have the people to launch this grand initiative. Also, "we are operating in the most incorruptible neutral country in the world," he reminded the spymaster. The Swiss ignored his small "discreet" intelligence missions; they would be up in arms if he turned their country into an aircraft carrier for launching a clandestine war with Germany. Even if he had the personnel and Swiss cooperation, Dulles argued that the window for this kind of operation had long closed. The networks Donovan envisioned must be organized before war broke out. After the fighting starts, a totalitarian state like Germany locks down. OSS agents now parachuting in would have no safe houses and friendly civilians to sustain them as they did in France. Donovan's advisers in Washington tended to agree with Dulles. Germans by and large would be hostile to Allied operatives, their communities "mobilized for war and literally linked house by house, if not person by person, to the secret police," one of their memos warned. At this point the best intelligence out of the Reich will come not from foreign agents swooping in, Dulles argued, but rather from Germans already in the country, like Kolbe and Gisevius, who are willing to bring out information.

Donovan knew full well the hurdles, but remained undeterred. He now wanted to find his Bern station chief to pump him up on penetrating Germany. Dulles, who also wanted to hook up with Donovan (albeit for a different reason), crossed the border into France the first week of September and trekked with a French guerrilla team to a hideout east of Lyon. He hoped to catch a flight there to London, then to Washington where he thought Donovan was. Several days later, an OSS officer knocked on the door of the hideout and told Dulles that Donovan, who had been looking for him, had a plane waiting at an airstrip south of Lyon, ready to fly them both to London.

As the DC-3 warmed its engines on the Lyon strip, Donovan greeted his Bern station chief like a long-lost relative. The two men climbed into the transport plane, Dulles paying little attention to a young officer who introduced himself as Lieutenant Casey and followed them up the ladder. Casey buckled into his seat and sat silently as the aircraft took off from the grass strip and pointed northwest along the River Loire, just below the retreating German army, heading for the English coast. He occasionally looked out the window nervously, hoping a stray Luftwaffe fighter didn't dip south to attack their defenseless plane, which had no armed escort. Meanwhile, Dulles, shouting over the noise in the cabin, updated Donovan on recent details he had picked up on the July 20 plot. The purge had been bloody, he told Donovan, but he still believed a German opposition movement remained, which the OSS could exploit. Donovan nodded but quickly got to the point Dulles had braced himself to hear. "I wonder if the time isn't ripe for penetration en masse" of Germany, he asked Dulles. "Agent drops from England—the way we infiltrated France."

Casey said nothing while for the rest of the flight Dulles rolled out his arguments for why the idea had little chance of success. After all, he was next to the man who had become as much a celebrity in the intelligence world as Donovan; it did not seem appropriate for an officer so junior to chime in. Besides, Casey already knew Donovan would pay no attention to Dulles's objections. In the locked briefcase chained to the lieutenant's wrist were plans he and Bruce had been polishing at Donovan's request the past few weeks for the infiltration of agents—en masse—into Germany.

The DC-3 landed in London the afternoon of September 8. That evening, Donovan, Dulles, and Bruce repaired to the Savoy Hotel bar for drinks, which were soon interrupted by the first of the German V-2s slamming into the city, puncturing Chiswick with a huge crater and killing three. During the nights that followed, when the air raid alarm sounded Donovan parked himself on the rooftop of the OSS station at Grosvenor Square to watch for more of Hitler's "vengeance weapons" streaking by.

Casey, who had been a rooftop gawker for the earlier jet-powered V-1 buzz bombs, headed to the bunker with the arrival of these monster missiles that were six times heavier. His days and nights were now consumed with brainstorming how the spy bureaucracy in the London station would have to be rearranged to make penetration of Germany the high priority Donovan wanted it to be. Dulles remained hostile to the idea and tried to smother it with alternatives, but Donovan was now listening to his young aide in London instead of his star station chief from Bern. A rift had grown between Donovan and Dulles. The two men did not particularly like each other. Two years of Dulles cabling occasionally presumptuous foreign policy recommendations and subtle critiques of Donovan's administration had begun to grate on the OSS chief. He thought Dulles wanted his job, which wasn't far from the truth.

Donovan had also concluded that Dulles was a poor administrator—ironic because Donovan was a chaotic manager. But more importantly, he believed Dulles lacked leadership qualities needed to command the loyalty of those under him. (Donovan certainly had them.) During their drinks at the Savoy, Donovan had broken the news to his Bern chief that he would be denied the prize he most coveted. Dulles had heard rumors Bruce wanted to return to Washington; he wanted to replace him as chief of the all-important London station with the soon to be expanded responsibility of supervising OSS operations for continental Europe. Donovan told both men at the bar he wanted them to stay put; Bruce would continue as London chief and take over European operations while Dulles remained in Bern. Casey was relieved when he learned the news later. He had heard gossip about Dulles's poor administrative skills and did not want him becoming his London boss.

Donovan tried to sugarcoat the bitter pill for Dulles by claiming that he just couldn't afford to lose him in Switzerland. When the war ended and Bruce returned home, Donovan added, he wanted Dulles to lead the OSS mission moving into occupied Germany. He did not tell Dulles that he would have preferred Bruce for that job and Dulles serving under him.

Dulles was devastated, though he should not have been surprised that he would be leading the postwar German mission. For the past six months, Ferd Mayer and Donovan had been cabling him to start thinking about how he would organize a spy operation in Germany after it collapsed. Leaving Gaevernitz in charge of the Bern station, Dulles flew back to Washington with Donovan on September 15 to dutifully begin work on his two new assignments—penetrating Germany during and after the war.

The sleepy southern town Dulles had left two years ago now burst at the seams with busy civilian administrators, military staff officers, and every hotel room and vacant office space taken up by the avalanche of government programs and bureaucrats who came with the war effort. Though he professed to miss his family, Dulles allotted only one day to Clover and the children during his two-week visit. The rest of the time he spent conferring with OSS colleagues in the New York office and at headquarters in Washington, where he was assigned a room and phone. Aides practically lined up at the door for a glimpse or chat with the man now famous for his intelligence triumphs in Switzerland—among the visitors an OSS historian who began interviewing Dulles to preserve a record of what he had accomplished. "The best thing we did can't be told now; however, we were able to penetrate the

Abwehr pretty successfully, turning it anti-Hitler," he told the historian, inflating what actually happened. Dulles also made the rounds in the Kremlin and at the Pentagon, briefing senior officials on his ideas for setting up a postwar mission in Germany and penetrating the country while it was still fighting—although he thought the second mission was futile and gave them a long list of reasons why.

Casey paid a visit to Washington around the same time Dulles did. Unlike Dulles, Casey did not ignore his family. He caught the first train he could to New York to reunite with Sophia and sixteen-month-old Bernadette, who were staying with her family. If Casey and Dulles got together during their Washington sojourn, neither man recorded it. But Dulles did drop by Richard Helms's office. The Navy lieutenant, who read Dulles's Bern cables closely, had been making a name for himself as a headquarters operations officer for Central Europe and Scandinavia. Dulles soon placed Helms on a list of key aides he wanted for his German mission.

The Bern station to which Dulles returned in October 1944 eventually bustled with new staffers and operations. He did not take well to the expansion. It was "a most disturbing transformation," Mary Bancroft wrote in her memoirs. "I never again saw the Allen Dulles I had watched operating with such consummate skill when he was cut off from all outside influences and just acting on his own. . . . The sparkle and charm went out of Allen's personality." Another attack of gout added to his gloom—exacerbated by Bern's rainy fall, he was sure—and when the affliction spread to his right elbow he had to stop writing. He began to complain more to headquarters and London about his heavy administrative load, the lack of trained officers being sent to relieve it, and stateside visitors on junkets wasting his time. Washington fired back with its complaints about Dulles's administrative shortcomings. Donovan began scribbling caustic notes on the side of Dulles cables. Officers newly arrived in Bern found the station chief hard to deal with and uncommunicative.

Back in London, Casey, on the other hand, was winning accolades for his administrative prowess. Five admirals stood in a room to watch the Bronze Star medal pinned to his uniform in late fall, he proudly wrote Sophia. He and a roommate also moved into a plush new apartment at 87 Harley House. It had a statuary, several fireplaces, tiger and lion skins on the floors,

1

The son of a Presbyterian minister, Allen Welsh Dulles was born with a clubfoot, which his parents had a surgeon repair. A bright, precocious young boy, interested in foreign affairs at an early age, young Allie wrote a book on the Boer War at age eight.

2

Richard McGarrah Helms was born into a prominent banking family on his mother's side. In 1929, Richard's father moved the family to Europe, where the young boy learned French and German at Switzerland's exclusive Le Rosey school. Helms later said his early education groomed him to be a spy.

William Egan Colby traced his family back to the Massachusetts Bay Colony settlers who landed at Salem in 1630. The son of an Army officer, Bill's constant family moves opened a window to the world for him. During their 1929 posting in Tientsin, China, the nine-year-old boy tried on a local costume.

Weighing a staggering fourteen pounds at birth, William Joseph Casey hailed from scrappy Irish Catholic roots in New York. His early family life orbited around the Church and Democratic politics. A voracious reader determined to educate himself as he saw fit, Bill infuriated the nuns who taught him when he acted smart-alecky in class.

Dulles learned the basics of intelligence work as a young State Department diplomat, spying on the Germans during his World War I posting in Switzerland and collecting information on the Russians after the Armistice as an envoy in Turkey.

5

The first in his family to attend college, Casey enrolled in Fordham University in the Bronx. His grades improving by his senior year, Casey joined the debate team, impressing his coach with his ability to assemble facts for an argument. But he mumbled when he spoke.

6

Taking ROTC classes at Princeton University, Colby followed in his father's footsteps and, after graduating, was commissioned in August 1941 as an Army second lieutenant. Desperate to see action after the Japanese attack on Pearl Harbor, he talked a military doctor into overlooking his poor eyesight during a physical so he could become a paratrooper.

Disenchanted with social work after he graduated from college, Casey earned a law degree and eventually became a budget expert in Washington for the Research Institute of America, a think tank that churned out reports advising businesses on how to land defense contracts. But after Pearl Harbor, Casey wanted to do more for the war effort than just push paper.

A standout at Williams College, Helms chose journalism rather than the law after he graduated and found a job with United Press as a cub reporter in Berlin during the mid-1930s. Above is the press card the Nazis issued him. Helms's biggest scoop was attending a lunch for a handful of reporters with Adolf Hitler, who impressed him as intent on war.

10

Six months before Pearl Harbor, Franklin Roosevelt appointed William J. "Wild Bill" Donovan, a World War I hero and top Wall Street Republican lawyer, to be his spymaster and form what was eventually called the Office of Strategic Services. The OSS, which spied on the Axis, was the forerunner of the CIA and the place where Dulles, Helms, Colby, and Casey learned to be secret warriors.

11

At first reluctant to join Donovan's agency, Dulles eventually signed on with the OSS after Pearl Harbor and set up a satellite office in New York to mine the intelligence potential of its émigré community. He was given an identification card for the Washington headquarters, but spent little time there. Instead he got Donovan to transfer him to neutral Switzerland, where he set up a station to spy on the Nazis.

12

Sealed off in Switzerland and operating largely on his own, Dulles's OSS station in Bern became one of Donovan's most important during the war. Dulles succeeded in recruiting key agents in the Third Reich, who provided him with a wealth of political, economic, and military intelligence on the Nazis.

13

Among the important operatives who worked for Dulles in Bern was Gero von Schulze-Gaevernitz, left, a handsome international financier who was the son of a Weimar legislator. Gaevernitz became Dulles's prized door opener, introducing him to contacts in the German intelligence service and resistance movement.

14

Among Dulles's diplomatic gambits, he secretly arranged for the surrender of German forces in Italy in an operation code-named "Sunrise." Because of delays on both sides, however, the capitulation did not take place until May 2, 1945, six days before the entire German army surrendered. Pictured here are the German participants in Sunrise, with Gaevernitz second from left: General Hans Roettiger, deputy commander of German forces in Italy, far left; General Heinrich von Vietinghoff, commander of German forces in Italy, third from left; and General Karl Wolff, Waffen-SS chief for Italy, far right.

LEFT: Desperate to see action, Colby joined a secret OSS program, code-named "Jedburgh," to parachute three-man teams behind the lines in France after D-Day. The teams organized French Resistance attacks against the Germans. The Jedburghs trained at Milton Hall, a country estate in Peterborough north of London.

RIGHT: Colby's three-man team that dropped into France was code-named "Bruce." Its leader was Ca-mille Lelong, a dashing French army lieutenant who became a close Colby friend during and after the war.

16

BELOW: The OSS organized a massive effort to aid the French Resistance, parachuting in not only Jedburgh teams but also tons of arms and supplies like that shown in this airdrop. The Resistance harassed the Wehrmacht but never posed a strategic threat to the Nazi occupation force.

The Germans carried out brutal reprisals for French Resistance raids, torturing and executing the guerrillas and Jedburgh commandos they caught and wiping out French villages. Here French guerrillas have German prisoners dig up the mutilated bodies of Resistance operatives the Nazis murdered so they could be given proper military funerals.

The Nazis ran a ruthlessly efficient counterespionage operation in France to penetrate French Resistance cells. Hugo Bleicher, who had recruited key moles in the Resistance network that Colby worked with southeast of Paris, was one of the Abwehr's top spy catchers.

Casey, shown here with his wife, Sophia, and their daughter, Bernadette, was eager to break loose of the Research Institute of America and join the fighting. He at first did not impress the Navy as officer material, but eventually the sea service commissioned him as a lieutenant junior grade and put his RIA experience to work in its shipbuilding program.

Quickly bored with Navy procurement, Casey lobbied the OSS to hire him. Impressed with his administrative skills, Donovan's senior advisers sent him to London to manage the OSS station's flow of paperwork. Soon Casey, on the left with two other officers in front of the Queen Victoria Memorial and Buckingham Palace, was dabbling in almost every secret operation the station ran.

A year after Casey arrived in London, Donovan made him chief of secret intelligence for Europe with the mission to penetrate Germany with OSS agents. Scrambling to launch the difficult espionage program, Casey loved to tour the front lines and visit agents who had returned from missions— although he usually arrived in mismatched battle garb.

After the Jedburgh operation in France, Colby led a commando team into Norway to blow up key sections of a rail line the German occupiers used. The mission, code-named "Rype," was extremely dangerous, with Colby's men fighting Norway's harsh winter as much as the Nazis. He is seen here, battle-hardened and gaunt (second from the right), with a fellow commando and Norwegian officers after the country's liberation.

Flying conditions for the pilots infiltrating Colby's special operations team into Norway were nightmarish. Half the planes for the mission crashed or had to turn back because they got lost in the winter weather. Colby held a military funeral at a crash site for four of his commandos and eight airmen who had died in one wreck.

25

After Pearl Harbor, Helms joined the Navy and was assigned to a New York office, plotting courses American vessels could take to avoid German U-boats in the Atlantic. A friend approached him about joining the OSS, but he declined. Eight months later, however, the agency got the Navy to reassign him to its Washington headquarters so his knowledge of Germany and fluency in the language could be put to use in intelligence operations.

26

After nearly a year and a half in Washington working as a staffer planning and overseeing intelligence operations from OSS headquarters, Helms (right) made it to London in January 1945 as the Allies made their final push against the Third Reich. Helms was put to work under Casey helping to infiltrate OSS agents into Germany.

27

Helms, seen here with his helmet and field jacket in a war zone, did not think Casey's operation to infiltrate agents into Germany accomplished much in the way of useful information. As the war neared its final months he detached himself from that program and began planning the OSS's intelligence mission for an occupied Germany after its defeat.

28

After the Nazi surrender, Dulles, at right, led the OSS mission in occupied Germany. He is pictured here with Navy commander Frank Wisner, the mission's aggressive secret intelligence chief, who went on to become a legend in the young CIA. In addition to hunting for war criminals and Nazi subversives who might have gone underground, Dulles's mission began spying on what quickly became America's new enemy, the Soviet Union.

Helms, pictured here on the far right with Dulles center and other OSS staffers, became a key member of the OSS mission's Berlin base, where he oversaw espionage operations increasingly targeting the Russians in their occupation zone. Helms, who eventually took charge of the Berlin base, found the jovial, pipe-smoking Dulles hyperactive, demanding, and "into everything."

30

Believing covert operations were an important part of American foreign policy, Dulles, at right, as CIA director ran the agency much as he had his OSS station in Bern, immersing himself in the clandestine programs that interested him and ignoring the ones that bored him. After the war, Casey set out to make his fortune as a venture capitalist before he returned to government service.

The administrative shortcomings Dulles had shown as OSS station chief in Bern caught up with him when he ran the CIA. Dulles's biggest blunder came with the CIA-led invasion of Cuba's Bay of Pigs in April 1961. Fidel Castro's army had little trouble sweeping up the 1,300 Cuban exiles who landed at the beach. Four months later, President John Kennedy fired Dulles for the botched operation. The day before Dulles left office on November 29, Kennedy visited the CIA's new headquarters in Langley, Virginia, to award him the National Security Medal as a fig leaf.

32

Appointed CIA director by Lyndon Johnson, Helms, far right, earned a seat in the president's inner circle of national security advisers. Richard Nixon kept Helms as his CIA director but did little to conceal his disdain for the agency and its spy chief.

33

By spring 1967, Helms and his first wife, Julia, had drifted apart and Helms decided to end the marriage. Being walled out of a large part of her husband's life because of the secrecy that came with the job had grated on Julia. In December 1968 Helms married British socialite Cynthia McKelvie, pictured here, whom he had met on the diplomatic dinner circuit.

34

After World War II, Colby earned a law degree and worked briefly in William Donovan's New York firm, then the National Labor Relations Board in Washington. But itching to be on the front lines of America's new Cold War, he joined the CIA in 1950 and rose quickly through the ranks. By 1953 he was running Dulles's largest covert political action program, to prevent the communists from winning national elections in Italy. An admiring Donovan visited Colby and his family in Rome.

As CIA director, Colby became a pariah among many in his agency for turning over to congressional investigating committees the "Family Jewels" report, which chronicled agency dirty tricks during the 1950s, 1960s, and 1970s, and for testifying candidly on the controversial operations. Considering him a liability for the 1976 presidential race, President Gerald Ford fired Colby in November 1975.

As CIA director, William Casey confers with Ronald Reagan in the Oval Office. Hard of hearing, Reagan often had difficulty understanding Casey's briefings because his spy chief mumbled. The Iran-Contra scandal stained Casey's legacy and imperiled the Reagan presidency.

LEFT: William Casey spoke at a 1983 Veterans of OSS dinner with Helms on the left and an iconic photo of Wild Bill Donovan as the backdrop. For Casey, Helms, Dulles, and Colby their service in Donovan's OSS had a huge impact on their lives.

RIGHT: William Casey, sitting in front of a shot of the CIA's Langley, Virginia head-quarters, hung two photos in his office—Ronald Reagan's and William Donovan's.

and "a wonderful bed which is as wide as it is long," he told her. The work now is "more challenging and more fascinating than anything I've ever tackled before," he wrote in another letter. "I'm operating on the ambassador and general and minister level, all of Europe is the territory, and I have almost complete freedom of decision and movement."

Casey made another trip to France on October 13, zipping across the English Channel in a PT boat to Cherbourg, where he took a bouncy ride in a jeep to Paris. He gazed in awe at the massive Allied convoys along the way, stretching as far as his eye could see. "It makes you proud of Americans," he wrote Sophia. Casey checked into the Royal Marceau Hotel, which boasted hot water for the rooms. He marveled at how its chefs could whip up exquisite dinners with Army rations, cheese sauce, garlic, and cooking wine. The London station had begun emptying out, with 350 of the more than 3,400 people Bruce commanded so far in Paris and many more looking for excuses to transfer to it.

Casey found the City of Light "glorious," he wrote Sophia. He was less impressed with the OSS officers who had staked out posh offices with balconies overlooking the Champs-Élysées. Too many of them were deadwood "making fools of themselves," he complained in the same letter. "It makes one awful mad to go up front and see little white crosses and then go back and see a lot of guys hitting the nightlife so that they're no damn good on the job the next day." The OSS outpost was in a funk, Casey found, much of its work now mundane—accounting for agents left over from the French campaign or picking up stray German spies left behind. Bruce had ordered him to shake things up, which he intended to do. The changing tide of battle compelled it.

Feeding the Paris doldrums that Casey found had been a widespread belief in American and British intelligence that they would not have Germany as a combatant to spy on much longer. Even Casey had told Sophia he would be surprised if the war lasted through the winter. MI6 reported German officer morale seriously deteriorated. An OSS survey of 170 POWs found most believed Germany would be defeated and the war would be over soon. Donovan sent the poll results to Roosevelt along with an OSS study of German newspaper obituaries showing that more of the country's teenagers and older men were dying in battle—indicating the Wehrmacht was running low on the ideal manpower pool of ages twenty to thirty. Dulles cabled Washington tips from his sources that leading German industrialists and Wehrmacht generals now wanted to end the war quickly. Cracks had even begun appearing in the top Nazi leadership, his informants claimed. Göring was making plans to fly to South America, one said, though Dulles admitted "this may be a fairy story." Other sources reported Hitler suffered from a serious throat malady (to explain the drop in public appearances), malnutrition, deafness from the July 20 attack, and what is now called bipolar disorder.

Dulles did caution that Hitler "remains the führer and his iron will is felt in every domain," but the caveat was drowned in a sea of long-standing optimism. Even before the Normandy invasion Eisenhower's staff had ordered up studies on how a conquered Germany should be administered. By August Donovan's headquarters had drafted detailed plans for the intelligence operation it would set up in Germany in case of an early surrender by the Third Reich. Casey and Dulles both worked on "Twilight," the code name for an operation devised in July to rush agent teams called T-forces into Berlin and four other key cities immediately after Germany's collapse.

Operation Market Garden soon doused any delusions the Germans had no more fight left in them. Hastily conceived by Montgomery and launched on September 17, the bold plan called for parachute divisions to drop into the Netherlands and clear a corridor for the 2nd British Army to seize a bridgehead over the Rhine, overrun V-2 launch sites terrorizing England, trap a quarter million enemy soldiers, then lunge east toward the Ruhr in a "full-blooded thrust" to end the war quickly. The execution, however, suffered from timing too split-second (divisions did not arrive or seize bridges and towns at appointed hours), command cocksureness (Montgomery was having his portrait painted when the attack began), and faulty Army intelligence (caught by surprise when the Germans rushed in 85,000 battle-ready soldiers to turn back or overrun attackers). During five days, the Allies lost seventeen thousand men in what one British officer called "an epic cock-up." Casey thought it was a debacle. For the OSS, the operation had already begun to rouse the London and Paris stations from their lethargy. After Market Garden, the Allies soon realized prospects were dim for ending the war in 1944. Donovan's agency faced the far more daunting mission of penetrating a hostile Germany rather than one that had capitulated.

Before boarding the PT boat to cross the English Channel Casey had cabled a nine-page memo to Washington on October 12, titled "OSS Program for Germany." Donovan circulated it among his senior staff. Their mission in France had succeeded, Casey's memo began, and now "the center of gravity has shifted to operations in Germany" and the penetration of a country still fighting. Gestapo security controls are still tight, but the Allied advance on the ground and pounding from the air are breaking them down and increasing public "dissatisfaction with the Nazi regime," he predicted. Casey proposed to infiltrate one hundred agents from England, Switzerland, and Sweden to collect military intelligence on Wehrmacht forces as well as political and economic intelligence on the Nazi regime. The agents would also sabotage Reich operations and spread subversive propaganda. The branches already set up in the London station can be harnessed, he told Donovan, but it will take "top caliber staff work" to organize them for this ambitious enterprise. Casey's memo did not state who should be assigned the job of bringing all these moving parts together. But it was clear the person he had in mind was himself.

CHAPTER 18

NORWAY

_____

After finishing his Team Bruce report, Colby took the train south to London in October and checked into the Cumberland. The hotel was a short walk from Grosvenor Square where he spent the next few days roaming the halls of the OSS town houses looking for a job. Finally he cornered Gerald Miller, a portly, forty-one-year-old Detroit banker in civilian life who had recently taken over the station's special operations branch and was more preoccupied now with shutting down Jedburgh missions in France than being a career counselor to commandos looking for more action. Colby could transfer to Asia, Miller told him. Even though he had lived in the Far East, that didn't sound too appealing. The other choice was Norway. Miller's tiny and largely neglected Scandinavian section needed an officer to take command of nearly eighty men in the Norwegian Special Operations Group (NORSO). They will drop into the country to sabotage rail lines.

It was a politically sensitive operation. "We need someone who won't fuck it up," Miller told Colby.

Colby immediately accepted the assignment. Though he spoke not a word of Norwegian and knew nothing about the country save for what Norwegian American friends in the United States had told him, he calculated this was the quickest way to get back into the fight rather than waiting months for a transfer to Asia.

"By the way," Miller asked as they wrapped up, "do you ski?" It was the only way to travel in Norway's snow-packed mountains. He did, Colby assured the special ops chief. From his high school days in Vermont he had become a fairly accomplished skier.

. . . .

It was a thousand-mile-long, largely barren country off Europe's beaten path with harsh winters, less than 3 percent of its land under cultivation, and just three million people speaking many dialects. Norway's isolation and inhospitableness had made it secure from foreign conquerors. Roman emperors sought its furs and tall blond men for their praetorian guards but not its land for occupation. During the Middle Ages, its shipbuilding and seafaring had expanded with storied Norwegian Vikings raiding and plundering large parts of Europe and some of America. By the early twentieth century, Norway was a thriving yet insular country uninterested in Europe's political rivalries and untouched by its militarism and economic crises. The nation struggled to maintain neutrality during World War I, but had no military force to speak of for defending it. Roused out of its semi-isolation afterward, Norway engaged more in international affairs and became active in the League of Nations. Yet it remained oblivious to the growing Nazi threat of the mid-1930s. After war broke out in 1939, the Western powers pressured the country to join their side but Norway, along with the rest of Scandinavia, insisted on remaining neutral.

On April 14, 1939, Roosevelt demanded assurance from Hitler that he would not attack the country, whose defenses had fallen into a deplorable state. But increasing German belligerence should have alerted Norwegians that an invasion was coming. U-boats began sinking Norwegian ships, while German vessels laden with Swedish iron ore used Norway's jagged coast to hide from British patrols and scores of Nazi espionage agents began slipping into the country. In December 1939, Vidkun Quisling, a heavyset former defense minister with a jaundiced complexion from too much drinking who now headed a Nazi-like fringe party called Nasjonal Samling, paid a secret visit to Hitler to sell him on the idea of invading Norway.

In the early morning hours of April 9, 1940, the first wave of ten thousand German paratroopers and amphibious soldiers rushed in to capture

Oslo and five other key cities. Quisling announced on the radio that the government had been removed and he was now in charge. Nazi propaganda proclaimed the invasion had been launched to save Norway from the mining of its coastal waters, which Britain and France had announced the day before to block German shipping. A brass band followed the first German troops entering the Norwegian capital, the soldiers truly shocked to discover their protection was not welcomed. The invasion eventually cost the Wehrmacht 63,000 casualties. Norway's tiny army, navy, and air force fought gallantly for two months—proud they had held out longer than Poland, France, or the Low Countries—but German reinforcements poured in and spread out to secure other cities and towns. Norway's armed forces chief formally surrendered on June 10. King Haakon VII, Crown Prince Olav, and the government's ministers evacuated to London along with the gold that had been stored in the Bank of Norway. They left a country stunned and grief-stricken by the invasion, as well as angry that their leaders and the Allies had been powerless to prevent it.

Some 300,000 enemy soldiers eventually occupied Norway. Hitler appointed Josef Terboven, the ruthless Nazi *Gauleiter* of Cologne who had married Goebbels's former mistress, to be *Reichskommissar* for Norway with a force of six thousand Gestapo men, SD agents, and Norwegian Nazi thugs under him to bully the populace. With much fanfare, on February 1, 1942, Terboven formally designated Quisling "Minister President" to head a puppet government that became as tyrannical as its German overlords. A preacher's son who considered himself a prophet come to lead Norway to national socialism, Quisling was allowed to keep the Hird, a paramilitary force of some 8,500 in his Nasjonal Samling that he used to terrorize his subjects. As in France, the Germans also had the help of collaborators in Norway—as many as 48,000 by postwar counts who informed on fellow countrymen or helped the Nazis build defenses. Another five hundred Norwegians volunteered for an SS guard battalion.

Hitler's generals had not wanted to invade Norway. But once in, the Wehrmacht found the country a rich source for war industry raw materials, such as nickel, copper, and iron ore, as well as a strategically important base for U-boats and reconnaissance aircraft. The Nazis set about to plunder the nation, carting off not only valuable minerals but also grain, fish, and thousands of forced laborers for work gangs in the Reich. And as they did in other occupied countries, the Germans stepped up their terror tactics in Norway as the years dragged on. Arrogant Wehrmacht officers routinely caned civilians on sidewalks. Gestapo or Hird agents increased late-night raids on homes to carry off and torture dissidents. More than nineteen thousand Norwegians were sent to the dreaded Grini detention center west of Oslo.

The resistance movement took a while to form. Norwegians were as unprepared for an insurgency against their occupiers as they had been for the German invasion. Organizing a nationwide opposition was difficult in a country so thinly populated. Communities were small, which meant clandestine activity became quickly known among townsfolk and could spread to snitches the Gestapo laced among them. The subarctic mountain ranges were also far too inhospitable and devoid of food sources to sustain guerrilla base camps. But gradually a "white war" against the Germans gained traction.

The national resistance began with what came to be called an "ice front"—men and women individually becoming more impolite, more unfriendly, more uncooperative toward enemy authorities. Defying a German ban on demonstrations, Norwegians on the first anniversary of the April 9 invasion stopped their cars, their work in factories, and teaching in schools for a half hour of silence. A vibrant cultural life of music, book publishing, and patriotic newspapers went underground. Norwegian soldiers and seamen who had surrendered got hold of transmitters to begin radioing intelligence on Nazi fortifications to London. Secretaries showered with looted jewelry by their German bosses spied on their employers for resistance networks. Chauffeurs diverted their Quisling government cars to drive resisters escaping labor drafts to Sweden. Guerrilla attacks, at first spontaneous, eventually became organized. Norwegian officers who had been released from German POW camps on a promise not to fight the occupation broke their promise, dividing the country into zones and setting up in each of them "Milorgs"—secret military organizations made up of former soldiers, sports and shooting team enthusiasts, and even Boy Scouts—all directed by a clandestine central command in Oslo that reported to the exiled government in London. The Milorg's fighting strength reached as high as 25,000.

British agents, who had begun slipping into Norway before the invasion, infiltrated its porous coastline of fjords and firths by the hundreds afterward. Norwegian agents for the SOE helped as spotters of the mighty German battleship *Bismarck* before it was sunk in 1941. A series of SOE sabotage raids eventually crippled the Norsk Hydro heavy water plant near Vemork, which had been feeding the nascent German nuclear program. Anglo-Norwegian tensions simmered, however. SOE officers griped that their Norwegian counterparts in the field were too trusting and chatty among friends who might be Nazi informants. Norwegian resistance leaders complained the SOE commandos were often too headstrong, launching raids that only invited harsher Nazi reprisals. The Germans responded to the attacks by bringing in one thousand more Gestapo agents to crack down on the resistance and drafting fifteen thousand Norwegians to build defenses for the Allied invasion they expected to follow this increased guerrilla activity.

Churchill, in fact, had toyed with the idea of an invasion of Norway, but the Allied command eventually chose Normandy for its landing site. The SOE, however, could not ignore Norway; to do so might tip off the Germans to Normandy, it feared. From 1942 to 1943, British agents kept up their pressure with deception operations and sabotage attacks so Hitler would keep his 300,000 soldiers in Norway instead of transferring divisions to the defense of France. Dulles's Bern sources reported the ruse appeared to be working. Berlin authorities feared British and American troops would launch from Scotland and Iceland to land on the coast of central Norway, he cabled in August 1943.

• • • •

Seven months after the Pearl Harbor attack, Donovan had been mulling the idea of forming a company of Norwegian American commandos to get in on the action in Norway. Knowing Roosevelt had shown interest in the country, he sent the White House maps and summaries his research analysts had prepared on Norwegian rail and sea traffic. But the idea of an OSS commando force met a chilly reception from the Norwegian government in exile, which already had its hands full with exuberant SOE operations in the country, and British officials, who did not want American interlopers spoiling relations they had struggled to improve with King Haakon and his ministers. Donovan's Norwegian Americans, an SOE memo concluded in 1942, would "undoubtedly be more trouble than they are worth."

Allied hostility had not deterred Donovan in the past and it didn't in this case. In January 1943, Lieutenant Colonel Ellery Huntington, a former Yale all-American quarterback who was Donovan's special operations chief in Washington, flew to London with an ambitious plan for OSS sabotage operations in Norway. His meeting with Sir Charles Hambro, the imposing chief of SOE, and Major General Wilhelm von Tangen Hansteen, the ramrod commander in exile of the Norwegian armed forces, could not have been frostier. Stretching the truth a bit, Huntington claimed the U.S. high command was anxious to mount operations in Norway to protect Eisenhower's northern flank. America's Midwest had "a large population" of Norwegian Americans fluent in their native tongue who were "clamoring" to join the fight to liberate the homeland, he told them. Realizing Donovan would not be stopped, Hambro and Hansteen reluctantly agreed—but only after laying down ironclad conditions. No American commando would set foot in Norway unless the SOE and exiled government approved. The OSS team would operate in a remote, and pretty unappealing, part of central Norway, north of where British and indigenous units fought in the south. And the Norwegian Americans must be led by a "responsible" officer, Hambro insisted, someone with a level head who would not cause trouble. Donovan's representatives agreed.

In April, OSS recruiters flew to Camp Hale in Colorado's Eagle River valley near Denver, where eight hundred Norwegian Americans trained in mountain warfare for the 99th Infantry Battalion. The recruiters picked ten officers and sixty-nine enlisted men who skied and spoke Norwegian (although many not fluently or with a heavy American accent) and flew the volunteers to the East Coast for OSS commando training. Eight months later, the seventy-nine newly minted guerrillas, some of whom had been stranded Norwegian seamen when the war broke out, sailed to the United Kingdom for more special operations instruction from the British in Scotland and parachute training at Ringway. Then they languished at Brock Hall, a country estate near Harrington Field. The British had no mission for them in Norway. Eisenhower's staff, meanwhile, scoured for commandos they could find in addition to the Jedburghs for operations after D-Day. The Norwegian Americans were dropped into southern France, where they fought for three months.

By the time Colby took command of the guerrillas in late October, Norway had lost much of its value for the Wehrmacht. It had become increasingly difficult for German ships to slip past Allied blockades to deliver the country's raw material to Reich war industries. Occupation troops felt increasingly isolated and fearful of being cut off forever from the Fatherland. Through the ranks spread the sentiment that it was time to evacuate, a British intelligence summary reported, "whilst the going is good."

The morale of the Norwegian Americans Colby had been ordered to lead was not much better. The special forces headquarters in London told him to train the men for guerrilla attacks in Norway although it had no immediate mission for them. OSS officers began to suspect the British would make sure none materialized. Donovan began to wonder if NORSO would ever see Norway. The Norwegian American commandos were now a battle-tested yet decidedly cynical group. Month after month they had been diddled on the assignment for which they had volunteered—to liberate their homeland. If they were deployed now, they muttered among themselves, would it be just for politics' sake? So Wild Bill Donovan could boast that he had a force in the country?

But if the order did come, this Army major named Colby appeared competent to lead them, the men decided among themselves.

CHAPTER 19

ASSIGNMENT EUROPE

Confusion prevailed. The London station, which up to late fall 1944 had been focused on France, had little idea how to mount the ambitious penetration operation Donovan now wanted for Germany. It would need a large staff to organize such a program and it had none. There were hardly any trainers to instruct agents in the difficult job of spying inside the Reich, few German-speaking OSS officers to dispatch operatives and watch over them when they were in the field. The unit that had been set up to run the Sussex intelligence mission in France had been disbanded; everyone had assumed after the liberation that the war would soon be over and German operations would not be needed. Even if the Sussex managers had been around, their expertise was France not Germany. Casey began cataloguing the bureaucratic thicket that had to be cleared and all the decisions he and Bruce had to make. The station's intelligence, special operations, and propaganda sections, which had begun small initiatives on their own to target Germany, had to be reorganized so they no longer worked at cross-purposes. For the expanded program Donovan demanded, Casey sent Bruce a long list of items "we are short on"—equipment, clothing, and false documents for agents, planes to fly them deep into Germany, safe houses to hide them when they get there.

Up to now, the British program to penetrate Germany had been as paltry as Donovan's. Both MI6 and the Special Operations Executive had considered the Third Reich too tough to crack and not worth the effort. Casey found British intelligence officers practically snobby about the idea of joining their cousins in German spy operations—"not intimate," as he diplomatically put his relations with MI6 in one report. Early September 1944, Bruce's station and the SOE did manage to mount "Downend," the code name for a joint mission that parachuted an OSS spy into Sögel, Germany, just across the Dutch border in order to scout out an espionage and sabotage network to attack arms factories in the Ruhr. Otherwise, among the best the SOE could come up with was Operation Periwig, which amounted to a virtual sabotage program for Germany. Several agents would be dropped in to create an imaginary insurrection. "Think of German resistance in much the same way Voltaire thought of God," an SOE report explained. It would drive the Gestapo nuts and convince the German public "there really was some organized resistance." Periwig flopped. But when Major General Colin Gubbins, a battle-seasoned guerrilla organizer who took over the SOE from Hambro in the fall of 1943, learned that Donovan was organizing a major German penetration effort, he ordered his reluctant Baker Street staff to gin up one as well.

The OSS's part in the Downend mission had been run by an outfit in the London station that would hardly have been expected to mount infiltration operations into Germany—the Labor Division. But as he sorted through the bureaucratic tangle in September Casey discovered to his surprise that this small and largely ignored unit was doing the most work to send spies and saboteurs into the country. While Dulles was still in the New York office preparing to transfer to Switzerland, Arthur Goldberg had boarded a Pan Am Clipper to England in September 1942 to open lines to exiles in London representing European trade unions and what remained of the labor movement in Germany. They might have members willing to spy for the OSS in enemy territory, he believed. After three months of networking, Goldberg had racked up many contacts and begun setting up an office in the London station to recruit agents with the help of the unions. Donovan had him made a major in the Army so he would have some rank in dealing with the military for his project. He told Goldberg if that didn't work with senior officers he should take off his uniform and pretend to outrank them as a civilian.

While the rest of the London station occupied itself the next year and a half with infiltrating agents and commandos into France, Goldberg's little Labor Division, like a neglected stepchild, set out to put together its own organization for training and equipping European refugees from factories, rail yards, and merchant vessels to be spies who would leapfrog into Germany. The patrician Bruce, as had his Republican colleagues in the Washington headquarters, suspected at the outset that Goldberg was assembling a band of leftist union agitators to threaten capitalism after the war. Donovan, however, remained enthusiastic about his labor lawyer's work, sending Roosevelt regular updates on the unit.

As Casey began inventorying in the fall of 1944 what the London station could produce in the way of operations to penetrate Germany, Goldberg went home. Donovan agreed to let him process out of the Army. Goldberg's family finances were depleted, a major's salary was not enough to pay the bills, and he mistakenly believed the war would soon be over. But he left behind the seed for Casey's soon to be expanded initiative. It was a project code-named "Faust," after the tragic character who makes his pact with the devil in Johann Wolfgang von Goethe's play.

A half dozen Labor Division officers in London, along with the aides Goldberg had hired for the OSS office in New York, began recruiting Faust agents in January 1944. They found them among French and Low Country workers who had fled Nazi slave labor gangs in Germany but were willing to return to spy, sailors and stowaways on neutral merchant vessels who might slip away from their ships when they docked at German ports, and German refugees who might return posing as Wehrmacht officers. The Faust team also began collecting the addresses of friendly German safe houses the agents could use to make contact with the remnants of trade unions that were still resisting the Nazis and might be willing to collect intelligence or sabotage defenses facing invading Allied armies.

By early June 1944, twenty prospects had been recruited and sent to "Milwaukee," the code name for two adjoining London town houses where fake identities were prepared for the prospects and instructors trained them on spying inside Germany. (For one class, the men, posing as Wehrmacht prisoners, were sent to British POW camps so they could mingle with real captives in the cages to rehearse their cover stories and vacuum information on life in Germany.) When Casey found Faust in the fall, the project, operating on a shoestring budget of $46,784, had SHAEF's approval to infiltrate three-man teams (two spies and a radio operator) into Berlin and nine other major German cities.

Through their contacts in the International Transport Workers' Federation, the Faust team also found a woman willing to spy in Germany—a twenty-nine-year-old Berlin office clerk active in the anti-Nazi underground who had fled to Sweden in 1940. "She is intelligent, slight of build, not likely to be conspicuous in any respect, appears to be well balanced and not easily excited," noted a memo Goldberg sent to Donovan. The plan called for the woman to stow away on a Scandinavian ship and sneak off the vessel when it docked at Hamburg. Staying with German literature, her mission was given the code name "Goethe."

. . . .

Through the fall and winter, Dulles continued to inundate Washington with cables on the enemy. Kolbe made it to Bern in January 1945 with two hundred diplomatic documents crammed onto microfilm. A United Press reporter tipped Dulles off to outbreaks of diphtheria and scarlet fever in the southern part of Germany. Traffic snarls in the rest of the Reich, according to another source, were "approaching catastrophe," making it nearly impossible to distribute food supplies. To maintain home front morale Hitler had done his utmost to keep it well supplied with food and consumer goods, but now Germans could not buy staples with their ration cards. Dulles's reports on Asia also increased. The Japanese embassy in Berlin had begun relocating its intelligence section to Zurich, which will become "their European observation point for the coming years," he wrote to the State Department. One of his officers had struck up a conversation with Kojiro Kitamura, a Japanese director at the Bank of International Settlements in Basel, who passed along bleak predictions for Tokyo: "There will be no big naval engagement" in the Pacific "because one third of the Jap fleet is sunk and another one third is undergoing slow repairs" and the "Jap air force [is] insufficient to protect [the] remainder." Japan was also facing serious food shortages while Army Air Forces general Curtis LeMay's "bombardment by incendiaries" was proving far "more damaging than explosives." Dulles also became attentive to his press clippings, cabling Donovan after a *Reader's Digest* article on the Allied air strike on Peenemünde that he should be given credit as one of the agents who sent intelligence on the Nazi rocket center.

He continued, as well, to dabble in unconventional missions. An OSS propagandist arrived in October pretending to be a "special correspondent" for the *New York Herald Tribune*, a controversial cover because it put all journalists in jeopardy of being suspected government agents. Dulles, how-ever, had suggested the ruse and immediately put the man to work on psy-chological operations against the Germans. At the behest of Cordell Hull, the Bern chief got his hands on the diaries of the late count Galeazzo Ciano, Italy's disreputable foreign minister whom Mussolini had dismissed and the Germans had marched off to a firing squad even though Ciano was his son-in-law. His widow, Edda Mussolini Ciano, had fled to Switzerland with the diaries and now wanted to cash in on the material by having it published in the West. Dulles, who found the glamorous countess a testy fascist to work with, helped arrange a deal with the *Chicago Daily News*. The diaries cov-ered Ciano's service under Il Duce from 1939 to early 1943 and were chock-full of embarrassing gossip on Hitler, but Edda proved to be such a difficult contract negotiator the revelations did not appear in American papers until after Europe's war had ended.

Dulles's orbit of confidants in Bern continued to grow. Fritz Molden, a courageous Vienna agitator the Gestapo had briefly detained when he was just fourteen, had arrived in the summer to serve as a conduit between the OSS and the struggling Austrian underground. Dulles found the now twenty-year-old Molden "extraordinarily mature," he cabled Washington, more experienced as a covert operative than many of his seasoned agents. Molden brought out information on the location of Göring's and Himmler's Austrian hideouts as well as secret storage sites in Salzburg for Nazi archives. In 1948, he would become Dulles's son-in-law, marrying his daughter Joan. (Six years later, Dulles helped arrange Joan's divorce from Fritz, who turned out to be a philanderer like his father-in-law.)

Dulles's stable of mistresses expanded as well. Arturo Toscanini had long since become disillusioned with Mussolini, finally refusing to conduct the Fascist anthem for the dictator and emigrating in the 1930s to the United States, where he resettled in Riverdale, New York. The seventy-seven-year-old maestro now led the NBC Symphony Orchestra, recording propaganda broadcasts on the side for the Office of War Information. Meanwhile, his daughter, Countess Wally Castelbarco, an aristocratic and stunning divorcée with jet-black hair and piercing dark eyes, had taken up residence in Switzerland, where she funneled money to refugees and partisans from northern Italy. Dulles helped transfer funds from Toscanini to a Lloyds Bank account in Lausanne, which Wally regularly tapped for the antifascist underground. Soon he shared her bed, which irritated Mary Bancroft, who thought Dulles should be a one-mistress man.

Juggling women, however, now became an avocation for him. In November Dulles began making arrangements for Clover to join him in Bern. He truly missed his wife and wrote her "it would be grand to have you here." Clover needed no convincing. Securing all the visas and travel permits to cross what was still considered a war zone in France took a considerable amount of help from her husband's pals in the State Department. For the first leg from the Iberian Peninsula to Paris, Clover worked as a relief driver for a half dozen cars the department was delivering to the French capital. From there she hitched a ride in an Army car an officer was driving southeast, munching cold K rations along the way. She arrived in Bern in January 1945.

Dulles quickly introduced Mary Bancroft to Clover, who just as quickly surmised that Mary was her husband's lover. Astoundingly, the two women became friends. Clover had long reconciled herself to Allen's infidelity. She also soon craved companionship. Dulles once more proved to be an absentee husband, consumed with his spying and leaving his wife to fend for herself in Bern. "I want you to know I can see how much you and Allen care for each other," Clover finally told Mary. "And I approve." Mary soon introduced Carl Jung to Clover, who unloaded on the psychiatrist's staff the troubles in her marriage. Dulles thought the psychoanalysis would do her good.

The media reported in February that Helmuth von Moltke, the leader of the Kreisau Circle, had escaped Nazi custody and fled to Sweden. Dulles, who had tried in vain to spring him from the gallows, soon learned the reports were untrue. Moltke had been executed in January. Dulles received better news on Hans Gisevius that month. Late Saturday night, January 20, the doorbell for the West Berlin apartment the Abwehr agent was hiding in rang. Gisevius, who felt practically brain dead from a half year of hiding, opened the door to see a black car speed away and a thick envelope stuffed in the mailbox. Emptying it inside he soon realized an OSS courier had delivered the envelope, as Dulles had long ago promised. It contained the thick metal badge of a Gestapo executive officer, a passport with his picture identifying him as a Mr. Hoffman, and a special pass and letter from Gestapo headquarters instructing anyone he confronted to help in his secret mission to Switzerland. The forgers in the London station had produced works of art.

Gisevius bought a railroad ticket that night and Sunday evening boarded a southbound train. Ironically a senior SS officer was also a passenger, which enabled Gisevius to flash his phony Gestapo badge pretending to be a member of the general's traveling party. When the train finally stopped early morning on January 23 at the border town of Konstanz, Gisevius, hungry, thirsty, and exhausted from the strain of the journey, walked the last mile to a frontier post on the German side of the road. The Gestapo guard and customs officer inside inspected his credentials and lifted the gate. Gisevius shot out his arm in a Hitler salute and walked across to Kreuzlingen, Switzerland. That evening, he sat in the den of Herrengasse 23, his nerves "shattered," Dulles would report in a cable to London the next day thanking the station for the phony credentials. The Abwehr officer, his hair turned gray, hunched over in the easy chair beside the fireplace, unable to say more than "Thank you" for the first twenty minutes.

When he finally found his voice, Gisevius recounted the long, sad tale of how the July 20 plotters had failed. Dulles cabled the lengthy story to Washington, where Donovan passed it on to Roosevelt. The Abwehr man also settled historical scores with Stauffenberg, who was no longer alive to defend his legacy. He claimed the colonel would have established a "workers and peasants regime in Germany" allied with the Soviet Union if the coup had succeeded. Gisevius then secluded himself to finish his manuscript, filling in the last chapters on Valkyrie. Dulles eventually helped him find a publisher.

• • • •

Since August, Hitler had been telling his retreating generals in France to prepare for a return to the offensive when winter clouds and snows made it difficult for enemy airpower to control the skies. The plan the führer dreamed up by September—it in fact had supposedly come to him in a fever dream when he was afflicted with jaundice—was code-named "Herbst-nebel" for Autumn Mist. It called for thirty rebuilt divisions in Field Marshal Walter Model's Army Group B to counterattack west through the dense Ardennes to seize the Meuse River bridges, sever Montgomery's 21st Army Group from the Americans in the south, eliminate the threat to the Ruhr, destroy a third of the British-American force, and ultimately recapture Antwerp. Hitler envisioned Churchill and Roosevelt then forced to sue for peace, freeing up Wehrmacht divisions for the east to block the Russian winter offensive.

Model and other top generals in the field tried their best to talk Hitler out of Autumn Mist—arguing that the depleted armies they actually had in the west would be far too weak and stretched thin for such an ambitious counterattack—but the dictator refused to change hardly a word in his order. On December 16, as Bradley enjoyed a champagne dinner in Eisen-hower's villa quarters outside Paris to celebrate the news that Ike would receive his fifth star, 200,000 German soldiers moved out in deep snow toward the Americans at Ardennes. Autumn Mist lost momentum in ten days. The weather cleared for Allied air cover, Patton's 4th Armored Division relieved the 101st Airborne Division encircled at Bastogne, and Montgom-ery's January 3 counterattack restored the old lines within two weeks. Hitler lost about 100,000 men, succeeding only in delaying the West's advance into Germany while more than 180 Red Army divisions that had massed in the east launched their attack. But Ike and his generals had no cause for gloating over the führer's "last gamble," as it came to be called. American casualties totaled seventy thousand, including about eight thousand taken prisoner when two U.S. regiments surrendered in what came to be known as the Bat-tle of the Bulge.

The surprise offensive in the Ardennes was also the worst intelligence failure for the Americans since Pearl Harbor. Watching from London, where dazed panic swept through the Grosvenor Square command centers, Casey wrote later that Bradley, Eisenhower, and their field commanders had "grown complacent" that Ultra would alert them to any surprises from the Germans. The radio intercepts did not in this case because the Wehrmacht kept communications about Autumn Mist off the air. Officers for the 1st Army in the Ardennes, meanwhile, had long ago kicked out the OSS detachment assigned to collect intelligence from resistance elements ahead of the force, believing the unit was not needed. Donovan, who had been in Paris several days before Christmas, had rushed to Patton's headquarters. Along the way, the spy chief ordered his aides to root through the OSS's reports filed before December 16 to see if any had contained intelligence that the Germans would launch a counteroffensive. His officers found precious little, save for several cables on interrogations of German POWs and civilians in Luxembourg who noted large numbers of well-armed enemy convoys traveling at night before the attack. The OSS and Britain's services clearly were not producing enough information from behind Wehrmacht lines. Dulles thought the OSS director deserved some of the blame for that shortfall. Donovan, however, saw opportunity in the failure. "He sensed immediately that getting caught flat-footed in the Ardennes would create for the first time a clamor to get agents inside Germany," Casey recalled.

It would, although by the end of 1944 Casey had little to show for the penetration operation Donovan had ordered three months earlier. "Intelligence coming out of Germany is extremely meager," he admitted to Donovan in a December 29 memo. Only four American agents had been planted inside the country (one in Berlin) but none had radios to quickly send back any useful information. The London station had been reorganized to focus on Germany and had about a hundred spies and radio operators on hand for the mission, but Casey still lacked the planes to fly them into enemy territory, and the shortage of safe houses to receive them once they arrived was still a nagging problem.

Since they first met on the Lyon airstrip in September, Casey and Dulles had been taking subtle swipes at each other. Casey dismissed Dulles's making the rounds of different Allied headquarters that fall "peddling his line that more attention should be paid to indigenous German resistance." Dulles sent condescending cables to Washington on Casey—one, for example, pointing out his "misunderstanding" of a Bern station mission inside Germany. It explained why a promotion Donovan gave Casey on December 1 did not sit well with Dulles.

Before he transferred back to the United States, Bruce had cabled Donovan on November 27 recommending that he appoint Casey chief of secret intelligence for all of Europe with blanket authority to organize operations inside Nazi Germany. Bruce realized Casey was "young in years," but he was the only person in the London station who knew everything about the German operations and who had the "complete confidence of his associates," he wrote Donovan. Dulles thought such an important position should be given to someone more senior in the OSS than a thirty-one-year-old Navy lieutenant. But Donovan agreed with Bruce that Casey was the man to put the penetration of Germany on a fast track. He quickly approved the appointment. Because his new European intelligence chief would have military officers with higher ranks working under him and he would have to haggle with British and American generals to get operations launched, Donovan arranged for Casey to be processed out of the Navy so he could serve as a senior civilian. His salary was bumped up to $6,750 a year. Casey marched over to Selfridges three blocks from Grosvenor Square and picked out two gray suits, six shirts, four ties, two pairs of shoes, a fedora, and an overcoat, signing for them on the account the London station kept with the department store.

On December 10 he took a moment to pen a letter to Sophia and let her know there had been "startling developments in my military career." He couldn't tell her what they were, but two weeks earlier he thought it was a toss-up whether "I'd get a big job or come home," he wrote her. "I can confess only to you that the hope that I'd be turned down and could see you quickly kept rising." But "I got the job." Now he was "rushing about furiously" from early morning to 1 a.m. each night on work he would explain to her when he returned home.

CHAPTER 20

CASEY'S SPIES

Finally, Richard Helms broke free from Washington. The first week of January 1945, he arrived in London. Julia and the children remained in South Orange, New Jersey, near his parents. For her, Helms's transfer marked simply the beginning of another sad year of loneliness without her husband.

London clung to its seedy look. Christmas had been dreary for the city and New Year's Eve practically absent of booze for its somber residents. Jute sandbags stacked around government buildings had become rotted by rainy weather and smelly from dogs peeing on them—some with grass sprouting, others waterlogged and burst open. But the protection was still needed. Three weeks after Helms arrived, Britain suffered its worst attack of V-2s, with thirteen rockets slamming down on January 26.

The Board of Trade office in London issued him a clothing coupon book although others in the OSS station thought Helms hardly needed it. This model young lieutenant, always walking down hallways with long strides, never appeared in public unless he was immaculately attired in his crisply pressed Navy uniform. Colleagues also noticed Helms soon took up Bruce's hobby—prowling London's antique shops on weekends hunting for treasures.

The organized chaos Helms found in the London station offended his sense of order. He discovered the bright creative minds darting about

Grosvenor Square's hallways to be not much different from the crop that permeated OSS headquarters in Washington—men like Norman Pearson, a Yale American literature professor who worked in German operations, and Richard Ellmann, a future James Joyce biographer who worked for Pearson—and as in Washington some of them did not impress him. He thought Arthur Schlesinger, with whom Casey had bonded, was an academic effete.

Helms had been sent to London with orders to begin organizing the OSS mission Dulles would lead in Germany after the war ended. The Ardennes counteroffensive made clear to everyone in the station that it would be a while before Helms needed to worry about that assignment—"a colossal failure" of American intelligence, Casey grunted when they shook hands the first time. Instead of planning operations after the Germans surrendered, Casey dragooned Helms for his organization launching missions while they were still fighting—a far more dangerous undertaking, Helms realized. He marveled that Casey, who had held the same military rank he did and was just seventeen days older, now commanded such a big operation, but he didn't hesitate for a moment in agreeing to serve under him.

In fact, he felt lucky. Apartments were still scarce in London and the job came with an offer from Casey to share the one he now rented at 87 Harley House, a short walk from Grosvenor Square. The third roommate in the flat was Milton Katz, a Harvard Law School professor who had roamed Central Africa on an anthropological expedition and served as a New Deal attorney for Roosevelt. Though their politics were polar opposite, Casey thought the New Yorker was "one of the finest guys" he had ever met, he wrote Sophia. "I've learned more about being a nice person from him than from anybody since you started teaching me." Katz, now a Navy lieutenant commander, relieved Casey of some of his crushing workload training and dispatching agents into Germany. He soon made the legal scholar, who could be as overbearing as Casey at times, his trusted deputy.

Helms knew a lot about Casey's German operations before he showed up in London—many of Casey's memos to headquarters had been routed through him—and he knew this former Navy lieutenant had become one of Donovan's protégés. Donovan was easy for Helms to figure out—a war hero, born leader, a man who commanded instant loyalty. Casey, not so easy. He lived like a slob, Helms thought. He walked out of the apartment each morning with something always askew—his necktie, his shirt, his coat jacket, whatever. He had some kind of speech defect, Helms decided. He was forever asking Casey, "What did you say?" when he uttered what sounded like, "Mphmphmphmph." Yet Helms could see that Casey commanded the intense loyalty of his German operations staff, he had a brilliant energetic mind, he read voraciously, he worked nonstop, and he was definitely a risk taker. He was also chatty. When Casey arrived at the apartment late at night he invariably took another hour to fill Helms and Katz in on the high-level gossip he had picked up during the day.

Casey, however, soon began spending fewer nights at Harley House, Helms found. On January 23, Casey hopped aboard a plane with Colonel J. Russell Forgan, a close Dulles friend and former New York banker who had replaced Bruce as the overall OSS chief for Europe. They flew to the headquarters for the American armies in the field to poll their intelligence officers on what they needed from OSS agents in Germany. The fighting might last until fall 1945 and the Ardennes counteroffensive had made all the commanders painfully aware that "we are going blind into Germany," Brigadier General Edwin Sibert, Bradley's 12th Army Group intelligence chief, told the two men. Scouting patrols and aerial reconnaissance could tell commanders what lay just ahead of their front lines, but they needed agents farther east of the Rhine radioing back information on troop movements at key German transport centers, Sibert and the other intelligence officers said, along with operatives dropped even deeper inland to report on enemy reinforcements being sent to the front. "Thousands of men a day are being killed along the front," lectured General Eugene Harrison, the top intelligence officer for the 6th Army Group, whose divisions had landed at southern France. Don't "hesitate to take risks with your agents." Forgan assured all the generals that he and Casey had "already decided to abandon any caution."

Back in London, Casey mapped out his missions for Germany. They were ambitious. He wanted espionage teams trained in the makeup of the enemy's army dropped in to observe and radio back Wehrmacht troop movements through the militarily important rail centers at cities such as Hanover, Mainz, and Munich. Agents posing as laborers would parachute into industrial towns such as Darmstadt, Koblenz, and Karlsruhe to worm their way into factories and report back on arms production schedules, technological innovations, and plant layouts for Allied bombers to attack. Spies versed in guerrilla organizing would parachute into Berlin to hunt for remnants of the anti-Nazi movement and into Bavarian cities for evidence that the Nazis themselves were preparing an underground force to battle the Allies after the war. And as American and British armies overran cities he planned to have men and women posing as Germans infiltrate their civilian populations to spot trouble for occupation soldiers.

Casey cabled headquarters in Washington that he needed more staff officers, secretaries, and clerks for his operation. Donovan quickly approved each personnel request. Within a couple of months Casey had 330 people working for him. He set up the headquarters for his growing enterprise in town houses on Grosvenor Street and nearby Mount Street with telephone and teleprinter lines installed to connect them to the radio station near London designated Victor that received agent transmissions from Germany and to the BBC World Service in central London's Bush House, which could broadcast coded messages to the operatives. Casey also organized outposts in France, Belgium, the Netherlands, and other liberated countries to recruit and screen prospective agents who would be sent to London for spy training.

This would not be a lethargic bureaucracy, he decreed. No longer would the London station be "conservative in laying on missions" into Germany, Casey ordered in a February 22 memo. The OSS officers Donovan assigned to him were among the agency's most seasoned and energetic. George Pratt, the National Labor Relations Board lawyer who had served under Goldberg in New York and now ran the London station's labor division overseeing Faust, became chief of Casey's new Intelligence Procurement Division, which recruited, trained, and dispatched agents. (In addition to Faust, Pratt's division also took control of the German penetration operations the London station's French, Belgian, Dutch, Polish, Czech, and Scandinavian sections had been struggling to put together.) To be Pratt's deputy, Casey brought in Major Hans Tofte, a hard-charging Danish American who cut his teeth on covert operations by infiltrating into Yugoslavia for the OSS to funnel arms to its partisans. William Jay Gold, who had been managing editor of the

Virginia Quarterly Review before he joined the London station as a research analyst and who could read out of only one eye, became head of Casey's Reports Division, which made sure the intelligence the agents radioed in was distributed quickly to the field commanders who needed it. Robert MacLeod, a Swarthmore College psychology professor, had joined the OSS in Washington as a psychological warfare expert and risen to be a senior intelligence officer for Europe. He now led Casey's Division of Intelligence Direction, in charge of selecting German targets and briefing the spies on how to collect information on them. It became a difficult job. With so few contacts or safe houses on the ground, MacLeod's analysts had to research areas intensely so agents parachuting in blind had a fighting chance when they landed. Among the intelligence targets his experts found: Panzer refitting depots in Magdeburg and Grafenwöhr, intermediate communications centers in Giessen and Münster, equipment-loading stations in Cologne and Bingen.

Casey also had two of the OSS's most resourceful officers manning his important outposts in France. Commander Thomas Cassady had served as a naval attaché in Vichy, helping the OSS spirit downed British pilots back to England. After the Americans landed in North Africa and the Wehrmacht swept through southern France, Cassady was interned at Baden-Baden, Germany, where with bluffs and bribes he eventually managed to escape to Lyon. There he set up his own sabotage network. The Gestapo eventually caught him, but Cassady managed to convince them to arrange an exchange of diplomatic prisoners through Swiss intermediaries, which enabled him to return to the United States. He was now back in France in charge of Casey's Paris office, which worked with de Gaulle's intelligence service recruiting French agents to sneak across the border into Germany.

The grandson of an American insurance magnate, Henry Hyde had been born in Paris, educated at Harvard Law School, and recruited into the OSS by Dulles, who knew the agency would prize his fluency in French and German. At the young age of twenty-eight, the boyish-looking Hyde had organized highly successful agent operations into southern France from his base in North Africa. He next led the OSS detachment assigned to Patch's 7th Army as it marched north, and when the force neared the German border, Hyde recruited forty German-speaking agents for Casey (some were disgruntled Wehrmacht POWs) and sneaked them into the Reich. Casey pronounced the high-strung and quick-thinking Hyde "the most productive single human we have."

The war moved swiftly in January. The western Allies had 3.7 million soldiers protected by 18,000 warplanes along a 729-mile front now crossing the German border. Pratt and Tofte calculated that they would need as many as 175 spy students in the training pipeline in order to end up with 100 qualified agents who could have some chance of success in the Reich. Casey believed they had to move quickly to infiltrate operatives, particularly into Berlin, during the nights in February and March when the moon would be full and pilots could better see drop zones for their parachutists. But though his armies on the Western and Eastern Fronts could no longer halt the Allied and Soviet advances, Hitler's grip inside his country remained iron-tight. Casey pored over OSS estimates on the strength of the Gestapo, SD, and other intelligence services in Germany. It was still overwhelming.

Finding safe houses continued to be a headache for Casey. Some agents refused to parachute into Berlin unless they had in their pockets the address of at least one home considered friendly. The rapid movement of refugees and Wehrmacht troops in some areas made them "disorganized cauldrons." Aerial reconnaissance photos taken one day showing a field empty for an agent's parachute drop often had soldiers swarming over it the next night when the American plane arrived. A unit code-named "Bach" had been organized in the Milwaukee town houses for the Faust operation to create believable life stories, print phony identifications, and find German clothes for agents working in one of the world's most efficiently ruthless police states. Pratt's Intelligence Procurement Division took over Bach and made it a self-sufficient enterprise, no longer relying on the British or other foreign services for cover material. Lazare Teper, a Russian Jew whose family had emigrated to the United States, had been a Johns Hopkins University economist and research director for the International Ladies' Garment Workers Union when the OSS plucked him from Army basic training. The agency sent him to London to read Nazi journals and clip German newspapers for trivia on how the Reich's citizens lived, how they traveled and dressed, what ration cards, identity documents, and work permits they carried—all of which later became valuable information for the agent covers he now created as leader of the Bach unit.

An intricate set of regulations, like no other in the world, governed daily German life. The Nazi racial records system perfected over twelve years had compiled ancestry history on citizens going back five generations. Teper's analysts calculated that the average German citizen had up to eighteen different basic identity documents the Bach unit would have to forge. A Wehrmacht officer could carry as many as thirty. Teper's men scoured London's paper mills for ones that could produce stock nearly resembling what the Germans manufactured, then sent the sheets to a lab where chemists treated the paper so it matched. Different-colored dyes were found in the city or imported from the United States to duplicate the ink. Foreign workers recently returned from Germany and Wehrmacht soldiers captured in the Ardennes counteroffensive were emptied of their identity documents and interrogated on their nuances to help forgers duplicating them. And the nuances were multiple. The all-important *Arbeitsbuch*, the labor conscription card an agent needed to pose as a foreign worker, had an obscure number code on it designating the region in which the laborer could seek employment. Nazi eagle-and-swastika symbols looked right for some documents, left for others; a document with the eagle looking the wrong way was a dead giveaway it was phony.

Bach interrogators also found war prisoners a rich source of trivia. A German POW would clam up when asked about military matters but saw no harm in answering questions about how easy it was to travel in Berlin, how often his papers were checked, how clerks treated him in stores, what kind of ration coupons he used to buy meat, how a letter must be posted if it was being mailed overseas—all vital information for an OSS operative. Covers took weeks to craft and had to be individualized so the phony life story an agent gave authorities dovetailed somewhat with the agent's real background or physical makeup and made sense to the person checking his papers. Captured German telephone books became valuable; they contained addresses that could be used for these stories. German cigarettes, Bach found, could be bought in Belgium. From war prisoners and the closets of homes and the shelves of shops in German border towns the Allies had captured, Teper's scavengers collected for their male and female agents hundreds of German uniforms, civilian suits, ties, shirts, shoes, socks, overcoats, hats, dresses, ladies hose, panties, bras, cigarette lighters, toothbrushes, razors, tubes of toothpaste, and lipstick. The clothing and phony documents fooled the enemy for the most part. But Bach had its slipups. German security officers noticed that the identity cards for two agents, although supposedly issued from different towns, had the same handwriting. The ration cards given to other agents had expired so they were no good for buying food. Sometimes an item from England slipped into a spy's German wardrobe, such as the billfold in his back pocket or the comb and case tucked in his jacket. Resourceful Gestapo officers also found ways to strip through a cover, such as ripping off a suspect's clothes to see if he had bruises on his chest or thighs—the spots where parachute straps yanked at him when his chute unfurled.

Even with the elaborate covers Bach created, finding the spies themselves proved no easy task for Casey and his officers. He was willing to pay well by the day's standards: $200 a month while an agent was in training, $331 monthly after he was sent in, plus a $3,675 death benefit for his widow if the Germans killed him. Casey wanted quality over quantity. The ideal spy, he decided, was an older man or woman (females, in fact, would "have less difficulty . . . getting around Germany," he said), someone who already knew how to operate a radio and had experience "in underground work" so it wouldn't take long to train him, and a person with "strong ideological or grudge motives for the job." That talent pool was small, he quickly discovered. German American OSS officers would be clueless about the country under Nazi rule and their accents would likely give them away. Able-bodied native Germans dropped in would immediately raise a question with the Gestapo: why weren't they in the army at the front? Ardent anti-Nazis were an endangered species; Himmler had scooped most of them up after the Valkyrie plot. There was a universe of Germans with "unsavory backgrounds," as one memo to Donovan put it—Nazi prostitutes from occupied countries, former German officials trying to ingratiate themselves with the Allies, Wehrmacht criminals from penal units the Americans captured, juvenile delinquents cast out of the Hitler Youth, and an assortment of closet socialists or dissident Nazi rightists—but they all had their drawbacks. That left the three most fruitful groups for Casey to canvass: POWs, foreign laborers, and German communists.

As of the beginning of January, the OSS estimated the Allies had more than a million German soldiers in their POW camps. A debate had percolated in military circles since November over whether a select few of these men could be used as spies. The Geneva Convention and War Department regulations clearly forbade it. But the Army's provost marshal (which ran the military police and oversaw the incarceration of enemy prisoners), the service's G-2 intelligence section, and Donovan's senior advisers in Washington saw no problem with enlisting Wehrmacht prisoners for espionage work if they were willing. Casey ordered Helms to investigate the legalities. He came back with an artfully worded memo that essentially recommended don't ask, don't tell. Any official request to use German POWs as spies "would be disapproved" by the Joint Chiefs, Helms wrote, so do not submit one. Instead, Hyde in France and OSS and British officers in Italy have been quietly visiting prisoner cages, interrogating Germans, and, with a wink and nod from the camp commanders, taking away the agreeable ones to train as spies. No paperwork was sent up the chain of command. Casey should do the same at POW camps in England and the United States, Helms advised, and not "attempt to straighten it out formally with [the] military authority."

As it was, Casey decided he did not need the POWs as spies until after Germany's surrender when they would be sent in as informers for the occupation armies. For the wartime espionage he found he had enough recruits from the other two groups: foreign laborers and communists. To toil in Reich factories, by D-Day Germany had drafted eight million workers or POWs from France, Belgium, Luxembourg, the Netherlands, Scandinavia, Czechoslovakia, the Soviet Union, and Poland. Men from these nations, posing as foreign workers, would have reason to be in Germany but not in its army. Casey's officers searched for prospects among refugee camps and the resistance forces of many of these countries. Communists, however, gave Casey and other hard-liners in his unit pause. In Paris, Cassady had found a number of German communists who had taken refuge with the Comité Allemagne libre pour l'Ouest, or CALPO, a Moscow-backed group that had fought with the French Resistance during the occupation. The State Department wanted CALPO kept at arm's length, while the British Home Office, already nervous about the OSS bringing Germans to England for spy training, was even more antsy about German communists arriving. Instead of returning to the Fatherland they might just as easily remain in the United Kingdom as Soviet agitators, the Home Office feared. Donovan, however, was willing to work with anyone ready to fight the Nazis. He ordered Casey to bite his lip and recruit the communists.

Katz investigated whether their operation should set up a psychological assessment program as headquarters had in the United States to carefully screen prospects for their spy potential. He decided there wasn't enough time. They would just have to throw recruits into training and hope they had the mental makeup for espionage work. Casey agreed. Almost overnight, Pratt's men set up training and briefing centers at five secret sites in England and one in Poissy northwest of Paris. Security officers watched the neighborhoods surrounding the facilities for anyone suspicious and erected innocuous-looking barriers around training buildings to keep intruders from getting too near and peering into windows. Elaborate background checks were conducted for the staffs at each site—down to the charwomen who cleaned the rooms—to make sure Axis spies did not infiltrate them. Students were kept mostly quarantined, save for occasional times they were allowed out for visits to the hospital or dinner at a restaurant, and only then under escort. Casey often motored to Area F, a walled estate in the suburb of Ruislip northwest of London, where his agents received their basic spy training. In addition to tradecraft classes, instructors drilled their students on German military organizations, war equipment, convoy procedures, road signs, uniform insignias, as well as Nazi slang and problems the agents might encounter at Gestapo checkpoints. Casey lived vicariously through these brave men and women who would be dropping into danger he could not imagine. "Give these guys anything they want," he usually told the trainers when he left. "They're the kings around here."

. . . .

Casey's life became a blur of one meeting after another on Grosvenor Street, lunches with the foreign officers at Claridge's, late nights at his desk, ducking into shelters for Nazi rocket attacks, or darting off in what practically became his personal plane to inspect his outposts in England and on the continent. Some station colleagues sniped that his new position swelled his head, made him a braggart, full of himself. But no one could deny that he had a talent for untangling bottlenecks, browbeating sections to work together, and making the machinery of putting spies into Germany speedier and more efficient. It took weeks but he eventually solved his transportation problem. After France's liberation, agent parachute operations atrophied. Relations between the OSS and what remained of the Carpetbaggers in the 492nd Bombardment Group had grown poisonous. Through cajoling and threats Casey finally got the planes he needed—although even then the vagaries of winter weather over Germany many times kept aircraft grounded, or pilots carelessly dumped spies in the wrong spot. "Look, you're not dropping bombs, you're dropping human beings!" Casey at one point shouted to an air group leader not particularly bothered by the foul-ups.

A breakthrough came with Joan-Eleanor. It was the name Lieutenant Commander Steve Simpson, a hard-driving former RCA scientist, had given to a lightweight compact radio with long-life batteries that Casey's agents could now take into the field to transmit directly to an OSS officer in a high-flying plane circling overheard. Joan came from a WAC major Simpson admired and Eleanor came from the wife of his co-developer in RCA's Long Island lab. The radio signal shot upward on a narrow beam that made it nearly impossible for German direction-finding equipment on the ground to locate the sender. Simpson began testing the top secret communications system in October with a speedy British De Havilland Mosquito carrying the receiver flying at thirty thousand feet over an agent in the field. He finally got it to work. A team still needed the old suitcase-sized wireless telegraph sets for much of the two-way communications with London, the lone Mosquitos could not fly over areas infested with enemy antiaircraft defenses, the BBC had to alert a team when a plane was in the area, and elaborate code words had to be used because the agent transmitted in the clear. But an operative could radio in twenty minutes over Joan-Eleanor what often took a day to send over the wireless telegraph. Time wasn't wasted having to retransmit Morse code messages that had arrived garbled; the officer in the plane could have the agent repeat what he said until he heard it correctly. The conversation was also recorded in the aircraft so London had a record of what was said. And for a lonely spy in hostile Germany Joan-Eleanor was a much appreciated friendly voice.

Despite many setbacks, Casey began to see progress. By the end of March, fifty-three teams had infiltrated into Germany and the portion of the Netherlands the Wehrmacht still occupied—five of them already overrun by advancing Allied armies. Another fifty teams were being readied to parachute in during April. "It mattered little to us or to the generals we served that in retrospect the war seemed almost won," he recalled. Demand for intelligence on what lay ahead of the Allied armies "inside Hitler's fast crumbing Reich" remained insatiable.

. . . .

Helms often drove out to Harrington Field on cold forbidding nights to oversee the dispatch of agents to Germany. Casey wanted him there as his eyes and ears when he couldn't attend. The ritual was almost always the same, Helms found. He met the agents in a London apartment, bare except for a few desks, where a staffer from the Bach section, acting like a Gestapo thug, grilled the men one last time on their cover. Helms wondered how long the phony life stories or meticulously prepared documents would keep a spy alive. Bach could not change the records stored in German archives; even a perfunctory check with the department from which the forged document supposedly came would likely reveal it was illegitimate, Helms worried. And as German administration ahead of the Allied advance began to fall apart, harried Gestapo or SS officers might not even bother with a records check; they would simply shoot a suspect on the spot. These men and women likely will die if they are stopped, Helms believed. He had heard stories that the suicide capsule they all carried to spare them from agonizing torture did not always work; just as bad, overly anxious agents, according to reports reaching London, had been known to gulp down their L tablet in situations that turned out to be not as dangerous as they first thought and to kill themselves needlessly.

A "Joe handler," the name for the conducting officer assigned to escort the team and cater to its last wishes (like a favorite meal, groceries for a family left behind, or a final fling with a prostitute), joined them for the two-hour car ride to Harrington. Helms said little to the agents along the way. He thought the odds of these missions succeeding were slim and he thought the spies knew they were slim. No one was in the mood for chitchat. At Harrington's dressing hut, the Joe handler, clutching a long list, performed his final inventory of the items each agent would have hanging from him or stuffed in two battered suitcases—sets of clothing, radio equipment, one knife, a grenade, a pistol with three clips, his false documents, and spy gadgets each might need such as miniature cameras camouflaged as match-boxes, digestible paper, cloth for invisible messages, shaving brushes with hidden compartments in the handles, leather belts with secret pockets, or capsules to shove up rectums for hiding microfilm. The Joe handler also made a final check of the clothing to make sure it was German, of the agent's head and hands to make sure the cut of hair and condition of the fingers matched the cover story. (If he was supposed to be a manual laborer his hands should be rough and the nails dirty.)

With coveralls over them (not only so the gear hanging from their bod-ies wouldn't snag on parachute lines but also so the civilian suit they wore wouldn't be muddied and look to a policeman like they had just jumped into a field) the agents waddled to their planes. As they climbed aboard, Helms always wondered how much self-control these men and women would have when they landed at a site with no one friendly around. Would an operative take the time, as instructed, to dig a deep hole to bury his parachute and coveralls, then gather sticks and leaves to cover the freshly dug dirt? Or would he run as fast and as far away from the drop zone as he could, for fear of the authorities stumbling onto him and asking what he had in the suit-cases? Helms knew his first instinct would be to flee quickly. He admired the courage of the spies who remained to cover up their landings.

Helms spent much of the night waiting in Harrington's cramped control tower until the plane that had carried his agents returned and the pilots re-ported to him that they had parachuted out. He usually made it back to the Harley House apartment by early the next morning bleary-eyed while Casey was eating his breakfast.

"A successful drop," was all he said most times if the news was good. Casey always grunted, with a look of relief on his face, and returned to his powdered eggs.

• • • •

Early Sunday morning, March 18, a driver, with Casey in the backseat, motored to Grendon Hall, a secluded manor house in Northamptonshire that his officers had designated part of Area O for quartering spies before they were delivered to Harrington Field seventeen miles away. The agents also had access to the firing range at nearby Castle Ashby to test their pistols before infiltrating. Seeing off spies was always an emotional experience for Casey. Unlike the taciturn Helms, he compensated for the agony he felt inside by being chatty with the operatives before they boarded their planes. This evening he was seeing off the teams code-named "Doctor" and "Painter." His Belgian desk had recruited them to parachute into two different spots around Munich to organize espionage networks among Belgian workers in the city and to scout out drop zones and safe houses for agents Casey planned to infiltrate later into the Bavarian city. Doctor's two agents would parachute into an empty field fifty miles southeast of Munich in Austria's Tyrolean Alps and make their way to the good friend of one of the team members who might shelter them in his house at the border town of Kufstein. Painter's two operatives would parachute to a safe house near Trostberg east of Munich, which was owned by the Catholic Church.

Unlike some of the teams, these four men were experienced espionage agents. Thirty-three-year-old Alphonse Blonttrock, who went by the alias Jean Denis and was Doctor's radioman, had worked in the Belgian Air Ministry as a telegraph operator and served with a sabotage unit near his country's German border until September 1944. A short man with an oval face, receding hairline, and a scar down his right cheek, Blonttrock would never be accused of being brilliant but he was a serious-minded spy student at Area F, who retained well what he learned, was punctual to class, and conscientious about security. Because his cover was as a Belgian mechanic drafted for garage work in Munich, his OSS trainers sent him to auto repair school. Jan Smets, Blonttrock's twenty-four-year-old partner who served as the team's spy, had been a student all his life, specializing in catalytic chemistry at the University of Brussels until he joined the Belgian resistance in 1944. Going by the alias Jan Bloch, Smets was the opposite of Blonttrock, whom he didn't particularly like. Erect and self-centered with a ruddy complexion, Jan had been a quick study at F school, but he was lazy, arriving to classes late, skipping morning physical training, and interested more in London's women and nightlife than his course work. He barely passed spy training. For Smets's cover, he was a Belgian laborer who had worked in a Munich factory until it was bombed out and now he was looking for employment elsewhere.

The Painter team's spy was twenty-five-year-old Emil Jean Van Dyck, who had joined the Belgian army in 1939, escaped to England after the Nazis overran his country, then returned to Belgium twice for espionage missions as an SOE agent. With his horn-rimmed glasses and hair swept back he looked more like a young librarian than a secret warrior, but Van Dyck, who had accumulated seven cover names (for the different countries he had infiltrated), was an exuberant and strong-willed man who "likes action and danger," his Area F instructors reported. His politics worried the trainers—"sentimental left" and sympathetic to the Soviet Union, they noted—but Emil more than made up for it by his deep hatred of the Germans. François Flour, his radioman and about the same age, had been a university student in classical philology until he joined the Belgian merchant navy and later his country's secret service after the Nazis invaded. Handsome with his mustache cropped close like Hitler's, François (who used the last name Fouget for his cover) had been imprisoned by the Germans but freed after Brussels was liberated in October 1944; he spent the next two months behind the lines in the Netherlands for the SOE. With seven forged identity documents each, both agents planned to pose as Belgian workmen. In addition, Emil had 109,000 reichsmarks in his money belt along with letters of introduction from Belgian Jesuits to convince the Catholic Church's Alexian Brothers east of Munich to hide them in one of their half dozen sanctuaries while they built their espionage network. The prearranged sentence Emil would recite to prove to the Alexians that he and François were Belgian agents and not Nazi plants: "I am coming from Aachen where I saw the Jesuit Fathers and I am bringing news of Père Faust."

By the time Casey arrived at Grendon Hall on March 18, the agents were in a surly mood. Casey had planned to dispatch the Doctor team at the end of December 1944 and the Painter team two months later but the dates kept slipping because of frustrating air transport delays. The four men had been cooling their heels at Area O's country cage the past three days and had begun clamoring with their Joe handlers to either put them on a plane for Germany or let them spend their nights in London's pubs. To the relief of the handlers, who had run out of ways of keeping Doctor and Painter entertained at Grendon, their flight was definitely set for mid-morning that Sunday. A plane would take the four men to Dijon in eastern France where they would hop aboard another plane that would fly them to Munich.

At Harrington, Casey watched as the Joe handlers rechecked the leather suitcases each man would carry with their weapons, clothes, and radio equipment. Bavaria was still frigid in March so they packed heavy with thick overcoats, snow boots, and an extra ration of food in case they had to survive in the mountains or forests longer than planned. Casey watched as the bomber lifted off with the agents and their escorts precisely at 11 a.m. Jan Smets appeared jaunty and carefree as he climbed into the aircraft. Casey thought it was an act. The tight-lipped and grim look of the other three men more accurately mirrored their mood—and likely how Smets felt inside, Casey believed.

Back at the London station, Casey received a cable in the wee hours of Tuesday morning that drove him to distraction as all the previous ones like it had. The plane with the Painter and Doctor teams had taken off from Dijon with no problem but the pilot lost his bearings when he had to evade antiaircraft flak south of Kufstein and was forced to return to base with the two teams. Painter finally parachuted in during the early morning hours of Wednesday, March 21. Doctor did not drop until three days later. Casey's Belgian desk ordered the Victor radio receiving station to keep a close watch of the frequencies on which the two teams would transmit and to report to the London station "immediately" when it received the first message from Doctor or Painter.

Doctor was the first to come on the air March 26. The short Morse code transmission informed London that it had landed safely and asked the BBC to radio a test message with the sentence: "The Reich is the armory of the enemy through cruelty." Casey immediately alerted Shepardson in Washington that Blonttrock and Smets had infiltrated into Germany.

The Doctor team landed five miles from the designated drop zone southeast of Kufstein, which turned out to be a lucky break. Smets and Blonttrock probably would have been killed if the pilot had dropped them in the right spot. German mountain soldiers had been conducting maneuvers in that field during the day and planned to return the next day. They would surely have noticed tracks in the snow-covered meadow and could easily have tracked the team. But Smets and Blonttrock faced the problem all agents did when they parachuted into the wrong place: they had no idea where they were. Finding out was made more difficult by the fact that with snow covering practically everything that night the men had no way to orient themselves. Fortunately, Smets had landed only fifty yards away from Blont-trock. The plane's dispatcher had shoved out the three containers with their equipment and clothing, then Smets had jumped through the Joe hole and his partner had followed. They had agreed ahead of time that Smets would stay put and Blonttrock would look for him.

Smets gathered his billowing chute, pulled the flask out of his jacket, took a swig of cognac, and collapsed. It took Blonttrock only five minutes to find him. It took both men about three hours to locate the three containers, which had landed about 250 yards away. With their dark coveralls and suits, the agents stood out in the snow illuminated by the clear moon, so they cut up one of the white parachutes to cover their bodies for camouflage and began digging holes to bury the other chutes and their three containers near where they landed. They had been dropped on the top of a mountain that looked out to the Kitzbühel Alps. Smets guessed it was about three thou-sand feet to the valley below; they didn't have the equipment or experience to climb down. The snow ranged from three to twelve feet deep in places. So they climbed to a rise that gave them a view of any Germans who might show up from below. Smets unrolled his sleeping bag, drained the rest of his cognac from his flask, and crawled in. Blonttrock took the first watch.

The second stroke of good luck arrived several hours later as dawn broke. Blonttrock nudged his partner to wake him. Through his binoculars he had spotted three figures trudging up the mountains toward them. Blont-trock and Smets kept their pistols trained on them. But the intruders turned out to be friendly, the agents discovered to their relief. The three men were Tyrolean deserters from the German army. The day before, they had spread a large red-and-white Austrian flag in the exact spot on which the Doctor team had landed, hoping to signal to Allied planes passing by that friendly partisans were in the area and receive airdrops of supplies to help them form a resistance group. When they heard the B-24 Liberator with Doctor flying low over the area the previous night, they set out at dawn to see if the plane had left a parachute load.

The Tyroleans helped Smets and Blonttrock dig up their containers and lug them to a nearby hut where they had been hiding out and where they had bread, meat, and hot tea to feed the Belgians. Later that night, the de-serters helped the two agents make the exhausting four-hour climb down the mountain to a farmhouse in the village of Scheffau, which was just south of Kufstein. The next morning Blonttrock unpacked his radio and sent his first message to let London know that Doctor had arrived and was ready to go to work. Casey's analysts had given Smets a list of more than three dozen targets around Kufstein to check out—weapons factories, parts depots, airfields, SS garrisons, suspected concentration camps, villas for top officials like Göring, and arms caches fanatical Nazis might have hidden to fight with after the surrender. Doctor's orders were to stay in the field spying and radioing back what they found until the war's end.

From Painter, nothing but silence—always frustrating for Casey. Van Dyck and Flour had also been dropped in the wrong place in the early morning hours of March 21—about a dozen miles from their intended spot near Trostberg. They immediately gathered up their parachutes, quickly stripped off their coveralls, and found a place in the woods to hide them in one of the containers that had dropped nearby. Grabbing the suitcases with the rest of their equipment they began laboriously walking northwest until daybreak when they took cover in the woods for the rest of the day. Flour's right heel throbbed with pain. He had injured it in January after a parachute jump and his subsequent jumps, like last night's, had only made it ache even more. Late the second night they set out on a northwest trek once more, but this time with half their equipment. Carrying everything was too difficult, particularly with Flour's bad heel, so they buried one of the two wireless telegraph sets they brought instead of Joan-Eleanor, one of their two batteries (it had been cracked from last night's landing and was probably useless, Flour believed), and their two Sten guns (which wouldn't be much good in holding off any Germans they encountered, the men decided).

By the next morning, Van Dyck and Flour had reached the outskirts of Trostberg. They decided to bury the second radio set and the rest of the equipment in the woods there and walk the final leg along the road leading into the city. Van Dyck tracked down the address there of an Alexian Brothers sanctuary he had been told might provide them shelter. The Brothers fed the two agents but their charity stopped with the meal. A Hitler Youth center sat next door to the sanctuary. The Alexians were terrified it would be only a matter of time before the fanatical teens discovered the sanctuary was harboring subversives.

Van Dyck and Flour set out once more, by foot and by train, until they finally reached Munich Saturday night, March 24. They sat in an all-night café until the next morning, sipping coffee and trying to look inconspicuous. Then they took a bus to the next address on Van Dyck's list of prospective safe houses—this one an apartment a Belgian mechanic rented over a military garage the SS used. He introduced himself only by his last name, Van Geel, but he was much friendlier than the Alexians. Van Geel's problem, however: he knew practically no one in Munich so he would be no help to the agents in setting up a spy network among other Belgian laborers. Van Geel did know a lot about living conditions in the city—he filled Van Dyck and Flour in on them the rest of that Sunday—and he did have one friend, who found them lodging with another Belgian couple willing to take the agents for the night. Bright and early Monday morning, March 26, Van Dyck and Flour walked into Munich's Arbeitsamt (the Employment Exchange) and registered as refugees looking for work. It was their first step into a month-long quagmire of oppressive Nazi security controls and bad luck.

• • • •

The preparations for the end had begun in earnest by the first week of February. Churchill, Roosevelt, and Stalin convened in the limestone and marble Livadia summer palace at the Crimean resort town of Yalta on the Black Sea to decide how Germany would be demilitarized, denazified, and carved into zones occupied by the victors, how the war-torn nations of Europe would be reconstituted when the fighting ended, and how the three powers would move to crush the Japanese empire in Asia. After his failed Ardennes counteroffensive, Hitler moved his headquarters to Berlin to ride out what remained of the war in the deep underground Führerbunker near the Reich Chancellery. While Eisenhower's armies established a bridgehead to his west, to his east the Red Army, whose advance in January had been slowed only by supply trains not catching up, now stood at the Oder ready to begin the final advance on the capital of the Reich that the Nazis proclaimed would flourish for a thousand years.

Helms flew to Paris on March 20, booking a comfortable room in the Parc Monceau Hotel near the Arc de Triomphe, and began organizing the

OSS mission that would move into Germany with the occupation army. Shepardson had alerted Donovan and Dulles in November that with his reporting stint in Berlin and his "very considerable" knowledge of the German language and culture the Navy lieutenant was ideally suited for setting up the administrative machinery of the postwar intelligence operation. Helms left London with an uneasy feeling about Casey's drive to quickly plant agents inside the Reich. He was a meticulous man by nature and if his year and a half in the spy world had taught him anything it was that carefully planned intelligence missions produced far more than hurried derring-do. Casey's German operation had too much of the latter, Helms feared. Missions had been organized slapdash and teams had been rushed into Germany with too little preparation, he thought. Time was of the essence, he knew, but he also knew that agents got killed when corners were cut.

But Helms could not dwell on that now. He had thousands of details to attend to in putting together the spy mission for a defeated power. Within two weeks he had recruited small teams of OSS intelligence officers to enter Cologne, Frankfurt, Nuremberg, Bremen, Munich, Stuttgart, and Berlin when they were liberated. Helms planned to join the five men he had rounded up so far for the Berlin team.

• • • •

Within a year after he had arrived in Bern, Dulles had begun cabling Washington with his thoughts on how a postwar German government should be set up and the role the OSS should play in it. "Germany should be decentralized" after the war, he advised in a December 1943 radiotelephone call, "and Prussia divided up into its constituent pre-Bismarck parts, and the capital removed from Berlin. . . . The principal reason for the liquidation of Prussia is the fact that the reactionary forces in Germany, which helped the Nazis into power, had their stronghold there." Besides Nazi holdouts, the enemy of a peaceful and democratic Germany will be the Soviet Union, he believed. During his visit to Washington in October 1944, Dulles took time to pen a lengthy memo to Donovan, which predicted—correctly as it turned out—a future Cold War. "Russia now believes that she is entitled to a dominating position in Eastern and Southeastern Europe," he wrote. In areas such as Poland, eastern Germany, Hungary, Czechoslovakia, and the Balkans "Russia does not intend to impose a strictly Communist regime" but it will expel, liquidate, or subordinate political elements in those countries considered hostile and install "leftist regimes . . . pledged to cooperate primarily with Moscow," Dulles predicted. Stalin knows "we will not try to prevent Russian domination by force and hence we should not bluff about it." But Stalin also "does not wish a clash in Europe with the United States or England at the present time." So for countries like Germany—particularly in the territory the Red Army will occupy—Dulles believed Russia's clandestine services will use psychological warfare, subversion, and political intimidation to establish a pro-Soviet government. Therefore, "the German people will need sound guidance politically in order to develop a democratic system after the collapse," he wrote in another memo—guidance he was prepared to give.

Dulles cabled to Donovan, Mayer, and even Helms lists of "useful Germans" for the postwar government—labor leaders, socialists, scientists, and intellectuals he had met during his Bern tour as well as survivors of the Valkyrie plot like Gisevius and Waetjen. He began brainstorming as early as November 1943 on the team of officers he wanted with him to fly into Berlin when the Americans or Soviets took it. Goldberg sent him long lists of German union members, German Americans in the U.S. Army fluent in the language, and key people in the London station's labor division, such as George Pratt and Lazare Teper, who could help organize what was left of the German labor movement after hostilities ended.

On January 4, 1945, Dulles flew to Lyon to huddle with Donovan on the assignments his postwar German mission would have. The unit's spies and experts will collect and analyze military, political, economic, and even "sociological" intelligence in the zone the Americans will occupy, they decided. Its counterespionage officers will root out subversive Nazis gone underground to mount a guerrilla war. Teams will hunt for the technology, hardware, and German scientists who developed Hitler's secret weapons, such as rockets and chemical and biological agents. There was one other highly secret mission the two men discussed. Donovan wanted Dulles to send spies into the zones Russia and Great Britain will occupy in Germany. He assumed the Soviet and British intelligence services will try to penetrate the American zone. Donovan wanted the OSS doing the same in their sectors.

CHAPTER 21

TO GERMANY

The Doctor team spent its first five days hidden in the Scheffau farmhouse of the three Austrian deserters. The trio's leader, who identified himself as Rudolf Steiner, summoned sixteen other deserters to the farm. They were all eager to take up arms against the Nazis and they now became the nucleus for Smets and Blonttrock's espionage network. On day six, the Austrians and the OSS agents moved to a cabin high up in the mountains, which farmers used in the summer to guard grazing cattle and which afforded the team more security for storing their equipment and transmitting messages. Blonttrock radioed London on March 29 that he needed food, medicine, weapons, and uniforms of the German mountain infantry to equip a guerrilla band of twenty. A plane delivered the supplies in eight parachuted containers three days later along with explicit orders that did not sit well with the partisans: the weapons were to be used to protect the team, not to attack the Germans, which the partisans dearly wanted to do. Such attacks would only invite reprisals, London feared.

Though the region was infested with SS, Blonttrock and Smets needed little protection. They rarely mingled among villagers in the valley, except to occasionally buy black-market food with the reichsmarks they brought with them. (The pair soon realized the identity documents the Bach section manufactured for them had errors and would not survive close inspection.)

A number of villagers knew the Americans were in the mountains but never informed on them. The Austrians around Kufstein had long since become fed up with arrogant German officers and were decidedly anti-Nazi. Blonttrock's only close call came one afternoon as he transmitted from a partisan's house in the Alpine village of Ellmau south of Kufstein. Field Marshal Robert Ritter von Greim, who had succeeded Göring as Luftwaffe commander on April 26, had decided to relocate his headquarters to Ellmau. A haughty staff officer rapped on the door of the partisan's home looking for suitable quarters for his field marshal. The quick-thinking partisan showed the adjutant around, except for a bedroom where he said his four children were sleeping. (Blonttrock was in the room with his radio.) Satisfied, the adjutant left and later commandeered the house for Greim to occupy.

Doctor became one of Casey's most productive teams. Over forty-five days, Blonttrock radioed fifty-two messages with intelligence Smets and his guerrilla gang collected on the deployment of Wehrmacht mountain battalions, artillery batteries, antiaircraft emplacements, and Volkssturm civilian militia around Kufstein, as well as the location of a war factory, an oil depot, Himmler's private train on a rail track, and a section of the Autobahn southeast of Munich being used as a runway for a nearby jet plane base—all rich targets for Allied bombers. Smets also discovered two POW camps— one with twelve thousand Russian soldiers south of Stuttgart, the other with about fifty prominent captives at the thirteenth-century Itter Castle in North Tyrol. They included former French premiers Édouard Daladier and Paul Reynard, French army commander Maurice Gamelin, and Stalin's son. (London ordered Smets not to try a guerrilla raid to free the VIPs; just keep collecting information.) On May 5, three days before the German surrender, Smets set out on foot from Scheffau and walked west in the dark for two hours until he ran into a forward battalion of the American 36th Division. During the next week, he led GIs to the addresses of Nazi bigwigs so they could be arrested—including Field Marshal von Greim, snug in his Ellmau village quarters.

• • • •

From March into April the weeks became frenetic for Casey and his men racing to place spies inside Germany—"a chess game against the clock," he later recalled. Their war room at 70 Grosvenor Street became a madhouse as radioed reports poured in, espionage teams streamed out (fifty-eight from March 17 to April 24), and pins on maps hanging from the walls moved hourly as battle lines inched forward and planes dropping agents rushed to stay ahead of moving fronts. The Allied and Soviet drives left a narrower nation in the center under Hitler's control. Advancing forces like the 3rd Army overran more spy teams. "General Patton is screwing up all my operations," moaned one of Casey's dispatchers. To complicate matters even more, the full moon period began on March 20 with all of Western Europe blanketed by dense clouds; Casey eventually ordered pilots to make their way to Germany as best they could and drop agents in blackness. When an exhausted Army captain asked for two days off at the end of March, Casey huffily rejected it. "The war may be too nearly over for that kind of nonsense," he told the officer. But the pace was wearing everyone down, Casey included. Pushed to fly dark night after dark night, Carpetbagger aircraft and their crews neared the breaking point. One navigator, spent from eight missions in seven days, broke down on the tarmac after the last one and cried like a baby.

The communists Casey found so distasteful turned out to be his most daring and resourceful agents. The London station's labor division organized the German refugees, drawn from the Soviet-backed resistance movements in Western Europe, and gave each team a code name after a tool. Among the tenacious was Hammer, one of several teams Casey tapped for his most hazardous mission—parachuting into Berlin. Paul Lindner, a thirty-four-year-old machinist who fled Berlin in 1935 when his underground labor organizing caught the attention of the Gestapo, had eventually ended up in England where British authorities kept a close watch on him because of his work with the Moscow-aligned Free Germany Movement in Great Britain. Small and wiry, Lindner struck Casey's trainers as a driven anti-Nazi, full of nervous energy, who might be a valuable spy. His partner, a thirty-three-year-old printer named Anton Ruh, had also escaped Berlin after being jailed seven months as a union agitator and had also eventually made it to England and joined the Free Germany Movement. As smart as Lindner, Ruh also had "a stolid kind of courage" the OSS trainers thought would "keep the mission on an even keel" in dangerous Berlin. Flown in a speedy A-26 Invader light bomber, the two men parachuted to a spot just northwest of the capital in the early morning hours of March 2, each with a $500 diamond in his pocket in case the 14,000 reichsmarks they carried did not impress a Nazi as a bribe.

Hammer's mission was to form an espionage network with a wide circle of friends the two men still had in Berlin and radio back intelligence with their Joan-Eleanor set. It became practically an impossible assignment. The day after they landed, the team reached a vacant bungalow Lindner's parents owned, but little else worked in their favor. Berlin still had the tightest security controls of any German city—their phony documents identifying them as skilled laborers were routinely checked by the SS. Constant Allied air raids meant a trip across the devastated city could take as long as six hours ducking into shelters or dodging explosions along the way; during their fifty-five days in Berlin they had only two bomb-free nights. Lindner and Ruh could find no safe place where planes could parachute in supplies. They soon ran out of forged ration cards to purchase food and had to buy bread on the black market with their reichsmarks and American cigarettes (still a valuable barter commodity in Germany). Most of the anti-Nazi friends they hoped to enlist as informants had died in the army or concentration camps. From the few they found still alive they managed to collect bits of information on Wehrmacht troop movements but their first two attempts at transmitting their reports to a circling plane failed. They finally made contact with an aircraft on March 26, reporting that arms factories still operated around Berlin and the Klingenberg power station still delivered electricity to these plants. The city railroad was also the only transportation system working, Lindner added; if bombers disabled that, all traffic would stop.

He could have talked for hours, but the pilot had to leave. The BBC later sent a coded message to the team asking it to find out if tank factories were still producing around Berlin. Within a week, Lindner and Ruh discovered that some were miraculously still operating along with smaller plants manufacturing tank parts, but Allied bombers forced Lindner to rush into an air raid shelter when the plane carrying the Joan-Eleanor arrived and he never had a chance to deliver his report. No more radio planes showed up to receive their messages, just around-the-clock Allied bombing that had reduced Berlin's city center to a heap of rubble.

Travel now became extremely difficult for Lindner and Ruh as civilians fled the few houses left standing and Wehrmacht soldiers moved into them to take up positions for the final defense. Another BBC message came on April 22 advising that one of the two men should flee to the American lines with his intelligence while the other remained in the city until the liberators arrived. Lindner tried but SS troops closed the western defense ring and threatened to shoot any Berliner who did not take up arms against the Red Army closing in from the east. Trapped, both men waited for the Russians, who now fired artillery shells into the city at the rate of one every five seconds. They met their first Soviet soldiers on April 24 and the next day found a Russian commander who hustled them off to a counterespionage detachment when Lindner and Ruh told him they were OSS agents. The Soviet intelligence officers, however, showed no interest in the maps and reports the men had on Wehrmacht defenses. Their only question was whether the team knew where Hitler was. Lindner and Ruh had no idea.

The OSS considered the Hammer mission a success, not for the little intelligence the team delivered but rather because it had simply survived in Berlin until the end. But for the two agents the success proved pyrrhic. The Soviets snatched their codebooks, placed Lindner and Ruh under arrest, and did not return them to the Americans until June 16. With the European war over and the Cold War beginning, OSS and British security officers treated the two communists as if they had a contagious disease, suspicious about why the Red Army had held them so long. Had they become double agents?

Casey had other innovative spies. Joseph Allard and Paul L'Hoest, two seasoned Brussels operatives from the Chauffeur team parachuted into Regensburg, a Bavarian city with a Messerschmitt aircraft factory and oil refinery, in the early morning hours of April 1. Volkssturm grenadiers arrested them at one point, an SS patrol fired on L'Hoest, and Allard was eventually wounded by the artillery shrapnel of approaching American units. But operating from a dairy near Regensburg the men managed to radio information on defenses and POW camps around the city and on the fighting quality of its Wehrmacht and SS troops. One of the sources Chauffeur used were two French girls forced to work in a German brothel who enticed military secrets between the sheets from their Wehrmacht customers as Allard took notes while hiding in the closet. Frederick Mayer, a husky Brooklyn Army sergeant whose Jewish parents had fled Nazi Germany, parachuted on February 26 to a glacier near Innsbruck, along with a young Dutch American and an Austrian lieutenant the OSS recruited from a POW camp in Italy who had been born in the city. Dressed in German army uniforms the team, code-named "Greenup," recruited an assortment of dissident Wehrmacht soldiers, Volkssturm converts to the Allied cause, police snitches, and Gestapo traitors, who helped them collect intelligence on German convoys moving through the strategically important Brenner Pass. On April 20, Gestapo officers still loyal to the Reich arrested Mayer and began brutally torturing him, but the OSS officer kept quiet. Mayer eventually managed to talk the region's Nazi *Gauleiter*, who was looking for a way to save his skin, into surrendering Innsbruck to an American division at its western outskirts on May 3. It avoided a bloody fight with German forces dug in for a last-ditch defense.

Other initiatives produced disappointing results. Casey and Pratt had high hopes for Project Eagle, which recruited forty German-speaking Polish soldiers. With the Reich having so much Polish slave labor, these agents were considered ideal for setting up espionage networks there. The men got the best training, equipment, and phony documents available. Sixteen teams, all given code names after cocktails, were dropped into fifteen German cities. None produced any valuable intelligence. The lateness of their arrival was one reason; the war ended before many could get started. But Casey claimed the agents also "were generally inferior in native intelligence and ability," and their enthusiasm for the missions deflated considerably after the February Yalta conference ceded a sizable chunk of Poland to the Soviet Union. The two members of the Highball mission lost their nerve almost immediately after they landed in Kassel in central Germany and headed straight for the American lines. Cuba Libre's two disreputable agents made little effort to spy in Göttingen southwest of Berlin and instead squandered the cash and diamonds they had been given.

Other brave Eagle Project operatives were intent on doing their jobs but simply became victims of bad luck. Leon Adrian with the Martini team was a street-smart agent and a keen observer of German military hardware. He parachuted into Augsburg northwest of Munich on March 19, made a quick sketch of the nearby military airfield, and was eager to send the intelligence back to London when a rail bureaucrat in the station at Altenburg farther north noticed a slight discrepancy in his identity documents and called the police. Before four Gestapo agents dragged him off to an interrogation center in Halle to the east, Adrian managed to shred his map and swallow it. Suspecting he had ingested incriminating evidence, the Gestapo thugs injected Adrian with a solution to make him throw up, knocked out his front teeth with a rifle butt, and poured another vomit-inducing concoction down his throat, then rolled two cylindrical pins up and down his body to force everything out of his stomach. When they found bits of paper in his vomit they beat him mercilessly with rubber clubs the next five days to force him to confess he was a spy and talk. Adrian never did. On the sixth day when he expected to be executed, one of the bombs from a B-17 raid over Halle blew open the door to his cell. Crippled from his beatings, Adrian staggered out and finally reached the American lines on April 15. For the next three weeks, he helped an Army counterintelligence team round up Gestapo officers in the region. Among a group of prisoners the GIs had collected and placed in a room, Adrian spotted two of the goons who had tortured him. He pulled a revolver out of the holster of a guard and calmly pumped two bullets into each of them.

By late April, Casey had dispatched 103 teams. Sixty-nine were still operating in the field, and he had twenty more being prepared for infiltration. But there were teams missing in action. One that he still had not heard from since it left on March 20 was Painter.

．．．．

The Nazi regulations Van Dyck and Flour had to navigate could not have been more maddening. Van Geel, their friendly Belgian mechanic, agreed to temporarily hide their radio equipment in the Munich military garage he worked in and the SS used. But obtaining the necessary government travel passes and making the train trip back to Trostberg to retrieve one of the radio sets they had buried in the woods and return to Munich consumed two weeks. Next they had to register as foreign workers with the Munich police and be given a job, ration cards, and a place to live. The police told them they would be put in a workers camp, which would make it impossible to set up their radio for transmissions to London. Van Geel came to the rescue once more arranging with the police for the two agents to work in his garage and to live in employee barracks next to it.

Those quarters were only slightly better than the camp's. The barracks was divided into tiny rooms, three yards by three yards, with thin plywood for walls so Van Dyck and Flour's neighbors could hear them cranking up the radio, which they hid under a trapdoor they rigged for the floor. Transmitting at night was out of the question because the barracks was full then and during the day Van Dyck and Flour were busy with their garage job, which turned out to be arduous. The German bosses made them work ten-hour shifts and their sleep most nights was interrupted when they had to trudge down into the shelter because of Allied air raids. It left them exhausted for any spying. Flour could pretend to be sick and transmit from the room during a weekday while the others were at work, but that proved to be dangerous as well; SS officers often dropped by the barracks to chat with anyone there.

The OSS agents eventually recruited five informants to feed them information on military installations around Munich. Flour finally unpacked the radio to make his first transmission on Sunday, April 15, when the barracks happened to be empty. But he discovered he had a serious problem. He could hear London's Victor station on his set, but he realized Victor could not hear him because their operators made no reply to his transmission. Frantically he tried radioing on other frequencies. Still no reply. Flour made three more tries that week and another three the next week but Victor never picked up his transmission. Either the set had been damaged during the parachute drop or the team's signal just could not be heard from this barracks. They had no practical way of getting off work and obtaining all the permits needed to retrieve the second set they had buried. The agents looked for alternate transmission sites for the set they had, such as one of the thousands of vacant homes wrecked by the bombing or perhaps a cemetery. But foreign workers were forbidden from entering bombed-out zones and their radio set with its antenna would be noticed in a cemetery. Painter was stranded in Munich.

Their frustration became even more painful when an intelligence windfall fell into their laps. Karl Frey had been sent to the Dachau concentration camp in 1933 for his left-wing activities. For the past year, however, he had been working in Munich's Gestapo headquarters as a trusty supervising thirty other Dachau prisoners assigned to menial duties in the building. Frey met Van Dyck and Flour and told them he had much information they could use. More important, Frey arranged for the two agents to meet Emil Weil, who for the past twelve years had been the executive secretary for the Gestapo in Munich. Weil, it turned out, had also been investigating evidence that spies had infiltrated into the area, but he was not interested in arresting the Painter agents. The Gestapo man could see that it was only a matter of time before the Americans reached the city and he was already plotting how to ingratiate himself with his new conquerors. In return for the German's help, Van Dyck told him he would arrange for the OSS to help Weil and his family escape to South America—a promise Van Dyck never intended to keep.

The Painter agents spent two days grilling Frey and Weil to size them up and find out exactly how much intelligence they could provide. It turned out to be a lot. Their two snitches gave them the names of some fifty Gestapo officers who worked in all parts of the Munich headquarters and who, like Weil, now wanted to switch sides. Van Dyck began questioning the turncoats one by one. He wanted to know the Gestapo's activities the past two months and whether German security services and party leaders had received orders from Himmler to go underground in Munich after the Allies arrived and continue the fight.

From his many interviews and payroll lists Weil supplied, Van Dyck assembled a complete roster of the Gestapo officers serving in Bavaria. And the Nazis so far had made no plans for a resistance movement in Munich, as near as he could determine. This was important intelligence. But Van Dyck had no way to radio it to the Allied force marching toward the city.

CHAPTER 22

SUNRISE

Since 1944, Allen Dulles had been sending Donovan a steady stream of cables warning that after Germany's defeat the Nazis would establish a guerrilla enclave in the Bavarian and Austrian Alps to continue an underground war against the Allies. Donovan subscribed to the redoubt theory and forwarded many of Dulles's cables predicting it to Roosevelt and the Pentagon along with the OSS's plans to root out and destroy the Reich's last bastion. Headquarters pressed Casey's team to have its agents hunt for evidence in the areas they infiltrated of the Nazis storing arms and equipment for a last stand. Eisenhower and his staff, along with Army intelligence in Washington and the British spy services in London, were convinced there would be a redoubt, although none had hard evidence—only deductions, like Dulles's, assuming fanatical Nazis must be planning one. Tantalizing hints fanned fears. Himmler publicly announced that "Werewolf" guerrillas—as many as 800,000 of them according to Italian sources—would harass Allied forces in the areas of Germany they occupied. Dulles received reports the SS chief had sent his family to an Alpine hunting lodge in Austria where he would join them to direct the last resistance.

Allied armies making their way through Germany did encounter scattered acts of Nazi sabotage and pockets of rabid party holdouts. But the Alpine redoubt turned out to be a myth, fueled by German deception, as well as an intelligence failure for Dulles, the OSS, and the other Allied services. To prepare for a postwar guerrilla force meant admission of defeat—a heresy in the Nazi psyche. Hitler signed an eleventh-hour order on April 20 to begin building an enclave, but it came far too late. Helms eventually realized the notion of a national redoubt was nonsense. So did Casey, whose spies could find none being built. But even if he could turn up no proof of German soldiers moving into the Alps to serve as a redoubt force, Dulles believed there was always the danger that the large Wehrmacht element holed up in North Italy would be sent there to protect that last bastion. And in February 1945, he was engaged in the most sensitive diplomatic negotiations of his intelligence career to prevent just that from happening.

. . . .

Nazi peace feelers made their way to Dulles at the beginning of 1945, but they could not have been from a more despicable source—Heinrich Himmler, the ruthless, ultraracist, homophobic, and Germanophilic mass murderer who had assumed near total control of the Reich's national security apparatus after the July 20 plot. Switzerland's intelligence chief alerted Dulles that General Walter Schellenberg, the head of the SS's foreign intelligence department, wanted to meet the OSS officer to deliver the message that Himmler was open to negotiating a cease-fire if "the Anglo-Americans were disposed to modify their stand on unconditional surrender." A Viennese SS agent arrived in Bern with a message from General Ernst Kaltenbrunner, chief of the Reich Main Security Office and the second most powerful man in the SS: Himmler was anxious to end the fighting and "contemplating liquidating the warmongers within the Nazi party" to do so, but first he wanted to make contact with the Allies. Dulles ignored both approaches, "believing that this might be a trap to cause trouble between [the] Russians and ourselves," he cabled Washington.

Dulles remained just as suspicious when Gaevernitz told him that Alexander Constantin von Neurath, the German consul in Lugano, Switzerland, was "discreetly taking soundings" for an Allied peace deal with the Nazi military leadership for Italy. A German consul was hardly a senior position, but Neurath, whose father had been a foreign minister in Hitler's early cabinet, routinely rubbed shoulders with high military officers. He reported to

Gaevernitz in February that he had talked privately to the three top Germans for North Italy—Field Marshal Albert Kesselring, who commanded the Wehrmacht occupation force, his Waffen-SS chief, General Karl Wolff, and Rudolf Rahn, the German ambassador to Mussolini's puppet regime that the Nazis established in the north after Italy's King Victor Emmanuel III ousted Il Duce in 1943. All three, Neurath claimed, were prepared to negotiate a surrender "if the Allies can make it worth their while." Donovan forwarded Dulles's updates on the Neurath contacts to Roosevelt and the Joint Chiefs, but warned that all these peace feelers, including ones even passed by Vatican intermediaries, smelled to him like they came from the same source—Himmler. Dulles agreed.

The Allied Mediterranean command in Caserta, Italy, however, was intensely interested in any intelligence Dulles had that Kesselring might be ready to quit. The Americans and British had suffered nearly 300,000 casualties in the eighteen-month Italian campaign, whose advance north crept at a far slower pace than the race east through France. After giving up Rome two days before the Normandy invasion, Kesselring succeeded in stalling the Allied breach of the fortified Gothic Line north of Florence until the fall of 1944. By February 1945 he still held the industrial-rich north and the key cities of Genoa, Milan, and Turin with twenty-three German divisions, four fascist Italian divisions, plus four SS divisions and 150,000 Italians of the National Republican Guard under the command of Wolff. The German soldiers under both men remained blindly loyal to their führer and determined to fight to the death. Meanwhile, British field marshal Sir Harold R. L. G. Alexander, the Allied commander in Italy, had been forced to turn over divisions to Eisenhower for his offensive. Italian partisans also had been shortchanged arms so the French Resistance could be better supplied. Italy had been relegated to a secondary theater. The stately Alexander, who had been wounded charging from the trenches of World War I, had the unappealing mission of pinning down as many Axis divisions as he could in a bloody stalemate so they could not be shifted to the Western Front. No wonder he was eager for any way to end his ugly war in North Italy quickly.

It was far from clear that the three Germans in Dulles's cables could deliver Sir Harold that victory. Handpicked by Hitler to keep close watch on the mercurial Mussolini, Ambassador Rahn had the ear of Kesselring and Wolff, but the cease-fire plan he had in mind was unrealistic. Rahn envisioned that Wehrmacht forces in Italy, disarmed except for officers' sidearms, be allowed to return to Germany to quell unrest among its foreign slave laborers. Kesselring, whom the Americans nicknamed "Smiling Albert" because he appeared in public always buoyant, was a ruthlessly efficient officer who had commanded both Luftwaffe and ground forces. But Kesselring's interest in negotiating a surrender might not be as strong as Neurath believed. Though the field marshal realized by the beginning of 1945 that Germany had little chance of winning the war, he clung to the naive belief that if Hitler did not pull off a military miracle he would at least negotiate a political deal with his enemies to avoid the Fatherland's annihilation. Kesselring was also obsessed with keeping his military record clean of any stain that he had betrayed his country or its führer.

Solidly built with swept-back blond hair, blue eyes, and Nordic good looks well preserved as he entered his mid-forties, Karl Friedrich Otto Wolff had been chief of Himmler's personal staff, serving as a liaison between the SS and Hitler. He became one of the führer's favorites and not shy about exploiting it for his own ends. When Himmler forbade Wolff from divorcing his wife to marry a countess, Wolff went around his back to obtain permission from Hitler. Installed by Himmler with the high rank of *Obergruppenführer* for the SS, police, Gestapo, and counterintelligence units in Italy, Wolff controlled all the repressive instruments of intimidation, torture, and murder the occupiers had at their disposal. He was clearly a war criminal.

By the end of January, Wolff finally realized the war was lost and Hitler did not have the force or a wonder weapon to alter that fact. He did not have at the outset the noblest of motives, believing the dictator could split the Alliance and stave off defeat by extending a peace offer to the West. Wolff broached that idea with Hitler in a February 6 meeting in the Führerbunker. To his surprise Hitler did not fly into a rage as he had when others suggested negotiations. Wolff took the fact that the führer politely heard him out and remained noncommittal as a green light to approach the Americans or British in Bern.

Back at his Lake Garda headquarters just west of Verona, Wolff ordered his senior officers to alert him to any possibility of making contact with the Allies. He would deal with the approach himself. The *Obergruppenführer* also ordered that his combat engineers not carry out the scorched-earth decree from Berlin to destroy heavy industries and utilities from territory the Wehrmacht ceded to the Allies unless he personally approved it.

The third week of February a senior SS officer under Wolff dispatched an Italian industrialist named Baron Luigi Parrilli to Switzerland to make contact with the OSS. Parrilli had worked for an American appliance company before the war and during the war had accumulated extensive North Italy manufacturing interests under the fascists that he did not want destroyed by more fighting. He found Professor Max Husmann, an old friend who ran a private school near Lucerne, to introduce him to Major Max Waibel, a cigar-smoking Swiss intelligence officer. Switzerland was keenly interested in any peace deal that rescued its extensive business interests in North Italy from destruction and could keep hordes of Wehrmacht soldiers from crossing its border as they fled an Allied offensive. Waibel immediately contacted Dulles. Over an excellent trout dinner in a Lucerne restaurant the night of February 25, the Swiss officer told his OSS friend of his meeting with an industrialist bearing another peace feeler from the Italian Front. Waibel urged Dulles and Gaevernitz, who had also joined the two for the meal, to meet Parrilli that night.

The OSS station chief was immediately wary. Peace feelers continued to trickle in from intermediaries for Himmler, who was now more interested in saving himself than Germany. Dulles took the next train back to Bern and left Gaevernitz in Lucerne to meet with this Italian he had never heard of in a room at the city's Hotel Schweizerhof. Gaevernitz reported back to Dulles the next day that the station chief had good reason to be suspicious. Parrilli seemed a likable enough fellow during their long conference at the Schweizerhof. Short, slightly built, and bald, the baron spoke Italian, French, and German and had an annoying habit of interlacing whatever language he was uttering with phrases from the other two. Gaevernitz immediately wondered how this man, who seemed to him like an ingratiating innkeeper trying to sell him a room, could possibly be an envoy for Field Marshal Kesselring. Parrilli kept hedging when Gaevernitz pressed him on who exactly he represented; he mentioned only the names of two officers who served under Wolff and did not appear to Gaevernitz senior enough to make such a surrender happen. The baron did say that "all was not as it seemed" with the

German occupation force in Italy. The SS was more open-minded than Kesselring's Wehrmacht to the idea of a negotiated peace. Gaevernitz remained courteously noncommittal, but he was convinced this would be the last they saw of Parrilli and went off on a skiing trip after he briefed Dulles.

Dulles dutifully reported Gaevernitz's meeting to Washington, then dumped the cable into his bulging "Peace Feelers" file. The Parrilli approach, however, immediately drew high-level attention. Eisenhower was alerted and in turn notified the British Chiefs of Staff that peace feelers had come from "one or more senior German officers." Startled MI6 officials immediately demanded details on what their American cousins were up to. Dulles quickly moved to douse everyone's expectations. "It is going too far to designate this move as [a] 'peace feeler from German generals,' " he cabled Washington on March 1. The next day Dulles would discover that he was wrong.

Parrilli returned to Wolff's Lake Garda headquarters and delivered a far more optimistic report than his meeting with Gaevernitz deserved. On March 2, Wolff secretly dispatched Parrilli back to Switzerland along with two of his trusted aides: SS colonel Eugen Dollmann, a bright, cosmopolitan, and cunning officer well versed in Italian affairs who was Himmler's personal liaison to Mussolini, and SS captain Guido Zimmer, a devout Catholic, something of an intellectual, and an aesthete who wanted to save Italy's art and religious treasures from destruction. Late that night, Waibel phoned Dulles at Herrengasse that Parrilli had returned to Lugano with two SS men. Dulles still did not think the affair looked promising enough to summon Gaevernitz back from his Davos ski trip. Instead, he decided to send Paul Blum from his Bern staff. An American Jew, Blum would be ideal for sizing up these two Nazis, Dulles thought.

Waibel set up Blum's meeting with Parrilli, Dollmann, and Zimmer for the afternoon of March 3 in the private dining room above the Ristorante Biaggi in Lugano, which the local Rotary Club used for its lunches. Blum arrived at the *sala* shortly after four o'clock, conflicted during the train ride to Lugano about whether he should shake the hands of two members of the despised SS. He decided to extend his hand, which the Germans took. Dollmann, with his dark good looks and jet-black hair slicked back with a little curl over his ears, struck Blum instantly as the slippery type. Zimmer seemed to him the obvious subordinate because he said nothing. The four decided to converse in French. Fully aware of the extreme delicacy of this meeting and the danger that he might be walking into a trap, Blum had jot-ted down on a notepad what he wanted to say to open the meeting. He now recited it from memory: "The material and moral destruction in Europe caused by this war is so gigantic that the Allies will need the help of every available man of goodwill in the work of reconstruction. Everyone who helps shorten the war gives us proof of his goodwill." Beyond that, Blum's instructions from Dulles were to listen to what these Germans had to offer and determine if they were serious.

Dollmann asked if the Allies would be willing to negotiate with Himmler if he backed a separate peace for North Italy.

Blum reverted to English for his answer: "Not a Chinaman's chance."

Blum sensed that Dollmann appeared pleased with the reply. The colonel revealed that he was a member of Wolff's staff and that he would advise the SS general to personally visit Switzerland to continue the talks if Wolff could be guaranteed a meeting with Dulles. Blum said nothing in reply. Instead, he passed across the table to Dollmann a slip of paper with the names of two Italians written on it: Ferruccio Parri, one of the leaders of the Italian resistance who had operated under the pseudonym "General Maurizio," and Antonio Usmiani, one of Dulles's best intelligence agents operating in North Italy. The SS had captured both men, sending Parri to a Verona dungeon and Usmiani to a jail in Turin. Dulles had ordered Blum ahead of time to demand that Parri and Usmiani be released to the OSS as evidence that these emissaries were serious and had the authority to deliver in such important negotiations. Parri and Usmiani were prize catches for the Ger-mans. Only an officer with Wolff's rank could release them and even then at great risk; Dulles guessed that Mussolini and perhaps even Hitler knew of Parri's arrest. Dollmann appeared to Blum almost to gasp at the thought of giving up a prisoner as valuable as Parri. After he recovered from his initial shock the SS colonel said he would do everything in his power to meet the demand. The OSS would hear from him "in a few days," Dollmann assured Blum. Dulles was sure that would be the last they heard from the colonel. Blum wasn't so sure. He didn't like Dollmann, he was sure the Nazi knew more than he was telling, but on the subject of halting the bloodshed in North Italy, Blum told Dulles he was impressed with the German's "earnest-ness."

On March 8, Gaevernitz, still in his ski suit, had just come off the legendary Parsenn Downhill Run at Davos when the phone rang in his hotel room. On the line was Waibel, who did not want to risk calling Dulles's office in Bern and having who knows who listening in. "Gero, are you standing or sitting?" the Swiss intelligence officer began. "Because if you're standing you might fall over when you hear the news." Waibel told Gaevernitz to send Dulles a message over a secure line that "Parri and Usmiani are here. They were delivered safe and sound a few hours ago to my man at the Swiss-Italian frontier at Chiasso." Zimmer had driven the two guerrillas across the border and one of Waibel's lieutenants was already on the way to Zurich with them. The Swiss major had a second piece of startling news. General Wolff, Baron Parrilli, Dollmann, Zimmer, and Wolff's adjutant, Major Eugen Wenner, had also crossed the Swiss border shortly after the Italian guerrillas and wanted to meet with Dulles. Waibel had immediately piled Wolff's party into a private compartment with the curtains drawn on a train now speeding to Zurich. Even though the Germans all wore civilian suits Wolff was taking an incredible risk. His photo had occasionally appeared in Italian newspapers. Any enterprising reporter would immediately question what the SS commander for Italy was doing in Switzerland.

Shortly before 10 p.m. on March 8 came a knock on the door of the apartment Dulles rented at the end of Zurich's Genferstrasse facing a corner of Lake Zurich. It was an ideal safe house for sensitive meetings, tucked away on the ground floor of a bleak-looking building with three locked doors that had to be opened to reach the flat. Gaevernitz, who had rushed to Zurich by train, had helped stoke a blaze in the library's fireplace—Dulles's favorite prop for putting visitors at ease. Wolff stood at the doorway with only Professor Husmann, Parrilli's friend from the Lucerne school. A short, stocky man with a shock of gray hair, Husmann had visited the Genferstrasse apartment earlier carrying what amounted to a lengthy résumé complete with character references from prominent Italians, which Wolff wanted Dulles to read before their meeting to show that he was not like the other SS butchers. Wolff said he had released prominent Italians from prison, rescued precious works of art from destruction, and with Kesselring saved Rome from German bombardment. (He omitted from the papers the villages his SS goons had wiped out and the partisan hostages they had tortured or killed.) Dulles ordered Husmann to return only with Wolff and to tell the general he wanted only to hear his plan for the "unconditional surrender of the German armies in Italy. Nothing else."

Before Dulles arrived in Zurich, he had cabled Donovan, who alerted Roosevelt that Wolff, if he was really working with Kesselring, might be in Switzerland to "effect an unconditional surrender" of German forces in North Italy. Dulles had also kept an irritated Wolff cooling his heels in Husmann's apartment so he could first visit a fancy Zurich clinic. Parri and Usmiani, who thought their SS guards had dragged them out of their prison cells to deliver them to Germany or a firing squad, were totally baffled why they were now sitting in this hospital room registered by Husmann as patients not to be disturbed. Dulles intended to keep them in the dark and out of sight so their release did not expose the secret negotiations with Wolff. He convinced the two guerrillas, who tearfully hugged him, to remain incommunicado for a week or two.

Dulles and his two visitors settled into stuffed chairs around the fireplace with glasses of Scotch Gaevernitz passed out. Wolff sat stiffly in his, silent at first. He spoke no English and Dulles's German was only passable. Husmann, with Dulles's consent, began by summarizing the discussion he had already had with the general. Wolff conceded that the war "was irrevocably lost for Germany and that the Western Allies could not be divided," Husmann recounted. The general nodded in agreement. Wolff had also assured him that neither Hitler nor Himmler knew he was approaching the Americans, Husmann said. (That would later turn out not to be true.)

"What are you now prepared to do?" Dulles interrupted, looking at Wolff.

"I control the SS forces in Italy," the general replied, "and I am willing to place myself and my entire organization at the disposal of the Allies to terminate hostilities." But to end the war there, Wolff quickly added, the Wehrmacht's commanders would have to agree to lay down their arms. He said he had good relations with Kesselring and had acted at times as his political adviser. The field marshal had not been won over yet, but Wolff was confident he could talk him into surrendering, and when he did, Hitler and Himmler would be powerless to stop them. Ambassador Rahn will also be helpful with the field marshal, the SS officer said. (Wolff did not tell Dulles that Rahn had already approached Kesselring the week before about the peace initiative they were launching, but Smiling Albert had given only a cryptic response: "I hope your political plans succeed.")

If Dulles could assure him that he had a secure line of communication to the Allied high command, Wolff said he would do his best to arrange for Kesselring or his deputy to come to Switzerland to discuss a surrender.

Dulles said he was "in direct contact with Allied headquarters."

Appearing immensely relieved that he now had established a channel to the West, Wolff later ticked off for Gaevernitz the next steps he planned to take. He would meet Kesselring over the weekend and obtain his commitment to join the peace talks in Switzerland. He would draft with the field marshal a declaration conceding the futility of further fighting, announcing an end to hostilities in Italy, and calling on their military commanders to dissociate themselves from Hitler and Himmler. Radio messages would be broadcast and leaflets dropped to spread the message to Germans in the field. A joint announcement by Wolff and Kesselring would have a domino effect, Wolff predicted, prompting other generals on the Western Front, "waiting for someone to take the lead," to surrender their forces. Wolff also planned more confidence-building measures besides the release of Parri and Usmiani. He would immediately halt SS attacks on Italian guerrillas, release several hundred Jews interned at Bolzano, assure the safety of 350 American and British POWs at Mantua, and arrange for Italian officers held in Germany to be returned home.

The meeting ended. Dulles made no commitments, but he was impressed with Wolff. So was Gaevernitz. Dulles immediately reported the conference's details to Washington, telling Donovan he thought Wolff was an SS moderate and likely the "most dynamic personality in North Italy." Wolff left Zurich dazzled as well with his cultivated American interlocutor. "Why didn't anyone tell me there were Americans like Dulles?" he later said over and over.

Dulles also cabled the meeting's details to Field Marshal Alexander in Caserta. Eager for any alternative to slugging it out with a still powerful German force in North Italy, Sir Harold immediately asked the Combined Chiefs of Staff, made up of top American and British officers, for permission to send two major generals—his deputy chief of staff, Lyman Lemnitzer, a West Pointer who had risen to that high rank by his early forties, and

Terence Airey, a British intelligence officer expert in European affairs and the German culture—to Switzerland to await Wolff's return with Kesselring. The Combined Chiefs approved, but the two aides—and particularly Dulles—must be kept on a short leash, the British staff chiefs insisted. Churchill's War Office warned him in a top secret memo that this approach by Wolff, who "is very close to Himmler," was "suspicious." The SS general might be a plant to split the West from Stalin. Furthermore, the United Kingdom had broader interests in the Mediterranean region that she did not want disrupted by the Americans going off on their own with these negotiations. But as long as the Russians were notified, the War Office saw "no harm" in pursuing the Wolff approach. Feeling one-upped, the SOE tried to horn in and contact Wolff. Sir Harold demanded that Dulles handle these talks. The Baker Street Irregulars backed off.

When Dulles returned to Bern with Gaevernitz on March 12—the two got lost during the overnight drive on snow-covered roads—a cable awaited him from Caserta. His talks with Wolff had been given the code name "Sunrise." The British assigned them the code name "Crossword"—Dulles guessed because Churchill believed it "was indeed to be a puzzle." Alexander's headquarters agreed that the number of people who know about the negotiations must be kept to the "absolute minimum." Dulles continued to keep Parri and Usmiani, who already were becoming restless in their hospital quarters, under wraps. Wally Castelbarco, who was a close friend of Parri's, begged Dulles "to do something to try to rescue him" from the Germans. He could not tell his mistress that he already had.

Sunrise sparked a slow-burning fuse with the Russians. The day Dulles returned to Bern, London ordered its ambassador in Moscow to inform the Kremlin that Alexander would be sending two officers to Switzerland to negotiate the surrender of the Germans in Italy if Wolff's offer were bona fide. The Soviet government asked to send three of its senior officers to Bern to join the negotiations, a request the British Foreign Office deemed reasonable. The Pentagon's Joint Chiefs did not. This was a German force on a British-American front proposing to surrender. The Russians had no business being there. American diplomats agreed. If it were a Wehrmacht army on the Eastern Front offering to surrender, argued W. Averell Harriman, the U.S. ambassador in Moscow, the Soviets would never let the British or

Americans be present for the negotiations. Allowing the Russians to come to Bern would be read by the Kremlin as a sign of weakness, Harriman added, and would invite only more unreasonable demands from Stalin. The State Department had Harriman inform the Soviet government with polite diplomatic language that its officers would be welcome to attend "as observers" the final talks and inking of a surrender document at Caserta, if that ever occurred, but not any preliminary discussions in Bern.

The Russians were outraged—and the British Foreign Office privately believed they had a right to be. It took little to stoke Stalin's paranoia that Churchill and Roosevelt secretly wanted to sell him out. The capitulation of more than thirty Axis divisions in Italy, Stalin feared, only made it easier for Eisenhower's army to advance more quickly and gobble up more territory in Europe for the capitalists while the Soviets, who had already suffered more than twenty million dead, slowly trudged forward on the Eastern Front. Vyacheslav Mikhaylovich Molotov, Stalin's hard-line foreign minister, demanded that the talks with Wolff "be broken off." Even London thought that was unreasonable. On March 21, Molotov fired off a nasty telegram to the British Foreign Office and U.S. State Department complaining that "in Bern, for two weeks behind the backs of the Soviet Union, which is bearing the brunt of the war against Germany, negotiations have been going on between representatives of German Military Command on the one hand and representatives of the English and American Command on the other. Soviet Government considers this completely impermissible."

London was shocked by Molotov's language. For starters no negotiations had even begun in Bern. Churchill huddled four days later with Eisenhower, who was outraged over Molotov's charge that the Americans were operating in bad faith. As a military commander, Ike told Churchill, he had the right to "accept the unconditional surrender of any body of enemy troops on his front, from a company to the entire Army." "I do not see why we should break our hearts if, owing to mass surrender in the West, we get to the Elbe or even further before Stalin," Churchill wrote his foreign secretary. He decided "we should send no answer to the insulting letter from Molotov." But it would not be the last they heard from the Soviets.

Wolff ran into trouble the minute he crossed back into Italy on March 9. A telegram awaited him at the Italian customs station from Kaltenbrunner,

Himmler's top man, who had found out from his snitches in the Italian command that Wolff had sneaked into Switzerland. He wanted to meet the *Obergruppenführer* in Innsbruck. Wolff begged off, cabling him a cover story that he had made the trip to swap Parri for German POWs. Kaltenbrunner didn't buy it and sent Wolff a second cable ordering him to halt the contacts he knew the SS general had with Dulles. Kaltenbrunner claimed he and Himmler "were extremely anxious to end the war" and did not want Wolff's peace feelers disrupting theirs. By this point, however, Dulles appeared willing to sabotage anything Himmler was up to. In a March 14 radiotelephone call to Washington—which he knew the Germans would monitor and perhaps reveal to Hitler—Dulles warned the OSS headquarters to be prepared for a final German peace offensive "if Himmler can persuade Hitler to let him put it on." Dulles added that Himmler was preparing to offer up Jews and other concentration camp prisoners in exchange for favorable peace terms.

When he arrived at Kesselring's command post in Recoaro northeast of Verona to convince Smiling Albert to join the peace talks, Wolff discovered more bad news. Parrilli later relayed it to Dulles. Kesselring was not there and would never return. Hitler had summoned the field marshal to Berlin, where he ordered him to replace Rundstedt, who had lost the führer's confidence as commander of the Western Front. On his way back to his Lake Garda headquarters to the west, Wolff's car was shot up by an American fighter-bomber. He had Parrilli deliver to Dulles a burnt piece of his uniform along with a message that the SS commander intended to talk Kesselring's replacement, Heinrich von Vietinghoff, into joining the surrender talks. Wolff was good friends with the Panzer colonel general. Vietinghoff was a stiff, broad-shouldered Westphalian with a clipped mustache and hair parted down the middle in the style of the last century, who had fought doggedly in Eastern Europe and Italy. He was one of Hitler's most nonpolitical generals and had never given the slightest thought to not carrying out Berlin's orders to fight on. Dulles grew pessimistic and cabled Caserta on March 13 that Sunrise was in trouble. But clinging to what little optimism he could find, Alexander decided to send Lemnitzer and Airey to Switzerland anyway. They arrived in Bern disguised as Army sergeants.

On March 17, Baron Parrilli returned to Switzerland with news that

Sunrise had been revived. Wolff and his party would arrive at the Swiss border early on the morning of the 19th for surrender talks with Dulles and Alexander's aides. Instead of Bern, Dulles selected as the site for the meeting property Gaevernitz's brother-in-law owned at Ascona on Lake Maggiore just north of Switzerland's border with Italy. It was ideal for such a secret conference. Screened from intruders by trees, mountains, and water, the Ascona estate had two villas—one on the lakeshore, the other on the hillside—so the two sides could be kept separate until brought together for direct talks. Gaevernitz had it stocked with food and liquor and brought in tough-looking armed guards posing as tourists. Dulles came with Clover, who had become restless in Bern. He had Waibel's friendly wife keep her occupied with a long rowboat ride on Lake Maggiore.

Monday morning, March 19, broke clear and sunny with spring beginning to bloom on the southern side of the Alps. A good omen, Dulles thought. Wolff arrived promptly at the lakeside villa with Husmann, Waibel, Parrilli, Captain Zimmer, and his adjutant, Major Wenner. He left Colonel Dollmann back at his headquarters to keep watch for any meddling communications from Himmler or Kaltenbrunner. Lemnitzer and Airey remained at the hillside residence while Dulles sat down in the lake villa's living room, before an antique octagonal table that took up almost the entire space, to prepare the ground with Wolff.

Settling into his chair, the *Obergruppenführer* began with a recital of the problem posed by Kesselring's abrupt departure. Dulles pressed Wolff for details on his successor. Vietinghoff was an old friend, Wolff insisted, but having just assumed command of the German army in Italy it was unlikely he'd be ready to give it up immediately to the enemy. Wolff said it would take some time to convince the colonel general to surrender.

Dulles did not think Wolff had that kind of time, he told the SS man. If the Germans wish to surrender, they should do so quickly. Wolff said he didn't have the power to arrange by himself the capitulation of all the Axis forces in Italy. Of the soldiers he commanded, only about fifteen thousand of them were actually Germans he could count on to follow his order to lay down their arms. The rest were Italians, Russians, Serbs, Slovenians, and Czechs not particularly dependable. In any surrender, Wolff would be the "persuader" talking other German army generals "into realizing the futility of further fighting." He told Dulles he planned to drive to Kesselring's headquarters on the Western Front and secure his backing for the surrender in North Italy. If Kesselring went along with the plan, Vietinghoff "would be easier to handle."

Dulles raised a technical matter. Parrilli had been a loyal courier but events were now moving quickly and messages would need to be transmitted between the two sides faster than the baron could carry them back and forth across the border. Dulles proposed installing an OSS radio operator, who spoke perfect German and could pass for a Wehrmacht soldier, in Wolff's headquarters with a wireless set to transmit and receive coded telegrams with the Allied command in Caserta. Wolff agreed, promising to keep the man safe.

While the Germans broke for lunch, Dulles motored to the hillside villa to brief Lemnitzer and Airey on the morning meeting. Both Allied generals were inclined to agree that Wolff should travel to Germany immediately to see Kesselring. But they both wanted to meet Wolff to size up what kind of character he was and judge with their own eyes whether he could pull off what would obviously be a tricky maneuver. Airey, however, had one condition. "I'm quite willing to meet Wolff and to discuss with him the means of getting a German surrender," he told Dulles, "but you must understand that I will not shake hands with an SS general."

Dulles thought he could work around that protocol by having Gaevernitz usher the two Allied generals into the living room from the kitchen door while Dulles brought Wolff in from the terrace on the opposite side. The large table in the center would separate the two sides so physical contact would be impossible. But no sooner had Dulles made the introductions than Wolff darted around the room, squeezed through the narrow gap between the table and the wall and grabbed Airey's hand and then Lemnitzer's to shake them. The startled Brit and American reluctantly went along.

Dulles introduced the two senior officers only as his "military advisers," giving Wolff neither their names nor ranks—although the SS man could easily guess that they were senior Allied officers. Lemnitzer opened the session. He said he realized the problems Wolff faced by Kesselring's departure, but Wolff, as a soldier, would "understand that speed in any operation of this character was a vital factor." The Allies, he continued, are interested only in unconditional surrender. There would be no use in the Germans coming to Caserta unless they "agreed to such terms." What do you think Kesselring can accomplish for you? Lemnitzer asked.

If his mission is successful, Kesselring will tell Vietinghoff "to go ahead" with the surrender. Wolff would return to the colonel general's Recoaro headquarters with the backing of the supreme commander for Germany's Western Front behind him to arrange the capitulation. "I cannot tell how long this will take," Wolff said. "I am no prophet. With good luck, and if the Allied bombers do not get me"—he looked at Dulles for a brief pause—"I might make the trip in five days, or a maximum of seven."

"Possibly Kesselring, too, would feel the urge to surrender on the Western Front if he had a good chance," Gaevernitz suggested. Wolff did not respond, but the same thought was on his mind. Dulles, Lemnitzer, and Airey wondered as well if Wolff could pull off a magic trick for both fronts.

The next day, Dulles cabled a top secret report to Donovan on the Ascona meeting, giving Wolff the code name "Critic" and Kesselring "Emperor." Dulles would not predict success, but Critic "gave [the] impression of being determined," he wrote. The OSS director immediately forwarded the cable's details to FDR and other top administration officials. Airey thought Wolff had a "crafty appearance," but he and Lemnitzer were encouraged enough to remain in Switzerland after sending an optimistic telegram to Caserta. A little more than a week later, Dulles cabled London that it was "becoming more and more apparent" that Hitler planned to use his army in North Italy to defend his Alpine guerrilla enclave after Germany's collapse— although it was obvious only in Dulles's mind, not from any concrete intelligence he had. If Wolff succeeds in defanging the Wehrmacht in North Italy, it might "defeat" the redoubt, he optimistically speculated.

What Dulles did not realize when he sent his cable to London—in addition to the Alpine redoubt being a myth—was that Sunrise was in danger of coming to a grinding halt. Dodging Allied bombers along the way, Wolff finally reached Kesselring's western headquarters at Bad Nauheim north of Frankfurt on March 23. The command post was a madhouse. The Allied armies were little more than nine miles away. Wolff managed to wedge in private time with a busy Kesselring to present his surrender plan. The field marshal refused to have his western force join it. He was surrounded by a new staff of "strangers," he told Wolff, many of them Himmler cronies, whom he did not trust to carry out a capitulation order even if he was inclined to give it. Wolff sensed that Emperor was practically a prisoner in his own headquarters. Kesselring did tell Wolff that he agreed with the Italian surrender and the SS general should advise Vietinghoff that he did. Or at least that's the impression Wolff had. It was unclear exactly how much Kesselring would actually help Wolff in convincing the colonel general. Wolff, far more optimistic than he should have been, motored south to the Recoaro headquarters instructing Zimmer to message Dulles that, though there had been "technical difficulties" with Kesselring, he hoped to get Vietinghoff on board and be back at Ascona by April 2. He would come with "Glazier" (the code name for Vietinghoff) or one of his staff officers.

But first Wolff had to keep an appointment in Berlin with Heinrich Himmler. The SS *Reichsführer*'s suspicions had grown white-hot. Though Himmler was not prepared to punish Wolff he did demand an accounting of what his SS chief for Italy had been doing in Switzerland. Carrying out the führer's secret order to explore peace talks with the Allies, Wolff baldly replied. Himmler, who continued to have intermediaries pepper Dulles with feelers, knew it was highly unlikely that Hitler had issued such an order, but he could not be sure. He allowed Wolff to return to Italy—under orders not to set foot in Switzerland again. Easter Sunday morning, April 1, Himmler phoned Wolff to let him know "your wife and children are now under my protection" in a village near Salzburg.

Sunday night, Wolff finally caught up with Vietinghoff at Recoaro and told him Kesselring endorsed his surrender. To Wolff's surprise, the colonel general, just back from an inspection tour of the Italian front, agreed it was "nonsense to go on fighting." But as long as Hitler remained in charge, Vietinghoff refused to capitulate. His soundings among commanders and soldiers in the field convinced him they still had not accepted the reality of defeat. If Vietinghoff tried to surrender now, he feared his troops would not follow him. Wolff could see that returning to Ascona Monday, as Zimmer had promised Dulles, was out of the question. He was sure Gestapo agents loyal to Himmler had him under surveillance in Italy. One false move and the SS *Obergruppenführer* knew he and his family would be corpses. When Bern received the news that the April 2 meeting would not happen, Lemnitzer said quietly: "It's not half as bad as it looks." But it was.

Sunrise was also under diplomatic siege. Stalin stewed as his intelligence service continued to send him reports of Dulles's exchanges with Wolff. Roosevelt had decided he could not leave Molotov's belligerent telegram of March 21 unanswered and three days later had Harriman deliver a secret letter to Stalin to set the record straight on the "misunderstanding" his foreign minister had over Sunrise. Washington and London had dutifully informed Moscow that Dulles was exploring the possibility of a German surrender in North Italy, FDR explained, but that "investigation" so far had not resulted in a meeting between "competent German officers" and Alexander at his Caserta headquarters "to discuss details of the surrender." If such a meeting is held, Roosevelt wrote, he would be "pleased" to have Stalin's officers attend, "but I cannot agree to suspend investigation of the possibility because of objection on the part of Mr. Molotov for some reason that is completely beyond my understanding."

The March 24 letter began one of the most acrimonious exchanges Stalin and FDR had during the war. The Soviet leader fired back a letter five days later, claiming that Dulles's negotiations will enable Hitler to shift his Italian force to face the Soviets. The Germans "have already made use of the negotiations" to move three divisions from North Italy to the Eastern Front. "This circumstance is irritating the Soviet Command and creates ground for distrust," Stalin complained.

Not so, Roosevelt responded on March 31. The United States will not engage in negotiations with the Germans "which would permit them to transfer elsewhere forces from the Italian front." As for the three German divisions Stalin cited, they were moved before the Sunrise talks ever began, Roosevelt pointed out. Stalin delivered his next blast April 3. "It may be assumed that you have not been fully informed," his letter began condescendingly. Stalin wrote that his generals have told him the Sunrise negotiations have already resulted in Kesselring agreeing to open his Western Front "and permit the Anglo-American troops to advance to the East" in exchange for concessions at the peace talks.

Stalin's accusation, which could not have been further from the truth, shocked the White House and Pentagon. Outraged, Roosevelt wrote back the next day that it was "astonishing that a belief seems to have reached the Soviet government" that he would reach such a sleazy deal with the Germans. "It would be one of the great tragedies of history if at the very moment of the victory, now within our grasp, such distrust, such lack of faith should prejudice the entire undertaking after the colossal losses of life, material and treasure involved," Roosevelt angrily stated. "Frankly I cannot avoid a feeling of bitter resentment toward your informers, whoever they are, for such vile misrepresentations of my actions or those of my trusted subordinates." His ears pinned back, Stalin wrote back two days later with as close to an apology as he would ever give: "I never doubted your honesty and dependability." The Sunrise missives ended.

Parrilli showed up in Ascona April 2 to brief Dulles, Lemnitzer, and Airey on the problems with Himmler and Vietinghoff and to relay Wolff's message that he needed at least "ten more days." The American and British generals returned to Caserta and told Alexander "there is only a slight chance of surrender of German forces in North Italy." Dulles suspected Wolff was stalling for time until the Allied advance into Austria created enough chaos that his family could escape reprisal when he acted.

Wolff, however, plowed forward with Vietinghoff and by April 8 had convinced him to agree to unconditional surrender, except for one condition the colonel general demanded—that the capitulation be on "honorable military terms." Some of those terms were symbolic, such as permitting Germans to stand at attention when the Allies arrived, but others Caserta firmly rejected, such as allowing the soldiers to return to Germany with Vietinghoff's command post intact instead of being marched off to a British or American POW camp. Moreover, by the second week of April the tide of battle in North Italy had turned decisively in the Allies' favor with Alexander's 8th Army breaking out of the Argenta Gap to Ferrara and his 5th Army plunging into the Po Valley west of Bologna. A peace deal became less important to Sir Harold.

With Wolff not delivering, Dulles perhaps should have abandoned Sunrise. But he remained fascinated by the diplomatic game and for the moment his superiors let him continue playing it. He borrowed Little Wally, a valuable German-speaking radio operator in Henry Hyde's organization, and sent him to the SS general's headquarters. Little Wally was the cover name for twenty-six-year-old Václav Hradecky, a short, rather uncommunicative Czech survivor from Dachau who set up his radio in Zimmer's Milan office so Dulles could have instant communications with Wolff. On April 10, one of Donovan's aides asked Grace Tully, FDR's secretary, to pouch down to the president in Warm Springs, Georgia, a memo with Dulles's cable reporting that Vietinghoff wanted a surrender with "military honor." Tully did not know if Roosevelt ever read it.

Donovan flew to Paris the evening of April 12, checking in to the suite

Hermann Göring once used at the Ritz Hotel and planning a brutal schedule of nonstop meetings that would begin the next morning with Casey's update over breakfast on the German penetration operations. He went to bed at midnight not knowing that the White House shortly before 6 p.m. Eastern Standard Time had released a bulletin to the press. The spymaster was shaving in the bathroom the next morning when an aide rushed in with the news that Roosevelt had died at Warm Springs. Casey arrived for his briefing to find Donovan sitting on the side of the bed in his suite, his head slumped over, muttering to himself: "This is the most terrible news I've ever heard." Roosevelt had protected his spy agency from powerful enemies in Washington. Donovan hardly knew Harry Truman and could not count on him to shield his OSS or to support his plan for a postwar central intelligence agency. The spymaster soon recovered and listened intently as Casey described his missions that had succeeded or failed.

The next morning, April 14, Donovan was just as eager to hear from Dulles, who arrived at the Ritz and over dark coffee and fresh croissants recounted how Sunrise appeared derailed for the moment because of Vietinghoff's points of honor. Donovan filled Dulles in on the acidic letters Roosevelt had exchanged with Stalin. Dulles was surprised that Donovan nevertheless remained enthusiastic about the surrender negotiations and pressed his Bern chief to do all he could to bring them to a successful conclusion. As he walked through the Ritz's dimly lit corridor late that evening after their conference finally ended, Dulles was startled when a stranger approached him and asked for "110." That was Dulles's code number on secret documents. Had he been discovered and this man knew what he was up to at the Ritz? He quickly recovered before blurting out, "You're talking to him," and realized the man was hunting for his room number, which happened to be 110. Back in Bern, Dulles was almost as surprised when Zimmer showed up in Lugano with a three-page handwritten letter from Wolff offering his "sincere and deeply felt sympathy" over Roosevelt's death.

The day after FDR's passing, Churchill sent a note to Stalin hoping that the "Crossword misunderstanding may now be considered at an end." The British prime minister, indeed, was eager to put the subject behind them. Though they were not prepared to end the talks, Alexander's advisers had grown more suspicious that Wolff was just stringing Dulles along. Churchill's Foreign Office, which had never seen the point in excluding the Soviets from the early negotiations, now fretted over the political fallout the talks were having with Stalin; with Crossword/Sunrise going nowhere, it was an unnecessary sore spot, his diplomats believed. Churchill agreed and sent a "Personal and Top Secret" message to the new American president recommending that the negotiations be shut down. Otherwise, Stalin will just spin more conspiracies in his head and make new unreasonable demands, "which we cannot tolerate."

Unaware of the momentum building on the Allied side against him, Wolff continued to lobby Vietinghoff and enlist other senior officers in the colonel general's command to join the surrender. But hurdles continued to pop up in front of Critic. A mysterious man in civilian clothes turned up at the Genoa intelligence section for the Ligurian Corps, one of the Italian fascist units attached to the Wehrmacht, and claimed he was a British major with a message from Alexander that Vietinghoff should break off talks with Dulles and negotiate directly with the United Kingdom. Dulles suspected the man, whose message spooked Vietinghoff when he heard it, was a Russian plant sent to make the colonel general think the whole world knew he was mulling surrender. Himmler also summoned Wolff to Berlin once more and this time he ended up in the Führerbunker on April 18 to explain himself to Hitler. Wolff left behind a "personal statement," which amounted to a will, that he ordered Parrilli to deposit with Dulles.

With the Red Army's final drive on Berlin begun, at 4 a.m. Wolff was ushered into a briefing room across the hall from Hitler's private quarters several stories below ground. The führer, who aides feared was near a nervous breakdown, appeared bent and shaky with sunken features, bloodshot eyes, and his right hand trembling constantly. According to Wolff's account provided later to Dulles, Hitler was irritated but not unfriendly, complaining that Wolff's approach to the Allies, of which Kaltenbrunner had already informed him, was a "colossal disregard of authority." But the dictator did not accuse Wolff of acting behind his back. Instead, he appeared more miffed that his SS *Obergruppenführer* for Italy might muck up his broader plan for dealing with the Allies by negotiating a peace on one front.

Looking Hitler directly in the eye with sincerity painted on his face, Wolff calmly reviewed his negotiations in Italy, insisting that he was only following his führer's order from February 6 to explore contacts with the Allies and that he now had succeeded in establishing a direct contact with Churchill and the president of the United States if Hitler wanted to use it.

Hitler said he understood—although it was unclear whether he really did. He asked Wolff what the surrender terms for the Italian Front would be. Unconditional, the *Obergruppenführer* replied. Hitler asked him to return around 5 p.m. to give him time to take a nap and mull over what Wolff was doing. When Wolff returned, Hitler instructed him to fly back to Italy, "give my regards to Vietinghoff," stall the Americans, and win better terms than unconditional surrender. But sign nothing until he ordered it. Hitler believed he could hold out in Berlin for as long as eight weeks. In the meantime, as his delusional mind saw it, fighting would erupt between the Western Allies and Russia. "Then I shall join the party which approaches me first," Hitler said. "It makes no difference which." Wolff reached his head-quarters on April 20, breaking open a bottle of champagne with Dollmann and Parrilli to celebrate "that his head was still attached" to his neck.

But though he didn't know it, staying alive was all he could celebrate. That day the Joint Chiefs ordered the OSS to shut down Sunrise. The Ger-mans in North Italy have "no intention of surrendering," the chiefs con-cluded in their order; the talks were only aggravating the Russians. The Combined Chiefs of Staff issued the same directive to Alexander. Exasper-ated, Dulles cabled Washington that he realized "orders are orders," but in two long messages to headquarters on April 21 he listed all the problems he could think of in following this one. For starters, Little Wally was planted in Wolff's headquarters and Dulles now had to find a way to extract the OSS agent safely. The Swiss had gone to great lengths to arrange these talks and Dulles did not want to alienate them in breaking them off. Sunrise could checkmate a future Alpine redoubt. While cooperating with the Russians was important, the United States should not pass up a quick capitulation to save lives. Moreover, if the Germans in North Italy don't surrender to us they will to the Russians, Dulles predicted. "We are breaking this contact a couple of days too soon," he argued. Knowing his subordinate's proclivity to test the edge of the envelope on orders, Donovan sent Dulles a pointed cable that he expected him to comply with the Joint Chiefs' command "in the strictest manner." Dulles promised he would.

But on Monday, April 23, he faced an even knottier predicament in doing so. Wolff, who had finally browbeaten Vietinghoff into accepting capitulation (albeit with watered-down conditions Vietinghoff still hoped for), crossed the Swiss border that day and parked himself at Waibel's villa in Lucerne. With him were his adjutant, Major Wenner, and Lieutenant Colonel Viktor von Schweinitz, one of Vietinghoff's senior staff officers who had an American-born grandmother, spoke English fluently, and carried with him written authority to join Wolff in signing a surrender document on the colonel general's behalf in Caserta. Waibel had phoned Dulles with the astounding news that morning.

Dulles rushed to Lucerne with Gaevernitz. He assured Washington he would not meet with Wolff, making the excuse that he should be in the city in case Waibel fished any intelligence from the Germans that should be passed on to OSS headquarters. Dulles clearly was exploiting any ambiguity he could find in the Joint Chiefs' ban in order to keep Sunrise alive. Alexander, meanwhile, pleaded with London and Washington to reverse the directive and told Dulles to "parry for time." Stricken with another bout of gout in his knee that became so painful Gaevernitz had to find a doctor to inject him with morphine, Dulles huddled with Waibel, Husmann, and Parrilli Monday night to reveal that the Allies had halted the surrender talks; but he told them to ask the Germans to be patient. Wolff agreed to wait a day or two.

By Wednesday evening, April 25, with Dulles still keeping his distance, the SS general returned to his Lake Garda headquarters, leaving Wenner behind with full powers to surrender the SS force if the Allies agreed to bring the major and Schweinitz to Caserta.

Dulles sent more cables to Washington pleading for a change in orders. He sat and waited. The hours dragged on. "We are in an absolutely impossible situation," Waibel complained to him. "We will be ridiculed for centuries if we don't manage this properly." By now the diminished German army had less of Italy to surrender. Sunrise would save lives but at this point with Alexander's force well on the offensive they would be more German lives than British and American. For Dulles it was his most frustrating point in the negotiations, everything "about to end in hopeless confusion," he recounted later—with only silence coming from the Joint Chiefs.

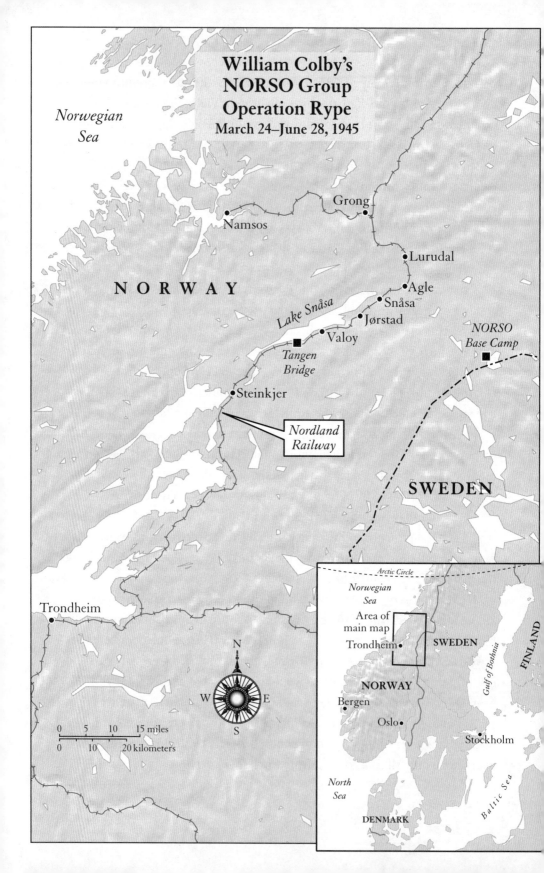

William Colby's
NORSO Group
Operation Rype
March 24–June 28, 1945

*Norwegian
Sea*

Grong

Namsos

Lurudal

Agle

Snåsa

N O R W A Y

Lake Snåsa

Jørstad

Valoy

*NORSO
Base Camp*

Tangen
Bridge

Steinkjer

*Nordland
Railway*

SWEDEN

Trondheim

N
W   E
S

| 0 | 5 | 10 | 15 miles |

| 0 | 10 | 20 kilometers |

Arctic Circle

*Norwegian
Sea*

Area of
main map

Trondheim •

SWEDEN

FINLAND

Gulf of Bothnia

NORWAY

Bergen •

Oslo •

Stockholm •

*North
Sea*

Baltic Sea

DENMARK

CHAPTER 23

FLIGHT OF THE RYPE

Bill Colby sat scrunched and tense on the hard-backed seats of the bouncing B-24 Liberator. The more than four hours of flying over Scotland, across the black, forbidding North Sea, and now into Norwegian airspace had taken its toll on him and the other three commandos in the cabin. Despite layers of heavy gear and wind-resistant, white parkas covering each of them they were cold and miserable. Beside Colby huddled three Scandinavian Americans: Alf Paulson, Fred Johanson, and Sverre Aanonsen. A North Dakota farm boy whose Norwegian mother had drilled her native language into him, Paulson was a conscientious thirty-two-year-old Army corporal, but with a little more than eight years of schooling, five months of it to learn a trade, his OSS trainers did not consider him officer material. Johanson was the team's sole medic—a twenty-year-old stock clerk in civilian life whose Swedish parents had emigrated to Brooklyn, where he was born. A sturdy, thirty-four-year-old blacksmith's helper, Aanonsen had even less formal education than Paulson, but like his comrade spoke Norwegian fluently and could be counted on to carry out any assignment without question. Crammed into the belly of the B-24, and seven other planes like it flying into Norway, were ninety-six containers weighing ten tons and packed with explosives, food, machine guns, pistols, ammunition, forty-eight pairs of skis, fifteen ski toboggans, thirty-two rucksacks, and several radio sets.

Colby also had strapped to him a leather case with a small Kodak movie camera inside to record their operation on film.

Eight Liberators with Colby and the other thirty-one commandos in his team took off from Harrington Field the afternoon of March 24, stopping at the Kinloss Royal Air Force Base in north Scotland to refuel. Conditions after the planes left the Moray Firth that night could not have been worse for the pilots. Natural hazards presented more dangers than German air defenses in Norway. Its terrain changed from narrow valleys to tall mountains abruptly so flying over or through them could be tricky. Meteorologists found it difficult to forecast its bad weather and navigators had few reliable maps to guide them. Ice easily covered wings weighing planes down while severe updrafts or downdrafts sent them on roller-coaster rides. Snow covered practically all of the country (even in early spring) and Norwegians turned their lights off at night making it hard for pilots to find landmarks to guide them. Only a little more than half the British and American parachute drops into Norway had been successful.

The uniqueness of this mission and his commandos impressed Colby— the first combined ski and parachute operation American forces were attempting in Norway. Their assignment, Colby told his men, came directly from Eisenhower—to keep the German army bottled up in Norway, or at least do their part in containing the Wehrmacht. They came as did Vikings of old (this time in metal planes rather than wooden ships)—men like Einar Eliassen, a blunt-talking shipbuilder born in Norway who landed at Ellis Island in 1931; Leif Oistad, a skilled skier stranded on a Norwegian tanker when the Germans invaded his country, and who enlisted in the U.S. Army to return and rescue his parents; Knut Andreasen, a tough Norwegian merchant marine captain who stoically accepted a lower rank as an OSS radio operator; Matti Raivio, a Finnish auto mechanic transplanted to Brooklyn who had fought the Russians and calculated that the only way he would kill Nazis was to join this unit parachuting into Norway.

Their B-24, and Colby assumed the other seven Liberators following close by, flew up the Norwegian-Swedish borderline, over stark fjords, between Aurora-haloed white mountains, past the city of Trondheim, to a region almost 150 miles from the Arctic Circle. It was midnight. The pilot radioed to Colby over the intercom that they had veered twenty-five miles off course over neutral Sweden but he would now angle left and plunge down to approach the drop zone. Colby and the three commandos clipped their parachute static lines to the hooks. Paulson and Aanonsen helped the dispatcher hoist the plywood door off the Joe hole. Colby could see the shaved forest demarcating the two countries, then the ice- and snow-covered lake that the Norwegians called Gjevsjøen for their side and the Swedes spelled Jävsjön for their half. Wisps of snow swirled through the mountain passes around the lake and a faint mist shrouded the light from the full moon, but he managed to spot through the Joe hole the four blazing piles of wood on the hard-packed lake arranged like an L—the signal for their drop zone from the reception committee on the ground.

"This is it," he shouted to the pilot over his intercom mike. The four men along with a dozen containers the dispatcher shoved tumbled out of the Liberator's hole.

Even wearing a facemask, Colby was stunned by the frigid blast. Europe had experienced its coldest winter in forty years. Though spring had started, the night air above Norway was twenty degrees below zero Fahrenheit. The mission had begun—code-named "Rype" (the Norwegians pronounced it "Reepay") after a local bird that changed colors with the season.

· · · ·

After the Germans' failed Ardennes counteroffensive in December 1944, Eisenhower worried that Hitler would bring home some of his 315,000 soldiers, sailors, and airmen in Norway, making the Allied offensive into Germany even more difficult. Ike had reason to be fearful. In January 1945, Berlin ordered 150,000 battle-hardened mountain ski troops who had pillaged Finnmark, Norway's northernmost county (or *fylke*, as the Norwegians call each of them), to begin moving rapidly south for redeployment to the Fatherland. The rest of the occupation army, Allied intelligence speculated, would remain in Norway to conduct a scorched-earth campaign or perhaps turn the nation into a postwar redoubt like the Nazis allegedly planned in Austria and Bavaria.

By the end of 1944, Donovan's NORSO commandos finally had their mission. Eisenhower wanted them, along with British and Norwegian guerrillas, to block or slow the evacuation of northern German units (particularly the ones from the crack Finnmark force) by attacking the single-track Nordland Railway that ran south into Trondheim off the Norwegian Sea near the center of the country. Once the nation's capital and considered a holy city where Norwegian kings were crowned in its medieval cathedral and a shrine to the patron saint Olav stood, Trondheim had been a resistance hotbed because it had also become home to a key submarine and ship base for the Germans. Crippling the rail line would force the Wehrmacht either to plow through roads nearly impassable with snow or take sea routes off the western coast making them vulnerable to air and naval attacks.

An ideal spot for Allied special forces to create this transportation bottleneck was the swath of territory in the center of Norway just north of Trondheim where the land narrowed in the *fylke* of North Trøndelag. Settled by farmers during the stone age, North Trøndelag had vast stretches of unpopulated spruce forests, barren mountain ranges along its western Norwegian Sea coast and eastern border with Sweden, and some of the best salmon rivers in Europe. Speaking an Old Norse dialect called Trøndersk, its sparse population of some 100,000 congregated in coastal fishing villages or along the main inland roads and the Nordland rail line. The Norwegian resistance command in Oslo had begun setting up Milorg guerrilla bases in North Trøndelag's forests and mountains in January. Keeping the remote outposts resupplied with arms and food proved difficult, but the territory now became critical for the guerrilla war Eisenhower wanted ramped up. The Nordland Railway, one of the three most important in the nation for the German evacuation, snaked over North Trøndelag's wild, hilly land from Trondheim in the south to the village of Grong 137 miles away in the north, where one branch of the line veered west to the coastal town of Namsos and the other branch continued farther north up the country. Along the North Trøndelag section, the track wound around sharp curves, up steep gradients, across unguarded bridges, and through dark tunnels—perfect places for Colby's commandos to bring train traffic to a crashing halt with sabotage.

· · · ·

In December 1944, Colby had moved his NORSO commandos to Dalnaglar, a dreary, dank, and isolated castle in the snow-covered Glenshee of central

Scotland. The roomy Victorian hunting lodge, gone to seed and designated Area P, had few amenities save for food far more digestible than the early fare at Milton Hall. By January, Colby had ruthlessly weeded out twenty-five of the men he considered unsuited for Norwegian operations, sending them back to the Army or to Asia for OSS operations in that theater. He put the three officers and fifty enlisted men who were left through a brutal training schedule that placed heavy emphasis on skiing and climbing the mountains around Dalnaglar with heavy loads on their backs. "Don't hot dog around!" Colby barked at them on the slopes. "If you find yourself skiing too fast, sit on your rump. Anyone injured will be left behind." The hulking Scandinavians found their 130-pound commander a rigorous taskmaster. The men nicknamed him "Bones and Guts." Colby had to be tough. By the end of January with Scotland's snow melting, he rated his men as just barely qualified for the demanding skiing they would undertake.

Early in February, Lieutenant Colonel Hans Skabo, Colby's boss in the OSS Scandinavian Section, made the long drive from his Oxford Square office in London to Dalnaglar, carrying satchels full of documents and photos for towns, train stations, and practically every mile of the Nordland Railway track in North Trøndelag. A Norwegian American somewhat rough around the edges, Skabo was old-school Army and not afraid of pushing back when British special operations staffers tried to keep Operation Rype grounded in England because they still resented American meddling in what they considered their territory.

Colby and Skabo found an empty room in the castle where the lieutenant colonel could spread out his material. American and British intelligence officers had interviewed exiled rail officials from Norway's State Railways to assemble reams of information on the system's tracks, locomotives, and freight cars in order to determine vulnerabilities. Blueprints had been collected for every important bridge and tunnel. German units were now traveling on the Nordland Railway's train through North Trøndelag at the rate of about one battalion, or five hundred men, a day, a top secret OSS report Skabo brought with him estimated. Colby and his men were ordered to paralyze rail service on the section of Nordland track stretching south from the Grong station to Steinkjer, an old Viking village whose historic buildings Luftwaffe bombers had flattened during the invasion of Norway.

Two tunnels in one curvy leg of that section—from the village of Formofoss south to the village of Lurudal—should be attacked simultaneously, Skabo told Colby. They were the Røhylla tunnel, which Skabo's engineers said was already crumbling from poor concrete construction, and the northern tunnel of the Svartfossan series whose cut through the mountain had weak supports that explosives could easily topple. After that, Skabo wanted the NORSO team to scout out and blow up the difficult-to-reach Grana River bridge that trains crossed farther south, then destroy the railroad track at different points between Lurudal and the tiny Jørstad village off the southern coast of Lake Snåsa.

When Skabo wanted to send Colby a coded message over the BBC, he would begin it with the phrase: "From Henrik to Rype." Otherwise, Colby was under strict orders to keep his force hidden and make no contact with the civilian population, which was laced with Nazi informants. British intelligence sources estimated the Germans had several thousand soldiers in the North Trøndelag area housed in an assortment of barracks, pillboxes, observation posts, radio relay stations, artillery battery emplacements, and machine gun nests. Platoons of about two dozen men each went out with itchy trigger fingers to patrol practically every mile of the rail tracks while others were stationed in guardhouses at key bridges like the Grana's. Skiing and fighting a guerrilla war against all of them in snow as deep as six feet will "be one bitch of a job," an aide to Skabo told him before he drove up to Dalnaglar to deliver Colby the mission. The lieutenant colonel agreed.

From the fifty-three men he had available, Colby picked his thirty-five best skiers for the mission. He put in an order for nine planes, each to carry four commandos. The other men would continue training at Dalnaglar and join them after the spring thaw when skiing wasn't so important for the operation. But things began to go wrong from that point on. The Army Air Forces would cough up only eight planes so Colby had to cut four more men to bring his force down to thirty-two. To scout out the targets, he had also planned to send in a three-man reconnaissance team ahead of the main party, led by one of his best officers—Lieutenant Tom Sather, a tall, lanky Norwegian who ended up in California in 1940 and eventually joined the 99th Infantry Battalion at Camp Hale as a platoon leader. Sather kept secret from Colby the four back vertebrae he injured in an earlier parachute jump for fear he'd be cut from the Rype operation. But bad flying weather during

February and early March when the moon was full forced a cancellation of his recon mission.

Next came a security leak either in England, Norway, or Sweden. Colby and Skabo never determined where, but Norwegian agents radioed London that a German patrol was swarming over the parachute drop zone planned for the Rype mission. Then a Free Norwegian newspaper published in London reported that the Germans had put as many as fifty extra guards at the tunnels and bridges along the Formofoss-to-Lurudal section of the Nordland track that the commandos wanted to attack first. Colby changed their drop zone to Lake Gjevsjøen. The two tunnels in the Formofoss-to-Lurudal leg were dropped as targets. Instead, the team would start with the bridge over the Grana River. Because the terrain around it was so rugged, it would take the Germans longer to bring in equipment to repair the structure after an attack and restore the severed Nordland line. But it would also take first-class skiers to reach the bridge, set the charges, and escape. Colby built a model of the Grana bridge at Dalnaglar so his men could rehearse how to destroy it. The night before the Rype raiders boarded the bombers on March 24, the men left behind threw a raucous party for them at the castle.

• • • •

A number of other guerrilla operations were under way to disrupt road and rail traffic as Colby and the other American paratroopers drifted to land. Agents had launched a large-scale attack on the Railway Administration Offices in Oslo. Rype's was one of fifteen sabotage or espionage missions the Milorg command in Trondheim was overseeing for the North and South Trøndelag *fylker.* Farther north, forty Norwegian paratroopers had been dropped to attack the Nordland rail line. But in the early hours of March 25, as Colby's boots touched frozen Lake Gjevsjøen, none of the operations was as fouled up as his.

The roar of the bombers faded quickly and a deathly quiet fell over the lake as Colby gathered his parachute, took out his pistol, and made his way toward the light of the signal bonfires he could see in the distance through the ground mist. About a half dozen local men stood around the fires when Colby approached. He gave the prearranged password in broken Norwegian: "Is the fishing good in this lake?"

The response was supposed to be: "Yes, particularly in the winter." But one of the men by the fire looked at him quizzically and answered: "To tell you the truth, it's not good at all." Before Colby cocked his .45, one of his commandos recognized a Norwegian Resistance Army officer in the group. Colby realized the reception party either forgot the password or had never received it. He lowered his pistol. These were the right men.

But only fifteen of Colby's commandos, from his plane and three others, eventually showed up at the bonfires. Having no idea what happened to the other half of his force, Colby and his truncated team began looking for their equipment from at least the four bombers. It became an exhausting and frustrating exercise. One container crashed through the lake ice into the water underneath, a second one came apart in the air, destroying its contents, while a third and fourth were forever lost. The rest were scattered over thirty-six square miles of forests and fjords. In the two and half years he had served as a paratrooper, Colby thought this was the worst airdrop he had ever seen. In one plane, the dispatcher (whom Colby thought should be disciplined) simply tossed out the containers without bothering to hook their static lines so the packages plummeted to earth with chutes unopened and burrowed into snow as deep as fifteen feet in places. The only shred of good news: just one man was injured from the jump with a sprained knee— Oddberg Stiansen, a Norwegian fisherman who had reached New Jersey in 1941 to work as a deckhand.

The NORSO commandos spent the rest of Palm Sunday, March 25, hunting for their equipment and hiding the containers in the snow. It was backbreaking work even with the horses and sleds the Norwegians on the ground provided. Each man ended up carrying eighty-three pounds on his back. Colby was outraged to discover that someone at the loading station in England pilfered cigarettes, candy, and soap from his men's packs.

One of the team's radio sets survived, damaged but workable. Borge Langeland, one of their radio operators and also one of the few Norwegian Americans in the group short and wiry like Colby, managed to start up the transmitter Sunday evening and tap out a message to London that only four bombers with sixteen men had made it to the drop zone. Their equipment had been "badly scattered and much will be lost," he telegraphed. They needed the rest of the planes with their men and arms so this operation did not end in failure. The next day, headquarters radioed back with details on just how disastrous the infiltration had been. One plane developed engine trouble before it reached the Norwegian coast and had to return to Scotland. Finding no landmarks on the snow-covered ground to guide them, the pilots of the two other bombers could not find Lake Gjevsjøen to make the drop and flew back to base with their men and equipment. The fourth plane managed to shove out its commandos and containers, but they all landed about forty miles from the lake in Sweden where authorities immediately interned the men. Headquarters promised to send four aircraft with the rest of Colby's team as soon as it could.

The NORSO commandos spent the first week gathering and inventorying the last pieces of scattered equipment. The losses from the four planes were tolerable but Colby wanted more arms and explosives from the other aircraft to begin their raids. After sleeping out in the bone-chilling cold for several nights he decided to move his men into a warm, dry farmhouse off Lake Gjevsjøen. The farm's owner, Alfred Andehsson, evacuated his family to Sweden then returned to serve as a guide. Corporal Paulson put his farm experience to work and kept the cows in the barn milked. A local Lapp herder also agreed to sell Colby a reindeer each week to help feed his team.

Glenn Farnsworth, one of Colby's lieutenants and a demolitions expert, began putting together the explosive charges they would use for the Grana bridge. The isolated lakeside farm was about as secure a base camp as Colby could find for this work. The mountainous area around it was largely uninhabited. Even so, there was always the danger of constantly prowling German patrols, particularly ones with radio-direction-finding gear, locating their hideout. Also, Easter weekend neared when Norwegians—and hostile Quislings among them—strapped on skis for sports outings in these hills. The team's first scare came Good Friday when a vacationing party of eleven skiers stumbled onto the farmhouse. Colby's Norwegian guides kept them away from the inside of the buildings so they never saw the Americans.

Later in the day after the intruders left, Langeland received a radio message from headquarters: four planes would arrive late that night with the other sixteen men and their equipment, to be dropped at the northeast corner of Lake Gjevsjøen. Colby and a receiving party hid near the lakeshore until the early morning hours of March 31 when they lit the signal fires. At one point they could hear the sound of bomber engines overhead but a sleet storm, thick clouds up to eight thousand feet, and low mist had just rolled in, making it impossible to see any aircraft. Easter morning, Langeland received the discouraging news from London. The foul weather made the drop zone's lights impossible to see and forced the pilots of the four planes to return home with their loads. One did not make it back to Kinloss. The aircraft crashed in the Orkney Islands north of the Scottish coast after two of its engines died, killing seven crewmen and six of Colby's commandos. Colby sent a Norwegian courier to Sweden, where the OSS had secretly stockpiled supplies, with a list of weapons and food he hoped the man could bring back, including canned pineapples as a morale boost for the local guides who hadn't seen the fruit in years. Meanwhile, London promised another try at getting planes to Lake Gjevsjøen.

The next sortie failed as well, however. Four planes bearing the commandos and their equipment prepared to take off from Scotland the night of April 6. One of the planes, however, was grounded for mechanical trouble. Again, Colby's men at Lake Gjevsjøen heard aircraft noise above but saw no parachutes in the sky. Langeland also radioed headquarters that the NORSO team heard what sounded like an explosion they guessed was about fifteen miles west of their camp. London radioed back that the pilots again could not find the drop zone in the bad weather and the team might well have heard an aircraft crashing because one of the planes with four commandos aboard never made it back to Scotland.

The accumulation of failed sorties and deadly air accidents had reached scandalous proportions, as far as OSS officers were concerned. The Germans had not fired a shot and Colby had lost half his force with six men killed and four missing. The failures with the parachute drops "represent a sad chapter in the history of our air activity," Skabo's boss in the Scandinavian Section reported to Donovan. Recriminations in London came quickly and they were harsh. Missing a drop zone by several miles was common, but how do you miss a country, as the airmen did with the landing in Sweden, one OSS officer asked. Skabo angrily complained that some of the planes had been substandard or their American aircrews unqualified for this difficult operation. He had pleaded for better British bombers and Norwegian crews used to flying far north. His request had been turned down.

London decided it could not afford to waste more lives. No flights would be made to the NORSO men until the air forces could find planes and crews suitable for the mission. Colby would have to fight with what he had.

Three more Norwegian resistance operatives joined Colby's base camp on April 8. His guerrilla army now numbered twenty-six. Colby had already dispatched his chief scout—Hans Liermo, who was one of the best Norwegian hunters in the region—to check out the Grana bridge. Liermo reported back that it was heavily defended by about two dozen Germans posted in guardhouses at both ends of the bridge and underneath it near the river. As many as two thousand Germans were also garrisoned at the nearby village of Snåsa. Just as problematical, the crust on the top of the snow approaching the bridge crackled when skis ran over it, so the guards would be alerted when they approached. Colby devised a plan to take down the bridge that looked like it had come out of a Wild West movie. At a considerable distance south of the structure, his men would hijack an empty train traveling north to pick up more Wehrmacht troops. The commandos would ride the train to the bridge, stop it at the guardhouses, and overwhelm the unsuspecting Germans. His men would then slap their charges to the bridge, back up the train, blow the bridge, and ride south to a more favorable area for them to make their escape. Then they would send the empty train back up the tracks so that it crashed into the river at the severed bridge, making a mess that would take the Germans forever to repair.

London agreed that he should try his daring sabotage scheme with the men he had on hand. But headquarters realized Colby's chance for success faced long odds. Elbridge Colby, still on the staff of Hodges's 1st Army, paid a visit to the OSS station during a trip to London. Aides in the Scandinavian Section were at first reluctant to talk to him—even though he had the security clearance and an obvious interest in learning how his son was faring— but eventually they agreed to brief the colonel on the Rype mission's status at that point. Elbridge walked away from Grosvenor Square realizing Bill was in "grave danger."

By the time Colby parachuted into Norway, the morale of the enemy occupation force had plunged. Defeatist literature from Allied propagandists gained wider circulation in German ranks. Courts-martial had increased along with the number of Wehrmacht soldiers marched off to firing squads. Two thousand German troopers had been sentenced to POW camps in Norway, where guards treated them more harshly than the Russian prisoners. Nevertheless, the Nazis in Norway remained a deadly force. Even with the Wehrmacht evacuation, one OSS intelligence report estimated there were still in the country "as many able bodied male Germans as there are able bodied male Norwegians—approximately 250,000." It meant the balance of power still remained with the Germans, who were far better armed. Crown Prince Olav paid a secret visit to Washington to warn Pentagon officials of severe food shortages in his country, made worse by foraging German soldiers. Before Colby's arrival the Nazi and Quisling security services had stepped up their terror campaign of mass arrests and executions to crush the resistance. Prisons overflowed; one in the Nordland *fylke* north of Colby's base camp held some 68,000. Nazi reprisals became savage—the SS executed thirty-five Norwegian civilians after guerrillas attacked an ore-mining facility in North Trøndelag that had been supplying German war factories—and interrogations took on a new level of sadism, with Gestapo thugs drunk on cognac having beating orgies that made it impossible for captives to confess even if they wanted to.

More troubling, Norway's infestation of collaborators informing to the Gestapo became such a problem that the SOE, at the request of the Norwegian high command, assembled a four-man team to begin assassinating them. (The death squad, code-named "Bittern" and trained in silent murder, poison potions, and break-ins, infiltrated in but never carried out any hits.) The most notorious of the collaborators was Henry Rinnan and his gang of snitches in South and North Trøndelag where Colby's team operated. A small, hump-backed, and sickly-looking man who drove a truck for the Norwegian army before the invasion and afterward became an eager Nazi informant, Rinnan's ring helped the Germans arrest more than one thousand Norwegians and execute about a hundred.

On April 9, Colby and nineteen of his NORSO men and Norwegian guerrillas set out from the base camp for Grana bridge. A dozen rail attacks were planned by different resistance groups during that month. Donovan kept close track of them, sending the Joint Chiefs updates on the successful ones. The five-day, forty-mile trek to the bridge was brutal. Each man carried a fifty-pound rucksack along with his rifle, and they took turns dragging three *pulks*, small toboggans with sixty pounds of explosives and supplies on each. The first day they skied through a driving rainstorm, which turned their uniforms into sheets of ice, and holed up that evening in one of the many summer huts dotting the Norwegian mountains. This well-equipped *seter* belonged to a Nazi sympathizer. After drying their clothes and gear, the men warmed their insides with liquor the turncoat had hidden behind the baseboard of his piano.

The next two days, a snowstorm raged so fiercely the Norwegian guides convinced Colby to keep his men in the *seter* because a mountain crossing would be too dangerous. Thursday morning, April 12, Colby could not stand being cooped up in the hut any longer and ordered the men to buckle on their skis and push out, even though the blizzard had let up only slightly. The going that day was tough. In zero temperature they forded icy streams, having to stop after each crossing to dry their skis because they would not slide through the snow easily when they were wet. The men had to take off their skis to climb the ice-covered and boulder-strewn Imsdals Mountain. Next they had to circle south around Flat Mountain to avoid a German observation post atop the hill just north from spotting them. Late that evening they found another deserted hut and collapsed inside it.

The next afternoon, after another day of exhausting skiing over broken and steep terrain through Rokt Valley, Colby left most of the group at a spot near Grana River and took his Norwegian guide and three commandos with him to scout out the bridge. Peering through binoculars from afar he counted the Germans at both ends of the structure and spotted another machine gun nest at its south end. He sat in a snowbank and watched for a while. A train soon came by loaded with freight. The bridge was far more heavily defended than he imagined—too many enemy soldiers for his small force—and his idea of seizing a locomotive to ride up with guns blazing seemed wildly impractical, Colby realized. Who knew when the next train would roll by for them to seize. After another day of scouting the area, he decided they would attack the smaller Tangen bridge, which was on his list of alternates and stood just south of the train station for the village of Valoy. With no permanent guards, that bridge would be easier than Grana's to take down, but hardly a cakewalk. Enemy patrols passed by frequently. Valoy farther north had ten Germans, who Colby's scouts could see had been alerted for trouble.

The sky still dark, Colby's team reached the cliffs over the long downward slope toward the railroad track and Tangen bridge by 4:30 Sunday morning. They took off their skis and Colby and Langeland crept ahead as carefully as they could to reconnoiter the bridge. Glimmers of sunlight peeked above the horizon for what looked to be a clear day in the quiet forest around them. The sound of their feet crunching the crusted snow could be heard far away, they feared. Atop a small hill overlooking the track, which skirted Litløyingen Lake, Colby and Langeland spotted a small house they thought might be a useful spot for gathering the men before the attack. They could see no ski tracks around the hut. It appeared empty. But as they tiptoed to it, they could hear sounds inside. Machine guns drawn, the commandos kicked down the door and found huddled inside a terrified family that had fled the Nazi rape of Finnmark in the north. The family was friendly, updating Colby on the German patrols that came by Tangen bridge regularly, but he nevertheless had Langeland keep his weapon pointed at them while he made his way down the rest of the slope to take a look at the bridge. No sign of any enemy around it, as far as he could see.

Langeland radioed back for the main party to join them. They scampered quickly down the slope. Colby placed five men near the north end of the bridge and four at the south end to serve as sentries. Sather kept a four-man assault party as a reserve along the height overlooking them, ready to counterattack if an enemy patrol showed up. (Along the way, Sather's team spotted another farmhouse and cut its phone line so whoever was inside couldn't alert anyone after he heard the blast.) Those fighters in place, Farnsworth, their demolition expert, rushed to the bridge with four men and the eighty pounds of explosives they had planned to use at Grana.

That was more than enough to obliterate the smaller Tangen bridge. The thirty-six-foot structure had four I beam stringers, each about forty feet long and made of inch-thick steel. Farnsworth's men quickly slapped on the charges and ran back to Colby's position. Then they waited. Colby hoped to blow the bridge when a southbound train came by so there would be even more damage for the Germans to repair.

But none showed up. At 6:30 a.m., Colby ordered Farnsworth to detonate the charges. In the still morning air the deafening blast echoed back and forth among the mountains. When the smoke cleared he could see nothing left of the bridge. Colby ran down to the wreckage and placed shoulder patches with American flags sewn on them around it. It would tell the Germans who had done the damage and, he hoped, spare the local population from reprisal.

Now they had to move quickly. Every German in the area knew guerrillas had struck and they would surely fan out to catch the saboteurs and shoot them on the spot. Colby's team gathered up their skis and hurriedly climbed back into the mountains toward Litløyingen Lake. There he let them wolf down a breakfast and rest for a few hours; the men had eaten little nor slept for a day. Late afternoon, the sound of a spotter plane overhead awakened them. They never saw the aircraft but assumed it was looking for them so the men strapped on their skis to move out once more. To deceive the Germans he knew would be following them, Colby decided on a circuitous route back to the base camp that would take them to the Swedish border, then cut back to Lake Gjevsjøen. It was a wise move because three enemy ski patrols had immediately begun the hunt for them after the explosion.

Colby soon spotted one of them—ten Germans trudging along their trail from the railroad. His exhausted men were in no condition to stand and fight. The Germans could easily radio for hundreds of reinforcements in the area. The only hope for the NORSO men and Norwegian guerrillas was to stay ahead of the enemy. To slow their pursuers, Farnsworth rigged a couple pounds of plastic explosives to a tripwire and buried the booby trap in their ski trail along the downslope of a steep hill. When the Wehrmacht patrol's leader glided down the hill the blast crippled him. After another of their men broke his leg on a particularly rough patch of land, the discouraged patrol gave up the chase. But by then it was late Monday afternoon, April 16, and, on the move now for two days through the worst terrain Colby had ever seen with little more than two-hour breaks and their dried rations run out, his men neared physical breakdown. When they reached an empty mountain hut that night at about ten o'clock he told his raiders they could flop down in it until the next morning. Colby, meanwhile, radioed a Norwegian resistance officer who was on his way south to meet their group. The officer had alarming news: a combined German and Norwegian Nazi patrol hunting for the American commandos (the resistance officer counted twenty-five of them and they were all accomplished skiers) was now just a few thousand yards from the mountain hut where Colby's men snored.

After only two hours of sleep, Colby roused his guerrillas once more and gave them his unpleasant order to move out. Cold, hungry, and seriously weakened from fatigue, they set off before dawn for another climb, this one several miles long and at a brutal forty-five-degree angle over another snow- and ice-covered mountain identified on Colby's map as Sugartop. They nicknamed it "Benzedrine Hill" because practically all the men had to gulp down the stimulant pills for artificial energy to reach the peak. By daybreak they stood at the summit, out of range of the German patrol, which never saw them scaling the slope in darkness. They gazed at glorious Sweden ten miles away. The ski trip down went far faster. Near the Norwegian border Colby deposited his team at a camp the underground maintained, where the men rested and feasted on roasted elk covered in gravy. After sleeping sixteen hours, Colby left his men at the hideout for another two days to re-cuperate while he, Langeland, and two Norwegian guerrillas skied the final leg back to Lake Gjevsjøen so his radioman could send their report on the successful mission to London.

Good news awaited him when he reached the farm. His men who had been mistakenly dropped in Sweden were there, dressed like Norwegian hunters. With the help of Swedish intelligence agents, OSS officers had managed to spring them from an internment camp north of Stockholm and spirit the men to Norway. His army of NORSO and Norwegian fighters now swelled to thirty-four—although Colby remained bitter over his manpower shortage. A Norwegian family of three also arrived to bake bread for his men—he paid them 100 kroner—and one of his sergeants bought a cow from a local farmer for 400 kroner so they would have extra milk. A few days later, a Swedish courier rode in on a sled packed with explosives and supplies (including the canned pineapples they requested).

But it was only a matter of time before the enemy found their base camp, Colby realized. With so many American bombers flying over them trying to drop reinforcements, the Germans were bound to suspect that Allied commandos lurked near Lake Gjevsjøen. The NORSO men had destroyed one of the Wehrmacht's prized bridges and severely wounded a soldier with a booby trap. Enraged over the sabotage all along the Nordland track,

Terboven, the *Reichskommissar*, wanted to execute ten thousand Norwegians. Word of Colby's raid spread quickly among the villages and Norwegians began showing up at the base camp wanting to volunteer as fighters. One of them was sure to tell the Germans he had been to the hideout, Colby knew. Just as irksome, it took the Germans only about a week to repair the rail cut and restore twice-daily service on the Nordland line. The NORSO commander planned his next attack.

The two miles of track that looped from the old Norse village of Lurudal near the edge of Snåsa Lake was a key slice for the Germans' freight trains barreling south on the Nordland line. Before he left England, Colby and Skabo had decided that cutting the track at multiple points gave the Wehrmacht practically as much a headache as blowing a bridge like Tangen's thirty miles south because repair crews had to be sent to so many difficult-to-reach points to reconnect the line. With Langeland and a Norwegian guide at his side, on Wednesday morning, April 25, Colby peered over a snowbank, his white parka camouflaging him, and gazed at the track snaking from Lurudal. The spring thaw, which brought mercifully higher temperatures, still ended up making the two-day ski trek to Lurudal for his twenty-five-man team a grind. With higher temperatures, skiing over the thirty-one miles of wetter snow became more laborious, while three lakes along their route to Lurudal had to be circumvented because their softened ice rendered travel over them with heavy-equipment *pulks* too hazardous.

Colby could see no Germans along the Lurudal track, but he knew many would descend on it quickly after the explosions. His intelligence reports told him forty Wehrmacht soldiers were garrisoned at Lurudal while the Plutten tunnel and three other villages nearby had sixty more. The two thousand Germans at Snåsa farther south could also make it to Lurudal in ten minutes.

After sketching on a sheet of paper the points along the track that they would strike, Colby and his two comrades skied five miles back to the vacated hut at Skjorsjohaugen where his other men bivouacked. As the full moon appeared above the horizon that night, eight groups of three or four men each skied away from the hut at staggered times, so they all would arrive simultaneously at their designated spots along the two-mile stretch of track six miles away. Each team carried thirty rail charges. For his group,

Colby had a Norwegian scout and Corporal Sivert Windh, a husky former Brooklyn waiter and one of the NORSO men mistakenly dropped into Sweden who now hefted, in addition to his share of the explosives, a heavy Browning Automatic Rifle with extra ammunition.

The eight teams reached the edge of the track at 11:30 p.m. The temperature had dropped to zero and a west wind howled through, but otherwise the night was silent. They had not been discovered. The men moved forward like a long chorus line to plant the charges—talking only in whispers as they placed a pair of explosives each at the alternating fishplates that bolted together the thirteen-yard-long rails. That way, each team could be sure that its thirty charges would tear up about two hundred yards of rail. They worked quickly—two men to strap the charges to the rail, the third to hook the firing system to the charges. Colby had instructed them before they set out that he would shoot a green flare into the air at precisely 11:45 p.m. to signal them to detonate the charges. If they didn't see a flare they were under orders to start the explosions exactly five minutes later.

Every team finished on time except for one—Colby's. A tunnel guardhouse that he hadn't spotted with Germans inside stood just thirty yards from the northern tip of the section his group was blowing up. It had forced them to work slower so they didn't alert the enemy soldiers and Colby never had time to shoot his flare. At 11:50 on the dot, explosions on the track quickly erupted one after another to a deafening crescendo as teams raced from one pair of charges to another firing them off individually.

Like bees whacked from a hive, the enemy for miles around fired aimlessly into the air and lit up the black sky with flares. Worried the guardhouse nearby would spill out with angry Germans, Colby ordered Windh to set up his BAR across the track to give them covering fire as he and his Norwegian guide ran along their section to spark the charges. It took only a couple of minutes but as Colby pulled the last time-delayed detonator and started back, he saw to his horror that his Norwegian guide stood right next to the last rail that in ten seconds was about to be blasted.

He yelled at the guide, but the Norwegian, who spoke no English, looked at him bewildered. Colby ran to the man, lunged at him, knocking him down with Colby on top as the charge exploded, sending shards of steel over their heads.

Germans from the guardhouse opened fire. Most of their shots sprayed wildly. But one struck near, kicking up dirt and a pebble into Colby's forehead. He and his two comrades hopped up and ran with all their might through the snow and away from the track.

With no trouble, the eight teams reached the assembly point Colby had designated after they finished their mission—another empty hut they broke into near Snåsa's Skartnes farm. Quickly, they tabulated the damage. One hundred and nine of the double charges had successfully detonated destroying 218 rail sections, or about a mile and a half of the Nordland line. But they had no time to celebrate except for quickly gulping down cups of hot coffee to keep them awake. Colby and the others could hear the noise of enemy patrols closing in on them. Strapping on their skis they pushed out toward Lake Gjevsjøen thirty-five miles away.

They reached the base camp by four o'clock Thursday afternoon, never taking a break of more than a few minutes along the way. Colby saw no Luftwaffe spotter planes overhead as they made the trip while another snowstorm all but wiped out their tracks for the fifty Germans sent out to hunt them. But back at their hideout he posted extra guards at its perimeter and waited for an enemy response. The only one, however, came from a friendly Norwegian agent, who reported that a Wehrmacht officer had told him the terrorists who wrecked the line at Lurudal were "a very brave and resourceful group." Intelligence officers in London estimated that for the month of April seven German mountain divisions would reach southern Norway, but they clogged there because mines and Allied warships off the North Sea coast made ocean travel to Hamburg nearly impossible. The Wehrmacht forced Russian slaves to patch up the Lurudal track to continue the overland flow, but the prisoners did so poorly and the stretch continued to have breakdowns after the attack.

The soggy ground turning to mush by the end of April, the living at Lake Gjevsjøen became harsh. With more Norwegian volunteers trickling into the camp, the NORSO commandos began to run out of food. They stumbled upon a German cache of flour and looted French champagne. With their weekly supply of reindeer halted, Colby let one of his men venture out and shoot one—which cost him 130 kroner to keep quiet an angry herder who claimed the animal was his. Otherwise, no more supplies would be coming soon from Sweden or the United Kingdom, headquarters told him. The physical wear and tear took its toll. Sivert Windh, the BAR man during the Lurudal rail attack, doubled over in pain from appendicitis and had to be bundled onto a sled a Norwegian volunteer drove to a Swedish hospital. Colby lost a toe and the tip of a middle finger to frostbite.

Also as April's end drew near, the Norwegian resistance's high command, realizing German capitulation in Central Europe could not be far off, was preparing for what it hoped would be a peaceful return of the country. The Wehrmacht might, however, try to hold out, the Norwegians feared. If that happened, they knew the Allies would have no troops to spare for an invasion. That was why the resistance did not want any guerrilla operation to imperil a quick and quiet settlement with their occupiers. "In view of the tense German situation," headquarters radioed Colby on May 1, his mission now was "to make small and frequent attacks" on the rail line rather than "larger scale" strikes that would arouse the enemy. In particular, London wanted Colby to abandon a grand scheme he had been pushing in messages to headquarters for several weeks.

It came to be called the "Lierne Plan" after a thousand square miles of salient jutting into Sweden northeast of the Lake Gjevsjøen base camp. Lierne hosted cross-country ski races each year over its many mountains and had a little more than two thousand Norwegians scattered in fewer than a half dozen villages. With the help of arms coming in from Sweden, Colby wanted to seize the municipality, plant an American flag on it, and declare Lierne liberated by the Allies so Norwegians would flock to it and establish a guerrilla enclave independent of the Germans. Colby's plan had a few backers in London's Scandinavian Section but not Skabo nor anyone else in the special forces command or SHAEF, who thought the brash young major needed to calm down. Neutral Sweden's support was critical for the Allies at the moment and they did not want the Stockholm government put in the embarrassing position of appearing to back a major operation against Germany with supplies pouring into Lierne. A large Wehrmacht force would have little difficulty swooping in to wipe out this redoubt and inflict brutal reprisals on Lierne's Norwegians, London warned. Colby also did not know that SHAEF was in the middle of delicate negotiations with the German High Command to have the Wehrmacht turn over Norway peacefully. His escapade would blow up those talks. London radioed its NORSO commander that the "Lierne Plan cannot be executed now for obvious reasons."

The reasons did not seem obvious to Colby, who continued to argue for his idea. "We can help liberate Norway more by organizing and preparing a guerrilla force" to battle the Germans if they resist or the Quisling paramilitary force if it tries to start a civil war if the Germans do surrender, he messaged back on May 2. "Lierne is easy to take and equally easy to defend." Headquarters fired back with a sharply worded order: stay in hiding. Any attempt to start the Lierne plan "will subject you to immediate disciplinary action." Much later in life, Colby admitted in his memoirs that "headquarters was right." His "flamboyant" proposal, he acknowledged, would have upset "the delicate procedure of securing the surrender of the remaining Germans in Norway."

Colby also discovered at the end of April what happened to the bomber whose crash his men had heard in the early hours of April 7. A reindeer herder arrived at the base camp on April 26 and informed him that he had found the wreckage of a plane on the west side of Plukketjern Mountain fifteen miles north. Three days later after a storm had passed, Colby took a patrol to the site and found scattered over a large area hundreds of pieces of the Liberator, supply containers broken open, and the burned or mutilated bodies of eight airmen and four of his commandos. Several men in the patrol who had been interned in Sweden recognized the aircrew as the same one that had mistakenly dropped them there. They had obviously gone to their deaths determined to make good on this sortie after the failed one. From the position of the wreckage, Colby surmised that the B-24 had been circling west to make its drop over Lake Gjevsjøen when it hit the top of the tree-barren Plukketjern Mountain and bounced down the slope.

The frozen ground was too hard to dig graves. Colby had his men wrap the bodies in the parachutes they found in the area then cover them with rocks at a slight knoll overlooking Lang Lake. He placed a small American flag on the rock pile, said a short prayer, and his men fired three volleys over the gravesite. He also had a commando snap photographs of the makeshift ceremony to send to the families of the fallen.

The patrol returned to Lake Gjevsjøen with Colby still fearful the Germans would soon discover their hideout.

CHAPTER 24

VICTORY

Finally, the Joint Chiefs reversed themselves and notified Donovan shortly before noon on Thursday, April 26, that Dulles could resume Sunrise. An hour later, Donovan sent a top secret cable to Bern for Dulles's eyes only with precise instructions the Pentagon wanted followed. There will be no more negotiations in Switzerland. The Germans must proceed to Caserta to sign the surrender document "at once or [the] entire deal is off," Donovan told his station chief. The Russians have also been notified to send their representative to the Allied command in Italy. No freelancing, Donovan warned Dulles. "We must carry out these instructions literally."

Dulles scrambled to round up the Germans. When Donovan's cable arrived, Wolff's adjutant, Major Wenner, and Vietinghoff's senior staff man, Lieutenant Colonel Schweinitz, had already hopped in a car and were somewhere on the road from Lucerne to the Italian border. By Saturday, Dulles succeeded in intercepting the two officers and redirecting them. He cabled Donovan that Schweinitz and Wenner were scheduled to arrive at General Alexander's headquarters that day with "full powers" from their bosses to sign the surrender—or at least Dulles hoped they had that authority. Schweinitz is a "capable" officer, he assured Donovan. Wenner was not a "forceful character" but Dulles believed he could be counted on to rubber-stamp the SS's part of the surrender. If a last-minute glitch arose and they needed to reach Wolff, Little Wally, disguised in an SS uniform the general provided the OSS man, would sit in Wolff's headquarters with his radio tuned to Caserta's.

Alexander's comfortably appointed C-47 rushed to Annecy, France, near Geneva. It took off from there at noon on Saturday with Schweinitz and Wenner for the flight through a rainstorm to Caserta. Dulles remained in Bern. He had become a celebrity in the region from his cover as FDR's personal representative and worried that war correspondents at the Allied headquarters might recognize him and blow the operation's security. Gaevernitz boarded the plane in his place to serve as translator and fixer for any problems.

The Allies' Mediterranean headquarters was housed in a grand Caserta castle Neapolitan kings once used, with a lush waterfall tumbling down behind it from a hill terraced with pools, fountains, Baroque statues, and eighteenth-century English gardens. Shortly after three o'clock a car with Schweinitz and Wenner pulled up to the entrance for a separate barbed-wire-encased and heavily guarded compound with Quonset huts and bungalows that sat atop the hill with a spectacular view of the Bay of Naples and the white houses along the blue Tyrrhenian Sea's coastline. Large sheets of olive drab canvas, however, were fastened to the trees to prevent the Germans from recognizing their sylvan surroundings and the location of the Allies' headquarters.

The first official meeting took place in the compound's conference room promptly at six o'clock, presided over by Lieutenant General Sir William Duthie Morgan, Alexander's chief of staff, who sported a bushy white mustache and silver hair swept back. On one side of the long conference table Lemnitzer and Airey (both now in their general's uniforms) sat with three other senior Allied officers and Sir William. Gaevernitz sat at one end to interpret while Schweinitz and Wenner sat on the other side. A Russian major general, Aleksey Pavlovich Kislenko, who served as the Soviet liaison officer in Rome (and spy for the GRU), was in the compound but not invited to this first session.

With no pleasantries to start, Morgan curtly introduced himself along with the senior officers on his side of the table and then demanded that the two German officers produce their credentials authorizing them to sign the surrender on behalf of Wolff and Vietinghoff. Wenner slid across the table his sheet with a short sentence and Wolff's signature underneath permitting him to sign. The credentials Schweinitz passed forward, however, contained a condition, which the lieutenant colonel now explained. "Within the frame of the instructions" Vietinghoff had given him, Schweinitz said, he had "full powers" to sign. But it was possible that "propositions might be made" in the surrender terms that "would be outside" Schweinitz's instructions and they would have to be referred to Vietinghoff directly for a decision. Sir William ignored Schweinitz's caveat, although he should not have. Among the instructions Vietinghoff had given his lieutenant colonel: he wanted written into the surrender a provision allowing his soldiers to march back to Germany instead of to a POW camp—which the Allies would never accept. Morgan, instead, pushed across the table to Schweinitz and Wenner three copies of the twenty-page Instrument of Surrender with appendices. He told them they had three hours to read the documents and return ready to declare whether they accepted their terms.

The Germans returned at 9 p.m., stunned by the cold, uncompromising language they hastily read in the lengthy document. Kislenko and his translator attended this meeting. For several hours Schweinitz and Wenner haggled with Morgan over the terms. Sir William was willing to make minor concessions—such as allowing the officers to keep their sidearms to maintain order until they entered prison camps—but he adamantly refused Vietinghoff's condition that his army be allowed to return to Germany. The best the British general would offer was to attach his own personal statement to the document that, although he could make no promises, he expected most of the German soldiers would be held near Italy instead of being interned in the United States or other far-off sites for a long time.

Through the night and into early Sunday morning back at their quarters, the unhappy Germans argued over the terms with Gaevernitz, who finally put their choice in stark terms. "Don't you realize," he said exasperated, that every minute you quibble here over the document's sentences means more Wehrmacht soldiers in Italy killed and "further destruction, further air raids on German cities, further death!" Wenner was willing to sign. Airey arrived shortly to let the Germans know it would be impossible for the Allies to wait while they tried to reach Vietinghoff for his approval of the surrender document. An exhausted Schweinitz finally agreed to sign without his general's final consent. The formal surrender was fixed for May 2 at noon, Greenwich time.

At 2 p.m. Sunday, a groggy Schweinitz and Wenner were ushered into the ballroom of the nearby Royal Summer Palace, squinting their eyes because of the floodlights turned on for movie cameras recording the event. In addition to the senior Mediterranean Command officers, Kislenko and his translator, and Gaevernitz, a small group of American and British newspaper and radio correspondents stood by a long, polished conference table on which seven copies of the surrender documents (five in English, two in German) sat. The newsmen had agreed not to print or broadcast their stories until after noon on May 2.

Morgan signed for Alexander, then Wenner fixed his name to the sheets. Before he lifted his pen, Schweinitz paused to make a statement, more as a final gasp. "I have received powers from General von Vietinghoff, which have certain limits. I am taking it on my own responsibility to exceed these limits. . . . I assume that my commander-in-chief will approve my action, but I cannot give an absolute assurance to this effect." Gaevernitz shot Lemnitzer a quick glance. Did this make Schweinitz's signature worthless?

Morgan thought not. "We accept that," he said quietly with a nod.

. . . .

Alexander expected the Germans to broadcast surrender orders over their military radio channels the morning of May 2, followed by leaflet drops on their soldiers and an advance party from Vietinghoff's headquarters appearing at the Allied front lines carrying a white flag. That was the plan, but Sir Harold had no idea if the enemy would follow it. Would their commanders accept terms agreed to by two midlevel German officers, one of whom blurted out at the last minute that he might not have the authority to sign? Dulles worried as well.

Both men, it turned out, had reason to fret. Anything that might derail the surrender happened at this point. Schweinitz and Wenner, who had flown to Bern after the signing, were held up by the Swiss from crossing the border to Italy with copies of the surrender documents for their bosses until Dulles intervened. After they received the papers, Wolff and Vietinghoff quarreled with other senior Nazis. Kaltenbrunner tried to block the surrender to peddle his peace offer. With Hitler still alive on April 29, Kesselring also intervened to try to halt Vietinghoff's capitulation. For a coup de grâce, American warplanes bombed Vietinghoff's headquarters that night. Dulles wired Caserta to halt the sorties.

But Wednesday morning, May 2, Donovan messaged Truman that despite "every possible vicissitude" the surrender appeared set for that day. With Hitler's suicide on April 30, Kesselring no longer ran interference. Vietinghoff's headquarters began radioing orders Tuesday night for its troops to lay down their arms the next day. Alexander followed, publicly announcing the armistice at 6:30 p.m. on Wednesday. Dulles broke out bottles of champagne for his Bern staff. Kesselring next cabled Alexander, interested in surrendering his front to Eisenhower. Smiling Albert obviously wants to "get on [the] bandwagon," Dulles cabled Donovan. The Bern chief envisioned a silver lining—Sunrise starting a cascade of capitulations on other fronts.

. . . .

Dulles juggled other pressing matters as Sunrise unfolded. He learned to his relief that the Stauffenberg family had survived after the July 20 plot. The Allies found the family alive, along with other prominent concentration camp prisoners. Canaris did not survive. The Abwehr admiral who had supported the assassination attempt was beaten savagely at the Flossenbürg concentration camp, then hanged by wire on April 9, 1945. After the war, Dulles hunted for Canaris's diary, which he knew would contain a trove of insights on the Third Reich, but he never found it.

Fritz Kolbe arrived in Bern on April 3. His boss, Karl Ritter, had arranged for him to drive the ambassador's mistress and her two-year-old daughter in a Mercedes to his house in Bavaria where they would be safe. After dumping the pair off in the southern town of Kempten, Kolbe took the train west to the Swiss capital with his final cache of documents and photos. The material painted a grim picture of Germany since mid-March. Government and Nazi Party agencies in Berlin had been ordered to begin burning their archives and the German railway system had "broken down completely," he reported. Berliners had become eager listeners of Voice of America broadcasts and privately rejoiced when Allied bombers flattened Goebbels's Propaganda Ministry building. Elite Soviet troops entering Germany behaved well, the Foreign Office informant said, while poorly trained Soviet Asiatic soldiers "kill, loot and rape." Kolbe's final delivery capped one of the most successful espionage hauls the Allies had during the war—although it took far too long, Helms thought, for the U.S. government to recognize the agent's legitimacy and the value of his intelligence.

Dulles decided to keep Kolbe at his Herrengasse apartment performing odd jobs, such as compiling lists of "good Germans" in the Foreign Office who could work in a postwar government and paying a visit to the German ambassador in Bern to persuade him to stop burning documents revealing Nazi financial holdings in Switzerland.

Kolbe also brought with him in his last batch intelligence on Japan, which Washington could not get enough of. Kolbe arrived with diplomatic reports that Japanese soldiers were dug in for a long fight in northern Luzon and southern Burma but that Tokyo's leaders had become more unpopular.

Perhaps because of that growing unrest, in early May Dulles began receiving peace feelers from Japanese who considered him an ideal conduit after his Sunrise triumph. The first came from Per Jacobsson, an old friend and prominent Swedish economic adviser at Basel's Bank of International Settlements, who acted as an intermediary for two Japanese officials at the BIS, Kojiro Kitamura and Tsuyoshi Yoshimura. The other came from Dr. Friedrich Hack, a German expat widely traveled in Asia and a pal of Gaevernitz's, who said he spoke for Lieutenant Commander Yoshiro Fujimura, the Japanese naval attaché in Bern. Fujimura, Hack claimed, had "excellent connections" back home. Dulles met separately with Jacobsson and Hack through late summer. Above all, Kitamura, Yoshimura, and Fujimura wanted to preserve the emperor's status as a constitutional monarch in any peace deal. The lieutenant commander sent more than twenty cables to his superiors in the Japanese navy (many of which the Allies' Magic system intercepted and decoded) urging them to initiate peace talks with Dulles. In his messages Fujimura inflated Dulles's diplomatic prowess and his willingness to strike a deal. Dulles was convinced the Japanese wanted to surrender, but never knowing if anyone in Tokyo was paying attention to these so-called emissaries, he simply sat and listened in most of his meetings with their front men. He finally told Hack in June that if Fujimura was serious about peace he should have his navy send to Switzerland a senior officer, such as an admiral, with full powers to begin talks. None arrived.

Through April and early May, Dulles vacuumed all signs he could find of the Third Reich's final death throes. The officer corps' personal oath to Adolf Hitler chained it to the dictator and was now reason for their "stubborn" yet futile resistance, he told Washington in a radiotelephone call, but he could see cracks everywhere. Party bigwigs were fleeing Berlin, but Hitler forbade the evacuation of the capital's three million hapless residents, Dulles cabled headquarters. Around-the-clock Allied bombing of Berlin seemed to Dulles senseless at this point, only hardening its citizens toward the West. Eisenhower wanted the German border with Switzerland sealed and Dulles to report on Nazis slipping into the country. The Bern chief cabled Washington on April 20 that for the first time since the führer assumed power the swastika flag was not flown over the German legation that day to celebrate his birthday. Hitler's whereabouts became a subject of intense debate with Molden reporting to Dulles that the dictator had a bulletproof plane ready to fly him to the Middle East or South America and Dulles speculating in January that he would evacuate to the Bavarian Alps for his last stand. By April both Dulles and Casey had reports from sources that Hitler was holed up in the Führerbunker—suffering from depression and working only at night, a Swiss officer told Dulles. After the Allies entered Munich at the end of April, Donovan ordered Dulles and Casey to have their agents hunt for Hitler's fingerprints on file in the city's municipal records to be used if the dictator tried to switch with an impostor in the bunker.

Swamped with millions of refugees from the Russian advance, its train station platforms "black with people" (as one intelligence memo described it), by April Berlin's misery was difficult for Casey's agents to put into words. Bread and potato supplies were "virtually exhausted" sparking food riots, they reported. Overcrowded hospitals lacked "the simplest medicines," potable water was scarce, sanitation was nonexistent, and a deadly flu virus was spreading quickly. Even with the Red Army's artillery shells reaching the city center by April 20, blasting the Tiergarten stables and sending its horses galloping on fire, Berlin remained tough for the Soviets to crack. The Waffen-SS command ordered hundreds of thousands of battle-weary soldiers, weak old men, and brave young boys to fight to the death.

With the Soviets just a quarter mile from the Führerbunker, Hitler had one of his doctors test on his favorite German shepherd the poison he would take. The dog died instantly. After dictating his last political testament on April 29 and firing Himmler for his peace feelers to the Allies, Hitler married his longtime mistress, Eva Braun, rounding up a startled municipal officer from the barricades to perform the ceremony. The next afternoon, Hitler led Eva to his private quarters where they swallowed cyanide capsules and he put a bullet from his service pistol into his head. After the Soviets recovered the couple's charred corpses, Donovan ordered Dulles to send the Russians Hitler's dental records, which OSS officers had retrieved from his captured SS dentist, so they could identify his body.

. . . .

By the end of April, Norway's resisters and their German occupiers had the same goal—self-preservation. Rumors of Himmler's peace offers to the West swept through the country, bringing out cheering demonstrators to Oslo's streets. Not knowing how the Wehrmacht there would react, the resistance command immediately issued a terse directive to the civilian population: "Dignity—quiet—discipline." "No one must by ill-advised actions imperil the possibility of an orderly unrolling of the German occupation of Norway," the exile government in London advised in another radio message. Their occupiers were spooked enough. Panicked by the rumors of Himmler's peace offer, Quisling released political prisoners and floated the idea of his heading a transition government to "save the country from civil war." On May 2, Wehrmacht commander General Franz Böhme declared no intention to end the occupation: "We shall, proud and loyal, continue our unbroken vigil in Norway." The next day, Grand Admiral Karl Dönitz, whom Hitler had designated his successor, summoned Böhme, Terboven, and occupation officials for Denmark to receive new orders, prompting rumors in Oslo that Norway would be surrendered or used as a bargaining chip in an overall peace deal. London broadcast orders to Norway's resistance and the foreign commando units like Colby's to remain calm, to take no actions provoking the enemy, and, at the same time, to be on the lookout for renegade Germans trying to start a fight. What happened to Operation Rype on May 2, after Colby's burial party had returned from Plukketjern Mountain, was exactly what headquarters wanted to avoid.

A five-man German patrol had wandered to the crest of the hill over-looking the Lake Gjevsjøen farm and decided to ski down to check it out. One of the patrol members noticed several people outside the farmhouse. In a radio message to London the next day, and in lengthier after-action reports and press interviews later, Colby recounted what happened next: The Germans (four armed with machine pistols, the fifth with a rifle) "slid down the hill rapidly," Colby reported to headquarters, and surrounded three of the NORSO commandos (all unarmed) and one of their Norwegian guides, Karle Berre, who happened to have a pistol and now pointed it at the enemy intruders.

Sergeant Marinus Myrland, one of the NORSO soldiers, "coolly and deliberately informed [the Germans] that they could shoot him but that there were enough men here to get all of them," Colby wrote his superiors. By then, commandos had rushed out of the farmhouse with their Thompson submachine guns cocked and aimed at the Germans. The German sergeant, seeing he would lose this standoff, "stated that he would surrender," Colby recounted. But when Berre lowered his pistol, the *Feldwebel* shot him in the stomach. The sergeant's machine pistol jammed so he could not fire another shot, according to Colby, and "the five Germans, still armed and with weapons in hand, were immediately shot down by our men before they could fire further." Fred Johanson, Colby's medic, pumped Berre full of penicillin and sent him by sled to Sweden.

Colby's report traveled quickly up the OSS chain of command in London. But was it accurate? Many decades later, Norwegian investigators found evidence the five Germans might not have died in a shootout. Berre was quoted in a 2001 history of North Trøndelag's guerrilla operations, written by Kåre Olav Solhjell and Friedrich Traphagen, as stating that he had a slight scuffle with the German sergeant when the patrol leader's machine gun went off, wounding him. Colby's men and Norwegians in the farmhouse poured out with their Tommy guns and soon disarmed the five Germans, according to Berre, who was taken inside to be treated by Johanson. While the medic dressed his wound, Berre said he heard shots outside. "It's our guns," Berre quoted Johanson as telling him. Other German soldiers who dug up the five buried bodies after the war told Traphagen each of them had a bullet wound to the neck, indicating they had been executed. All those involved in the incident are dead and no documents remain in Wehrmacht or OSS records that give this version. "It's no longer possible to find the correct description of what happened," Solhjell and Traphagen wrote. When Traphagen asked Colby about the incident, the historian wrote that Colby told him only that "commando soldiers do not take prisoners."

The Germans certainly would have tortured and executed the NORSO team if the tables had been turned. Colby worried that more Wehrmacht soldiers might quickly follow this patrol. Dragging along prisoners while on the run would have been difficult. Yet the war would be over in five days. The enemy soldiers could have been sent to Sweden. If Colby did order the execution of five Germans in uniform it would be a clear violation of the "international code of conduct in warfare," Solhjell and Traphagen wrote. Skabo was suspicious that Colby had not given him the whole story. After the war he wrote a memo to his boss recommending "that investigation be made of the encounter between a German patrol of five men and our Rype party." No records exist in the OSS files to indicate that such an investigation was ever conducted.

Two Norwegian guerrilla parties arrived at the Lake Gjevsjøen base camp after the May 2 incident warning that more German patrols were out hunting for the NORSO men. Colby had more soldiers to fight them off—the two Norwegian groups increased his manpower to forty-five—but he now had a more pressing problem than the Germans—lack of food for his growing army. London radioed him that resupply was impossible at this point. Melting snow and ice had turned North Trøndelag into a muddy bog, making transportation difficult. The team had already killed three cows for meat (paying farm owner Andehsson for them) and was subsisting now on *grut*, a foul-tasting gruel from the grain left in Andehsson's storehouse. Colby's scouting parties spotted long gray lines of bedraggled Germans marching south through North Trøndelag along with three or four trains a day on the Nordland line carrying Wehrmacht equipment. "We will run out of food soon," Colby radioed London on May 4, increasingly irritated that headquarters appeared to be ignoring his pleas for supplies. The next day he sent another cable to London proposing that he and Langeland ski with a white flag to the German garrison at Steinkjer and negotiate its surrender to the Allies so his team could have access to its stores. The response from headquarters came quickly this time: "Stay in hiding" and "stand by for additional orders. Any unauthorized contact by you with [the] enemy . . . will subject you to immediate disciplinary action."

. . . .

Early May, Bill Casey hit the road once more touring liberated territory in the Netherlands, Germany, and Czechoslovakia. He hunted for his spy teams that had been overrun by the Allied advance and in one instance encountered Red Army officers at a point where the American and Soviet forces met. During a visit to liberated Munich, he tracked down the Painter team. Flour and Van Dyck ushered him into their tiny cramped room in the employee barracks next to the SS garage and told him the story of their mission from beginning to end. Late into the night, Casey listened raptly.

The evening of May 1, the two agents had finally been able to reach American intelligence officers who had arrived in Munich with the 7th Army. They handed over the long lists they had compiled of Gestapo officers for Munich and Bavaria along with last-minute plans Berlin had cabled for the German agents to go underground. When Casey arrived, Flour and Van Dyck were helping Army counterintelligence officers mop up the city's senior Gestapo officers and their underlings so they could be charged with war crimes. Among the more than sixty arrested was Emil Weil, Munich's Gestapo executive secretary, who betrayed his comrades to Flour and Van Dyck. Weil discovered the two agents recommended that he be sent not to South America with his family, as they promised, but instead to a prison camp with the other war criminals.

. . . .

Many capitulations followed Vietinghoff's and Wolff's in Italy on May 2. Berlin's commander surrendered that same day to the Soviets. Occupation forces in Denmark and the Netherlands surrendered on May 4. Sunrise's success "placed the German troops just to the north of Italy in an equally impossible situation," Eisenhower recalled in his memoirs. For the first time Kesselring made up his mind quickly and surrendered his Army Group G to General Jacob Devers's 6th Army Group on May 6. The same day, Admiral Dönitz ordered the German High Command to surrender all forces unconditionally.

At 2:30 a.m. Monday, May 7, Allen Dulles, hobbled by another attack of gout, stood on crutches wedged among Allied officers, war correspondents, newsreel photographers, and hot klieg lights. They were crowded around a large oak table in the stuffy second-floor room of a schoolhouse Eisenhower used as his forward headquarters in the ancient city of Reims northeast of Paris. Dulles had come to SHAEF's headquarters to brief Eisenhower on the OSS's postwar operation for Germany and had been invited by his chief of staff, Walter Bedell Smith, to witness the signing ceremony for the surrender of all German forces. Flanked by Allied and Russian officers around three sides of the table, Smith sat with copies of the five-paragraph "Act of Military Surrender" before him. A British colonel, who had been an actor and theater manager in civilian life, had hastily written its text three days earlier, cribbing from the surrender document Alexander used in Italy for Sunrise. *Generaloberst* Alfred Jodl, Dönitz's chief of the Wehrmacht operations staff dispatched to sign the surrender, was called in a minute later with two of his aides. Each clicked their heels and bowed slightly. Smith waved them to the unoccupied seats facing him. The signing consumed only ten minutes—the German surrender to take effect fifty-nine minutes before midnight on May 8. Tears running down his cheeks, Jodl was led to Eisenhower's office where the supreme commander brusquely told the German he would "personally be held responsible if the terms of the surrender are violated." Jodl said he understood.

"That is all," Ike said, dismissing the officer like a private.

The next day Helms drove from Paris to Reims to join Dulles, a man he hardly knew at that point, to help with briefing SHAEF on the mission the OSS would now send into Germany. Casey was touring Augsburg in southwest Bavaria when he heard Churchill's voice on the radio announcing the end of the war in Europe. "Now that perhaps the greatest military feat in history has been achieved," he wrote Sophia and his daughter, Bernadette, "I'm consumed with a frantic desire to return to you two and never leave again."

Church bells rang nonstop in Bern on May 8. Smoke no longer billowed from the German embassy's chimney from documents being burned, its employees clicking their heels smartly and offering coffee to a Swiss Foreign Office team entering the compound to inspect it. After a torrential downpour May 8, London's streets jammed with cars, trucks, and buses honking

their horns. Thousands filled Parliament Square and Leicester Square singing and dancing. Harrods in Knightsbridge draped a sign outside proclaim-
ing "God Save the King" and bonfires blazed in Green Park and Hampstead
Heath. That night street lighting glared throughout the city, making business
more difficult for prostitutes who had enjoyed the blackout. Later, all the
combatants would have to come to terms with the sixty million persons
killed in both the European and Asian theaters.

Among the German cast of characters in Sunrise, on May 21 the Allies
nabbed Himmler, disguised as an army sergeant; he died two days later after
swallowing a poison capsule. Kaltenbrunner peddled the line after his capture that he was the hidden hand behind the Sunrise negotiations. The Allies
weren't buying and executed him for his war crimes. Kesselring served five
years in prison for war crimes in Italy. Vietinghoff was released as a POW in
September 1947. Dulles worked from afar to try to protect Wolff, who expected to be spared prosecution for past war crimes because of his key role
in Sunrise. Public pressure mounted to bring Wolff to justice, however, and
he eventually served seven years in prison.

Dulles and Gaevernitz visited Caserta on May 5 and were met with a
hero's welcome. Congratulatory telegrams poured in from Donovan and
senior Allied officers. If they knew about the secret talks, "countless thousands of parents would bless you" for the lives Sunrise saved in North
Italy, cabled John Magruder, one of Donovan's deputies. Considering it his
greatest achievement of the war, Dulles believed that Sunrise resulted in the
surrender of one million German and fascist soldiers and forestalled a Nazi
redoubt in the Alps. Some of Dulles's officers in Bern, however, believed
Sunrise deserved only minor billing. The capitulation in North Italy ended
up coming just six days before the surrender of the entire German army.
The redoubt was always a myth and the Axis forces that gave up in North
Italy likely numbered 500,000 or less, not one million. Italian property and
art treasures no doubt had been spared destruction. The lives saved at that
point probably numbered in the hundreds or low thousands and they were
mostly German lives because Alexander's army was taking far fewer casualties. In his memoirs Eisenhower credits Alexander's "brilliant campaign,"
not Dulles's negotiations, with bringing an early halt to the fighting. What
Sunrise did demonstrate was that a covert operation to achieve an end to

war on one front could become exceedingly complex and fraught with diplomatic pitfalls.

Dulles plotted a postwar press strategy with Donovan to make sure
he and the OSS received public credit for Sunrise. Glowing news articles
resulted. Even *True Comics* ran a strip on the secret surrender. The Italian
government bestowed on Dulles the Order of Saints Maurizio e Lazzaro
for chivalry. At Donovan's request, Dulles eventually received the Medal
of Merit, a civilian award he richly deserved for his World War II service.
Dulles feigned modesty over the medal, but behind the scenes he lobbied
quietly to make sure the War Department approved it and his name was
spelled correctly on the citation. He took a week's vacation after the Reims
surrender to write with Gaevernitz a detailed Sunrise history for the OSS
so their spin could be put on the talks. The negotiations helped to inflate
Dulles's reputation as a secret agent, and much later as CIA director they
further fueled his faith in the capability of covert operations like Sunrise to
change the course of history. After he retired from the CIA, Dulles wrote a
book on the secret talks and worked with Hollywood on a movie treatment
of the story.

Dulles was not shy about taking credit for his other successes in Bern.
He wrote another book in 1947 on his work with Germany's underground.
He had reason to be proud of what he accomplished. His station became
one of Donovan's most important during the war. Sealed off in Switzerland
and operating largely on his own, Dulles opened a window for Washington
to the Third Reich with key agents feeding him material from inside Germany's Foreign Office, Abwehr, and resistance movement. The volume and
quality of the political and economic intelligence he collected was first-rate
while his military intelligence improved over the years. He cabled rumors
and unverified information, to be sure. At times he misjudged the course of
events. The intelligence he supplied also ended up having little direct impact
on the policy decisions of Roosevelt and his senior advisers. Yet Donovan
distributed his reports widely in the White House and among cabinet agencies. What Dulles established in Bern—a mini–central intelligence agency
uncovering secrets, hatching psyops schemes, launching covert operations,
and supplying analysis on subjects far and wide—was unprecedented and
unlikely to be repeated. From his colleagues and rivals he earned grudging
respect. Stewart Menzies, chief of MI6 and a man not given to gushing,

particularly over Americans, judged Dulles the "Koh-i-noor" diamond of Allied intelligence.

. . . .

After the surrender, Casey sat down and wrote a lengthy memo evaluating his operation. In all, more than 150 agents had been sent to Germany from London, France, and the Low Countries for 102 different missions. The results had hardly been spectacular, he admitted. Only fifty-seven of the missions were considered successful. Twenty-six had failed. And as of the end of July, Casey could not determine what happened in the rest. Penetrating Germany "was not really as hard as it was believed to be," Casey decided. Agent casualties (about three dozen) were far lower than he expected. Moreover, "a great many by-products accrued" besides intelligence, he believed. A few teams, like Mayer's in Innsbruck, persuaded German commanders to surrender, while several teams, like Painter's, penetrated the Gestapo or SD. And even if they could not radio back intelligence, teams overrun by Allied armies were able to provide the advancing units tactical intelligence on the enemy just ahead or help identify local Nazis in captured towns. The real problem, as Casey saw it: Europe's war ended just as his agents began to show results. "There is no getting away from the fact that it does take anywhere from three weeks to three months for a clandestine team to become really productive," Casey wrote. "If these operations had started to roll two months earlier, really substantial and significant results would have been achieved."

Helms was not persuaded. "I don't think it did very much good," he said later when asked about Casey's operation. "These were very brave men who dropped in there . . . but to say that it had any effect on the outcome of the war would be to exaggerate." Dulles too believed Casey ended up producing minimal results. The only one with firsthand experience parachuting into a hostile environment, Colby thought penetrating Germany was far more difficult than Casey made it out to be. Much later in life Casey was far more circumspect about what he had achieved. "We probably saved some lives," was all he would say.

J. Russell Forgan, who had replaced Bruce in London, recommended that Casey be awarded the Legion of Merit for the German penetration operation. The Navy decided the Bronze Star he had already received was enough. Both men thought they had the last laugh. A French officer dropped by Forgan's office with a bag full of five Croix de Guerre medals for the station chief to pass out to OSS agents. Forgan peeked into the paper sack, turned to Casey, who was in the room, and asked, "Who should we give the other three to?"

. . . .

Under orders from Dönitz, Böhme surrendered his force in Norway on May 8. Desperate to get away from his base camp and find food for his starving men, Colby radioed headquarters on May 10 that he had rations left to keep them alive for only several more days. "Morale is sinking rapidly," Colby messaged London in another angry cable. Well-fed Allied troops had begun arriving in Oslo, hailed as liberators, while the commandos who did the fighting wasted away in the hills. The next day headquarters finally approved Colby's plan to evacuate his men from the camp to find food at Snåsa, then to arrange for the surrender of the German garrison at Steinkjer farther south.

The trip to Steinkjer posed new dangers. Immediately after the German surrender Norway was a tense, confused, and unstable country with no civilian government in charge. Quisling and most of his top ministers had been arrested along with collaborators like Rinnan and his gang in Trondheim. Many Gestapo, Abwehr, and SD officers fled like rats to neutral Sweden. Meanwhile a quarter million German soldiers, airmen, sailors, and SS troops remained in Norway fully armed—most "behaving correctly," according to one Allied intelligence report, but many in an ugly mood, with isolated instances of shots still being fired between them and resistance forces. Tens of thousands of Wehrmacht soldiers now filled North Trøndelag with orders to surrender. Would they do so peacefully to tiny bands of Allied commandos like NORSO's? Colby worried they would do something stupid that could get his men killed.

Thankfully, he found the German commander at Snåsa passive while its joyous villagers welcomed him with food for his emaciated men. At Steinkjer, whose enemy garrison had swelled to six thousand, Colby brought with him the two biggest commandos in his unit to the front gate of the Wehrmacht barracks. The rest of his NORSO men covered the three from farther back. The German commander, however, appeared more nervous than Colby and willingly surrendered. More delicate disarmament duty followed. Colby's team was sent to the coastal town of Namsos, where groups of its ten thousand Wehrmacht soldiers brushed his commandos' shoulders on narrow sidewalks with insolent looks on their faces and the crews of five German warships circled the harbor chanting "*Sieg Heil!*" Colby, who knew nothing about ships, boarded the five vessels with three of his commandos who had been merchant mariners and pretended to be an expert inspecting them. The show of bravado impressed on the Germans that they had lost and ended their defiant behavior.

After weeks of boring occupation duty, interrupted with parade marches for Norway's returning royal family and exiled government, Colby and his NORSO commandos finally booked passage on crowded planes that took them back to London in late June. Though gaunt and exhausted, he arrived at the nearly deserted OSS station on Grosvenor Street eager for another operation, such as one he suggested to destabilize Franco's fascist regime in Spain. The London station ignored the idea and instead ordered him to settle up his expense account for NORSO and write his final report on Rype. Operating under the harshest environment he could imagine, Colby believed the team did its part to slow the German evacuation from Norway. But his unit was small, able to launch just two raids that disabled the Nordland Railway only temporarily, and it spent as much time surviving in the wild and running from Germans as it did fighting the enemy. With a larger force he could have mounted continuous attacks to keep the rail line "out of operation completely," he argued. After he retired from the CIA Colby, like Casey, took a harsher view of what he accomplished—at the cost of ten of his men dead. "I don't think we changed the course of the war very much," he told an interviewer.

But in early July 1945, when he boarded a British merchant ship crammed with planes and GIs for the eleven-day voyage to New York, Bill Colby was bursting with optimism and patriotic pride. He wrote his mother that he wanted to visit his grandfather in St. Paul and then head to Vermont to "do some swimming" and chase "American girls" before he shipped out to Asia where the war with Japan continued. "It will be wonderful to get back to the U.S.," he wrote her. The more countries he saw overseas, "the higher stands the U.S. in every way," he had decided.

PART THREE

COLD WAR

CHAPTER 25

HOME

Casey felt like a potentate touring Europe after the war. At his disposal were cars with drivers, a plane with a crew of four to fly him, OSS châteaux for his overnight stays, "and hundreds of people at my beck and call," he wrote Sophia. "I may never again be such a B.S. (big shot) or VIP (very important person)." He city-hopped in Europe for six weeks to close down his German penetration operation—a job taking more time and effort than he first realized. Accounts had to be settled for money due agents. Casey worked to secure bonuses for prized teams like Doctor and Painter. Each returning agent must be thoroughly interrogated "as to his entire experiences" in the field, George Pratt, Casey's intelligence procurement director, had advised him at the end of April. Every report an agent radioed as well as everything he said in after-action interviews had to be checked against what the OSS now learned as it entered Nazi Germany. Each spy then had to be returned "to the life from which he was recruited"—a tricky exercise that might take as long as six months because some operatives might not want to go back and, if forced to, they might start divulging secrets out of "ill will," Pratt warned. Casey set up rules for foreign agents who wanted to settle in the United States after the war. He did not want the OSS turning into an immigration agency sponsoring agents, but a foreign operative who applied for admission could write on his application that he worked for the spy agency, Casey decided.

Casey also became part of a massive Allied intelligence effort to account for agents the Germans sent to concentration camps. It was for this reason, after his stop in Munich to visit the Painter team, that he took a short drive to the quaint village of Dachau, where one of the Reich's earliest prison complexes had housed over 200,000 inmates, more than 30,000 of whom died in captivity. Captured OSS officers, British SOE agents, and foreign resistance fighters had passed through Dachau or had been tortured, executed, or left to rot there.

On his tour of the former gunpowder factory, Casey, who had reports in his briefcase on concentration camps the Allies were searching for intelligence agents, roamed among some thirty thousand gaunt inmates still wandering about the compound and inspected piles of shoes and clothes. He turned up no evidence of his operatives' internment. He saw Army graves teams disposing of thousands of naked, decomposing bodies stacked like cordwood in the camp's storerooms and thirty-nine boxcars along the nearby railroad track. It sickened and enraged him as it had the GIs who liberated the camp. "I'll never understand how, with all we knew about Germany and its military machine, we knew so little about the concentration camps and the magnitude of the holocaust," he later wrote. What Casey did not realize, or chose to ignore, was that Donovan's organization showed little interest in investigating reports it received on the genocide because the OSS's principal customer, Franklin Roosevelt, showed little interest in the intelligence. Casey left Dachau hardened in his conviction that the evil of Nazism would continue with the communists unless they were now stopped.

Back in London, Casey and the staff he had assembled to penetrate Germany during the war turned their attention to the secret intelligence operation that would have to be mounted in the conquered nation. He sent Dulles, who would lead the OSS's mission in Germany, the names of officers in London who could help mount postwar intelligence operations. Dulles sent Casey a list of forty "good Germans" he and Gaevernitz had compiled— men like Fritz Kolbe and Hans Gisevius who had helped the Bern chief in Switzerland and would now be useful for the German mission. Kolbe, for example, could sift through Foreign Office documents the occupiers in Berlin seized. Casey assigned Helms to manage the "Crown Jewels," as these

Germans soon came to be called. The London station also revived plans to recruit willing German soldiers held in Allied POW camps to spy for the OSS mission. Helms forwarded to Casey a proposal for a covert operation, code-named "Duo," to enlist secret agents from among the 25,000 Spaniards working in German industries. Casey and the others agreed that an important target for these spies—although they decided to put little about this mission on paper—would be the Soviets and the zone of Germany their Red Army would occupy.

Curiously, Casey declined Donovan's offer to make him Dulles's chief of intelligence in the German mission. He said he had "no special knowledge" of Germany—an odd excuse considering that he had just spent every waking hour the past six months spying on the country. Instead, Casey told Donovan that he wanted to return to the United States and after a brief reunion with his family ship out to Asia for the war against Japan—a country he knew even less about. The more likely reason for his begging off was that he thought postwar duty in Germany would be unimportant and he did not want to serve there under Dulles, who had ended up being his wartime rival. Early July, Casey and Forgan hopped a ride to Washington with Donovan aboard his personal plane. The three men played gin rummy on the long flight back and talked about the work left in the Far East.

· · · ·

The SS *Empire MacAndrews* deposited Colby and its other GIs at a New York City dock. The next day he took the train to Washington and reported to the Congressional Country Club, which had become a holding pen for OSS officers from Europe preparing to transfer to Asia. Compared to Norway, Area F's food was haute cuisine. Breakfast was pushed forward to a luxurious 7:30 a.m. First-run movies played after dinner each night for 15 cents a ticket. Donovan had also begun allowing generals to play golf on the club's beat-up course.

Colby was one of fifteen NORSO commandos classified as "essential" to the OSS. The agency wanted to assign him to China to instruct and lead native units in sabotage missions behind Japanese lines. But before receiving his orders, he had to endure another interview from one of Congressional's psychiatrists. He was declared amply fit for duty in Asia. The doctor concluded Colby had been "an outstanding officer, as a Jedburgh and on the Norwegian mission." His men, some of whom waited at the club for reassignment, praised his stamina, leadership, and courage. The only note of caution from the interviewer: when asked for his attitude toward the OSS, Colby was "generally admirable, but critical of the incompetents in the higher positions."

. . . .

While Colby relaxed at the country club, Casey and Forgan worked with Donovan in drafting plans for turning the OSS into a postwar central intelligence agency, which the general wanted to continue leading. By that point, however, it looked like Donovan's political enemies in Washington had succeeded in making it a wasted exercise. A copy of his secret proposal setting up a postwar CIA had been leaked in February of 1945—probably by J. Edgar Hoover, although it was never proved—to the rabidly Republican McCormick-Patterson newspaper chain, which published inflammatory stories accusing Donovan of wanting to set up a Gestapo-like organization. That was enough bad publicity for Roosevelt to shelve the idea. Truman had little in common with Donovan and did not particularly like the Wall Street lawyer. When Truman became president, Hoover and the Pentagon ganged up once more, feeding the White House highly derogatory information on the OSS and its director's personal life.

After the atomic bombs were dropped on Hiroshima August 6 and Nagasaki August 9 and Japan announced its surrender six days later, Casey saw no need to go to Asia. He also did not want to remain in the OSS or its successor if there was one—at least for now. He had mingled with the powerful of his country and of other nations. But he was not of their class. What he had achieved he had done by determination and skill, not by birthright. He wanted one day to be a part of America's national security leadership and he intended to do so by following the path Wild Bill Donovan, another Irish Catholic street kid from his state, had taken. He would return to New York to make enough of a fortune so he could join the moneyed elite who moved easily between business and public service, as Donovan did. He put it more plainly to a close friend: He wanted to be rich so he would have "fuck you money" when he returned to Washington.

Suffering from a mild case of jaundice, Casey turned in his resignation papers to leave the OSS on August 31. Donovan was not surprised by his protégé's decision but he was pained to see him leave. He had never hesitated to hand big jobs to young men like Casey if they had intelligence and drive. "You took one of the heaviest loads, which any of us had to carry at a time when the going was roughest," Donovan wrote him, "and you delivered brilliantly." Casey felt like a deserter leaving the old man. He promised always to be on call for Donovan and the OSS if they needed him—and he meant it. Donovan had often interrupted his Wall Street business for brief excursions into the spy world. Casey wanted to do the same.

. . . .

After Japan surrendered, Colby moved out of the Congressional Country Club and found a temporary apartment in Washington. Whatever peacetime intelligence agency remained likely would have no need for the paramilitary skills he had honed in the war, Colby decided. He could remain in the Army as his father had. He had orders to attend the service's Command and General Staff School at Fort Leavenworth, Kansas, and then return to the Artillery Corps at Fort Sill. But Colby felt out of place in a conventional military he thought too conservative and rigid-thinking for his tastes. He decided to return to Columbia Law School in the fall and resume his coursework to become an attorney.

Colby also decided to marry Barbara Heinzen. The two had hardly pined for each other during the war years. Bill had phoned as many as a half dozen girls when he returned to the United States. Barbara happened to be the only one who picked up the line, so he resumed his romance with her. The day the *Empire MacAndrews* docked in New York she had a date with a West Point instructor that evening. She had known Bill since 1940, but it had never been love at first sight, Barbara realized, although she was sure they would be happy with each other. She was swept up by the excitement she and her girlfriends felt with the war being over and young men returning and proposing. Bill as well thought this was what men home from the front and his age did—they got married.

Whatever their reasons, Elbridge was delighted with the union. In a rare display of praise he wrote his son how pleased he was that "at this important moment" Bill was "accepting new responsibilities and going on to new happiness in the difficult world which lies ahead." On September 3 Barbara's mother announced her daughter's engagement to a war hero and twelve days later the couple married in New York's St. Patrick's Cathedral—about a month and a half after Colby had returned to the United States. Before he arrived at the cathedral, Colby stopped at another Catholic church to confess the sins he had committed on leave as a paratrooper in Europe.

They found a cramped apartment for $80 a month near Columbia. The GI Bill paid Colby's tuition and rent but it left them with only $10 a month for food. To cover their other expenses, Barbara continued working as a freelance copywriter, now for an industrial bulletin reporting on bills of interest that the state legislature in Albany passed. Colby, who soon made the law review, told Barbara little about what he had done in the war beyond what she could read in press accounts. But she surmised that it had been dangerous from the decorations he soon received. The Oslo government bestowed on him the Royal Norwegian Order of St. Olav for chivalry in the NORSO operation. On September 28, Colby put on his Army uniform for the last time and took the train to Washington to listen to Donovan's farewell speech and join thirteen other OSS operatives at the ceremony receiving medals from the old man. The Army had awarded him the Silver Star for "gallantry in action" during Operation Rype.

That muggy, hot Friday evening, more than seven hundred OSS spies, commandos, research analysts, and headquarters staffers crowded into the Riverside ice skating rink, which had been converted into office space near the agency's headquarters on Navy Hill. Donovan's bureaucratic enemies in Washington had finally succeeded in convincing Truman to disband the OSS at the end of September and parcel its functions to the Pentagon and State Department. Donovan had bitterly fought the executive order Truman signed eight days earlier and the employees who gathered in the skating rink now had glum looks on their faces. "We have come to the end of an unusual experiment," the general now told the men and women sitting in rows of chairs before him like relatives at a funeral service. "This experiment was to determine whether a group of Americans constituting a cross section of racial origins, of abilities, temperaments and talents could meet and risk an encounter with the long-established and well-trained enemy organizations.

How well that experiment has succeeded is measured by your accomplishments and by the recognition of your achievements." A friend at headquarters mailed Casey a copy of the farewell address.

After his speech, Donovan walked down the line of operatives waiting to receive medals. Colby stood next to an officer who had fought for the agency behind Japanese lines in Thailand. The last time Colby had seen Donovan was for his short interview during Jedburgh training nearly three years earlier. The general's hair had since grown whiter and he looked his sixty-two years. As he pinned the Silver Star on Colby's chest and congratulated him, Donovan stopped for a moment and said, as if musing to himself, "That's a fine decoration. I never earned that." True, but he had won practically every other award, including the nation's highest. "I'm sure it would look very good next to your Medal of Honor, sir," Colby said sheepishly. Donovan smiled and moved down the line.

Thoughts swirled in Colby's mind as the OSS director pinned awards on other agents. It struck him that he was damned lucky to be alive. If the Liberator had been even more off course and dropped him on the German garrison at Montargis, if Roger Bardet had betrayed him, if he had been on one of the planes that crashed off the Scottish coast or in Norway, if a German patrol had caught him after the Nordland Railway attacks. His OSS experience had been more than an adventurous episode, he pondered as he stood in the line. Its impact on him had been tremendous. Rather than serving as a cog in the conventional military machine rolling across Europe, he had been a "remarkably free" unconventional operator in the field, even with London's tight leash. He had entered the Army a shy young student. He now left the OSS a confident man who knew he could face danger and hold his own "in a company of free spirits," he later wrote. He had been impulsive at times as a commando, but ultimately, he thought, his OSS service had taught him that bravery and commitment by themselves were not enough. "If they are not accompanied by wisdom, they can lead to futile, and fatal, wastage," he decided. His OSS experience also convinced him of the importance of personal and political freedom. The fact that he had survived the war defending these liberties gave him hope that if he fought for them in the future he would succeed.

CHAPTER 26

BERLIN

Dulles took his time getting to Germany after the surrender. In addition to a week's vacation to write his Sunrise report with Gaevernitz, he left Clover and his daughter Joan under Mary Bancroft's care and flew to Washington and then to New York to confer with Donovan and his partners at Sullivan & Cromwell. His gout continued to bother him on the trip. The law firm stopped paying his salary as of July 1 so Dulles started drawing a paycheck from the OSS. It amounted to $850 a month. He had part of it sent to Clover in Bern, where she remained with Joan while he worked in Germany. On his return to Europe, the British gave him royal treatment during his London stopover, taking him to Churchill for a private visit and thank-you. Finally on July 6, 1945, he turned over the Bern station and his Herrengasse apartment to Robert Joyce, a Yale-educated foreign service officer who had worked Balkan operations for the OSS. Dulles flew to Wiesbaden the next day wearing a baggy Army uniform with no insignia on it. Donovan asked that he be given a civilian rank equal to a general since he now had a general's-size job. His mission would oversee OSS intelligence not only for Germany but also for Austria, Czechoslovakia, and Switzerland. The Pentagon balked. But it did grant him quarters fit for a general.

Dulles continued to be under surveillance by his rivals. Spies for the Pond, the military espionage unit set up behind Donovan's back, reported to their leader, Major John Grombach, that Dulles planned to use a government plane as many as three times a month to visit his family in Bern. Meanwhile, gossips in the OSS believed Donovan sent Dulles to Wiesbaden to get him out of the way. If so, the plan wasn't going to work. Dulles did not intend to stay long in the mess the Nazis had left behind.

When he arrived in Wiesbaden, the United States had just over three million troops in Europe, 1.6 million of whom were in Germany to join Soviet, British, and French forces occupying zones delineated by the February Yalta conference. The number of German soldiers who had laid down their arms was about eleven million. The violence did not end on V-E Day. Much of war-torn Europe after the May 8 surrender descended into anarchy with institutions demolished, governments exiled, borders dissolved, banks closed, law and order absent. The continent lived as if in the Middle Ages with 1,700 Soviet cities and towns destroyed, one-third of Greece's forests lost, a millennium of Polish architecture wiped out, and just 2 percent of Germany's industrial capacity left standing. Up to 40 million lay dead, 27 million of them Soviets, with vast swaths of once thriving Europe devoid of humans and in Germany the rotting corpses of many of the six million killed still spread freely among the rubble. Europe became a continent of war orphans, more than one million of them in Germany, where homeless children roamed in crime gangs like wild animals. As many as forty million displaced persons went on the move—many, such as slave laborers in Germany, trying to return to their countries, others, such as Germans, bombed out of their homes or forcibly evicted from East European communities. Vengeance swept far and wide. Civil wars and ethnic cleansing broke out, while the victors arrested, beat, enslaved, or murdered the conquered across the continent. Red Army savagery toward German civilians became so intense, Stalin, fearing a backlash, finally issued orders to scale it back.

After three weeks in Paris screening OSS officers for postwar Germany— he had a list of nearly fifty who spoke the language as well as he did—Helms moved to Luxembourg with the advancing Allied armies on April 5, setting up a temporary headquarters there for the mission under the cover name "Economic Analysis Unit." On June 1, he flew to Biebrich, a suburb south of Wiesbaden, where an advance party had established its permanent headquarters in the Henkell Trocken Champagne Factory. In addition to undergarments and spare uniforms, Helms stuffed his duffel bag with survival items he thought he would need, such as medicine, tea bags, and candy.

The unit, however, ended up comfortably quartered, with an ample supply of booze. On the Rhine west of Frankfurt, the spa city of Wiesbaden, which also became Bradley's command post for his 12th Army Group, had largely escaped destruction by Allied bombers—its casino and theater still intact along with hot sulfur baths that had rejuvenated the Reich's wealthy. In the Biebrich suburbs, filled with well-appointed villas and lush gardens, the Henkell factory had been bombed but still boasted a well-stocked cellar and continued producing sparkling wines. Helms requisitioned eight homes (some with servants) and an apartment building near the factory for the staff's billets. With several other officers he shared one of the villas they nicknamed the "Horned Rabbit Club" because mounted animal trophies hung from the walls, on one of which the taxidermist had affixed horns to a rabbit's head. They set up their spy offices, sealed off with locked doors and barbed wire, in the factory's administrative building, which retained the sweet scent of champagne. The OSS agents first swilled the bubbly for free, then eventually set up an officers club they called the "Battle Cloud" and paid the factory 10 cents a glass.

As he had in Switzerland, Dulles organized a full-service spy operation in Wiesbaden bringing in espionage officers to recruit foreign informants and collect intelligence throughout Germany, research analysts like Arthur Schlesinger from London to evaluate what the operatives found, counterintelligence agents to penetrate other services like the Soviets', plus a full contingent of medical, communications, and administrative officers to back up the enterprise. Helms, by now a lieutenant commander, served as the deputy for the espionage section, which was called the Production Division and run by Lieutenant Colonel Ides van der Gracht, a punctilious Austrian American who before joining the OSS had been the chief design architect for the Pentagon and at the London station had run spy operations in the Netherlands. Van der Gracht and Helms quickly set up espionage outposts, called "P Units," not only in Wiesbaden, but also in Berlin, Bremen, Heidelberg, Kassel, Munich, Nuremberg, and in the British and Soviet occupation zones.

Among the Bern hands to arrive, Gaevernitz became a Dulles political confidant as he had been in Switzerland. His hair turned white from his har-rowing escape after the July 20 plot, Gisevius helped hunt for the few fellow conspirators left in Germany who might now aid Dulles's mission. Kolbe, who ended up blacklisted by his country's postwar governments for helping the Allies during the war, had an OSS-supplied car and Berlin apartment by late July to run undercover operations for Dulles against the Soviets and German communists. Mary Bancroft, however, declined Dulles's invitation to join him in Berlin. The Bern station job had left her physically, psycho-logically, and emotionally exhausted. "I never wanted to hear the words 'intelligence work' again," she recalled.

To serve as his intelligence chief after Casey turned down the job and to supervise van der Gracht's and Helms's espionage unit, Dulles brought in a Navy commander named Frank Wisner. A stocky and intense Mississippian who excelled in track at the University of Virginia and enjoyed watching the muscles in his thick arms ripple when he made fists, Wisner grew bored as a Wall Street lawyer and joined the Navy six months before Pearl Harbor. In the OSS he developed an intense hatred of the Nazis and an equal moral outrage over the Soviets whose brutal occupation tactics he witnessed while stationed in Bucharest after the Red Army took over Romania in early fall 1944. A workaholic and hard partier, Wisner had a sense of right and wrong that was crystal clear and an enthusiasm for clandestine operations—particularly now against the Russians he so hated—that bordered on reli-gious fervor. Helms marveled at how Wisner would prop a foot on his desk drawer, spread the first two fingers of both hands and slide them down the sides of his mouth as he sorted out a knotty spy problem in his mind. He didn't know at the time that Wisner likely suffered from manic depression, a mental illness that would end with his suicide in 1965.

Dulles was delighted to have Wisner as his secret intelligence chief. Casey also thought he was the best man for the job. An efficient and de-manding administrator, which Dulles was not, the Navy commander was not shy about disciplining slackers. Wisner, however, had a distant relation-ship with Dulles, who enjoyed the limelight while Wisner shunned it. He grew far closer to Helms, whom he considered a protégé. Despite the fact that the two could not have had more different personalities, they remained close friends for as long as Wisner lived.

During those early months at the champagne factory, Helms proved adept at setting up the mission's complicated spy machinery throughout Germany. With a broad knowledge of the country and its language he demonstrated "an exceptional degree of balance, judgment and ability to inspire the confidence of his associates," according to his officer's fitness report. Much of his time at Biebrich and later Berlin was also spent cleaning up the garbage of Nazi crime and corruption. Helms collected evidence of and hunted for war criminals on the Allies' "automatic arrest" lists. Though he sought to protect Germans who fed him secrets and helped in the Sunrise talks, Dulles cared nothing about the other suspects. He turned over to Nuremberg prosecutors incriminating documents the OSS collected at Wiesbaden on the Nazis—Donovan particularly wanted the ones who tortured and killed his agents hanged—and lent the attorneys Gisevius and Kolbe to build legal cases against the culprits.

Wiesbaden also became one of several American collection points for thousands of paintings and precious art objects the Germans had bought at bargain prices for investment or stolen from museums, Jews, or other private collections of conquered nations. Roosevelt had formed a commission in 1943 to protect Europe's art and a year later Donovan had organized an art looting unit to help FDR's "Monuments Men" and to interview art advisers for captured Nazi chiefs like Göring, the Reich's biggest thief, to track down caches. Helms joined in the hunt—an exercise embarrassing for more than postwar Germans. In countries the Soviets occupied much of the stolen art ended up just changing hands from the old plunderer to the new one. American dealers had bought on the cheap modern works Hitler deemed degenerate. Some sticky-fingered GIs pilfered art objects to sell back home. The U.S. government also toyed briefly with the idea of making art a war trophy and forcing the Germans to pay reparations with the works they stole or legitimately owned.

. . . .

On July 20, Dulles flew to Potsdam on the southern outskirt of Berlin. Truman, Stalin, Churchill, and Clement Attlee (who soon took over after Churchill's defeat in Britain's general election) had begun their conference there three days earlier in the mock Tudor Cecilienhof Palace of Crown Prince

"Little Willi." Stalin was intent on establishing a Soviet sphere of influence in Eastern Europe while making Poland and the chunk of Germany his army controlled a buffer against future invasion across his western border. The dictator insisted the governments in that region remain friendly to the Soviet Union. To a degree, Churchill had sympathized with "Uncle Joe," while Truman, echoing his predecessor's view, insisted on the right of nations ravaged by the war to self-determination. The new president, however, did not intend to press his cause to the point of starting another war with Russia over eastern Germany and Eastern Europe. Dulles, like Donovan, was critical of American concessions made to the Soviets, but he was now in Potsdam with a different subject on his mind—the Japanese. Dulles pulled aside Henry Stimson, Roosevelt's war secretary who had stayed on with Truman, to brief him on the Japanese peace feelers he had received in Bern. Stimson thanked him for the information and sent him away. He did not let Dulles in on the news, which Truman learned on the way to the conference, that scientists in New Mexico had just successfully tested a nuclear device. Dulles was in Berlin when news came of the atomic bombs having been dropped. He wondered if the Japanese negotiators had come to him sooner whether the horrors of Hiroshima and Nagasaki, which he privately abhorred as mistakes, could have been avoided.

The Cold War would come soon after Potsdam. Stalin's paranoia over a resurgent Germany and freely elected governments in Eastern Europe, coupled with his visceral suspicion of American motives, made any possibility of the United States working with him remote. A key pawn in the emerging struggle between East and West became Berlin. Dulles, Helms, and a P Unit espionage team Helms would lead relocated to the former Reich capital in August. Almost as soon as he arrived, Helms realized America's clandestine war with the Russians was on, and he wanted to be part of it as he had against the Nazis. He entered Berlin with a .32 caliber pistol, shoulder holster, and helmet that he took with him whenever he walked the city's streets. In his field jacket pocket he had a permit to drive an Army jeep anywhere along with special SHAEF passes ordering American military police not to interfere with his movements. But his paperwork had little pull with the Russians in Berlin, who were in an excellent position to make his life difficult.

At the time of the Reims surrender on May 7, advancing Allied forces had crossed into 16,400 square miles of German territory the Yalta conference had designated for the Soviets to control after the war. The crafty Red Army commander, Marshal Georgy Zhukov, eventually talked the Americans and British into agreeing to evacuate from that territory on July 4 in exchange for the Soviets allowing the Western forces to begin on July 3 occupying the 185 square miles of Berlin allotted to them. General Lucius Clay, a long-nosed Southerner who was Eisenhower's deputy and a savvy political officer, later regretted making that deal. Stalin and Zhukov stalled the Red Army's evacuation of West Berlin until July 12 to finish stripping its American, British, and French sectors of much of their industries.

When Dulles and Helms arrived, they discovered that the delay also gave the Soviets time to impose communist control over practically every aspect of Berlin life. Clocks had been changed to Russian time and street signs had been put up calling on residents to "salute the glorious Red Army." Waves of German communists exiled in Moscow poured in to take over city administration. Realizing that with an international spotlight shining on it Berlin could not be openly communist at this point, the clever Soviets placed harmless local bureaucrats at the head of municipal agencies with German "Muscovites" installed under each of them as deputies to call the shots. Informants alerted the American mission that Zhukov also moved quickly to neuter Berlin's independent political parties and censor their newspapers. Soon Soviet propaganda in the Russian zone became as omnipresent as it had been under Goebbels, with communist newspapers, radio broadcasts, and strict control over films, the performing arts, and school curriculums.

Helms took jeep rides and long walks to reacquaint himself with the noisy bustling city he had inhabited ten years earlier. He found little remained of what he remembered. Berlin was eerily silent, save for the sound of *Trümmerfrauen* ("rubble women") tapping on bricks to clear debris. Soviet artillery and 75,000 tons of Allied bombs had left only 300,000 of its 1.5 million homes undamaged, the city center reduced to eleven square miles of rock pile. In the stifling August heat he encountered, tens of thousands of decomposing corpses still strewn among the rocks or floating in sewage-polluted canals and lakes bred billions of flies and mosquitoes and created a stench nauseating to breathe. Only twenty of the city's eighty fire stations operated. Electricity was beginning to be restored but with three thousand breaks in mains, drinkable water was a long way off. Rail, bus, and subway transportation was largely absent. U-Bahn tunnels had gaping holes from bombs. Bridges destroyed in the final month of aerial attacks left the city a sprawling cluster of medieval-like villages. The only vehicles moving about were military ones like Helms's, which he had difficulty driving through roads blocked or cramped with debris. The Berliners he encountered, weak and cowed, had tense, furtive, or dazed looks on their faces, still not yet recovered from the shock of the battle for their capital. The city, which before the war had 4.3 million people, now had 2.3 million—mostly starving women and children, homeless old men, pathetic-looking teenagers in tattered Wehrmacht uniforms, and refugees fleeing Russian hordes from the east. American forces entering the city were quickly overwhelmed by the lack of food, medicine, or shelter for civilians now dying at a rate of about a thousand per day.

Helms located the shattered remains of his old apartment on Bayreutherstrasse near Wittenbergplatz. From one of its broken-out windows on the ground floor he could scan through the dust the flat rubble for three blocks in every direction. To his surprise, he found still standing the grand Adlon Hotel, his favorite watering hole with fellow journalists. Several shells had wrecked its roof, the livable space had been converted to a field hospital, and Russian soldiers had carted off brass instruments, Bokhara rugs, and 65,000 bottles of claret from its cellars.

In the six boroughs that made up the U.S. sector in West Berlin, only 5 percent of homes left standing had furniture in them. The Russians emptied the rest. American officers took over the furnished residences in the upper-class Dahlem neighborhood of the Zehlendorf district, which had been untouched by Allied bombs, giving their owners two choices—vacate in twenty-four hours or move into the servants' quarters and wait on the new occupants. Dulles was assigned one such villa, a small one on ImDol Street in Dahlem. Helms and the espionage team, which would soon number more than thirty, took over a three-story brick office building with several more levels below ground at No. 19 on the quiet, tree-lined Föhrenweg Strasse. It had once served as headquarters of General Beck, one of the July 20 plotters, when he led the German General Staff.

The immediate problem Helms faced when his team moved into the Föhrenweg building: nowhere to buy what he needed to set up shop. Helms drew up long lists of personal supplies that would have to be flown in for his staff: cigarettes, candy bars, coffee, sugar, cases of C rations, toothpaste and brushes, toilet paper, and liquor. Particularly liquor; "send soonest," he cabled. The station also became desperate for automobile tires, Scotch tape, and secretaries and stenographers for the clerical work. Off-the-shelf items for spying had to be imported: six bicycles so his German agents could ride around town, one hundred milligrams of penicillin to save the life of one of his valuable contacts, plus barter items such as cameras, wristwatches, and women's stockings for bribing local officials. Then there were safe houses—a vital espionage commodity. Bombed-out Berlin had few homes or apartments available.

In daily meetings at Föhrenweg and breakfasts every morning at the Dahlem villa, Helms got to know Dulles. The first impression he formed of the man at the Reims surrender—a tweedy, virile Mr. Chips type with that carefully trimmed mustache, rimless oval glasses, ever present pipe, and jovial manner—was reinforced now in Berlin. Helms also quickly discovered that Dulles was hyperactive—pulling a chess set out of his briefcase to occupy himself if he had to wait a few minutes for an appointment—and a busybody—"into everything, intelligence and otherwise," Helms recalled— and a demanding taskmaster. He peppered his morning meals with "take-care-of-this" orders for the lieutenant commander—often to look out for his Crown Jewels. Much later Helms would realize Donovan was correct in his verdict that administration was not Dulles's strong suit. For his part, Dulles thought Helms was an American version of Gaevernitz: tall, handsome, sophisticated, worldly, and terribly efficient in anything he did.

As he had in Bern, Dulles operated the Föhrenweg base under light cover, reasoning that he would never be able to keep it secret from the Russians. He permitted his officers to mingle freely with local professional people, artists, and businessmen to develop contacts. Among the early jobs he assigned Wisner, Helms, and the Berlin operatives: helping retrieve Casey's missing agents, such as the Hammer team's Lindner and Ruh, who had been taken by the Russians, and hunting for survivors of the July 20 plot and their families. They found the widow and two sons of Count von Moltke safe and in good health at their Kreisau estate. Dulles wanted to be a key player in shaping postwar Germany. Helms and others in the mission helped him track down more "good Germans" for his expanding Crown Jewels list, both to provide intelligence to the Americans and to form the nucleus for future German governments. The Crown Jewels initiative, however, produced mixed results. The quality of its intelligence proved to be uneven and Dulles never became the postwar kingmaker he wanted to be, Helms thought. The American military command was the early power broker but eventually "the Germans were running their own affairs pretty much," Helms later said.

Helms spent as much time looking for bad Germans as the good ones. The OSS conducted a secret study of Nazi occupation tactics in France for lessons in how to control Germany's population after the Allies moved in. Dulles had agents scour the country for signs its intelligence organizations would try to revive. Army counterespionage agents launched operations with code names like "Choo Choo," "Nursery," and "Grab Bag" to hunt for German subversives riding trains, hiding in villages, or stowed aboard ships. The agents found few of them. Save for scattered instances of vandalism, graffiti on walls, GI muggings, and angry Hitler Youth fanatics, Germans after the surrender were docile—"disgustingly servile" to any American uniform, as one OSS report contemptuously put it. Instead of a hostile secret service, Dulles's counterintelligence agents found Abwehr and SD officers eager to ingratiate themselves and turn their networks over to the Americans "to embroil us with the Russians," according to another top secret OSS report.

Even so, Dulles's mission joined the mammoth effort to eradicate from German government and business twelve million Nazi Party members. Within a year the Americans and British had interned 136,500 Nazis. The Russians had investigated a half million cases in their zone. The Russian, American, and British occupiers eventually lost interest in denazification. Minor functionaries or Germans only loosely connected to the party were easily rounded up while bigger fish had the money to vanish. The backlog of cases quickly overwhelmed Allied courts trying to separate innocents from the ones deserving punishment. The Americans, according to one Army history, also soon realized that if they swept all Nazis out of the government they would have only old men to run chaotic Germany "until the next generation grew up." As with other American agencies in the zone, Dulles's mission had to fire several German civilians hired for menial work after his officers discovered their Nazi pasts. "You can't run the railroads without taking in some Nazi Party members," Dulles later complained. Helms agreed.

At first, General Clay, who headed the entire American mission in Berlin, held out hope he could work with the Russians, so he kept a tight leash on Dulles's spying for fear it might spoil relations with them. Though Donovan had no illusions that the Soviet Union would not be a postwar rival and he wanted to spy on it as he would any foreign country, the OSS director also thought at first that Washington might be able to work with Moscow. So did Dulles. Berlin was a fluid city in the early months of occupation with each army able to move about the other's sector while OSS officers sipped drinks in bars and mingled with foreign intelligence officers, including the Soviet Union's. (Zhukov did order that his Russians always have a superior officer at these mixers and do more listening than talking.) The freedom gave Dulles a chance to crawl over rocks and wander down into the abandoned Führerbunker in the Soviet sector; he scooped up documents and medicines to take back to his research analysts. Helms sneaked into what was left of the nearby Reich Chancellery and in the debris strewn on the banquet hall's floor snatched four plates from Hitler's dinnerware. He earlier retrieved a handful of the führer's personal stationery and penned his son, Dennis, a touching note on the tan paper with its swastika and eagle embossed on a corner: "The man who might have written on this card once controlled Europe—three short years ago when you were born. Today he is dead, his memory despised, his country in ruins."

It did not take long for Clay, Dulles, and everyone else in America's Berlin outpost to sour on the Russians. The Soviets began to quibble more about American air flights over their zone to supply Berlin's U.S. sector, to hassle Army Graves Registration teams from entering eastern Germany to find U.S. war dead, and to erect barriers in the capital to keep the other three powers out of the Russian sector. Signs soon sprouted everywhere marking boundaries in four languages. Meanwhile, Soviet agents continued sneaking into West Berlin to kidnap German dissidents they considered a threat. To protect vulnerable citizens, British guards beat up the Russian thugs they found and dumped them back into the eastern sector, while American

MPs often shot them. Soviet propaganda also began targeting the Americans. TASS published an article alleging that U.S. officials had no interest in ridding their zone of Nazis. German communists published a virulently anti-FDR book, one chapter titled "Roosevelt—Dictator of Democracy." Russian writers eventually took aim at Dulles, alleging he toadied to German and American financiers during his World War II service in Bern. Dulles found the personal attacks amusing for the most part, but Allied leaders soon worried that anti-American screeds spewing from outlets such as the Soviet-operated Radio Berlin were beginning to sway Germans.

Though Washington did not formally designate them the prime target, spying on the Russians quickly became the priority for Dulles's mission and the U.S. military's security officers in Germany. Army agents packed up hundreds of pages of captured Nazi documents on the Soviets' war industry and flew them to the Pentagon for analysis. In his safe at Wiesbaden, Wisner had a secret list of more than fifty "Intelligence Objectives" for his agents in the Russian zone—from compiling detailed dossiers on senior Soviet officials in eastern Germany to calculating the strength of each Red Army unit in the country to measuring the quality of the boots and uniforms its soldiers wore. When Dulles and Helms arrived in Berlin, a cable from OSS headquarters awaited them with instructions to begin vacuuming information on the names and ranks of Soviet officers in their East German mission, the chain of command they followed to Moscow, and the location of supply depots, planes, and airfields in their sector that they were keeping secret from the Americans. Helms and the other officers began recruiting informants from labor agitators and Georgian and Lithuanian separatists they found in East Germany. Dulles launched Project Caviar to penetrate the Russian intelligence service in Vienna. Caviar cost about 10,000 Austrian schillings a month to pay eight Soviet turncoats and twenty-three Austrian informants.

Accoutrements for spying on the Russians had to be developed from scratch. Dulles's counterespionage agents fortunately discovered among captured SS stores two truckloads of printing equipment, phony Soviet identity documents, rubber stamps with the signatures of senior Red Army officers, and phone books for Russian towns, all of which they put to good use in creating covers for American spies. A Soviet indoctrination manual the Nazis had for their operatives was translated and employed for training the mission's agents. Clothing for operatives plus suitcases and briefcases with secret compartments for them to carry stolen documents were flown to Helms. A cover unit in the German mission also quickly began printing its own identity passes that agents could flip out to get past security checkpoints in the Soviet zone—with mixed results. Russian guards soon became more expert at spotting fabricated papers.

Helms was open-minded yet pragmatic with his early postwar spying. Informants in ravaged Berlin could be bought for pocket change. Helms would push a little money to one of his officers and say, "Go play with it." He had no fantasies the petty cash would turn up startling secrets. When asked if he thought a dangle would succeed he usually said, "I don't know, but let's see if it works." Like Dulles, he looked for snitches anywhere they could be found, casting his net out to German opposition party members who survived Nazi purges. Wisner tried to do favors for Germany's papal nuncio in exchange for tidbits. Helms and other officers tried to arrange for an unofficial Catholic envoy code-named "Beechnut" to pass them information he picked up in the Russian sector. The operation never succeeded, but they tried.

Under increasing pressure to deliver intelligence on the Russian zone, Helms launched a manhunt for Soviet defectors to be spies. He discovered a rich pool of recruits—as many as one thousand Red Army deserters hiding in Berlin wearing civilian clothes, along with thousands more Soviets the Nazis had held as POWs or forced laborers, whom the NKVD now distrusted. Clay, who had promised Soviet commanders he would turn over to them any deserters and criminals his soldiers found, at first tried to frustrate the effort but eventually relented. "We looked for someone who would be useful," recalled Rolfe Kingsley, who worked with Helms, "not just common Soviet soldiers who didn't know anything."

In Wiesbaden Schlesinger was queasy about the mission hiring former Nazi intelligence officers to spy on the Soviets. Dulles, Helms, and Army counterespionage officers were not. They launched a widespread effort to recruit their former enemy against the new one. A German counterespionage officer the Russians released, code-named "Zigzag," had the names of more than a dozen Abwehr colleagues who would be useful. A woman identified in classified documents as Barbara Güttler, a former Abwehr naval intelligence analyst, fed Helms's unit secrets from a job she landed as a newspaper reporter in the Russian zone. Dulles found an SS aide who helped Wolff in the Sunrise talks willing to cooperate. Army agents separately recruited Major General Reinhard Gehlen, a top Abwehr officer who incurred Hitler's wrath because of his pessimistic reports from the Eastern Front and was now eager to reconstitute his old spy network for the Americans. Later after the CIA took over Gehlen's operation, Dulles and Helms became chummy with the sly general, which Helms eventually regretted. Soviet propaganda had a field day painting the Gehlen organization, the genesis for the West German intelligence service, as a warmed-over Nazi agency, which was not far from the truth. Russian agents also had no trouble penetrating the spy ring, whose reports to the Americans were often fabricated.

In its early months, the OSS mission's reports painted a grim picture for Washington of the ruthlessly efficient takeover of East Germany and Eastern Europe by the Soviet army and its intelligence organs. Dulles's men assembled dossiers on scores of compliant Germans the Russians screened for senior government jobs. They reported on the NKVD's moves to control Berlin's police department and Zhukov's reopening of six universities in his zone with admission preference given to communists. Considering that so many of their soldiers had been starved to death or executed in Nazi POW camps, the Russians believed it their right to treat Wehrmacht prisoners as brutally. All the Allied powers hated the Germans for the kind of war they fought. Yet Helms and the other officers in the mission found the scope and cynicism of Moscow's retribution breathtaking. They filed scores of reports on it. Trains carted millions of German soldiers and civilians to slave labor camps in the Soviet Union. The Russians also packed more than 100,000 military and political prisoners into reopened Nazi concentration camps, treating them as harshly as the old guards would. At the old Sachsenhausen-Oranienburg camp in Brandenburg, German men, women, and children, many wearing the same striped clothes the Nazis issued, were dying at a rate of 150 a day from "starvation and disease," Dulles's mission reported. Meanwhile, German intelligence officers were recruited, or sometimes forcibly drafted, to train the Soviets in Gestapo techniques useful for Eastern Europe.

Both the East and the West laid claim to Germany's economic and scientific resources. Helms and the mission's other officers watched closely as the Soviets replaced German track with the broad Russian gauge so their trains dragging long lines of freight cars could transport dismantled industries, businesses, and food stocks to the USSR. What could not be hauled away fed the Soviet military in place, with factories in Magdeburg turning out tank parts for the Red Army, the OSS reported, and Russian admirals ordering heavy fittings there for submarine engines. Dulles's mission found French officers pillaging their zone as eagerly as the Russians did in the east, throwing local officials in jail if they did not deliver food, fuel, and plant equipment on time for France's battered economy. Great Britain shipped out factory equipment for client states like Greece. Meanwhile, the Americans moved quickly to strip their portion of the Reich of its technology, flying nearly 1,500 tons of research documents to Washington. Helms and the other mission officers joined in Operation Paperclip, the broad Pentagon and State Department initiative to spirit away some one thousand German scientists and technicians involved in rocket, aviation, space medicine, and weapons of mass destruction programs. Paperclip ignored the long Nazi pedigrees many of the scientists had as well as the thousands of innocents worked to death as slave laborers in their plants or murdered as guinea pigs in gruesome experiments.

. . . .

Dulles, Wisner, and Helms were under top secret orders to spy on their friends as well. The three men drew up programs to watch the British and French as the British and French helped the OSS watch the Russians. Informants in Great Britain's zone, for example, kept the Americans posted on British programs to restart mines and orders giving German police authority to shoot looters. Van der Gracht organized for Wisner a unit code-named "Triangle," to set up a network of agents in the French zone. For Project Marietta, Dulles's men planted a Czech secretary in the French intelligence service's Austria office to keep Washington "informed of all their activities," according to one secret memo. Among the information the snitches passed along: German government graft was on the upswing in France's zone, French officers there were hoarding raw materials the Americans and

British urgently needed for their zones, and French intelligence agents had former Abwehr officers on their payroll just as the Americans did.

· · · ·

When they arrived in Berlin, Dulles and Helms found a Russian intelligence operation laps ahead of them. The NKVD and NKGB, run by the ruthlessly efficient Colonel General Ivan Alexandrovich Serov out of a former Nazi training center and a hospital in East Berlin's Karlshorst neighborhood, ruled the eastern zone with the same terror and intimidation tactics Russian citizens faced at home. In addition to loyalists planted in the American sector's municipal agencies, the NKVD recruited block informants throughout the western part of the city to report to them. For the next three months Clay found it impossible to replace all the communist bureaucrats while Dulles's men hoped to identify as many neighborhood snitches as they could and convince them to switch sides. From one of the informants they turned, Dulles's officers learned that by September the priority for Soviet spy services had changed from hunting Nazis to targeting the Americans and British. Soviet espionage and counterespionage agencies already knew more about the OSS than Donovan's operatives knew about them and now they began to dig deeper. Dulles's mission reported an uptick in Russian agents approaching American GIs and their commanders during September. Soon a favorite NKVD scam: recruit a former Abwehr officer to cross into the American sector and convince Dulles's mission he had been forced to work for the Russians but now wanted to spy for the Americans. The Soviets could play rough when they wanted to, sometimes kidnapping and beating up the American informants they identified. Early on, Helms's Berlin bureau drafted anyone available in the office, including secretaries posing as streetwalkers, for duty trailing agents to make sure they weren't being followed.

By mid-October, Dulles's mission had sixty-four counterespionage operatives in Berlin and a half dozen other German cities battling Russian penetration. The work was time-consuming and tedious, made more difficult by the fact that the Soviet services, far more compartmentalized and disciplined than the Nazis', were tough to crack and few of Dulles's men spoke Russian. His counterintelligence officers planted informants in Berlin nightclubs with orders to keep their ears open, while some of the agents the NKVD sent to West Berlin genuinely did not want to work for their employer and immediately switched sides.

Spy-versus-spy games became elaborate. Heinz Krull, a former Reich security officer, was a bird-dog for Helms's Berlin bureau, on the hunt for Abwehr and Gestapo officers useful for penetrating the Soviets. One day, Krull ran into an old friend named Hans Kemritz, a bird-dog for the NKVD with a different way of snaring his quarry. A lawyer, Kemritz invited old intelligence cronies to his East Berlin office, where after a friendly chat NKVD officers would tail the subjects and arrest them as they were about to leave the Soviet sector. Krull had been on Kemritz's list for an approach. But the two met in West Berlin instead of East and Krull brought along one of Helms's counterespionage officers who talked Kemritz into defecting and feeding the Americans information on the targets that interested his NKVD handlers. To keep the Soviets happy and trustful, one secret memo explained, Helms's bureau gave Kemritz an "occasional small fry" from the Abwehr or Gestapo that he "played into Russian hands."

By the end of September, Dulles's entire German mission had more than 280 intelligence officers, counterespionage agents, research analysts, file clerks, and secretaries. The mission's informants in the field had delivered to them more than a thousand reports during the month, their quality improving and focus on the Russians increasing as time went on. For Helms and others in the Berlin bureau, the job was exhausting with long hours stretching late into each night. Their base worked hard and played hard. Liquor flowed at parties into the early morning and drunken operatives raced their jeeps through empty Berlin streets. Many of the men took German girlfriends or, if they were married, mistresses. Somewhat prudish, Helms didn't approve of officers who cheated on their wives. But the others were in good company. Despite early attempts by commanders to curb GI fraternization, about fourteen thousand American soldiers brought home German brides and far more enjoyed routine one-night stands with desperate German women willing to sell their bodies for as little as a chocolate bar. The occupation Army's venereal disease rate soared.

. . . .

The military transport plane carrying Peter Sichel and his German shepherd, Rex, landed at Tempelhof Airport in south-central Berlin mid-morning on October 1. Sichel helped his dog down the plane ladder and retrieved his luggage. He spotted Helms on the tarmac, standing beside a Buick with an Army driver. After loading his bags in the trunk and Rex jumping into the front seat with the driver, Sichel climbed into the backseat with Helms for the ride to the city center, then west to the Zehlendorf district where the Berlin base was located. The sight of *Trümmerfrauen* clearing rubble along the way—many of them wearing high-heeled shoes with a scarf over their head—struck Sichel as odd. Probably all they had to wear, he thought.

Helms spoke to him in French so the driver would not understand what he was saying. Sichel was fluent in the language, and like Helms, in German as well. The son of a well-off German wine merchant family that had fled Nazi terror, Sichel had been drafted into the Army medical corps after Pearl Harbor and soon was spotted by the OSS, which eventually put him to work as finance man for the agency's detachment with the 7th Army invading southern France. After the French campaign, Sichel ran agents into Germany for Henry Hyde, then manned the Heidelberg outpost for the German mission when Helms summoned him to Berlin to put his expertise in money matters to work once more.

"You know, Peter, the private driving us has much more money than you and I," Helms began, "and he probably made it in the last few weeks in Berlin." The Reich capital had become lawless. Looting, petty thefts, and assaults by gangs of displaced persons, homeless children, former POWs, freed slave laborers, and foreign soldiers roaming Berlin had grown to epidemic proportions. Drunken marauding Red Army soldiers had become such a problem that Soviet military police had begun shooting them on the spot. The spike in pilferage, robberies, and murders among American GIs alarmed General Clay. A popular line started spreading among city residents: "An American is just a Russian with his trousers pressed." Helms's men suspected Soviets dressed in U.S. Army uniforms carried out some of the street attacks on Germans to sour them on the West.

Black-marketing was out of control. Stands, filled with contraband liquor, medicines, nylons, watches, cameras, gasoline, and even Army cars, stretched from the burned-out Reichstag to the Brandenburg Gate to the

Tiergarten. From the lowliest privates to American officers enjoying the good life black marketers peddled American cigarettes, soap, chewing gum, and coffee at inflated prices to desperate Germans. It was the reason Helms had brought Sichel to Berlin—to lance the scandal infecting his own spy bureau.

It began on September 20 when Army criminal investigators nabbed two OSS officers in the Munich airport—Captain Gustave Mueller, who ran the 3rd Army's OSS detachment in the city, and Major Andrew Haensel, who was a member of Helms's P unit in Berlin—and found 138 watches in their baggage that Mueller had brought from Switzerland. The pair tried to talk their way out of the jam, claiming their watches were for spy operations, but the Army agents were convinced, rightly so, that they planned to sell them on the Berlin black market in violation of military regulations and Swiss export laws. With the local currency worthless, the P outfit, which also came to be known as the Peter Unit, used more than two dozen types of barter items—from fountain pens to razor blades to marmalade—to pay German snitches or bribe Russian officials for information. Haensel and its other members were handed bags of largely unaccounted-for cash to buy a lot of these items. But the Peter team did not need this many watches.

Haensel, a naturalized American citizen since 1930 who had been born in Germany to Russian parents and was valued by Dulles's mission because of his fluency in Russian, was transferring back to the United States. But before he left he had managed to slip away for a few days to Munich to meet Mueller, an old friend and another naturalized U.S. citizen whose parents were Swiss, to receive the watches. Mueller often visited relatives in Switzerland with wads of OSS cash mixed in with large amounts of his personal funds. Haensel had no business being in Munich with Mueller, who was not a member of the Berlin team, but Louis Dups, a decorated Army major who was Haensel's boss in the Peter Unit, turned out to be a sloppy manager and had okayed the trip. When he got word of the arrest, Wisner knew immediately the two men had no spy duties that would put them together and that he had not approved bringing in 138 watches. Neither had his intelligence production chief, Ides van der Gracht. Helms, van der Gracht's deputy, had been duped as well. Buried among the mounds of paperwork crossing Helms's desk had been unusual cash requests from Dups for the Peter Unit, such as 12,000 rubles for bribing Russians. Helms demanded more reports from Dups accounting for his money but never sensed there was any financial chicanery going on in the unit.

Proving guilt in court would be difficult because of the case's complexity. The investigators found it almost impossible to sort OSS funds from personal cash the two officers used. But it was pretty clear that Mueller was smuggling the watches out of Switzerland, then selling them to Haensel at an inflated price, and that Haensel planned to sell the ones Dups did not need for legitimate espionage operations to other customers with another price markup. And Dups, who steadfastly defended Haensel in the face of strong evidence he was engaged in something shady, had just as clearly overstepped his authority in approving financial transactions for the Peter Unit's barter items. He had also trusted Haensel too much.

Dulles at first considered the two officers' black-marketing a "minor" irregularity. Compared to Berlin's vast illegal trade, 138 watches certainly was. He cabled Washington on October 12, downplaying the problem: "Certain men with fine combat and pre-V day records have tended to go to seed morally and otherwise." He soon discovered the Haensel-Mueller case was the tip of the iceberg. Many of the Peter Unit officers, roaming Berlin freely with barter items and cash, were earning nest eggs on the side from the tools of their trade. Dulles succeeded in fending off demands from angry superiors in the military that the Army audit his mission and kept the investigation of the Haensel-Mueller affair in-house. Dups received a reprimand. An OSS board recommended that Haensel and Mueller be court-martialed. The two were later allowed to quietly resign from the service. Although it never came, Dulles also bore some blame for lax administration over his mission—a flaw dogging him from Bern. So did the normally meticulous Helms, who let himself be fooled by Dups's assurances that the unit's financial transactions were legitimate.

Dulles and Helms wanted to move fast to weed out the corrupt officers— which was now Sichel's assignment, Helms explained to him during their car ride to the Zehlendorf headquarters. The twenty-three-year-old Army captain almost immediately realized he faced a big job. After a lunch Helms arranged to introduce him to the Peter Unit's members, Sichel sat down with another Army captain who he had been told would be his deputy. The officer looked admiringly at the watch Sichel wore on his wrist. It could easily fetch a thousand dollars if his new boss wanted to sell it on the Berlin black market, the captain told him. Sichel quickly went to work cleaning house.

. . . .

The black market fiasco's timing could not have been worse for the German mission's managers. The Cold War was heating up and the OSS was shutting down. Helms felt blindsided by Truman's order closing Donovan's agency at the end of September and, in effect, cashiering the general. Donovan cabled Dulles and his other station chiefs around the world that as of October 1, the War Department would oversee their spying under a new organization called the Strategic Services Unit. It would be headed by Brigadier General John Magruder, a thin and nervous man with trembling hands who had been Donovan's meticulous deputy. Helms feared "take-over artists in the War Department" would soon target Magruder and liquidate the SSU. The brigadier general, however, was intent on preserving as much as he could of the old agency for the new Cold War. He asked Dulles, Wisner, and Helms to stay on in Germany and continue spying on the Russians. But budget cuts would force them to carry on their clandestine battle with less than a quarter of the intelligence officers and analysts they had under the OSS—barely enough to keep the Soviets their priority target.

Dulles consolidated operations, closed P Units in several German cities like Bremen and Pilsen, and laid off unproductive agents in spy programs such as Triangle's for the French zone. Remarkably, the number and quality of reports sent to Washington dipped only slightly at least for the month of October. But budget cuts and the transfer to the Pentagon soon played havoc on the German mission. Dulles found it nearly impossible to plan future operations. His outfit went on hold. Magruder could not guarantee permanent jobs for the sixty operatives and support personnel who remained in the country. He could only assure Dulles in a cable that if those men and women stuck it out for three more months he would give them "preferential consideration for employment" in a permanent spy agency he hoped the Truman administration would organize. Hardly job security. Helms and the others wondered if they had any future in intelligence. Dulles worried he would have trouble retaining the sixty through December. With this new

Strategic Services Unit viewed as on life support many would simply go home with the war over or drift away to other government agencies. Like vultures, Army intelligence outfits in Germany began approaching Dulles's officers and secretaries with job offers at two to three times the salaries he could pay them.

Productivity soon plummeted. The NKVD and NKGB remained aggressive, but an SSU inspection team sent to Germany the first week of November reported back to Washington that "practically no operations of a [counterespionage] nature were being conducted in Germany." Dulles's mission was "clearly the worst victim of the post-hostilities 'get home' psychology," the team concluded.

The most important talent drain was Dulles himself. He left Germany on October 10, telling Magruder he would resign from the spy service the first week of December. As was his style, Dulles made it a long trip back to the United States, stopping in Naples, Algiers, and Casablanca to visit friends before settling up his accounts in Washington with the government. Perhaps a permanent central intelligence agency would be established one day, Dulles thought, but he did not see it in the immediate future. He wanted to return to his law firm, maybe write a book on his nearly four years of spying. He returned to Bern to spend Christmas there with Clover, the children, and his sister Eleanor. Dulles cared to remember little about his time in Germany. But he missed Switzerland. His wartime service there would likely be the best years of his life, he decided.

Dulles left bitter feelings among Helms and the other managers in Germany. They did not appreciate the further disruption of him bailing out so quickly after the OSS closed. Helms took command of the Berlin spy base, finally stepping out of the shadows of others in the agency. But the base was disorganized and aimless after Dulles's departure. He reorganized the trimmed-down detachment so its intelligence and counterintelligence functions began producing once more. By now Helms knew his way around Berlin better than any officer under him. The paper flow to and from his desk moved quickly. Cerebral and focused intently on the spy mission, he gave precise instructions, expected his subordinates to carry them out precisely, and when they did not he could be quick-tempered. But he was also attentive to the dispirited officers who remained in the Föhrenweg Strasse headquarters, hosting them at a Thanksgiving dinner in his apartment. Morale improved dramatically. His superiors in the Strategic Services Unit were struck by his calm decisive manner in what had become a front line in the new Cold War. The lieutenant commander, they could see, commanded respect in a quiet way.

The overworked base also managed to turn up an interesting historical find on his watch. Frederick Stalder, one of Helms's energetic staffers who had been born in Switzerland and was fluent in three languages, located Erna Flegel, a nurse on duty in Hitler's bunker. In a long interview he recorded her observations of the führer's final days. Until the end Hitler ate a special diet of fresh vegetables from Holland, always taking his meals alone, Erna told Stalder. He doted on Goebbels's children and let them bathe in the bunker's only tub reserved for him. The dictator required no medical care but with his hair graying he looked to her like a man twenty years older than his age. "He shook a good deal, walking was difficult for him, his right side was still very much weakened as a result of the attempt on his life," yet he could still fill a room "entirely with his personality" and "up to the end, it was impossible to turn away from his eyes." When she and the others learned that the führer planned to marry Eva Braun, they knew the end was near. Hitler would never have married his mistress—"a completely color-less personality," she said—if he thought the Third Reich would continue. At 12:30 a.m. on April 30, Erna and some thirty others in the bunker, who she said were now "like a big family," were ushered into Hitler's quarters. He shook each person's hand, an aide whispering into his ear the names of the secretaries and cleaning women he did not know. After the suicide, an SS captain fetched gasoline from the shelter's garage and Hitler's body was burned in the garden outside. "We were told that now we were released from our oath," Erna recalled, "and everyone was permitted to choose his own fate." She remained in the bunker until the Russians arrived.

Helms finally left Germany on December 11. He was anxious to return to his family. He had also become bored with the Berlin job. A cold, cruel winter was descending on the city, which had little fuel to heat homes left standing or food to spread on Christmas tables. One hundred and sixty-seven Berliners would give up that season and commit suicide.

Helms took the eighteen-hour plane ride back to the United States with

Wisner, who was transferring to Washington. Once home Helms received a military form letter thanking him for serving "in the greatest Navy in the world"—ironic because he had never set foot aboard a ship and did not intend to do so now. He mustered out of uniform in January 1946. He also had no interest in returning to the *Indianapolis Times*, whose executives were eager to have him back. He wanted, instead, to continue being a spy.

CHAPTER 27

THE DIRECTORS

Allen Dulles found his Sullivan & Cromwell work lucrative but maddeningly dull. His interests remained with the war he had just fought and the new one with the Soviets. He kept up with old spy pals like Frank Wisner, reminiscing with them over long lunches, and attended postwar reunion parties with Donovan, OSS veterans, and French resistance operatives. The July 20 plot against Hitler never strayed far from Dulles's mind. He celebrated its anniversaries with the conspirators who had survived like Gisevius and continued to do favors for the families of the ones who died. Gaevernitz helped him begin researching his book on Breakers and Valkyrie. Dulles had a wealth of information but he proved to be a boring writer and his manuscript needed considerable editing.

Though he remained always cordial with Donovan, the two men kept a somewhat distant relationship after the war. Dulles did join Donovan in lobbying Congress on legislative language granting Truman the authority to establish the Central Intelligence Agency in 1947. The new CIA, in most respects, mirrored Donovan's vision for a postwar spy organization. It also employed many men and women who had been in the OSS.

Dulles's family went its separate ways. Now independently well off with an inheritance from her parents, Clover grew closer to Jungian teachings as she pulled further away from her husband. Dulles became even more distant from Allen Macy until the young man suffered a debilitating head wound in the Korean War, from which he never recovered. Allen Macy's traumatic brain injury pained his father, who finally displayed some compassion toward his son. Dulles eventually promised his daughter Joan he would be a more attentive father and grandfather. She was skeptical.

Mary Bancroft divorced Jean Rufenacht in 1947. She continued a lively correspondence with Dulles, sending him books she authored, advice on his writing, condolence letters when there were deaths in the family, and compliments when she saw him on television. Their affair had ended. Dulles always referred to Mary as "a very old friend," which she now was, not only to him but also to Clover. Wally Castelbarco arrived in New York in 1947 to restart their affair. It flickered only briefly. Hoover's agents, who suspected Dulles was a Donovan shill leaking derogatory information on the FBI to the press, continued to collect information on his other women and the strains in his family life.

. . . .

With the same brash energy he displayed infiltrating agents into Germany, Bill Casey set about to make his fortune, eventually earning millions writing tax shelter guides and investing in media, real estate, and finance as a venture capitalist. He bought Mayknoll, a Victorian bayside mansion in the Long Island village of Roslyn Harbor, and learned to play golf, a staple for business networking. He became president of Veterans of OSS, which looked out for his comrades' interests after the war, and dined occasionally with Donovan. He also sent him Research Institute of America reports on U.S. security and traded long letters with him on world affairs. Like Donovan in his younger years, Casey craved recognition from America's foreign policy cognoscenti as he amassed his fortune. He initially faced rejection. The prestigious Council on Foreign Relations turned him down the first time he tried to join it in 1967.

Politics—the hard-line anticommunist version—became important to him. Sichel thought his old friend too paranoid about the Soviets, but Casey found OSS allies like Donovan. He joined the general in organizing American Friends of Russian Freedom to help East Europeans flee the Communist Bloc. Among the business ventures Casey backed: a new conservative publishing house run by Henry Regnery, who he was delighted to see breaking the monopoly he thought liberal New York elitists had on the book industry.

. . . .

Richard Helms occupied a nearly bare office in Room 1249 of the Q Building on Navy Hill, not far from where he had worked during his OSS days at headquarters. The Strategic Services Unit had taken over the Kremlin as well as a patchwork of ramshackle buildings drafty cold in winter and stifling hot in summer alongside the Reflecting Pool fronting the Lincoln Memorial. The agency's senior officials were delighted they had been able to talk the capable former naval officer into taking a leap of faith and sticking with an organization they feared Truman might shut down at any moment. At an annual salary of $7,070, soon to be raised to $8,179.50, thirty-three-year-old Helms was the SSU's youngest division chief, overseeing some 260 field operatives and headquarters aides targeting the Soviets in the vast region of Central Europe and Scandinavia. He occasionally dropped by the Sullivan & Cromwell office to bring his old boss news on the agency's Cold War. Sometimes he wrote Dulles to verify whether Germans who claimed they worked for Dulles during the war actually did. Dulles, in turn, passed along the names of old OSS hands he thought might be useful for the SSU.

Julia located a house for them in the Chevy Chase, Maryland, suburb north of the District. Both thrived in the close-knit, almost incestuous, spy world they now entered, where men and women worked in secret and socialized mostly with one another because outsiders did not have the security clearances to mingle among them. The mandarins of this service fascinated the couple. Men like Bronson Tweedy, a Princetonian who returned to spying after a brief stint in boring Madison Avenue advertising and car-pooled with Helms to work; Desmond Fitzgerald, an Asia expert and Helms tennis partner; and James Jesus Angleton, an oddball Rome operative for Donovan who Helms thought was a brilliant mole hunter for the agency now. The Helms home became a favorite for elegant black-tie parties. Angleton devised a complicated game of charades to test their brains, clouded after rounds of cocktails, with T. S. Eliot lines nearly impossible to act out like: "Garlic and sapphires in the mud, Clot the bedded axel-tree."

. . . .

Nine months after her wedding, Barbara Colby gave birth to a boy they named John. He would be the first of five children in the family. Carl, born in 1951, was given the middle name Bruce, after the code name for his father's operation in France. Colby was a caring but somewhat remote father physically because he was away a lot on secret business.

Occasionally, he flew to Louisiana to reminisce with Camille Lelong, who settled there after the war. On several European vacations, Colby also took the family to Montargis, finding the place where Team Bruce parachuted to and retracing his steps to the ditch where they hid from the Germans the next day.

After Columbia Law School, he joined Donovan's firm in New York. Briefly he wore his Silver Star lapel pin on his suit coat until someone in a bar made the snide remark: "I see you have the officer's good conduct medal." He never wore it again. As with other young attorneys Donovan hired after the war, he put Colby to work helping with corporate clients and serving as a de facto aide-de-camp when he pursued foreign policy or intelligence interests on the side. The general occasionally invited Bill and Barbara to sit with him at Columbia football games. The university was also Donovan's alma mater.

But Colby thought he would be miserable earning his riches as a corporate lawyer. He was also a liberal Democrat (campaigning for Truman's reelection) in a law firm whose principal partner was a conservative Republican. In 1949, Colby moved to Washington to revive his interest in labor law and become an attorney for the National Labor Relations Board. "Don't forget us here in New York," Donovan told him when he cleaned out his desk. Despite their political differences the general admired the former commando and his beautiful wife.

. . . .

Though as a loyal Republican Allen Dulles campaigned in 1948 for New York governor Thomas Dewey, he had grown close to Harry Truman, who had approved his Medal of Merit and even sounded him out if he might be interested in an ambassadorship. Considering it political heresy, Foster talked Allen out of taking any such appointment. But Allen, who kept his itch for international affairs and coauthored a report for Truman critical of the new CIA in its growing pains, accepted an offer in 1950 to run the agency's clandestine operations. Soon he became the CIA's deputy director under General Walter Bedell Smith, Eisenhower's ruthlessly efficient staff chief during World War II. Clashes between the two men were inevitable. Not cut out to be anyone's subordinate, Dulles ran the agency's espionage program as he saw fit. Donovan meddled with ideas for covert operations; Dulles usually mailed back a form letter saying only that he would "keep them in mind." Smith, who expected CIA officers to stand at attention when he entered a room as military subordinates had, came to distrust Dulles's secretive nature and concluded his deputy was "not a bad administrator—he is simply innocent of administration."

Always deliberate in his career calculations, Richard Helms's decision after the war that spying was his calling proved correct. He rose quickly in the young CIA, overseeing all the agency's intelligence collection operations by early 1951. Less than two years later he was promoted once more—to chief of operations, involved in both intelligence collection and worldwide covert actions against hostile nations like Russia.

· · · ·

By fall 1950, each morning Colby began walking not toward the National Labor Relations Board headquarters on Independence Avenue when his car pool dropped him off downtown, but instead to the ramshackle barracks along the Reflecting Pool. Gerald Miller, who had given him command of the Norwegian unit during the war and had joined the CIA afterward, phoned his OSS comrade within weeks after Colby moved to Washington and over lunch sounded him out about returning to clandestine work. Fresh to his labor job, Colby begged off, but within a year he phoned Miller back and accepted. NLRB work was dull and Colby longed to return as a soldier at the vanguard of the new Cold War. In his memoirs, Colby wrote that he and Barbara talked about the job change before he made it. Barbara recalled it differently. She said she learned that her husband had joined the CIA when one of the car poolers told her she noticed Bill walking away from the NLRB building when they dropped him off one morning. She asked him that evening what was going on.

Colby became part of what was considered a glamorous, exotic, and patriotic service peopled by bright, enthusiastic men and women like him, politically liberal for the most part and many from the finest Ivy League campuses. Colby never considered himself part of the "cult" of intelligence—he disparaged insular officers like Helms who worked and partied with the same clique—but visitors to his house soon became other CIA officers instead of neighbors who knew only that he had some kind of job in government.

As he had in World War II, Colby wanted to "march to the sound of the guns," running paramilitary operations in the Korean War. His heart sank when the agency returned him to Scandinavia for two years to organize guerrilla cells that would fight behind the lines if the Soviets invaded Western Europe. Though he kept her in the dark about his true work, Barbara became the perfect diplomatic wife for his cover job as a political attaché in the Stockholm embassy. Colby, who practiced appearing so gray and inconspicuous he couldn't attract a waiter's attention in a restaurant, used family vacations in the countryside as masquerade to deliver radios to CIA partisans. He left the region in 1953 wondering if the stay-behind networks he built ever stood a chance in the unlikely event the Russians attacked.

• • • •

When Eisenhower became president in 1953, he made Beetle Smith an undersecretary of state to keep an eye on his new secretary of state, John Foster Dulles. Allen Dulles considered himself the natural heir to the CIA's directorship, not the beneficiary of nepotism. But the good word Foster put in for his brother with the president-elect helped considerably. Dulles's Senate confirmation as Director of Central Intelligence was cheered by CIA officers and he was hailed by *The New York Times* as the "right man for the job." Smith opposed Dulles replacing him, believing Allen's enthusiasm for covert operations would make trouble for Eisenhower. Donovan, who had drafted surrogates to lobby Ike to appoint him CIA director, predicted to friends that his Bern station chief would now screw up the agency.

Dulles ran the CIA as he did the OSS station in Bern. He set up his office in the old OSS headquarters on Navy Hill as if it were Herrengasse 23, with multiple access doors and waiting rooms so callers, particularly spies under deep cover, could be kept separate from one another. Yet Dulles, who enjoyed Ian Fleming's James Bond novels, wanted the CIA visible as his Bern station had been. He had his home number and address listed in the phone book and posted a sign at Navy Hill's front gate identifying it as the CIA's headquarters. Every cabbie in town knew it was the spy agency's home so why keep it a secret, he reasoned. Dulles believed, as he had in Switzerland, that intelligence was an important part of American foreign policy and that the network of associations, the breadth of vision, and the daring he had displayed in the war against Nazism would succeed in the new war against communism. He continued to envision spying as a gentleman's pursuit, practiced in the shadows by and among "men of affairs" like him, who were competent to bend ethics or cut legal corners for a higher cause. He organized the agency so deputies were responsible for every major undertaking, leaving him free to dabble in the clandestine operations that interested him and to ignore the ones that bored him. As in Bern, he was obsessed with precision and attention to detail in the CIA, berating officers if they were just minutes late to an appointment. Yet his agents, for the most part, revered him. Dulles's tweedy pipe-smoking cordiality charmed them as it had informants in Bern. He kept his door open to spies just returned from the field, having them brief him on their missions before they briefed their supervisors. Throughout his CIA tenure, he remained "the great case officer," recalls Arthur Lundahl, an aerial photography expert for the agency.

Though he never talked about Donovan when swapping war stories with his agents, Dulles's operating style mirrored the general's in many respects. Like Donovan with the OSS, Dulles showed no interest in managing the CIA's inner workings yet he infuriated midlevel managers by bypassing them to meet an agent or phone a lower-level analyst. Before arriving at overseas stations he memorized the names of officers and their wives, as Donovan had, to make them feel like old friends. He also proved to be as adept as the general in cultivating Congress and the press. Though he deferred to Foster as the senior official who shaped American foreign policy, Dulles, like Donovan, still wanted to be a player with the covert operations he launched. He routinely made world tours of his stations acting like a secretary of state. Dulles, as well as Helms, shared Donovan's interest in the seamier dark arts, such as testing mind-altering drugs on unwitting subjects. Dulles, who had plotted to kill Hitler during the war, also had no qualms about targeting hostile leaders in peacetime. With Eisenhower's encouragement, Dulles gave his men the okay to try to kill Congolese leader Patrice Lumumba and Cuban dictator Fidel Castro.

Six months after taking over the CIA, Dulles made the cover of *Time* magazine, which proclaimed him "a new phenomenon in the U.S." Eisenhower was delighted with his spymaster, carving out for him the first time slot at his weekly National Security Council meetings in the Cabinet Room to give a tour de horizon of world developments. Dulles delivered concise reports larded with anecdotes to hold the president's interest. His priority for intelligence penetration and covert action became the Soviet Union, whose nuclear arsenal was growing to the point that an all-out war with the United States, he feared, would mutually assure the destruction of both nations. Instead, he saw Russia bent on world domination through other political or economic means and he was eager for his CIA warriors to battle the Soviet empire and communism in every corner. "The whole communist movement is too important and too dangerous to be neglected," he wrote an OSS friend. America's youth should be taught its evil beginning in high school, he believed. Casey became one of his enlistees, agreeing to put money into a private fund to help financially strapped agents pay for their kids' college education.

Driving a beat-up Plymouth to work each day, Helms put in brutally long hours for Dulles overseeing operations against the Soviets—with mixed results. Among their successful recruits was Pyotr Semyonovich Popov, a Soviet intelligence officer who for six years slipped the agency Russian military secrets that saved the Pentagon hundreds of millions of dollars in weapons research. From Israeli intelligence, Angleton obtained a copy of Soviet premier Nikita Khrushchev's 1956 Communist Party Congress speech denouncing Stalin, which Dulles, as he had with Count Ciano's diaries, leaked to the press. But operations to infiltrate agents across borders into the Communist Bloc failed for the most part and Dulles eventually closed down a program to build a resistance force there. His operatives successfully dug a tunnel into East Berlin to tap Soviet phone cables, only to learn later that the Russians knew about the project all along from a mole in Britain's MI6 and decided the information the agency gleaned from the calls did no serious damage.

A few months after Dulles had become the CIA's director, Helms walked into his office with an outgoing cable to the overseas stations for him to read and sign. Dulles made a few edits to the message and put his name to it, but as Helms rose from his seat to leave the boss motioned him to stay. It was a busy morning but from his time with Dulles in Berlin, Helms wasn't surprised by the impromptu brainstorming session he wanted to have. "A word about the future," Dulles began, adding with a pause for effect, "the agency's future." The CIA had two missions, he continued: to collect intelligence to prevent another Pearl Harbor surprise and to launch covert operations to secretly affect the course of events overseas. Foreign intelligence collection programs were proceeding nicely, he thought, but under his directorship the CIA would focus on the second mission, which had equally held his interest during the war: covert operations to shape foreign affairs with the American government's hand never seen in the deed. The Eisenhower White House has "an *intense interest* in every aspect of *covert action*," he said emphasizing the two points. Dulles wanted his clandestine department on board— especially Helms, although he didn't tell him directly that he needed to get with the program. Helms had become a skilled intelligence collection officer yet he retained some skepticism of the value of covert action.

It did not take Helms long to see the course Dulles was setting for the CIA. The agency organized coups to oust Prime Minister Mohammad Mossadegh in Iran and President Jacobo Árbenz in Guatemala. The White House had deemed both leaders inimical to American political and business interests. Colby became a star in Dulles's new war with a plum assignment after Scandinavia—running the CIA's largest covert political action program in Rome from 1953 to 1958, which secretly funneled up to $30 million a year to Italian center democratic parties with the aim of preventing the communists from winning national elections. Ensconced in an apartment near the Colosseum, their five years in Rome were among the happiest for Bill and Barbara, whom the Italians called *la bella figura*. Donovan made a point of visiting them for a Sunday lunch. Colby knew full well the CIA's interference in the political affairs of another nation was highly illegal, but with Moscow pumping $50 million a year into the Italian Communist Party by the CIA's estimate he considered his agency's meddling morally justified.

Helms, who toned down other covert action projects crossing his desk, was suspicious of the value of these "high-risk" power plays—his caution justified later. The friendlier Mohammad Reza Shah Pahlavi the CIA strengthened in Iran was a despot eventually ousted by a Shi'a-led revolution in 1979. Árbenz's removal ushered in decades of brutal military rule over Guatemala. In Italy, the covert money ended up achieving little for Washington or Moscow. The 1958 vote totals for all the parties—including the communists with 22 percent—changed little from the 1953 tally. Helms's early recalcitrance, which others in the agency could plainly see, made him an outsider in the fraternity of covert action enthusiasts surrounding Dulles. Helms had also earned a reputation among colleagues for being indecisive. Over a sandwich lunch in Dulles's office during the fall of 1958, the spy chief informed his Berlin protégé he would not be promoted to deputy director for plans, a bland-sounding title for the top person under Dulles who oversaw all the CIA's clandestine intelligence gathering and covert operations overseas. Instead, Dulles picked Richard Bissell, largely because he had successfully developed the U-2 spy plane program. A brilliant Yale economist, Bissell was also a covert action apostle largely naive to the complexities and hazards of clandestine work. A bitter Helms soldiered on, eventually considering himself vindicated when Dulles much later admitted to him that Bissell had been a bad choice.

The administrative shortcomings Dulles had shown since World War II became apparent to Eisenhower during his second term. Sixty-seven years old by 1960, Dulles had begun to slow down physically—unable to keep track of everything in the vast CIA organization. Bissell pioneered aerial reconnaissance with the high-flying U-2, but Eisenhower and an inattentive Dulles let him launch one too many flights over Russia to photograph its strategic weapons sites. The Soviets shot down the aircraft in May 1960, capturing its pilot, Francis Gary Powers, and forcing an embarrassed Ike to admit he had been spying after his administration publicly denied it at first. Dulles's biggest blunder, however, came nearly eleven months later when some 1,300 Cuban exiles landed on the western shore of Bahía de Cochinos, or as it came to be known in English, the Bay of Pigs. Dulles, who was giving a speech in Puerto Rico when Bissell launched the misadventure, watched in horror as Castro's defense forces swept up the poorly armed invaders at the beach by the second day. At a press conference where he took responsibility for the debacle, President John Kennedy quoted what he thought was an old saying that "victory has a hundred fathers and defeat is an orphan." The line, likely unknown to the new president, came from the Ciano diaries Dulles had captured during World War II.

Colleagues whispered in the hallways that the Bay of Pigs would not have happened if Helms had been deputy director for plans. Perhaps. The White House would still have forced the CIA to do something to topple Fidel Castro, an agency historian later concluded, but it was unlikely Helms would ever have launched a covert operation "anywhere near as large and unwieldy" as the one Bissell concocted. After an appropriate interval, the president fired his CIA director in August 1961. Dulles spent his final months on the job overseeing the building of a permanent headquarters on 140 acres of farmland outside Washington in Langley, Virginia—important work at that point considering Kennedy reportedly told an aide he wanted to break the agency "into a million pieces."

. . . .

Colby thought the Bay of Pigs fiasco looked like a larger version of his aborted plan to dynamite the Grana bridge in Norway. If Dulles had taken the time to scout his target as Colby had his—in the director's case, it would have meant consulting experts—he could have saved his job. Colby made this observation halfway around the world in Vietnam, whose growing communist insurgency Dulles had mostly ignored. The agency sent him there in 1959, reasoning that his fluency in French (the language imposed by the nation's colonizer) and three years in China as a boy prepared him well for the Saigon station. It did not. Colby joined thousands of Americans who went to Vietnam noble in their ideals yet naive to the alien culture they entered. Vietnam, however, would define Colby as much as World War II had. The nation he came to love became his obsession.

He began his intelligence assignment with the right approach, touring the countryside with his family and cultivating contacts in the Saigon government. Quickly concluding that the U.S. government's conventional military strategy for rolling back the communist insurgency was misguided, Colby got his opportunity to implement his ideas for winning in Vietnam when he was promoted to chief of the Saigon station in 1960. For a project code-named "Tiger" he infiltrated South Vietnamese agents into the communist North. Realizing the contest lay at the village level in the countryside, he devised a strategic hamlet program, which herded villagers into thousands of militia-defended enclaves—encircled with barbed wire, bamboo stakes, and moats—to wall out the Viet Cong. Project Tiger failed. Ho Chi Minh's agents in the North had little difficulty killing most of Colby's spies or turning the ones left alive into doubles against the South. So did the strategic hamlet program, which the Saigon government mismanaged and communist insurgents easily penetrated.

Colby seriously underestimated the power of the Viet Cong and the unwillingness of the corrupt regime in Saigon to provide a better future for the villagers. He grew too close to Ngo Dinh Diem, South Vietnam's president, and his brother Ngo Dinh Nhu, who headed the government's thirteen security services, wearing blinders to the fact that Diem was an eccentric colonial-era puppet alienated from his people while Nhu was a scheming opium addict who admired Adolf Hitler. Other CIA officers in his station became far more pessimistic about Vietnam and critical of Diem. Colby grudgingly allowed their cables to be wired to headquarters, but in his monthly reports he always delivered a positive spin. Now considered one of the CIA's most promising officers, he transferred back to Washington in the summer of 1962 to be deputy director of the agency's growing Far East Division. Colby left Vietnam brimming with optimism for its future and proud of what he had accomplished. He was crushed sixteen months later when the Kennedy administration gave the green light for a generals' coup that ended with Diem and Nhu assassinated. Colby's conviction that the pair were the only ones who could save the country from the communists remained unshakable. Diem's overthrow, Colby later insisted, was "the worst mistake of the Vietnam war." He asked Barbara to say a prayer for the brothers at mass.

· · · ·

In 1966, Richard Helms took over the CIA, which now had about twenty thousand employees and a $1 billion budget. His pseudonym in agency cable traffic was Fletcher M. Knight. After the Bay of Pigs disaster, Bissell had been fired and Helms replaced him as deputy director for plans, overseeing Operation Mongoose, the seamy project the Kennedy brothers encouraged, which failed to eliminate Castro by coup or popular uprising. When Lyndon Johnson appointed Admiral William Raborn, a Texas political crony, to be CIA director in 1965, he made Helms his deputy to compensate for the seaman's ignorance of intelligence matters and foreign affairs. Colby expected to replace Helms in the third spot as the clandestine service director. The Far East Division, which Colby now headed, had a quarter of the agency's undercover officers running operations in Vietnam, Laos, Thailand, Indonesia, the Philippines, Singapore, Japan, Korea, mainland China, and Taiwan. Not now, Helms told him. "Your time will come later." Helms and Colby's relationship had grown complicated. They lived near each other, shared the same OSS heritage, and kept their emotions in rigid check. Each man also respected the other and treated the other politely. But they were never personally close. Helms eventually promoted Colby to more senior positions because of his ability, not from friendship. Always, Helms was the intelligence-oriented thinker and planner, Colby the paramilitary-oriented man of action.

Like Dulles, Helms talked little to friends and family about Donovan after the war. But they could see that the old man and the OSS experience had a considerable impact on the way Helms now ran the CIA. He was not a feet-on-the-desk director like Dulles who enjoyed spinning yarns with agents, noted a CIA historian. Senior aides "had to work to get to know" him. He was a demanding taskmaster who left a clean desk when he departed the office each day, usually before 7 p.m., and he expected others to be as efficient. Unlike Dulles, Helms shunned publicity though he cultivated reporters in private, as Donovan had, and became adept at courting congressmen. He easily grew irritated with his security detail, however, bothered that the guards hovering around him made him stand out when a good intelligence officer should be inconspicuous.

Helms assumed the directorship with no vision for recasting the CIA as Dulles had. Johnson once told him to "shake things" up at the agency, but Helms had no idea how that might be done. He thought the organization now ran pretty smoothly as is. His hands-off approach eventually drew grousing from subordinates, who thought the "old boys club" of former OSS officers in the agency did need shaking up. Though he professed to want to keep his distance from old spy pals so he wouldn't be seen as playing favorites when he became the director, Helms did play favorites. He pulled OSS officers' children who had joined the CIA out of meetings to give them a special welcome in his seventh-floor office. He often balked at firing veterans who misbehaved overseas, instead finding out-of-the-way jobs for them in headquarters. He allowed Angleton, a Donovan favorite in the OSS, to run amok as the CIA's top counterintelligence officer, disrupting legitimate intelligence operations because of his fear that they might harbor Soviet moles.

Helms's strength, as it had been in postwar Berlin, resided in management not innovation. Determined to keep the CIA out of the headlines, he ordered his division heads to scrub covert operations overseas for security and shut down the ones in danger of being exposed. Station chiefs free to take risks under Dulles were now told to be cautious. Helms did increase the number of overseas spies roaming free of U.S. embassies and under deep cover as businessmen instead of posing as diplomats. His men trained more than 700,000 foreign military and police officers to fight communism, ignoring the unsavory regimes that also used the newly acquired skills to suppress their own people. But otherwise, if Helms had an overarching mission it was that there be no surprises on his watch.

It explained his irritation at Colby when LBJ hit him with a surprise in early 1968. Out of the blue at the national security team's Tuesday White House lunch, Johnson told Helms he wanted Colby detached from the CIA to be the deputy for CORDS, the Civil Operations and Revolutionary Development Support program set up to win "the other war" among South Vietnam's rural population. Robert "Blowtorch Bob" Komer, a former CIA analyst and hard charger in the Johnson White House, led CORDS, which roped all U.S. counterinsurgency and pacification programs under his management. Helms suspected that Colby, who was eager to return to Vietnam and thought CORDS finally put the Americans on the right track to victory at the village level, had engineered the appointment behind his back.

Even with these hiccups, by the last year of the Johnson presidency Helms was at the top of his game. Though the Soviet invasion of Czechoslovakia that year had caught the CIA by surprise, in 1967 the agency's analysts predicted that Israel would win its war with the Arabs in less than two weeks. The conflict lasted six days. Helms had earned a seat in Johnson's inner circle.

But his private life was in turmoil. Helms decided in spring 1967 to end his marriage to Julia. She was a quick-witted and, at times, sharp-tongued woman who relatives thought overly domineering and his CIA colleagues noticed had grown distant at parties over the years. Julia had a right to be unhappy over Helms spending so much time away from her on spy business. The secrecy, being walled out of such a large part of her husband's life, grated on her. Helms admitted it was "probably" his fault that they had drifted apart. After a Tuesday luncheon in April, he slipped into the Oval Office and asked Johnson if the divorce he was planning would cause the president "any political complication." "It will not be a problem for me," Johnson said and excused his spymaster so he could take his afternoon nap.

At a Lebanese embassy dinner the year before, Helms had sat next to Cynthia McKelvie, a red-haired British farm girl who had steered vessels in harbors as a member of the Women's Royal Naval Service during World War II and was now married to a prominent Scottish surgeon in Washington who ignored her. The spymaster and the British socialite hit it off immediately, talking nonstop throughout the meal. The two ran into each other at more dinner parties on the Georgetown circuit. Helms seemed to Cynthia genuinely interested in every word she had to say. He was relieved to find this tablemate, with sophisticated good looks in her early forties, who wanted to talk about subjects other than his secret work. Soon they fell in love. After their divorces, Dick and Cynthia married in December 1968. They found an apartment at the Irene just north of the District of Columbia line in Chevy Chase. Within months, foreign government spies, who had little difficulty locating the newlyweds' address, rented flats in the building.

Richard Nixon decided to keep Helms as his CIA director, though the Republican president did little to conceal his disdain for the agency and its spy chief. It was a hostility Nixon had nursed since 1960, when he suspected Dulles and liberals in the CIA secretly slipped the Democrats intelligence that helped Kennedy's campaign. Helms, who had found Nixon to be a studious vice president but completely devoid of charm, nevertheless remained as loyal to the new chief executive as he had been to the old one—too loyal in some instances. At LBJ's behest he launched Operation Chaos to investigate the burgeoning antiwar movement to determine if communist agents funded or influenced it. Helms continued the program for Nixon but his officers found no evidence of any significant foreign involvement. Helms later admitted Chaos violated the CIA's charter forbidding it from spying on Americans.

His fortune made, Bill Casey turned to Republican politics, serving as an unpaid adviser for Nixon in 1960, making his own unsuccessful bid for a New York congressional seat in 1966, and when Nixon ran again in 1968 raising money and writing a quickie issues book for the campaign that caught the president-elect's eye. Wildly unrealistic, Casey expected to be rewarded with a cabinet post or ambassadorship. The best Nixon offered was the deputy's job under Helms at the CIA. Casey liked Helms, but considered him an intelligence bureaucrat. Working under a man who had been his subordinate in the OSS would be insulting, Casey thought. He sulked back to his New York business.

Nixon finally offered Casey a job in 1971 that he would accept: chairman of the Securities and Exchange Commission. Senate Democrats complained that a venture capitalist sued in the past for violating securities laws was hardly suited for overseeing Wall Street, but Casey surprised skeptics and tackled business regulation with the enthusiasm he displayed spying in Europe. Nixon rewarded him two years later with the job of undersecretary of state for economic affairs. It turned out to be not much of a reward. Henry Kissinger, who became Casey's boss in 1973 when he took over the State Department, seemed to have little interest in international economics and ignored him. A year later, Casey escaped Kissinger and became president of the Export-Import Bank. On overseas trips for Ex-Im Bank he enjoyed booking dinners with European colleagues from the war to relive old spy adventures.

• • • •

Colby joined Komer's CORDS team in March 1968. Because it was a program run jointly by the military and the State Department's Agency for International Development, Colby had to change payrolls and temporarily leave the CIA, which he did not mind doing. Convinced that CORDS would succeed where the strategic hamlet program had failed, he plunged into the work, overseeing the distribution of a half million weapons to villagers in

South Vietnam. But the problem as always: corruption ran rampant in the provinces and in Saigon's government, now headed by Nguyen Van Thieu, one of a line of army generals who ran the country after Diem. All Colby could do was bring cases of graft to the attention of Thieu, who did little to stop it. Eight months after arriving in Saigon, Colby replaced Komer as CORDS director and was given the rank of ambassador. At the age of forty-eight, he had become the general of the other war in Vietnam with a helicopter and plane at his disposal.

By the time he assumed the top job, Colby could rattle off a stream of statistics to prove CORDS was succeeding, which he fed to American reporters in Saigon. The program indeed had begun to show progress in pacifying South Vietnam's countryside, but State Department officials and CIA analysts at Langley did not believe it was enough. When he paid attention to the war, which was not a whole lot, Helms leaned toward the pessimists. Later, in his memoirs, he described Vietnam as his "nightmare for a good ten years." As CIA director he invited Williams College students to his office to debate them on Vietnam. He vanquished their arguments against American involvement but only because he had mounds of analytical data at his disposal to argue for it. He was not an enthusiastic debater. His son, Dennis, and his nephew, Gates Hawn, phoned occasionally with accounts of the growing unrest they saw on college campuses. Helms was interested in the reports but told Gates it was useless to pass them on to the president. Nixon was not interested in his views.

After three years of his being away in Vietnam, tension had begun to build between Bill and Barbara Colby. She had been left in Washington to deal by herself with a slow-building family crisis. Their oldest daughter, Catherine, who had been born in 1949, suffered from epilepsy as a girl and now depression and anorexia nervosa in her early twenties. With her condition not improving, Bill returned to Washington in June 1971. For him, the nation's capital had become a hostile city because of his Vietnam service. He was jeered in public, awakened in the morning with threatening phone calls to his home, and heckled by antiwar protesters when he testified before Congress. The peace movement had targeted Colby as a war criminal for what it considered one of the most repugnant programs the American government ever sponsored in Vietnam.

In response to Viet Cong assassinations and kidnappings, Komer had convinced Thieu to get on board with "Phung Hoang," a pacification project named after a mythical Vietnamese bird, which in English roughly translated as Phoenix. Its stated goal, which Colby backed enthusiastically when he returned to Saigon, was to capture Viet Cong operatives and use the intelligence they provided to dismantle the communist infrastructure embedded in the villages. But Phoenix, manned principally by some five thousand CIA-trained Provincial Reconnaissance Unit operatives (many of them criminals or South Vietnamese army deserters), ended up with assassinations as a by-product. In congressional testimony, Colby eventually admitted that more than twenty thousand VC had been killed in Phoenix. He insisted most died in legitimate combat operations but it was clear that many in that number included Viet Cong members as well as innocent South Vietnamese peasants executed by PRU terror squads. CIA and CORDS officers found victims of Phoenix raids with ears, noses, and even heads cut off. The program understandably quieted the VC for a time but did not make them disappear. As he had during his first tour in Vietnam, Colby again misread the real conflict in the country. Whether led by Diem or Thieu or the succession of warlord presidents between them, South Vietnam's government was irrevocably undemocratic, corrupt, and incapable of winning any kind of war—conventional or unconventional—against the North.

Nearly two years after he returned to Washington, Catherine, emaciated, died when internal organs in her body began shutting down. Her psychiatrist thought she had been improving, but brave and shy Catherine, red-haired like her mother, eventually succumbed to the eating disorder. Barbara was devastated. It was the only time the other children ever saw their always reserved father break down and cry.

. . . .

Nixon fired Richard Helms in November 1972. Long frustrated with what he considered a bloated and inefficient intelligence community, populated by East Coast elitists who flooded him with useless or biased reports, Nixon wanted "a real shakeup in CIA" and had lost confidence that Helms could accomplish it. Helms believed he was dismissed because he refused to have the CIA take the fall for the burglars who broke into the Democratic Party headquarters at the Watergate complex six months earlier. His first instinct always to do a president's bidding, Helms had been cooperative up to a point. His CIA officers provided one of the burglars, E. Howard Hunt, who had once worked for the agency, equipment to break into the Beverly Hills offices of Daniel Ellsberg's psychiatrist. Analysts at Langley had prepared a psychological profile of Ellsberg, who had leaked the Pentagon Papers on Vietnam to the press. And caving to White House pressure, Helms allowed his deputy to try to wave off the FBI in its Watergate probe with the excuse that it would tread on a CIA operation. But Helms balked when Nixon aides wanted him to pay the burglars hush money from agency funds. As a consolation prize, the president nominated Helms to be ambassador to Iran, but he squeezed the last bit of mean-spiritedness he could from the episode by forcing Helms to leave the CIA early at the expense of his retirement income and letting him learn from a radio report that he would be replaced by James Schlesinger, an Office of Management and Budget deputy who had written a top secret report for Nixon on reforming the CIA and other intelligence agencies. During his final days at Langley, Helms destroyed transcripts of sensitive office conversations he had secretly tape-recorded along with records of the agency's drug testing program. He left the CIA defiant and not one bit ashamed of its controversial record. Agency employees jammed the main entrance hallway when he departed, many weeping.

At his February 7 confirmation hearing for the Iran ambassadorship, Helms lied under oath before the Senate Foreign Relations Committee. When a panel member asked if the CIA had passed money to opponents of Salvador Allende and had tried to overthrow the government of Chile, he responded that the agency had not. In fact, since 1964 the CIA, at the behest of the White House, had been pumping money into Chilean elections to prevent Allende from winning the presidency. After the Marxist candidate gained a plurality of the popular vote in the first round of the 1970 election, Nixon had ordered the covert political warfare ratcheted up and the agency had tried, unsuccessfully, to foment a military coup to prevent Allende from winning a majority in the second round of balloting by the Chilean congress. Helms flew with Cynthia to Tehran convinced he had not committed perjury. Most of the senators at the hearing were not authorized to hear the truth, he concluded, and even if they had the security clearances Nixon had ordered him not to talk to anyone outside of a select group in the White

House and CIA about the agency's backing a military coup in Chile. Lying to protect the agency's secrets, and American national security, did not constitute a crime, Helms reasoned. He was only doing his job.

Five months after Helms arrived in Tehran, Allende, who remained a target of CIA covert action, committed suicide in his presidential palace on September 11, 1973, rather than allow Chilean generals to capture him in a coup they had staged.

. . . .

Coldhearted at the office yet a gentle bird watcher at home, Schlesinger arrived at the CIA intent on cleaning house the first day. Within months he fired some 1,500 officers, delivering most of the dismissal slips to the clandestine service. Colby, who left the OSS angry over incompetents above him, convinced Schlesinger to appoint him deputy director for plans (soon renamed the Directorate for Operations) making the argument that as an insider he knew best how to purge the agency of its deadwood. Colby and many others in the CIA agreed the flotsam needed to be fired. Schlesinger became so unpopular that guards had to keep watch on his portrait eventually hung in a headquarters corridor to prevent it from being defaced. The CIA's old hands and retirees like Helms, however, detested Colby even more. One of their own had betrayed them to an outsider.

Schlesinger, whose temper could be volcanic, erupted when newspapers reported that the CIA had provided White House burglars with tools to break into the office of Ellsberg's psychiatrist. Colby talked him out of firing more people, Schlesinger's first inclination, and instead agreed to his boss's demand that all agency employees report to the front office any questionable activities they witnessed in the past. The result: a 693-page report, which became known as the "Family Jewels," that catalogued practically all the CIA's dirty tricks, such as Operation Chaos, the bugging of American journalists, mail intercepts, mind control drugs, and assassination plots. Surprisingly, the list appeared to Colby to be less damaging than he anticipated. Colby briefed the senior members of the congressional committees overseeing the CIA on its contents. Most agreed to let past skeletons remain in the closet on Colby's promise that abuses would not be repeated. Helms was outraged Schlesinger and Colby had allowed such an odious document to be compiled. An unprecedented breach of security, he thought.

Soon after the Family Jewels report was compiled, Nixon moved Schlesinger to the Defense Department as its secretary in a shake-up of his cabinet because of the Watergate scandal. Colby was shocked when Nixon nominated him to be his CIA director. The president hardly knew him, he thought. But Nixon did know Colby. He had sent him a handwritten condolence note when Catherine died. He considered Colby a safe, apolitical choice Congress would approve—and a faceless bureaucrat the White House could control, as it hadn't been able to with Helms in the end. The Senate overwhelmingly approved his nomination, although posters sprouted everywhere in Washington with a likeness of Colby superimposed on an Ace of Spades announcing he was "wanted" for murder in the Phoenix program. Harassing telephone calls to his home resumed. When one persistent man kept phoning at all hours and just breathing heavily over the line, Colby had the phone company track down his name and number. The next time the breather called, Colby addressed him by his name. The man gasped, hung up, and never called again. Colby guessed he was terrified a CIA hit team would come after him.

His OSS experience had a huge impact on Colby, who liked to putter around his Bethesda, Maryland, home wearing his old floppy Army fatigue cap from World War II. It had been "a seminal period of his life," said his oldest son, John, shaping how he ran the CIA. Although his father soon demonstrated, John added, that "he hadn't drunk the Kool-Aid." Colby took on Everyman airs as CIA director, driving his own car to work, eating with employees in the cafeteria, calling in young analysts to compliment them on their reports, then suggesting ways their work could be improved, and finding time in his schedule to listen to any employee walking in with a complaint. He pushed for more women and African Americans in the senior ranks. With advances in technical intelligence gathering, Colby viewed the human spy as a "contributor, but not the sole actor." Yet he increased the number of informants recruited among Soviet delegations around the world, improved the quality of the information his Operations Directorate produced, and demanded better packaging of reports his analysts delivered to consumers. Young officers appreciated the changes; many senior hands resented them, grumbling that Colby could be stubborn and single-minded. He polled his senior staff on the idea of distributing intelligence reports in a daily, classified newspaper format that top officials could leaf through to find what interested them. They opposed it. He launched it anyway, the publication becoming the *National Intelligence Daily* with a circulation of about sixty. Enemies and even some allies in the ranks found Colby officious, pedantic, a cold fish, difficult to understand—a "very strange guy," as one put it, who "went his own way."

A political firestorm broke after *The New York Times* revealed Operation Chaos on December 22, 1974, as well as the CIA's mail intercepts and surveillance of thousands of American citizens. Gerald Ford, who assumed the presidency after Richard Nixon's resignation, fanned the flames when he blurted out to *Times* editors during a private lunch that the CIA had plotted assassinations. Ford appointed his vice president, Nelson Rockefeller, to chair a blue-ribbon presidential commission to investigate what the public feared was a rogue agency. Congress was no longer content to let the Family Jewels stay on Langley's shelf. Investigating committees chaired by two Democrats, Idaho senator Frank Church and New York representative Otis Pike, demanded that Colby turn over the report, as well as other documents, and testify before the panels. Colby cooperated, convincing the panels to agree to security ground rules he hoped would channel their requests so the CIA could still keep important secrets from making their way to Capitol Hill.

For months Colby kept up a grueling schedule, testifying before Congress during the day and running the CIA in the evening. On touchy subjects like assassinations, he patiently explained to the committees what the CIA had done and not done. Before pulling up to the witness table he paid a visit to Bernard Knox, an old Jedburgh comrade and classics scholar, to test-market his thoughts with him. The White House believed its CIA director was out of control. Old-timers at Langley still loyal to Helms were furious that Colby was allowing Congress to meddle in what they deemed the president's intelligence activities. Helms considered Colby's cooperation and testimony an act of betrayal against the agency as well as the country. Barbara picked up the phone one day to hear an undertaker tell her an unidentified man had called to inform him her family would need his funeral home's services soon for Bill. Colby had a thick skin and his combat tour in Europe had given him an inner courage and resolve never to back down before anyone. But privately the vilification—particularly among colleagues in the CIA—hurt him deeply.

Theories abounded for why he appeared so candid before Congress. Detractors accused him of being an overgrown Boy Scout, a misguided Jesuit at confessional. Some OSS veterans traced it back to his World War II upbringing as a paramilitary commando oriented to noisy action; Colby was never attuned to keeping secrets quiet as an intelligence collector as Helms would be. Colby, who always tucked a miniature copy of the Constitution into the breast pocket of his coat, posited loftier motives in his memoirs. The CIA was an integral part of a democracy, he maintained, subject to checks and balances. His duty was to convince a public, traumatized by the Vietnam War and Watergate, that there was still value in having an intelligence agency by lifting slightly the veil of secrecy cloaking it. Colby's real reason for turning over the Family Jewels, however, was more legally prosaic, he confided to his son Paul, a fellow attorney. As a lawyer Colby knew that if he did not make a good faith effort to comply with a court's discovery order in an antitrust case an angry judge would seize everything in his client's office. In this standoff, the judge was Congress. Colby had to convince that body he was making a good faith effort to produce what its committees wanted in their discovery. All the while, he tried to put the material he turned over in its proper context in order to paint the CIA in the most favorable light. If he hadn't done it, the legislative branch, no longer deferential to executive privilege, would have carted off every secret with a flood of congressional subpoenas. Helms never understood that, he thought. Colby's hard-boiled assessment of the best way to proceed proved correct. The agency would likely have been torn apart had he stonewalled. Instead, Congress clamped down with tighter oversight of the CIA, but ultimately concluded that a strong intelligence service remained in the national interest.

Colby's approach never convinced Casey, who watched in horror the scandal's unmasking from afar. When a friend later pointed out to him that Colby had no choice but to answer truthfully under oath a question put to him by a member of Congress, Casey responded icily: "He didn't have to understand the question."

Considering him a liability for the 1976 presidential race, Ford fired Colby on November 2, 1975. After introducing George H. W. Bush, his successor, to the CIA workforce gathered in the Langley headquarters' auditorium on January 30, 1976, Colby slipped away to his aging Buick Skylark in the visitors' parking lot, a few employees in the hallway applauding as he made his exit.

. . . .

Helms, whose name appeared on practically every CIA document related to misdeeds the committees were investigating, flew back to Washington sixteen times from Tehran to testify more than one hundred hours. A molten fury built inside him as he dodged questions from what seemed to him grandstanding, hypocritical congressmen deliberately playing dumb to how the CIA must be used by a president to combat dangers in the world.

But Helms reserved a special loathing for Colby, the man he thought he had mentored. Congress was not the only government body demanding access to the Family Jewels. The Justice Department wanted a look as well and under pressure from his Langley staff Colby reluctantly turned over to Justice CIA files in the Chile operation so the department could investigate whether Helms had committed perjury in his congressional testimony. Helms eventually agreed in November 1977 to plead no contest to not testifying "fully, completely and accurately" before Congress. He remained defiant after a federal judge slapped him with a two-year suspended sentence and $2,000 fine. "I don't feel disgraced at all," he told reporters as he left a Washington courthouse. Retired CIA officers took up a collection to pay his fine.

The CIA split bitterly between Helms loyalists who considered Colby a traitor and mostly younger generation officers, in the minority, who believed he had done the right thing. At a 1981 banquet in New York's Waldorf-Astoria hosted by the Veterans of the OSS, the cocktail party the two men attended before the dinner demonstrated the divide. The ballroom, full of World War II operatives and current CIA officers, divided down the middle with Helms and his supporters on one side and the pro-Colby group on the other. At MacArthur Beverages, a Washington liquor store, Colby's son John watched from the car as his father walked to the store and ran into Helms coming out with a case of wine. The two men said nothing as they passed each other, exchanging only slight frigid nods. When his father returned to the car, John gave him a quizzical look. "Don't ask," Colby said. "Just drive home."

. . . .

Bill Casey was captivated by Ronald Reagan's warmth, sure-footedness, and talent for drawing people to him, but shocked at first by his shallowness and malleability. Like other Reaganites, Casey would come to admire the man and adamantly insist that the former B-movie actor and California governor was smarter than people gave him credit for. Casey took over management of Reagan's troubled presidential campaign in February 1980 after the New Hampshire primary and turned it around. When Reagan trounced incumbent Democrat Jimmy Carter in the fall, Casey was credited with being the victory's architect. He expected to be made secretary of state or defense as his reward. But appalled by his sloppy dress and table manners, Nancy Reagan thought Casey not presentable as America's top diplomat. Retired general Alexander Haig, a former Nixon and Ford chief of staff, had the inside track for State, while Caspar Weinberger, a member of Reagan's California kitchen cabinet (which Casey was not), would be secretary of defense. Reagan was surprised when Casey at first acted cool to his offer of the CIA directorship. Casey quickly came around, however, after consulting with OSS friends and calculating that the agency was an ideal perch for promoting Reagan's hard-line anticommunist agenda.

Most of the officers who had served under Donovan were jubilant with Casey going to the CIA. Even the liberal Arthur Schlesinger was pleased to see him take the agency helm. Casey came from Donovan's intelligence collection ranks, not the paramilitary forces, whose operators created so much trouble for the CIA after the war, Schlesinger reasoned. Other OSS veterans were uneasy about the choice. Colby and Helms worried that Casey would be a loose cannon at Langley.

After Casey's successful Senate confirmation, Helms began dropping by his office or lunching with him at restaurants away from the CIA campus. He offered advice on problems he believed lingered in the agency, recommended OSS vets Casey should hire, and acted as a sounding board for the new director's ideas. Casey kept a soft spot for his former OSS assistant. He arranged for Reagan to present Helms with the National Security Medal, which had been awarded to Donovan and Dulles. Colby also sent letters offering advice on how Casey should organize the CIA to spy on future threats and enclosing articles he had written on intelligence. Casey ignored the mail and never invited Colby to his office or to lunch.

As had been the case throughout his life, Casey made a poor first impression walking into the Langley headquarters. Now sixty-seven, he was tall, stoop-shouldered, and jowly, with wisps of white hair flying from his balding head. He always wore expensive suits but looked like he'd slept in them, he used paperclips to pick his teeth, and he chewed on the end of his silk tie in meetings. Agency officers, particularly the young ones, initially brushed him off as a political hack with a shady business past, whom Reagan appointed because he owed him a favor. They quickly realized their new boss had a razor-sharp mind, he was a voracious reader keeping several books on his desk at all times, he could speak "the language of intelligence," and he had as much experience running espionage operations from his OSS days as many of the pros at Langley. And he made up for what he did not know about current agency programs with a boundless enthusiasm for the business the CIA conducted. His energy quickly galvanized his employees and made them want to work hard for him—which Casey expected. As subordinates in London discovered during the war, Casey could be a stimulating but confounding boss. He spent long hours at the office during the week and on weekends, much of the time early on reading CIA files on countries and cases to catch up. Senior aides felt forced to give up their Saturdays and Sundays to follow suit. Like Donovan, he was a quick decider who did not agonize over decisions afterward. He demanded fast turn-around on assignments and expected employees to know what he wanted without his having to waste time telling them what he wanted. Like the general, he delegated and micromanaged at the same time, which added to the frustration. And he never handed out compliments—only more work.

Casey hung two photos on the wall of his seventh-floor office—Ronald Reagan's and Wild Bill Donovan's. He soon commissioned a statue of Donovan, which was placed in the CIA entrance hall. His reverence for the old man went far beyond symbols. Casey ran the CIA the way he thought the general would. Like Donovan with the OSS, he kept his door open to all ideas for operations, even the wacky ones. He hated bureaucracy, circumvented the chain of command, and poked his head into offices rungs below. He was proud, as Donovan had been with his agency, of the vast array of

Ph.D.s working at Langley and he reached out to experts in corporations, think tanks, and universities for infusions of new ideas. Like Donovan, he loved to tour his overseas stations, not only to boost morale and size up the field officers who worked for him but also to escape Washington's political wars. When he returned he always delivered vivid trip reports to Reagan, just as Donovan had done with Roosevelt.

Yet Casey's relationship with his president was as complicated as Donovan's with FDR. Though he had been given cabinet rank and he snared a space for himself in the Executive Office Building next to the White House, he was not personally close to Reagan. He did his best to cultivate Nancy, but was only an infrequent social guest at the White House. He never openly disparaged Reagan but he knew the president had narrow interests, a limited attention span, and only a rudimentary knowledge of foreign policy. Reagan, who was hard of hearing, often could not understand anything Casey said during briefings because he mumbled. Friends suspected the CIA director turned on the scrambler when he did not want Reagan or Congress to comprehend what he was doing in sensitive operations.

Casey did not emulate his mentor in other ways. Unlike Donovan he despised the Washington press corps and showed a contempt the general never would have for Congress, routinely referring to members of the oversight committees as "these fuckers." Reporters became hostile and legislators returned the disdain in kind. Barry Goldwater, the conservative Republican chairman of the Senate Select Committee on Intelligence, called Casey "flapper lips." A seasoned analyst and writer from his Research Institute of America days, Casey became a demanding editor sharpening mushy CIA reports to administration officials so they came to a point. Agency analysts soon complained that Casey crossed the line, bullying them to slant reports to conform to his hard-line ideology and driving independent-minded experts out of the organization.

Casey arrived at the CIA believing communism was as dangerous to American interests as Nazism had been during World War II. He was intent on using his agency to wage war against the Soviet Union as Donovan had used his against the Axis. Just as the OSS had helped resistance movements in Nazi-occupied Europe, the CIA would now increase its aid to foreign governments or guerrillas battling the communists, he decided. Their days of moping after Vietnam, Watergate, and the Church Committee were over, Casey told his officers. He intended to shake things up and rebuild. The rough-around-the-edges, can-do culture of the OSS was back at Langley under his watch. The CIA's covert action capability would roll back Soviet and communist gains around the world. More polished senior officers warned him that covert action had been a highly overrated weapon against the Soviets. Casey ignored them. The CIA's budget jumped to $3 billion. Convinced his Operations Directorate had grown flabby and complacent, he shuffled personnel to make room for gung ho OSS types and revved up clandestine battles against the communists in spots like Afghanistan, El Salvador, and Poland. The agency would win the war, he decreed, not settle for stalemate or détente.

For Casey, Nicaragua (he always pronounced it "Nica-wa-wa") became the critical test for how *contrarrevolucionarios* would defeat the nation's Marxist Sandinista regime as World War II partisans had overcome Nazi occupiers. His operation eventually threatened to bring down an American president. Casey set up a program Reagan approved to train thousands of "contra" rebels at secret camps in Honduras and Costa Rica with tens of millions of CIA dollars to overthrow the Managua government. Circumventing regular CIA channels, as Donovan did with the OSS, Casey had covert action enthusiasts running the program report directly to him. When Congress, fearing another Vietnam, eventually blocked further funds for the CIA's covert operation to aid the rebels, Casey arranged for the White House to secretly take up a collection behind lawmakers' backs from the friendly governments of Saudi Arabia, Brunei, and Taiwan to keep the contras intact. His principal agent for this end run became Oliver North, an overeager Marine lieutenant colonel on the National Security Council staff whom Casey treated as a rambunctious son.

The young naval officer who had been Donovan's standout in Europe was now in deep enough trouble as CIA director. He had clearly violated congressional directives prohibiting him from soliciting third-country funding for the contra rebels. With Iran, he would dig his hole far deeper. Reagan had become obsessed over the kidnapping of Americans in Lebanon by Iranian-backed Shi'a extremists. Casey found the torture and murder of one of the Americans—the CIA's Beirut station chief William Buckley—as revolting as the Nazi executions of his OSS agents during the war. Reagan, who had pledged never to "make concessions to terrorists," gave Casey, North, and his White House national security adviser, Robert McFarlane, his approval to sell TOW antitank and Hawk antiaircraft missiles to Iran for hostages in Beirut. The transfers were arranged through an assortment of shady Middle East brokers. Reagan also ordered Casey not to brief Congress on the covert operation as required by law, which Casey was only too happy to oblige. By summer 1986 senior CIA officials believed that trading arms for hostages and not telling Congress was "suicidal" for the agency. Speaking from experience, Helms had told Casey earlier "the only thing you can't tell Congress about are operations you shouldn't be doing in the first place." Casey was not bothered by the deception, nor by the fact that the enterprising Iranians replaced the two hostages released with more captives to keep the arms flowing. The operation, in his mind, was merely a play one made in the great international game, the cost of failure just a few hundred missiles and their spare parts. He was oblivious to the larger price paid with Congress and the public trust. Most Americans were disgusted when they learned of the deal.

The enterprise next included a scheme North hatched to divert to the contras millions of dollars from profits earned selling the Iranians arms at inflated prices. Admiral John Poindexter, who succeeded McFarlane as national security adviser, claimed he approved the diversion but never told the president. The entire sordid affair inevitably began seeping out in press stories. A shaken Ronald Reagan followed by his attorney general, Edwin Meese, went public on November 25. Meese revealed that as much as $30 million in Iranian arms sales profits might have gone to the contras. Reagan announced that North had been fired and Poindexter had resigned. North later testified that Casey knew of the Iranian profits being funneled to the contras and was enthusiastic about it. Congressional committees investigating the scandal believed the lieutenant colonel, but the evidence of Casey's actual involvement in the diversion was not clear-cut. Even if North had not included him in that part of the deal, the other parts Casey had participated in, together with the lies he told Congress to cover it up, would have been enough for him to face criminal charges. He was clearly guilty of undermining the Reagan presidency. He also came close to tearing back down the CIA he had been so determined to rebuild after the dark years of the 1960s and 1970s. Iran-Contra indelibly stained what he hoped would be his legacy.

The shadow wars Allen Dulles, Richard Helms, Bill Colby, and Bill Casey waged against Adolf Hitler were messier than the greatest-generation portraits would have them painted. Espionage and sabotage always are. Yet their battles did have an underlying clarity and nobility that could not be denied. All four had fought tenaciously, resourcefully, and heroically. They had more than done their part to defeat tyranny and oppression. They returned home, invigorated with high hopes, affected profoundly by their service in the OSS, determined to take up arms against communism in the way they had learned to wield those weapons against Nazism. It made it all the more tragic that their Cold War after the guns of Europe fell silent finished so badly for each of them. Dulles's end came on a swampy beach along Cuba's coast, Helms's in a courtroom striking a plea deal to avoid a felony conviction, Colby's as a pariah to many in his agency, and Casey's as a target of accusation and ridicule. It was a sad ending for all four.

EPILOGUE

A little more than a month before Allen Dulles died, Gero von Schulze-Gaevernitz wrote him in a touching letter that he had a vivid dream about his Bern comrade the night before. "The most important years of my life have been spent in the blessed and delightful cooperation with you, which I shall never forget," the German wrote.

Dulles spent his years after the CIA writing his books with Gero's help, making numerous television appearances (defending his actions in the Bay of Pigs for many of the interviews), and traveling abroad. He paid a visit to Colby in Vietnam in 1962. Dulles had visions of becoming an elder statesman summoned for advice on intelligence matters, but the CIA and Kennedy White House never called after his resignation. Intent on rehabilitating him somewhat, Johnson put Dulles on the Warren Commission probing Kennedy's assassination and sent him to Mississippi to show that the administration intended to hunt down the murderers of three civil rights workers. Frail with his health deteriorating, Dulles returned to the Langley headquarters in March 1968 for the unveiling of a bas-relief bust Helms had commissioned of him for the building's main lobby. He had first been wary of posing for the work, fearing the sculptor would not carve a good likeness of him. But the artist had and Dulles was delighted with the result.

After Dulles succumbed to pneumonia on January 29, 1969, Eric Sevareid eulogized on the *CBS Evening News* that he "was an old fashioned American in character and original in mind, and more than anybody else, originator of a new experience for the American government." Helms, who had a miserable cold the day of the funeral, escorted Clover up the aisle of Georgetown Presbyterian Church to the coffin. Afterward, she flew to Switzerland—the country of her spiritual awakening with Jung—to clear her head once more. Helms remained devoted to the Dulles family. Later he would be with Joan consoling her at Clover's burial in 1974.

Bill Casey never had an opportunity to fully defend himself in the Iran-Contra scandal. On December 11, 1986, Helms had attended a testimonial dinner with him in Philadelphia for Robert C. Ames, a CIA analyst killed in the 1983 terrorist bombing of the U.S. embassy in Beirut. Casey offered Helms a ride back to Washington on his CIA plane. Helms was shocked that Casey could barely hold up his cocktail glass during the flight. When he arrived home that night Helms bounded up the stairs to the bedroom and told Cynthia: "Something is wrong with Casey!" She had rarely seen her husband so agitated.

The next day Helms phoned Robert Gates, Casey's deputy, and told him to get his boss out of Langley and into a doctor's office. Gates already knew he had a problem. Casey's security detail had reported to him that the director had been falling down or bumping into furniture at his home. Preparing on the morning of December 15 for another grueling round of Senate testimony, Casey collapsed from a seizure after an agency physician had taken his blood pressure. Paramedics wheeled him out on a stretcher. Georgetown University Hospital's neurological team concluded Casey suffered from brain cancer. Surgeons removed what they could of the tumor and Casey was transferred from intensive care to a private room on January 6, but his brain did not heal. A little more than three weeks later, Casey ended his directorship. A tearful Sophia signed the resignation letter addressed to Reagan for him because he could not with his enfeebled hand.

She took him home to Mayknoll on March 27. He died in a Long Island hospital on May 6. Controversy dogged Casey to his grave. At his funeral mass in St. Mary's Roman Catholic Church near his home, the bishop presiding denounced the American-backed contra war in his sermon, enraging family and friends in the pews.

William Colby joined a law firm after he left the CIA. He wrote two books that were memoirs, traveled the world as a consultant, and continued to dabble in intelligence matters on the side. He remained a staunch defender of his operations in Vietnam and lobbied on behalf of Vietnamese boat refugees fleeing the country. Colby also pursued a host of liberal causes, supporting, for example, the nuclear freeze movement to halt the atomic arms race between the United States and the Soviet Union, opposing Reagan's plan for a Star Wars missile defense shield, and backing the legalization of marijuana use.

And he grew tired of Barbara. As with Helms and Julia, CIA life had taken its toll on the Colby marriage with Bill unable to talk about his work and away for long stretches and Barbara left to deal with Catherine's deteriorating health on her own. The couple drifted apart. Barbara became more consumed with family and the Catholic Church, while Bill felt he could no longer intellectually connect with his wife. During his second tour in Vietnam he became infatuated with a married Egyptian woman in Saigon, but he never acted on it. In 1982, he fell in love with Sally Shelton, a Fulbright Scholar and former State Department diplomat who worked with him in an international business consulting firm. Barbara was shocked when Bill asked for a divorce in May 1983—deeply bitter that he ended up not as loyal to her as he had been to the CIA. After the split she earned a master's degree in liberal studies from Georgetown University.

Bill married Sally in Venice in November 1984. After the wedding he stopped attending regular Catholic Church services, disgusted with the Vatican's conservative policies.

Saturday evening, April 27, 1996, Colby was enjoying a plate of mussels and a glass of wine by himself at the couple's Cobb Neck cottage on the shore of Maryland's Neale Sound. Weekenders like Colby usually departed Sunday evening so curious neighbors who spotted his sport utility vehicle still parked in his driveway at sunset on the 28th dropped by to check on him. They found his door unlocked, the plates from his dinner in the sink, his wineglass on the table, his radio and computer turned on, and his canoe missing. A resident discovered the canoe tipped over at Rock Point less than a quarter mile away. Searchers finally found Colby's body floating off marsh weeds near there on May 6. Conspiracy theories proliferated on how the former spymaster had died: Soviet or Chinese agents or vengeful CIA officers assassinated him, Colby committed suicide because of guilt over his role in the Vietnam War, or because he was distraught over Catherine's death. The coroner's autopsy concluded the most mundane explanation was the accurate one. Apparently deciding to take a short ride in the sound after a pleasant dinner, he suffered a stroke or heart attack, fell out of the canoe, experienced hypothermia in the chilly water, and drowned.

After his burial in Arlington National Cemetery near the graves of his mother and father, Sally said she received about ten letters from men identifying themselves as CIA officers who told her Bill Colby "had it coming to him."

Refusing to accept a court's judgment that he had fallen from grace, after his conviction Richard Helms formed an international consulting business, shrewdly invested in the stock market, continued to travel the world with Cynthia, and became a regular on the Washington tennis and cocktail circuit. Keeping a safe distance from inquiring reporters and admonishing Cynthia to do the same, he remained closed-mouthed about both his CIA and OSS service until he began writing his autobiography after the Berlin Wall collapsed and the Cold War ended. He then hosted dinners with former KGB officers to swap stories.

In 1993, Helms learned he had multiple myeloma, a cancer of the plasma cells that produce antibodies. Typical of his nature, he ordered Cynthia to keep the ailment secret from friends and the rest of the family. He did not want people pestering him with questions about his health. He continued to live a vigorous life the next eight years, traveling with Cynthia to far-off places like eastern Russia and the Arctic Circle. In his final year, his condition seriously deteriorated and Cynthia eventually had to bring in a nurse to help care for him. He died in his home on October 23, 2002, at age eighty-nine.

At Helms's funeral, then CIA director George Tenet eulogized him as "the complete American intelligence officer." Washington's Old Guard led the cortege to bury his ashes in Arlington Cemetery. It marked the passing of the last of the disciples.

SELECTED BIBLIOGRAPHY
FOR SOURCE NOTES

MANUSCRIPT COLLECTIONS

Abbreviations are used for manuscript collections in the source notes.

CA	Churchill Archives Centre
	CHAR Chartwell Papers
CCWM	Carpetbagger Covert Warfare Museum, Harrington, Northamptonshire
CMH	U.S. Army Center for Military History
COR	Cornell University Law Library, Donovan Archive
DDEL	Dwight D. Eisenhower Library
FBI	Federal Bureau of Investigation, Freedom of Information Act, File on Allen Welsh Dulles, Request No. 1187433-000
FDRL	Franklin D. Roosevelt Presidential Library
	OF Official File
	PSF President's Secretary File
	WSP Whitney H. Shepardson Papers
GU	Georgetown University Library Special Collections Division

	CEP	Cornelius van H. Engert Papers	RHP	Richard Helms Papers
	CHP	Cynthia Helms Papers	WHP	William Hood Papers
	LCP	Larry Collins Papers	MQP	Martin S. Quigley Papers

HIA   Hoover Institution Archives

    CBP   Carl Bertram Papers   JDP   James B. Donovan Papers

    CCP   Charles M. Carman Papers   JLP   Jay Lovestone Papers

    GP   Hermann Göring Papers   JPP   Joseph E. Persico Papers

    GGP   Gero von Schulze-   NAP   Norwood F. Allman Papers
        Gaevernitz Papers

    GSP   Ginetta Sagan Papers   RFP   J. Russell Forgan Papers

    HGP   Hugh S. Gibson Papers   RSP   R. Harris Smith Papers

    HRP   Henry Regnery Papers   WJCP   William J. Casey Papers

LOC   Library of Congress

    AGP   Arthur Goldberg Papers   HVP   Hoyt S. Vandenberg Papers

    CAP   Carl W. Ackerman Papers   MDP   Martha Dodd Papers

    GMP   George C. Marshall Papers   RMP   Robert McNamara Papers

    HBP   Henry Brandon Papers   WDP   William Edward Dodd Papers

MHI   U.S. Army Military History Institute, Army War College

    WJDP   William J. Donovan Papers

NA   National Archives and Records Administration

    M1656   SSU Intelligence Reports (for Germany and Soviet Union) 1945–1946

    RG59   General Records of the Department of State, 1763–2002

    RG65   Records of the Federal Bureau of Investigation, 1896–2008

    RG218   Records of the U.S. Joint Chiefs of Staff

    RG226   Records of the Office of Strategic Services

        A-3304   Original Microfilm of Washington Director's Office

        M1623   History of the London Office of the OSS

        M1642   Microfilm of Washington Director's Office Administrative
            Files

    RG263   Records of the CIA

        GP   Records of the Grombach Organization ("the Pond")

        TTP   Thomas Troy Papers

    RG319   Records of Army Staff, 1903–2009

    RG331   Records of Allied Operational and Occupation Headquarters, World
        War II

    T-77   Records of Headquarters, German Armed Forces Command

    T-78   Records of the OKH, German Army High Command

    T-84   Miscellaneous German Records Collection

T-120	Records from the German Foreign Office Received from the Department of State
T-175	Records of the SS and Chief of the German Police
T-1745	Records of the Reich Leader of the SS and Chief of German Police

NAUK   The National Archives United Kingdom

HS	Records of the Special Operations Executive
KV	Records of the Security Service

NCM   National Cryptologic Museum Archives, David Kahn Collection

NPRC   National Personnel Records Center

RHNR	Richard M. Helms Navy Personnel Records
WCNR	William J. Casey Navy Personnel Records

NSA   National Security Archive

ADP	Allen Dulles Papers
RED	Russian and Eastern European Archive Database

PU   Public Policy Papers, Department of Rare Books and Special Collections, Princeton University Library

AWDP	Allen W. Dulles Papers	HAP	Hamilton Fish Armstrong Papers
AWDD	Allen Dulles Digital Files	WECP	William E. Colby Papers

UA   Archives of University at Albany-SUNY, Joseph Persico Papers

UD   University of Delaware Library Special Collections, George S. Messersmith Papers

WHS   Wisconsin Historical Society

LLP	Louis P. Lochner Papers	SSP	Sigrid Schultz Papers

PERSONAL COLLECTIONS

BCS	Bernadette Casey Smith	TCB	Theodore C. Barreaux
CBC	Clive Bassett	PC	Paul Colby
GMH	Gates McGarrah Helms	SS	Sim Smiley

REMINISCENCES

Abbreviations are used for the oral history collections. For example, the reminiscences of Jane Smith in the Columbia University Oral History Research Office Collection will be listed in the source notes as "Smith, COH, page number."

COH: Columbia University Oral History Research Office Collection. Reminiscences of Mary Bancroft, Richard M. Bissell Jr., Leo Cherne, Clarence Douglas Dillon, Eleanor Lansing Dulles, Eleanor Lansing Dulles (Eisenhower Administration series), Robert H. Jackson, James P. Killian, Arthur C. Lundahl, and Jane Smith.

DOHP: The John Foster Dulles Oral History Project, Princeton University Library. Reminiscences of Allen Dulles, Eleanor Lansing Dulles, and Margaret Dulles Edwards.

FAOH: The Foreign Affairs Oral History Collection of the Association for Diplomatic Studies and Training, American Memory from the Library of Congress, http:// memory.loc.gov. Interview with Morton A. Bach.

OHP: OSS Oral History Project, National Archives and Records Administration, Record Group 263, Records of the CIA. Interviews with Raymond Brittenham, David Crockett, Richard Helms, Charles P. Kindleberger, Gertrude Legendre, Fritz P. Molden, Eloise Page, Arthur Schlesinger Jr., and John K. Singlaub.

OTHER ABBREVIATIONS USED

AG	Arthur Goldberg	JEH	J. Edgar Hoover
AMD	Allen Macy Dulles	JFD	John Foster Dulles
AWD	Allen Welsh Dulles	JWF	John Watson Foster
B	Box for an entry or collection	OCD	O. C. "Ole" Doering
COI	Coordinator of Information	OSS	Office of Strategic Services
CTD	Clover Todd Dulles	P	Part in a collection
DDE	Dwight David Eisenhower	R	Microfilm reel
DKEB	David K. E. Bruce	RG	Record Group for a collection
E	Entry for a collection	RL	Robert Lansing
EFD	Edith Foster Dulles	RMH	Richard M. Helms
FDR	Franklin Delano Roosevelt	S	Series in a collection
FLM	Ferdinand L. Mayer	SHAEF	Supreme Headquarters Allied
FR	Frame on a microfilm reel		Expeditionary Force
FW	Frank Wisner	SI	Secret Intelligence
GG	Gero von Schulze-Gaevernitz	SKC	Sophia Kurz Casey
GM	Gates McGarrah	SOE	Special Operations Executive
GSM	George S. Messersmith	SSU	Strategic Services Unit
HHH	Herman Henry Helms	WEC	William Egan Colby
HSG	Hugh S. Gibson	WJC	William Joseph Casey
HST	Harry S. Truman	WJD	William Joseph Donovan
JCS	Joint Chiefs of Staff	WS	Whitney Shepardson

AUTHOR INTERVIEWS

In the source notes only the last name of the interviewee will be listed followed by the date of the interview. For example, author interview with Joan Dulles Tally on August 4, 2012, will appear in the source notes as Tally, Aug. 4, 2012.

Theodore C. Barreaux, Clive Bassett, Russell K. Bond Sr., Yvonne Lelong Bordelon, Barbara Colby, Carl Colby, John Colby, Paul Colby, Sally Shelton Colby, Edward Cox, Kenneth E. deGraffenreid, Joseph DeTrani, Norman "Dick" Franklin, Christine Colby Giraudo, Gates Hawn, Alberta Helms, Cynthia Helms, Dennis Helms, Gates McGarrah Helms, Bill Hood, Cordelia Hood, Fisher Howe, Gregory Hutchison, Will Irwin, Jack Jolis, James Albert Jolis, Paul Jolis, Robert Kehoe, Rolfe Kingsley, John Lenczowski, Elizabeth McIntosh, Hugh Montgomery, Betty S. Murphy, Thomas Polgar, Peter Riddleberger, Ginni Lelong Sears, Peter Sichel, John Singlaub, Bernadette Casey Smith, Owen Smith, Stanley Sporkin, Joan Dulles Talley, William J. vanden Heuvel, Jenonne Walker, and Frank G. Wisner.

BOOKS, PERIODICALS, DISSERTATIONS, AND GOVERNMENT REPORTS

A work's full citation is given here. In the source notes it will appear as second reference.

Alsop, Stewart, and Thomas Braden. *Sub Rosa: The OSS and American Espionage.* New York: Harcourt, Brace, 1964.

Ambrose, Stephen E. *Band of Brothers: E Company, 506th Regiment, 101st Airborne from Normandy to Hitler's Eagle's Nest.* New York: Simon & Schuster, 1992.

Andrade, Dale, and James H. Willbanks. "CORDS/Phoenix: Counterinsurgency Lessons from Vietnam for the Future." *Military Review,* March–April 2007, pp. 9–23.

Andrew, Christopher, and Vasili Mitrokhin. *The Sword and the Shield: The Mitrokhin Archive and the Secret History of the KGB.* New York: Basic Books, 1999.

Atkinson, Rick. *An Army at Dawn: The War in North Africa, 1942–1943.* New York: Henry Holt, 2002.

———. *The Guns at Last Light: The War in Western Europe, 1944–1945.* New York: Henry Holt, 2013.

Axtell, James. *The Making of Princeton University: From Woodrow Wilson to the Present.* Princeton: Princeton University Press, 2006.

Bancroft, Mary. *Autobiography of a Spy: Debutante, Writer, Confidante, Secret Agent. The True Story of Her Extraordinary Life.* New York: William Morrow, 1983.

Banks, Charles Edward. *The Winthrop Fleet of 1630.* Baltimore: Genealogical Publishing Co., 1976.

Beavan, Colin. *Operation Jedburgh: D-Day and America's First Shadow War*. New York: Penguin, 2006.

Berg, A. Scott. *Wilson*. New York: Putnam, 2013.

Bessel, Richard. *Germany 1945: From War to Peace*. New York: Harper Perennial, 2009.

Bordo, Michael D., Alan M. Taylor, and Jeffrey G. Williamson, eds. *Globalization in Historical Perspective*. Chicago: University of Chicago Press, 2003.

Bradsher, Greg. "A Time to Act: The Beginning of the Fritz Kolbe Story, 1900–1943." *Prologue: Quarterly of the National Archives* 34, no. 1 (Spring 2002).

Brown, Anthony Cave. *The Last Hero: Wild Bill Donovan*. New York: Vintage, 1982.

Burke's Genealogical and Heraldic History of the Landed Gentry. London: Burke's Peerage, 1939.

Casey, William J. "The Clandestine War in Europe (1942–1945)." *Studies in Intelligence*, Spring 1981, pp. 1–7.

———. "OSS: Lessons for Today." *Studies in Intelligence*, Winter 1986, pp. 55–66.

———. *The Secret War Against Hitler*. Washington, D.C.: Regnery, 1988.

Chalou, George C., ed. *The Secret War: The Office of Strategic Services in World War II*. Washington, D.C.: National Archives and Records Administration, 1992.

Chernow, Ron. *The House of Morgan: An American Banking Dynasty and the Rise of Modern Finance*. New York: Atlantic Monthly Press, 1990.

Clay, General Lucius D. *Decision in Germany*. New York: Doubleday, 1950.

Colby, Elbridge. *Army Talk: A Familiar Dictionary of Soldier Speech*. Princeton: Princeton University Press, 1942.

———. "The Battle for Thompson's Point." *The George Washington University Magazine*, August 1969, pp. 10–13.

———. *English Catholic Poets: Chaucer to Dryden*. Milwaukee: Bruce Publishing, 1936.

———. *Theodore Winthrop*. New Haven: College & University Press, 1965.

Colby, James. *History of the Colby Family with Genealogical Tables*. Brockton, Mass., 1895.

Colby, William, with Peter Forbath, *Honorable Men: My Life in the CIA*. New York: Simon & Schuster, 1978.

Colby, William, with James McCarger. *Lost Victory: A Firsthand Account of America's Sixteen-Year Involvement in Vietnam*. New York: Contemporary Books, 1989.

Colby, William. "OSS Operations in Norway: Skis and Daggers." Center for the Study of Intelligence, https://www.cia.gov/library/center-for-the-study-of-intelligence.

Colvin, Ian, ed. *Colonel Henri's Story: The War Memoirs of Hugo Bleicher, Former German Secret Agent*. London: William Kimber, 1954.

Cookridge, E. H. *Set Europe Ablaze: The Inside Story of Special Operations Executive—Churchill's Daring Plan to Defeat Germany Through Sabotage, Espionage, and Subversion*. New York: Thomas Y. Crowell, 1967.

Crane, Conrad C. *Bombs, Cities, and Civilians: American Airpower Strategy in World War II*. Lawrence, Kansas: University Press of Kansas, 1993.

Cruickshank, Charles. *SOE in Scandinavia*. New York: Oxford University Press, 1986.

Delattre, Lucas. *A Spy at the Heart of the Third Reich: The Extraordinary Story of Fritz Kolbe, America's Most Important Spy in World War II*. New York: Grove, 2003.

Donovan, William J. "A Central Intelligence Agency: Foreign Policy Must Be Based on Facts." *Vital Speeches,* May 1946, pp. 446–48.

Dreux, William B. *No Bridges Blown.* Notre Dame, Ind.: University of Notre Dame Press, 1971.

Dulles, Allen. *The Craft of Intelligence.* New York: Harper & Row, 1963.

———. *Germany's Underground: The Anti-Nazi Resistance.* New York: Da Capo, 2000.

———. *The Secret Surrender: The Classic Insider's Account of the Secret Plot to Surrender Northern Italy During WWII.* Guilford, Conn.: Lyons Press, 2006.

Dulles, Eleanor Lansing. *Chances of a Lifetime: A Memoir.* Englewood Cliffs, N.J.: Prentice Hall, 1980.

Dunlop, Richard. *Donovan: America's Master Spy.* New York: Rand McNally, 1982.

Eisenhower, Dwight D. *Crusade in Europe.* New York: Garden City Books, 1948.

Foot, M. R. D. *Resistance.* New York: Granada, 1978.

———. *SOE in France.* London: Whitehall History Publishing, 1966.

Ford, Harold. *William E. Colby: As Director of Central Intelligence, 1973–1976.* Washington, D.C.: CIA History Staff, released August 2011.

Ford, Roger. *Steel from the Sky: The Jedburgh Raiders, France 1944.* London: Weidenfeld & Nicolson, 2004.

Franklin, Dick. *Jedburgh: A Recollection.* Self-published, 1999.

Fuller, Jean Overton. *The German Penetration of SOE: France 1941–1944.* London: William Kimber, 1975.

Gardner, Lloyd C., Arthur Schlesinger Jr., and Hans J. Morgenthau. *The Origins of the Cold War.* Waltham, Mass.: Ginn-Blaisdell, 1970.

Gates, Robert M. *From the Shadows: The Ultimate Insider's Story of Five Presidents and How They Won the Cold War.* New York: Simon & Schuster, 1996.

Gilbert, Martin. *The Second World War: A Complete History.* New York: Henry Holt, 1989.

Gill, Anton. *A Dance Between Flames: Berlin Between the Wars.* New York: Carroll & Graf, 1993.

Gisevius, Hans B. *To the Bitter End: An Insider's Account of the Plot to Kill Hitler, 1933–1944.* New York: Da Capo, 1998.

Gjelsvik, Tore. *Norwegian Resistance, 1940–1945.* London: C. Hurst, 1979.

Grose, Peter. *Gentleman Spy: The Life of Allen Dulles.* New York: Houghton Mifflin, 1994.

Halbrook, Stephen P. *The Swiss and the Nazis: How the Alpine Republic Survived in the Shadow of the Third Reich.* Philadelphia: Casemate, 2010.

Hall, Roger. *You're Stepping on My Cloak and Dagger.* Annapolis, Md.: Naval Institute Press, 1957.

Harding, Steve. *Gray Ghost: The R.M.S. Queen Mary at War.* Missoula, Mont.: Pictorial Histories Publishing, 1982.

Hathaway, Robert, and Russell Jack Smith. *Richard Helms: As Director of Central Intelligence.* Washington, D.C.: Center for the Study of Intelligence, CIA, 1993.

Heimark, Bruce H. *The OSS Norwegian Special Operations Group in World War II.* Westport, Conn.: Praeger, 1994.

Helms, Cynthia. *An Intriguing Life: A Memoir of War, Washington, and Marriage to an American Spymaster*. New York: Rowman & Littlefield, 2013.

Helms, Richard. *A Look over My Shoulder: A Life in the Central Intelligence Agency*. New York: Ballantine, 2003.

Henry, Thomas R. "The White War in Norway." *National Geographic Magazine* 88, no. 5 (November 1945): 617–40.

Hoffmann, Peter. *The History of the German Resistance, 1933–1945*. London: McGill-Queen's University Press, 1996.

Holman, Mary Lovering. *Ancestry of Charles Stinson Pillsbury and John Sargeant Pillsbury, Volume I*. Higginson, 1938.

Hoyt, David W. *The Old Families of Salisbury and Amesbury Massachusetts*. Camden, Maine: Picton Press.

An Index of Ancestor and Roll of Members of the Society of Colonial Wars: The Honor Roll Services of Members of the Society During the World War, 1917–1918. Albany: General Assembly of New York, 1922.

"Interview: William Colby, former director, Central Intelligence Agency." *Special Warfare* 7, no. 2 (April 1994): 40–43.

Irwin, Will. *The Jedburghs: The Secret History of the Allied Special Forces, France 1944*. New York: PublicAffairs, 2005.

Jackson, Julian. *France: The Dark Years, 1940–1944*. New York: Oxford University Press, 2001.

Jackson, Wayne G. *Allen Welsh Dulles as Director of Central Intelligence, 26 February 1953–29 November 1961, Volume 1*. Washington, D.C.: Historical Staff, Central Intelligence Agency, July 1973.

Jacobsen, Annie. *Operation Paperclip: The Secret Intelligence Program That Brought Nazi Scientists to America*. New York: Little, Brown, 2014.

Jeffery, Keith. *MI6: The History of the Secret Intelligence Service, 1909–1949*. New York: Bloomsbury, 2010.

Jolis, Albert. *A Clutch of Reds and Diamonds: A Twentieth Century Odyssey*. New York: Columbia University Press, 1996.

Kahn, David. *Hitler's Spies: German Military Intelligence in World War II*. New York: Macmillan, 1978.

Keegan, John. *The Second World War*. New York: Viking, 1989.

Kehoe, Robert R. "Jed Team Frederick 1944: An Allied Team with the French Resistance." *Studies in Intelligence*, 1997, pp. 15–50.

Kelly, Richard M. "The NORSO Mission." *Bluebook: A Magazine of Adventure for Men, by Men*, January 1947, pp. 34–43.

Kinzer, Stephen. *The Brothers: John Foster Dulles, Allen Dulles, and Their Secret Cold War*. New York: Henry Holt, 2013.

Kladstrup, Don, and Petie Kladstrup. *Wine and War: The French, the Nazis, and the Battle for France's Greatest Treasure*. New York: Broadway, 2001.

Ladd, Brian. *The Ghosts of Berlin: Confronting German History in the Urban Setting*. Chicago: University of Chicago Press, 1997.

Lankford, Nelson D. *The Last American Diplomat: The Biography of Ambassador David K. E. Bruce*. New York: Little, Brown, 1996.

———. *OSS Against the Reich: The World War II Diaries of Colonel David K. E. Bruce*. Kent, Ohio: Kent State University Press, 1991.

Larsen, Karen. *A History of Norway*. Princeton: Princeton University Press, 1948.

Larson, Erik. *In the Garden of Beasts: Love, Terror, and an American Family in Hitler's Berlin*. New York: Crown, 2011.

Laurie, Clayton D. "Black Games, Subversion, and Dirty Tricks: The OSS Morale Operations Branch in Europe, 1943–1945." *Prologue: Quarterly of the National Archives* 25, no. 3, (Fall 1993): 259–71.

Lebor, Adam. *Tower of Basel: The Shadowy History of the Secret Bank That Runs the World*. New York: PublicAffairs, 2013.

Lewis, S. J. *Jedburgh Team Operations in Support of the 12th Army Group, August 1944*. Fort Leavenworth, Kans.: Combat Studies Institute, 1991.

von Lingen, Kerstin. *Allen Dulles, the OSS, and Nazi War Criminals: The Dynamics of Selective Prosecution*. New York: Cambridge University Press, 2013.

Lochner, Louis P., ed. *The Goebbels Diaries*. New York: Charter, 1948.

Longerich, Peter. *Heinrich Himmler*. New York: Oxford University Press, 2012.

Lowe, Keith. *Savage Continent: Europe in the Aftermath of Word War II*. New York: St. Martin's, 2012.

Luck, J. Murray. *History of Switzerland: The First Hundred Thousand Years: Before the Beginnings to the Days of the Present*. Palo Alto, Calif.: Society for the Promotion of Scholarship, 1985.

Ludewig, Joachim. *Rückzug: The German Retreat from France, 1944*. Lexington: University Press of Kentucky, 2012.

MacDonogh, Giles. *After the Reich: The Brutal History of Allied Occupation*. New York: Basic Books, 2007.

Mauch, Christoff. *The Shadow War Against Hitler: The Covert Operations of America's Wartime Secret Intelligence Service*. New York: Columbia University Press, 1999.

Merrill, Joseph. *History of Amesbury*. Haverhill, Mass.: Press of Franklin P. Stiles, 1880.

Meyer, Herbert E. *Scouting the Future: The Public Speeches of William J. Casey*. Washington, D.C.: Regnery, 1989.

Molden, Fritz. *Exploding Star: A Young Austrian Against Hitler*. New York: William Morrow, 1978.

Montague, Ludwell Lee. *General Walter Bedell Smith as Director of Central Intelligence: October 1950–February 1953*. University Park: Pennsylvania State University Press, 1992.

Morgan, Edward P. "The Spy the Nazis Missed." *True*, July 1950, pp. 21–22, 98–108.

Mosley, Leonard. *Dulles: A Biography of Eleanor, Allen, and John Foster Dulles and Their Family Network*. New York: Dial, 1978.

Moyar, Mark. *Phoenix and the Birds of Prey: the CIA's Secret Campaign to Destroy the Viet Cong*. Annapolis, Md.: Naval Institute Press, 1997.

Mueller, Michael. *Canaris: The Life and Death of Hitler's Spymaster*. Annapolis, Md.: Naval Institute Press, 2007.

Murphy, David E., Sergei A. Kondrashev, and George Bailey. *Battle Ground Berlin: CIA vs. KGB in the Cold War*. New Haven: Yale University Press, 1997.

Nicholas, Lynn H. *The Rape of Europa: The Fate of Europe's Treasures in the Third Reich and the Second World War*. New York: Vintage, 1995.

O'Donnell, Patrick K. *Operatives, Spies, and Saboteurs: The Unknown Story of the Men and Women of WWII's OSS*. New York: Free Press, 2004.

The Overseas Targets: War Reports of the OSS. Volume 2. New York: Walker, 1976.

Parnell, Ben. *Carpetbaggers: America's Secret War in Europe*. Austin, Texas: Eakin Press, 1987.

Persico, Joseph E. *Casey: The Lives and Secrets of William J. Casey: From the OSS to the CIA*. New York: Viking, 1990.

———. *Piercing the Reich: The Penetration of Nazi Germany by American Secret Agents During World War II*. New York: Barnes & Noble Books, 1979.

———. *Roosevelt's Secret War: FDR and World War II Espionage*. New York: Random House, 2001.

Petersen, Neal H. *From Hitler's Doorstep: The Wartime Intelligence Reports of Allen Dulles, 1942–1945*. University Park: Pennsylvania State University Press, 1996.

Petropoulus, Jonathan. "Co-Opting Nazi Germany: Neutrality in Europe During World War II." *Dimensions: A Journal of Holocaust Studies*. Anti-Defamation League's Braun Holocaust Institute, http://www.adl.org/braun/dim_14_1_neutrality_europe.asp.

Phillips, David Atlee. *The Night Watch*. New York: Atheneum, 1977.

Pierce, Robert M. "The Airborne Field Artillery: From Inception to Combat Operations." Master of Military Art and Science thesis, Fort Leavenworth, Kansas, 2004.

Powers, Thomas. *The Man Who Kept the Secrets: Richard Helms and the CIA*. New York: Alfred A. Knopf, 1979.

Prados, John. *Lost Crusader: The Secret Wars of CIA Director William Colby*. New York: Oxford University Press, 2003.

The Probate Records of Essex County, Massachusetts: Volume I, 1635–1664. Salem, Mass.: Essex Institute, 1916.

Province, Charles M. *Patton's Third Army: A Daily Combat Diary*. New York: Hippocrene Books, 1992.

Pryser, Tore. *USAs Hemmelige Agenter: Den Amerikanske Etterretningstjenesten OSS I Norden under Andre Verdenskrig*. Norway: Universitetsforlaget, 2010.

Read, Anthony, and David Fisher. *Berlin: The Biography of a City*. London: Hutchinson, 1994.

———. *The Fall of Berlin*. New York: Norton, 1992.

Richie, Alexandra. *Faust's Metropolis: A History of Berlin*. New York: Carroll & Graf, 1998.

Robarge, David S. "Overview." *A Life in Intelligence: The Richard Helms Collection*, CIA Publication.

Rosenau, William, and Austin Long. "The Phoenix Program and Contemporary Counterinsurgency. Santa Monica, Calif.: RAND Corp., 2009.

Ruffner, Kevin Conley. "You Are Never Going to Be Able to Run an Intelligence Unit: SSU Confronts the Black Market in Berlin," *Journal of Intelligence History*, 2 (Winter 2002), pp. 1–20.

Salter, Michael. *Nazi War Crimes, U.S. Intelligence and Selective Prosecution at Nuremberg*. New York: Routledge-Cavendish, 2007.

Schlesinger, Andrew, and Stephen Schlesinger. *Journals: 1952–2000, Arthur M. Schlesinger, Jr.* New York: Penguin, 2007.

Schweizer, Peter. *Reagan's War: The Epic Story of His Forty-Year Struggle and Final Triumph over Communism*. New York: Anchor, 2002.

Sheehan, Neil. *A Bright Shining Lie: John Paul Vann and America in Vietnam*. New York: Random House, 1988.

Shirer, William L. *Berlin Diary*. New York: Alfred A. Knopf, 1941.

Sichel, Peter. Draft of a manuscript provided to the author.

Silverman, Jeff. "Spies in the Clubhouse." *2011 U.S. Open: The Official Magazine of the Championship*, United States Golf Association, pp. 79–82.

Singlaub, John K., with Malcolm McConnell. *Hazardous Duty: An American Soldier in the Twentieth Century*. New York: Summit, 1991.

Smith, Bradley F. *The Shadow Warriors: O.S.S. and the Origins of the C.I.A.* New York: Basic Books, 1983.

Smith, Bradley F., and Elena Agarossi. *Operation Sunrise: The Secret Surrender*. New York: Basic Books, 1979.

Smith, Richard Harris. *OSS: The Secret History of America's First Central Intelligence Agency*. Guilford, Conn.: Lyons Press, 1972.

Solhjell, Kåre Olav, and Friedrich Traphagen. *Fra Krig Til Fred: Fokus på Snåsa Nord-Trøndelag*. Norway: Boksima, 2001.

Srodes, James. *Allen Dulles: Master of Spies*. Washington, D.C.: Regnery, 1999.

Stebenne, David L. *Arthur J. Goldberg: New Deal Liberal*. New York: Oxford, 1996.

Stein, Jeff. *A Murder in Wartime: The Untold Spy Story That Changed the Course of the Vietnam War*. New York: St. Martin's, 1992.

Sudoplatov, Pavel, and Anatoli Sudoplatov, with Jerrod L. and Leona P. Schecter. *Special Tasks: The Memoirs of an Unwanted Witness—A Soviet Spymaster*. New York: Little, Brown, 1994.

Thomas, Evan. *The Very Best Men: The Daring Early Years of the CIA*. New York: Simon & Schuster, 2006.

Trevor-Roper, Hugh, ed. *Final Entries 1945: The Diaries of Joseph Goebbels*. New York: Putnam, 1978.

Van Young, Sayre. *London's War: A Traveler's Guide to World War II*. Berkeley: Ulysses Press, 2004.

Waller, Douglas. *Wild Bill Donovan: The Spymaster Who Created the OSS and Modern American Espionage*. New York: Free Press, 2011.

War Report of the O.S.S. (Office of Strategic Services). New York: Walker, 1976.

Warner, Michael. "The Office of Strategic Services: America's First Intelligence Agency." Washington, D.C.: Center for the Study of Intelligence, CIA History Staff, 2000.

———. "Reading the Riot Act: The Schlesinger Report, 1971." *Intelligence and National Security.* Vol. 24, No. 3, June 2009, pp. 387–417.

Wehrle, Edmund F. *Catoctin Mountain Park: A Historic Study.* National Park Service, http://www.nps.gov/history/history/online_books/cato/hrs.htm.

Weinberg, Gerhard L. *A World at Arms: A Global History of World War II.* New York: Cambridge University Press, 2005.

Weiner, Tim. *Legacy of Ashes: The History of the CIA.* New York: Doubleday, 2007.

Weinstein, Allen, and Alexander Vassiliev. *The Haunted Wood: Soviet Espionage in America—The Stalin Era.* New York: Modern Library, 1999.

Weis, Frederick Lewis. *The Colby Family in Early America: Early Generations of the Descendants of Anthony Colby of Boston, Cambridge, Salisbury and Amesbury, Massachusetts, 1595–1661.* Concord, Mass., 1970.

Winks, Robin W. *Cloak and Gown: Scholars in the Secret War, 1939–1961.* New Haven: Yale University Press, 1987.

Woods, Randall B. *Shadow Warrior: William Egan Colby and the CIA.* New York: Basic Books, 2013.

Woodward, Bob. *Veil: The Secret Wars of the CIA, 1981–1987.* New York: Simon & Schuster, 1987.

Ziegler, Phillip. *London at War.* New York: Alfred A. Knopf, 1995.

Ziemke, Earl F. *The U.S. Army in the Occupation of Germany, 1944–1946.* Washington, D.C.: Center of Military History United States Army, 1990.

SOURCE NOTES

In many instances a source note covers several paragraphs. Each source note lists material cited up to the previous source note. Some box numbers may have changed as archivists reconfigure their collections.

PROLOGUE

2 *"a role that was"*: "Funeral Services Are Held in Capital for Gen. Donovan," *Buffalo Evening News*, Feb. 11, 1959; excerpts from the sermon delivered by the Right Rev. John K. Cartwright, Feb. 11, 1959, Unnumbered Box, "World War I. Political Campaigns, Etc." WJDP, MHI; Cathedral of St. Matthew the Apostle website, http:www.stmatthews cathedral.org; "Gen. William J. Donovan," *Buffalo Evening News*, Feb. 9, 1959; Jane Smith, COH, p. 48; Dunlop, p. 4; Brown, p. 834.

3 *he erected:* Instructions for honorary pallbearers, WJD file, WSP, FDRL; Grose, pp. 325–26; Mary Bancroft interview July 16, 1980, pp. 25–26, Unnumbered Box, "Interviews—Bancroft to Sherwood 1945—undated," WJDP, MHI; Talley, Aug. 4, 2012; Bancroft, COH, pp. 236, 242–43, 249, 252; Lundahl, COH, p. 490; "The Voyager," B: 2. AWDP, PU; Sichel, March 11, 2013; Molden, pp. 177–78; Bancroft, p. 133; Kingsley, Jan. 1, 2008; Howe, Dec. 20, 2007, and March 12, 2012.

4 *character for life:* "William J. Donovan and the National Interest," by Allen W. Dulles, *Studies in Intelligence*, Summer 1959, B: 10, E: 27, RG263, NA; Grose, pp. 245–47, 409, 484, 490.

4 *often ineffective:* "Associates Gather at CIA to Mourn Donovan," *Buffalo Evening News*, Feb. 12, 1959; Powers, pp. 38–39, 140; Cynthia Helms, July 18, 2012.

5 *bedtime neared:* Montgomery, July 17, 2012; McIntosh, July 12, 2012; Howe, July 12, 2012; Dennis Helms, Aug. 19, 2012; Powers, pp. 2, 24; Cynthia Helms, pp. 96–98; Robarge, p. 18.

6 *be a spy:* Hawn, Aug. 18, 2012; Alberta Helms, July 18, 2012; Cynthia Helms, pp. 15, 96–98; Dennis Helms, Aug. 19, 2012. Richard Helms, OHP, pp. 11–12, 28–34; Cynthia Helms, July 18, 2012; Powers, p. 54.

6 *in the margins:* Persico, *Casey*, p. 99; Bernadette Casey Smith, Aug. 24, 2012; Montgomery, July 17, 2012; Page, OHP, p. 27.

7 *"than I could":* Bernadette Casey Smith, Aug. 24, 2012; "How to Read a Book," WJC/bsm, Sept. 18, 1982, TCB; Sporkin, Oct. 12, 2012; Barreaux, Aug. 6, 2012; Meyer, p. 3; James Jolis, Sept. 17, 2012; Jack Jolis, Sept. 20, 2012; Sporkin, Oct. 12, 2012; Howe, Dec. 20, 2007, and July 12, 2012.

7 *of his life:* Persico, *Casey*, p. 86; DeTrani, Nov. 9, 2012; "The Clandestine War in Europe," *Studies in Intelligence,* Spring 1981, p. 1, B: 7, E: 27, RG263, NA; Barreaux, Aug. 6, 2012.

8 *Donovan had died:* William Colby, *Lost Victory*, pp. 19–22, 30, 52; William Colby, *Honorable Men*, pp. 142, 146, 148–50; Powers, pp. 66, 165; John Colby, July 30, 2012; Dunlop, p. 4.

9 *in his mind:* Barbara Colby, July 16, 2012; "Intelligence in the 1980s," by William E. Colby, *Studies in Intelligence,* Summer 1981, B: 8, E: 27, RG263, NA; Carl Colby, July 16, 2012; Powers, p. 9; Paul Colby, Sept. 9, 2012; Cox, Sept. 22, 2012.

10 *big enough for two:* John Colby, July 30, 2012; Phillips, pp. 244, 279–80; Sally Shelton Colby, July 27, 2012; Paul Colby, Sept. 9, 2012; Cox, Sept. 22, 2012; John Colby, July 30, 2012; Carl Colby, July 16, 2012; Howe, July 12, 2012.

11 *done before:* Dennis Helms, Aug. 19, 2012; Gates Helms, Aug. 18, 2012; Talley, July 14, 2012; Sporkin, Oct. 12, 2012; Bernadette Casey Smith, Aug. 24, 2012; Meyer, pp. 296–97; Barbara Colby, July 16, 2012; Sally Shelton Colby, July 27, 2012; John Colby, July 30, 2012; Carl Colby, July 16, 2012.

CHAPTER 1: ALLEN WELSH DULLES

15 *recalled Eleanor:* Eleanor Dulles, DOHP, pp. 9, 35; Edwards, DOHP, pp. 34, 60; "Mrs. Allen Dulles Expires in Auburn," *The Post Standard,* June 9, 1941; Srodes, pp. 9–10; Grose, p. 9; Eleanor Dulles, pp. 8–10; Mosley, pp. 13–17.

16 *in 1915:* "John Watson Foster: An Appreciation," B: 120, AWDP, PU; Grose, pp. 5–6; Eleanor Dulles, pp. 2–4, 11; Srodes, pp. 21, 42, 46–47; Mosley, pp. 20, 35–38.

17 *message poorly:* Edwards, DOHP, pp. 15, 17; Eleanor Dulles, DOHP, pp. 3, 40; "Rev. Allen Macy Dulles, D.D.," B: 120, "Notes from Washington," *Our Paper,* October 1887, B: 18, AWDP, PU; Eleanor Dulles, pp. 8–9, 19–25; Srodes, pp. 10–16; Grose, pp. 5–9.

17 *overpowering rage:* Talley, July 28, 2012; Bancroft, COH, p. 162; Mosley, p. 21; Eleanor Dulles, p. 15; Bancroft, p. 139; Grose, p. 13.

18 *foreign affairs:* Eleanor Dulles, DOHP, p. 36; Edwards, DOHP, p. 30; Description of Henderson Harbor, Foreword for draft written by AWD, B: 80, AWDP, PU; Eleanor Dulles, pp. 2–5, 7, 12; Grose, pp. 12–15; Talley, July 28, 2012.

19 *was "infantile": The Boer War: A History* by Allen Welsh Dulles, and original manuscript, B: 63, John Welsh Dulles letter to AWD April 5, 1902, B: 23, EFD undated letter to AWD, B: 19, JFD letter to AWD March 22, 1902, B: 19, "To Help the Boers," *Washington Post,* April 6, 1902, AMD letter to AWD March 21, 1902, Letter from the private secretary to the Speaker of the House to JWF April 17, 1902, B: 63, AWDP, PU; Grose, pp. 13–14; Eleanor Dulles, p. 15; Eleanor Dulles, DOHP, pp. 106–7; Mosley, pp. 15–17.

20 *class of ninety-four:* Edwards, DOHP, p. 20; Eleanor Dulles, DOHP, pp. 22, 36; "Rev. Allen

Macy Dulles, D.D.," B: 120, École Alsacienne report card of AWD, B: 112, AWDP, PU; Allen Dulles, DOHP, pp. 3–4; Grose, pp. 10, 15–17; Eleanor Dulles, p. 4; Axtel, pp. 1–3, 35, 50–59, 71–73, 112; Berg, pp. 196–97; FBI confidential report on Allen Welsh Dulles, Jan. 14, 1941, NK File No. 118–1654, FBI; Srodes, pp. 34–35; Mosley, pp. 26, 32.

20 *Ewing Christian College:* Henry Brandon interview with AWD, B: 16, HBP, LOC; Foreword for draft written by AWD, B: 80, AWD letter to AMD May 24, 1914, B: 18, AWD letters to EFD June 20 and July 2, 12, 21, 24, and 28, 1914, B: 19, AWDP, PU.

21 *another week:* AWD letters to EFD July 27 and Oct. 19, 1914, AWD letters to EFD Aug. 13 and Nov. 20 and 24, 1914, B: 19, AWDP, PU.

23 *on May 22:* AWD letters to EFD Aug. 2 and 13, 1914, March 16 and 30, April 9, May 13, June 20, July 5–20 and July 18, 1915, B: 19, AWD letters to JWF Jan. 8, 1915, May 17, 1915, B: 26, AWD letter to AMD Feb. 26, 1916, B: 18, Foreword for draft written by AWD, B: 80, AWDP, PU; Grose, pp. 19–20; Srodes, p. 50.

CHAPTER 2: WILLIAM JOSEPH CASEY

26 *nearby Corona:* Waller, pp. 9–12; Application for Employment and Personal History Statement for William Joseph Casey, B: 112, E: 224, RG226, NA; Persico, *Casey*, pp. 10–13, 17; Bernadette Casey Smith, Aug. 24, 2012; Certificate of Baptism at Church of Our Lady of Sorrows for WJC, WCNR, NPRC; Certificate and Record of Birth for WJC, B: 460, WJCP, HIA.

27 *Saturday afternoons:* Application for Employment and Personal History Statement for WJC, B: 112, E: 224, RG226, NA; Persico, *Casey*, pp. 10–17; Bernadette Casey Smith, Aug. 24, 2012.

28 *other students:* Application for Employment and Personal History Statement for William Joseph Casey, B: 112, E: 224, RG226, NA; Persico, *Casey*, pp. 14–18, 25–26; Bernadette Casey Smith, Aug. 24, 2012; Report of Physical Exam March 17, 1943, for WJC, WCNR, NPRC; Barreaux, Aug. 6, 2012.

28 *he admitted:* WJC letter to SKC circa 1934, BCS; WJC's Application for Commission or Warrant, U.S. Naval Reserve, Fordham University college transcript for WJC, WCNR, NPRC; Persico, *Casey*, pp. 22–24.

29 *batch of liquor:* Application for Employment and Personal History Statement for William Joseph Casey, B: 112, E: 224, RG226, NA; Persico, *Casey*, pp. 26–27; Bernadette Casey and Owen Smith, Aug. 24, 2012; WJC letter to SKC Oct. 2, 1933, BCS.

29 *"can imagine":* WJC letters to SKC April 3, Oct. 2 and 3, 1933, and circa 1934, and Dec. 12, 1936, BCS; Persico, *Casey*, pp. 26–30; Bernadette Casey Smith, Aug. 24, 2012.

30 *to Sophia:* Fordham University college transcript for WJC, WCNR, NPRC; WJC letters to SKC Oct. 2, 1933, and circa 1934, BCS; Persico, *Casey*, pp. 23–24, 29, 31.

32 *welfare department:* WJC letters to SKC Sept. 26 and 29, Oct. 7, 1934, Jan. 1 and 11, Feb. 11, March 30, and May 6, 1935, BCS; Persico, *Casey*, pp. 36–37; Catholic University of America transcript for WJC, WCNR, NPRC.

33 *more than two years:* Persico, *Casey*, pp. 37–39; WJC's Application for Commission or Warrant, U.S. Naval Reserve, and Medical Questionnaire for WJC, St. John's University

School of Law transcript for WJC, WCNR, NPRC; Bernadette Casey Smith, Aug. 24, 2012; Application for Employment and Personal History Statement for WJC, B: 112, E: 224, RG226, NA.

34 *"the election"*: Application for Employment and Personal History Statement for WJC, B: 112, E: 224, RG226, NA; Persico, *Casey*, pp. 40–45; Cherne, pp. 1, 369–71, COH; Meyer, pp. 1–2, 280; WJC's Application for Commission or Warrant, U.S. Naval Reserve, WCNR, NPRC.

34 *pushing paper*: Application for Employment and Personal History Statement for WJC, B: 112, E: 224, RG226, NA; Casey, *The Secret War Against Hitler*, pp. 3–4; Meyer, pp. 3–4; Persico, *Casey*, p. 46; Atkinson, *An Army at Dawn*, p. 8.

CHAPTER 3: RICHARD MCGARRAH HELMS

35 *him "Governor"*: Autobiographical material on Richard McGarrah Helms, P: 4, B: 1, Helms Biography Material, P: 3, S: 7, B: 7, RHP, GU; "Gates McGarrah, Famed Banker, Dies in New York," *Chicago Tribune*, Nov. 11, 1940; "Magnificent McGarrah," *Time*, Feb. 3, 1930, p. 25; RMH Application for Commission in U.S. Naval Reserve March 12, 1942, RHNR, NPRC; Cynthia Helms, July 18, 2012; Hawn, Aug. 18, 2012.

36 *his funeral*: Gates Helms, Aug. 18, 2012; Richard Helms, p. 2, OHP; Cynthia Helms, July 18, 2012; Hawn, Aug. 19, 2012; Dennis Helms, Aug. 19, 2012; "The (Really) Quiet American," *Washington Post*, May 20, 1973, p. C2; HHH letters to RMH Friday undated, June 25, 1930, July 7, 1932, Jan. 7, 1932, P: 1, S: 1, B: 1, RHP, GU.

36 *outside friends*: Gates Helms, Aug. 18, 2012; Dennis Helms, Aug. 19, 2012; Hawn, Aug. 18, 2012; Cynthia Helms, July 18, 2012; Autobiographical Material on Richard Mc-Garrah Helms, P: 4, B: 1, Helms Biography Material, P: 3, S: 7, B: 7, RHP, GU.

37 *father-in-law*: Autobiographical Material on Richard McGarrah Helms, P: 4, B: 1, Helms Biography Material, P: 3, S: 7, B: 7, RHP, GU; Hawn, Aug. 18, 2012; Richard Helms, p. 1, OHP.

37 *team manager*: Helms, *A Look over My Shoulder*, p. 14; Cynthia Helms, July 18, 2012; Hawn, Aug. 18, 2012; RMH Application for Commission in U.S. Naval Reserve March 12, 1942, RHNR, NPRC; Dennis Helms, Aug. 19, 2012; Gates Helms, Aug. 18, 2012.

38 *of his life*: Autobiographical Material on Richard McGarrah Helms, P: 4, B: 1, Helms Biography Material, P: 3, S: 7, B: 7, GM letters to RMH May 20, 1930, P: 3, S: 1, B: 2, May 31, 1932, and Oct. 1, 1931, P: 1, S: 2, B: 4, March 16, 1932, P: 1, S: 2, B: 4, RMH letter to "Wuz," Tuesday undated, P: 3, S: 1, B: 1, Le Rosey report cards for RMH November 1929, May 1930, P: 1, S: 2, B: 4 and P: 1, S: 7, B: 19, RHP, GU; Hawn, Aug. 18, 2012; Dennis Helms, Aug. 19, 2012; Helms, *A Look over My Shoulder*, pp. 14–15; Gates Helms, Aug. 18, 2012; Cynthia Helms, July 18, 2012; Lebor, pp. xviii–xix, 13, 21, 28–34, 38–43; Bordo, pp. 515–25; Chernow, pp. 311–12; RHP, GU.

39 *that fall*: Helms, *A Look over My Shoulder*, p. 15; Cynthia Helms, July 18, 2012; RHM "Qualification and Experience," B: 326, E: 224, RG226, NA; Helms Biography Material, P: 3, S: 7, B: 7, RHP, GU.

40 *situation unprepared*: Cynthia Helms, July 18, 2012; Gates Helms, Aug. 18, 2012; RMH

Application for Commission in U.S. Naval Reserve March 12, 1942, Bureau of Naviga-tion news release material for RMH July 1, 1942, RHNR, NPRC; Helms, *A Look over My Shoulder*, pp. 16–17; Helms Biography Material, P: 3, S: 7, B: 7, RMH letter to Priscilla Taylor Aug. 8, 1994, P: 1, S: 2, B: 9, "Campus Character No. 5: Richard McGarrah Helms," *The Williams Purple Cow*, June 1935, Williams College transcript for RMH, Nov. 5, 1934, P: 1, S: 7, B: 19, "Eight Honorary and 141 B.A. Degrees Given at Graduation," *The Williams Record*, June 17, 1935, p. 1, P: 1, S: 7, B: 19, "Twenty Members of Junior Class Tapped by 'Gargoyle' Society," *The Williams Record*, June 1, 1934, P: 1, S: 11, B: 24, Annual Initiation Banquet: Alpha Theta of Chi Psi 1932, Williams College Class Elections, P: 3, S: 7, B: 8, RHP, GU; Dennis Helms, Aug. 19, 2012.

40 *he thought:* Cynthia Helms, July 18, 2012; Helms, *A Look over My Shoulder*, pp. 16–19; Helms Biography Material, P: 3, S: 7, B: 7, RMH Certificate of Registration Sept. 17, 1935, P: 4, B: 1, RHP, GU.

41 *there was terror:* HF note to RMH undated, P: 1, S: 2, B: 9, RHP, GU; Helms, *A Look over My Shoulder*, pp. 18–19; Cynthia Helms, July 18, 2012; Gill, pp. 4, 90–99, 104–7, 190–93, 214–15, 234–37; Read, *The Fall of Berlin*, pp. 22–23; Read, *Berlin*, p. 206; Richie, pp. 458–60, 474.

42 *"Germania":* Read, *Berlin*, pp. 204–8; Hoffmann, pp. 4–5; Larson, pp. 46–54, 278; Gill, pp. 86, 133–35, 216, 246; Richie, pp. 432–36; Hoffmann, pp. 4–5; Read, *The Fall of Berlin*, pp. 18–21.

43 *covered Hitler:* German General Rental Agreement for apartment at Bayreutherstrasse 34, Helms Approval Notification for the Bayreutherstrasse 34 apartment, Helms press pass for a reception at the Römer, Frankfurt am Main, March 16, 1936, P: 1, S: 2, B: 4, Helms Biography Material, P: 3, S: 7, B: 7, Ed Beattie letter to Doktor Nov. 4, 1939, P: 1, S: 2, B: 4, RMH letter to Gatesy Dec. 30, 1936, P: 3, S: 1, B: 1, RHP, GU; Application for Federal Employment for Frederick Cable Oechsner Nov. 2, 1942, B: 569, E: 224, RG226, NA; Int. 11, 2/4/72, CIA HQ Washington, No. 246, B: 27, UA; American Press Correspondents in Berlin, FR: 229–30, R: 58, LLP, WHS; Ladd, p. 112; Helms, *A Look over My Shoulder*, pp. 18–19; Gates Helms, Aug. 18, 2012.

44 *they despised:* Larson, pp. 53–55, 201; Dennis Helms, Aug. 19, 2012; Wallace Deuel letters to Chief of the Bureau of Navigation March 5 and 7, 1942, William L. Shirer letter to the Chief of the Bureau of Navigation March 9, 1942, RHNR, NPRC; Cynthia Helms, July 18, 2012; Helms, *A Look over My Shoulder*, pp. 18–19; GSM memo to the Secretary of State May 12, 1933, S: II, B: 2, UD; Sigrid Schultz diary entry Dec. 26, 1936, B: 32, SSP, WHS; undated "Society" column item on Berlin Foreign Press Association Ball, B: 2, MDP, In-vitations Extended for Reception for Anglo-American Press and Staff, Wednesday, Jan. 1, 1936, WDP, LOC; Gill, pp. 13, 242–44.

44 *the führer:* Helms, *A Look over My Shoulder*, pp. 19–20; Cynthia Helms, July 18 and 20, 2012; Larson, pp. 7, 12, 21–25, 40–41, 61, 113–19, 125–27, 154, 160–62, 183, 218, 254, 264, 338, 355; Martha Dodd kept a lengthy address and phone book and kept all the in-vitations and calling cards she received in Berlin. Helms's name does not appear in any of them. See B: 1, MDP, LOC.

44 *releasing them:* GSM letter to J. Pierrepont Moffat Jan. 19, 1935, S: II, Box 4, GSM; memos
to the Secretary of State May 22, Aug. 8, and Sept. 1, 1933, S: II, B: 2, Voluntary Report:
German Press, Radio, Film and Theatre as a Political Instrument of the Hitler Government Sept. 8, 1933, S: II, Box 3, UD; Journalists who were ordered to leave Germany
(1933–1937), FR: 220–21, R: 58, LLP, WHS; "Unfair Sensation Mongering," Editorial,
Berliner Börzeitung, Oct. 21, 1936, S: II, B: 7, UD; Larson, pp. 16, 33, 67–69, 94; Richie,
pp. 415, 430; Gill, pp. 239, 252; Shirer, p. 45.

46 *of this man:* Dennis Helms, Aug. 19, 2012; Helms, *A Look over My Shoulder,* pp. 20–21;
Int. 11, 2/4/72, CIA HQ Washington, No. 246, B: 27, UA; "Hitler & Mars, Inc.—Local
Interviewer Sees Fuehrer as Consummate Politician," RMH copy for the *Indianapolis
Times,* March 15, 1938, P: 1, S: 6, B: 17, RHP, GU; Cynthia Helms, July 18, 2012; Shirer,
pp. 48–53; Richie, pp. 26–27.

46 *"monkey sports":* Gill, pp. 208–11, 252–54; Richie, pp. 464–65; Helms, *A Look over My
Shoulder,* p. 26; Dennis Helms, Aug. 19, 2012; Cynthia Helms, July 18, 2012; Ladd, pp.
142–43; Read, *The Fall of Berlin,* pp. 12–13.

48 *toward war:* Helms, *A Look over My Shoulder,* pp. 22–25; Richie, p. 429; Powers, p. 21;
Cynthia Helms, July 18, 2012; Invitation from Dr. O. Dietrich to RMH for lunch with
Hitler, Sept. 12, 1936, P: 1, S: 1, B: 1, RMH notes on Key Quote from Hitler Interview,
B: 2, Helms Biography Material, P: 3, S: 7, B: 7, RHP, GU; Int. 11, 2/4/72, CIA HQ Wash-
ington, No. 246, B: 27, UA.

49 *the* Indianapolis Times: RMH letter to HHH Oct. 19, 1936, Harry Payne Burton letter to
RMH June 8, 1937, Hugh Baillie letter to RMH Nov. 27, 1936, Letter from George to RMH
Dec. 11, 1936, P: 1, S: 2, B: 4, Note from Arnold Gingrich, *Esquire* editor, P: 1, S: 1, B: 9, Wal-
lace Deuel letter to Carroll March 1, 1937, HHH letter to RMH March 13, 1936, P: 1, S: 1, B: 1,
RHP, GU; Helms, *A Look over My Shoulder,* pp. 26–27; Dennis Helms, Aug. 19, 2012.

50 *eligible bachelors:* Helms, *A Look over My Shoulder,* p. 27; Louis D. Young letter to RMH
March 4, 1942, RMH Application for Commission in U.S. Naval Reserve March 12, 1942,
Bureau of Navigation news release material for RMH July 1, 1942, RHNR, NPRC; "The
(Really) Quiet American," *Washington Post,* May 20, 1973, p. C2; Free . . . This Book tells
The Secret of Smartness advertisement, Learn to be *Charming* advertisement, P: 1, S: 2,
B: 9, Earl J. Johnson letter to RMH Feb. 17, 1938, P: 1, S: 2, B: 4, Mark Ferree letter to the
Chief of the Bureau of Navigation, March 2, 1942, P: 4, B: 1, Joseph H. R. Moore letter to
RMH Oct. 24, 1939, RMH letters to Gatesy Wednesday and Monday undated, P: 3, S: 1,
B: 1, RHP, GU; Hawn, Aug. 18, 2012; Cynthia Helms, July 18, 2012.

51 *only grow:* Dennis Helms, Aug. 19 and Sept. 10, 2012; Alberta and Gates Helms, Aug. 18,
2012; Richard Helms, *A Look over My Shoulder,* p. 29; Bureau of Navigation news release
for RMH July 1, 1942, RHNR, NPRC; Hawn, Aug. 18, 2012; Cynthia Helms, *An Intriguing Life,* p. 184; "The (Really) Quiet American," *Washington Post,* May 20, 1973, p. C2;
Earl J. Johnson letter to RMH July 8, 1939, P: 1, S: 2, B: 4, RHP, GU.

CHAPTER 4: WILLIAM EGAN COLBY

53 *in 1660*: Banks, p. 65; *The Probate Records of Essex County*, pp. 407–9; Society of Colonial Wars, Office of the Secretary, Preliminary Application by Paul Lawrence Colby, PC; Holman, pp. 137–38; Weis, pp. 3–4; James Colby, p. 18; Hoyt, p. 103; Paul Colby, Sept. 3, 2012; Barbara Colby, July 16, 2012; John Colby, July 30, 2012.

54 *two daughters*: Society of Colonial Wars, Office of the Secretary, Preliminary Application by Paul Lawrence Colby, PC; Merrill, p. 107; *An Index of Ancestor and Roll of Members of the Society of Colonial Wars*, p. 113; Weis, p. 8; James Colby, pp. 76, 85; Certificate and Record of Death for Charles Edwards Colby, PC; Woods, pp. 9–11, 20; Barbara Colby, July 16 and 30, 2012; William Colby, *Honorable Men*, p. 27.

55 *Colby family*: State of New York Certificate of Birth for Colby Oct. 17, 1891, Return of the Given-Name of an infant that was born Oct. 4, 1891, to Office of Registration for Elbridge Atherton Colby, PC; "Col. Elbridge Colby, 91, Dies; Headed GW Journalism Dept.," *Washington Post*, Dec. 28, 1982, p. B2; William Colby, *Honorable Men*, pp. 27–28; John Colby, July 30, 2012; Barbara Colby, July 16 and 30, 2012; Paul Colby, Sept. 3, 2012; Elbridge Colby—An Appreciation, B: 12, WECP, PU; Marriage License and Certificate, State of Minnesota for Elbridge Colby and Margaret Egan, Nov. 5, 1917, PC; *Burke's Landed Gentry*, pp. 26–27; Woods, pp. 10–12.

55 *Thompsons Point, Vermont*: City of St. Paul Record of Birth for WEC Jan. 4, 1920, PC; William Colby, *Honorable Men*, pp. 26–27; Woods, pp. 12–13; Paul Colby, Sept. 3, 2012; Sally Colby, July 27, 2012; Prados, pp. 19–20; William E. Colby Army personnel card, B: 133, E: 224, RG226, NA; Elbridge Colby—An Appreciation, B: 12, WECP, PU; Elbridge Colby, "The Battle for Thompson's Point," pp. 10–13; Elbridge Colby, *Army Talk*, p. ix; Elbridge Colby, *Theodore Winthrop*, front matter; Elbridge Colby, *English Catholic Poets*, p. ix; Barbara Colby, July 16 and 30, 2012; John Colby, July 30, 2012.

56 *his father*: An Appreciation, B: 12, WECP, PU; John Colby, July 30, 2012; Barbara Colby, July 16 and 30, 2012; Paul Colby, Sept. 3, 2012; Carl Colby, July 16, 2012; Sally Colby, July 27, 2012; Personal History Statement for WEC, B: 12, WECP, PU; Prados, pp. 23–24; William Colby, *Honorable Men*, pp. 27–29; Woods, pp. 13–14.

57 *ever experienced*: Personal History Statement for WEC, B: 12, WECP, PU; Prados, pp. 21–23; Woods, pp. 14–18; Sally Colby, July 27, 2012; John Colby, July 30, 2012; Paul Colby, Sept. 3, 2012; Barbara Colby, July 16 and 30, 2012; William Colby, *Lost Victory*, p. 19; Carl Colby, July 16, 2012.

58 *ahead of schedule*: Personal History Statement for WEC, B: 12, WECP, PU; "Local Bicyclists Pedal 753 Miles," *Burlington Free Press*, July 31, 1935; Paul Colby, Sept. 3, 2012; Barbara Colby, July 16 and 30, 2012; Woods, p. 19; John Colby, July 30, 2012.

59 *"the planet"*: Axtell, pp. 14–16, 114–22, 181–85, 345–46; John Colby, July 30, 2012; Paul Colby, Sept. 3, 2012; William Colby, *Honorable Men*, pp. 29–30; Sally Colby, July 27, 2012; Carl Colby, July 18, 2012; Prados, pp. 25–26; Barbara Colby, July 16, 2012.

60 *detested communism*: Personal History Statement for WEC, B: 12, WECP, PU; Prados, p. 26; Sally Colby, July 27, 2012; William Colby, *Honorable Men*, pp. 30–31; John Colby, July 30, 2012; Paul Colby, Sept. 3, 2012; Carl Colby, July 16, 2012.

60 *Democratic candidates:* Personal History Statement for William Egan Colby, B: 12, WECP, PU; Prados, p. 27; John Colby, July 30, 2012; William Colby, *Honorable Men*, pp. 31–32; Paul Colby, Sept. 3, 2012; Barbara Colby, July 16 and 24, 2012; Woods, p. 28; Giraudo, July 24, 2012.

61 *be soon:* Personal History Statement for WEC, B: 12, WECP, PU; "People: Barbara Comes Back," *Wheeling News Registrar*, Oct. 16, 1963; Barbara Colby, July 24 and 30, 2012, and April 8, 2013; "Interview: William Colby, former director, Central Intelligence Agency," *Special Warfare*, p. 40; Prados, p. 27; William Colby, *Honorable Men*, pp. 31–32.

CHAPTER 5: WAR CLOUDS

64 *like Penfield:* Talley, July 28, 2012, AWD letters to EFD June 24, July 13, and 27, 1916, and undated in July 1916, B: 19, Pleasant A. Stovall letter to the Secretary of State, B: 112, AWD letters to JWF Dec. 17, 1916, and May 2, 1917, AWD letters to RL Jan. 17 and Aug. 24, 1918, B: 37, AWDP, PU; Grose, pp. 22–25; Srodes, pp. 51, 58, 62; Mosley, pp. 38–39; Dulles, *The Craft of Intelligence*, pp. 73–74.

65 *military attaché:* AWD letter to EFD undated July 1916, RL letter to AWD April 18, 1917, B: 37, AWD letters to EFD April 13 and 23, 1917, AWD letters to EFD Sept. 3, 1917, April 7, 23, and May 7, 1918, and undated letter to EFD, B: 19, AWD letter to Pleasant Stovall April 30, 1918, B: 53, AWD letter to Henry March 4, 1918, B: 24, AWDP, PU; Srodes, pp. 70, 77–78; Mosley, pp. 44–45; Grose, pp. 34–35; Berg, p. 405.

65 *highbrow manners:* AWD letter to RL, B: 37, AWD letters to EFD Sept. 3, 1917, May 21, 1918, undated letter to EFD, B: 19, AWD letter to H. Remsen Whitehouse Aug. 14, 1918, B: 58, AWDP, PU; Srodes, pp. 70–71, 78–79; Grose, pp. 27–29.

66 *other tables:* AWD letters to EFD Dec. 31, 1917, and April 7, 1918, undated letter to EFD, B: 19, AWD letter to Harry B. Hawes June 1, 1918, B: 31, AWDP, PU; Eleanor Dulles (Eisenhower Administration), COH, pp. 102–4; Dulles, *The Craft of Intelligence*, pp. 1–4; Grose, pp. 27–28.

66 *"of Switzerland":* AWD letter to EFD April 7, 1918, undated letter to EFD, B: 19, AWDP, PU; Dulles, *The Secret Surrender*, pp. 9, 13.

67 *from Dulles:* Notes of Four Lectures Delivered before the Foreign Service School by A. W. Dulles, Aug. 10–13, 1925, B: 3, CEP, GU; AWD letter to Karl W. Ackerman Aug. 18, 1918, B: 27, CAP, LOC; AWD letter to EFD March 19, 1918, B: 19, AWDP, PU; Srodes, pp. 84–85; Grose, pp. 32–33.

68 *most suspicious:* AWD letters to EFD June 10 and Dec. 31, 1917, and Sept. 4, 1918, B: 19, AWD letter to Henry March 4, 1918, B: 24, AWDP, PU; Mosley, pp. 46–48; Talley, July 28, 2012.

68 *near Switzerland:* Mosley, pp. 45–46; Rasmus Rasmussen letter to H. Wilson Aug. 14, 1918, AWD letter to E. B. Harran Sept. 21, 1918, letter to The Hague July 25, 1919, AWD letters to John C. Wiley and Pleasant Stovall Aug. 4, 1919, John Wiley letter to AWD Aug. 7, 1919, L. Lanier Winslow letter to AWD Sept. 9, 1919, B: 48, AWDP, PU.

69 *was building:* Allen Dulles, DOHP, p. 32; AWD letter to EFD Nov. 5, 1918, B: 19, Polk

memo to American Delegation Bern Dec. 7, 1918, B: 37, AWD letter to J. C. Hughes Nov. 29, 1919, B: 32, AWD letters to AMD Nov. 26, 1918, and April 6, 1919, AWD letter to CTD June 25, 1925, B: 18, Alexander Kirk letter to AWD Nov. 3, 1919, B: 36, AWDP, PU; Kinzer, pp. 26–27; Grose, p. 51; Dulles, *The Craft of Intelligence*, pp. 1–4.

70 *do just that:* AWD letter to Alexander Kirk Nov. 13, 1919, B: 36, AWD letter to Grant Smith March 2, 1920, B: 29, AWD letter to Ellis Dresel Feb. 20, 1920, AWD letter to AMD April 5, 1920, B: 18, AWD letters to EFD Feb. 8 and 29, 1920, B: 19, AWDP, PU; AWD letter to HSG March 19, 1920, B: 22, HGP, HIA; Grose, pp. 66–69; Mosley, p. 62.

70 *been cheated:* AWD letters to AMD Nov. 26, 1918, and April 5, 1920, B: 18, AWD letters to EFD Feb. 8 and March 7, 1920, B: 19, AWDP, PU; Allen Dulles, DOHP, p. 30.

71 *with Foster:* CTD letter to mother and father Feb. 8, 1919, B: 120, CTD *Washington Post* and *Washington Star* photos undated, B: 18, Henry Alfred Todd biography, AWD letter to Mrs. Todd July 22, 1920, B: 119, AWDP, PU; Kinzer, p. 28; Eleanor Dulles (Eisenhower Administration), COH, pp. 104–5, 107–10; Mosley, pp. 3, 64–66; Bancroft, pp. 241–42; Srodes, pp. 119–20; Talley, July 28, 2012; Grose, pp. 73–75; Eleanor Dulles, *Chances of a Lifetime*, pp. 80–81.

71 *civil war:* Woodlands by Mrs. Allen W. Dulles, B: 18, "Miss C. Todd Engaged," *New York Herald*, Aug. 4, 1920, AWD-CTD wedding invitation Oct. 11, 1920, CTD letters to mother and father Aug. 9 and Sept. 3, 1921, CTD letter to father Dec. 13, 1920, CTD letter to Grandma Jan. 26, 1921, B: 120, AWD letters to Mother Todd Jan. 5 and Feb. 16, 1921, B: 119, AWD letters to EFD Nov. 5, 1920, Jan. 4 and 18, 1921, and March 16, 1921, B: 19, AWDP, PU; AWD letter to C. van H. Engert Nov. 7, 1921, B: 2, CEP, GU; AWD letter to HSG May 6, 1921, B: 22, HGP, HIA; Srodes, pp. 121–25; Grose, pp. 76–78.

72 *be the case:* Betty Carp letter to CTD July 26, 1922, AWD letter to CTD undated 1921, B: 18, AWDP, PU; Srodes, pp. 124–28; Talley, July 28 and Aug. 4, 2012; Grose, pp. 82–85.

72 *wander aimlessly:* AWD letters to CTD July 2 and 20, 1923, undated Sunday 1923, Aug. 2, 1924, undated letter, B: 18, AWD letter to JFD Dec. 18, 1925, B: 19, AWDP, PU; Grose pp. 84–86; Srodes, p. 136; Mosley, pp. 3, 73–74.

73 *disarmament delegations:* AWD letter to F. Lamont Belin Sept. 24, 1926, B: 7, Department of State letter to AWD May 31, 1927, AWD letter to Frank B. Kellogg Sept. 22, 1926, B: 35, "The Daily Washington Merry Go Round," by Drew Pearson and Robert S. Allen, *Daily Mirror*, Oct. 10, 1934, B: 106, AWDP, PU; Allen Dulles, DOHP, p. 34; AWD letters to HSG April 26, 1927, and Jan. 7, 1930, B: 22, HGP, HIA; Srodes, pp. 142–47, 152–53, 190–91; Talley, July 28, 2012; Grose, pp. 98, 112, 129; Sichel, March 11, 2013; Associates and Contacts, Westrick contacted Dulles 6/29/40 (65-10325-37, p. 6A), Sponsored Visa of Alfred Weiss 10/21/41 (61-7566-2762) (61-7466-1898) (40-17545), Activities and Organizations, Associations Against Dulles by Mrs. Robert Whitney Imbrie 2/21/41 (100-13781-1), The Fight for Freedom Committee 4-8-41 (100-24467-44), Confidential memo on AWD Jan. 19, 1953 (62-83338-8), FBI.

74 *"years hence":* "Davis Busy in Berlin," by Frederick T. Biechall, *New York Times*, April 9, 1933, p. 26; AWD letter to CTD April 11, 1933, B: 18, Memorandum of Conversation

Between German Chancellor Adolf Hitler and Mr. Norman Davis April 8, 1933, 4 p.m., Enclosures, Norman Davis account of the meeting, AWD Memorandum Oct. 27, 1933, B: 42, Cordell Hull letter to AWD March 17, 1933, B: 32, FDR draft letter to Norman Davis undated, B: 49, AWD letters to CTD Sept. 25, 1933, and March 19, 1939, B: 18, AWDP, PU; AWD letters to HSG Oct. 26 and Dec. 8, 1932, B: 22, HGP, HIA.

74 *father's absences:* Talley, July 28 and Aug. 4, 2012; Srodes, pp. 128–30, 169, 181, 192–93; Mosley, p. 74; Grose, p. 107.

75 *in Germany:* Brandon interview with AWD, B: 16, HBP, LOC; Allen Dulles, DOHP, p. 45; AWD letter to Wendell Willkie July 5, 1940, B: 58, AWD brochure as Republican Candidate for Delegate to the Constitutional Convention, AWD campaign material for 1938 Congressional Republican Primary, AWD letter to FDR March 6, 1932, B: 49, AWDP, PU; AWD letter to Walter Lippmann May 30, 1933, B: 24, HAP, PU; Dunlop, pp. 203–4; Mosley, pp. 88–98, 100–2; Talley, July 28, 2012; Grose, pp. 117, 121–25, 130–31; Dulles, *The Secret Surrender,* p. 9.

76 *spy agency:* Dulles, *The Secret Surrender,* pp. 9, 113–17; Waller, pp. 69–80, 146; Grose, pp. 139–40; J. P. Warburg letter to WJD Sept. 3, 1941, with enclosure on AWD, 8-26-41, R: 120, FR: 738–39; DKEB memo to WJD Dec. 1, 1941, R: 100, FR: 1217–19, M1642, RG226, NA.

CHAPTER 6: WASHINGTON

80 *in 1943:* Waller, p. 83; Notes on WJC, B: 1, JPP, HIA; Application for Employment and Personal History Statement for WJC, WJC Personnel Data, B: 112, E: 224, RG226, NA; WJC letters to SKC Jan. 25, 1943 and circa 1941, BCS; Attachment to the New York State Bonus Application WJC, B: 460, WJCP, HIA; Bernadette Casey Smith, Aug. 24, 2012.

81 *of ensign:* Application for Employment and Personal History Statement for WJC, B: 112, E: 224, RG226, NA; Placement Questionnaire for WJC, Report of Physical Examination for WJC for the U.S. Army, W. T. Tutt letter to WJC April 10, 1943, B: 460, WJCP, HIA; WJC letter to John Wittin with enclosures March 31, 1943, WJC letter to John W. Engle April 13, 1943, F. Eberstadt letter to Leo Cherne Jan. 7, 1943, Jeanne Gaines letter to Blanche Casey March 23, 1943, B: 460, WJCP, HIA; Bernadette Casey and Owen Smith, Aug. 24, 2012; Endorsement Summary for WJC by C. G. Collins, First Endorsement for WJC by W. F. Berberich, Report of Physical Examination for William Joseph Casey June 14, 1943, Application for Commission or Warrant for William Joseph Casey, William F. McMahon letter to Bureau of Naval Personnel March 27, 1943 (one of many recommendation letters for Casey), Chief of Naval Personnel memo to WJC May 7, 1943, Request for Assignment of Service Personnel for WJC Feb. 12, 1943, Charles K. Mallory memo to Chief of Procurement and Material March 4, 1943, Appointment in Naval Reserve for WJC May 10, 1943, WCNR, NPRC.

81 *in the door:* Transcript of DCI William Casey interview with David Kahn Jan. 18, 1982, NCM; Casey, *The Secret War Against Hitler,* pp. 4–5; Meyer, pp. 284–85; Report of Compliance with Orders for WJC June 15, 1943, WCNR, NPRC; Bernadette Casey Smith, Aug. 24, 2012; Waller, pp. 73, 93; Persico, *Casey,* pp. 51–54.

82 *of interviews:* Waller, pp. 73, 93, 97; Casey, *The Secret War Against Hitler,* pp. 3–5; Persico,

Casey, pp. 51–54; WJC letter to Jerome Doran Sept. 4, 1943, OCD letter to the Senate Committee on Banking, Housing and Urban Affairs March 5, 1971, B: 460, WJC notes for OCD memorial dinner April 24, 1980, B: 543, WJCP, HIA.

83 *he waited:* Waller, pp. 73, 93; Casey, *The Secret War Against Hitler*, pp. 4–5; Montgomery, July 17, 2012; Barreaux, Aug. 6, 2012; Persico, *Casey*, pp. 54–55; WJC letter to Jerome Doran Sept. 4, 1943, B: 460, WJCP, HIA; L. L. Rafferty memo to Charles Vanderblue Oct. 18, 1943, B: 94, E: 92A, SO Personnel Interview Data Sheet for WJC Sept. 1, 1943, B: 112, E: 224, RG226, NA.

83 *lived well:* Randall Jacobs memo to WJC Nov. 2, 1943, Charles K. Mallory memo to the Chief of Procurement and Material Oct. 28, 1943, Ward P. Davis memo to Chief of Naval Personnel Oct. 12, 1943, Request for Assignment of Service Personnel for WJC Oct. 6, 1943, WCNR, NPRC; WJC letter to Joseph Persico Oct. 20, 1978, UA.

84 *military capabilities:* Casey, *The Secret War Against Hitler*, pp. 5, 13; Persico, *Casey*, pp. 55–57; Casey, "The Clandestine War in Europe," p. 2; Bernadette Casey and Owen Smith, Aug. 24, 2012; Waller, pp. 93–97; WJC letter to Joseph Persico Oct. 20, 1978, UA; David H. Winton memo to Kelly O'Neil Oct. 29, 1943, H. S. Prescott memo to Gerald E. Miller Sept. 24, 1943, Gerald E. Miller memo to Security Office Sept. 23, 1943, B: 94, E: 92A, WJC memo to WJD Oct. 21, 1943, R: 79, FR: 11–15, WJC memo to James G. Rogers Oct. 22, 1943, R: 11, FR: 709–12, M1642, OCD letter to DKEB Nov. 7, 1943, B: 320, E: 190, RG226, NA.

85 *to be there:* Transcript of DCI William Casey interview with David Kahn Jan. 18, 1982, NCM; Notes on WJC, B: 1, JPP, HIA; Persico, *Casey*, p. 57; Barreaux, Aug. 6, 2012; Casey, *The Secret War Against Hitler*, pp. 12–13; OCD interviews, B: Oral History Interviews O. C. Doering Jr., Activities in Europe 1941–89, WJDP, MHI; Bernadette Casey Smith, Aug. 24, 2012; Leonard J. Cushing memo to Chief of Naval Personnel Nov. 3, 1943, Randall Jacobs memo to WJC Nov. 2, 1943, WCNR, NPRC.

CHAPTER 7: JEDBURGH

88 *his application:* Paul Colby, Sept. 3, 2012; John Colby, July 30, 2012; Barbara Colby, July 16, 2012; Colby, *Honorable Men*, pp. 32–33; SO Officers' Data Sheet for War Diary on WEC, B: 2, E: 101, OSS personnel file duty stations for WEC, B: 133, E: 224, RG226, NA; "Interview: William Colby, former director, Central Intelligence Agency," *Special Warfare*, p. 40; Pierce, pp. iii, 31.

89 *on the sheet:* Colby, *Honorable Men*, pp. 32–33; SO Officers' Data Sheet for War Diary on WEC, B: 2, E: 101, OSS personnel file duty stations for WEC, B: 133, E: 224, RG226, NA; Pierce, pp. 31–33, 81; "Thousands of Officers, Enlisted Men Taught Complexities of Modern Battle in This Vast 150,000 Acre Classroom," Oct. 1, 1942, p. 9, "Post's History Depicts Rapid Growth of Army," Nov. 12, 1942, p. 1, "Post's 'Good' Old Days When Things Were Really Tough Are Revived by Fort Historian," p. 2, "Expert Rigger Made in Parachute School," p. 4, "Paratrooper Frowns on 'Glamor Boy' Title," p. 5, Nov. 12, 1942, *Ft. Benning Bayonet*; Singlaub, July 20, 2012; Ambrose, p. 35. John Colby, July 30, 2012; Paul Colby, Sept. 3, 2012; Sally Shelton Colby, July 27, 2012.

91 *troubled nation:* Recruiter notes for interviews with Jedburgh candidates, Memo on Special Recruitment, Jedburgh Plan Oct. 8, 1943, Edward J. Gamble memo to J. Hoag Oct.
16, 1943, B: 280, E: 92, J. M. Scribner memo on Meeting on Special Recruitment, Jedburgh Plan Oct. 1, 1943, J. A. Hoag memo to the Adjutant General (Officer's Branch) Oct.
9, 1943, Franklin O. Canfield memo to Colonel Connely Oct. 11, 1943, J. A. Hoag memo
to AC of S, G-1 Oct. 9, 1943, C. S. Williams memo to Mr. Scribner Oct. 14, 1943, B: 264,
E: 146, Personnel Requirement for SO/SOE D Day Plan, B: 355, E: 190, SO Personnel Interview Data Sheet for WEC Oct. 20, 1943, B: 133, E: 224, RG226, NA; Singlaub, July 20,
2012; Singlaub, OHP, pp. 1–3, 10; Irwin, pp. 40–41; War Diary, SO Branch, OSS London,
Vol. 4, Jedburghs, Preamble . . . to 1 January 1944, B: 359, E: 190, M1642, R: 8, RG226,
NA; Beavan, pp. 47–49, 57; Colby, *Honorable Men*, p. 35; Paul Colby, Sept. 3, 2012; Sally
Shelton Colby, July 27, 2012.

92 *in the war:* Julian Jackson, pp. 1, 81, 118–19, 123–29, 140–43, 181, 215, 221, 227–28;
Weinberg, pp. 139–40, 514–15; Cookridge, p. 102; Foot, *SOE in France*, p. 121.

93 *"horizontal collaborators":* Lessons from the Resistance to the German Occupation of
France June 1945, B: 741, E: 190, RG226, NA; Julian Jackson, pp. 1, 151–96, 219–29,
230–43, 292–98, 334–35; Keegan, pp. 281–85; Foot, *Resistance*, p. 20.

94 *London headquarters:* Julian Jackson, pp. 216–17, 239–43, 389–403; AWD letter to Larry
Collins Jan. 10, 1964, B: 49, AWDP, PU; The French Intelligence Services 1942–1943
Jan. 13, 1944, B: 38, E: 99, WJD letter to Colonel Passy Aug. 2, 1943, and Passy response,
DKEB cable to WJD Oct. 22, 1944, B: 349, E: 210, OSS Aid to the French Resistance
in World War II: Origin and Development of Resistance in France, Summary, Lessons
from the Resistance to the German Occupation of France June 1945, B: 741, Summary
of Developments Within France Since 1940, April 4, 1944, B: 44, E: 190, RG226, NA;
Cookridge, pp. 1–7, 14–20, 52–59; Beavan, pp. 10–17; Foot, *SOE in France*, pp. 121–26;
Atkinson, *The Guns at Last Light*, pp. 34–35.

94 *"future government":* Summary of Developments Within France Since 1940, April 4,
1944, B: 44, Lessons from the Resistance to the German Occupation of France June 1945,
B: 741, France: The Present Value and Tempo of Resistance Memorandum by S.O.E.
Oct. 9, 1943, B: 329, SO War Diary, Vol. 3, Preamble . . . to 1 January 1944, pp. 57–64,
B: 360, E: 190, RG226, NA; The Rise of France with the Aid of the U.S. Army, European Theater of Operations, Office of the Chief of Military History, CMH; Foot, *SOE in
France*, pp. 122, 209; WJD Lecture for the Army-Navy Staff College March 12, 1945, B:
119A, WJDP, MHI; Beavan, p. 18; O'Donnell, pp. 143–44; Julian Jackson, pp. 7, 386–87,
395–97, 400, 408–56, 469–75, 505; Ludewig, p. 27; Irwin, pp. 86–87; Cookridge, p. 131.

95 *of France:* Lessons from the Resistance to the German Occupation of France June 1945,
B: 741, France: The Present Value and Tempo of Resistance Memorandum by S.O.E.
Oct. 9, 1943, B: 329, Organization of Resistance Nov. 17, 1943, B: 448, E: 190, RG226,
NA; Cookridge, pp. 16–17; Beavan, pp. 20, 22, 43, 103; Foot, *SOE in France*, p. 131; *The
Overseas Targets*, p. 178.

96 *radio operators:* Co-Operation of Activities Behind the Enemy Lines with the Actions of

Allied Military Forces Invading N.W. Europe April 6, 1943, HS 8/288, NAUK; Memorandum on the Co-Operation Between the S.O.E. and Military Forces in the Event of a Re-Invasion of the Continent March 18, 1943, B: 355, E: 190, Memo to G. B. Guenther with enclosure July 21, 1942, R: 8, FR: 781–85, M1642, SO Officers' Data Sheet for War Diary for Franklin Canfield, B: 2, E: 101, War Diary, SO Branch, OSS London, Vol. 4, Jedburghs, Preamble . . . to 1 January 1944, R: 8, M1642, B: 359, E: 190, RG226, NA; Roger Ford, pp. 9–10; History of Jedburghs in Europe 1942–1944, S.O.E. History 12, Vol. 1, pp. 7–8 with attachments, HS 7/17, NAUK; Beavan, pp. 26–31.

97   *the best men:* Aide to the Resistance SSU Report 1961, B: 740, E: 190, Memo to G. B. Guenther with enclosure July 21, 1942, R: 8, FR: 781–85, Ellery Huntington memo to R. Davis Halliwell, June 22, 1943, R: 4, FR: 558–61, M1642, Introduction for OG training and organization, B: 45, E: 99, Ellery Huntington memo to Scribner, Sept. 4, 1943, B: 280, E: 92, War Diary, SO Branch, OSS London, Vol. 1, pp. xxx–xxxviii, B: 359 and 360, Jedburghs, AD/E/603, Dec. 20, 1943, B: 339, E: 190, War Diary, SO Branch, OSS London, Vol. 4, Jedburghs, Preamble . . . to 1 January 1944, B: 359, E: 190, R: 8, M1642, RG226, NA; Joint Psychological Warfare Committee Jedburghs, Note by the Secretary with enclosure, Aug. 21, 1942, W. B. Smith memo Sept. 3, 1942, 11. Jedburghs (J.P.S. 35/11/D), DDE memo to AGWAR Sept. 16, 1942, B: 8, Central Decimal File, RG 218, NA; Waller, pp. 88, 96, 202; History of the Jedburghs in Europe 1942–1944, S.O.E. History 12, Vol. 1, pp. 8, 13–14, HS 7/17, Co-Operation of Activities Behind the Enemy Lines with the Actions of Allied Military Forces Invading N.W. Europe April 6, 1943, HS 8/288, NAUK; Irwin, pp. 37–40, 235; Beavan, pp. 42–43; *War Report of the O.S.S.,* p. 210.

98   *Congressional Country Club:* Jedburghs, AD/E/603, Dec. 20. 1943, B: 339, E. F. Connely memo to the Adjutant General (Officer's Branch) Oct. 13, 1943, B: 355, E: 190, RG226, NA; Co-Operation of Activities Behind the Enemy Lines with the Actions of Allied Military Forces Invading N.W. Europe April 6, 1943, HS 8/288, NAUK; Singlaub, pp. 25–26; Singlaub, OHP, pp. 3–4; Singlaub, July 20, 2012; Beavan, pp. 59–62; Kehoe, p. 17.

101   *of training:* Silverman, pp. 79–82; Hall, pp. 24–27; Kehoe, Oct. 26, 2012; Kehoe, p. 18; Irwin, pp. 45–46; Beavan, pp. 62–64; Singlaub, pp. 27–30; Sally Shelton Colby, July 27, 2012; Paul Colby, Sept. 3, 2012; Report on Seventy-five SO Agents (Mostly Jedburghs) Dropped by Parachute into France, B: 69, WJCP, HIA; Singlaub, OHP, pp. 4–6; Carl Colby, July 16, 2012; Singlaub, July 20, 2012; Waller, pp. 93, 151–52.

101   *to halt:* "You Can't Visit Camp David . . . But You Can Get Close," by Richard Dunlop, *Ambassador TWA,* May 1978, p. 70; WJD memo to JCS July 30, 1942, R: 3, FR: 1333–54, M1642, RG226, NA; Hall, p. 34; Wehrle, pp. 1–8; Franklin, p. 143; Kehoe, p. 18.

102   *his parents:* Franklin, Oct. 24, 2012; Franklin, pp. 144–46; Singlaub, pp. 31–33; Beavan, pp. 71–75; Singlaub, OHP, pp. 5–10; Dreux, pp. 17–18; Singlaub, July 20, 2012; Irwin, pp. 46–50; Special Orders No. 253, Headquarters and Headquarters Detachment OSS Nov. 6, 1943, B: 280, E: 92, RG226, NA; Barbara Colby, July 16, 2012.

103   *"Some shit!":* C. S. Williams memo to Mr. Howland Oct. 8, 1943, B: 280, E: 92, RG226, NA; Franklin, p. 146; Beavan, pp. 39–42, 62–64; Colby, *Honorable Men,* pp. 35–36; War-

ner, "The Office of Strategic Services"; Irwin, pp. 46–50, 193; Franklin, Oct. 24, 2012; Report on Seventy-five SO Agents (Mostly Jedburghs) Dropped by Parachute into France, B: 69, WJCP, HIA; Singlaub, p. 33; Singlaub, July 20, 2012.

103 *and D-Day:* Franklin, p. 146; Singlaub, OHP, pp. 5–10; F. O. Canfield cable to Gerald Miller Nov. 17, 1943, B: 355, E: 190, RG226, NA.

104 *and vomit:* Irwin, pp. 50–54, 134; Kehoe, pp. 18–19; Singlaub, July 20, 2012; Woods, pp. 36–37; Beavan, pp. 78–84; Harding, pp. 1–2, 31; Franklin, Oct. 24, 2012.

CHAPTER 8: TRADECRAFT

106 *United Press colleagues:* Helms, *A Look over My Shoulder,* pp. 29–30; Aero Mayflower Transit Co. manifest March 3–4, 1942, RMH Application for Commission in U.S. Naval Reserve March 12, 1942, reference letters from Wallace R. Deuel, Russell J. Ryan, Hubert Hickam, et al., early March 1942, RHNR, NPRC.

106 *never dropped:* Report of Physical Exam for RMH March 13, 1942, Randall Jacobs memo to RMH April 17, 1942, Adolphus Andrews memo to Chief of the Bureau of Navigation April 24, 1942, J. T. G. Stapler memo to Chief of the Bureau of Navigation March 26, 1942, Kenneth G. Castleman memo to Chief of the Bureau of Navigation June 12, 1942, Report of Medical Examination for RMH Sept. 8, 1951, F. P. Olds memo to RMH June 5, 1942, RMH Appointment in Naval Reserve as Lieutenant J.G. June 6, 1942, RHNR, NPRC.

107 *the request:* My Early Years in Intelligence, notes by RMH, P: 1, S: 1, 3, B: 10, RHP, GU; "The (Really) Quiet American," *Washington Post,* May 20, 1973, p. C2; Chief of Naval Personnel memo to RMH June 16, 1942, Record of Compliance with Orders Aug. 29, 1942, C. A. MacGowan memo to RMH Aug. 28, 1942, and MacGowan memo July 1, 1942, RMH Reports on the Fitness of Officers April 1–Aug. 11, 1943, and Aug. 29, 1942– March 31, 1943, RMH memo to Chief of Naval Personnel May 3, 1943, RHNR, NPRC; Robarge, pp. 14–15; Sichel, March 11, 2013; Sichel manuscript; Gates Helms, Aug. 18, 2012; Helms, *A Look over My Shoulder,* pp. 29–30.

108 *wasn't interested:* Malcolm A. Crusius memo to John O'Keeffe June 3, 1942, Wallace Deuel memos and letters to WJD May 18, Aug. 25, and Sept. 26, 1942, and to Fred Oechsner Aug. 20, 1942, R: 77, FR: 167–76, M1642, Report to Executive Committee on MO Organization, Personnel and Operations Aug. 20, 1943, B: 126, E: 136, WJD General Order No. 9, Jan 3, 1943, with attachments, B: 188, E: 139, Frederick Oechsner Oath of Office Nov. 27, 1942, Director of Personnel memo on Frederick Oechsner Nov. 16, 1942, OSS Director's Office Personnel Action Request for Frederick Oechsner Nov. 2, 1942, Frederick Oechsner Application for Federal Employment Nov. 2, 1942, B: 569, E: 224, RG226, NA; Helms notes on being recruited by Fred Oechsner Oct. 9, 1996, B: 2, WHP, GU; Waller, pp. 150–51; Helms, *A Look over My Shoulder,* pp. 30–31; Powers, p. 22; Dennis Helms, Aug. 19, 2012.

109 *its track:* Helms Biography Material, P: 3, S: 7, B: 7, RHP, GU; Naval Message 17059, Pers-3155-HA from BuPers to T. R. Cooley July 31, 1943, Request for Assignment of Service Personnel from OSS July 9, 1943, IBM punch card for RMH June 20, 1942, Randall

Jacobs memo to RMH Aug. 7, 1943, Report on the Fitness of Officers for RMH Aug. 16, 1943 to March 31, 1944, RHNR, NPRC; Helms, *A Look over My Shoulder*, pp. 31–32; Helms, OHP, pp. 2–3; Gates Helms, Aug. 18, 2012; Cynthia Helms, July 18, 2012.

110 *told him:* Desk Indoctrination Memo for O.S.S. Basic Course, B: 265, James O. Murdock memo to J. A. Patterson June 1, 1944, B: 235, E: 146, N. F. Allman memo to Mr. Katz Sept. 30, 1943, B: 48, E: 92, Brochure Concerning the Schools and Training Branch, B: 135, E: 99, Instructions for Recruits Jan. 19, 1944, B: 161, E: 136, RG226, NA; Helms, *A Look over My Shoulder*, pp. 31–32.

110 *into classrooms:* Brochure Concerning the Schools and Training Branch, B: 135, E: 99, L. B. Shallcross memo to John O'Hara with excerpts from History of Schools and Training, OSS, Feb. 1, 1951, B: 7, E: 161, Kenneth P. Miller memo to G. Edward Buxton June 29, 1943, Willis C. Reddick memo to E. C. Huntington, Jr. Sept. 3, 1942, B: 161, Schools and Training October 1943, B: 158, E: 136, RG226, NA.

111 *students attended:* WJD memo to J. R. Hayden Jan. 3, 1942, R: 56, FR: 761, Brooker memo to WJD Dec. 18, 1942, R: 36, FR: 578–81, Garland H. Williams memo to WJD July 21, 1942, R: 107, FR: 479–80, M1642, R. P. Heppner memo to WJD June 22, 1942, B: 327, E: 210, RG226, NA; Helms, *A Look over My Shoulder*, pp. 31–32.

111 *he explained:* Training manuals for Area E students, B: 3 and 4, E: 161, Instructions to Students, B: 161, E: 136, RG226, NA; Helms, *A Look over My Shoulder*, pp. 31–32.

112 *and interrogated:* Waller, pp. 101–2; Qualifications for Agents December 1942, B: 161, Basic SI-SO Course of Instruction March 13, 1943, with course schedule for Class No. E-56 Sept. 20–Oct. 8, 1943, B: 163, E: 136, Division 19 Program as of Dec. 1, 1943, Louis P. Zelenka memo to Charles R. Buell July 18, 1944, H. J. Anderson memo to Stanley P. Lovell May 2, 1944, B: 207, R. Mazzarrini memo to H. P. De Vries June 2, 1944, B: 366, E: 210, William H. Vanderbilt memo to Dr. Rogers Oct. 17, 1942, Enclosure: Amendments to O.S.S. 1942 Catalogue of Material, R: 14, FR: 1352–89, 1776–77, Sylvester C. Missal memo to WJD Feb. 16, 1942, R: 73, FR: 201–2, Copy of Message received from Capt. Benson Oct. 12, 1942, R: 8, FR: 1065–68, M1642, Complete Cipher Course All Areas OSS: Double Transposition Cipher, B: 3, E: 161, RG226, NA; Helms, *A Look over My Shoulder*, pp. 31–32.

114 *smiling Fairbairn:* Helms, *A Look over My Shoulder*, pp. 31–32; Dennis Helms, Aug. 19, 2012; Cynthia Helms, July 18, 2012; My Early Years in Intelligence, notes by RMH, P: 1, S: 1, 3, B: 10, Helms Biography Material, P: 3, S: 7, B: 7, RHP, OSS Symposium Remarks by RMH Sept. 20, 1986, B: 1, WHP, GU; Kenneth P. Miller memo to G. Edward Buxton July 27, 1943, Résumé of Services of Lt. Col. William E. Fairbairn, B: 591, E: 190, Area F's Interview Report for W. E. Fairbairn, WJD memo to Adjutant General April 5, 1945, B: 226, E: 224, "Gutter Fighting," Part II, "Unarmed," 2nd Revision SI: March 25, 1944, B: 11, E: 90, RG226, NA.

115 *his arm:* Helms, *A Look over My Shoulder*, pp. 31–32; Cynthia Helms, July 18, 2012; Waller, p. 94; My Early Years in Intelligence, notes by RMH, P: 1, S: 1, 3, B: 10, Helms Biography Material, P: 3, S: 7, B: 7, RHP, GU; George A. Barnes letter to Patrick Dolan

Nov. 18, 1943, R: 106, FR: 853–57, Kenneth H. Baker memo to WJD March 27, 1943, R: 116, FR: 1230–46, Ellery C. Huntington memo to WJD Nov. 27, 1942, R: 116, FR: 1193–1202, M1642, Brochure Concerning the Schools and Training Branch, B: 135, E: 99, H. L. Robinson memo to Ezra Shine Nov. 18, 1942, Kenneth P. Miller memo to Philip Allen Aug. 20, 1943, Copy of the phony White House letter with Jonathan Daniels's signature Aug. 17, 1943, "Inside Washington," *Chicago Sun*, Aug. 23, 1943, Philip Allen memos to Col. Rehm April 28, 1944, and to Ainsworth Blogg Feb. 24, 1944, Area "E" Outline of Revised One Day Scheme, Pittsburgh Scheme Class E-86 May 8–10, 1944, B: 163, E: 136, RG226, NA.

116 *staff hatched:* RMH letter to Calvin B. Hoover Sept. 22, 1965, P: 1, S: 1, B: 5, RHP, GU; Julia McWilliams Change in Status Jan. 29, 1944, U.S. Civil Service Commission memo to OSS on Julia McWilliams Nov. 7, 1942, Edna Stonesifer memo to J. C. Byrd Oct. 29, 1942, Julia McWilliams résumé May 17, 1943, B: 513, H. L. Robinson memo to Director SSU March 20, 1946, B: 262, E: 224, OSS Archives, Washington PS-OP-4, B: 33, Henry Leir letter to OSS Nov. 17, 1943, and RMH response Nov. 22, 1943, B: 34, E: 144, RG226, NA; Cynthia Helms, July 18, 2012; Dennis Helms, Aug. 19, 2012; Helms, *A Look over My Shoulder*, pp. 32–33; Report on the Fitness of Officers for RMH Aug. 16, 1943–March 31, 1944, RHNR, NPRC.

117 *Third Reich:* AWD letters to FLM June 10 and July 19, 1919, FLM letter to Secretary of State undated, FLM letter to Edwin Watson undated, B: 40, AWDP, PU; John Hughes memo to Weston Howland, B: 17, E: 160A, Hugh Wilson memo to Mr. Howland Nov. 16, 1942, B: 32, FLM memo to Chief, SI, Dec. 13, 1943, B: 419, E: 210, Francis Miller memo to Kenneth Hinks Aug. 24, 1943, B: 32, Whitney Shepardson memo to I. R. H. Goddard Aug. 1, 1944, FLM memo to Special Funds Branch May 10, 1945, B: 32, E: 92A, Maurice Fatio memo to Robert deVecchi July 15, 1943, B: 101, E: 92, RG226, NA; Richard Harris Smith, p. 49; Waller, p. 158; Helms, *A Look over My Shoulder*, pp. 32–33; Helms, OHP, p. 5.

118 *Allen Dulles:* Helms Biography Material, P: 3, S: 7, B: 7, RHP, PU; RMH memo to Chief, SI, Dec. 28, 1944, B: 32, E: 92A, RMH memo to J. E. O'Gara Oct. 12, 1944, B: 46, E: 92, JEH memo to Attorney General Dec. 13, 1944, B: 349, WJD cables to Forgan Oct. 20 and 21, 1944, WJD letter to Harold George Oct. 22, 1944, Harry Kelleher letter to E. J. Putzell Nov. 3, 1944, B: 349, FLM memo to Chief, SI, Dec. 13, 1942, B: 419, E: 210; OCD memo to WS June 15, 1944, A. van Beuren memo to John O'Gara Oct. 9, 1944, B: 48, E: 92, RG226, NA; Notes on RMH, B: 27, UA; Helms, OHP, p. 5; Persico, *Piercing the Reich*, pp. 239–40; Cynthia Helms, July 18, 2012.

CHAPTER 9: SWITZERLAND

120 *for secrets:* The New York Office, Dec. 16, 1944, B: 64, The New York Office of the Director of Strategic Services Dec. 7, 1942, B: 513, E: 210, Spencer Phenix memo to Weston Howland Jan. 21, 1943, B: 226, E: 146, DKEB memo to AWD March 7, 1942, B: 101, E: 92, RG226, Office of the Coordinator of Information circa January 1942, B: 1, OCD letter to

Thomas Troy, B: 7, TTP, RG263, NA; Office Information Dec. 9, 1941, B: 19, AWD letter to CTD Jan. 28, 1942, B: 18, AWDP, PU; Talley, July 28, 2012; Waller, p. 84; Grose, pp. 140–42.

121 *Axis-occupied countries:* To: George, Re: New Organization, B: 218, John O'Keeffe memo to G. Edward Buxton Jan. 3, 1945, The New York Office, Dec. 16, 1944, B: 64, E: 210, WJD memo to FDR Feb. 17, 1942, R: 22, FR: 1036, M1642, RG226, NA; Waller, pp. 97–98; Mosley, pp. 113–14.

122 *lifted it:* The New York Office, Dec. 16, 1944, B: 64, The New York Office of the Director of Strategic Services Dec. 7, 1942, B: 513, AWD memo to Hugh Wilson April 17, 1942, B: 389, E: 210, AG memo to AWD July 30, 1942, B: 40, E: 211, AG memo to AWD Aug. 12, 1942, B: 374, AG memos to AWD July 1 and 2, 1942, B: 391, Murray I. Gurfein personnel card, B: 300, Lithgow Osborne Application and Personal History Statement, B: 577, Betty Carp personnel card, B: 108, Matthew Woll letter to WJD Jan. 13, 1942, and Alexander Lipsett Application and Personal History Statement, B: 456, E: 224, Betty Carp memo to AWD Oct. 8, 1942, R: 67, FR: 143–52, WJD memo to FDR June 1, 1942, R: 23, FR: 469–72, Sigrid Schultz memo Oct. 2, 1942, R: 52, FR: 90–112, M1642, Duncan Lee memos to WJD Nov. 11, 1942, to Col. Rehm Nov. 20, 1942, and to OCD Nov. 16, 1942, OCD letters to Col. Buxton Oct. 6, 15, and 20, 1942, B: 189, E: 146, RG226, NA; AWD letter to Spencer Phenix Dec. 11, 1942, B: 44, AWDP, PU; Waller, pp. 62–70, 122.

123 *"most secret" reports:* Duncan Lee memo to files Nov. 3, 1942, B: 189, E: 146, William Whitney memo to WJD Jan. 8, 1942, R: 13, FR: 427–32, M1642, AWD memo to DKEB Oct. 31, 1942, B: 262, The New York Office, Dec. 16, 1944, B: 64, E: 210, RG226, A. A. Berle memo to Mr. Dunn Nov. 18, 1940, B: 2, TTP, RG263, NA; DKEB memo to WJD March 28, 1942, B: 139A, WJDP, MHI; Waller, pp. 62–70, 122.

124 *secret war:* Stebenne, pp. 4–11, 15, 20–23, 29–31; Notes on AG, B: 2, JPP, HIA; Adlai Stevenson letter to AG Dec. 13, 1941, B: 22, AGP, LOC.

124 *sabotage devices:* The New York Office of the Director of Strategic Services Dec. 7, 1942, B: 513, E: 210, AWD memo to WJD April 8, 1942, R: 45, FR: 810, M1642, RG226, NA; Gerhard Van Arkel interview Nov. 11, 1983, B: 11, RSP, HIA; AG memo to WJD with enclosure Feb. 23, 1943, B: 27, UA; Stebenne, pp. 31–32; Jolis, p. 94.

125 *soon concluded:* AG memo to WJD with enclosure Feb. 23, 1943, B: 27, UA; The New York Office of the Director of Strategic Services Dec. 7, 1942, B: 513, The New York Office, Dec. 16, 1944, B: 64, Leslie Fossel memo to Col. Buxton March 4, 1942, B: 376, AG memo to AWD July 6, 1942, B: 389, Edwin Hartrich memo to E. C. Huntington July 27, 1942, AWD memos to George Bowden Aug. 28 and Sept. 15, 1942, James Kirk memo to George Bowden Oct. 2, 1942, Russell D'Oench memo to K. H. Baker Oct. 26, 1942, Kenneth Baker memo to Russell D'Oench Nov. 26, 1942, Louis Cohen memo to Kenneth Baker Nov. 23, 1942, B: 401, E: 210, George Pratt Application and Personal History Statement, B: 617, David Shaw Application for Federal Employment Dec. 9, 1944, B: 700, E: 224, Edward Buxton memo to WJD Aug. 31, 1942, WJD memo to AWD Sept. 20, 1942, B: 640, E: 190, Weston Howland memo to Hugh Wilson Sept. 19, 1942, Spencer Phenix memo

to Weston Howland Jan. 21, 1943, B: 226, E: 146, Leigh Hoadley letter to Spencer Phenix March 4, 1942, AWD memo to DKEB March 9, 1942, A. D. Hutcheson memo to David Williamson April 23, 1942, Spencer Phenix memos to Francis Miller May 27, 1942, and to Robert Cresswell June 5, 1942, Francis Miller memos to Roland Sept. 10, 1942, and to WS April 14, 1943, File WN24907, E: 216, RG226, Gene Tunney letter to Thomas Troy Aug. 6, 1969, TTP, RG263, NA; Stebenne, p. 33; AG letter to WJD Aug. 15, 1946, B: 5, AG memo to George Pratt Oct. 2, 1942, B: 22, AGP, LOC.

126 *on his payroll:* Memos to Mr. Nichols 40-35274 on 9/17/42, 40-34540 on 9/17/42, 65-29488-171, p. 12 on 4/5/48, 100-64082-21 on 7/2/43, 65-55553-A on 12/24/48, 100-344378-19 on 10/11/46, 65-59140-3 on 6/10/42, 62-64427-383 on 7/29/42, 100-74840-155 on 9/11/42, 100-162169-1 on 9/10/42, and 62-64427-255 on 3/5/42, A. H. Belmont memos to D. M. Ladd Jan. 19, 1953, FBI; Srodes, p. 213; Mosley, pp. 123–25.

127 *the schoolmaster:* Waller, pp. 123–24; Winks, pp. 116–23, 150–76; Donald Downes letter to Col. Rehm Jan. 11, 1942, B: 197, E: 224, George Bowden memo to Col. Buxton and Col. Rehm Sept. 11, 1942, Donald Downes memo to DKEB with enclosure Oct. 15, 1942, B: 5, "Strategic Services," B: 8, E: 136A, RG226, NA.

127 *him quiet:* Waller, pp. 110–11; Grose, pp. 145–47; Winks, p. 175; SAC New York memo to Director, FBI, Sept. 23, 1954, B: 201, SAC New York memo to Director, FBI, Jan 10, 1956, Memo on Frederick William Taylor with enclosure NH 105-1177, July 31, 1956, B: 201, E: A1-36M, RG65, Memorandum for A. D. April 13, 1942, B: 5, E: 136A, AWD memo to WJD Sept. 24, 1942, B: 130, Memo to A. D. May 14, 1942, B: 45, E: 92, AWD memo to Hugh Wilson May 29, 1942, B: 346, E: 210, George Bowden memo to Donald Downes with enclosures Oct. 19, 1942, B: 4, E: 136A, DeWitt Poole memo to John Wiley May 22, 1942, R: 51, FR: 107–9, M1642, OSS files on Gottfried Treviranus and T-Plan, B: 1, E: 183, RG226, NA.

128 *than Donovan:* The New York Office, Dec. 16, 1944, B: 64, The New York Office of the Director of Strategic Services Dec. 7, 1942, B: 513, AWD memo to WJD April 16, 1942, B: 346, E: 210, DeWitt Poole memo to WJD with enclosure March 1, 1943, R: 18, FR: 454–58, M1642, RG226, NA; X memo to AD/E June 22, 1943, HS 6/703, NAUK.

129 *the transfer:* Waller, p. 146; USTRAVIC London cable to COI Sept. 17, 1942, AWD memo to DKEB Oct. 21, 1942, B: 101, E: 92, Confidential for Mr. Dulles, Memorandum IDS #9 Sept. 17, 1942, B: 9, E: 215, Hugh Wilson memo to R. G. D'Oench Sept. 25, 1942, B: 7, E: 214, AWD memo to WJD with attachment July 30, 1942, R: 105, FR: 1208–9, M1642, AWD memo to Hugh Wilson May 12, 1942, B: 399, E: 210, RG226, NA; Talley, July 28, 2012; Mosley, p. 114; Dulles, *The Secret Surrender*, p. 9; Grose, p. 149; Lankford, *OSS Against the Reich*, p. 195.

129 *special assistant:* SOE history, Italy, Switzerland and Mediterranean Section October–December 1942, "Allen Dulles Returning to Bern," HS 7/262, NAUK; WJD letter to G. Howland Shaw July 18, 1942, B: 203, E: 224, W. E. DeCourey memo to Mr. Kimbel July 27, 1942, AWD memo to William A. Kimbel July 29, 1942, AWD memo to George Bowden Aug. 21, 1942, File 22, B: 101, E: 92, RG226, NA.

129 *told them:* Agent's Check List for Burns, B: 101, E: 92, AWD memo to George Bowden Oct. 10, 1942, Dries Defee letter to Father Damiaan Letter No. 2, Memorandum re: contact first referred to by Drum in his Report No. 8, B: 7, E: 214, DeWitt Poole memo to AWD Aug. 4, 1942, B: 9, E: 215, First Boston Corporation letter to AWD Sept. 25, 1942, B: 101, E: 92, RG226, NA.

131 *two years later:* Dulles, *Secret Surrender*, pp. 11–13; Grose, pp. 149–52; Dulles, *Germany's Underground*, p. 125; Burns cable for Victor Nov. 10, 1942, B: 121B, WJDP, MHI.

132 *the evenings:* Srodes, p. 227; Burns cable for Victor Nov. 10, 1942, B: 121B, WJDP, MHI; AWD cable to WJD May 17, 1944, B: 266, E: 134, RG226, NA; AWD letters to CTD Nov. 28, 1942, and March 7, 1943, B: 18, AWDP, PU.

132 *the shelf:* Luck, pp. 469, 473, 719, 747, 765, 771; Petropoulus, pp. 1–4, 8; Atkinson, *The Guns at Last Light*, p. 213; Halbrook, pp. 1–4, 11, 19–33, 76–82, 95–99, 108–35, 155–69, 192, 233, 236, 243–45, 304; Weinberg, p. 397; Delattre, p. 80; "First Detailed Interrogation Report, HQ Intelligence Center, Military Intelligence Service in Austria, KV 3/244, NAUK; WJD memo to FDR July 10, 1944. and FDR response July 13, 1944, R: 24, FR: 132–33, R: 30, FR: 866–69, M1642, Wilmarth Lewis memo to F. L. Belin May 29, 1942, B: 389, E: 210, RG226, NA; (translated) The Situation in neutral states relating to the wartime economy October/December 1944, Dec. 27, 1944, R: 522, FR: 1692905–11, T-77, NA.

133 *least hoped:* Halbrook, pp. 76–77, 199; Persico, *Piercing the Reich*, p. 45; Bancroft, p. 130; Dulles, *Germany's Underground*, pp. 125–26; Gerhard Van Arkel interview Nov. 11, 1983, B: 11, RSP, HIA; Axis Agents in Switzerland, August 1943, KV 3/246, Axis Intelligence Activities in Switzerland Oct. 21–Nov. 21, 1943, KV 3/245, JFC letter to D. G. White Nov. 20, 1942, KV 3/244, NAUK; Joseph Dasher memo to WS with attachment March 14, 1945, B: 2, E: 19A, Bern cable to 109 and Jackpot March 15, 1944, B: 469, E: 210, Thomas Dunn memos to John McDonough March 7, 1944, and James Murphy April 7, 1944, B: 21, E: 211, RG226, NA; Appendix: Schellenberg's relations with the Swiss Intelligence Service, B: 1, ADP, NSA; Bach, FAOH, p. 7; Halbrook, pp. 111, 239–40, 272, 283; Delattre, p. 91; Sudoplatov, pp. 119, 138; Andrew, p. 102; Dulles, *The Craft of Intelligence*, pp. 109–10.

134 *later wrote:* Petersen, pp. 1, 7, 10, 31–33, 117–18, 350–51; OSS History Office transcripts of interviews with OSS Officers, Allen Dulles on Sept. 22 and 28, 1944, B: Unnumbered 4th and 3rd from the end of the collection, WJDP, MHI; Dulles, *Germany's Underground*, pp. xi, 126, 132–33; Chalou, p. 273; Edward Bigelow memo to W. Lane Rehm March 16, 1944, B: 203, E: 224, David Crockett memo to Edward Glavin Sept. 20, 1944, R: 83, FR: 180–83, Bern cable to OSS headquarters Aug. 19, 1945, R: 106, FR: 817–19, Bern cable to OSS headquarters May 13, 1944, R: 52, FR: 2–5, M1642, Bern cable to OSS headquarters Dec. 9, 1943, B: 332, Bern cable to OSS headquarters Nov. 18, 1943, B: 170, E: 134, RG226, NA; AWD letter to Susan Klein Dec. 14, 1965, B: 110, AWD letter to CTD Nov. 28, 1942, B: 18, AWDP, PU; SOE War Diary: Italy, Switzerland and Mediterranean Section July–December 1943, "No" for C., p. 360, HS 7/263, NAUK; Dulles, *The Secret Surrender*, pp. 13–14; Dulles, *The Craft of Intelligence*, p. 7; Bancroft, COH, p. 238.

135 *Dufourstrasse 24:* Bach, FAOH, pp. 7–8; AWD letters to CTD Dec. 9, 1942, and March 7, 1943, B: 18, AWD letter To Whom It May Concern July 5, 1945, B: 44, AWDP, PU; Dulles, *The Secret Surrender,* pp. 13, 80; Bancroft, p. 130; Talley, July 28, 2012; Srodes, pp. 228–30; Mary Bancroft interview July 16, 1980, B: (unnumbered) "Interviews—Bancroft to Sherwood 1945—undated," OSS History Office transcripts of interviews with OSS Officers, Allen Dulles on Sept. 22, 1944, B: Unnumbered 4th and 3rd from the end of the collection, WJDP, MHI; Gerry Mayer letter to AWD March 24, 1947, AWD letter to WJD April 25, 1947, Statement of War Service of Gerald Mayer April 25, 1947, B: 40, AWDP, PU; Bancroft, COH, pp. 233–34; Petersen, pp. 5–6; Delattre, p. 95; Bradsher, "A Time to Act."

135 *decoding messages:* AWD letter to DKEB Dec. 7, 1950, B: 9, AWDP, PU; Cable from Jackpot and Carib to 110 June 28, 1943, B: 332, Cable from 284 to SI Aug. 11, 1943, B: 171, E: 134, WJD memo to JCS Sept. 26, 1944, R: 83, FR: 161, M1642, RG226, NA; Srodes, pp. 220–21, 230; *The Overseas Targets,* pp. 273–74; Petersen, pp. 4, 6, 9, 69.

136 *cook prepared:* Burns cables to Victor Nov. 14 and 20, 1942, B: 121B, WJDP, MHI; Bern cable to SI May 7, 1943, B: 449, Elizabeth Wiskemann letters to Dulles Dec. 11 and 30, 1942, Feb. 20 and March 21, 1943, E: 210, RG226, NA; 105 cable to Burns Jan. 4, 1944, B: 2, ADP, NSA; Petersen, pp. 12, 41–42, 129, 176–77; Dulles, *The Craft of Intelligence,* p. 27; *The Overseas Targets,* p. 275; Dulles, *Germany's Underground* pp. 119–20; Molden, p. 178; Bancroft, p. 141.

137 *the opportunity:* Transcript of Henry Brandon interview with AWD, B: 16, HBP, LOC; SOE War Diary 42, Italy, Switzerland and Mediterranean Section, July–December 1943, McCaffrey Suggests a House and a Car, pp. 359–60, HS 7/263, SOE War Diary 41, Italy, Switzerland and Mediterranean Section, July 1942–June 1943, Dulles, pp. 83–84, NAUK; Telegram dated 3rd December (Copy), Dec. 4, 1942, B: 7, E: 214, Bern cable to SI Dec. 17, 1944, 110 and 399 cables to Reddick Jan. 6 and 16, 1945, B: 133, E: 134, RG226, NA; Cookridge, p. 20; Delattre, pp. 79, 111; Srodes, pp. 231, 234; OSS History Office transcripts of interviews with OSS Officers, Allen Dulles on Sept. 22, 1944, B: Unnumbered 4th and 3rd from the end of the collection, WJDP, MHI; Petersen, pp. 221, 285–86, 352–53; Talley, July 28, 2012; Bancroft, COH, pp. 236, 239; Dulles, *The Craft of Intelligence,* pp. 173–74, 201; "The World of Cloak & Danger," by Henry Brandon, London *Sunday Times,* April 28, 1963, p. 13; AWD letter to CTD Dec. 9, 1942, B: 18, AWDP, PU; Jeffery, p. 509.

138 *naive prediction:* Bern cable to SI Jan. 22, 1944, B: 265, Bern cables to SI Aug. 31 and Oct. 26, 1943, B: 264, Bern cable to SI Aug. 27, 1943, B: 332, 109 cable to Joyce and 110 May 16, 1945, B: 194, E: 134, John Hughes memo to F. L. Mayer, B: 101, E: 92, Bern cable to SI Aug. 12, 1943, B: 79, E: 210, Raymond L. Brittenham memorandum for the files June 30, 1943, Raymond Brittenham memo to Henry Morgan Aug. 25, 1943, E: 94, RG226, NA; AWD handwritten scripts for flashes, B: 4, AWD letter to CTD March 7, 1943, B: 18, AWDP, PU; Bancroft, pp. 135, 138, 145; Delattre, p. 77; Dulles, *The Secret Surrender,* p. 16; OSS History Office transcripts of interviews with OSS Officers, Allen

Dulles on Sept. 22, 1944, B: Unnumbered 4th and 3rd from the end of the collection, WJDP, MHI; O'Donnell, p. 71; Petersen, p. 149; Talley, July 28, 2012.

138 *practically anybody:* (translated) German memo May 4, 1943, on Telegram from Bern to Washington, State Department, Mr. Burns, from 7 April 43, R: 458, FR: 2975006-47, T-1745, AWD memo to BRL on Egon Winkler, B: 355, E: 210, Bern cable to SI Nov. 21 1943, B: 332, E: 134, RG226, NA; AWD letter to W. L. Clayton Dec. 3, 1946, B: 51, AWD letter to Eliot Coulter March 26, 1946, B: 57, AWDP, PU; B. H. Townsland note to White with attachment Feb. 1, 1944, KV 3/246, NAUK; OSS History Office transcripts of interviews with OSS Officers, Allen Dulles on Sept. 22, 1944, B: Unnumbered 4th and 3rd from the end of the collection, WJDP, MHI; Bancroft, COH, p. 242; Hood, Dec. 12, 2008; Grose, pp. 156–62; Petersen, pp. 147, 261–67.

139 *"be prospering":* Excerpt from article by Ferruccio Lanfranchi, B: 4, ADP, NSA; GG biography, WJD letter to GG Oct. 1945, GGP, HIA; JEH letter to Harry Hopkins July 26, 1943, DOJ Rpt. No. 2361-A, OF 10B, FDRL; Srodes, pp. 247–48; Grose, pp. 171–73; Kindleberger, OHP, p. 9; Dulles, *The Secret Surrender,* pp. 14–15; Mary Bancroft interview July 16, 1980, pp. 31–32, B: (unnumbered) "Interviews—Bancroft to Sherwood 1945— undated," WJDP, MHI; Talley, July 28, 2012.

140 *phone calls:* Srodes, p. 269; Bancroft, pp. 8–15, 26, 33–34, 55–60, 64–84, 91–96, 110–12, 121–29; Bancroft, COH, pp. 1–3, 20–21, 43, 61–64, 196–97, 202, 226, 230–31, 339–40; Hood, Dec. 12, 2008; Talley, July 28, 2012; "P. M. Hamilton Asks Divorce," *New York Times,* July 24, 1946, p. 3; "Dulles Days," by Mary Bancroft, *Washington Post,* Feb. 1, 1969.

141 *wartime mistress:* Bancroft, pp. 129–37, 151–61; Bancroft, COH, pp. 7, 103, 245; Mary Bancroft interview July 16, 1980, p. 12, B: (unnumbered) "Interviews—Bancroft to Sherwood 1945—undated," WJDP, MHI.

142 *depress her:* AWD letters to CTD April 19 and May 23, 1943, and Jan. 26, 1944, George Gordon letter to CTD Sept. 27, 1943, B: 18, AWDP, PU; Talley, Oct. 24, 2013; WS memo to WJD with enclosures May 11, 1943, Jimmy Dunn letters to Hugh Wilson July 13 and Aug. 14, 1943, John Hughes letter and memo to Hugh Wilson July 22, 1943, Hugh Wilson memo to John Hughes July 15, 1943, B: 101, E: 92, RG226, NA; Talley, July 28, 2012.

142 *injudicious conclusions:* Bern cable to Director Aug. 31, 1943, B: 264, 154 cable to 110 March 3, 1944, B: 165, E: 134, Jackpot cable to 110 April 28, 1943, R: 150, A-3304, RG226, NA; Hood, Dec. 12, 2008; Richard Harris Smith, p. 7; Grose, p. 180.

143 *to Washington:* Bern cable to SI Dec. 9, 1943, Jackpot cable to Bern July 29, 1943, SI cable to Bern Aug. 12, 1943, SI cable to Bern May 12, 1943, B: 332, Bern cable to SI Oct. 2, 1943, Bern cable to SI Oct. 28, 1943, Bern cable to 105 Sept. 14, 1943, Bern cable to SI July 7, 1943, B: 264, OSS HQ cable to Bern May 26, 1944, B: 266, Bern cable to SI Nov. 13, 1943, B: 170, Jackpot cable to 110 May 20, 1944, 110 cable to Jackpot March 28, 1944, B: 165, E: 134, WJD memo to FDR July 10, 1944, R: 24, FR: 83–84, R: 104, FR: 399–43, M1642, RG226, NA; Petersen, pp. 6–7, 75, 99–101, 113, 121, 173–76, 197–98, 211–12, 232, 316–17, 327–28, 380, 393; *The Overseas Targets,* p. 281.

144 *believe otherwise:* (translated) memo by SS-Hauptsturmführer Ahrens on Dulles, Roo-

sevelt's Special Envoy in Switzerland with enclosure April 30, 1943, R: 458, FR: 2975006-47, T-1745, Abwehr counterintelligence (III) report on British and Allied "intelligence agents" integrated into diplomatic and consular missions abroad Aug. 6, 1942, R: 357, FR: 264449-76, T-120, (translated) Secret Commando Matter of the OSS Dec. 5, 1944, R: 705, FR: 35–51, Report by V-Man "Wittich" on Anglo-American strategic planning, based on a conversation with AWD, June 8, 1943, R: 539, FR: 423–29, T-78, AWD letter To Whom It May Concern Feb. 27, 1946, R: 114, FR: 699–704, M1642, Special Interrogation of Schellenberg 15 and 21 September, B: 2, E: 125A, NA; National Archives and Records Service, Record Group 1048, Report on Kaltenbrunner message to Martin Bormann Nov. 29, 1944, B: 106, AWDP, PU; Memo for 110 Oct. 20, 1943, B: 1, Carib cable to 110 March 31, 1944, B: 2, ADP, NSA; Gisevius, p. 482.

144 *valuable intelligence:* Petersen, pp. 148–49; OSS History Office transcripts of interviews with OSS Officers, Allen Dulles on Sept. 22, 1944, B: Unnumbered 4th and 3rd from the end of the collection, WJDP, MHI; OSS Personnel Action Request for Clover T. Dulles, Clover T. Dulles assignment in OSS with biography, B: 203, E: 224, Kappa cable from 110 May 25, 1944, B: 519, Bern cable to 105 Nov. 30, 1944, B: 451, Bergen memo to 110 Feb. 7, 1945, B: 262, E: 210, WJD cable to AWD Feb. 18, 1944, B: 265, E: 134, RG226, NA; Vassilliev Notebook, Wilson International Center for Scholars, CWIHP, White Notebook #3, Maxim delivered from Wash. on 13.6.44 "Mary's" report, p. 23, Report dated 4.4.45, p. 27, Yellow Notebook #4, p. 99; Memo on Penetration and Compromise of OSS in Switzerland and Western Europe (Allen Dulles) May 4, 1948, B: 56, HVP, LOC; Watch. for 109 and Jackpot Dec. 11, 1943, B: 1, ADP, NSA; *The Overseas Targets*, p. 180; Murphy, pp. 4, 456; Weinstein, p. 240; Petersen, pp. 167, 431; Mosley, pp. 147–48.

145 *war ended:* Bern cable to MO Sept. 11, 1943, B: 264, E: 134, RG226, John Grombach memo to Chief MIS June 7, 1945, B: 18, Monograph on the OSS, pp. 4–5, B: 18, Switzerland OSS, April 1945, B: 27, Memorandum to Miss Wells March 22, 1945, Memo for Chief, MIS on OSS Activities in Switzerland June 30, 1945, B: 18, E: P12, File on AWD, B: 1, E: P19, GP, RG263, NA; Halbrook, pp. 83–84; Delattre, p. 80; Bradsher, "A Time to Act"; Talley, July 28, 2012; Srodes, p. 216; Bancroft, pp. 140–41; Grose, p. 181; Memorandum to Mr. Nichols, "Dulles Importance Overrated in German Circles," 11/9/45 65-55559, FBI.

146 *saving it:* Talley, July 28, 2012; Persico, *Piercing the Reich*, pp. 49–52; Mosley, pp. 138–39; Gisevius, pp. vii–xiv, xxi, xxvi, xxxi–xxxii, 227, 331–32, 456–58, 478–79; Dulles, *Germany's Underground*, pp. 126–34; Srodes, p. 255.

147 *Adolf Hitler:* AWD letter to Tiny Sept. 4, 1947, B: 29, AWDP, PU; Telegram No. 2174 to Bern Aug. 1, 1943, B: 1, ADP, NSA; USTRAVIC, London cable to Bern Feb. 14, 1944, B: 453, E: 210, AWD letter To Whom It May Concern Feb. 27, 1946, R: 114, FR: 699–704, M1642, RG226, NA; Petersen, p. 217; Hoffmann, p. 121; Bancroft, pp. 161–65, 166–68, 188–95; Dulles, *Germany's Underground*, pp. 130–34; Dulles, *The Craft of Intelligence*, pp. 203–4; Jeffery, p. 380–2.

147 *of Germany:* Helms Biography Material, B: 7, P: 3, S: 7, RHP, GU; F. L. Mayer memo to

Chief, SI, Dec. 13, 1943, B: 419, E: 210, RG226, NA; Helms, *A Look over My Shoulder*, pp. 33–37; Report of Fitness of Officers for RMH April 1, 1944 to Jan. 8, 1945, RHNR, NPRC; Cynthia Helms, July 18, 2012.

148 *personal business:* AWD memo on conversation with George Wood, Aug. 31, 1943, 19430831_0000031385, Correspondence—General—English 1942–1974-and-undated 1940s, AWDD, PU: Bradsher, "A Time to Act"; Delattre, pp. 5, 9–18, 35–51, 60–73, 110–11.

152 *September 25, 1900:* Delattre, pp. 7, 9–24, 28–29, 85–91, 91–110, 115–17; F. L. Belin memo to WJD Oct. 12, 1943, R: 36, FR: 659–61, M1642, Norman Holmes Pearson memo to DKEB Nov. 23, 1943, B: 435, E: 210, RG226, NA; Alias George Wood by Anthony Quibble, B: 4, ADP, NSA; Morgan, pp. 98, 100–101.

153 *in watchcases:* Bern cables to SI Aug. 21 and 26, 1943, B: 451, Method of Control of Boston Series Material Feb. 29, 1944, Special Procedure for the Handling of "Kappa" Intelligence March 24, 1944, B: 435, W. A. Kimbel memo to Chief, SI, Feb. 20, 1946, B: 350, Bern cables to SI Oct. 11 and 16, 1943, B: 451, E: 210, The Story of George, B: 7, E: 190C, AWD cable to 105, 109 and Jackpot Oct. 9, 1943, B: 332, E: 134, RG226, NA; Petersen, pp. 8, 109, 140; Alias George Wood by Anthony Quibble, B: 4, ADP, NSA; Morgan, p. 102; AWD court deposition Jan. 15, 1948, B: 36, AWDP, PU; Mosley, p. 149; Delattre, pp. 118–19, 146–48, 165–66, 193–95.

154 *such games:* Morgan, p. 104; Delattre, pp. 111–27; Helms Biography Material, B: 7, P: 3, S: 7, My Early Years in Intelligence, B: 10, P: 1, S: 1, RHP, GU; Claude Dansey letter to DKEB Aug. 25, 1943, Norman Holmes Pearson memo to DKEB Nov. 23, 1943, Questions to Be Asked Source Feb. 1, 1944, B: 435, 110 cable to Carib and Jackpot April 26, 1944, B: 451, Bern cable to Jackpot Dec. 29, 1943, B: 453, E: 210, AWD cable to 105, 109 and Jackpot Oct. 9, 1943, B: 332, E: 134, RG226, NA; Alias George Wood by Anthony Quibble, B: 4, ADP, NSA; Helms, *A Look over My Shoulder*, pp. 33–37; Mosley, pp. 157–58; Grose, pp. 189–91.

155 *"this war":* The Story of George, B: 7, E: 190C, RG226, NA; AWD court deposition Jan. 15, 1948, B: 36, AWDP, PU; Boston Series No. 6: Treatment of Italian Jews, No. 123: Nazi Plane Losses over England, No. 609: Manufacture and Development of Japanese Aircraft, No. 23: Airfields in England, B: 431–33, Bern cable to SI (London) Jan. 10, 1944, B: 451, Alfred McCormack memos to Lt. Dunn Dec. 28, 1944, and May 23, 1945, Thomas Dunn memo to J. R. Murphy March 11, 1944, B: 435, Ferdinand Mayer memo to WS Dec. 28, 1944, B: 350, E: 210, Wood cables—Evaluation of Kapril and subsequent series Aug. 7, 1944, Saint London memo to Saint Washington May 11, 1944, B: 22, E: 124, RG226, NA; W. S. Stephenson letter to WJD Nov. 15, 1944, B: 1, RFP, HIA; Delattre, pp. 127–99, 131–36, 139–45; Petersen, pp. 183–86, 189.

156 *to Switzerland:* WJD memo to FDR Jan. 10, 1944, R: 23, FR: 708–35, Hugh Wilson memo to WJD Oct. 20, 1943, R: 102, FR: 96–98, WS memo to Edward Buxton with enclosure Jan. 26, 1944, R: 62, FR: 1010–16, M1642, Cable from Regis, Carib, Jackpot, 140 and everyone Dec. 24, 1943, SI cable to Bern Dec. 11, 1943, B: 265, SI cable to Bern March 14, 1944, B: 165, Carib and Jackpot cable to 110 Dec. 30, 1943, B: 332, E: 134, RG226, NA.

CHAPTER 10: LONDON

158 *become testier:* WJC letter to SKC Nov. 16, 1943, BCS; Short Guide to Grosvenor Square, B: 22, E: 92, RG226, NA; Leonard J. Cushing memo to Chief of Naval Personnel Nov. 3, 1943, WJC Application for Commission or Warrant, WJC flight schedule from New York to Prestwick Nov. 13–14, 1943, WCNR, NPRC; Meyer, pp. 116–17; Casey, *The Secret War Against Hitler*, p. 12; Barreaux, Aug. 12, 2012; Ziegler, pp. 4–8, 19, 42, 50–51, 67–68, 120–23, 161–71, 189; Lowe, p. 6; Van Young, pp. 4–16.

159 *classical records:* Short Guide to Grosvenor Square, B: 22, E: 92, RG226, NA; WJC letters to SKC Nov. 11 and 23, 1943, BCS; Ziegler, pp. 31, 73, 107–8, 115, 118, 133, 155–56, 234–36, 241–42, 282; Van Young, pp. 2, 31, 127, 224, 250, 295; Casey, *The Secret War Against Hitler*, pp. 23–24.

160 *"under Eisenhower":* Short Guide to Grosvenor Square, B: 22, E: 92, OSS list of restaurants in London, B: 10, E: 92A, RG226, NA; WJC letter to SKC Nov. 17, 1943, WJC letter to Mary Kurz Nov. 17, 1943, BCS; Barreaux, Aug. 12, 2012; Ziegler, pp. 74, 90, 183, 216–17, 221–26, 233–34, 242–52, 268; Lankford, *OSS Against the Reich*, p. 17.

160 *the idea:* Interview with OCD 1977, pp. 162–63, B: Oral History Interviews—O. C. Doering Jr., Activities in Europe 1941–89, Interview with DKEB Jan. 29, 1945, B: Interviews—Bancroft to Sherwood 1945—undated, WJDP, MHI; Howe, Dec. 20, 2007, July 12, 2012; Kingsley, Jan. 1, 2008; Lankford, *The Last American Aristocrat*, pp. 7–25, 48–59, 66–67, 82–86, 94–104, 111–13, 124–25, 133–37, 151–53; Lankford, *OSS Against the Reich*, pp. 4–9, 12–13, 20; War Diary: SI Branch, OSS London, Vol. 1, pp. 1–2, R: 4, FR: 542–1305, R: 5, FR: 2–962, M1623, DKB letter to WJD Feb. 18, 1944, B: 229, United States Federal Officers in London May 26, 1943, B: 247, E: 190, DKEB memo to WJD Oct. 13, 1942, R: 92, FR: 1188–90, M1642, RG226, NA.

161 *his assistant:* Montgomery, July 17, 2012; WJC letters to SKC Nov. 25 and Dec. 5, 1943, Jan. 7 and 10, 1944, circa late November or early December 1943, and undated 1944, BCS; Howe, July 12, 2012; Jolis, p. 108; Lankford, *The Last American Aristocrat*, pp. 163–76; "Col. Bruce Free Friday, Wed Monday," *Times Herald*, April 25, 1945, B: 130, E: 99, WJD letter to G. Howland Shaw July 15, 1942, R: 36, FR: 379–82, M1642, OCD letter to DKEB Nov. 7, 1943, B: 320, E: 190, RG226, NA.

162 *Bible verse:* Short Guide to Grosvenor Square, B: 22, E: 92, Edward Buxton memo to JCS with enclosure Jan. 27, 1944, R: 62, FR: 1003–5, Ellery Huntington memo to WJD March 26, 1943, R: 69, FR: 1040, OCD memo to C. W. Barnes Sept. 26, 1942, R: 69, FR: 1015–16, M1642, United States Federal Officers in London May 26, 1943, B: 247, Thomas Upton memo to Maj. Hornaday May 26, 1944, B: 455, E: 190, RG226, NA; Author tour of Grosvenor Square Dec. 12, 2012; Casey OSS badge and "For God and Country" card, B: 460, WJCP, HIA; Ziegler, pp. 215–17; Van Young, pp. 133–37, 156; War Diary: SI Branch, OSS London, Vol. 1, opening Chronological Summary and p. 1, R: 4, FR: 542–1305, R: 5, FR: 2–962, M1623, RG226, NA; Lankford, *The Last American Aristocrat*, p. 135; Hall, p. 125.

162 *Schlesinger served:* WJC letter to SKC Dec. 3, 1943, BCS; London Office OSS Security

Instructions, B: 48, E: 92, WJD letter to Chief of Naval Personnel Aug. 8, 1942, Junius S. Morgan letter to Edward Buxton April 11, 1944, J. Robert Rubin letter to WJD March 16, 1944, Frederick Spencer memo to WJD June 1, 1944, R: 101, FR: 1215–24, M1642, Preston E. James memo on Arthur Schlesinger Request for Discharge Nov. 15, 1945, B: 683, E: 224, RG226, NA; WJC Priority Certificate for Air Travel June 26, 1944, WCNR, NPRC; Richard Harris Smith, p. 14; Casey, *The Secret War Against Hitler*, pp. 22–23; Barreaux, Aug. 6, 2012; Schlesinger, pp. 504, 513.

162 *so expensive:* WJC letters to SKC Nov. 17 and Dec. 2, 1943, undated letter likely 1944, BCS; Bernadette Casey Smith, Aug. 24, 2012; Ziegler, pp. 42, 63; WJC letter to Cdr. R. Guest Nov. 21, 1944, Rules and Regulations for the Wine Mess, WCNR, NPRC.

163 *the Americans:* WJD letter to Stewart Menzies July 28, 1943, and Menzies's response July 29, 1943, R: 34, FR: 645–53, Ellery Huntington letter to WJD Nov. 16, 1943, R: 45, FR: 1382–85, Summary of Agreement between British SOE and American SO, R: 111, FR: 1333–45, John Wilson memo to WJD May 6, 1944, R: 69, FR: 1164–70, M1642, H. Redman memo to Captain Royal with enclosure Oct. 7, 1943, B: 545, E: 190, War Diary: SI Branch, OSS London, Vol. 1, pp. 12–13, 16, R: 4, FR: 542–1305, R: 5, FR: 2–962, M1623, RG226, NA; Minute Sheet D.B. p. 38, Reference SF.50/6/143, KV 4/149, NAUK; Ziegler, p. 61; Foot, *SOE in France*, p. 26; Lankford, *The Last American Aristocrat*, pp. 138–39; Casey, *The Secret War Against Hitler*, pp. 22, 31–32; Casey, "OSS: Lessons for Today," p. 57.

164 *in Washington:* E. J. Putzell letter to WJC Jan. 29, 1944, B: 230, E: 190, WJC letter to Ensign Putzell March 4, 1944, B: 187, E: 146, WJC memo to Executive Committee March 17, 1944, Executive Committee minutes for March 30 and April 6, 1944, and Agenda for April 24, 1944, B: 18, E: 168, RG226, NA; WJC memo on semi-monthly report to Theater Headquarters Feb. 25, 1944, WJC memo to Robert Alcorn Feb. 19, 1944, John Mitchell letter to Otto Tolischus June 27, 1944, Walter Giblin memo to Lt. J. G. Emmons June 23, 1944, WJC and Leo Cherne telegrams July 25 and Aug. 3, 1944, Leo Cherne letter to WJC July 26, 1944, WCNR, NPRC; Barreaux, Aug. 6, 2012; Letter to E. J. Putzell Jan. 20, 1944, B: 460, WJCP, HIA; Montgomery, July 12, 2012.

165 *as well:* Letter to E. J. Putzell Jan 20, 1944, B: 460, WJCP, HIA; WJC letters to SKC Nov. 11, 1943, and Feb. 12, 1944, BCS; Casey, *The Secret War Against Hitler*, pp. 22–23, 40–46, 63, 65; Montgomery, July 12, 2012; Barreaux, Aug. 6, 2012; Persico, *Casey*, p. 60; Report on the Fitness of Officers for WJC Nov. 3, 1943–March 31, 1944, WCNR, NPRC; WJC memos to Col. Giblin May 20 and June 5, 1946, WJC letter to OCD June 9, 1944, B: 232, E: 190, RG226, NA; Montgomery, July 12, 2012; Lankford, *The Last American Aristocrat*, p. 137; Casey, "OSS: Lessons for Today," pp. 57–58.

166 *American magazines:* WJC memo to DKEB April 13, 1944, B: 224, E: 190, Executive Officer, MO Branch memo to WJC Feb. 29, 1944, Shepard Morgan memo to Acting Director, Strategic Services, May 2, 1944, B: 338, E: 210, Theater Officers Pouch Report July 28, 1944, The Harvard Plan, B: 12, E: 99, WJC memo to Rae Smith and Fred Shoninger July 31, 1944, DKEB memo to WJD with enclosure April 11, 1944, B: 229, E: 190, Robert Thrun letter to WJC Oct. 25, 1944, R: 45, FR: 1035, M1642, RG226, NA; Shepard Morgan

letter to DKEB April 28, 1944, WJC memo to Col. Giblin May 3, 1944, B: 67A, WECP, PU; Casey, *The Secret War Against Hitler*, pp. 24, 40, 181; WJC letter to SKC Nov. 22, 1943, BCS; Montgomery, July 12, 2012; Lankford, *The Last American Aristocrat*, pp. 139–41; Casey, "The Clandestine War in Europe," pp. 1–2; Persico, *Casey*, p. 61; Van Young, pp. 140–41; Ziegler, pp. 195–96, 256.

167 *"big guy"*: WJC letters to SKC Nov. 23, 1944, Jan. 5, 10, and 27, 1944, and May 1944, WJC letter to Bernadette Feb. 21, 1944, BCS.

CHAPTER 11: MILTON HALL

170 *and England:* Roger Ford, p. 15; Colby, *Honorable Men*, p. 36; Singlaub, July 20, 2012; Singlaub, p. 34; Irwin, p. 53; War Diary, SO Branch, London, Vol. 4, Preamble to 1 January 1944, R: 8, M1623, B: 359, Franklin Canfield memo to Joseph Haskell, Dec. 10, 1943, B: 356, E: 190, RG226, NA; Kehoe, p. 19; Franklin, pp. 19, 150–52; Kehoe, Oct. 26, 2012; John Colby, July 30, 2012; Colby, *Honorable Men*, p. 36; Jedburghs, AD/E/603, Dec. 20, 1943, History of the Jedburghs in Europe 1942–1944, S.O.E. History 12, Vol. 1, HS 7/17, NAUK; Elbridge Colby letter to Richard Van Wagenen Nov. 12, 1943, B: 2, WECP, PU.

170 *"a Jedburgh":* Franklin Canfield memo to Joseph Haskell, Dec. 10, 1943, B: 356, Training Section History of the SO Branch by O. A. Pitre and I. A. Verschoor, B: 345, E: 190, Jedburgh Board Report for WEC, B: 10, E: 128, War Diary, SO Branch, London, Vol. 4, Preamble to 1 January 1944, R: 8, M1623, B: 359, E: 190, RG226, NA; Formation of Jedburgh Teams, pp. 1–3, 1943, p. 11, and Jedburgh Board sample report card, History of the Jedburghs in Europe 1942–1944, S.O.E. History 12, Vol. 1, HS 7/17, NAUK; Roger Ford, p. 15; Singlaub, July 20, 2012; Irwin, pp. 57–59; History of the Training Section of the SOE, 1940–1945, p. 59, History 30, HS 7/51, NAUK.

171 *joke funny:* Report on Seventy-five SO Agents (Mostly Jedburghs) Dropped by Parachute into France, B: 69, WJCP, HIA; FM/US memo to DR/US Jan. 5, 1944, AD/A memo to MT Dec. 15, 1943, B: 450, Training Section History of the SO Branch by O. A. Pitre and I. A. Verschoor, B: 345, E: 190, RG226, NA; Franklin, pp. 177–79; Beavan, pp. 106–7; Kehoe, p. 21; Singlaub, July 20, 2012; Singlaub, pp. 35–38.

171 *on instructors:* Training Section History of the SO Branch by O. A. Pitre and I. A. Verschoor, B: 345, Jedburghs, AD/E/603, Dec. 20, 1943, B: 339, E: 190, RG226, NA; Reich Central Security Office report, June 13, 1944, on spy- and saboteur-training facilities operated by the Allies, R: 488, FR: 196–205, T-84, NA; Kehoe, p. 20; Singlaub, July 20, 2012; Jedburghs, AD/E/603, Dec. 20, 1943, I. Origins and Objects, p. 10, History of Jedburghs in Europe 1942–1944, S.O.E. History 12, Vol. 1, HS 7/17, NAUK.

173 *in hand:* The Camus Project: The History of Castor, Ailsworth, Marholm, Upton and Sutton—and the Milton Estates, 2004, Chapter 22, Milton Park and the Fitzwilliam Family, by William Craven, pp. 227–31; Author tour of Peterborough and Milton Hall, Dec. 21, 2012; War Diary, SO Branch, London, Vol. 4, January–July 1944, R: 8, M1623, B: 359, E: 190, RG226, NA; Singlaub, July 20, 2012; Alsop, pp. 141–43; Kehoe, p. 20; Irwin, pp. 61–64; Cookridge, pp. 27–28; Dreux, pp. 49–50; Franklin, p. 170; History

of the Training Section of the SOE, 1940–1945, p. 126, History 30, HS 7/51, NAUK; Milton Hall photos, B: 7, CCP, HIA; Jedburgh scrapbook (Feb. 1, 1944–December 1944), CBC.

173 *its master:* European Theater of Operations Report, January 1944, B: 121, E: 99, Robert Dodderidge memo to Commanding Officer, S.O. Branch, OSS London, Feb. 11, 1944, B: 356, Henry Coxe memo to Commanding Officer, S.O. Branch, OSS London, Feb. 14, 1944, B: 450, E: 190, RG226, NA; History of the Jedburghs in Europe 1942–1944, S.O.E. History 12, Vol. 1, III. Training, p. 6, HS 7/17, NAUK; Beavan, p. 104; Kehoe, Oct. 26, 2012; Singlaub, July 20, 2012; Franklin, pp. 153, 170; Dreux, p. 22; Alsop, pp. 148–49; Dreux, p. 57.

174 *their eyes:* Beavan, pp. 84–87, 92–93; John Colby, July 30, 2012; Carl Colby, July 16, 2012; Report on Seventy-five SO Agents (Mostly Jedburghs) Dropped by Parachute into France, B: 69, WJCP, HIA; Cyrus Manierre memo to CO US Contingent, Training Detachment, M.E. 65, April 15, 1944, Statements by Major Fuller–U.S. Army April 15, 1944, and by Maj. Johnson, F.P., British Army, Lt. Col. Musgrave memo to Carleton Smith April 16, 1944, B: 9, E: 128, European Theater of Operations Report, January 1944, B: 121, E: 99, Henry Coxe memo to Commanding Officer, S.O. Branch, OSS London, Feb. 14, 1944, B: 450, E: 190, Franklin Canfield memos to Commanding General, HQ, ETOUSA, Oct. 9, 1943, and to Joseph Haskell Jan. 11, 1944, B: 280, E: 92, RG226, NA; Franklin, Oct. 24, 2012; Franklin, p. 165.

174 *a major:* Henry Coxe memo to Commanding Officer, S.O. Branch, OSS London, Feb. 14, 1944, B: 450, Training Section History of the SO Branch by O. A. Pitre and I. A. Verschoor, B: 345, E: 190, Franklin Canfield memo to Chief, SO Branch, Jan. 10, 1944, B: 280, E: 92, H. K. Lenocker memo to European Theater Officer May 1, 1944, E: 224, War Diary, SO Branch, London, Vol. 4, January–July 1944, R: 8, M1623, B: 359, E: 190, RG226, NA; Kehoe, Oct. 26, 2012; Beavan, p. 108; Lewis, pp. 11, 13; Roger Ford, pp. 21–22; History of the Jedburghs in Europe 1942–1944, S.O.E. History 12, Vol. 1, II. Formation of Jedburgh Teams, insert after p. 7, HS 7/17, NAUK; Dreux, p. 164.

175 *laughed nervously:* Role of Jedburghs: Summary of the speech by Brigadier E. E. Mockler-Ferryman to Jedburgh students on Feb. 24, 1944, script of his address to Jedburghs, B: 356, E: 190, RG226, NA; Beavan, pp. 108–11; Alsop, p. 143.

175 *the program:* Statement by O.C., M.E. 65, April 15, 1944, Lt. Col. Musgrave memo to Carleton Smith April 16, 1944, Statement by Lt. Konrad Dillow–U.S. Army, DAB memo to DR/JED April 26, 1944, B: 9, E: 128, European Theater of Operations Report, March 1944, B: 122, E: 99, RG226, NA.

176 *beyond that:* Lewis, p. 11; Dreux, pp. 55–56; Franklin, p. 166; Prados, pp. 10–11; Kehoe, Oct. 26, 2012; Singlaub, July 20, 2012.

176 *"Milton Hall animals":* History of the Jedburghs in Europe 1942–1944, S.O.E. History 12, Vol. 1, Syllabus of Training: 6 Week Course, Living Off the Land: A Memorandum on the More Valuable and Common Wild Foods of Europe, HS 7/17, NAUK; Irwin, pp. 61–64; Beavan, p. 112; Singlaub, OHP, pp. 13–14; Singlaub, p. 55.

177 *the flirting:* Carl Colby, July 16, 2012; Paul Colby, Sept. 3, 2012; Franklin, Oct. 24, 2012; Franklin, pp. 164, 170–73; Bassett, Dec. 21, 2012; Beavan, p. 114.

177 *in France:* Barbara Colby, July 16 and 30, 2012, and April 8, 2013; Colby, *Honorable Men,* p. 37; Sally Colby, July 27, 2012; Ziegler, pp. 220–21.

179 *to lieutenant:* Beavan, pp. 112–13; War Diary, SO Branch, London, Vol. 4, January–July 1944, R: 8, M1623, B: 359, E: 190, RG226, NA; Dreux, p. 62; WEC letter to Rene de Monseignant March 7, 1988, B: 2, WECP, PU; Bordelon, Oct. 25, 2012; Sears, Nov. 20, 2012; Alsop, p. 150; Sibley Cooley interview with Camille Lelong, Team "Bruce" WWII France TRT 42:16, Veteran & Military Television; Sears, Nov. 20, 2012; 27 FFC for Camille Lelong, Confidential Questionnaire for Candidate No. 9, Jacques Favel, HS 911/5, Briefing Office report with photos of members for Team Bruce, HS 6-489, NAUK; Carl Colby, July 16, 2012; Sally Colby, July 27, 2012; Colby, *Honorable Men,* pp. 25, 37–38; John Colby, July 30, 2012; Irwin, p. 142.

179 *became "Berkshire":* Glossary, Jedburgh Codes, B: 741, Jedburgh Teams. Cross Index. Team Names, B: 455, E: 190, RG226, NA; Beavan, p. 113.

180 *their orders:* Beavan, pp. 112, 115; Singlaub, July 20, 2012; Training Section History of the SO Branch by O. A. Pitre and I. A. Verschoor, B: 345, E: 190, Jedburgh Board Report for WEC, B: 10, E: 128, John Tyson memo to Major Canfield, Warning Order: Exercise "Spur," Narrative Exercise "Spillout," B: 356, Reeve Schley memo to Chief, Western European Section, May 2, 1944, B: 450, E:190, RG226, NA; Irwin, p. 65; Singlaub, p. 40; Franklin, pp. 171–72; History of the Jedburghs in Europe 1942–1944, History 12, Vol. 1, III. Training, p. 5, HS 7/17, NAUK; Singlaub, OHP, p. 16; War Diary, SO Branch, London, Vol. 4, January–July 1944, R: 8, M1623, B: 359, E: 190, RG226, NA; Singlaub, OHP, pp. 19–22; Singlaub, pp. 39–40; Casey, *The Secret War Against Hitler,* pp. 74–75; Kehoe, Oct. 26, 2012.

CHAPTER 12: D-DAY

182 *"Little Blitz" increased:* Atkinson, *The Guns at Last Light,* pp. 5, 12, 18; Keegan, p. 370; Ludewig, p. 31; Weinberg, pp. 665–67; Bern cable to SI April 12, 1944, B: 451, E: 210, NA; Memo to the Secretary, Chiefs of Staff Committee, Office of the War Cabinet on Operation "Overlord," July 15, 1943, B: 46, E: 23, RG331, NA; Ziegler, pp. 267–73; Stebenne, p. 39.

183 *to Argentina:* WJC letters to SKC April 16, 23 and May 1944, BCS; Casey, *The Secret War Against Hitler,* pp. 90–93; Lankford, *OSS Against the Reich,* pp. 106, 113; Richard Harris Smith, p. 167; David Kahn interview with WJC Jan. 18, 1982, NCM; Edward Buxton memo to Henry Stimson with enclosure June 13, 1944, R: 50, FR: 409–10; JCS Memorandum of Information No. 258, Activities of the Office of Strategic Services in Theaters of Operation, June 28, 1944, R: 8, FR: 1135–72, M1642, K. D. Mann memo to Kay Halle with enclosure July 29, 1944, B: 88, E: 99, WJC memo to Col. Forgan May 24, 1944, B: 230, E: 190, RG226, NA; Laurie, pp. 263, 267; Casey, "The Clandestine War in Europe," p. 3; Casey, "OSS: Lessons for Today," p. 60.

184 *through France:* Casey, *The Secret War Against Hitler*, pp. 109–10; War Diary, SI Branch, OSS London, Vol. 1, Chronological Summary, pp. 14–26, Vol. 3, Chronological Summary, pp. 6–10, 68, 206–7, 215, R: 4, FR: 542–1305, R: 5, FR: 2–962, M1623, Charles Cheston memo to JCS Sept. 1, 1944, R: 81, FR: 288–92, M1642, WJC memo to Lt. Armistead March 20, 1944, B: 299, E: 190, RG226, NA.

185 *from the air:* Memo to the Secretary, Chiefs of Staff Committee, Office of the War Cabinet on Operation "Overlord," July 15, 1943, B: 46, E: 23, RG331, Tactical Problems of an Invasion of North-West Europe May 1943, B: 330, E: 190, RG226, NA; Beavan, p. 98; Irwin, pp. 67–68; Meyer, pp. 233–34; Jackson, pp. 533, 551; Atkinson, *The Guns at Last Light*, p. 85; Casey, *The Secret War Against Hitler*, pp. 72–76, 83–88; Richard Harris Smith, pp. 164–65.

186 *a bonus:* John Bross memo to Chief, SO Branch, Feb. 10, 1944, Memo to Joseph Scribner on Tonnage of Supplies furnished Resistance Groups Jan. 1–June 30, 1944, July 7, 1944, SHAEF Operational Directive to SOE/SO March 23, 1944, B: 329, SO War Diary, OSS, Vol. 3, January, February, March 1944 and April, May, June 1944, B: 359, 360, 375–76, E: 190, WJD memo to FDR July 8, 1944, R: 24, FR: 56, M1642, RG226, NA; Casey, *The Secret War Against Hitler*, pp. 73, 87–88; Foot, *SOE in France*, p. 311; *The Overseas Targets*, pp. 197–99; Meyer, p. 234; Jackson, pp. 534–35, 541; Beavan, p. 117; Atkinson, *The Guns at Last Light*, p. 13; Ludewig, pp. 27–28.

186 *philatelist-in-chief:* Bern cables to B. Homer Hall March 1 and April 18, 1944, B: 169, Bern cable to SI May 5, 1944, B: 192, E: 134, Bern cable to SI April 12, 1944, B: 451, E: 210, RG226, NA; Petersen, pp. 5, 243–44, 255–56, 289–90, 305.

188 *"final downfall":* Bern cables to SI April 11 and 12, 1944, B: 451, E: 210, RG226, NA; David Kahn interview with WJC Jan. 18, 1982, NCM; Atkinson, *The Guns at Last Light*, pp. 82–83; Delattre, pp. 144, 158–59, 161–66, 172–75; Dulles, *The Craft of Intelligence*, p. 184; Petersen, pp. 65–66.

188 *be ignored:* Part XXXVI, Sept. 10, 1943, Comment on Hitler's Speech, Part XLIII, Report on Conversation Dec. 31, 1943, R: 109, FR: 643–45, 705–8, WJD memos to FDR with enclosure April 15 and 19, 1944, R: 23, FR: 856–64, M1642, Bern cable to B. Homer Hall Jan. 31, 1944, B: 169, E: 134, Bern cable to SI April 17, 1944, B: 451, E: 210, RG226, NA; John Weckerling memo to the Chief of Staff April 16, 1944, Edward Buxton memos to the Chief of Staff with enclosure April 15 and 19, 1944, R: 14, FR: 283–93, GMP, LOC.

189 *quit on him:* SI cable to Bern Feb. 1, 1944, B: 265, E: 134, James Lay memo to T. J. Betts with enclosure Aug. 21, 1944, R: 11, FR: 162–74, M1642, RG226, NA; Casey, "The Secret War Against Hitler," p. 101.

190 *the invaders:* John Bross memo to Chief, SO Branch, Feb. 10, 1944, DR/G 1 memo to DR/US May 29, 1944, B: 329, OSS Aid to the French Resistance in World War II, Missions, F-Section, p. 27, B: 740, SOE/SO Planning Survey as at May 1, 1944, with appendices, B: 330, SO War Diary, OSS, Vol. 3, April, May, June 1944, B: 359, 360, 375–76, E: 190, Minutes of Executive Committee Meeting May 4, 1944, B: 18, E: 168, RG226, NA; WJC letters to SKC May 1944, June 3, 1944, BCS; Casey, "OSS: Lessons for Today," p. 60; Ludewig, p. 26; Interview with Gen.

Walter Warlimont July 28, 1945, A Garland Series: World War II Germany Military Studies, Vol. 2, pp. 6–8, MHI; Gilbert, p. 521; Casey, *The Secret War Against Hitler*, p. 100; Waller, pp. 235, 240; Ziegler, pp. 278–81; Lankford, *OSS Against the Reich*, p. 98.

191 *"of Bolshevism"*: Atkinson, *The Guns at Last Light*, p. 29; SO War Diary, OSS, Vol. 3, January, February, March 1944 and April, May, June 1994, B: 359, 360, 375–76, E: 190, Bern cable to SI June 6, 1944, B: 266, Bern cable to B. Homer Hall June 6, 1944, B: 169, E: 134, RG226, NA; Weinberg, pp. 684–91.

191 *to London:* French Desk, SI, memo to Stephen Penrose April 23, 1945, Justin O'Brien memo to Chief, SI, with enclosures, March 1, 1945, B: 16, E: 99, John O'Gara memo to WJD with enclosure Oct. 21, 1944, R: 80, FR: 1193–1208, M1642, War Diary, SI Branch, OSS London, Vol. 3, pp. 16–17, 209, 219–21, 228, R: 4, FR: 542–1305, R: 5, FR: 2–962, M1623, RG226, NA; Petersen, pp. 301–2; Waller, pp. 243–46.

192 *first day:* WJD letter to James Forrestal June 14, 1944, R: 19, FR: 1074–75, M1642, RG226, NA; Casey, "The Clandestine War in Europe," p. 4.

CHAPTER 13: FRANCE

193 *early wave:* Exercise "Lash," Index 2, B: 356, E: 190, History of the Jedburghs in Europe 1942–1944, III, Training, p. 5, HS 7/17, NAUK; War Diary, SO Branch, OSS London, Vol. 4, January–July 1944, B: 359, E: 190, R: 8, M1623, RG226, NA; Franklin, p. 186.

193 *the ground:* Nominal Roll of Jedburghs July 24, 1944, B: 455, E: 190, RG226, NA; Beavan, pp. 127, 311; War Diary, SO Branch, OSS London, Vol. 4, April, May, June 1944, B: 359, E: 190, R: 8, M1623, RG226, NA.

194 *used precipitously:* Summary of French Resistance June 6–Aug. 31, 1944, B: 16, E: 99, RG226, NA; Franklin, p. 186; Alsop, pp. 151–52; Beavan, pp. 164–65; Singlaub, July 20, 2012; Colby, *Honorable Men*, p. 37; History of the Jedburghs in Europe 1942–1944, VI. France, p. 11, Jedburghs, AD/E/603, Dec. 20, 1943, HS 7/17, NAUK; Ford, pp. 29–30; Casey, *The Secret War Against Hitler*, pp. 93–95.

195 *of crowds:* Bern cable to B. Homer Hall June 9, 1944, B: 169, Bern cable to SI June 10, 1944, B: 226, Bern cable to OSS HQ June 23, 1944, MO cable to Bern June 21, 1944, B: 226, E: 134, WJD memo to FDR July 10, 1944, R: 30, FR: 855–56, WJD memo to FDR July 21, 1944, R: 24, FR: 165–67, M1642, RG226, NA; Atkinson, *The Guns at Last Light*, pp. 82–86, 100, 104–6; Keegan, p. 388; Ludewig, pp. 23, 32–33; Weinberg, p. 691.

196 *decisive one:* A. Military Value of the Resistance July 7, 1944, B: 440, OSS Aid to the Resistance in World War II, Missions, F-Section, pp. 28–31, B: 740, E: 190, RG226, NA; Memo to Prime Minister on Action by the Resistance in support of Operations at Normandy June 20, 1944, B: 329, E: 190, European Theater of Operations Report June 1944, OSS Activities, including European Theater, June 44–Sept. 45, Washington History Office, B: 123–25, E: 99, War Diary, SO Branch, OSS London, Vol. 3, April, May, June 1944, B: 359, E: 190, R: 8, M1623, RG226, NA; Julian Jackson, pp. 541, 544–45, 550–56; Atkinson, *The Guns at Last Light*, pp. 96–97; Meyer, p. 234; Foot, *SOE in France*, pp. 314, 349–51; SOE History 90A, France, Participation of the F.F.I. in the Liberation of France,

pp. 779–80, H 7/127, H 7/7, H 7/129, H 7/130, H 7/132, NAUK; French Forces of the Interior–1944, War Department Special Staff Historical Division File No. 8-3 FR (Vol. 1), p. 508, CMH; Ludewig, pp. 25, 29, 101.

196   *"well repaid"*: French Forces of the Interior–1944, War Department Special Staff Historical Division File No. 8-3 FR (Vol. 1), p. 1586, CMH; WJD memo to General Marshall July 12, 1944, B: 17, E: 99, War Diary, SO Branch, OSS London, Vol. 3, April, May, June 1944, B: 359, E: 190, R: 8, M1623, RG226, NA; Ludewig, pp. 28–29.

197   *he believed:* Casey, *The Secret War Against Hitler*, p. 108; WJC notes to Theodore Barreaux on Intelligence/Unanswered Questions, TCB; Schlesinger, OHP, p. 23.

198   *"absolutely maddening"*: Memo to Prime Minister on Action by the Resistance in support of Operations at Normandy June 20, 1944, B: 329, A. Military Value of the Resistance July 7, 1944, B: 440, E: 190, OSS photos of bodies at Oradour, B: 2, E: 101, WJD memo to FDR July 8, 1944, R: 50, FR: 460–63, M1642, European Theater of Operations Report July 1944, OSS Activities, including European Theater, June 44–Sept. 45, Washington History Office, B: 123–25, E: 99, War Diary, SO Branch, OSS London, Vol. 3, April, May, June 1944, B: 359, E: 190, R: 8, M1623, RG226, NA; Fuller, pp. 148, 172–75; Irwin, p. 112; Beavan, pp. 145–46; Lankford, *OSS Against the Reich*, pp. 142–50; Foot, *SOE in France*, p. 346; Julian Jackson, pp. 546, 556; Cookridge, pp. 218–19.

198   *of Tarbes:* E. R. Kellog memo to WJC with enclosure Jan. 15, 1945, R: 47, FR: 1093–1115, M1642, Paul Cyr biographical sheet, Report of the Activities of Team George Aug. 23, 1944, Horace W. Fuller biographical sheet, DKEB memo to Commander, U.S. Naval Forces in Europe, Dec. 22, 1944, "Bugatti" Report, Serial No. 12, B: 9–11, E: 128, RG226, NA.

199   *in Europe:* Beavan, pp. 128–29; Irwin, p. 181; C. Beaudry memo to A. B. MacLaren April 27, 1945, Jed Team-Ian, Maj. John Gildee, 1/Sgt. L. Bourgoin Killed in action, Report of Team "Ian" by Maj. Gildee, James R. Forgan memo to Commanding General, European Theater of Operations, June 28, 1945, Report on Captain Manierre, U.S., Field Name Rupert, F. E. Rosell memo to Col. Haskell Aug. 16, 1944, Roderick McKinnon memo to Archibold van Beuren Jan. 8, 1945, B: 9–11, E: 128, RG226, NA.

199   *"ask for it"*: War Diary, SO Branch, OSS London, Vol. 4, April, May, June 1944, B: 359, E: 190, R: 8, M1623, RG226, NA; Franklin, p. 185; Singlaub, pp. 41–42.

CHAPTER 14: BREAKERS

202   *military families:* 512 chronology, Jan. 13, 1943, entry, Burns cable for Victor Jan. 14, 1943, B: 9, E: 190C, RG226, NA; Hoffmann, pp. xiv, 7, 10–14, 20–21, 28, 31–35, 225, 295, 298; Dulles, *Germany's Underground*, pp. 81, 88–89, 109; Gisevius, pp. 430–35; Waller, p. 191; OSS biography of Count von Moltke Nov. 2, 1943, B: 18, E: 99, RG226, NA.

203   *backed off:* Gisevius, pp. ix, 168–69, 277–78, 288–89, 292–97, 303–19, 327–28, 435–38, 450–52, 462–63; Keegan, p. 482; Dulles, *The Secret Surrender*, p. 29; Hoffmann, pp. 43–46, 54–55, 69–70, 79–82, 90, 109–10, 264, 271; Dulles, *Germany's Underground*, pp. 24–33, 61.

204   *the Germans:* John Wiley memo to J. R. Hayden with enclosure Jan. 14, 1942, R: 49,

FR: 1111–14, Hugh Wilson memo to WJD with enclosure, R: 52, FR: 813–23, John Wiley memos to WJD Aug. 20 and 23, 1943, R: 104, FR: 1305–7, M1642, Memo from Broadway for December 1942, B: 22, E: 124, RG226, NA; Gisevius, pp. 376–82, 448; Hoffmann, pp. 153–55, 161, 167, Weinberg, p. 469.

204 *for Overlord*: Waller, pp. 54, 191–93; Hoffmann, p. 226; Hermann Plan Exposé, WJD memo to JCS April 2, 1944, WS memo to WJD March 2, 1944, Irving Sherman memo to WJD March 9, 1944, R: 52, FR: 314–95, M1642, RG226, NA.

205 *"state secrets"*: Mauch, p. 114; Petersen, pp. 107, 128–29; WJD letter to Sumner Welles April 6, 1943, R: 19, FR: 47–48, M1642, DKEB cables to Bern Aug. 1, 9, and 11, 1943, B: 9, E: 190C, RG226, NA; Bancroft, COH, p. 272; Dulles, *Germany's Underground*, pp. 70, 75; Weinberg, pp. 448–49.

206 *to hear*: Basic German Text of 512's Account March 29, 1945, B: 18, 512 chronology Nov. 12, 1943, entry, B: 9, E: 190C, E: 99, Jan. 26, 1942, memo, Report No. 10423, E: 16, British memo, "Double Agents," B: 251, E: 210, Wilmarth Lewis memo to Hugh Wilson re: S.A. #8560, Report No. 18363, E: 16, RG226, Canaris Vortraganotiz für Chief OKW, April 29, 1941, and October 1941, FR: 601–5, 611–16, R: 705, T-78, NA; Erika Canaris letter to AWD Aug. 24, 1947, B: 11, AWDP, PU; Erika Canaris letter to WJD Nov. 15, 1945, Vol. XVII, Part 1, COR; Testimony of Erwin Lahousen, B: 68, AWDP, PU; Gisevius, pp. 421–25, 439–45; Dulles, *Germany's Underground*, pp. 71–78; Srodes, p. 234; Petersen, p. 163; Kahn, pp. 226–34.

207 *as "Breakers"*: Bern cable to B. Homer Hall Feb. 11, 1944, B: 169, Bern cable to B. Homer Hall, B: 16, E: 134, Breakers Personalities File, Bern cables for Carib and Jackpot Jan. 20 and 29, 1944, Carib and 154 cable to 110 Jan. 26, 1944, B: 235, E: 146, RG226, NA; Mauch, p. 116; Hoffmann, p. 237; Dulles, *Germany's Underground*, p. 93; Bancroft, p. 202.

207 *"with events"*: Breakers code names, B: 234, Bern cable to Carib and Jackpot Jan. 27, 1944, B: 235, E: 146, Bern cable to OSS HQ Jan. 27, 1944, B: 265, E: 134, NA.

208 *already read*: Bern cable to London June 12, 1944, B: 18, E: 99, RG226, NA; Petersen, p. 345; Lankford, *OSS Against the Reich*, p. 125.

208 *to say*: Bern cable to Carib and Jackpot Jan. 27, 1944, Carib and 154 cables to 110 Feb. 1 and 2, 1944, B: 235, E: 146, RG226, NA; Dulles, *Germany's Underground*, pp. 134–35; Persico, *Piercing the Reich*, p. 62; Casey, "OSS: Lessons for Today," p. 58.

209 *the gang*: Basic German Text of 512's Account March 29, 1945, B: 18, E: 99, 512 chronology for Feb. 4, 1944, Telegram relayed to Secstate Washington from Bern Feb. 23, 1944, B: 9, E: 190C, Bern cable to SI Feb. 24, 1944, B: 265, E: 134, Bern cable In-4442 March 5, 1944, B: 235, E: 146, Bern cable to SI April 6, 1944, B: 219, E: 134, Bern cable to SI April 7, 1944, B: 235, E: 146, RG226, NA; Petersen, pp. 254–55; Dulles, *Germany's Underground*, p. 80; Gisevius, pp. 425, 479–81; Hoffmann, pp. 235–36, 293–95.

210 *"Nazi ruse"*: Bern cable to Jackpot and 109 May 12, 1944, Carib and 154 cable to 110 April 11, 1945, Bern cable to Carib, Jackpot, and 109 May 13, 1944, B: 235, E: 146, RG226, NA; Casey, *The Secret War Against Hitler*, p. 63; Hoffmann, p. 245; Dulles, *Germany's Underground*, p. 139.

210 *on Dulles:* Bern cable to Carib, Jackpot, and 109 May 13, 1944, B: 235, E: 146, G. Edward
    Buxton memo to Cordell Hull with enclosure May 17, 1944, R: 125, FR: 649–54, R: 19,
    FR: 733, M1642, Carib and 154 cable to 110 May 17, 1944, B: 235, E: 146, RG226, NA.

211 *country afterward:* Bancroft, pp. 206–8; Gisevius, pp. 427–28, 491–94; Hoffmann, p. 239.

212 *Roosevelt and Hull:* Bern cable to SI and WJD July 13, 1944, B: 18, E: 99, WJD cable to
    Cordell Hull with enclosure July 18, 1944, R: 113, FR: 1107–8, M1642, Bern cables to SI
    July 12 and 15, 1944, Bern cable to SI July 12, 1944, B: 235, E: 146, Bern July 12, 1944,
    cable forwarded to Secstate Washington, B: 9, E: 190C, RG226, NA; Persico, *Roosevelt's
    Secret War*, p. 323.

CHAPTER 15: VALKYRIE

214 *with the Soviets:* Gisevius, pp. xv–xvii, 495, 503–11; Petersen, p. 348; Basic German Text
    of 512's Account March 29, 1945, Bern cable to SI July 25, 1944, B: 18, E: 99, RG226, NA.

217 *be killed:* Hoffmann, pp. 90–91, 140, 243–44, 251–60, 272, 278–89, 298, 301–9, 322–44,
    370–77, 514–21; Mauch, p. 118; Gisevius, pp. xv–xx, 310–11, 393–95, 409–11, 483–85,
    519–21; Lochner, p. 554; Longerich, p. 699.

217 *with Hitler:* Basic German Text of 512's Account March 29, 1945, B: 18, E: 99, RG226, NA;
    Hoffmann, pp. 359–69, 377–88; Dulles, *Germany's Underground*, pp. 3–4, 175; Gisevius,
    pp. 498, 521–34.

221 *in danger:* H. Buchholz letter to AWD July 1, 1946, B: 33, *New York Times* printout
    July 21, 1944, of Hitler radio address, B: 66, AWDP, PU; Gisevius, pp. 536, 540–47, 550,
    554, 560–75; Hoffmann, pp. 391–92, 397–41, 455–56, 460–72, 479–503, 507–8, 511;
    Special Interrogation Series No. 10, Miss Johanna Wolf, May 31, 1945, Vol. XCIX, COR;
    Bancroft, pp. 203, 205.

221 *open line:* Bern cable to B. Homer Hall July 20, 1944, B: 169, E: 134, RG226, NA; Phone
    Nr. 180 July 20, 1944, Correspondence-Phone Calls-1943–1945, AWDD, PU.

222 *to Roosevelt: New York Times* photos July 23, 1944, of Wolf's Lair bomb site and Adolf
    Hitler shaking hands with Benito Mussolini, B: 68, AWDP, PU; Bern cable to B. Homer
    Hall July 24, 1944, B: 169, E: 134, WJD memo to FDR July 26, 1944, B: 18, E: 99, RG226,
    NA.

223 *and Churchill:* WJD memos to FDR July 22 and 26, 1944, SI cable to London July 25,
    1944, B: 18, E: 99, London cable to Bern July 21, 1944, B: 9, E: 190C, Bern cable to Lon-
    don Aug. 15, 1944, B: 219, E: 134, Subject: Background information on Breakers July 22,
    1944, Bern cable July 21, 1944, B: 22, E: 124, London cable to 154 July 24, 1944, B: 235, E:
    146, RG226, NA.

223 *prove true:* Bern cable to B. Homer Hall July 21, 1944, B: 169, E: 134, RG226, NA.

224 *of the loop:* London cable to 154 July 24, 1944, B: 235, London cable to 109 and 154
    July 22, 1944, London cable to Bern July 28, 1944, B: 234, E: 146, Bern cable to SI July
    21, 1945, Bern cables to London July 23 and 24, 1944, London cable to Bern July 26,
    1944, London cable to SI July 26, 1944, B: 219, E: 134, SI cable to London July 25, 1944,
    B: 18, E: 99, RG226, NA.

224 *a deal:* London cable to 154 July 24, 1944, B: 235, E: 146, 109 cable to Bruce July 28, 1944, B: 18, E: 299, Bern cable to B. Homer Hall July 22, 1944, B: 169, Bern cable to London July 26, 1944, B: 219, E: 134, WJD memo to FDR Aug. 2, 1944, R: 24, FR: 237–38, M1642, RG226, NA; Weinstein, pp. 249–50; Petersen, p. 351; Mauch, p. 120.

224 *escape Germany:* Bern cable to B. Homer Hall July 22, 1944, B: 169, Bern cables to SI July 22, Aug. 11 and 18, 1944, B: 219, E: 134, RG226, NA.

225 *German resistance:* Bern cable to B. Homer Hall July 22, 1944, B: 169, E: 134, RG226, NA; Casey, *The Secret War Against Hitler,* pp. 114, 116, 120; Atkinson, *The Guns at Last Light,* p. 138.

225 *opposition sympathizers:* The Attempt on Hitler's Life and Its Consequences. R&A No. 2387, July 27, 1944, B: 18, E: 99, Bern cable to W. A. Kimbel July 29, 1944, B: 169, E: 134, RG226, NA; Longerich, pp. 698–702, 746–47.

225 *preparations for it:* Erika Canaris letter to WJD Nov. 15, 1945, Vol. XVII, Part 1, COR; Bern cable to SI Aug. 5, 1944, B: 219, E: 134, Bern cable to Washington Aug. 3, 1944, Nazis Post Reward for Capture of Arthur Nebe Aug. 7, 1944, B: 235, E: 146, Bern cable to SI July 25, 1944, B: 18, E: 99, RG226, NA; Longerich, pp. 696–97; Hoffmann, pp. 511–19; Gisevius, pp. 582–88; Petersen, pp. 379–80; Mueller, pp. 243–46.

226 *to Dachau:* Bern cables to SI Aug. 10, 11, 24, 26 and Sept. 15, 1944, B: 219, E: 134, Bern cable to Bari Aug. 25, 1944, B: 235, E: 146, USTRAVIC London cable to OSS Aug. 25, 1944, B: 18, E: 99, Bern cable to W. A. Kimbel Dec. 1, 1944, R: 30, FR: 433–36, M1642, RG226, NA; Hoffmann, pp. 16–17, 512–16, 519–21, 525–29, 720; Dulles, *Germany's Underground,* pp. 82–83; Longerich, pp. 697–98.

226 *escape Germany:* Bern cable to SI Aug. 11, 1944, B: 219, E: 134, Raymond L. Brittenham memo to John Haskell July 23, 1944, B: 22, E: 124, RG226, NA; Delattre, pp. 180, 183; Gisevius, pp. 567–69, 582–87.

227 *with Jackpot:* Basic German Text of 512's Account March 29, 1945, Bern cable to SI undated from 476 to 110, B: 18, E: 99, Bern cable to SI Oct. 23, 1944, B: 235, E: 146, Certain Industrial and Wehrmacht Leaders Desire Early Cessation of Hostilities Nov. 8, 1944, R: 30, FR: 734–35, WJD memo to Secretary of State Oct. 12, 1944, R: 20, FR: 124, Walter C. Langer memo to WJD July 26, 1944, R: 52, FR: 23–27, M1642, Bern cable to B. Homer Hall July 21, 1944, B: 169, E: 134, RG226, NA; Petersen, pp. 14, 373, 396; Mauch, pp. 119–20.

227 *Shepardson cabled:* Petersen, p. 9; 110 cable to 109 Aug. 2, 1944, B: 219, E: 134, 109 cable to Bruce July 28, 1944, B: 18, E: 99, USTRAVIC London cable to Bern July 23, 1944, B: 219, Bern cable to SI July 25, 1944, B: 193, E: 134, RG226, NA.

CHAPTER 16: THE YONNE DEPARTMENT

229 *for London:* Procedure for the Despatch of Jedburgh Team, R, 203, HS 8/288, NAUK; Colby, *Honorable Men,* pp. 38–39; Irwin, pp. 5–11; E.M.F.F.I. Operation Order No. 34 Aug. 8, 1944, Jedburgh Procedure ADE/900 Oct. 12, 1943, B: 356, E: 190, Morning Sick Report for WEC Aug. 2. 1944, B: 133, E: 224, RG226, NA.

230 *Jedburghs offered:* A Short History of E.M.F.F.I. Sept. 21, 1944, HS 7/126, NAUK; Atkinson, *The Guns at Last Light,* pp. 111–16, 123, 145, 149–52; Roger Ford, p. 259; Beavan, pp. 140–41, 166, 171, 198–202, 214–21; Ludewig, pp. 36–37, 95, 101–2; Casey, *The Secret War Against Hitler*, pp. 128–29; Julian Jackson, pp. 554–55; Province, pp. 19–20, 295; Waller, pp. 174–75.

231 *7th Armies:* E.M.F.F.I. Operation Order No. 34 Aug. 8, 1944, Jedburgh Procedure ADE/900 Oct. 12, 1943, B: 356, Operation Orders list numbers 1–47, B: 449, E: 190, RG226, NA; Colby, *Honorable Men*, pp. 38–39; Julian Jackson, p. 555; Roger Ford, p. 192; *The Overseas Targets*, pp. 191–92.

231 *the room:* Procedure for the Despatch of Jedburgh Team, R, 203, HS 8/288, NAUK; Kehoe, pp. 23–24; Colby, *Honorable Men*, p. 39; War Diary, SO Branch, OSS London, Vol. 13, Miscellaneous, pp. 2–10, B: 361, E: 190, RG226, NA; History of the Jedburghs in Europe 1942–1944, Vol. 1, II. Formation of Jedburgh Team, III. Training, pp. 9–10, IX. Despatch, pp. 1–3, HS 7/17, NAUK; Dreux, pp. 72–78; Lewis, pp. 12, 21.

232 *"weinführers":* Team Bruce Report, pp. 840–61, SO War Diary, Vol. 4, July, August, September 1944, R: 18, M1623, RG226, NA; Colby, *Honorable Men*, pp. 25–26, 38–39; History of the Jedburghs in Europe 1942–1944, Appendix IX C., S.F.H.Q., Jedburgh Operation Instruction, Team Bruce Report in M. E. 65 Records: 79, Date of Despatch: 14/15 August 1944, HS 7/17, NAUK; Irwin, p. 135; Julian Jackson, pp. 247–50, 255, 287; Kladstrup, pp. 57–71, 137–38.

233 *"Nancy":* Team Bruce Report, pp. 840–61, SO War Diary, Vol. 4, July, August, September 1944, R: 18, M1623, Jean-Marie, Donkeyman background p. 23, B: 455, F-Section, Vol. 3, April, May, June 1944, SO War Diary, B: 359, E.M.F.F.I. Operation Order No. 34 Aug. 8, 1944, Jedburgh Procedure ADE/900 Oct. 12, 1943, B: 356, E: 190, RG226, NA; Colvin, pp. 128, 196–98; Cookridge, pp. 87–91, 103–5; Fuller, pp. 25–26; Foot, *SOE in France*, pp. 224–25; Irwin, p. 138; Jedburgh Operation Instruction, Team Bruce Report in M. E. 65 Records: 79, Date of Despatch: 14/15 August 1944, HS 7/17, The "British" Circuits in France, p. 10, HS 7/122, NAUK.

234 *the airfield:* Team Bruce Report, pp. 840–61, SO War Diary, Vol. 4, July, August, September 1944, R: 18, M1623, Col. Haskell memo to MMFI Aug. 10, 1944, B: 356, E: 190, RG226, NA; Foot, *SOE in France*, pp. 88–89, 109, 111; Fuller, p. 176; Colby, *Honorable Men*, p. 26; John Colby, July 30, 2012; Barbara Colby, July 16, 2012.

234 *in corners:* War Diary, SO Branch, London, Vol. 13, Miscellaneous, pp. 10–19, B: 361, E.M.F.F.I. Operation Order No. 34 Aug. 8, 1944, Jedburgh Procedure ADE/900 Oct. 12, 1943, B: 356, E: 190, OSS photo album of Training Areas in the United Kingdom, B: 7, E: 161, RG: 226, NA; History of the Jedburghs in Europe 1942–1944, Vol. 1, IX. Despatch, p. 1, HS 7/17, NAUK; Author tour of Station 61, Dec. 12, 2012.

235 *later wrote:* Colby, *Honorable Men*, p. 39; Foot, *SOE in France,* p. 60; Team Bruce Report, pp. 840–61, SO War Diary, Vol. 4, July, August, September 1944, R: 18, M1623, RG226, NA; List of British and French agents arrested and killed, Miscellaneous Aide Memoires 10, Vol. 2, F Section, HS 8/999, NAUK; Province, pp. 24–25; Atkinson, *The Guns at Last Light,* p. 162.

236 *the chinstraps:* Author tour of Harrington Field Dec. 18, 2012; "The Carpetbaggers: A History of the 801/492nd Bombardment Group (H) U.S.A.A.F.," by R. W. Clark, 1997, Harrington Field Map, CCWM; Harrington Field photos, CBP, HIA; Parnell, pp. xi–xii; Photos of Jedburgh teams in dressing room at Harrington, War Diary, SO Branch, OSS London, Jedburghs, Vol. 4, B: 359, Personal Equipment for J's Dec. 23, 1943, B: 356, E: 190, R: 8, M1623, Clothing sizes for WEC and J. Favel, B: 10, E: 128, RG226, NA; Photos of Jedburgh teams preparing to leave Harrington Field, Jedburgh (1st February 1944–December 1944) Milton Hall-M.E. 65, CBC; Operational Clothing-Equipment-Stores, IX B., History of Jedburghs in Europe, Vol. 3, HS 7/19, NAUK; Lewis, p. 1; Bond, April 15, 2013.

236 *cockpit window:* Colby, *Honorable Men,* p. 39; "The Carpetbaggers: A History of the 801/492nd Bombardment Group (H) U.S.A.A.F.," by R. W. Clark, 1997, CCWM; The Wartime Experiences of the Carpetbaggers in Still Photos, 788th/859th BSs, Ewart Crew, Data from original mission reports, participants, researchers and microfilm roll A5688-August 1944, http://801492.org.

237 *another flight:* Sebastian H. Corriere letter to WEC Nov. 4, 1991, B: 1, WECP, PU; Parnell, pp. 21, 27; John Colby, July 30, 2012; Atkinson, *The Guns at Last Light,* p. 351; Crane, p. 51; London SI War Diary, Vol. 12, German Operations, pp. 63–65, R: 4, FR: 542–1305, R: 5, FR: 2–962, M1623, RG226, NA; Parnell, p. 20; Bond, April 15, 2013; Biographical information on the eight Ewart crew members, Flight Report 1657 for Aircraft No. 262, 859th Squadron, Aug. 14–15, 1944, http://801492.org.

237 *next to impossible:* Biographical information on the eight Ewart crew members, http://801492.org; "The Carpetbaggers: A History of the 801/492nd Bombardment Group (H) U.S.A.A.F.," by R. W. Clark, 1997, CCWM; Parnell, pp. 13–16; Bond, April 15, 2013; Flight Report 1657 for Aircraft No. 262, 859th Squadron, Aug. 14–15, 1944, http://801492.org; London SI War Diary, Vol. 12, German Operations, pp. 83–89, R: 4, FR: 542–1305, R: 5, FR: 2–962, M1623, RG226, NA.

238 *long gone:* "The Carpetbaggers: A History of the 801/492nd Bombardment Group (H) U.S.A.A.F.," by R. W. Clark, 1997, CCWM; John Colby, July 30, 2012; Dreux, pp. 89–92; Kehoe, pp. 26–27; Bond, April 15, 2013; Parnell, pp. 22–23.

239 *no problem:* Flight Report 1657 for Aircraft No. 262, 859th Squadron, Aug. 14–15, 1944, http://801492.org; Colby, *Honorable Men,* p. 23; Parnell, p. 28; Bond, April 15, 2013; Foot, *SOE in France,* pp. 79–83; Irwin, pp. xvii, 19.

239 *five-hundred-foot jump:* Sally Colby, July 27, 2012; Dreux, p. 92; Franklin, p. 21.

241 *recalled later:* Team Bruce Report, pp. 840–61, SO War Diary, Vol. 4, July, August, September 1944, R: 18, M1623, RG226, NA; Specimen Programme of Operation, HS 8/288, NAUK; Sibley Cooley interview with Camille Lelong, Team "Bruce" WWII France TRT 42:16, Veteran & Military Television; Irwin, pp. 139–40; Sally Colby, July 27, 2012; John Colby, July 30, 2012; Colby, *Honorable Men,* pp. 23–27, 39–40; Ford, p. 191.

243 *guerrilla leader:* Team Bruce Report, pp. 840–61, SO War Diary, Vol. 4, July, August, September 1944, R: 18, M1623, RG226, NA; Province, p. 26; Sibley Cooley interview with

Camille Lelong, Team "Bruce" WWII France TRT 42:16, Veteran & Military Television; Colby, *Honorable Men*, pp. 39–41; Extract for P.F. 600,885 Bardet, Roger @ Roger etc., KV 2/1175, NAUK; The "British" Circuits in France, p. 10, HS 7/122, NAUK; Irwin, pp. 141–42; Colvin, pp. 86–87; Cookridge, p. 109.

243 *the Abwehr:* Singlaub, July 20, 2012; Sally Colby, July 27, 2012; Kehoe, Oct. 26, 2012; Beavan, pp. 186–91; Foot, *Resistance*, p. 63; Fuller, pp. 177–78.

246 *next department:* Hugo Bleicher profile, File No. F.F.600.861, S.I.S. Teleprinter Form, Serial No. LN 877s-25a, Query 1 Von Stahlen, Connection with GIS, Sept. 9, 1942, and October 1943 entries for Hugo Bleicher, KV 2/2127, Personal Particulars for Hugo Bleicher, File No. P.F. 600, 861, Photographs of Hugo Bleicher and Suzanne Laurent, M.I.5 Interim Interrogation Report on the Case of Hugo Bleicher, Camp 020, Sept. 6, 1945, Bleicher, P.F. 600,861, Extract from Camp 020 Monthly Summary-1.9.45, KV 2/166, S/Ldr. Beddard memos to Colonel Stephens on Bleicher @ Verbeck, KV 2/1175, G. P. Wethered memo to R. H. Warden Feb. 26, 1944, G. P. Wethered Note Nov. 24, 1943, KV 2/2127, Extract for P.F. 600,885 Bardet, Roger @ Roger etc., KV 2/1175, D. I. Wilson letter to Lt. Col. Roche July 17, 1945, KV 2/165, Louba/Gilbert report November 1943, G. P. Wethered memo, B. 1. Information (Captain Gwyer) Nov. 17, 1943, G. P. Wethered Nov. 13, 1943, B.1.B., Extract from Note on Golbert by Major Wethered, B.1.B., Nov. 9, 1943, G. P. Wethered letter to John Senter, Feb. 14, 1944, KV 2/2127, NAUK; Colvin, pp. 11–13, 17, 21–38, 45–46, 57, 61–63, 72–85, 90–95, 109–11, 120–26, 135–43, 158–77, 190–91; Cookridge, pp. 75–76, 107–14, 182–85, 190–95; Fuller, pp. 17, 33–35, 43, 101–2; Foot, *SOE in France*, p. 244, 259–71; Extract of L. R. C. Information Index re the contacts of Kiffer, Jan. 15, 1945, P.F. 600.885, Bardet, B: 2, E: 119A, RG226, NA.

249 *in the dark:* Team Bruce Report, pp. 840–61, SO War Diary, Vol. 4, July, August, September 1944, R: 18, M1623, Role of Charles Communications in Jedburgh Operations, B: 4, Circuits ETO July–Aug. 1944 diagram, B: 1, E: 103, OSS Aid to the Resistance in World War II, Missions, F-Section, p. 36, B: 740, E: 190, Ciphers and Codes, Jedburgh Plan, B: 4, Jedburgh and Special Forces W/T Messages and Field Reports, Vol. 111, Aug. 18, 19, and 20, 1944, Team Bruce reports, B: 2, E: 103, RG226, NA; Briefing Officer, Code Name: Bruce summary report with transmission times, HS 6/489, NAUK; Franklin, pp. 157–59; Kehoe, pp. 35–36, 39; Singlaub, pp. 45, 51; Irwin, pp. 7–9, 21–22, 86, 99–100, 125; Foot, *SOE in France*, pp. 95–101, 326–27; Dreux, p. 60; Ford, p. 192; Irwin, pp. 137–38, 143–44; Cookridge, pp. 190–91; John Colby, July 30, 2012; Carl Colby, July 16, 2012; Atkinson, *The Guns at Last Light*, p. 214; Julian Jackson, pp. 438, 475; Colby, *Honorable Men*, pp. 41–42.

252 *right flank:* Team Bruce Report, pp. 840–61, SO War Diary, Vol. 4, July, August, September 1944, R: 18, M1623, Jedburgh and Special Forces W/T Messages and Field Reports, Vol. 111, Aug. 22, 23, and 24, 1944, Team Bruce reports, B: 2, E: 103, Passwords to be used by secret army delegates for C in C or zone commanders contacting Allied forces, B: 455, E: 190, Lt. L'Hereault interrogation of WEC Aug. 26, 1944, Code name card No. C.78 for WEC on password question and response, WEC estimate of Resistance per-

sonnel operating in his area, B: 10, E: 128, RG226, NA; Colby, *Honorable Men*, pp. 42–43; Alsop, pp. 30, 119, 128–29, 177, 181–83; Beavan, pp. 179–83, 187, 224–32; Irwin, pp. xx, 145–50; Singlaub, p. 54; Ludewig, pp. 102, 153–56, 161–72; Roger Ford, p. 192; Province, pp. 31–32; Irwin, Sept. 29, 2012; Casey, *The Secret War Against Hitler*, pp. 126, 152–53.

253 *3rd Army:* WJC letters to SKC Sept. 16, 1944, and undated letters to SKC, BCS; WJC letter to Duncan Lee Sept. 29, 1944, Quinn Shaughnessy letter to O. C. Doering Aug. 4, 1944, B: 187, E: 146, Thomas Early memo to E. J. Putzell with enclosure Sept. 2, 1944, B: 565, E: 92, WJC memo to Mr. Shepardson Nov. 3, 1944, B: 91, WJC memo to DKEB et al., Sept. 3, 1944, B: 167, E: 190, WJC memo to DKEB and J. R. Forgan Aug. 21, 1944, B: 41, E: 99, RG226, NA; Edward Glavin letter to All Concerned Aug. 16, 1944, E: 126, SS; Persico, *Casey*, p. 62; Casey, *The Secret War Against Hitler*, pp. 131–33, 142, 150–54; Memos from Commander, U.S. Naval Forces Europe, to WJC on Temporary Additional Duty Aug. 3 and 5, 1944, WJC memo to DKEB Aug. 31, 1944, Travel Data Form for WJC Aug. 2–15, 1944, Tally-Out for WJC Dec. 18, 1944, WCNR, NPRC; Lankford, *OSS Against the Reich*, pp. 178–79; Prados, pp. 17–18.

254 *their advance:* Atkinson, *The Guns at Last Light*, pp. 181–82, 219–22; Summary of OSS Activities During August 1944, European Theater of Operations Report August 1944, OSS Activities, Including European Theater, June 1944–September 1945, Washington History Office, B: 123–25, E: 99, War Diary, SO Branch, OSS London, Vol. 4, Jedburghs, July–December 1944, B: 359, E: 190, R: 8, M1623, RG226, NA.

257 *old girlfriend:* Team Bruce Report, pp. 840–61, SO War Diary, Vol. 4, July, August, September 1944, R: 18, M1623, Jedburgh and Special Forces W/T Messages and Field Reports, Vol. 111, Sept. 1, 3, 7, 8, 9, 15, and 25, 1944, Team Bruce reports, B: 2, E: 103, Charles Neil memo to Bates Compton with 11th Special Forces Detachment comments on War Diary for June 25–July 24, 1944, B: 338, Ciphers Staff Report NR 102, Army Sitreps to 0800 26 Sept., Agent Report No. 4 from Bruce Sept. 22, 1944, B: 198, E: 190, Yankydoodle message to Watermark Oct. 15, 1944, B: 10, E: 128, Continental Bases, Paris: Living Quarters OSS Personnel, B: 23, E: 99, RG226, NA; History of the Jedburghs in Europe 1942–1944, Vol. 1, IX. Despatch, pp. 5–7, HS 7/17, NAUK; Alsop, p. 126; Beavan, pp. 197–98, 280, 289; Cookridge, p. 37; Province, pp. 36, 38, 41; Irwin, p. 166; Ludewig, p. 244; Atkinson, *The Guns at Last Light*, pp. 247–48; John Colby, July 30, 2012; Sally Colby, July 27, 2012; Colby, *Honorable Men*, pp. 43–44; Prados, pp. 18–19.

257 *March 9, 1945:* Jedburgh and Special Forces W/T Messages and Field Reports, Vol. 111, Oct. 10, 1944, Team Bruce reports, B: 2, E: 103, RG226, NA; Sibley Cooley interview with Camille Lelong, Team "Bruce" WWII France TRT 42:16, Veteran & Military Television; Irwin, p. 230; Colby, *Honorable Men*, p. 44.

257 *the press:* Special Forces HQ memo EEMF/3103 Oct. 25, 1944, Team James File 64, B: 9, E: 128, Memo to Gerald Miller Oct. 21, 1944, B: 448, E: 190, RG226, NA.

257 *to England:* D. L. G. Carleton-Smith memo to S. Millett, Jr. April 7, 1945, B: 450, E: 190, WEC notes on expenses for Team Bruce, B: 10, E: 128, RG226, NA.

258 *"was nil":* Julian Jackson, pp. 557–60; DDE letter to Col. Forgan May 31, 1945, R: 126,

FR: 238–39, M1642, RG226, H. B. Hitchens memo for D/A. C. of S., G-2, Oct. 30, 1944, 103.819/11-244, RG59, NA; Eisenhower, p. 296; Ludewig, pp. 25, 28; Irwin, pp. 237–39; Foot, *SOE in France*, p. 388; Lewis, p. 64; WJD Lecture of the Army-Navy Staff College March 12, 1945, B: 119A, WJDP, MHI.

259 *guerrilla morale:* Lewis, p. 64; Foot, *Resistance*, p. 5; Weinberg, p. 533; *The Overseas Targets*, pp. xii, 219–22; Cookridge, p. 245; History of the Jedburghs in Europe 1942–1944, Vol. 1, X. Summaries and Conclusion, pp. 1–8, HS 7/17, NAUK; Irwin, pp. 236, 242; Sibley Cooley interview with Camille Lelong, Team "Bruce" WWII France TRT 42:16, Veteran & Military Television.

259 *told his son:* Team Bruce Report, pp. 840–61, SO War Diary, Vol. 4, July, August, September 1944, R: 18, M1623, RG226, NA; WEC memo to Chief, Special Branch, OSS, Washington, May 23, 1945, B: 3, WECP, PU; "Interview: William Colby," p. 41; History of Jedburghs in Europe, Vol. 3, Team Bruce Summary of Achievements, HS 7/19, History of the Jedburghs in Europe 1942–1944, Vol. 1, X. Summaries and Conclusion, insert after p. 6, HS 7/17, NAUK; John Colby, July 30, 2012.

260 *end now:* DKEB recommendation for Bronze Star Medal for WEC Dec. 12, 1944, B: 133, E: 224, James Forgan recommendation for Bronze Star Medal for Camille Lelong June 26, 1945, B:13, E: 168A, RG226, NA; Report on Seventy-five SO Agents (Mostly Jedburghs) Dropped by Parachute into France, B: 69, WJCP, HIA; Irwin, p. xxii; History of the Jedburghs in Europe 1942–1944, Vol. 1, X. Summaries and Conclusion, p. 2, HS 7/17, NAUK; Beavan, pp. 289–90.

261 *in Yonne:* Team Bruce Report, pp. 840–61, SO War Diary, Vol. 4, July, August, September 1944, R: 18, M1623, H. N. H. Wild memo to T. A. Robertson Jan. 15, 1945, B: 2, E: 119A, RG226, Dupre Sassard memo to Counter Intelligence War Room, London Oct. 16, 1945, B: 77, E: (A1) B4-B, RG319, NA; M.I.5 Interim Interrogation Report on the Case of Hugo Bleicher, Camp 020, Sept. 6, 1945, Authorization to Travel out of Germany for Hugo Bleicher Oct. 13, 1945, KV 2/166, Case Officer VB5F on Bardet Jan. 14, 1945, P.F. 600,885, Bardet, June 7, 1945, H. W. Astor memo Feb. 2, 1945, Extract for File No. P.F. 600,885 on Roger Bardet, John Senter memo to Guy Liddell March 2, 1945, Top Secret and Confidential memos to Bardet/Kiffer Enquiry Feb. 15 and 21, 1944, W. J. E. Mathe memo to Capt. Kressman with enclosed interrogation report on Roger Bardet Jan. 2, 1945, W.R./D.S.D.O.C.-Capt. Le Man memo July 19, 1945, KV 2/1175, S/Ldr. Beddard memos to Lt. Col. Stimson July 8 and Aug. 10, 1945, Camp 020 memos on Hugo Bleicher interrogations July 16, Aug. 16 and 18, 1945, Extract from Camp 020 Monthly Summary Aug. 1, 1945 on Bleicher, PF. 600,861, KV 2/165, War Room Outgoing Telegram June 13, 1945, and June 6, 1945, memo on Bleicher alias Verbeck in Allied hands, KV 2/2127, NAUK; Colvin, pp. 178–94, 197; Julian Jackson, pp. 578–80, 588; Lowe, pp. 154–59; Beavan, pp. 194–95; Irwin, pp. 154, 229–30; Fuller, pp. 156–59, 168; Cookridge, p. 195.

CHAPTER 17: FORTRESS GERMANY

263 *his boss:* Bach, FAOH; X-2, Switzerland (Notes for writer of Swiss story), B: 9, AWDP, PU; Gerhard Van Arkel interview Nov. 11, 1963, B: 11, RSP, HIA; Paul Blum résumé and Personnel History Sheet, B: 62, Charles Tracey Barnes Theater Service Record June 7, 1945, Area F Interviewer's Report, Barnes Personnel History Sheet, Report of Mission Sainfoin Oct. 6, 1944, Barnes Recommendation for Award of Silver Star, March 6, 1945, Edward Stettinius cable Dec. 30, 1944, B: 37, E: 224, RG226, NA; Grose, pp. 204–5; Petersen, pp. 5, 13–14, 381; Bill Hood, July 14, 2012; Srodes, pp. 309–10; Delattre, p. 187; Persico, *Piercing the Reich*, pp. 92–93.

264 *of Germany:* WJD letter to Gen. Koenig Aug. 22, 1944, R: 103, FR: 1168–73, 1181–82, M1642, RG226, NA; Remembering 109—Recollections of OSSers, by Bayard LeRoy King, OSS Society newsletter, Fall 2003, p. 3; Waller, p. 264; Atkinson, *The Guns at Last Light*, p. 214; Casey, *The Secret War Against Hitler*, pp. 142–44.

264 *"industrial installations":* A.W.S. memo to WJD Nov. 2, 1943, Secretariat memo to WJD Nov. 2, 1943, R: 53, FR: 294–97, WJD cable to AWD Aug. 2, 1944, R: 81, FR: 15–20, M1642, RG226, NA; Lankford, *The Last American Aristocrat*, p. 150.

265 *out information:* USTRAVIC London cable to OSS HQ Sept. 1, 1944, R: 81, FR: 63–65, 89–90, R: 18, FR 975–77, M1642, RG226, NA; AWD memo to WJD Aug. 8, 1944, B: 3, ADP, NSA; OSS history office interview with AWD Sept. 22 and 28, 1944, Unnumbered boxes 3rd and 4th from the end of the collection, WJDP, MHI; Grose, pp. 210–11; Waller, pp. 267–68.

266 *streaking by:* WJD cable to AWD Aug. 2, 1944, R: 81, FR: 15–20, M1642, European Theater Office Report, Aug. 31, 1944, Cables, 2. 110, B: 11, E: 99, RG226, NA; Dulles, *The Secret Surrender*, p. 39; Petersen, p. 382; Casey, *The Secret War Against Hitler*, pp. 144–45; Grose, p. 205; Persico, *Casey*, pp. 62–64; Legendre, p. 12, OHP.

267 *under him:* WJC letter to Duncan Lee, B: 187, E: 146, WJD cable to Cheston Aug. 25, 1944, R: 81, FR: 54, War Diary, SI Branch, OSS London, Vol. 1, p. 29, R: 4, FR: 542–1305, R: 5, FR: 2–962, M1623, RG226, NA; Persico, *Casey*, p. 65; Grose, pp. 211–12; William J. vanden Heuvel interview, Unnumbered box "Interviews Teitelbaum to Withrow Jr. 1979 Undated," Mary Bancroft interview July 16, 1980, Unnumbered box "Interviews—Bancroft to Sherwood 1945—undated," OSS history office interview with AWD Sept. 22, 1944, Unnumbered boxes 3rd and 4th from the end of the collection, WJDP, MHI; vanden Heuvel, March 11, 2008; Srodes, pp. 313–17; Barreaux, Aug. 6, 2012; Kingsley, Jan. 1, 2008; Petersen, p. 13; Dunlop, pp. 2, 454.

267 *after the war:* European Theater Office Report Sept. 20, 1944, Cables, 2. 110 in Washington, B: 11, E: 99, RG226, NA; F. L. Mayer memo to Chief, SI, Dec. 30, 1943, B: 101, E: 92, Carib and 154 cable to AWD March 10, 1944, WJD cable to AWD June 17, 1944, B: 165, E: 134, RG226, NA.

268 *reasons why:* Security Office, Badges & passes memo on AWD Sept. 19, 1944, B: 101, E: 92, AWD memo on the German Mission Sept. 30, 1944, R: 81, FR: 67, 306–8, R: 82, FR: 509–22, 630–32, M1642, AWD memo to WJD Sept. 29, 1944, B: 428, AWD memo to

Climax, Paris Nov. 7, 1944, B: 270, E: 210, RG226, NA; Delattre, pp. 185–86; Grose, pp. 205–7; Srodes, p. 332; Petersen, p. 13; Mosley, pp. 165–66; OSS history office interview with AWD Sept. 22, 1944, Unnumbered boxes 3rd and 4th from the end of the collection, WJDP, MHI.

268 *and uncommunicative:* Joseph Persico notes on interview with RMH, B: 27, UA; Persico, *Casey,* pp. 62–65; AWD letters to CTD Nov. 22 and Dec. 13, 1944, B: 18, AWDP, PU; Letter to Saint from Bern Dec. 31, 1944, B: 494, E: 210, RG226, NA; Dulles, *The Secret Surrender,* p. 57; Grose, pp. 209–10; Bancroft, pp. 138–39; Petersen, pp. 392, 423–24; Waller, p. 270; Crockett, OHP, pp. 17, 43.

269 *compelled it:* Recommendation of the Award of the Legion of Merit for WJC June 30, 1945, B: 112, E: 224, RG226, NA; WJC letters to SKC Sept. 22 and Oct. 10, 1944, and circa October 1944, BCS; Helms, *A Look over My Shoulder,* p. 39; Meyer, p. 285; Casey, "OSS: Lessons for Today," pp. 62–63; Lankford, *OSS Against the Reich,* p. 190; Itemized Schedule of Travel and Other Expenses for WJC Oct. 13–19, 1944, WCNR, NPRC; Casey, *The Secret War Against Hitler,* pp. 171–77.

270 *bipolar disorder:* WJC letter to SKC circa October 1944, BCS; European Theater Office Report Sept. 20, 1944, Cables, 5. German morale, B: 11, E: 99, WJD memo to FDR Oct. 11, 1944, R: 23, FR: 653–57, WJD memo to FDR July 4, 1944, R: 24, FR: 24–25, Memo on Germany: certain Industrial and Wehrmacht Leaders Desire Early Cessation of Hostilities, Nov. 8, 1944, WJD memo to FDR Nov. 2, 1944, Bern cables to W. A. Kimbel Dec. 5, 1944, and Jan. 12, 1945, R: 30, FR: 286–87, 349–50, 448–49, 734–35, M1642, RG226, NA; Ludewig, p. 1; Atkinson, *The Guns at Last Light,* p. 354.

270 *Germany's collapse:* Bern cable to W. A. Kimbel Jan. 12, 1945, R: 30, FR: 286–87, WJD cable to DKEB Aug. 1, 1944, DKEB and Forgan cable to WJD Aug. 5, 1944, R: 81, FR: 21, 32–35, 49–50, M1642, H. K. Heuser and Z. W. Erne memo to R. S. MacLeod Aug. 12, 1944, B: 46, E: 115, C. B. Peters memo to AWD Oct. 16, 1944, B: 310, E: 190, RG226, NA; Casey, *The Secret War Against Hitler,* p. 62; Atkinson, *The Guns at Last Light,* p. 380; War Diary, SI Branch, OSS London Vol. 1, Introductory Survey, p. 40, R: 4, Vol. 5, pp. 276–82, Vol. 11, p. 30, R: 4, FR: 542–1305, R: 5, FR: 2–296, Labor Division, Field Base "C," Milwaukee Forward (Withdrawal Material from SI War Diary), pp. 3–4, B: 74, E: 210, RG226, NA.

271 *was himself:* Weinberg, pp. 701–2; Atkinson, *The Guns at Last Light,* pp. 244–46, 258–65, 271, 281–89; Casey, *The Secret War Against Hitler,* pp. 162–68; AWS buck slip to Dr. Langer Oct. 21, 1944, WJC memo to WJD with enclosure Oct. 12, 1944, B: 25, E: 1, B: 25, Appendix A, Action Taken and Immediate Plans, R: 81, FR: 486–516, M1642, RG226, NA.

CHAPTER 18: NORWAY

274 *accomplished skier:* Address list for Colby and other OSS officers in London, B: 449, War Diary, SO Branch, OSS London, Vol. 11, Biographies, p. 3, B: 361, E: 190, Apollo memo to Chief, SO Branch, March 3, 1945, B: 291, E: 210, RG226, NA; Colby, *Honorable Men,*

pp. 44–45; Prados, p. 28; John Colby, July 30, 2012; Persico, *Piercing the Reich*, p. 254; Carl Colby, July 16, 2012.

277 *August 1943:* Gjelsvik, p. ix–x, 1, 3, 10–14, 29, 44, 58, 66–76, 86–90, 110–11, 130; Larsen, pp. 3–4, 16–24, 35–36, 40–52, 154–55, 496–98, 505–12, 533–59; Heimark, pp. 6, 13, 15, 101; III Norway, Enclosure No. 8, The Quisling Regime, B: 377, Situation Report, General, Report on Principles of Organized Resistance in Occupied Norway, April 17, 1945, B: 340, War Diary, SO Branch, OSS London, Vol. 8, Scandinavia, pp. xiv, 27, B: 361, E: 190, RG226, NA; Norway: Gestapo success against the home front, OSS #30732, March 29, R: 76, FR: 1132–80, M1642, RG226, NA; Cookridge, pp. 14, 313–28, 331; Foot, *Resistance*, p. 65; Henry, pp. 617–18; Cruickshank, pp. 51–57, 91–92, 169, 173, Appendix 1; Petersen, pp. 105–6.

278 *"are worth":* WJD memo to Psychological Warfare Committee July 18, 1942, R: 76, FR: 1135, WJD memo to FDR July 7, 1944, R: 24, FR: 50, Ellery Huntington memo to WJD Dec. 12, 1942, R: 103, FR: 1123–24, M1642, RG226, NA; Cypher Telegrams Desp. to New York Oct. 20 and 24, 1942, G. M. from AD/U, SN memo to D/CD(O), SN/1868, Oct. 26, 1942, HS 2/134, NAUK.

278 *representatives agreed:* SN memo to AD/E on O.S.S. Projects in Norway June 24, 1943, HS 2/134, D/CD(O) memo to D/S Jan. 10, 1943, Summary of Proposed Psychological Warfare Undertaking in Norway, Precis of meeting held at Kindston House Jan. 11, 1943, to discuss O.S.S. activities in Norway, HS 2/219, Proposed Psychological Warfare Undertaking in Norway by O.S.S., note by S.O.E., March 8, 1943, HS 2/212, NAUK.

279 *three months:* Albert Lanier memo to WJD Nov. 6, 1944, R: 92, FR: 427–30, M1642, War Diary, SO Branch, OSS London, Vol. 8, Scandinavia, pp. xviii–xxv, 29, B: 361, E: 190, RG226, NA; Heimark, pp. xiii, 4–7, 17–18, 25–54.

279 *among themselves:* Situation Report, General, B: 340, E: 190, Special Orders No. 215, HQ & HQ Detachment, OSS European Theater, Dec. 15, 1944, B: 133, E: 224, Theater Officers Pouch Reports Dec. 27, 1944, and Jan. 3, 1945, B: 12, European Theater Office Report Dec. 22, 1944, Cables, 1. Norwegian OGs, B: 11, E: 99, War Diary, SO Branch, OSS London, Vol. 8, Scandinavia, p. 79, B: 361, E: 190, RG226, NA.

CHAPTER 19: ASSIGNMENT EUROPE

282 *one as well:* WJC memo to DKEB Sept. 11, 1944, R: 81, FR: 299–305, M1642, War Diary, SI Branch, OSS London, Vol. 1, pp. 30–32, Vol. 6, pp. 380–93, Vol. 12, German Operations—1945, pp. 2–5, 31–32, 385–86, 429–30, R: 4, FR: 542–1305, R: 5, FR: 2–962, M1623, Faust Plan, Special Projects, B: 23, E: 99, RG226, NA; Casey, *The Secret War Against Hitler*, p. 177; Minutes of the 8th Meeting of the German Committee Aug. 11, 1944, at 64 Baker Street, C.D. memo to D/S, F, LC, DH/T, EU/P, DP, AD/4, D/Q, Aug. 11, 1944, HS 6/260, S.O.E. History, German Directorate, Part II 1(a), Formation of German Directorate, Policy Relations with SHAEF, General Liaison with "C" and OSS, General Assessment, Part II, Section 1(g), Deception Scheme in Neutral Countries and Germany—Operation Periwig, Aug. 17, 1945, HS 7/147, NAUK; Casey, "OSS: Lessons for Today," p. 63; *The Overseas Targets*, pp. 308–9.

282 *as a civilian:* George Pratt memo to WS Aug. 22, 1944, R: 82, FR: 482–85, M1642, Walter Wellman memo to Chief, SI, OSS, Washington, D.C., on AG, WJD memo to the Director, Officer Procurement Service, May 13, 1943, B: 279, E: 224, RG226, NA; AG letter to Mildred Sept. 9, 1942, AG memo to AWD Sept. 21, 1942, B: 22, AG letter to WJD Aug. 15, 1946, B: 5, AGP, LOC; Notes on AG, B: 2, JPP, HIA; Stebenne, p. 33; Persico, *Piercing the Reich*, pp. 20–21.

283 *on the unit:* Notes on AG, B: 2, JPP, HIA; WJD memo to FDR R: 68, FR: 522–43, M1642, RG226, NA; Labor Division, London, pp. 1–2, Labor Division, Field Base "C," Milwaukee Forward (Withdrawal Material from SI War Diary), B: 74, E: 210, RG226, NA; Mauch, pp. 168–69; Persico, *Piercing the Reich*, pp. 22–23; Howe, Dec. 20, 2007; Lankford, *OSS Against the Reich*, p. 108; Donovan, "A Central Intelligence Agency," p. 447.

283 *Goethe's play:* Notes on AG, B: 2, JPP, HIA; M. Preston Goodfellow memo to Adjutant General, War Department, Sept. 22, 1944, B: 279, E: 224, RG226, NA; Casey, *The Secret War Against Hitler*, p. 178; Stebenne, p. 42.

284 *German cities:* Faust B Plan, B: 23, Theater Officers Pouch Report Sept. 9, 1944, Infiltration of P. W. Camp, B: 12, E: 99, Ezra Shine memo on Summary of Reports by Students Living with P/Ws in P/W cages with enclosure March 16, 1945, B: 209, E: 190, I. S. Dorfman memo to WJD Feb. 4, 1944, R: 69, FR: 1129–33, M1642, George Pratt memo to Allan Scaife Oct. 20, 1944, B: 38, Chief, Labor Section, memo to Executive Officer, SI, Jan. 8, 1944, B: 393, E: 210, CO, OSS Detachment, ETOUSA, memo to Supreme Commander, SHAEF, Aug. 18, 1944, B: 5, E: 128, RG226, NA.

284 *code name "Goethe":* Goethe Project, Faust B Plan, B: 23, E: 99, War Diary, SI Branch, OSS London, Vol. 6, Labor Division, pp. 270–71, R: 4, FR: 542–1305, R: 5, FR: 2–962, M1623, AG memo to WJD Oct. 2, 1944, with enclosed memo of I. S. Dorfman to Taylor Cole Sept. 7, 1944, B: 340, E: 210, RG226, NA.

285 *had ended:* Bern cable to SI March 21, 1945, B: 192, Bern cables to SI Nov. 19 and 20, 1944, B: 193, E: 134, Bern cable to SI Jan. 28, 1945, B: 519–20, AWD memo to WJD Oct. 5, 1944, B: 342, E: 210, Bern cable to SI (1) Jan. 7, 1945, B: 5, E: 211, David Williamson memo to Howard Baldwin Oct. 24, 1944, B: 7, E: 214, RG226, NA; 110 memo to Colonel Glavin or Rodrigo Dec. 10, 1944, Cordell Hull cable to AWD Oct. 22, 1944, 679 cable to 110 Feb. 12, 1945, AWD Acknowledgment Jan. 13, 1945, Re: ECDAR Matter Jan. 19, 1945, Box 1, ADP, NSA; Grose, pp. 218–20; Petersen, pp. 402, 407, 421–22.

285 *his father-in-law:* Petersen, p. 10; Persico, *Piercing the Reich*, pp. 94–100; Molden, OHP, pp. 1–51; Talley, July 28 and Aug. 4, 2012; Bern cables to OSS HQ Jan. 24 and 25, 1945, B: 192, E: 134, RG226, NA; John Sinai letter to AWD Jan. 30, 1954, and AWD response Feb. 3, 1945, B: 10, AWDP, PU.

286 *one-mistress man:* "American Women Spies," by Donald Robinson, p. 53, B: 73, WJCP, HIA; Robert DeVecchi memo to Earl Brennan Dec. 6, 1943, "Anti-Fascist Toscanini Makes Movie for OWI," *PM's Daily Picture Magazine*, Jan. 11, 1944, p. 18; B. H. Hall memo to Robert DeVecchi March 21, 1944, Robert DeVecchi memo to Homer Hall April 8, 1944, B: 7, E: 214, RG226, NA; Talley, July 28, 2012; Grose, pp. 198, 215–16;

Srodes, pp. 271–72; Mary Bancroft interview July 16, 1980, Unnumbered box "Interviews—Bancroft to Sherwood 1945—undated," WJDP, MHI.

286 *do her good:* AWD letters to CTD Nov. 29, Dec. 5 and 13, 1944, Photos & papers of itinerary C. T. Dulles Portugal & Switzerland (when Mrs. Dulles went to join her husband, chief of O.S.S., in Switzerland), CTD travel notes for the trip, B: 18, AWDP, PU; Letter to AWD Dec. 20, 1944, B: 264, E: 210, RG226, NA; Talley, July 28 and Aug. 4, 2012; Srodes, pp. 333–38; Bancroft, pp. 241–47; Grose, p. 224.

287 *twenty minutes:* OSS HQ cable to Taylor in Stockholm Feb. 20, 1945, B: 235, E: 146, USTRAVIC, London, cable to OSS HQ Feb. 26, 1945, Bern cable to SI Feb. 27, 1945, B: 18, E: 99, Cable to Secstate Washington March 8, 1945, 110 memo to Secstate Washington Jan. 24, 1945, B: 9, E: 190C, RG226, NA; Gisevius, pp. 589–98; Bancroft, pp. 207–8.

287 *find a publisher:* Charles Cheston memos to FDR Jan. 27 and Feb. 1, 1945, with enclosure, B: 18, E: 99, 110 cable to 154 May 11, 1945, B: 9, E: 190C, RG226, NA.

289 *Casey recalled:* Ludewig, pp. 107, 206–9; Atkinson, *The Guns at Last Light,* pp. 393–95, 412–19, 435–40, 487–89; Keegan, pp. 440–51; Weinberg, pp. 765–69; Casey, *The Secret War Against Hitler,* pp. 182–85; Smith, *The Shadow Warriors,* pp. 297, 300–301; Interview with James B. Withrow, Jr., July 1, 1980, B: Unnumbered, "Interviews Teitelbaum to Withrow Jr., 1979—undated," WJDP, MHI; Petersen, pp. 413–14; Philip Horton memo to Director's Office Dec. 26, 1944, R: 57, FR: 1179–87, M1642, RG226, NA.

289 *nagging problem:* WJC memo to Ernest Brooks and John Creedy July 12, 1945, B: 300, E: 190, War Diary, SI Branch, OSS London, Vol. 1, Chronological Summary, R: 4, FR: 542–1305, R: 5, FR: 2–962, M1623, RG226, NA; WJC memo to WJD Dec. 29, 1944, SS.

290 *department store:* 154 cable to 109 Nov. 27, 1944, B: 660, E: 190, WS memo to Chief, Special Funds Branch, Feb. 23, 1945, B: 46, E: 92, War Diary, SI Branch, OSS London, Vol. 1, p. 31, Vol. 12, German Operations-1945, pp. 1–2, R: 4, FR: 542–1305, R: 5, FR: 2–962, M1623, RG226, NA; Notes on WJC, B: 1, JPP, HIA; Casey, *The Secret War Against Hitler,* pp. 179, 185; Petersen, pp. 413–14, 426–27; Bernadette Casey Smith, Aug. 24, 2012; Lankford, *The Last American Aristocrat,* pp. 160–61; Meyer, p. 285; BuPers Naval Message Dec. 7, 1944, PERS-369-GVB-2B, on Lt. William J. Casey, Requisition form for WJC civilian clothes itemized, Dec. 6, 1944, Thomas McCoy memo to All Branch Supply Officers and Administrative Officers Aug. 22, 1944, WCNR, NPRC.

290 *returned home:* WJC letter to SKC Dec. 10, 1944, BCS.

CHAPTER 20: CASEY'S SPIES

291 *January 26:* Beneficiary slip for RMH File No. 170590, Jan. 2, 1945, RHNR, NPRC; Helms, *A Look over My Shoulder,* p. 38; Helms, OHP, pp. 9–11; Dennis Helms, Aug. 19, 2012; Ziegler, pp. 298, 308–9; Van Young, p. 286.

292 *under him:* Smith, Aug. 24, 2012; Services Clothing Book for RMH, B: 3, S: 4, RHP, GU; Vint Lawrence letter to Cynthia Helms April 17, 2003, B: 1, S: 1, P: 1, RHP, GU; Cynthia Helms, July 19, 2012; Helms, *A Look over My Shoulder,* pp. 39, 44–48; European-Mediterranean Pouch Review March 21, 1945, SI-ETO, B: 12, E: 99, RG226, NA.

293 *during the day:* WJC letter to SKC undated, circa 1945, BCS; Milton Katz (Biographical Sketch to April 1976), B: 3, JPP, HIA; Milton Katz Application for Employment and Personal History Statement, James Forgan memo to Commanding General, European Theater of Operations, June 27, 1945, Personnel Office SI Washington-Theater Service Record for Milton Katz Feb. 22, 1945, B: 393, E: 224, London SI War Diary, Vol. 9, pp. 25–26, R: 5, FR: 542–1305, R: 5, FR: 2–962, M1623, RG226, NA; Helms, OHP, p. 7; Helms, *A Look over My Shoulder*, pp. 39–44; Cynthia Helms, July 18, 2012; Helms, OHP, p. 8–9.

294 *occupation soldiers:* WJC memo to Ernest Brooks and John Creedy July 12, 1945, B: 300, E: 190, RG226, NA; Allan Dettman memo Subject: Orders to WJC Jan. 6, 1945, Travel Orders for WJC, HQ, 6th Army Group, Jan. 23, 1945, WCNR, NPRC; Richard Harris Smith, p. 107; London SI War Diary, Vol. 12, German Operations-1945, pp. 21–25, R: 4, FR: 542–1305, R: 5, FR: 2–962, M1623, RG226, NA; Casey, *The Secret War Against Hitler*, pp. 186–90.

294 *spy training:* WJC memo to George Graveson Feb. 8, 1945, B: 255, E: 190, London SI War Diary, Vol. 12, German Operations-1945, pp. 17–18, R: 4, FR: 542–1305, R: 5, FR: 2–962, M1623, Section V, Organization, B: 255, WJC memo to Robert Thompson with enclosure April 2, 1945, B: 305, 1945 Plans Jan. 3, 1945, B: 309, E: 190, RG226, NA; Casey, "The Clandestine War in Europe," pp. 3–4.

295 *and Bingen:* Hans Tofte Curriculum Vitae December 1945, B: 1, RFP, Hans Vilhelm Tofte biography, B: 23, NAP, HIA; London SI War Diary, Vol. 1, pp. 48–50, Vol. 12, German Operations-1945, pp. 9–14, 20, 410–12, 434, R: 4, FR: 542–1305, R: 5, FR: 2–962, M1623, Section V, Organization, B: 255, WJC memo to Robert Thompson April 2, 1945, B: 305, WJC memo to Field Detachment & Mission CO's Feb. 22, 1945, B: 305, Intelligence Objectives, WJC memo to Mr. Horton and Capt. Rositzke with enclosure Feb. 8, 1945, B: 255, E: 190, William Jay Gold COI Application and Personal History Statement Nov. 11, 1941, Letter to G. Edward Buxton Oct. 15, 1943, B: 2790, Robert MacLeod, Change in Status form June 14, 1943, James Forgan memo to Commanding General, European Theater of Operations June 25, 1945, COI Application and Personal History Statement for Robert MacLeod, B: 472, E: 224, RG226, NA; Persico, *Piercing the Reich*, pp. 35–36.

296 *"we have":* Section V, Organization, B: 255, E: 190, WS memo to Frank Ball July 13, 1945, Memorandum Concerning the Assignment of the Assistant Naval Attaché at Vichy, Lt. Thomas Cassady, to OSS Duty, WJD letter to Adm. Train Nov. 28, 1942, B: 112, James R. Forgan memo to Commanding General, European Theater of Operations, June 23, 1945, B: 360, E: 224, WJC memo to Col. Jackson Feb. 17, 1945, B: 255, E: 190, RG226, NA; Waller, p. 167; Bancroft, p. 203; Henry Hyde interview May 14, 1981, Unnumbered Box "Interviews—Bancroft to Sherwood undated," WJDP, MHI; Casey, *The Secret War Against Hitler*, pp. 190–91; Persico, *Piercing the Reich*, pp. 108–13.

296 *Bach unit:* Weinberg, pp. 799, 815–16; London SI War Diary, Vol. 6, Labor Division, pp. 139–52, Vol. 12, German Operations-1945, pp. 16–17, R: 4, FR: 542–1305, R: 5, FR: 2–962, M1623, George Pratt memo to R. H. Alcorn Dec. 21, 1945, B: 311, WJC memo to George Pratt Feb. 17, 1945, WJC memo to Pearson Feb. 26, 1945, B: 255, 1945

Plans Jan. 3, 1945, B: 309, WJC memo to Robert Thompson April 2, 1945, B: 305, WJC memo to John Bross Feb. 23, 1945, B: 255, WJC memo to James Forgan May 23, 1945, B: 311, E: 190, RG226, NA; Atkinson, *The Guns at Last Light*, p. 491; Ludewig, p. 11; Persico, *Piercing the Reich*, pp. 13, 31–33; Alsop, p. 28.

298 *chute unfurled:* Basic German Identity Documents, Dec. 18, 1945, B: 247, E: 190, Douglas Alden memo to Maj. Tofte Jan. 13, 1945, G. R. Hawthorne memo to W. C. Reddick et al., Information on Organization Todt, W. C. Reddick memo to William Jackson Dec. 15, 1944, Douglas Alden memo to George Pratt Jan. 11, 1945, B: 87, E: 148, Appendix F, Operations Report, Operational Supply Report, May 26, 1945, R: 80, FR: 574–696, M1642, London SI War Diary, Vol. 1, p. 15, Vol. 6, Labor Division, pp. 141–58, Vol. 12 German Operations, pp. 110–26, R: 4, FR: 542–1305, R: 5, FR: 2–962, M1623, B: 20, E: 211, Field Base "C," B: 74, E: 210, RG226, NA; *The Overseas Targets*, pp. 162, 306–8; Persico, *Piercing the Reich*, p. 2.

299 *"military authority":* Persico, *Piercing the Reich*, pp. 13–14; WJC memo to Field Detachment & Mission CO's Feb. 22, 1945, B: 305, Kauno Lehto memo to Richard Watt March 19, 1945, B: 194, E: 190, W. B. Kantack memo to WJD Feb. 6, 1945, B: 19, E: 99, European-Mediterranean Cable Digest, Estimate of German Casualties, March 26, 1945, B: 13, E: 99, Notes on Geneva Convention provisions, B: 314, E: 190, Caserta cable to SI Nov. 2, 1944, USTRAVIC cable to SI Jan. 3, 1945, R: 98, FR: 521, 613–14, M1642, RMH memo to WJC Jan. 9, 1945, B: 208, E: 190, RG226, NA.

300 *the communists:* J. L. Caskey memo to L. A. Coleman April 2, 1944, S. A. Callisen memo to Commanding Officer, OSS/ETO, March 10, 1945, B: 314, WJC memo with Attached Paper on Dissident Elements in Germany Feb. 28, 1945, B: 255, T. G. Cassady memo to WJC Dec. 29, 1944, B: 430, E: 190, Notes of meeting with WJD Jan. 4, 1945, B: 243, Cassady cable to Pratt Dec. 26, 1944, B: 204, E: 210, Preliminary Report on the Comité Allemagne libre pour l'Ouest (CALPO), Summary, B: 5, E: 128, London SI War Diary, Vol. 12, German Operations-1945, pp. 26–28, R: 4, FR: 542–1305, R: 5, FR: 2–962, M1623, RG226, NA; Enemy Aliens Brought to the U.K. for Training as Agents by S.I.S. or O.S.S., H. L. A. Hart memo to N. H. Pearson Jan. 24, 1945, Measures to Be Adopted by O.S.S. in Dealing with Aliens Whom They Are Importing into the U.K., KV 4/150, Minute Sheet, A.D.D. 4., p. 74, KV 4/149, History of the German Directorate Allied Missions Section, German Directorate History Part II, HS 7/147, NAUK; Casey, *The Secret War Against Hitler*, pp. 189–90.

300 *"around here":* WJC memo to E. C. Thompson April 2, 1945, Ezra Shine memo to WJC Dec. 6, 1944, B: 305, E: 190, Milton Katz memo to Plans and Operations Staff March 7, 1945, B: 94, C. C. Bowman memo to Ezra Shine Jan. 16, 1945, D. F. Anderson memo to E. Shine March 10, 1945, V. C. Wilson memos to Ezra Shine Feb. 8 and March 9, 1945, B: 91, Douglas Alden memo to All Desks March 28, 1945, General Orders No. 58, Disbandment of Areas, June 11, 1945, B: 95, E: 148, London SI War Diary, Vol. 12, German Operations-1945, pp. 91–92 with charts and photos, R: 4, FR: 542–1305, R: 5, FR: 2–962, M1623, RG226, NA; Persico, *Piercing the Reich*, p. 206; Persico, *Casey*, p. 75.

302 *remained insatiable:* WJC memo to All Concerned Jan. 10, 1945, WJC memo on MO-SI
Cooperation January 1945, B: 255, WJC memo to Richard Watts Jan. 1, 1944, B: 194, E:
190, RG226, NA; Persico, *Piercing the Reich*, pp. 157–65, 171–72, 196–200, 214, 302; Riddleberger, Dec. 14, 2012; Kindleberger, OHP, pp. 51–55; London SI War Diary, Vol. 12,
German Operations-1945, pp. 46–57, 131–32, 430–31, R: 4, FR: 542–1305, R: 5, FR: 2–962,
M1623, Communications Branch Progress Report March 15, 1945, B: 204, James Gall-
atin memo to Commanding Officer, Field Detachments and Missions Dec. 13, 1944, B:
429, Thomas Wilson memo to A. E. Jolis Dec. 25, 1944, B: 194, E: 190, Summary of OSS
Missions During March 1945, European Theater Operations Report March 1945, OSS
Activities, including European Theater, June 1944–Sept. 1945, Washington History Office,
B: 123–25, E: 99, RG226, NA; Brittenham, OHP, pp. 41–42; Casey, *The Secret War Against
Hitler*, pp. 186–87, 193–98; *The Overseas Targets*, pp. 285–87.

303 *powdered eggs:* WJC memo to James Forgan Jan. 21, 1945, B: 430, E: 190, SOP Oper-
ations, Equipment List of Agents, B: 46, E: 115, Final Arrangements, September 1943,
B: 356, E: 210, London SI War Diary (Redacted material), Vol. 1, Organization, pp.
37–38, Vol. 3, Authentication, Vol. 4, Special Weapons pp. 4–6, B: 20, E: 211, London
SI War Diary, Vol. 12, German Operations-1945, pp. 70–75, R: 4, FR: 542–1305, R: 5,
FR: 2–962, M1623, RG226, NA; Helms Biography Material, B: 7, S: 7, P: 3, RHP, GU;
Helms, *A Look over My Shoulder*, pp. 45–48; RMH remarks at the Heritage Foundation
reception May 31, 1989, B: 1, WHP, GU.

309 *bad luck:* Ezra Shine memo to Clinton Webb March 30, 1945, B: 91, R. L. Brittenham
memo to D. W. Alden Dec. 21, 1944, Douglas Alden memos to Maj. Tofte Dec. 27, 1944,
and Jan. 4, 1945, B: 97, Francis Hekking memos to Capt. Shine Dec. 29, 1944, and to Lt.
Alden Dec. 25, 1944, B: 98, Lt. Hekking memo to Capt. Shine Jan. 27, 1945, R. Brittenham
memo to D. Alden Feb. 15, 1945, Douglas Alden memo to Charles Mills Feb. 21, 1945,
William Grell memo to Capt. Shine March 15, 1945, Miguel Dainau memo to Lt. Aldon
Feb. 20, 1945, B: 97, E: 148, Lt. Van Essen memo to William F. Grell March 27, 1945,
Tofte & Beau cables to WJC, Pratt & Thompson March 20, 22, and 23, 1945, Grell cable to
Brittenham, Espinette, March 24, 1945, Bowman et al. cable to Cassady et al. March 24,
1945, Operations Office memo to Capt. Grell March 13, 1945, Espinette Mission, Project
"Doctor," April 18, 1945, R. L. Brittenham memo to George Pratt Jan. 20, 1945, B: 5,
Doctor Team, Jan Bloch and Jean Denis material and photos, Alphonse Blonttrock and
Jan Smets forged identity papers, Doctor Team: General Notes for Preparation of Cover,
R. L. Brittenham memo to A. M. Scaife Nov. 17, 1944, The Report of the Mission of the
team "Doctor" (Jean Denis and Jan Bloch), B: 1, Emil Van Dyke material, William Grell
memo to Communications Branch March 23, 1945, Fouget, François-Painter Team re-
port, B: 27, Deprocessing of team "Doctor"—Jan Bloch May 31, 1945, B: 41, E: 210, R. B.
MacLeod memo to George Pratt Jan. 13, 1945, Douglas Alden memo to Mr. Teper Feb. 2,
1945, William Grell memo to Communications Branch March 24, 1945, Pratt, Thompson
& Grell cable to Gamble, Cassady & Horton March 26, 1945, Cable to Reports Division
March 26, 1945, target list for Doctor team to observe around Kufstein, B: 36, E: 115,

European-Mediterranean Cable Digest March 28, 1945, 10. Doctor Project, B: 13, E: 99, London SI War Diary, Vol. 12, German Operations-1945, pp. 143–68, 192–204, R: 4, FR: 542–1305, R: 5, FR: 2–962, M1623, RG226, NA; Transcript of DCI William Casey interview Jan. 18, 1982, NCM; Persico, *Piercing the Reich*, pp. 189–91, 200–209, 302–5; Barreaux, Aug. 6, 2012; Casey, *The Secret War Against Hitler*, pp. 208–13.

309 *a thousand years:* Keegan, p. 514.

310 *Berlin team:* WS memo to WJD et al. November 4, 1944, R: 80, FR: 1237–1303, M1642, RMH memo to Lt. Cdr. M. Katz April 3, 1945, B: 300, E: 190, RG226, NA; Helms, *A Look over My Shoulder*, pp. 50–51; H. R. Stark memo to RMH March 17, 1945, RHNR, NPRC; Cynthia Helms, July 18, 2012; Powers, p. 24.

311 *their sectors:* Petersen, pp. 131–32, 218–21, 383–88, 440–41; Bern cable to B. Homer Hall Dec. 7, 1943, B: 169, E: 134, Notes on meeting Jan. 4, 1945, with WJD, B: 243, AG memo to AWD Sept. 20, 1944, B: 192, E: 210, Bern cable to SI, also routed to RMH, June 12, 1944, B: 235, E: 146, Bern cable to OSS HQ Nov. 29, 1943, B: 170, Bern cable to OSS HQ Jan. 6, 1945, B: 133, E: 134, OSS Rep. SHAEF memo to Col. Forgan with attachment Jan. 7, 1945, R: 81, FR: 802–4, M1642, RG226, NA.

CHAPTER 21: TO GERMANY

314 *village quarters:* Deprocessing of Team "Doctor"—Jan Bloch May 31, 1945, Bowman and Thompson cable to Gamlin and Cassady March 31, 1945, Report from London April 20, 1945, on Transport of Troops in Kufstein area, SASAC Paris cables to 6th, 7th, Washington, Caserta and SHAEF Forward April 20 and May 3 and 4, 1945, B: 41, Report of the Mission of the team "Doctor" (Jean Denis and Jan Bloch), J. R. Forgan memo to Commanding General, European Theater of Operations, May 26, 1945, B: 1, E: 210, London SI War Diary, Vol. 12, German Operations-1945, pp. 143–68, R: 4, FR: 542–1305, R: 5, FR: 2–962, M1623, RG226, NA; Persico, *Piercing the Reich*, pp. 202–5; Casey, *The Secret War Against Hitler*, pp. 208–9.

315 *like a baby:* WJC memo to Capt. Hayes March 28, 1945, B: 256, E: 190, London SI War Diary, Vol. 12, German Operations-1945, pp. 55–56, 132, 431–32, R: 4, FR: 542–1305, R: 5, FR: 2–962, M1623, Summary of OSS Activities During April 1945, OSS Activities, including European Theater, June 1944–Sept. 1945, Washington History Office, B: 123–25, E: 99, RG226, NA; Casey, *The Secret War Against Hitler*, pp. 198–201, 213.

317 *double agents:* London SI War Diary, Vol. 6, Labor Division, pp. 431–56, R: 4, FR: 542–1305, R: 5, FR: 2–962, M1623, Report on Mission "Hammer," B: 43, E: 148, Leonard Appel memo to Jacques Beau with enclosed Synopsis of Hammer Mission, B: 307, E: 190, Lawrence Levin memo to Leonard Appel June 9, 1945, B: 125, Labor Division London, pp. 5–11, Labor Division, Field Base "C," Milwaukee Forward (Withdrawal Material from SI War Diary), B: 74, E: 210, RG227, NA; Persico, *Piercing the Reich*, pp. 319–23; Read, *Berlin*, p. 239; Gill, pp. 230–31.

318 *been given:* M. Ledure memo to G. O. Pratt on Operation "Chauffeur" March 8, 1945, B: 5, E: 210, London SI War Diary, Vol. 12, German Operations-1945, pp. 168–91, 289–90, 335–36, 354–60, 428, R: 4, FR: 542–1305, R: 5, FR: 2–962, M1623, Alfred Ulmer

memo to Chief, German-Austrian Section, Feb. 10, 1945, Greenup Debriefing Report, Bland West memo to Lt. Col. Chapin May 6, 1945, B: 26, E: 124, WJC memo to WJD Dec. 17, 1948, B: 100, WJCP, HIA; The Eagle Project report by Louis Dups, B: 4, E: 128, RG226, NA; Casey, *The Secret War Against Hitler*, pp. 209–10; Persico, *Piercing the Reich*, pp. 217–23, 232–36, 249–50, 281–95.

319 *was Painter:* J. W. Raczkiewicz memo to Chief, X-2 Branch with Interrogation of Observer Adrian, "Martini" Team, May 23, 1945, B: 39, E: 115, London SI War Diary, Vol. 12, German Operations–1945, pp. 300–308, R: 4, FR: 542–1305, R: 5, FR: 2–962, M1623, European Theater of Operations Report, April 1945, I. General, A. Penetration of German-held Territory, OSS Activities, including European Theater, June 1944–Sept. 1945, Washington History Office, B: 123–25, E: 99, RG226, NA.

321 *the city:* Fouget, François–Painter Team report, Painter Mission report dictated by Emil Van Dyck May 22, 1945, J. R. Forgan memo to Commanding General, European Theater of Operations, May 26, 1945, Edward Dyro's Communication Deprocessing Form for Painter team May 21, 1945, B: 27, E: 210, London SI War Diary, Vol. 12, German Operations–1945, pp. 198–204, R: 4, FR: 542–1305, R: 5, FR: 2–962, M1623, RG226, NA; Persico, *Piercing the Reich*, pp. 304–5; Casey, *The Secret War Against Hitler*, pp. 210–13.

CHAPTER 22: SUNRISE

324 *from happening:* WJD memo to FDR Dec. 1, 1944, R: 24, FR: 853–56, OSS HQ cable to USTRAVIC London Aug. 14, 1944, R: 81, FR: 45–46, Joint Intelligence Committee Addendum to J.I.C. 208/M German Plans for Underground Operations Following Surrender with enclosure Aug. 10, 1944, R: 12, FR: 1127–33, Stockholm memo Sept. 3, 1944, OSS #38170, R: 81, FR: 79, M1642, Bern cable to OSS Feb. 27, 1945, B: 192, E: 134, RG226, NA; Petersen, pp. 15, 450–51, 485; Chalou, p. 286; Dulles, *The Secret Surrender*, p. 26; Weinberg, pp. 817–23; Trevor-Roper, p. 243; Longerich, p. 714; Atkinson, *The Guns at Last Light*, pp. 591–97; Kingsley, Jan. 1, 2008; Mauch, pp. 193–97; Helms, OHP, p. 18.

325 *Dulles agreed:* WJD memo to Secretary of State Feb. 9, 1945, R: 114, FR: 455–59, M1642, AWD cable to WS Feb. 4, 1945, B: 350, E: 210, WJD memo to FDR March 13, 1945, R: 114, FR: 455–59, 464–65, 480–89, 532, Charles Cheston memo to FDR Feb. 24, 1945, R: 113, FR: 1110–1393, Charles Cheston memo to JCS with enclosure Jan. 24, 1945, R: 22, FR: 333–34, M1642, RG226, NA; Dulles, *The Secret Surrender*, pp. 37–44.

326 *war criminal:* Caserta cable to Bern Feb. 24, 1945, B: 709, E: 190, RG226, NA; Smith, *Operation Sunrise*, pp. 26, 31–48, 60–65, 76–77; Dulles, *The Secret Surrender*, pp. 44–56, 69, 80–81; Atkinson, *The Guns at Last Light*, pp. 555–56; Mosley, p. 178.

327 *that night:* Transcript of PW interviews with Wolff and Domizlaf June 1, 1945, Vol. CVIII, COR; Dulles, *The Secret Surrender*, pp. 57–59, 68–71; Smith, *Operation Sunrise*, pp. 68–69, 73.

328 *was wrong:* Dulles, *The Secret Surrender*, pp. 57–62, 84–85, Hoffmann, p. 295; Cheston cable to 110 March 17, 1945, B: 709, E: 190, Bern cable to Director Feb. 28, 1945, B: 219, E: 134, USTRAVIC London cable to 109 Feb. 28, 1945, 110 cable to Cheston March 1,

1945, B: 709, E: 190, RG226, NA; DDE SHAEF Forward cable to Combined Chiefs of Staff and British Chiefs of Staff Feb. 27, 1945, PREM 3/198/2, NAUK.

330 *in Switzerland:* Dulles, *The Secret Surrender,* pp. 47–66, 74–76; Smith, *Operation Sunrise,* pp. 69–72; Smith, *OSS,* p. 21; Mosley, pp. 176–78; Notes on Personalities, PREM 3/198/2, NAUK; AWD letter to L. L. Lemnitzer Nov. 25, 1946, B: 38, AWD memo to WJD June 18, 1945, B: 44, AWDP, PU; Bern cable to OSS HQ March 5, 1945, B: 709, E: 190, RG226, NA.

332 *over and over:* AWD memo to WJD June 18, 1945, B: 44, GG letter to L. L. Lemnitzer March 10, 1945, B: 27, AWDP, PU; Bern cables to 109 March 9, 1945, B: 709, E: 190, WJD memo to FDR March 13, 1945, R: 114, FR: 455–59, 464–65, 480–89, 532, WJD memos to FDR March 8 and 9, 1945, R: 113, FR: 1110–1393, M1642, RG226, NA; "The Secret History of a Surrender," by Forrest Davis, *Saturday Evening Post,* Sept. 22, 1945, pp. 98–107; Alexander cable to Combined Chiefs of Staff and British Chiefs of Staff March 11, 1945, WO 204/40, NAUK; Dulles, *The Secret Surrender,* pp. 72–83; Petersen, pp. 465–66; Bancroft, COH, p. 240.

333 *already had:* Caserta cables to Bern March 9 and 11, 1945, Bern cable to Caserta March 13, 1945, WJD memo to FDR March 13, 1945, R: 114, FR: 455–59, 464–65, 480–89, 532, M1642, Glavin cables to 110 March 10 and 11, 1945, B: 709, E: 190, RG226, NA; A.M.S.S.O. memo to J.S.M. Washington March 9, 1945, C.I.G.S. memo to Prime Minister March 10, 1945, PREM 3/198/2, General Morgan cable to C.I.G.S. March 12, 1945, War Office cable to Freedom Reference No. 76086 CIGS, WO 204/40, NAUK; Dulles, *The Secret Surrender,* pp. 83–87, 90–91, 107–8; Smith, *Operation Sunrise,* pp. 5, 85.

334 *the Soviets:* A.M.S.S.O. telegram to J. M. Washington March 12, 1945, Memo to Prime Minister March 10, 1945, Memo to J. M. Martin March 13, 1945, J.S.M. memo to A.M.S.S.O. March 13, 1945, Archibald Clark Kerr memo to Chequers March 17, 1945, Moscow embassy telegram No. 837 to Foreign Office March 17, 1945, Most Immediate memo to Washington March 1945, Foreign Office to Washington memo on Moscow telegrams Nos. 837 and 850 March 1945, Telegram 921 from Moscow to Foreign Office March 22, 1945, Washington to Foreign Office telegram March 20, 1945, Churchill memos to Foreign Secretary March 24 and 25, 1945, Foreign Office memo to Prime Minister April 3, 1945, PREM 3/198/2, NAUK; Smith, *Operation Sunrise,* pp. 92–93, 101–4.

335 *Army sergeants:* Bern cable to SI Feb. 17, 1945, B: 133, E: 134, Bern cable to W. A. Kimbel March 14, 1945, R: 30, FR: 84, Donovan memo to FDR March 13, 1945, Heinrich von Vietinghoff profile, R: 113, FR: 1110–1393, M1642, RG226, NA; Dulles, *The Secret Surrender,* pp. 85–89, 92–99, 117.

338 *optimistically speculated:* Bern cable to Caserta March 12, 1945, Bern cable to 109 March 20, 1945, Bern cable to London March 28, 1945, B: 709, E: 190, WJD memo to Secretary of State March 21, 1945, R: 113, FR: 1110–1393, M1642, RG226, NA; Dulles, *The Secret Surrender,* pp. 97–106; Smith, *Operation Sunrise,* pp. 96–99; Mosley, pp. 181–83.

339 *But it was:* Bern cables to London and Paris March 26 and April 1 and 3, 1945, B: 709,

E: 190, Bern cable to SI April 5, 1945, B: 350, E: 210, RG226, NA; Dulles, *The Secret Surrender*, pp. 108–11; Smith, *Operation Sunrise*, pp. 112–15.

341 *missives ended*: FDR-Stalin exchange of letters March 24, 29, 31, April 3, 4, and 7, 1945, Map Room Files, Sextant Conference, B: 28, FDRL; David Crockett, OHP, pp. 16–17; Dulles, *The Secret Surrender*, pp. 124–27; Smith, *Operation Sunrise*, pp. 105–24.

341 *ever read it*: Alexander telegram to Combined Chiefs of Staff and British Chiefs of Staff, Reference No. FX-56050, WO 204/40, NAUK; Bern cable to 109 April 9, 1945, B: 709, E: 190, 110 cable to 106 and Cheston April 21, 1945, B: 523, E: 210, G. Edward Buxton memo to Grace Tully with enclosure April 10, 1945, R: 25, FR: 533–37, M1642, RG226, NA; Grace Tully letter to G. Edward Buxton with enclosures May 9, PSF, Subject File OSS, Reports April 1945, FDRL; Henry Hyde letter to AWD Nov. 7, 1966, B: 57, AWDP, PU; Smith, *Operation Sunrise*, pp. 118–27; Dulles, *The Secret Surrender*, pp. 119–21.

342 *Roosevelt's death*: Joseph O'Malley memo to Strategic Services Officer, ETO, May 3, 1945, B: 6, E: 99, 679 cable to Gamble or 110 April 18, 1945, B: 709, E: 190, RG226, NA; Waller, pp. 318–19; Casey, *The Secret War Against Hitler*, pp. 201–4; Mosley, p. 180; Dulles, *The Secret Surrender*, pp. 121–29.

343 *"cannot tolerate"*: Appendix: Schellenberg's relations with the Swiss Intelligence Service, B: 1, ADP, NSA; Churchill memo to Stalin April 13, 1945, Foreign Office memo to Prime Minister April 13, 1945, PREM 3/198/2, NAUK; Prime Minister telegram to President Truman April 15, 1945, CHAR 20-214-110-111, CA; Smith, *Operation Sunrise*, p. 127.

344 *his neck*: Dulles, *The Secret Surrender*, pp. 128–36, 142–51; Smith, *Operation Sunrise*, p. 128; Longerich, p. 734; Bern cable to Caserta April 24, 1945, B: 709, E: 190, RG226, NA.

345 *Joint Chiefs*: A. J. McFarland memo for the Director of Strategic Services April 20, 1945, Charles Cheston memos to JCS April 24, 25, and 27, 1945, R: 113, FR: 1110–1393, M1642, 110 cables to 106 and Cheston April 21, 1945, B: 523, E: 210, USTRAVIC London cable to OSS April 19, 1945, 109 cable to 110 April 24, 1945, B: 709, E: 190, RG226, NA; Combined Chiefs telegram to Alexander and DDE April 20, 1945, PREM 3/198/2, Personalities, Lt. Col. Viktor von Schweinitz, WO 204/40, NAUK; Dulles, *The Secret Surrender*, pp. 137–41, 151–58; Mosley, p. 186; Smith, *Operation Sunrise*, pp. 135–45, 163–69.

CHAPTER 23: FLIGHT OF THE RYPE

348 *been successful*: Kelly, pp. 34–43; Appendix No. II, Field Order No. II, SO Branch Scandinavian Section Feb. 12, 1945, B: 350, Henry Gossard memo to Chief, Supply Section, SO Branch, Jan. 31, 1945, B: 350, E: 190, WEC memo to Chief, Field Photographic Section, Nov. 20, 1944, B: 76, E: 148, Bio on Alf Harry Paulson, Theater Service Record for Alf H. Paulson June 22, 1945, Area F Interviewer's Report for Alf H. Paulson, B: 590, Extract from Service Record for Fred J. Johanson, Security Office Investigation Report Oct. 30, 1943, Theater Service Record for Fred J. Johanson, B: 374, Theater Service Record for Sverre B. Aanonsen, Area F Interviewer's Report for Sverre B. Aanonsen, B: 1, E: 224, Operating Staff of DIP, Vol. 12, German Operations-1945, p. 63, London SI War Diary,

R: 4, FR: 542–1305, R: 5, FR: 2–962, M1623, RG226, NA; "The NORSO Raiders Who 'Captured' Norway with Only 15 Men," Mark Sufrin, *Saga*, January 1964, Vol. 47, No. 4, p. 20; Colby, "OSS Operations in Norway"; Henry, pp. 636–38; Parnell, pp. 133, 209–10; Heimark, pp. 17, 70–74; Cruickshank, pp. 6–7, 91.

349 *with the season:* Colby, "OSS Operations in Norway"; James R. Forgan memo to Commanding General, European Theater of Operations, June 26, 1945, Theater Service Record for Einar A. Eliassen June 22, 1945, Area F Interviewer's Report for Einar A. Eliassen, B: 216, Separation Process for Knut Andreasen Sept. 11, 1945, Area F Interviewer's Report for Knut Andreasen, Theater Service Record for Knut Andreasen, B: 17, Personal History Statement for Matti Raivio, E: 224, RG226, NA; Heimark, pp. 3–9, 72–74; Kelly, pp. 34–43; Henry, pp. 636–38; Persico, *Piercing the Reich*, p. 160.

349 *and Bavaria:* J. S. Wilson memo to E. E. Mockler-Ferryman March 31, 1945, B: 340, R. W. Bean memo to Chandler Morse April 3, 1945, WEC memo to Commanding General, OSS, June 30, 1945, Charles Brebner memo to A. S. Andrew Thorne Jan. 31, 1945, B: 350, Broadway Intelligence (Norwegian Section) March 15, 1945, B: 302, Appreciation: Made in London by SFHQ 10 Jan. 45 on the action which can be taken to interfere with the movement of German Forces through and out of Norway, B: 351, E: 190, European-Mediterranean Pouch Review April 13, 1945, B: 12, E: 99, Scandinavian Activities (within SFHQ) April 2, 1945, R: 80, FR: 26–28, M1642, RG226, NA; Heimark, pp. 19–20; Gjelsvik, pp. 188, 200–201; Hall, pp. 194–95.

350 *with sabotage:* WEC memo to Commanding General, OSS, June 30, 1945, B: 350, Appreciation: Made in London by SFHQ 10 Jan. 45 on the action which can be taken to interfere with the movement of German Forces through and out of Norway, B: 351, Progress Report for SN Section for Period 1st–30th April 45, B: 341, Milorg "Bases" in Norway Jan. 10, 1945, An Appreciation of an Area North of Trondheim with a View to the Possible Disruption of Road and Rail Communications, B: 340, SHAEF Main Signed Eisenhower to SCOTCO G (OPS) 021835.A Dec., B: 329, E: 190, Scandinavian Activities (within SFHQ) April 2, 1945, R: 80, FR: 26–28, M1642, Trøndelag Fylke General Survey, Book I, pp. 2, maps after X., B: 21, E: 115, RG226, NA; Henry, pp. 629–30; Cruickshank, p. 13; Gjelsvik, p. 100.

351 *would undertake:* WEC memo to Commanding General, OSS, June 30, 1945, Charles Brebner memo to A. S. Andrew Thorne Jan. 31, 1945, B: 350, E: 190, OSS Training Areas in the United Kingdom, Area "P," B: 7, E: 161, George Hawthorne memo to Chief, S&T Branch, Feb. 25, 1945, Weekly Training Schedule for NORSO, B: 91, E: 148, SO War Diary, Vol. 8, October–December 1944, Scandinavia, pp. 91, 105–7, R: 9, M1623, RG226, NA; Heimark, pp. 61–62; Hall, p. 196; Sally Colby, July 27, 2012; Paul Colby, Sept. 3, 2012.

352 *colonel agreed:* WEC memo to Commanding General, OSS, June 30, 1945, Appendix No. II, Field Order No. II, SO Branch Scandinavian Section Feb. 12, 1945, Field Order No. I, SO Branch Scandinavian Section, Jan. 29, 1945, B: 350, S/14164, Norway's State Railways, B: 340, E: 190, Sections of the Norwegian State Railways, March 15, 1943, B: 8, E: 115, Photos of North Trøndelag, B: 29, E: 168, Intelligence Annex No. 2, Rec'd 7

Feb. 45, B: 51, Trøndelag Fylke General Survey, Book I, German defenses for Namsos, Grong, Formofoss, Steinkjer, and Formo, B: 21, Arne Brogger memo to Hans Skabo Feb. 1, 1945, B: 51, E: 115, SO War Diary, Vol. 8, January–July 1945, Scandinavia, p. 101, R: 9, M1623, RG226, NA; Heimark, pp. 62, 66–68, 123; Hall, pp. 191–95.

353 *at the castle:* Field Order No. I, SO Branch Scandinavian Section, Jan. 29, 1945, WEC memo to Commanding General, OSS, June 30, 1945, Charles Brebner memo to A. S. Andrew Thorne Jan. 31, 1945, Hans Skabo memo to Charles Brebner Feb. 3, 1945, B: 350, E: 190, Intelligence Annex No. 3, to Chief of Defense Ministry IV, p.t. London, Jan. 24, 1945, B: 51, E: 115, Gerald Miller memo to CO, Hq & Hq Detachment, OSS, European T of Opns., April 17, 1943, Application for Employment and Personal History Statement for Tom Sather, B: 63, E: 92A, SO War Diary, Vol. 8, January–July 1945, Scandinavia, p. 108, R: 9, M1623, RG226, NA; Kelly, pp. 34–43; Heimark, pp. 3–6, 73; Colby, *Honorable Men*, p. 45; Hall, p. 201.

353 *fouled up as his:* S.O.E. Council Minutes of Meeting March 30, 1945, HQ Files Committees SOE Council, Minutes, January 1945–December 1945, HS 8/202, District 22 Operations, HS 8/979, NAUK; Hans Skabo memo, Appendix to FO II, para III.X., SO Branch Scandinavian Section, March 2, 1945, B: 350, E: 190, RG226, NA; Cruickshank, pp. 30–31; Henry, pp. 636–37; Heimark, pp. 72–74; Colby, *Honorable Men*, p. 46.

354 *men's packs:* Appendix No. VIII, Operation Rype, Morning Report, WEC progress reports to Hans Skabo April 1 and 5, 1945, Hans Skabo memo to Chief, Scandinavian Section, April 10, 1945, B: 350, E: 190, Personal History Statement for Oddberg Stiansen, B: 747, E: 224, RG226, NA; Henry, p. 638.

355 *as it could:* Telegrams to and from Rype, No. 1-25 March, Hans Skabo memo to Chief, Scandinavian Section, April 10, 1945, Messages to Rype No. 2-26 March, No. 3-27 March, and No. 4-27 March, B: 350, E: 190, Borge Langeland bio for SO Branch, OSS, ETOUSA, B: 431, E: 224, RG226, NA; Parnell, pp. 133, 209–10.

355 *the Americans:* WEC memo to Commanding General, OSS, June 30, 1945, WEC progress reports to Hans Skabo April 1 and 5, 1945, B: 350, E: 190, RG226, NA; Kelly, pp. 34–43; Colby, "OSS Operations in Norway."

357 *"grave danger":* WEC progress reports to Hans Skabo April 1 and 5, 1945, B: 350, E: 190, Theater Service Record for Glenn J. Farnsworth, B: 229, E: 224, Report of Bridle Operation-Plane Blane No. 819, April 1, 1945, Statement from member of crashed A/C March 31, 1945, Hans Skabo memo to Chief, SO Branch, OSS (Main), April 4, 1945, B: 51, E: 115, SO War Diary, Vol. 8, January–July 1945, Scandinavia, pp. 108, 110–11, R: 9, M1623, Appendix IX, Telegrams to and from Rype, No. 4-28 March and No. 22-7 April, Messages to Rype, No. 6-30 March, No. 10-1 April, and No. 11-3 April, No. 17-6 April, No. 18-6 April, and No. 19-8 April, Hans Skabo memo to Chief, Scandinavian Section, April 10, 1945, Hans Skabo memo to G. Unger Vetlesen April 14, 1945, G. Unger Vetlesen memo to Gerald Miller April 10, 1945, Appendix No. VIII, Operation Rype Morning Report, B: 350, E: 190, RG226, NA; Kelly, pp. 34–43; Heimark, pp. 17, 81–82; Hall, pp. 202–4.

359 *inside it:* Special Forces HQ, Minutes of Meeting Held in the War Room Norgeby House

at 1030 HRS January 10, 1945, B: 340, Progress Reports for the SN Section for Periods 1st–31st March 45 and 1st–30th April 45, B: 341, Appreciation: Made in London by SFHQ 10 Jan. 45 on the action which can be taken to interfere with the movement of German Forces through and out of Norway, B: 351, S. P. Karlow memo to Col. Buxton with enclosure April 9, 1945, B: 646, WEC progress report to H. H. Skabo April 18, 1945, B: 350, E: 190, Request from WJD to Lt. Karlow to prepare for JCS report on Railway Sabotage in Oslo Fjord Area, B: 22, E: 99, Charles Cheston memo to JCS Jan. 13, 1945, R: 80, FR: 878–83, M1642, RG226, NA; Larsen, pp. 560–63; Gjelsvik, pp. 77–78, 178, 195, 201; Cookridge, pp. 341–42; Cruickshank, pp. 18–24; Kelly, pp. 34–43; Colby, *Honorable Men*, p. 47.

362 *to London:* WEC progress report to H. H. Skabo April 18, 1945, WEC memo to Commanding General, OSS, June 30, 1945, Appendix IX, Telegrams to and from Rype, No. 25-18 April, B: 350, E: 190, RG226, NA; Kelly, pp. 34–43; Colby, "OSS Operations in Norway"; Colby, *Honorable Men*, pp. 47–48; Heimark, pp. 80–87.

363 *next attack:* Appendix IX, Telegrams to and from Rype, No. 35-28 April, Appendix No. VIII, Operation Rype Morning Report, WEC memo to H. H. Skabo April 19, 1945, B: 350, E: 190, WEC memo to Special Funds Officer July 9, 1945, B: 51, E: 115, RG226, NA; Kelly, pp. 34–43; Colby, "OSS Operations in Norway"; Heimark, p. 102.

365 *after the attack:* WEC memo to H. H. Skabo April 19, 1945, WEC memo to Commanding General, OSS, June 30, 1945, WEC operation report to H. H. Skabo April 27, 1945, B: 350, E: 190, Intelligence Annex No. 3, to Chief of Defense Ministry IV, p.t. London, Jan. 24, 1945, B: 51, E: 115, James Forgan memo to Commanding General, European Theater of Operations, June 29, 1945, Theater Service Record for Sivert Windh, B: 845, E: 224, SO War Diary, Vol. 8, January–July 1945, Scandinavia, p. 113–14, R: 9, M1623, RG226, NA; Colby, "OSS Operations in Norway"; Heimark, pp. 87–91; Kelly, pp. 34–43; Colby, *Honorable Men*, pp. 48, 50.

366 *to frostbite:* WEC memo to Commanding General, OSS, June 30, 1945, B: 350, E: 190, WEC memo to Special Funds Officer July 9, 1945, B: 51, E: 115, RG226, NA; Colby, "OSS Operations in Norway"; Colby, *Honorable Men*, p. 49; Henry, p. 639; Heimark, p. 93; Sally Colby, July 27, 2012; John Colby, July 30, 2012; Carl Colby, July 16, 2012.

367 *their hideout:* Gjelsvik, pp. 201, 207; Appendix IX, Telegrams to and from Rype, No. 36-30 April, No. 38-2 May, Messages to Rype, No. 24-20 April, No. 30-1 May, and No. 31-3 May, WEC memo to Commanding General, OSS, June 30, 1945, A. W. Brogger memo to Chief, SO, OSS, UKB, with enclosure from Hans Skabo, June 13, 1945, WEC memo to Hans Skabo April 30, 1945, B: 350, E: 190, SN/NOR memo to WEC April 25, 1945, B: 51, E: 115, RG226, NA; Heimark, pp. 80–81, 94–97; Colby, *Honorable Men*, p. 49; Kelly, pp. 34–43.

CHAPTER 24: VICTORY

369 *"instructions literally":* A. J. McFarland memo to the Director of Strategic Services with enclosure April 26, 1945, R: 113, FR: 1110–1393, M1642, 109 cable to 110 April 26, 1945,

B: 709, E: 190, RG226, NA; General Lemnitzer message to ALCOM Rome Personal for Admiral Stone April 27, 1945, WO 204/40, NAUK.

370 *to Caserta's:* Charles Cheston memo to JCS April 27, 1945, WJD memo to HST April 28, 1945, B: 709, E: 190, RG226, NA; Dulles, *The Secret Surrender*, pp. 169–71.

372 *with a nod:* J. E. Bastion memo with minutes and other attachments April 28, 1945, Record of the Second Meeting Held with the German Plenipotentiaries at 2100 Hours of Saturday April 28, 1945, with enclosures, Record of the Third and Final Meeting Held with the German Plenipotentiaries in the Chief of Staff's Office at 1400 Hours with enclosures, April 29, 1945, WO 204/40, NAUK; Dulles, *The Secret Surrender*, pp. 171–79; Smith, *Operation Sunrise*, pp. 146–57.

373 *other fronts:* Field Marshal Alexander memos to Fifteenth Army Group April 30, 1945, to AGWAR for Combined Chiefs of Staff and British Chiefs of Staff May 2 and 4, 1945, and to SHAEF Forward for Eisenhower May 5, 1945, WO 204/40, NAUK; 110 cable to Paris April 30, 1945, WJD memo to HST May 2, 1945, 110 cable to 109 May 3, 1945, B: 709, E: 190, AWD memo to WS June 21, 1945, B: 427, E: 210, RG226, NA; AWD memo to WJD June 18, 1945, B: 44, AWDP, PU; Dulles, *The Secret Surrender*, pp. 179–89; Smith, *Operation Sunrise*, pp. 158–69.

373 *found it:* Translation of a part of a letter written by the wife of Admiral Canaris to a friend, B: 26, RG319, 110 cable to Carleton USFET Sept. 20, 1945, B: 152, E: 88, RG226, NA; Dulles, *The Secret Surrender*, pp. 72–74, 208–9; Hoffmann, p. 530.

374 *more unpopular:* Philip Horton memo to Lawrence Shallcross with enclosure April 13, 1945, B: 308, E: 210, 110 cables to OSS HQ April 4 and 5, 1945, 109 cable to 110 April 4, 1945, B: 5, E: 211, RG226, NA; Delattre, pp. 202–13; Helms, OHP, p. 31; Smith, *The Shadow Warriors*, pp. 224–25, 266; Dulles, *The Craft of Intelligence*, pp. 82–83; Petersen, p. 493.

375 *None arrived:* Supplement Report of July 29, 1945 with enclosure, Aug. 1, 1945, B: 34, AWDP, PU; Was the Atom Bomb Really Necessary? by Gero v. S. Gaevernitz, B: 27, Notes for NBC-Television Program on Japanese Surrender Negotiations, B: 53, AWDP, PU; Memos to HST May 12 and 31, June 4, July 13 and 16, and Aug. 2, 1945, B: 4, RG263, NA; "Magic"—Diplomatic Summary, No. 1176-June 14, 1945, and No. 1171-June 9, 1945, B: 3, MQP, GU; Dulles, *The Secret Surrender*, pp. 218–19; Petersen, pp. 464, 523–24.

375 *the bunker:* Bern cable to OSS HQ March 6, 1945, R: 30, FR: 62, Bern cable to OSS HQ March 2, 1945, R: 25, FR: 258–59, R: 30, FR: 21–24, 109 cable to 110 April 28, 1945, R: 5, FR: 1190, M1642, Roger Griswold memo to AWD May 2, 1945, B: 250, E: 210, Bern cable to OSS HQ April 20, 1945, B: 223, OSS HQ cable to 110 March 13, 1944, B: 165, E: 134, Germany: Military/Political, Hitler Reported in Berlin Bunker, Report for OSS London, April 25, 1945, B: 14, E: 119, RG226, NA; Petersen, pp. 425–26, 433, 466–67, 514–15; Read, *Berlin*, p. 240; Read, *The Fall of Berlin*, pp. 448–49.

376 *his body:* G. Edward Buxton memo to JCS April 13, 1945, R: 22, FR: 133–34, OSS HQ cable Aug. 7, 1945, with Hitler's and Goebbels's dental records and note from WJD, R: 54, FR: 1191–97, M1642, German: Political, Military, Economic and Medical, Scene in a Ber-

lin RR Station, OSS Report from Paris, March 23, 1945, Defense of Berlin, OSS London Report March 20, 1945, Conditions in Berlin in Mid-March 1945, OSS London Report April 17, 1945, Food and Health Conditions in Berlin, OSS London Report, April 19, 1945, B: 90, E: 145, RG226, NA; Read, *Berlin*, pp. 239–40; Gill, p. 267; Longerich, p. 730; Read, *The Fall of Berlin*, pp. 448, 453; Keegan, pp. 526–28.

377 *to Sweden:* Colby, "OSS Operations in Norway"; Progress Report for SN Section for Period 1st–31st May 45, B: 341, Scandinavian Region, Daily Summary No. 21 as at 1400 Hours 2 May 45, Daily Summary No. 24 as at 1400 Hours 5 May 45, B: 345, Appendix IX, Telegrams to and from Rype, No. 1-25 March, Appendix No. VIII, Operation Rype Morning Report, WEC memo to Commanding General OSS June 30, 1945, B: 350, E: 190, RG226, NA; Gjelsvik, p. 208; Larsen, p. 563; Heimark, pp. 97–98; Kelly, pp. 34–43.

378 *ever conducted:* Scandinavian Region, Daily Summary No. 23 as at 1400 Hours 4 May 45, B: 345, A. W. Brogger memo to Chief, SO, OSS, UKB with enclosed memo from Hans Skabo June 13, 1945, B: 350, E: 190, RG226, NA; Solhjell, pp. 178–87; Pryser, p. 123.

379 *"disciplinary action":* Kelly, pp. 34–43; Colby, "OSS Operations in Norway"; Appendix No. VIII, Operation Rype Morning Report, WEC memo to Commanding General, OSS, June 30, 1945, Appendix IX, Telegrams to and from Rype, No. 41-4 May, No. 42-5 May, No. 43-6 May, Messages to Rype, No. 44-11 May, B:350, E: 190, RG226, NA; Heimark, pp. 98–99.

379 *war criminals:* WJC letter to SKC May 24 and June 7, 1945, BCS; London SI War Diary. Vol. 12, German Operations–1945, p. 202, R: 4, FR: 542–1305, R: 5, FR: 2–962, M1623, Painter Team report dictated by Emil Van Dyck May 22, 1945, B: 27, E: 210, RG226, NA; Casey, *The Secret War Against Hitler*, p. 219.

379 *forces unconditionally:* Eisenhower, p. 424; Dulles, *The Secret Surrender*, p. 208; Smith, *Operation Sunrise*, p. 170.

380 *"leave again":* Eisenhower, pp. 425–26; Ziemke, p. 257; Grose, pp. 242–43; Atkinson, *The Guns at Last Light*, pp. 551, 623, 626; Helms, *A Look over My Shoulder*, pp. 51–52; WJC letter to Bernadette Casey May 14, 1945, BCS; Helms Biography Material, B: 7, Part 3, Series 7, RHP, GU.

381 *in prison:* Halbrook, p. 199; Ziegler, pp. 312–14; Van Young, pp. 323–29; Weinberg, pp. 894–95; Longerich, pp. 735–36; MacDonogh, p. 461; Salter, pp. 109–21, 176–77; L. L. Lemnitzer letter to AWD March 5, 1946, B: 38, AWD letter to L. L. Lemnitzer July 28, 1945, B: 38, AWDP, PU; Eugen memo to The Highest SS and Police Commander Italy O.U., May 7, 1945, R: 225, FR: 2763180-3, T-175, NA; von Lingen, pp. 3, 155–56, 199–205, 287–94.

382 *diplomatic pitfalls:* 109 cable to 110 May 2, 1945, L. L. Lemnitzer letter to WJD May 15, 1945, Magruder cable to 110 May 3, 1945, B: 709, E: 190, RG226, NA; Henry Brandon, "The World of Cloak & Danger," *Sunday Times*, April 28, 1963, p. 13; Notes for NBC-Television Program on Japanese Surrender Negotiations, B: 53, AWDP, PU; Gerhard Van Arkel interview Nov. 11, 1983, B: 11, RSP, HIA; Dulles, *The Secret Surrender*, pp. 1–2; Petersen, pp. 14–15; Smith, *Operation Sunrise*, pp. 182–85, 191; Eisenhower, p. 424.

382 *of the story:* Bern cable to OSS HQ May 11, 1945, 110 cable to 109 May 6, 1945, B: 709, E: 190, 476 cable to 110 June 16, 1945, R: 114, FR: 355–57, M1642, 110 cable to 109 and 154 May 8, 1945, B: 223, E: 134, E. J. Putzell letter to Capt. Dern Aug. 9, 1941, Edwin L. Sibert memo to Commanding General, Headquarters United States Forces, European Theater, Nov. 13, 1945, Anna Lesher letter to AWD Sept. 13, 1946, B: 203, E: 224, RG226, AWD letters to Stanley Woodward May 6, 1946, Stanley Woodward letter to AWD May 17, 1946, B: 72, Central Digital Files, RG59, NA; "O.S.S. Prepared Nazi Surrender of Italy Armies," *New York Herald Tribune*, Sept. 18, 1945; L. L. Lemnitzer letter to AWD Nov. 23, 1945, B: 38, AWD letter to John Magruder July 15, 1946, B: 40, DKEB letter to AWD March 22, 1946, AWD letters to DKEB March 27, April 16, 23, and 25, 1946, B: 9, *The Secret Surrender*: a motion picture treatment based on the book of the same name by Allen Dulles, B: 27, AWDP, PU; Smith, *Operation Sunrise*, p. 187.

383 *Allied intelligence:* Smith, *The Shadow Warriors*, pp. 189–90; Mauch, pp. 132–33; Petersen, pp. 16–20; *The Overseas Targets*, p. 180; DKEB letter to AWD Sept. 27, 1961, B: 9, AWDP, PU.

383 *"been achieved":* Chief, SI, ETO, memo to CO, OSS, ETO July 24, 1945, R: 80, FR: 555–72, M1642, RG226, NA; Persico, *Piercing the Reich*, pp. 333–35.

384 *"other three to?":* My Early Years in Intelligence, manuscript by RMH, B: 10, Part 1, Series 3, RHP, GU; James R. Forgan memo to Commanding General, United States Forces, European Theater, June 30, 1945, B: 112, E: 224 RG226, NA; Casey, *The Secret War Against Hitler*, p. 55; Persico, *Casey*, p. 83; Casey, "OSS: Lessons for Today," p. 64; Helms, OHP, pp. 6–7; Grose, pp. 212–13; Ross Collins memo to Commander, U.S. Naval Forces in Europe, June 13, 1946, Bronze Star Medal citation for WJC April 20, 1945, WCNR, NPRC; Meyer, pp. 285–86.

384 *farther south:* Scandinavian Region, Daily Summary No. 28 as at 1400 Hours 10 May 45, B: 345, Appendix IX, Telegrams to and from Rype, No. 49-8 May, No. 50-9 May, No. 51-10 May, No. 52-10 May, No. 55-11 May, Messages to Rype, No. 44-11 May, B: 350, E: 190, RG226, NA; Heimark, p. 102.

384 *men killed:* Norway, German Intelligence Activities, May 1945, B: 16, E: 190A, Scandinavian Region, Daily Summary No. 30 as at 1400 Hours 12 May 45, B: 345, Scandinavian Region, Daily Summary No. 31 as at 1400 Hours 14 May 45, B: 190, Progress Report for SN Section for Period 1st–31st May 45, B: 341, Gerhard Bolland memo to Chief, Scandinavian Section, June 13, 1945, B: 350, E: 190, Scandinavian Desk memo to Mr. Felps, July 14, 1945, with July 3, 1945, enclosure on Norway, B: 365, E: 210, RG226, NA; Heimark, p. 103; Gjelsvik, pp. 212–13; Larsen, pp. 563–64; Cookridge, p. 345; Sally Colby, July 27, 2012.

385 *defiant behavior:* Appendix IX, Telegrams to and from Rype, No. 55-14 May, WEC memo to Commanding General, OSS, June 30, 1945, B: 350, E: 190, RG226, NA; Colby, "OSS Operations in Norway"; Kelly, pp. 34–43; Heimark, pp. 103–5; Colby, *Honorable Men*, pp. 49–51; Paul Colby, Sept. 9, 2012; John Colby, July 30, 2012.

385 *an interviewer:* WEC memo to Commanding General, OSS, June 30, 1945, A. W. Brog-

ger memo to Chief, SO, OSS, UKB, June 13, 1945, with enclosed memo by Hans Skabo, B: 350, E: 190, Hoke McDonald memo June 21, 1945, B: 133, E: 224, RG226, NA; Colby, "OSS Operations in Norway"; Kelly, pp. 34–43; WEC memo to Chief, Special Branch, OSS, May 23, 1945, B: 3, WECP, PU; "Interview: William Colby, former director, Central Intelligence Agency," *Special Warfare*, April 1994, Vol. 7, No. 2, p. 41; Hall, p. 213; Carl Colby, July 16, 2012; Colby, *Honorable Men*, pp. 51, 54–55; Paul Colby, Sept. 9, 2012.

385 *had decided:* WEC letter to his mother July 6, 1945, B: 2, WEC letter to his mother June 23, 1945, B: 1, WECP, PU; Charles Brebner memo to Harrison Barrow May 21, 1945, B: 578, E: 92, RG226, NA; Hall, pp. 214–15.

CHAPTER 25: HOME

389 *Casey decided:* WJC letter to SKC June 7, 1945, BCS; Casey, *The Secret War Against Hitler*, p. 220; G. O. Pratt memo to WJC April 25, 1945, B: 311, WJC memo to Capt. Grell May 12, 1945, WJC memo to R. R. Dodderidge June 5, 1945, with enclosure to Branch Field Headquarters May 16, 1945, B: 430, E: 190, RG226, NA.

390 *now stopped:* Lowe, p. 83; Larson, p. 54; Atkinson, *The Guns at Last Light*, pp. 611–13; Casey, *The Secret War Against Hitler*, p. 218; Persico, *Casey*, pp. 81–82; Woodward, p. 53; Barreaux, Aug. 6, 2012; Cookridge, p. 24; Foot, *SOE in Paris*, p. 373; S. O. SCI Unit memo to SI Branch, HQ Detachment, and Paul Paterni memo to C. O. Company D, 2677th Regt. OSS (prov), June 7, 1945, B: 278, E: 210, F. O. Canfield memo to WJC May 5, 1945, B: 114, E: 148, Saint, London, to Saint, Washington, with interrogation brief of Rene Guiraud, June 18, 1945, B: 16, E: 190A, RG226, NA; "Liberating Dachau," by Flint Whitlock, *World War II*, March 2000, pp. 26–80.

391 *the Far East:* Edward Gamble memo to OPSAF-OSS, London, March 24, 1945, B: 203, Homer White memo through S. A. Callisen and RMH to WJC March 13, 1945, B: 348, FW memo to WJC April 9, 1945, B: 439, E: 210, WJC memo to FW May 1, 1945, R: 81, FR: 988–1005, M1642, WS memo to WJD May 15, 1945, B: 112, E: 224, RG226, NA; Grose, pp. 250–53; Casey, *The Secret War Against Hitler*, pp. 217–22; Barreaux, Aug. 6, 2012.

392 *"higher positions":* Hall, pp. 214–15; Area F OSS Reallocation Center pamphlet, B: 478, E: 190, Men Essential to OSS, Request for Procurement of Military Personnel for WEC Aug. 8, 1945, Area F's Interviewer's Report for WEC Aug. 6, 1945, B: 133, E: 224, RG226, NA; James Hodges memo to WJD May 25, 1945, B: 81B, WJDP, MHI.

392 *personal life:* Waller, pp. 303–14, 333–37; Russ Forgan letter to WJC Feb. 16, 1966, B: 100, WJCP, HIA.

393 *do the same:* Charles Ford letter to Special Funds Division with enclosure Sept. 7, 1945, B: 112, E: 224, WJD letter to WJC Sept. 27, 1945, B: 94, E: 92A, WJC letter to WJD Sept. 13, 1945, R: 40, FR: 78–79, M1642, RG226, NA; Persico, *Casey*, pp. 84–85; Barreaux, Aug. 6, 2012.

394 *in Europe:* M. P. Harper note on WEC Sept. 24, 1945, OSS Request for Domestic Travel Order for WEC Sept. 17, 1945, B: 133, E: 224, RG226, NA; Barbara Colby, July 10 and 16, 2012, Colby, *Honorable Men*, pp. 51–52, 61–62; Carl Colby, July 16, 2012; Sally Colby,

April 6, 2013; Elbridge Colby letter to WEC Aug. 27, 1945, B: 2, WECP, PU; "Barbara Heinzen, Major Colby, of Ski Paratroops, to Wed," *New York Herald Tribune*, Sept. 3, 1945.

395 *would succeed:* Graham Campbell to CO, HQ and HQ Detachment, OSS, Washington with Silver Star Citation of WEC Sept. 29, 1945, B: 133, E: 224, Remarks of WJD at final gathering of OSS employees Sept. 28, 1945, R: 69, FR: 441–43, M1642, RG226, NA; "Donovan Gives Farewell Talk to OSS Crew," *Washington Post*, Sept. 29, 1945; Remarks of WJD at final gathering of OSS employees Sept. 28, 1945, B: 460, WJCP, HIA; Barbara Colby, July 16, 24, and 26, 2012; Woods, p. 74; Colby, *Honorable Men*, pp. 52–54; Waller, pp. 1–6; Prados, pp. 36–37; Paul Colby, Sept. 3, 2012.

CHAPTER 26: BERLIN

398 *left behind:* WHM letter to HFA June 18, 1945, B: 25 HAP, PU; Letter to AWD, Diary-notes of events leading to the surrender June 4, 1945, B: 4, ADP, NSA; AWD memo to W. Lane Rehm June 20, 1945, B: 203, E: 224, Robert Joyce memo to Director, OSS/Washington, Aug. 23, 1945, B: 11, E: 99, WJD letter to Harrison A. Gerhart Sept. 5, 1945, John McCloy letter to WJD Sept. 24, 1945, Peter Pugliese memo to WJD Sept. 5, 1945, R: 21, FR: 839, R: 44, FR: 473–74, M1642, Black memo to Canfield Aug. 18, 1945, B: 151, E: 88, RG226, Subject: OSS, July 24, 1945, B: 27, E: P12, GP, RG263, NA; Petersen, pp. 452, 521–25; Grose, pp. 247–48; Smith, *OSS*, p. 141; Srodes, p. 362; Crockett, OHP, p. 50.

398 *it back:* Stalin memo to commanders of the 1st and 2nd Belorussian Front and 1st Ukrainian Front April 20, 1945, B: 9, RED, NSA; Survey of the Occupation of Germany through November 1945, Historical Division, HQ, EUCOM APO 757, CMH; Ziemke, p. 320; Lowe, pp. xiii–xvii, 5–16, 24–28, 48–49, 69–76, 367.

399 *a glass:* RMH memo to Chief, SI, Dec. 28, 1944, B: 57, E: 92, RMH memo to WJC June 8, 1945, B: 313, E: 190, OSS Mission to Germany Progress Report June 1945, B: 9, E: 99, RG226, NA; RMH card for Battle Cloud Officers' Club, B: 3, P: 2, S: 2, RHP, GU; Helms, OHP, pp. 13–15; Robarge, p. 15; Helms, *A Look over My Shoulder*, pp. 53–56; Atkinson, *The Guns at Last Light*, p. 587; Sichel, March 11, 2013; Polgar, March 19, 2013; Schlesinger, OHP, pp. 38–40; Crockett, OHP, pp. 22–23.

400 *she recalled:* Arthur Schlesinger Application for Federal Employment, B: 683, James Forgan memo to Commanding General, European Theater of Operations May 5, 1945, B: 798, E: 224, Memo on OSS Mission for Germany as of 30 September 1945, Oct. 4, 1945, B: 9, E: 99, Memo on conference between WJD, Col. O'Malley, Lt. Bastedo and Lt. J. G. Wilson April 21, 1945, B: 185, Peter Sichel memo to Chadbourne Gilpatrick April 26, 1946, E: 210, 110 cable to Bessermann Aug. 17, 1945, Black for Bratton cable to Levine, Black cable to 110 AMZON RE UR 923, B: 151, E: 88, RG226, NA; Persico, *Piercing the Reich*, p. 326; Delattre, pp. 214–16, 228–37; Bancroft, p. 264.

400 *Wisner lived:* Gerhard Van Arkel interview Nov. 11, 1983, B: 11, RSP, HIA; Helms Biography Material, B: 7, P: 3, S: 7, Polly Wisner letter to RMH, Sunday undated, B: 9, P: 1, S: 2, RHP, Appearance profiler Feb. 7, 1997, B: 1, WHP, GU; Gerhard Van Arkel Theater

Service Record, B: 797, E: 224, RG226, NA; Wisner, Oct. 18, 2012; Sichel manuscript; Thomas, pp. 10, 17–23, 39, 162, 320; Sichel, March 11, 2013; Brown, pp. 677–79; Waller, pp. 285–86; Dennis Helms, Aug. 19, 2012; Cynthia Helms, July 18, 2012.

401 *legitimately owned:* Helms, *A Look over My Shoulder*, p. 60; OSS Activities, including European Theater, June 44–Sept. 45, Washington History Office, European Theater of Operations Report May 1945, B: 123–25, E: 99, OSS Art Looting Unit Final Report May 1, 1946, B: 505, E: 92, James Plaut memo to R. E. Josephs June 30, 1945, B: 276, E: 108A, RG226, NA; RMH Officer's Fitness Report Feb. 26 to Aug. 31, 1945, RHNR, NPRC; Helms, OHP, pp. 18, 24; Jackson, COH, pp. 1236–37, 1290; Salter, pp. 8, 247–53; Nicholas, pp. 3–6, 34–35, 43, 62–68, 83–89, 103, 123–24, 145–47, 164–70, 222–26, 354–55, 376–77; Richie, pp. 610–12; *War Report of the OSS*, p. 196; OSS Consolidated Interrogation Report No. 2, Sept. 15, 1945, The Goering Collection, B: 1, GP, HIA.

402 *life difficult:* AWD letter to Edward Stettinius March 23, 1949, B: 106, AWDP, PU; Grose, p. 249; MacDonogh, pp. 417–96; Weinberg, pp. 836–41; Richie, pp. 604, 629–30; Gardner, pp. 7, 36–37, 47–61, 70–74, 86, 89, 96, 102; Eleanor Dulles, Eisenhower Administration Series, COH, pp. 122–23; Helms Biography Material, B: 7, P: 3, S: 7, John McCawley memo to All Concerned Nov. 24, 1945, B: 1, P: 2, S: 2, Louis Kubler memo on Authorization to Drive Government Vehicle, SHAEF Special Authorization for RMH April 9, 1945, B: 3, P: 2, S: 4, RHP, GU; Helms, *A Look over My Shoulder*, pp. 57–58; Helms, OHP, p. 29; Tally Sheet, Incoming for RMH Oct. 12, 1945, HRNR, NPRC.

404 *per day:* Notes on the German Communist and Social Democratic Parties in Berlin July–August 1945, B: 169, E: 108, RG226, Notes on the Press in the Russian Zone, R: 1, FR: 1217–19, M1656, NA; Richie, pp. 605, 609, 622–33; Ziemke, pp. 298–305, 347; Clay, pp. 21, 26–32; MacDonogh, pp. 11–12, 112–21, 228–30; Read, *Berlin*, pp. 243–45.

404 *General Staff:* My Early Years in Intelligence, manuscript by RMH, B: 10, P: 1, S: 3, RHP, GU; Read, *The Fall of Berlin*, p. 405; MacDonogh, pp. 97, 104, 118; Helms, OHP, p. 27; Helms, *A Look over My Shoulder*, pp. 57–58; Black cable to 110 and Morse, message no. 5, Black cable to 110 and Schmidt, message no. 12, B: 151, E: 88, RG226, NA; Building Roster Nov. 10, 1945, B: 1, P: 2, S: 2, RHP, GU; Read, *Berlin*, p. 251; Sichel manuscript; Polgar, March 19, 2013; Murphy, pp. 6–8; Sichel, March 11, 2013.

405 *anything he did:* Black cable to 110 and services, message no. 9 and 15, Peter, No. 10, cable to Van der Gracht and FW, message no. 145, B: 151, Helms cables to Black, Van der Gracht Nov. 26 and 29, 1945, Malcom and Gillette cable to Black Oct. 20, 1945, B: 152, E: 88, Requisition to supply officer Aug. 27, 1945, B: 194, E: 190, WJD memo to List S, General Order No. 75-4, B: 200, E: 139, RG226, NA; Sichel manuscript; Helms, *A Look over My Shoulder*, pp. 58–62; Helms, OHP, p. 21–22; Talley, July 28, 2012.

406 *later said:* Monthly Reports of Steering Division, SI/Germany Aug. 2, Sept. 5, and Nov. 5, 1945, B: 4, E: 214, Black cable to directors London and Paris and to 110 and Exec., WT NR 30, 110 cable to Bross Sept. 26, 1945, 110 cable to Suhling Aug. 11, 1945, B: 151, E: 88, Progress Report, R&A/Germany, Sept. 1, 1945, B: 9, E: 99, Cheston and 154 cable to 110 Feb. 27, 1945, R: 81, FR: 874–76, M1642, 154 and Tofte cable to Fleisher Dec. 7,

1945, B: 12, E: 211, RG226, NA; AWD letter to H. Bruening April 22, 1946, B: 9, AWDP, 110 cable to FW May 23, 1945, 19450523_0000031757, AWDD, PU; Sichel manuscript; Srodes, p. 309; Mauch, p. 206; Helms, OHP, pp. 12, 21–23.

407 *Helms agreed:* Lessons from the Resistance to the German Occupation of France, June 1945, B: 741, E: 190, Memorandum T-4031 A, Sept. 15, 1945, B: 489, E: 210, OSS/Mission of Germany Progress Report August 1–31, 1945, Security Branch Progress Report Sept. 1–30, 1945, B: 9, E: 99, Monthly Progress Report—X-2 Branch—May 1945, B: 276, E: 108A, RG226, NA; Survey of the Occupation of Germany through November 1945, Historical Division, HQ EUCOM APO 757, Occupation Forces in Europe Series, 1945–46, Law, Order and Security, Office of the Chief Historian, European Command, pp. 34–35, 69, CMH; Clay, p. 67; MacDonogh, pp. 349–50; Bessel, pp. 189–90; Ziemke, p. 381; Helms, *A Look over My Shoulder*, p. 82; Montgomery, July 17, 2012.

407 *"in ruins":* 110 cable to Canfield Sept. 3, 1945, B: 151, E: 88, WJD memo to Gen. Marshall Aug. 5, 1944, R: 20, FR: 492–94, WJD memo to HST May 5, 1945, R: 105, FR: 869–86, M1642, RG226, NA; Zhukov memo to commanders of the 1st Belorussian Front April 24, 1945, B: 9, RED, NSA; Dinner plate Helms retrieves from the Reich Chancellery, B: 6, P: 3, S: 5, RHP, GU; "How a Letter on Hitler's Stationery, Written to a Boy in Jersey, Reached the CIA," by Ian Shapira, *Washington Post,* Oct. 31, 2011; MacDonogh, pp. 115, 119; Murphy, p. 8; Clay, p. 29; Polgar, March 19, 2013; Sichel manuscript; Grose, p. 254; Richie, p. 606; Helms, *A Look over My Shoulder*, p. 60; Helms, OHP, pp. 19–20; Dennis Helms, Aug. 18, 2012; Rolfe Kingsley, Jan. 7, 2008; Mosley, pp. 226–28.

408 *sway Germans:* Sample of TASS (Soviet News Agency) Propaganda Techniques Feb. 6, 1945, R: 1, FR: 1228–29, Anti-American Literature April 1946, R: 2, FR: 79–80, Opinion Trends and Anti-American Propaganda in Bavaria Feb. 23–March 15, 1946, R: 1, FR: 1208–10, M1656, NA; AWD memo to JFD with enclosure April 24, 1947, B: 51, "Did Allen Dulles Play Footsie with Nazis?," *Democratic German Report*, Aug. 19, 1960, B: 28, AWDP, PU; Mosley, p. 228; Ziemke, pp. 281–82; Clay, p. 115, 119; Richie, pp. 629, 652; Murphy, p. 19.

408 *Austrian informants:* Monthly Reports of Steering Division, SI/Germany, Aug. 2 and Sept. 5, 1945, B: 4, E: 214, Monthly Progress Report for SI/Production Sept. 1–30, 1945, B: 9, E: 99, Captured German documents the War Department Intelligence Division sends to Washington, B: 256–57, E: 139, Nine Seven One to Paris and Caserta May 30, 1945, with Intelligence Objectives in Areas Occupied by the USSR, B: 439, E: 210, OSS SI cable to AMZON Aug. 1, 1945, B: 192, E: 134, Review of Project Caviar, B: 3, E: 216, RG226, NA; Helms, OHP, pp. 16, 19; Petersen, p. 525; Polgar, March 19, 2013.

409 *fabricated papers:* OSS Mission to Germany September Report, Progress Report, CD Germany, September 1945, OSS/Mission for Germany Progress Report August 1–31, 1945, B: 9, E: 99, Peter Sichel memo to Hoyt Irving July 16, 1946, Needed documents and cover information, June 25, 1945, B: 4, E: 214, RG226, NA.

409 *but they tried:* Interview with Bill Hood June 2, 1986, B: 14, LCP, GU; FW cable to 110

Sept. 11, 1945, B: 9, E: 211, AWD and FW cable to Chapin & Perry Aug. 8, 1945, and Chapin & Perry response Aug. 11, 1945, OSS Det. "A" memo on Padre E. Gehrmann's Mission, SASAC Vienna cable to SASAC AMZON Nov. 2, 1945, FW and Chapin cable to AMZON, Info: RMH, Berlin, Nov. 6, 1945, Rolfe Kingsley memo to RMH Nov. 8, 1945, and to Earle Carleton Jan. 17, 1946, Kingsley cable to Peter, Berlin, Feb. 2, 1946, and to Emma Paxon March 1, 1946, B: 160, RMH memo to George Pratt June 5, 1945, B: 283, E: 210, RG226, NA.

410 *often fabricated:* Kingsley, Jan. 7, 2008; Murphy, pp. 20–23; Schlesinger, OHP, pp. 35–36: Richard Cutler memo to Crosby Lewis Oct. 31, 1945, B: 2, Progress Report for X-2 Penetration Cases, September 1945, Report of SCI Operations for Week Ending 26 September 1945, B: 3, E: 213, Russian Deserters in the Berlin Area September 1945, B: 169, E: 108, RG226, Forging an Intelligence Partnership: CIA and the Origins of the BND, 1945–49, Vol. 1, B: 30, E: 22-19, RG263, NA; AWD letter to Philip Bonsal Sept. 9, 1968, R. Gehlen letter to AWD April 20, 1959, B: 28, Letter to RMH Sept. 11, 1968, B: 31, AWDP, PU; Gehlen signed photo with inscription for RMH, B: 9, P: 3, S: 12, RHP, GU; Sichel manuscript; Polgar, March 19, 2013; Grose, pp. 311–14; Helms, *A Look over My Shoulder*, pp. 61, 83–87, 90–91.

410 *Eastern Europe:* Stilt USCON cable to Tiger AMZON WT NR 75, Black cable to 110 and Morse Aug. 8, 1945, B: 151, E: 88, Saint memo to Saint, DB1, May 3, 1946, B: 1, E: 214, AB-51, AMZON, memo to AB-43, Munich, Aug. 7, 1946, B: 2, E: 213, Memorandum T-4031 A, Sept. 15, 1945, B: 489, E: 210, Report on Sachsenhausen Concentration Camp Nov. 5, 1945, B: 169, E: 108, Germany (Russian Zone) Military PW Officers March 1, 1946, B: 27, E: 108A, RG226, Universities in the Russian Zone February 1946, R: 1, FR: 1077–78, Recruiting of Wehrmacht Officers by Russian Agents May 1946, R: 3, FR: 1036, Russian Order for Requisitioning of Labor Dec. 22, 1945, R: 1, FR: 1225, M1656, NA; Lowe, pp. 70–71, 111–20; Read, *Berlin*, p. 245; MacDonogh, pp. 214, 420–21; Bessel, pp. 202–3; Richie, pp. 449–50.

411 *gruesome experiments:* Peter, Berlin, cable to Van der Gracht, AMZON Aug. 16, 1945, B: 151, E: 88, Memorandum T-4031 A, Sept. 15, 1945, B: 489, E: 210, Monthly Report of Steering Division Sept. 5, 1945, B: 4, E: 214, Russian Removal of Machinery from Germany and Berlin October 1945, B: 169, E: 108, Peter, USCON, cable to FW and Van der Gracht, AMZON, 098, B: 151, E: 88, RG226, Russians Placing Orders for Military Equipment Jan. 11–March 11, 1946, Production of Tank Parts for the Russians, March 1945, R: 1, FR: 1000 and 1192, M1656, NA; Helms, *A Look over My Shoulder*, p. 60; MacDonogh, pp. 207, 239–40, 259; Ziemke, p. 315; Jacobsen, pp. ix, 132, 142–43, 152–53, 160–61, 187, 191, 213, 241, 430–31.

412 *Americans did:* Memorandum T-4031 A, Sept. 15, 1945, B: 489, E: 210, Monthly Progress Report of SI/Production Division, Sept. 1–30, 1945, B: 9, E: 99, Monthly Progress Report of Steering Division, SI/Germany Aug. 2, 1945, B: 4, Acting Chief FBM and DH136 memo to Commanding Officer, SSU WD Mission to Austria Oct. 9, 1945, B: 2, E: 214, Notes on Meeting 4 January 1945, B: 359, Franklin Canfield memo to AWD June 7, 1945,

B: 203, E: 210, Project Marietta Progress Report Nov. 11, 1946, B: 2, Saint, AMZON, memo to Saint, Paris, Oct. 17, 1946, B: 3, E: 213, Public Opinion in French Zone of Berlin Aug. 27, 1945, B: 169, E: 108, RG226, Political Situation in the Russian and British Zones March 1946, Situation in the French Zone April 1946, R: 2, FR: 26–28, 329–30, M1656, NA.

412 *being followed:* AB 16, Saint, Berlin memo to AB 24, Saint, AMZON, Jan. 14, 1946, B: 1, Shanghai Incident (Project Cactus) March 5, 1946, B: 2, E: 213, Progress Report for X-2 Penetration Cases, November 1945, B: 3, Monthly Progress Report, X-2, September 1945, B: 9, OSS Activities, including European Theater, June 44–Sept. 45, Washington History Office, Mission for Germany September 1945, B: 123–25, E: 99, SSU/X-2 Counterintelligence Summary July 1, 1946, B: 314, E: 210, RG226, NA; Ziemke, p. 305; Richie, pp. 638, 647–49; Murphy, pp. 6, 30–34; Polgar, March 19, 2013; Montgomery, July 17, 2012; Sichel manuscript.

413 *"Russian hands":* Murphy, pp. 18–19, 408; Richard Cutler memo to Crosby Lewis Nov. 29, 1945, B: 1, Sidney Lenington memo to Chief, Counterintelligence Project, Berlin, April 29, 1946, B: 3, E: 213, OSS/Mission for Germany Progress Report Aug. 1–31, 1945, OSS Mission to Germany September Report, B: 9, E: 99, RG226, NA.

413 *rate soared:* Monthly Report of the Steering Division Oct. 4, 1945, B: 4, E: 214, Strategic Services Unit as of mid-October, 1945, B: 7, E: 99, RG226, NA; Sichel manuscript; Sichel, March 11, 2013; Cynthia Helms, July 18, 2012; Ziemke, pp. 324–25; Lowe, p. 42; Clay, p. 62; MacDonogh, p. 241.

417 *cleaning house:* Theater Service Record for Peter Sichel, Temporary promotion record for Peter Sichel Sept. 25, 1945, B: 709, Rumors in Russian Zone Nov.–Dec. 1945, B: 169, E: 108, Investigation of Smuggling of Watches from Switzerland Sept. 26, 1945, Security Office Investigative Report on Andrew Haensel Feb. 12, 1944, OSS Requisition by Name for Andrew Haensel March 23, 1944, Gustave Mueller Application for Employment and Personal History Statement, H. K. Lenocker memo to Gustave Mueller Sept. 17, 1943, Bronze Star Medal citation for Louis Dups, Peter memo to Chief, SI Production, Exhibit M (Item 3), SI Production memo to Supply Officer, Exhibit M (Item 1), FW memo to I. Van der Gracht and RMH, Exhibit M (Item 13), Peter memo to Chief, SI Production, Exhibit M (Item 14), Peter Requisition of 18 August 1945, Exhibit M (Item 16), FW memo to Louis Dups Sept. 9, 1945, Exhibit E, Peter, Berlin, memo to FW, Van der Gracht, AMZON Sept. 14, 1945, Exhibit H, Dups memo 22.9.45, Exhibit T, Thomas Bland sworn statement Oct. 9, 1945, Exhibit GG, Bland memo to MacPherson Sept. 4, 1945, Exhibit O, Special Order No. 37, Sept. 22, 1944, Exhibit A, A. W. Schmidt memo to FW Sept. 24, 1945, Exhibit N, Meetings and testimonies of the Board of Officers investigating the Haensel-Mueller case, Sept. 24–Oct. 15, 1945, B: 206, 303, 544, E: 224, 110 cable to Magruder Oct. 12, 1945, Suhling cable to Magruder Oct. 18, 1945, Magruder cable to Suhling Oct. 23, 1945, Edwin Black memo to Louis Dups Oct. 27, 1945, Edwin Black memo to Louis Dups Nov. 6, 1945, Donald Hays memo to Office of General Counsel Feb. 12, 1946, Edward Green memo to Chief of Staff, U.S. Forces, European Theater, Feb. 18, 1946, Edward Green memo to General Counsel—Washington, SSU, Feb. 20, 1946, Edward

Green memo to General Counsel, SSU/WD, Washington, March 30, 1946, AMZON cable to War Department SSU March 22, 1946, B: 7, E: 90, RG226, NA; Sichel, March 11, 2013; Sichel manuscript; Persico, *Piercing the Reich*, pp. 109–10; Occupation Forces in Europe Series, 1945–49: Morale and Discipline in the European Command, Historical Division, European Command, CMH; Lowe, pp. 46, 97–98, 109; Ziemke, pp. 276–77, 421–23, 349–54; Richie, pp. 639–40; MacDonogh, p. 206, 211, 373–76; Montgomery, July 17, 2012; Read, *Berlin*, p. 252; Hutchison, July 28, 2012; Clay, pp. 63–64; Helms, *A Look over My Shoulder*, p. 58; Polgar, March 19, 2013; Ruffner, pp. 1–20.

417 *priority target:* WJD cable to his overseas stations Sept. 27, 1945, B: 192, E: 134, Magruder cable to Bross Oct. 5, 1945, B: 521, E: 210, 110 cable to Cheston and Magruder Sept. 29, 1945, B: 193, Magruder cable to 110 and Suhling Oct. 4, 1945, B: 192, E: 134, Franklin Canfield memo to John Bross and Lewis Gable Sept. 11, 1945, B: 292, E: 190, RG226, NA; Helms, *A Look over My Shoulder*, pp. 61–62; Kingsley, Jan. 7, 2008.

418 *pay them:* 110 cable to Cheston and Magruder Sept. 29, 1945, B: 193, Magruder cable to 110 and Suhling Oct. 4, 1945, B: 192, E: 134, Monthly Report on Steering Division Nov. 5, 1945, B: 4, E: 214, 110, Morse, Black, Bastedo cable to O'Malley and Suhling Sept. 2, 1945, B: 151, E: 88, OSS Activities, including European Theater, June 44–Sept. 45, Washington History Office, Mission for Germany September 1945, B: 123–25, E: 99, RG226, NA; Murphy, p. 10.

418 *he decided:* Hubert Will memo to James Murphy Dec. 18, 1945, B: 3, E: 122, Germany cable to War Department SSU Dec. 19, 1945, AMZON cable to War Department SSU Dec. 18, 1945, B: 608, E: 88, S. P. Karlow memo to Douglas Dimond Dec. 10, 1945, B: 203, E: 224, W. G. Suhling memo to AWD Sept. 5, 1945, R: 74, FR: 237–41, M1642, RG226, NA; AWD letter to GG Dec. 10, 1945, B: 27, AWD letter to Laird Bell Dec. 27, 1945, B: 7, AWD letter to Royall Tyler Nov. 28, 1945, B: 106, AWDP, PU; Petersen, p. 525; Talley, July 28, 2012.

419 *quiet way:* W. G. Suhling memo to Gen. Magruder Dec. 7, 1945, B: 2, P: 1, S: 1, RHP, GU; Bill Quinn letter to RMH Nov. 12, 1992, B: 2, P: 1, S: 1, RHP, GU; Helms, *A Look over My Shoulder*, p. 63; Montgomery, July 17, 2012; Murphy, p. 10; RMH Officer's Fitness Report Aug. 3–Dec. 12, 1945, RHNR, NPRC; Sichel, March 11, 2013; Polgar, March 19, 2013; Dennis Helms, Aug. 19 and Sept. 10, 2012.

419 *Russians arrived:* Theater Service Record for Frederick Stalder, Stalder Qualifications and Experience, B: 736, E: 224, RMH letter to James Kahn Aug. 4, 1981, Interview with Erna Flegel—Report Attached Nov. 30, 1945, B: 447, E: 210, RG226, NA; F. J. Stalder letter to AWD Aug. 28, 1946, B: 68, AWDP, PU.

420 *being a spy:* AMZON cable to War Department SSU Nov. 21, 1945, B: 193, E: 134, RG226, NA; James Forrestal letter to RMH April 17, 1946, B: 1, P: 2, S: 2, Henry Manz letter to RMH March 4, 1946, B: 4, P: 1, S: 2, RHP, GU; Helms, *A Look over My Shoulder*, pp. 64, 67; Montgomery, July 17, 2012; Ziemke, pp. 407–10; MacDonogh, p. 497; Helms, OHP, p. 26.

CHAPTER 27: THE DIRECTORS

421 *in the OSS:* Henry Hyde letters to AWD July 1 and Aug. 10, 1954, B: 32, AWD letter to GG Feb. 13, 1946, B: 27, Note on the German Underground by AWD, Sept. 5, 1946, B: 33, AWD letter to John Magruder Dec. 27, 1946, B: 40, AWD letter to Elizabeth Parsons Aug. 9, 1954, AWD letter to Annaliese Goerdeler Sept. 4, 1947, Sept. 4, 1945, B: 44, AWDP, PU; AWD letter to WJD June 16, 1951, B: 1A, WJDP, MHI; Grose, pp. 257, 281–82; Srodes, pp. 381–82; Waller, p. 352.

422 *family life:* AWD letter to H. L. Pugh June 12, 1953, AWD letter to Wilder Penfield March 22, 1954, B: 18, Mary Bancroft telegram to AWD Dec. 12, 1946, and letters to AWD on May 24, 1959, Dec. 29, 1962, and July 2, 1963, B: 7, AWD letter to Mary Bancroft April 30, 1962, AWDP, Report on Allen Macy Dulles Nov. 29, 1952, B: 25, HAP, PU; Srodes, pp. 450–51; Talley, July 28, 2012; Grose, pp. 263–64; Mosley, pp. 247–48; Bancroft, p. 290; Memorandum for Mr. Tolson Re: Allen Dulles Aug. 7, 1953, R. R. Roach memo to A. H. Belmont Nov. 5, 1958, Memos to Mr. Nichols (62-80750-722) July 27, 1948, and (62-81909-11) on Dulles Close Connection with WJD Jan. 14, 1947, A. H. Belmont memo to D. M. Ladd Jan. 19, 1953, FBI.

423 *book industry:* WJD letter to WJC Feb. 1, 1949, WJC letter to WJD March 30, 1948, B: 100, WJD letter to WJC April 7, 1948, B: 461, WJCP, WJC letter to Henry Regnery Jan. 29, 1953, Henry Regnery letters to WJC Sept. 19, 1952, and March 3, 1960, B: 13, HIA; WJC letter to WJD Jan. 14, 1955, B: 9A, WJDP, MHI; Barreaux, Aug. 6, 2012; Bernadette Casey and Owen Smith, Aug. 24, 2012; Persico, *Casey*, pp. 87–94, 101–2, 132–33, 157; Woodward, p. 36; Sichel, March 11, 2013.

423 *"axel-tree":* Divisional Deputy, Europe, memo to James Q. May March 1, 1946, Request for Personnel Data and Leave Transcript for RMH Oct. 20, 1946, B: 326, E: 224, Telephone Directory SSU December 1945, B: 509, E: 210, RG226, NA; AWD letter to RMH May 20, 1948, RMH letter to AWD March 3, 1947, and AWD reply March 5, 1947, B: 31, AWDP, PU; Helms, *A Look over My Shoulder*, pp. 68–74, 153–56, 274–78, 452; Polgar, March 19, 2013; Grose, p. 258; Annual Fitness Report for RMH June 30, 1945, RHNR, NPRC; Powers, p. 64; Dennis Helms, Aug. 19, 2012.

424 *beautiful wife:* John Colby, July 30, 2012; Carl Colby, July 16, 2012; Barbara Colby, July 16 and 30, 2012; Bordelon, Oct. 25, 2012; Sally Colby, July 27, 2012; Paul Colby, Sept. 3, 2012; Colby, *Honorable Men*, pp. 62–64, 73–75; Walker, July 30, 2012.

425 *like Russia:* "Allen Dulles: An Appraisal," by Kenneth J. Campbell, *Studies in Intelligence*, Spring 1990, B: 11, E: 27, RG263, NA; WJD letter to AWD Jan. 2, 1951, and AWD response Jan. 8, 1951, B: 1A, WJDP, MHI; Grose, pp. 288–92, 308–9; Bancroft, COH, pp. 162–63; Petersen, p. 526; Wayne Jackson, pp. 14–16; Helms, *A Look over My Shoulder*, pp. 101–3; Srodes, 428–30.

426 *in government:* Colby, *Honorable Men*, pp. 75–78, 87; Barbara Colby, July 16, 2012; Sally Colby, July 27, 2012; Carl Colby, July 16, 2012.

426 *Russians attacked:* Grose, pp. 304–6; Colby, *Honorable Men*, pp. 81–84, 88–89, 98–103, 107; Carl Colby, July 16, 2012; Barbara Colby, July 16, 2012; Prados, p. 49.

426 *up the agency:* "The Right Man for the Job," *New York Times* editorial, Jan. 27, 1953; Grose, pp. 333–39; Montague, pp. 264–65; Waller, pp. 360–61; Srodes, p. 433; AWD transcript, John Foster Dulles Oral History Project, p. 69, PU.

427 *for the agency:* "Our Spy-Boss Who Loved Bond," by Allen Dulles, *Life,* Aug. 28, 1964; Petersen, pp. 19–20; Grose, pp. 319–20, 386–87, 430, 491–92; Srodes, pp. 452–55, 463–65; Dulles, *The Craft of Intelligence,* p. 6; Lundahl, COH, p. 491.

428 *Fidel Castro:* Talley, July 28, 2012; McIntosh, July 12, 2012; Kingsley, Jan. 7, 2008; Grose, pp. 326–27, 340–41, 390–96, 416, 429, 432, 497–98, 500–504; Mosley, pp. 370, 431, 461–63; Srodes, p. 484; "An Interview with Richard Helms by David Frost," *Studies in Intelligence,* Fall 1981, B: 8, E: 27, RG263, NA.

428 *college education:* "The Man with the Innocent Air," *Time,* Aug. 3, 1953, pp. 12–15; AWD letter to DDE Jan. 11, 1954, B: 281, White House Central Files, Official Files, DDEL; AWD transcript, John Foster Dulles Oral History Project, p. 63, PU; AWD remarks at the meeting of the Board of Trustees of the Practicing Law Institute Oct. 15, 1958, B: 28, AWD letter to James B. Donovan, B: 64, JDP, HIA; Grose, pp. 362–63, 386; Srodes, pp. 439–40, 465; Woodward, p. 293.

429 *covert action:* Hathaway, p. 60; Helms, *A Look over My Shoulder,* pp. 102–10, 125–32; Grose, pp. 419–24; Weiner, pp. 123–25; Mosley, pp. 375–78; Powers, p. 50; Murphy, pp. 214–37.

430 *bad choice:* Dulles, *The Craft of Intelligence,* p. 224; John Colby, July 30, 2012; Colby, *Honorable Men,* pp. 108–19, 135–36; Prados, pp. 59–60; Woods, p. 98; Grose, p. 378; Helms, *A Look over My Shoulder,* pp. 108, 121–22, 163–65, 197, 374; Powers, pp. 88–93, 100–10; Cynthia Helms, July 18, 2012; Srodes, p. 473.

431 *"million pieces":* Grose, p. 404–49, 450, 469–84, 529–34; Mosley, pp. 456–58; Weiner, pp. 159–60; Bissell, COH, p. 44; Dillon, pp. 49–57; Killian, COH, p. 40; Powers, pp. 130–31, 182; Polgar, March 19, 2013; Robarge, p. 15.

432 *at mass:* Prados, pp. 69, 79–81, 88, 90, 112–25; Grose, p. 410; Weiner, p. 213; Cox, Sept. 22, 2012; Polgar, March 19, 2013; Woods, pp. 168, 329–30; Colby, *Honorable Men,* pp. 143–45, 152–55, 161–62, 170–73, 178, 203, 217–20; Colby, *Lost Victory,* pp. 32–34, 42–44, 58–59, 101–2, 106, 136–52, 156; Sheehan, pp. 174–80, 338, 540; Rosenau, p. 6; Woods, pp. 138–39.

433 *of action:* Powers, pp. 11–12, 133–34, 149–61, 190–95, 216, 324; Helms, *A Look over My Shoulder,* pp. 196–209, 225; Colby, *Honorable Men,* pp. 189–90, 226–27, 242–45; Prados, pp. 91, 157–58, 163, 189; Colby photo with inscription to Helms, B: 5, CHP, GU; Cynthia Helms, July 18, 2012; Montgomery, July 17, 2012; Weiner, p. 264.

434 *on his watch:* Gates Helms, Aug. 18, 2012; Dennis Helms, Aug. 19, 2012; Montgomery, July 17, 2012; Howe, July 12, 2012; Cynthia Helms, July 18, 2012; Hawn, Aug. 18, 2012; Robarge, pp. 17–18; Prados, pp. 37, 315–17; Hathaway, p. 69; Robarge, pp. 17–18; Helms, *A Look over My Shoulder,* p. 248; Jack Jolis, Sept. 20, 2012; Weiner, pp. 278–80, 284.

435 *inner circle:* Helms, *A Look over My Shoulder,* pp. 298–300, 335; Colby, *Honorable Men,* pp. 239–40, 245–46; Woods, pp. 248, 261–62; Colby, *Lost Victory,* pp. 205–8; Robarge, p. 19; Powers, p. 202.

435 *the building:* Helms, *A Look over My Shoulder*, pp. 295–96; Polgar, March 19, 2013; Gates and Alberta Helms, Aug. 18, 2012; Hawn, Aug. 18, 2012; Thomas, p. 151; Cynthia Helms, July 18, 2012; Dennis Helms, Aug. 19, 2012; Hugh Montgomery, July 17, 2012; Cynthia Helms, pp. 4–11, 39–50, 66–76, 89–91.

436 *spy adventures:* Powers, pp. 178, 228–31, 283–87; Helms, *A Look over My Shoulder*, pp. 11–12, 279–81; Persico, *Casey*, pp. 114–25, 126–32, 135–45, 152–63; Barreaux, Aug. 6, 2012.

437 *his disposal:* Woods, p. 385; Prados, pp. 201, 206; Colby, *Lost Victory*, pp. 235, 243, 269; Colby, *Honorable Men*, pp. 246–47, 252, 257, 261–64; Sheehan, p. 743.

437 *in his views:* "Soft-Spoken Pacification Chief, William Egan Colby," *New York Times*, Feb. 14, 1969; Sheehan, p. 731; Colby, *Lost Victory*, pp. 269–70; Prados, pp. 210–11; Powers, pp. 197, 212–13; Helms, *A Look over My Shoulder*, pp. 309–22, 338; Dennis Helms, Aug. 19, 2012; Hawn, Aug. 18, 2012.

438 *and cry:* John Colby, July 30, 2012, and April 11, 2013; Barbara Colby, July 16 and 30, 2012; Paul Colby, April 7, 2013; Colby, *Lost Victory*, pp. 216–17, 318, 326–32, 362–66; Colby, *Honorable Men,* pp. 266–76, 289–90; Andrade, pp. 17–21; Moyar, pp. 224–32; Woods, pp. 331–33; Sheehan, pp. 18, 732–33; Rosenau, pp. vii, 1–14; Woods, pp. 288–89, 311–15, 433–35, 476–77; Prados, pp. 188, 195, 217–18; Stein, pp. 71–72, 121, 323, 360; Prados, pp. 220–21, 232–37.

439 *many weeping:* Warner, "Reading the Riot Act," pp. 387–417; Helms, *A Look over My Shoulder*, pp. 410–12, 425–26; Weiner, pp. 319–23; Powers, pp. 5, 279–82, 302–4, 314; Cynthia Helms, p. 123; Hathaway, pp. 187–211.

440 *had staged:* Helms, *A Look over My Shoulder*, pp. 398–407, 413–15, 442; Weiner, pp. 306–16; Powers, pp. 9–10; "An Interview with Richard Helms by David Frost," *Studies in Intelligence,* Fall 1981, B: 8, E: 27, RG263, NA.

440 *he thought:* Phillips, pp. 233–34; Helms, *A Look over My Shoulder*, pp. 424–27; Weiner, p. 327; Prados, pp. 254–63, 322–24, 329; Colby, *Honorable Men*, pp. 332–46.

442 *"his own way":* "Cooling Off with William Colby," by Paul Hendrickson, *Washington Post*, May 24, 1978, p. C1; Colby, *Honorable Men*, pp. 342–48, 352–63; Woods, pp. 361–62, 366; Carl Colby, July 16, 2012; Harold Ford, p. 7; James Crowley interview Washington, D.C., May 1987, B: 14, LCP, GU; Sally Colby, July 27, 2012; John Colby, July 30, 2012; Phillips, pp. 243–45; Prados, pp. 262, 272–75; Colby, "Intelligence in the 1980s," *Studies in Intelligence,* Summer 1981, B: 8, E: 27, RG263, NA; Polgar, March 19, 2013.

442 *him deeply:* Colby, *Honorable Men*, pp. 12–13, 389–91, 398–99, 401–12, 427–29; Prados, 293–96, 300–14; Powers, pp. 333–35; "Bernard Knox (1914–2010)," by Garry Wills, *New York Review of Books*, Sept. 30, 2010; Paul Colby, Sept. 3, 2012; John Colby, July 30, 2012; Carl Colby, July 16, 2012; Sally Colby, July 27, 2012; Barbara Colby, July 30, 2012; Dennis Helms, Aug. 19, 2012; "An Interview with Richard Helms by David Frost," *Studies in Intelligence,* Fall 1981, B: 8, E: 27, RG263, NA; Helms, *A Look over My Shoulder*, pp. v, 428–29.

444 *his exit:* Powers, p. 353; Colby, *Honorable Men*, pp. 7–14, 18–21, 407; Howe, July 12, 2012; Paul Colby, Sept. 9, 2012; Prados, pp. xii, 305, 318, 323–26, 330, 341–42; Sally Colby, July 27, 2012; Barreaux, Aug. 6, 2012; Woods, pp. 462–63.

444 *his fine:* Helms, *A Look over My Shoulder,* pp. 431–37, 441–45; Cynthia Helms, pp. 151, 155; Powers, pp. 2, 14–15, 135–36, 341–42, 349–53; Colby, *Honorable Men,* pp. 382–86, 396; Prados, pp. 291–93.

444 *"drive home":* Prados, pp. 164, 341; Woods, p. 399; Jack Jolis, Sept. 20, 2012; Paul Jolis, Sept. 20, 2012; DeTrani, Nov. 11, 2012; John Colby, July 30, 2012.

445 *anticommunist agenda:* Persico, *Casey,* pp. 179–90, 199–203; deGraffenreid, Nov. 21, 2012; Sporkin, Oct. 12, 2012; Jack Jolis, Sept. 20, 2012; Woodward, pp. 35, 41–42.

445 *at Langley:* Arthur Schlesinger letter to WJC Dec. 12, 1980, B: 565, WJCP, HIA; Woodward, pp. 152–53; Schlesinger, pp. 513–14; Polgar, March 19, 2013; Howe, Dec. 20, 2007; Sally Colby, July 27, 2012; Carl Colby, July 16, 2012; Cynthia Helms, July 18, 2012.

446 *or to lunch:* DeTrani, Nov. 11, 2012; Murphy, Sept. 19, 2012; Sporkin, Oct. 12, 2012; Persico, *Casey,* p. 243; WEC letter to WJC Dec. 11, 1980, B: 322, WJCP, HIA; WEC letter to WJC with enclosure Dec. 11, 1980, B: 1, WECP, PU; Woodward, pp. 42–45, 55–59; Barreaux, Aug. 6, 2012; Helms, *A Look over My Shoulder,* p. vi.

446 *more work:* DeTrani, Nov. 11, 2012; Gates, pp. 215–16; Persico, *Casey,* pp. 94, 207–10, 293; Sporkin, Oct. 12, 2012; deGraffenreid, Nov. 21, 2012; Woodward, pp. 99, 384; Murphy, Sept. 19, 2012.

447 *with Roosevelt:* Smith, Aug. 24, 2012; Barreaux, Aug. 6, 2012; Sporkin, Oct. 12, 2012; Montgomery, July 17, 2012; Lenczowski, Sept. 18, 2012; DeTrani, Nov. 11, 2012; Gates, pp. 200, 208; Casey, "OSS: Lessons for Today," p. 64; deGraffenreid, Nov. 21, 2012; Persico, *Casey,* pp. 3, 218–22, 265, 382–83; Woodward, pp. 106–7.

447 *sensitive operations:* Persico, *Casey,* pp. 227–28, 305–6; deGraffenreid, Nov. 21, 2012; Gates, pp. 216–19; Sporkin, Oct. 12, 2012; Woodward, pp. 403–4; Barreaux, Aug. 6, 2012.

447 *the organization:* Gates, pp. 202, 207, 214, 218; Persico, *Casey,* pp. 334, 352, 354, 388–89; Woodward, pp. 148–49, 281, 341; deGraffenreid, Nov. 21, 2012; "The CIA and the Perils of Politicization," by Melvin A. Goodman, International Policy Report, Center for International Policy, March 2008.

448 *or détente:* Remarks of William J. Casey before The Commonwealth Club of California April 3, 1984, B: 32, GSP, HIA; Casey, "OSS: Lessons for Today," pp. 64–66; Meyer, pp. xv, 235–41; Sporkin, Oct. 12, 2012; Gates, pp. 199, 208–9, 224–25; Persico, *Casey,* pp. 212–18, 225; deGraffenreid, Nov. 21, 2012; Lenczowski, Sept. 18, 2012; Woodward, pp. 111, 136; Weiner, pp. 381–82.

449 *of the deal:* Meyer, p. 237; Schweizer, p. 204; Gates, pp. 242, 315–16; Woodward, pp. 168–77, 205, 301, 315–16, 328–30, 399, 408, 434–35, 466–69; Persico, *Casey,* pp. 5, 274–76, 302, 335–37, 361–62, 370, 392–407, 432–33, 446–53, 472, 492, 506–26; Sporkin, Oct. 12, 2012.

450 *his legacy:* Persico, *Casey,* pp. 487, 494, 501, 530–44, 561–70; Woodward, pp. 465–67, 481–502; Weiner, pp. 399–405, 412; Sporkin, Oct. 12, 2012; Schweizer, pp. 267–68, 283; Weiner, pp. 407–8; Gates, 400–403.

EPILOGUE

451 *German wrote:* GG letter to AWD Dec. 2, 1968, B: 27, AWDP, PU.

451 *the result: Meet the Press* transcript for interview with AWD Dec. 31, 1961, B: 449, JLP, HIA; AWD letters to RMH Sept. 26, 1964, and Feb. 10 and April 21, 1968, RMH letter to AWD Aug. 6, 1966, and AWD reply Aug. 18, 1966, B: 31, AWDP, PU; Grose, pp. 561–64; Srodes, pp. 549–54; Talley, July 28, 2012.

452 *in 1974:* "Allen Dulles Dies at 75; Former U.S. Master Spy," by Thomas Nolan, Washington *Evening Star*, Feb. 30, 1969, p. 1; Transcript of Eric Sevareid eulogy for AWD, *CBS Evening News*, Jan. 30, 1969; Material for Allen Dulles funeral, B: 113, AWDP, PU; "Notables Pay Tribute at Funeral for Dulles," *Washington Post*, Feb. 2, 1969, D6; CTD letter to RMH Feb. 21, 1969, B: 1, P: 1, S: 1, RHP, GU; Talley, July 28, 2012.

452 *in the pews:* Cynthia Helms, p. 176; Gates, pp. 410–14; Persico, *Casey*, pp. 546–57; Meyer, p. 292; Material for WJC funeral May 9, 1987, Francis Sorg letter to John McGann May 22, 1987, TCB; "Contra Controversy Raised at Casey Funeral," by Steven V. Roberts, *New York Times*, May 10, 1987.

453 *marijuana use:* Woods, p. 472; Cox, Sept. 22, 2012; Sally Colby, July 27, 2012; Prados, pp. 338–39; Carl Colby, July 16, 2012; Paul Colby, Sept. 3, 2012; WEC letter to Robert McNamara Aug. 22, 1979, B: 4, RMP, LOC.

453 *conservative policies:* Barbara Colby, July 16 and 26, 2012; John Colby, July 30, 2012; Paul Colby, Sept. 9, 2012; Sally Colby, July 30, 2012, and April 6, 2013; Woods, pp. 475–76.

454 *"coming to him":* Prados, pp. 1–6; John Colby, July 30, 2012; Sally Colby, July 30, 2012; Barbara Colby, July 16 and 26, 2012; Paul Colby, Sept. 9, 2012; Woods, pp. 2–5; "William E. Colby, 76, Head of C.I.A. in a Time of Upheaval," by Tim Weiner, *New York Times*, May 7, 1996, B7; Post Mortem Examination Report, Office of the Chief Medical Examiner, State of Maryland, for WEC, Case No. 96-2443-017.

454 *swap stories:* Powers, p. 8; "An Interview with Richard Helms by David Frost," *Studies in Intelligence*, Fall 1981, B: 8, E: 27, RG263, NA; Helms, *A Look over My Shoulder*, p. vi; Hawn, Aug. 18, 2012; Cynthia Helms, pp. 167–73, 183; Dennis Helms, Aug. 19, 2012; Gates Helms, Aug. 18, 2012.

454 *the disciples:* Cynthia Helms, p. 182; Cynthia Helms, Sept. 13, 2012; Dennis Helms, Aug. 19, 2012; "The Agency's Farewell," by Dana Priest, *Washington Post*, Nov. 12, 2002, C1; Material on RMH funeral Nov. 20, 2002, GMH.

ACKNOWLEDGMENTS

I had been hunting for another topic after my book on General William J. Donovan, the leader of the World War II Office of Strategic Services. It had become a frustrating search. A biographer could not ask for a more compelling, controversial, and multifaceted subject than Wild Bill Donovan. He would be hard to match. Finally, Larry MacDonald, who was the National Archives' top expert on the OSS and who guided me through the millions of agency records stored in its College Park, Maryland, facility for the previous volume, suggested I write my next book on the four men who served under Donovan and who later became CIA directors—Allen Dulles, Richard Helms, William Colby, and William Casey. Thank you, Larry. You sent me on a journey into four characters as rich as Donovan's.

So many people came to my aid along the way. Kristine Dahl, my literary agent, good friend, and trusted adviser, instantly recognized that this was a story that needed to be told and, as with my previous books, she was invaluable in shaping the early concept for *Disciples*. I was blessed to have Alice Mayhew as my editor at Simon & Schuster. I treasured her wise counsel, her skillful and loving hand with my draft, and her enthusiasm for the project. It was an honor to join the authors she has taken under her wing. Assistant editor Stuart Roberts could not have been more helpful in whipping the manuscript into shape for publication. Copy editor Fred Chase went over my prose with a meticulous eye and sanded the rough edges.

Disciples benefited from the revealing memoirs Dulles, Helms, Colby, and Casey wrote and from previous biographies of these four men by Peter Grose, James Srodes, Leonard Mosley, Thomas Powers, John Prados,

Randall B. Woods, and Joseph E. Persico. A number of important histories
have been written on the OSS, which provided background for the tens of
thousands of government documents I collected in the United States and
overseas. They include the two-volume *War Report of the O.S.S.,* a surprisingly candid official history of Donovan's agency; Joseph Persico's *Piercing
the Reich,* which chronicles the OSS operations to penetrate Germany; the
histories Colin Beavan, Lieutenant Colonel Will Irwin (Ret.), and Roger
Ford wrote of the Jedburghs; *Operation Sunrise* by Bradley F. Smith and
Elena Agarossi; Lucas Delattre's *A Spy in the Heart of the Third Reich,* chron-
icling Allen Dulles's agent, Fritz Kolbe, and Neal H. Petersen's *From Hitler's
Doorstep,* an exhaustive compilation of Dulles cables from the OSS station
in Bern.

I also enjoyed the cooperation of family members of the four men: Joan
Dulles Talley, Gates Hawn, Alberta Helms, Cynthia Helms, Dennis Helms,
Gates McGarrah Helms, Barbara Colby, Carl Colby, Christine Colby Giraudo, John Colby, Paul Colby, Sally Shelton Colby, Bernadette Casey Smith
and Owen Smith. They endured hours of interviews, and countless emails,
and phone calls from me with follow-up questions. They also provided me
with valuable letters, documents, and memorabilia from their personal collections. In addition, numerous family friends and OSS, CIA, and administration colleagues of these men shared valuable insights with me.

Archives and libraries in the United States and England became my
second home for two years. I knew my way around the National Archives'
vast collection thanks to Larry MacDonald's guidance during the Donovan
research and tips from John Taylor (the dean of the OSS records) before he
died. (It had taken me about three months to learn how to navigate the complex filing system for the OSS material.) For *Disciples,* Timothy Nenninger,
chief of the reference section for the National Archives at College Park, was
a wise counselor and gracious lunch companion during my research. Paul
Brown, an expert on the captured German World War II records stored at
the archives, cheerfully helped me hunt for Wehrmacht, Foreign Office, Gestapo, and SD documents related to my four subjects.

Elsewhere, the staff at Princeton University Library's Department of Rare
Books and Special Collections helped me wade through hundreds of its
boxes for the Allen Dulles and William Colby papers. The staff at Columbia

University's Oral History Research Office brought me the reminiscences of nearly a dozen friends or associates of Dulles. Nicholas Scheetz and Scott Taylor at Georgetown University's Special Collections Division ably assisted in my search through Richard Helms's papers, Cynthia Helms's papers, and the papers of others who knew Helms. Carol Leadenham and the staff at Stanford University's Hoover Institution Archives were a big help in my search through William Casey's papers and the papers of other OSS officers housed there. The Library of Congress's Manuscript Division staff helped me unearth letters and documents on my four subjects from the papers of public officials and associates who knew them. Gregory Smith helped me retrieve documents at the Wisconsin Historical Society for two journalism colleagues who worked with Helms in prewar Berlin. The National Personnel Records Center in St. Louis provided me with the naval personnel files for Helms and Casey. More than five hundred pages of the FBI's file on Allen Dulles have been released under the Freedom of Information Act. The staff at the National Cryptologic Museum gave me a fascinating tour of their artifacts and provided me with an important interview from their David Kahn Collection. The Franklin D. Roosevelt, Harry S. Truman, and Dwight D. Eisenhower presidential libraries also had important records for my project, as did the U.S. Army Military History Institute, the National Security Archive, and the University of Delaware Library Special Collections.

Other authors generously shared with me research from their books. Rick Atkinson put up with emails from me mooching information on the European campaign from *The Guns at Last Light,* the superb third volume of his Liberation Trilogy. Erik Larson sent me good leads on Richard Helms's reporting days in prewar Berlin from his research for *In the Garden of Beasts.* Joseph Persico, who wrote a first-rate biography of William Casey, pointed me to important Helms interview notes he made, which are in his papers at the University of Albany-SUNY Archives. (The courteous staff there quickly fetched the boxes for me.) Will Irwin gave me helpful advice from the history he wrote of the Jedburghs.

Sim Smiley generously shared with me OSS files she had collected for the research she did for William Casey when he wrote his World War II memoir. Charles Pinck, president of the OSS Society, helped me track down relatives and World War II comrades of these four men. Sibley Cooley provided me with a video of an interview he conducted with Camille Lelong in 2008. I also owe a special debt of gratitude to Major Ole Christian Emaus with the Norwegian Army's special operations force, who gave me important leads for my research of William Colby's NORSO operation in Norway and helped with the translation of an important Norwegian history of that mission.

In England, the archivists and staff at the National Archives at Kew could not have been more helpful in locating important documents and war diaries for me that dealt with Dulles, Colby, and Casey from the Special Operations Executive and Security Service records. Historian Steven Kippax shared with me thousands of British World War II documents from his files, gave me addresses for key SOE and OSS sites in London, and introduced me to other military researchers in England. Among the valuable contacts he provided was Clive Bassett, who spent two days showing me around Peterborough, where the Jedburghs trained, and Harrington Field near Northampton, where the commandos took off for their missions to France. Clive also arranged for me a special tour of the Carpetbagger Covert Warfare Museum at Harrington, which had valuable research material in its files. I want to thank Sir Philip Naylor-Leyland for allowing me to tour the Milton Hall estate, which the Jedburghs used as their training facility, and William Craven from the estate office, who showed me the buildings and grounds and provided me his research into the history of Milton Hall. Drew and Emma Waller, my son and daughter-in-law, let me camp out in their home south of London as I roamed archives and World War II sites in England. Emma also helped me identify important landmarks in London from old photos I found.

I collected a number of foreign documents during my research. I want to thank Sabine Bridges, who translated German military, Foreign Office, and intelligence reports for me; Michele Magill, who translated a French school report card for Allen Dulles, and Vladimir Bilenkin, who translated Soviet Red Army cables I accumulated.

Military historians Gerhard Weinberg, Tim Nenninger, and Rick Atkinson and intelligence historians Michael Warner and David Robarge dutifully read my first draft and made important corrections and suggestions for improving the manuscript. I can't thank them enough. I am also grateful to Jeff and Johanna Mann for proofreading the galleys. Of course, the conclusions and any errors that remain in the book are all mine.

Finally, I could not have begun this book or completed it without the encouragement, advice, editing, incredible patience, and love of my wife, Judy. She took care of grandchildren on the first floor of our home while I toiled away on the manuscript on the third floor—and occasionally reminded me that I needed to keep my priorities straight and come help with the babies. It is to the latest three grandchildren to arrive in our family that this book is dedicated.

INDEX

PHOTO CREDITS

25. — Gates Hawn Collection

26. — CIA Photo

27. — CIA Photo

28. — Frank G. Wisner Collection

29. — CIA Photo

30. — Bernadette Casey Smith Collection

31. — John F. Kennedy Presidential Library

32. — CIA Photo

33. — Gates Hawn Collection

34. — Colby Family Collection

35. — White House Photo

36. — CIA Photo

37. — Bernadette Casey Smith Collection

38. — CIA Photo

ABOUT THE AUTHOR

A former correspondent for *Newsweek* and *Time*, Douglas Waller reported on the CIA for six years. Waller also covered the Pentagon, State Department, White House, and Congress. Before reporting for *Newsweek* and *Time*, he served eight years as a legislative assistant on the staffs of Rep. Edward J. Markey and Sen. William Proxmire. Waller is the author of the best-sellers *Wild Bill Donovan: The Spymaster Who Created the OSS and Modern American Espionage*; *Big Red: The Three-Month Voyage of a Trident Nuclear Submarine*; and *The Commandos: The Inside Story of America's Secret Soldiers*. He is also the author of *A Question of Loyalty*, the critically acclaimed biography of General Billy Mitchell. He lives in Raleigh, North Carolina, with his wife, Judy.